A HISTORY OF MEDIEVAL IRELAND

from 1086 *to* 1513

By the same Author

A HISTORY OF IRELAND

A HISTORY OF MEDIEVAL IRELAND

from 1086 *to* 1513

by

EDMUND CURTIS

M.A., LITT.D.

PROFESSOR OF MODERN HISTORY

TRINITY COLLEGE, DUBLIN

BARNES & NOBLE, Inc.

New York

METHUEN & CO. Ltd

London

First published (Maunsel and Roberts) in 1923
This enlarged and completely rewritten
edition first published by
Methuen & Co., Ltd., in 1938

Reprinted, 1968
by
Barnes & Noble, Inc., New York
and
Methuen & Co. Ltd, London

Printed in the United States of America

PREFACE

THE first edition of this work was published in 1923. As it has been long out of print, and as there is a demand for a history of this formative period of Irish history, I have thought it well to undertake a second edition. In doing so, I have carried my scope backwards to the eleventh century and so made my pages cover the whole period from 1086, when the supremacy over all Ireland founded by Brian Boru was still effective in the O'Brien High kings, on through to the Anglo-Norman Conquest and its sequel up to the death of Gerald 'the Great Earl' of Kildare in 1513, a date when the second English conquest of Ireland (the 'Tudor Reconquest') became imminent.

In preparing a second edition, I have completely revised, recast and indeed practically rewritten the whole work. Such a revision was necessary in view of my own continuous studies in a chosen field of Irish history and the contributions made by others to what was formerly a much-neglected period. In addition to the previous work of such scholars as Dr. Goddard Orpen and Professor John MacNeill, many younger students have turned their attention to the history of medieval Ireland. Their various publications are too many to mention here; suffice it to say that the fruits of their work have gone to the making of this book.

Much of the detailed information and some of the longer footnotes of my first edition are not reproduced *in extenso*; the enquiring reader is referred back to the pages of that book. The new matter which appears in this edition and that contained in the first edition between them form a large body of digested material and considered judgments on many aspects of our medieval history.

In the Appendices I have given a detailed study of three obscure subjects, namely the Ostmen, or hibernicized Norse settlers in Ireland, the towns of medieval Ireland, and the legal treatment of the native Irish, whether free or villein (betaghs), by the Dublin government and the Anglo-Norman colonists during the whole period, a point which I illustrate by some unpublished documents. Also, at the end of this book I give genealogical tables of the twenty or so chief dynastic or feudal families, Gaelic and Norman, of medieval Ireland. These have had to be carefully worked out and, save for a few lists in Orpen's

Ireland Under the Normans, I do not know any historical work which contains such pedigrees, which are a most essential aid to the understanding of the period. The maps of Ireland in 1160, in 1395, and in 1500, are similarly an aid to the understanding of medieval Ireland.

In conclusion, I may be permitted to quote what I say in the Foreword to my first edition.

> 'Dr. Goddard Orpen's *Ireland Under the Normans* (four volumes, covering the period 1166–1333) has been an invaluable guide for part of my period, and it is a pleasure to acknowledge my indebtedness to him. His work is, however, professedly devoted to the history of the Norman colonists, whereas I have devoted more attention to the native side. For the period after 1333 I may claim the merits, as I admit the shortcomings, of a pioneer in a stretch of our history where sources are little known, legends many, and guides almost non-existent. I have not only traced the main course of the political history but devoted much space to institutions, political and social, of the Anglo-Irish and Irish, and to the languages and culture of the races of medieval Ireland.'

Since this was written Dr. Orpen has passed away, but I am glad of an opportunity to repeat a tribute to the devoted student of medieval Anglo-Irish records. Among the living authorities on this subject I again wish to express my gratitude and debt to Professor John MacNeill, who is the acknowledged pioneer and exponent in a whole new and scientific study of the continuous Gaelic *ethos* of Ireland as it stood intact in 1100 and continued in part up to 1603.

It is a pleasure to be able to record that since the above-quoted words were written the study of our medieval institutions, culture, and history, both from the Anglo-Norman and the Gaelic side, is attracting the attention of a growing number of scholars trained in comparative and critical methods of research.

EDMUND CURTIS

TRINITY COLLEGE, DUBLIN
November 1938

CONTENTS

MAPS

ABBREVIATIONS

Alen's *Reg.*	Alen's *Register*, or *Liber Niger Alani* (Register of John Alen or Alan, abp. of Dublin, d. 1534); original MS. in the Diocesan Office, Dublin. Copy by Reeves in Library of Trinity College, Dublin (*MS.* 1061).

ANNALS, GAELIC

A.F.M.	*Annals of the Four Masters*, ed. O'Donovan.
Ann. Boyle	*Annals of Boyle* (ed. Charles O'Conor).
Ann. Clon.	*Annals of Clonmacnoise*, transl. into English by Conell Mageoghegan, 1627, ed. Denis Murphy, 1896.
Ann. Conn.	*Annals of Connacht*, now being prepared for publication by A. Martin Freeman for the Irish MSS. Commission.
Ann. L. Cé	*Annals of Loch Cé*, ed. Hennessy.
Ann. MacFirbis	*Annals of MacFirbis* (or Dudley Firbisse), ed. O'Donovan in *Miscell. Irish Arch. Soc.*, 1846.
Ann. Tig.	*Annals of Tighernach* (or Tigernach), ed. Whitley Stokes in *Revue Celtique*, 1895–7.
Ann. Ult.	*Annals of Ulster*, ed. Hennessy and MacCarthy.
Dublin Ann. Innisfallen	*Annals of Innisfallen* (see p. xviii).

ANNALS, LATIN

Clyn's *Annals* or *Clyn*	*Annals of Friar Clyn* (to 1349), ed. R. Butler in *Irish Arch. Soc.*, 1849.
Dowling's *Annals*	*Annals of Dowling* (*Thady*), ed. R. Butler in *Irish Arch. Soc.*, 1849.
Grace's *Annals* or *Grace*	*Annals of Grace*, ed. R. Butler, in *Irish Arch. Soc.*, 1842.
Laud Annals	*Laud Annals of Ireland, 1162–1370* (original among the Laud MS., Bodleian Library), printed in *Chartularies of St. Mary's Abbey, Dublin* (R.S.), II, pp. 303–98 (also called Pembridge's annals).
Ware's *Annals*	*Annals of Ware* (*Sir James*), *1485–1558*, printed in Dublin, 1664. Translated into English in Ware's *Antiquities and Hist. of Ireland*, 1705.

Berry, *Statutes*	Berry (H. F.), *Statutes of Ireland*, 3 vols, John–Edward IV.
Betham, *Dignities*	Betham, *Dignities, Feudal, etc.*
Book of Howth	*Book of Howth*, a volume in *The Calendar of Carew MSS.* (Lambeth), ed. Brewer and Bullen (1871).
Book of Rights	*Book of Rights* (*Leabhar na gCeart*), ed. O'Donovan.
Bryan	Bryan (Donough), *Great Earl of Kildare* (1933).

Cal. Carew MSS.	*Calendar of Carew Papers* (*C.S.P.*), 6 vols (1515–1624).
Cal. Close Rolls	*Calendar of Close Rolls, England* (*C.S.P.*), 1892 &c.
Cal. Just. Rolls	*Calendar of Justiciary Rolls*, Ireland (*C.S.P.*, ed. Mills), 2 vols., 1295–1307.
Cal. Ormond Deeds	*Calendar of Ormond Deeds*, ed. E. Curtis (for the Irish MSS. Commission), 4 vols. 1170–1547.
Cal. Pat. Rolls	*Calendar of Patent Rolls, England* (*C.S.P.*), 1891, &c.
Carew Miscell.	*Carew Miscellany*, a volume of *The Cal. of Carew MSS.* (contains *Book of Howth*).
Chartae, Privilegia, etc.	*Chartae, Privilegia et Immunitates* (Irish Record Commission, 1829–30).
Chart. St. Mary's Abbey	*Chartularies, etc., of St. Mary's Abbey, Dublin*, ed. Gilbert (*R.S.*), 1884, 2 vols.
C.S.P.	*Calendar of State Papers, England*

Conway	Conway (Agnes), *Henry VII's Relations with Scotland and Ireland* (*1485–98*).
Davies, *Discovery*	Davies (Sir John), *Discovery of the True Reasons why Ireland was never Subdued, etc.*, in his collected works by Grosart; or in *Ireland as described by Davies, etc.*, ed. Morley.
Dugdale, *Mon.*	Dugdale, *Monasticon Anglicanum*, 3 vols.
E.H.R.	*English Historical Review*, 1886.
Exch. K.R.	*Exchequer* (*King's Remembrancer*) *MS. Rolls, 18 Ric. II*, in Public Record Office, London (Submissions of Irish Chiefs to Ric. II).
Excheq. Mem.	*Exchequer Memoranda* (*Ireland*) numerous volumes of MS., transcripts of Exchequer rolls, &c., in the Public Record Office, Dublin.
Facs. Nat. MSS.	*Facsimiles of National MSS. of Ireland*, ed. Gilbert.
Foedera	Rymer, *Foedera, Conventiones, etc. . . . inter Reges Angliae et alios.*
Gilbert's *Viceroys*	*Viceroys of Ireland, History of* (*1170–1504*), by Sir John T. Gilbert.
Giraldus	Giraldus Cambrensis, *Expugnatio Hibernica* (*Conquest of Ireland*), in volume v of his collected works, ed. Brewer (*R.S.*).
Harris, *Collect.*	Harris, *Collectanea* (19 folio MS. volumes in National Library, Dublin, compiled by Walter Harris (*floruit*, 1686–1761); now calendared by Charles MacNeill in *Analecta Hibernica* (1934), vol. vi.
Hermathena	*Hermathena*, Journal of classical, &c., studies published by Dublin Univ. Press.
Hist and Mun. Docs.	*Historic and Municipal Documents of Ireland, 1172–1320*, (*R.S.*), ed. Gilbert.
Irish Exch. Mem. Rolls	*Irish Exchequer Memoranda Rolls* (ed. by Miss Bateson in *E.H.R.*, 1903, from Corpus Christi College MS.).
King's Council in Ireland	*A Roll of the Proceedings of the King's Council in Ireland, 1392–3* (*R.S.*) ed. Graves.
Leabhar Chlainne Suibhne	*Leabhar Chlainne Suibhne* (Book of the MacSweenys), ed. Paul Walsh.

Lib. Mun.	*Liber Munerum publicorum Hiberniae* (or, *Establishments of Ireland, 1152–1827*), ed. Lascelles, 2 vols. (1824–30).
Life of Malachy (Lawlor)	*Life of St. Malachy by Bernard of Clairvaux*, ed. J. H. Lawlor.
Lynch, *Feudal Baronies*	Lynch, *Legal Institutions, Feudal Baronies, etc., in Ireland.*
Miscell. Irish Arch. Soc.	*Miscellany of the Irish Archaeological Society.*
Orpen, *Normans*	Orpen, *Ireland under the Normans, 1166–1333* (4 vols., 1911–20).
P.R.I.A.	*Proceedings of the Royal Irish Academy.*
Reg. All Hallows	*Register of All Hallows, Dublin* (*R.S.*).
Reg. St. Thomas'	*Register of St. Thomas' Abbey, Dublin* (*R.S.*).
Rep. D.K.	*Reports of Deputy Keeper, Public Record Office, Dublin.*
Richard II in Ireland	*Richard II in Ireland and Submissions of the Irish Chiefs*, by E. Curtis (1927).
Rot. Parl.	*Rotuli Parliamentorum* (Rolls of Parliament, Edward I–Henry VII), 6 vols. (1767–77).
Rot. Pat. Canc. Hib.	*Rotulorum Patentium, etc., Cancellariae Hiberniae Calendarium* (Pat. and Close Rolls of Ireland, John–Henry VII), ed. Tresham, 1810.
R.S. (Rolls Series)	*Chronicles, etc., of Great Britain and Ireland* (published under direction of the Master of the Rolls).
R.S.A.I.	*Royal Society of Antiquaries, Ireland* (*formerly Kilkenny Archaeological Society*), *Journal of.*
Song of Dermot	*Song of Dermot and the Earl*, ed. Orpen, 1892.
Studies	*Studies*, (an Irish quarterly review).
Theiner, *Monumenta*	Theiner, *Vetera Monumenta Hibernorum et Scotorum historiam illustrantia, 1216–1547.*
Triumphs of Turloch or *Caithréim*	*Caithréim Thoirdhealbhaigh* (or *Triumphs of Turloch*), ed. S. H. O'Grady (Irish Texts Society).
Ussher, *Sylloge*	Ussher, *Veterum Epistolarum Hibernicorum Principum Sylloge* (1631); also in Elrington's *Works of Ussher*, vol. iv.

INTRODUCTION

THE monarchy or High kingship of Erin was founded about the year A.D. 390 by Niall of the Nine Hostages. From him descended a royal line called the Ui Néill (descendants of Niall), who preserved till A.D. 1000 a practically unbroken succession. This was then broken by Brian Boru, king of Cashel, but even after him the name, fact and authority of the kingdom of Ireland persisted, and a High king, no matter what province he came from, continued to represent the national unity.[1]

This unity under native Gaelic kings was shattered for ever by the Norman invasion; and, taking the period 1000 to 1170, we may attempt an estimate of the value of this ancient civilization and of the character of this native monarchy.

Extant memorials and contemporary evidence show that Ireland had at this time a culture, arts, and institutions of a highly organized nature, which were native and distinctive in type, and were at once developing from within and being influenced by contemporary Europe. The twelfth-century Renaissance was affecting Ireland, isolated though she was, and it was inevitable that in some way she would be brought into the circle of Continental politics and civilization.

There now existed and were developing a native form of romanesque architecture, a distinctive form of Christianity, a whole body of native law, which had been, or was being, written down in great books, a common language, and a corpus of literature in the Gaelic idiom which orally went back to the pagan, and in its written form to the earliest Christian, age. In the centuries since Ireland accepted Christianity the supreme examples of her art had been seen in the *Book of Kells*, the Ardagh chalice, the stone churches of early days, the round towers of later times; after the Norse invasions ended, there began the noble high stone crosses of Monasterboice, Kells, and other places, and in gold and silver work were wrought the processional Cross of Cong and other such triumphs of hereditary metalworkers. The influence of the Continent was shown in the stone cathedrals and churches which were built after the time of Brian Boru. This Irish romanesque architecture reached its most admirable point in the church of Killaloe, built by his great-grandson Murchertach O'Brien; in King Cormac's chapel at Cashel, built in 1130; in the cathedral

[1] Árd Rí is the Gaelic form of 'High king'. As well as being called king of Erin, he was called king of Tara.

door of Clonfert; and in the High king Turloch O'Connor's church at Tuam.

IRISH LITERATURE

What especially distinguished the Irish among all medieval races was an enthusiasm for the native language and native culture. Ireland had for centuries possessed a professional learned lay class, numerous and well endowed, whose generic name was the 'Filí'.[1] The preservation and cultivation of native letters, law, history, state and local records, was the occupation and privilege of this class which went back to the pagan past. The annals and historical tracts which came from them in these latter centuries are numerous; the national epics were collected together in *Lebhor na hUidhre* (*circa* 1100), the *Book of Leinster* (*circa* 1150), and other book-collections which have not survived; and such important State documents were compiled as the *Book of Rights* (*Leabhar na gCeart*), a record of the mutual obligations and prerogatives of the High king and the province-kings, drawn up first about A.D. 900 and revised about A.D. 1000. No country in Europe of that time maintained so large a class of *literati*, or one so influential. They were part of the ruling Gaelic caste which in the course of a thousand years had imposed its laws, its language, and its military and political supremacy over the whole island, and their influence was cast entirely on the side of the kings, the aristocracy, and the Gaelic tradition.

This learned and literary caste had been for some long time developing into hereditary, privileged, local families who attached themselves to the dominant local king and mainly served his interests. Their original function became differentiated into judges or brehons, chroniclers, scribes, physicians, bards. The poet in particular was destined to play a master part in Irish civilization till it ended, for the bardic order supplied the praise and incitement which kept the Gaelic king reminded of his heroic heritage; and not less did the patronage and extravagant rewards of the princes keep the bardic school in its prosperity and prestige. As such, they were the two foes which Tudor centralism later strove to destroy together.

There had always been inspired and anonymous poets; and semi-pagan *filí* and wandering monks or scholars of the monastic schools have left us a good deal that survives of the Gaelic muse. But after the Norse invasion and increasingly from the twelfth century onwards the *file* becomes the 'bardic poet.' For the most

[1] The singular of this word is 'file' (pronounced 'filla') meaning at first a seer and later a poet. The plural is 'filidh' or 'filí'.

part he was a poet of form, writing in elaborate, difficult, highly wrought metres on the familiar themes of chieftains and their glories, on religion, legendary tradition, and history. His language, though understood by the rest of the learned and the aristocracy, was of an artificial and static nature. From 1200 to 1600 there is almost no change either in the idiom or the themes of the bardic poets.[1]

The poets and *literati* wrote only one standard language for all Ireland. If this diminished the richness and freshness of their output, still it meant that our island in spite of its local divisions had one literary medium, and the 'man of learning' could go everywhere, be understood everywhere, and was welcome everywhere. A famous bard could eulogize and earn rewards from more than one great chief. In the older order and up to the time of such great monarchs as Brian Boru, an *ollamh* ('professor', or 'man of learning'), who had had a long training in the memorization of his craft, was attached to every royal court. Brian's chief *ollamh* was MacLiag, and MacLiag wrote or left materials for the historical tract *The War of the Gael and the Gall*, which commemorates the glories of his master, and wrote a poetic lament at his death.[2] For, from early times the 'man of learning' was skilled in putting a 'golden thread of verse' around his knowledge for mnemonic purposes, and indeed a poetical, rhetorical, imaginative cast is over all our native literature. An *ollamh* could compose a historical romance or a poem in *dán direach* (strict syllabic measure) as well as write a law tract. By the thirteenth century, however, the trade-unions of the bards, historians, physicians were well launched, and while Cathal Crovderg O'Connor, king of Connacht from 1202 to 1224, had in Muiredach Ó Dálaigh a real court poet, so later the O'Briens had a professional historian in Seán MacCraith, who wrote (*circa* 1350) *The Triumphs of Turloch.*

The Latin and theological culture of Ireland centred in the numerous monasteries which had been founded from St. Patrick's time onward. This culture was the preserve of the monk and the cleric, while Gaelic was the language of the poets and the learned laymen. Indeed there was much rivalry between the two castes at first. But by the eleventh century the monkish class itself embraced with increasing preference the cultivation and use of

[1] For the history, language, themes and importance of the Bardic schools of poets see Miss Eleanor Knott: *The Bardic Poems of Tadhg Dall O'Huiginn*, introd. pp. xxxiii–xxxiv.

[2] *The War of the Gael and the Gall* ('the War of the Irish with the Foreigners'), at first meaning the fight of the Irish with the Norsemen, has become a famous expressive phrase to describe the struggle of the native Irish race against the Norman and later English settlers.

the Irish language. The first form of the language, which had been written since 650, comes to an end about 950: this is Old Irish. Then succeeded till 1450 Middle Irish which, about the end of the medieval age, was gradually displaced by Early Modern Irish. The Norse ravages destroyed most of the manuscripts, and indeed mueh of the learning and civilization of the earlier age; it was partly at least in the monasteries that the task of reconstructing and writing down the old literature and traditional lore was undertaken. But in their place arose in the eleventh century permanent schools of learning controlled by, and meant for, the lay *filí*, scholars, and *literati*, in which the native literature was cultivated and preserved. Successively the hereditary literary families began and the functions of the learned branched away from one another. We may say that it was at the beginning of the thirteenth century, and after the first Norman onslaught had spent itself (about 1200), the bardic poets begin, and the schools of the learned are finally found everywhere in the Gaelic and even in the Norman-Irish parts of the island.

THE HISTORIANS

Our knowledge of Gaelic Ireland, and of its institutions, mentality, and history, right up to the ending of the native world under Elizabeth, has to be sought in the study of the native or Brehon laws, the poetry, the antiquarian tracts, the pedigrees, the semi-historic, semi-fictitious sagas such as *The War of the Gael and the Gall* or *The Triumphs of Cellachan of Cashel*, and, above all, in the historical annals, either in their drier and therefore more credible forms, or in their longer and more entertaining forms which merge into romance and panegyric.

We have thus mainly to depend from 1050 onwards upon the annals, those of the abbot Tighernach of Clonmacnois, ceasing in 1088 as his but continued to 1178; those of Ulster (431–1541); of Loch Cé (1014–1590); of Innisfallen (428–1321); of Clonmacnois (going to 1408); of MacFirbis (1443–68); of Boyle; of Connacht; and most famous of all, the Annals of the Four Masters, which begin with the legendary origins and end in 1616 with the whole Gaelic order.[1]

[1] Henceforth quoted as *Ann. Tig.*, *Ann. Ult.*, *Ann. L. Cé.*, *Ann. Innisfallen*, *Ann. Clon.*, *Ann. Boyle*, *Ann. Connacht*, *Ann. MacFirbis*, *A.F.M.* The 'true' annals of Innisfallen (in the Bodleian) have lately been reproduced by MacNeill and Best. There are 'pseudo-annals' of Innisfallen, an eighteenth-century compilation, the best MS. of which is in T.C.D. They have value, however, and material not in the 'true annals of Innisfallen', or in any other extant ones. We quote them as *Bodleian* and *Dublin Annals of Innisfallen* respectively. Those of MacFirbis and Clonmacnois survive only in a quaint English rendering.

At least the historians had created and circulated a legend of Irish unity and antiquity going back to venerable times. In the Scandinavian period a number of writers and poets, whom a great authority calls the 'Synthetic Historians', built up the concept of a history which goes back to the Flood, of the coming of the first ancestor of the Gaels, Milesius of Spain, and of the primeval monarchy of Tara, as equated with world-history. The *Leabhar Gabhála* ('Book of Invasions'), put into writing about 1050, summed up the fictions, traditions, and facts thus collected, and the whole fabricated story, which, if not history, contains many aids to history, had become fully accepted by the time the Normans came, and was unhesitatingly believed by Keating in the seventeenth century.[1]

Further, the poets had stamped upon the Irish mind a poetic conception of Ireland, symbolized as a woman, Éire, Fodhla, or Banba. Such a mixture of ancient pedigree and claim to the soil of Erin and the tenacious sentiment of race and pride in the Gaelic culture, which was now common with all the Gaelic princes, no matter how they fought between themselves, was to prove a stubborn barrier to the English conquest, which took over four centuries to achieve. Seldom has any native aristocracy been so proud and haughty, conservative and untemporizing, as the Gaelic aristocracy of Ireland and the *intelligentsia* which supported it. They took unquestioningly and solemnly their imaginative pedigree of three thousand years in this island, and to them every new-comer who entered it was a foreigner—*Gall*, a word they applied successively to Norsemen, Normans, and the later English settlers. In fact, the Goidelic Celts themselves had only entered Ireland between 500 and 300 B.C., to conquer and spread themselves slowly over the Bronze Age inhabitants. As a warlike race of conquerors they came, as a war-loving aristocracy they remained, never made 'civil' in the Roman or modern sense, and keeping up almost till the days of Shakespeare the tradition of the Hero-age as it exists in Homer and in the Teutonic and Celtic epics.

THE HIGH KINGSHIP

From A.D. 483 to 1000, for five centuries, with only one serious intermission, the Ui Néill had held the title of Árd Rí, the office alternately passing between the kings of the north and the kings of Meath, who alike sprang from the great Niall of the Nine Hostages, the name-giver. The fatal breach in this succession was made by Brian Boru who, beginning as petty king of the Dal Cais

[1] See Professor Eoin MacNeill in a chapter of his *Celtic Ireland* (1921).

(the Dalcassians) of Thomond, secured the throne of Cashel, then the sovereignty of the Southern Half of Ireland, then the High kingship of Tara itself. The hereditary sanction once violated, it was henceforth open to every province-king to enforce or win the homage of his equals and be recognized as Árd Rí. Brian's name and fame indeed enabled his descendants for a century to claim and for a period to secure the supreme monarchy, but the real struggle of 'kings with opposition' had in fact begun with his successful usurpation.

The rule of eligibility for the High kingship is stated thus in the annals of Clonmacnois under 1041: 'If the king of Leth Mogha (the Southern Half) can command Munster, Leinster and Tara (Meath) and in addition Connacht or Ulster, he is fit to be Árd Rí, but the king of Leth Cuinn (the Northern Half) need have only one other province at command, namely Leinster or Munster.'[1]

About the year A.D. 200 Eoghan, called also Mogh Nuadat ('devotee of the god Nuada'), king of Munster, had been the rival of Conn Céd-cathach, the ancestor of Niall of the Nine Hostages, and a treaty ended the contest by which Ireland was divided into Conn's Half and Mogh's Half, a division marked by a line of sandhills, the 'Escir Riada', stretching from Dublin to Galway. The division remained a permanent one, which even as late as 1642 made the Irish of Munster reluctant to accept the leadership of the northern O'Neills. From Eoghan Mór the kings of Munster were henceforth called the Eoghanacht till Brian Boru deposed this stock.

In the twelfth century any province-king from Meath, Leinster, Ulster or Cashel who could battle-axe his way into sufficient acceptance could become High king when a majority of the seven under-kings of Ireland had 'gone into his house' and done homage to him, a kind of feudal submission.[2] The next token of loyalty was the giving of hostages to the new Árd Rí, who thereupon distributed stipends of kine, horses, gold, and armour to his vassals.

[1] The *Book of Rights* (*Leabhar na gCeart*) as edited under Brian Boru, says that only the kings of Leinster, Meath, Aileach, and Cashel (Munster) are eligible for the High kingship.

The *Ann. Clon.*, which survive only in an English version of a lost Irish original by Connell Mageoghegan in 1627, are not too authentic, but the above tradition seems credible and worthy of respect.

[2] Thus in 1161 Murchertach MacLochlainn became Árd Rí by securing the homage of Leinster, Connacht, Meath, Brefni, Dublin. Actually native chroniclers accept five kings after Maelsechlainn (died in 1022) as 'kings of Ireland with opposition,' viz. Turloch O'Brien (1064–86), his son Murchertach, Domnall MacLochlainn, Turloch More O'Connor, Murchertach MacLochlainn, and Rory O'Connor (*Genealogiae Regum etc. by the Four Masters*, ed. Rev. Paul Walsh, 1937).

This was done during the 'circuit of the High king', in which the newly accepted monarch travelled sunwise round Ireland, spending some thirteen months on the journey and receiving everywhere the submission of the local chiefs, the promise of their military service, and 'the great tribute to the king of Erin' paid in tributes of food, cattle, swine, etc. While they showed their acceptance of him as supreme king by their tributes, homage and hostages, he emphasized their vassalage of him by gifts and stipends (*tuarasdail*). In theory an accepted High king could call out the whole military levy of Ireland. Rarely, however, did the whole island obey, and it is certain that had all Ireland obeyed the slogan in 1170 against Dermot MacMurrough and his thousand or two of Normans, the latter could scarcely have survived.[1]

A fatal defect in the monarchy of Erin was the lack of an acknowledged capital. Tara, the sacred centre which recalled the pagan ages, decayed after the reception of Christianity. The last royal feast or 'Féis' was held there by the half-pagan High king Diarmaid in 559. Nevertheless the sanctity of this hill, the site of kings from the Bronze Age, was always admitted; the local king of Meath was styled king of Tara right up to 1170; and the hill is called in the *Book of Rights* 'the supreme seat of the monarch of Ireland'. Instead of the old sites of Emain Macha, Rath Croghan, Dinn Righ, and Cashel, by the twelfth century the province-kings had moved to more stragetic capitals or sacred places such as Armagh, or had imposed themselves on the Norse cities of Dublin, Cork, Limerick.

The political structure of the Irish monarchy and sub-kingdoms is sketched in the *Book of Rights*, a remarkable tract in Irish which was drawn up first about A.D. 900, and then revised about 1000 by direction of Brian Boru and in order to serve his ambitions.[2] In the latter version the right of Cashel, the seat of the Munster kings, to full supremacy over Ireland is asserted, and her monarch may, if he is powerful enough, lawfully enjoy the High kingship in the same way as Aileach (Ulster), Tara (Meath), and Leinster already do. In other words, the ancient monopoly of the Ui Néill is abolished and the High kingship is thrown open to a competition to which Cashel is admitted. Ireland is represented as a heptarchy, composed of Munster, Leinster, Connacht, Meath, Aileach, Oriel, and Ulidia.[3]

[1] A prerogative and token of being High king also was to hold the *Aonach* (Fair or national assembly) of Tailten in Meath, as was done by Brian and Malachy in 1007, Turloch O'Connor in 1120, and Rory O'Connor in 1168.

[2] *Leabhar na gCeart*. This is scientifically discussed by Professor Eoin MacNeill in his *Celtic Ireland* (1921).

[3] Oriel (Airghialla) was a state founded in the fourth century by princes of the royal race of Connacht. Aileach was another founded early in the fifth

The *Book of Rights* details the *jura* of the Irish dynasts, the obligations of the province-kings and their states towards the Árd Rí, and the rents and services due to themselves from their underlords. The rents, tributes, and stipends are paid in cattle, jewels, slaves, weapons, garments, silver, but there is no mention of coin. 'The great tribute to the king of Erin' has to be paid to the supreme monarch at his accession and during his 'circuit of Ireland', but apparently only once and on that occasion. The Árd Rí, however, was also king of his own province, whence he received recurrent profits and services and in which he had, like all the Irish dynasts, royal or 'mensal' land for his support.

THE POWERS OF THE HIGH KING

Apart from the hostages, and the homage which was sworn on sacred relics, the Árd Rí had various ways of securing loyalty. He could invade a subject king's territory and set up another in his place, or have him deposed by some national assembly. He alone could call out the whole national army. The whole system of law had its apex in the High king. Every king of a petty state (*tuath*) presided over the cases in his country and his brehons made the awards. The province-king judged and ruled among the kings of the *tuatha*, and the High king judged among his vassals, the province-kings, and his royal brehon was the supreme jurisprudent for all Ireland.[1]

The strength of the Irish king consisted in his own demesnes and in his own province. Though the High kingship had much prestige, it had suffered much by the dispossession of the sacred Ui Néill by the usurping Brian Boru. He and his line tried to remedy this by an *entente* with Armagh, like that which the

century by two sons of Niall of the Nine Hostages, Eoghan and Conall. Ulidia represented all that was left of the great prehistoric kingdom of the Ulaidh or Ulster, reduced by attacks of its neighbours to the modern Antrim and Down. The state founded by Eoghan is variously called the kingdom 'of Aileach' (from its dún-capital), and 'of the North (*an Fochla*)'; its ruling race is called the Ui Néill of the North and 'Cinel Eoghain' ('Race of Eoghan'), and their particular domain was Tír Eoghain ('the land of Eoghan'). We prefer to use the name Tír Eoghan or Tyrone for this kingdom, which by 1170 had more or less overpowered Ulidia and Oriel, and Cinel Eoghain (Kinel Owen) for its ruling race.

[1] While making the best case for the monarchy of Ireland we must not overstate it. Even if we only compare the Gaelic Árd Rí and the Norman king of England in two details, we find that (1) the High king could not, on pain of forfeiture of their estates, call out the chiefs of Ireland to do military service as and where he wished to lead them, as the feudal king of England could with his barons, and (2) the Irish king was not *dominus terrae* (supreme landlord) as the English king was, who conferred lands and lordships, privileges and jurisdictions, by charter, and from whom, down to the humblest tenant in England, all titles to freehold land were ultimately derived.

Anglo-saxon house of Egbert established with Canterbury. In 1002 Brian had recognized the traditional supremacy of Armagh over all Ireland and laid a gift of gold on the altar of the great church there. The transaction is commemorated by an entry of his scribe in the *Book of Armagh*.[1] In 1103 Brian's descendant, Murchertach, again left a tribute of gold on the high altar of Armagh, and on his part the archbishop, Celsus, made the visitation of Munster and received tribute from the states of that kingdom.

THE PROVINCE-KINGDOMS

The election of Cathal Crovderg O'Connor as king of Connacht in 1202 gives us a glimpse into the history of the *aireacht* or council which elected and advised the monarch, and the rule of kingly succession among the Irish.[2]

The ceremony, which took place according to ancient ritual at Carnfree (Carn Fraoich) near Tulsk, is typical of the election (*righadh* or 'enkinging') of a provincial dynast. Twelve *coarbs* (ancient bishop-abbots) and twelve chief lords were present. These were the immediate electors; each had some hereditary office and some function to perform, for example MacDermot was O'Connor's marshal, and each received rich stipends after the event, while O'Mulconry, chief historian, completed the ceremony by putting the rod of office into O'Connor's hand. These lay chiefs who elected O'Connor were 'royal chieftains', that is, they were the heads of septs which were of close kin to him and sprang from the same kingly race, the Siol Muiredaigh, hence they were free of all duties save the hosting. But there were also present other vassals of the king, whose line had branched off from the royal line of Connacht many centuries earlier: among these 'free

[1] The ancient *Book of Armagh*, ed. Rev. Dr. J. Gwynn. The whole Latin entry is as follows: '*Sanctus patri[ci]us iens ad coelum mandauit totum fructum laboris sui tam babtismi tam causarum quam elemoisinarum deferendum esse apostolicae urbi quae scotice nominatur ardd macha. Sic reperi in bibliothecis Scotorum. Ego scripsi, id est Calvus perennis in conspectu Briani imperatoris Scotorum et que scripsi finivit pro omnibus regibus Maceriae.*'—('The holy Patrick, going to heaven, ordained that all the fruit of his labour both as regards baptism and causes ecclesiastical and questions of alms should go to the apostolic city of Armagh. So I have found in the books of the Irish. I, Maelsuthain, have written this in the presence of Brian, High king of the Gaelic race, and what I have written he has accepted for all the kings of Cashel.')

[2] The tract, *The Inauguration of Cathal Crovderg*, written down in 1315, is edited by O'Daly in the *Journal of the Kilkenny Arch. Soc.* (1853). The Síol Muiredaigh, of whom the O'Connors were the senior branch, descended from Muiredach, king of Connacht, about 700. The *aireacht*, right up to Elizabethan times, is called by the English 'yraght', 'urraght', etc., signifying a chief and the body of his immediate vassals.

and kingly clans' were O'Ruairc, O'Reilly, O'Hara, and other chiefs of Connacht.

This form of inauguration, which went back to pagan times, was observed in 1315 at Felim O'Connor's election. In similar fashion up to the end of the sixteenth century was O'Neill enkinged at Tullahoge. This ceremony of close aristocratic election emphasized from reign to reign the mere life-tenure of the king's office, and thus the elected O'Connor was set up in the eyes of all the ruling races of his province as representing that ancient founder's kin of Brion and later of Muiredach, from which their own blood had diverged.

The practice of enkinging in the open air has been described by various writers, Irish and foreign. Spenser, in his *View of Ireland*, speaks of it as still common in the sixteenth century. The last effective instance was in 1592, when Red Hugh O'Donnell was inaugurated lord of his country on the Rock of Doon near Kilmacrenan, 'in the legal way that was the custom of the royal race hitherto'.[1]

No such solemn and general inauguration was applied to the 'King of all Erin'. The Árd Rí became so by submission and acceptance, by taking of homage and hostages of the province-kings, receiving their tributes and giving them wages (*tuarasdail*) in token of their vassalage, and by doing the 'circuit of the High king'. There is little trace of consecration by the Church for any form of monarchy, which in Ireland was pagan rather than Christian. In 892, according to the annals of Ulster, Muirecan, abbot-bishop of Armagh, conferred the 'degree of king' upon Aedh, son of Domnall, but it was only as king of Aileach.

ELECTIVE KINGSHIP

The kingship of Ireland was politically divided into provinces or *cúigí* (from *cúige*, a fifth), a word which recalled the older pentarchy. Each of the dynasts was called a *Rí cúige* or province-king. The *tuath* (an ancient name for tribe or people, and so for the tribal territory) was the basis of the political organization. Roughly there were about a hundred of these in pre-Norman Ireland. Several of them might be grouped into *mór-tuatha* ('great tuaths'), each having its Rí. Thus Laighis or Leix formed one *mór-tuath* of seven *tuatha* under the royal race of Ó Mordha. The Árd Rí himself might well be chief of a 'great tuath', and the territory of Síol Muiredaigh (most of the modern county of

[1] *Life of Red Hugh O'Donnell*, by Lughaidh O'Clery (ed. Denis Murphy, 1895), pp. xliii, 43. The erenach O'Friel proclaimed him 'O'Donnell'.

Roscommon with portions of Galway and Sligo) was O'Connor's personal demesne as king of Connacht.[1]

Native Ireland had many 'kings', high and low. A cognate of the Latin *rex,* as applied to an Irish king the word 'rí' recalls more the petty kings of early Rome or primitive Europe than the imperial, crowned, and anointed 'Rex Angliae' or 'Franciae' of the great medieval countries. How far down in the scale the title descended in Milesian Ireland we cannot be positive, or how many centres of local inauguration there were; it is probable that by the twelfth century the title and inauguration ceremony were becoming limited to the greater monarchs. But tradition and survival are so strong in Irish society with its pedantic record-keepers, who went on repeating themselves, and our knowledge is so scanty as yet, that no clear dating or development can at present be essayed. In Cathal O'Connor's grant to Citeaux we note how his sub-kings call themselves *dux* or *comes.* This may be a concession to Continental ignorance of Irish kingship, but it seems probable that *tighearna* (lord) and *taoiseach* (chief) would eventually have become the designation of the less-than-kings.[2] But up till the Tudor age the 'urrighs' (*Oir-righthe* or 'under-kings') of Gaelic Ireland, vassals of the great O'Neill or MacCarthy More, etc., were a prominent feature, and it seems as if the Norman invasion of Ireland had the unlooked-for result of reviving the powers of the local chiefs as real petty kings.[3]

LOCAL GOVERNMENT

There was no parallel in native Ireland to the hundred and shire courts of the Anglo-Saxons, but there were periodical meetings either of provinces or districts for settling law cases and promulgating local or general ordinances. These were attended in great numbers by the free classes, and in Elizabeth's days it was noted

[1] A name corresponding originally, it would seem, to the *tuath* was *tricha cét* ('thirty hundreds'). The Normans equated this with the word 'cantred', which they introduced. It is clear, however, that by 1100 the *tricha céd* was generally much larger than the *tuath,* probably it represented the absorption of several *tuaths* in one larger unit. Giraldus evidently equates *tricha céd* and cantred (in Welsh *cantref*), for he defines the latter as consisting of a hundred villages (*villae*) with thirty families in each (i.e. three thousand families in all). (See Hogan, 'The Tricha Cét', *P. R. I. A.*, 1929.)

[2] *Meguidhir Fermanach,* an historical tract relating to the fourteenth century, though of seventeenth century recension (ed. Rev. P. Dinneen), shows Maguire, lord of Fermanagh, appointing the heads of the twelve *tuatha* which comprised that country (p. 75). But Maguire himself was vassal of O'Donnell and rose by his favour in the fourteenth century.

For Cathal O'Connor's charter, see p. 141 of the first edition of this book.

[3] 'Urragh' or 'urraght' (confused with *aireacht*) was the Anglo-Norman of this word. Henceforth we use the abbreviated form 'urrigh'.

how attached the Irish were to these 'parles upon hills', and how loyally they observed their own statutes. The kings held their *aireachta*, or courts of their vassals and electors, how frequently we know not. The lawsuits of the noble and the simple free classes were tried in courts corresponding to the tribal courts of all the Germans, Celts, and non-romanized races of Europe. The two chief marks of a freeman were to carry arms and have a vote in the tribal assembly.

The brehon class, the jurisconsults and experts in Irish law, who made their awards in the midst of the nobles and freemen, and were rewarded with part of the fines, were so numerous that every *tuath* must have maintained its own. The *breitheamh* (brehon) was a pleader, arbiter, and exponent of the law; every king, high or low, was there to preside over the trials, to impose the penalties and enforce them. The Irish Rí, great or small, received a personal demesne to support him in his office out of the 'royal land', from which his nearer kin had also to be provided for; along with that he got the tributes and military service of his country and the right to quarter mercenaries (*ámuis*) on the whole territory by the right of *buannacht* or billeting.

At the basis of all was the free family or kin, the 'Fine'.[1] Society was based on kinship, and a man should have his family group to answer for him in court or pay whatever penalties the court might impose upon him, and to be answerable for payment of tributes and services.

The law presupposed that the land of the free kin (*fine*) could not be alienated without consent of all its members, but in fact the possession of private land was sanctioned. The spoils of war, whether in acres or in booty, became hereditary and personal property, and the more a king or lord could win of land, wealth, and vassals, the greater his son would be. In the struggle for land and lordship, the greater kings had all the advantage. Feudalism thus grew and in time might have produced its own remedy, the feudal monarch.

'TRIBAL' IRELAND

An eminent authority combats the legend that Gaelic society was based upon tribalism or, as he calls it, the clan system.[2] But clearly it was a society based more upon the blood-tie and long

[1] 'Fine' is pronounced 'finna'. It had four branches, viz. *geil-fine*, *derb-fine*, *iar-fine*, and *ind-fine*.

[2] Eoin MacNeill in his *Phases of Irish History* and *Celtic Ireland*. A chapter in the latter book deals with the 'Law of Dynastic Succession' (pp. 230–2) and describes the *derb-fine* rule. Professor James Hogan has written the latest treatise on the subject in *P.R.I.A.* (1932), 'The Law of Irish Kingship'.

male ancestry than was Anglo-Norman England. The Irish medieval king, like the kings of England and France, legislated and governed 'by the advice of his barons', and his *aireacht* was a sort of *curia regis*. But in England the barons were territorial magnates of no antiquity, and often enemies to the Anglo-Saxons they governed, and it was possible for the Crown which had enfeoffed them also to depose them. In Ireland the Gaelic king's 'barons' were heads of powerful families allied in blood to the king himself, and associated by history and popular choice with the territory they governed.

The ruling races had all the Celtic pride of pedigree, for genealogies which proved a man's noble descent proved also his claim to kingship and land. That the king should be of kindred blood to his subjects, nearly or remotely, was essential, and an O'Connor, for example, foisted upon Meath ran the risk of being murdered by some partisan of the lawful O'Melaghlin as 'a stranger in sovereignty'.[1] That the primitive blood-tie and patriarchal lordship should endure more bindingly in Ireland than in England was natural, for almost alone of European nations the Irish Gaels had held their ancient seat and preserved their social structure for over a thousand years.

THE 'O' AND 'MAC' PATRONYMICS

From the year A.D. 900 had begun the general adoption of the patronymics formed with *Ua* (*O*) and *Mac*, meaning 'grandson' and 'son', combined with the name of some royal hero or founder of the line. The most famous early example is O'Neill, sprung from the High king Niall Glúndubh, who was slain in the battle of Dublin in 919, who himself was head of the old Ui Néill stock of the north. From Brian Boru came the O'Briens of Munster; from a Lochlann of the Cinel Eoghain the name MacLochlainn; from Maelsechlainn, the last High king of the old Ui Néill of Meath, the O'Melaghlins; while Taig 'an Eich Ghil' (of the bright steed), who died in 1030 as king of Connacht, was the first O'Connor, grandson of the name-giver Conchobar.

THE 'DERB-FINE' RULE

The right of succession to the kingship was by law limited to those who had the designation of *rigdomna* (meaning 'royal heir', or 'makings of a king') that is, the male descendants, down to the great-grandsons, of a reigning chief, who formed the *derb-fine* or

[1] See later, p. 20.

'true family'. Women and claims through women were disallowed in the kingship. Many an internecine war rose out of the custom, for if a *rigdomna* who was on the outside edge of his *derb-fine* failed by force or favour to become king in his own time his descendants were for ever excluded from the succession. On the other hand, if he were elected, he perpetuated a fresh *derb-fine*. An ambitious man would be tempted therefore to strive for the kingship even if his claims were small. It was the great defect of the rule; the merit of which was that, owing to the numbers of eligible heirs, the royal stock was seldom likely to expire.[1]

Much remains to be investigated on this question of Irish kingship, so unlike anything else in European history. But it would appear that the exercise of the kingship (*ríge*), which was the perquisite of a ruling race such as the Cinel Eoghain of Ulster (the senior descendants of the original conqueror Eoghan), presented a problem. The Cinel Eoghain had the right to the lands or demesnes of their lordship ('Tír' or 'Inis Eoghain'), and these they could easily apportion among themselves from generation to generation. But how was their kingship or *regnum* of Aileach to be divided? It appears that the ruling stock itself, that is, the immediate royal heirs, would meet upon a vacancy in the kingship and decide which of themselves, best fitted in seniority and mental and physical qualities, should be chosen king of Cinel Eoghain, because kingship cannot be divided like land. But inasmuch as a claim in the kingship belonged to them all jointly, they did not surrender a possible claim in themselves as 'royal heirs'. The king being once chosen by his own royal stock or cousins, it remained only for his chief vassals, some of whom were of close kin to the royal stock, and some further off from a time before the O' and Mac rule was established, to meet and accept him by inauguration in the open air according to ancient rites, the local abbots and bishops uniting with them after Christian times began; upon which their voice was confirmed by the applause or acceptance of the inferior classes who had come to witness the ceremony.[2]

As a theoretic law, this system of electoral choice out of a limited royal group seems reasonable and fair, but in fact an elective system which led to constant disputes and changes of succession from a chief to his nephew or his cousin worked badly. Lineal descent and primogeniture seemed to be winning ground with

[1] MacNeill in *Phases* (op. cit.) says that there is no evidence of *rigdomna* before 867, after which date the son generally succeeds and sometimes the grandson, i.e. hereditary succession was displacing the older free election.

[2] After the adoption of 'O' and 'Mac', it would be the narrowed royal stock of the O'Neills, senior of all the Cinel Eoghain septs, who chose the king first.

some royal families such as the race of Brian, but the *derb-fine* rule of free election had a way of asserting itself, and in the case of the O'Connors after 1270 led to such succession disputes as to ruin this distinguished family. When it came to clash with the Anglo-Norman law of succession in the eldest son, the advantages of the latter system were clearly displayed.

THE RANKS OF SOCIETY

The social grades of the ancient Irish and the features of their law are matters for experts, and though much neglected up to this they are now being scientifically studied.[1] It is enough here to say how much they resemble the institutions and codes of the other northern races which Rome did not conquer or influence. In the atonements for offences, for example, the *eric* or fine for homicide, the *enachlann* or 'honour-price', and the *corp-dire* or wergild, are very reminiscent of Anglo-Saxon law. It would appear that, while the Gaels boasted of their 'free citizenship', great masses, possibly a majority, of the population were unfree, a status ranging from house-slaves to servile tenants. The demesnes of kings, lords, and abbots were worked for them by serfs called *biataigh*, who appear to have been more depressed than the Anglo-Norman villein and were a very numerous and widespread class.[2] Noble freemen (*flatha*) and simple freemen (*céiles*) and semi-bond and servile tenants were characteristic of Irish as of Teutonic society.

There seems to be no reason for calling the Irish social structure 'democratic'. It was aristocratic from top to bottom, and it would be better to call it (that is to say, the free classes that counted in arms, property, politics, and law) 'aristocratic-republican', for the top structure of the nobility (the 'free races') elected and checked the kings, but themselves ruled Ireland like the original military conquerors that they were. To be put under tribute, legal inferiority, rent, and other galling conditions was to be the lot of them after the Norman invasion, but while and as long as they could resist such a *diminutio capitis* they did so.

The death penalty was seldom imposed in Irish law, and the severe and numerous punishments of English law shocked the

[1] Professor Eoin MacNeill's *Phases* (op. cit.) deals in original fashion with the *céile* tenants of Irish law, and the question of free citizenship, etc. Professor Thurneysen has contributed to the subject in German, and see Binchy and Dillon, 'Studies in Early Irish Law', *P.R.I.A.* (1936).

[2] For the 'betagh' class, see Appendix IV on 'Legal Treatment of the Irish'. O'Donovan (*A.F.M.*, III, p. 27) says the *biatach* (food-provider) held land on condition of providing *biadh* (food) to the lord or his retainers and that the *ballybetagh* (*baile biatach*) was a thirtieth part of the *tricha céd*.

Irish, but the treacherous murder of a king or chief was atoned for by a penalty ranging from mere execution up to burning alive. In such ways, as well as by ancient pagan tabus, was the sanctity of the royal person maintained.

INCIPIENT FEUDALISM

In its complete form, medieval feudalism, as perfected in England under the Normans, and extended later to Ireland, means the holding of land of a superior lord (who may be the king, in which case the holder is a tenant-in-chief or baron of the Crown) by military and allied services. With the holding of the land goes jurisdiction of some kind. The succession to the land is hereditary as long as the conditions are observed, and the descent is from father to eldest surviving son, but might go to females in default of male heirs. The land is held of the lord, hence sovereignty and the ultimate ownership of land is vested in some one above. In feudal society authority comes *from above*; but in patriarchal society, such as the Irish, *from the people*, that, is, from the ruling and free classes.

This form of feudalism was well established in England by 1100, but in native Ireland, though feudal *tendencies* pointed the way, the advance to a feudal *organization* was but small. When the clash came in 1170 between Norman feudalism and Celtic patriarchy, the victory of the former as a political and military machine was rapid.

To grant lands and privileges by charter was among the highest prerogatives of feudal monarchy. Something of this had existed for centuries in Ireland as part of the royal function. The consent of the lord of a *mór-tuath* was necessary to grants made in the *tuath*, confirmation by the province-king was essential within his kingdom, and grants made by a province-king needed the confirmation of the High king in virtue of his final overlordship.

As an example, in 1161 Murchertach MacLochlainn, king of Aileach and High king, gave a charter in Latin to the new Cistercian abbey of Newry in which as 'Mauritius mag Lochlain Rex totius Hiberniae' he addresses 'universis magnatibus suis, subregulis, principibus, ducibus, clericis et laicis omnibusque et singulis Hiberniensibus presentibus et futuris', and, by will and consent of the kings and magnates of Ulster, Oriel, and Iveagh, grants certain lands named to the abbey. The witnesses are the archbishop of Armagh, four Ulster bishops, eleven *reges* and *duces*, and many others, cleric and lay. Here the Árd Rí makes a grant in the territory of his vassal, the king of Iveagh, who gives his assent, and the bishops of all Ulster and the chiefs of a large part of the province attest the grant.[1]

Grants of this formal nature, however, which have come down to us are few and mainly of the twelfth century; they are obviously due to the influence of the foreign Cistercian monks recently introduced, and they attest the importation of feudal ideas. Moreover they are made to the Church, whereas English land-grants and charters had long since begun to include the laity also.

It might be argued that by 1100 the only chance of survival for an independent state in the west of Europe was to turn feudal. For Gaelic Ireland to survive otherwise would have required far greater unity, patriotism, and wisdom than her princes and bishops showed when the crisis of 1170 came. Anglo-saxon England, though on the way to feudalism, had succumbed completely a century before. The third of the insular kingdoms, Scotland, had shown how the problem in its case could be met. Of Malcolm III, king from 1057 to 1093, we are told that 'he made earls of the toparchs of the greater clans, who in Irish speech were called *mór-maers*; these toparchs were always of one and the same family'. Malcolm's son David, king of Scots from 1124 to 1153, turned the Gaelic chiefs (*mór-maers*) north of the Tweed into the seven hereditary feudal earls of Moray, Lennox, Fife, etc. and gave them charters for their fiefs. This was what Henry VIII did long after when he made earls of O'Neill and O'Brien. In Ireland the title 'Rí' was becoming limited to the provincial kings or at least the greater princes. The further step of turning the greater princes into earls under one supreme king of Ireland, however, was not to be achieved in Gaelic times.

Another power of monarchy, the legislative, was not lacking to Irish kings. Sometimes the monarch acted on advice of his council, sometimes he judged and legislated in the midst, and with the consent, of great national assemblies. In 858 we find Maelsechlainn, High king, and the bishop of Armagh presiding over a *Ríg Dáil maithe Erenn* ('royal gathering of the nobles of Erin') at Rath-Aedha, where 'peace was made throughout all Ireland and Cervall, king of Ossory, submitted to the High king according to the decision of the Successor of Patrick'.[2]

[1] Dugdale, *Monasticon Anglicanum* (1830), vol. VI, pt. II, p. 1133. For other such grants see that of Baldoyle by Dermot MacMurrough (p. 31); and O'Donovan, *Irish Charters in the Book of Kells* (*Miscell. Irish Arch. Society* (1846), pp. 127–58). Kenney, *Sources for the Early History of Ireland* (*Ecclesiastical*), pp. 754–6, fully describes them.

Subreguli, in MacLochlainn's charter, is an interesting translation of *oir-righte* ('urrighs').

[2] *Fragments of Irish Annals* (ed. O'Donovan), *sub* 858.

Thus, though the Irish monarchy was tardy in its growth, there was in a sense a national will and a central command. These national assemblies were often incomplete, for Munster always resented the supremacy of the north. Still, a strong king, acting as final arbiter, might in time through such assemblies and with such powers have enforced a central monarchy. Hereditary succession and unity in one dynasty, however, was needed and this, after 1014, could not be achieved. And it must be admitted that local pride, patriotism, and privileges offered a tenacious opposition to a centralizing autocracy. The king of England after 1066 was emphatically a monarch over subjects, the Irish king was only a suzerain over vassals. The Anglo-Norman kingdom was hereditary. The Irish king, no matter how powerful personally, was but an elected life-president, and there was no security for his province or his heir continuing in supremacy.

The weaknesses of the political system and of the rules of monarchic succession are obvious. Possibly had Brian Boru left a strong son behind him and he again a strong son, an hereditary monarch might have unified and saved Ireland. But the local resistance to centralism was great, and, for the creation of an Irish state in the modern sense, someone as great and ruthless as William the Conqueror would have had to appear, with competent successors, able to evolve a competent and impersonal machinery of government. The office of High king, which even such a strong man as Brian or Turloch O'Connor found it hard to make real, was normally checked by seven under-kings, the real rulers of Ireland. Within the kingdoms the land was divided again into divisions known as *mór-tuatha*, *tuatha*, and *tricha céd*. But even the boundaries of these fluctuated. By 1170 the *tuath* had become little more than the size of the parish with which the Normans often equated it. The *tricha céd*, which was an area of 'thirty hundreds' of population, was also disappearing as a unit. How little we know of the exactitude of figures relating to pre-Norman Ireland! In the *Book of Rights* Munster has twenty states in all, eight free and twelve tributary. In 1175 we find that Desmond or south Munster alone has thirty-one cantreds. How is one to equate all this?

THE MILITARY SYSTEM

An eminent authority maintains that the Irish, after St. Patrick ceased to be a military race and that effective organization for war was lacking until the Norse invasions. Even then, armour and an established military order did not appear till the thirteenth century and in answer to the feudal attack. In the early times 'a war as a rule meant a single battle, and in the early annals, which were written in Latin, the word *bellum*, which in Latin means a war, is always used to mean a single battle'.[1] However this view may be maintained, Ireland was certainly full of weaponed men and the annals abound in fights wherein many fell, *nobiles atque ignobiles*. The king or chief had mercenaries either to guard his person, to carry out forays and raids against his enemies and neighbours, or to collect his rents, and to quarter on his tenants by the rule of *coinmhe* (maintenance). The freemen all had the right and duty to bear arms, and when the levy of a kingdom was called out or, as at times, the whole national levy at the High king's command, the numbers were imposing and the subsequent encounter a notable one.

From the evidence, however, both of the Irish themselves and foreigners such as Giraldus Cambrensis, it is clear that the Irish were only amateur and occasional fighters. They came to battle on foot in linen tunics, wore no armour or helmets, unless some prominent hero assumed such for glory rather than protection, and they used only slings, skeins (knives), swords, javelins, small bows, and an effective but small axe wielded in a single hand. They were essentially light troops, like the later kerns, 'naked' (that is, unarmoured) men, and though the kings and nobles felt it a matter of honour to be slain rather than scatter, the mass of the infantry, mere farmers untrained in campaigns, thought it little shame to do so. We shall see how in September 1171 the High king's whole army was disgracefully routed by the professional Norman troops.

Apart from political and military weaknesses, several of what are considered the requisites of a true civilization were lacking in twelfth-century Ireland. There was no coinage, save among the Norsemen of Dublin and Waterford, and ring-money or pieces of gold and silver measured in ounces served for barter and tribute.[2] The Irish were not a naval race. Both on land and on sea they had ceased to be the raiding, warlike race of before St. Patrick's time. It was the Ostmen, or Irish-Norse people of the coast towns, who were Ireland's traders, carriers, pilots, seamen, and who, in their galleys propelled by oar and sail, served the Irish dynasts in war or traded freely with Britain and Scandinavia.

The real wealth and medium for exchange and the payment of fines, etc. was indeed in cattle. Ireland was a country of abundant

[1] MacNeill, *Phases*, pp. 224, 235, 251, 267, 325.

[2] There are extant coins of Ifars (Ivar), Norse king of Limerick in 993, and of Askel MacTorkel, earl of Dublin in 1159, and other Ostman rulers. (See Lindsay, *Coinage of Ireland*.)

flocks and herds, horses, oxen, sheep, kine, and swine. Her rich prairies, plentiful grass, and soft climate made her for this an ideal land. In a land so fertile as Ireland, which the contemporary Giraldus praised highly for her temperate climate, there was no lack of every kind of food, though the humidity was somewhat against the due ripening of corn and fruit. 'The tillage land', he says, 'is exuberantly rich, the fields yielding large crops of corn, herds of cattle graze on the mountains, the woods abound with wild animals.' But he adds that though the crops give great promise when in the grain, the yield is small, 'the barns are loaded with the produce, but the granaries only show scanty returns'.

Town life was alien to Irish civilization till the Norsemen arrived. The Gaels were a rural and open-air people, attached to the free life, and living in open raths, dúns, and cashels. In so far as they had towns, these were the monastic centres such as Glendaloch, Durrow, and Kildare, which are often called 'cities' (*civitates*). There were a considerable population in these monastic towns and many stone houses, for they were centres alike of learning, education, religion, art, and even trade, for fairs were held within their sanctuary. Thus in Armagh there were seven churches, and the city was divided into 'the Rath', 'the Great Third', 'the Third of Massan', and 'the Third of the Saxons', that is, the quarter anciently frequented by English students. Around these sacred places, and protected by their walls and holiness, hereditary craftsmen practised the metalwork which they carried to so high a level.

The Norse or Ostman fortresses of Dublin, Waterford, Wexford, Cork, and Limerick were the true towns of Ireland. Governed in the typical Scandinavian way by petty kings or earls (called by the Irish *mór-maers* or 'great stewards') and a thing or parliament of the free warriors, they had walls and stone houses, and a considerable population of traders and mariners within their gates. When the Normans came, the capture or submission of these strategic and fortified places, at the heads of the great rivers and bays, was very instrumental in securing the country for them.

Irish kings, high and low, lived in great earthen raths, dúns, and stone cashels protected by triple rings of earth or stone. On the inmost mound would be the king's or chief's wooden hall. There was as yet no stone architecture save in churches, and even the cashels were unroofed and open.

Roads connected the main centres of life. The five great highways which, since Conn Céd-cathach (*circa* A.D. 200), had stretched out on every side from Tara, namely Slighe Mór, Slighe Dála, Slighe Asail, Slighe Cualainn, and Slighe Midluachra were still in use. The numerous monasteries must have had roads leading to and from one another. The armies of the Normans found many highways available for their campaigns.

Nevertheless no great clearance of Ireland had ever been taken in hand, and Ireland was to prove to the invaders for centuries a very difficult country to traverse, with its mountains and forests, lakes, rivers, and boglands, affording great defence and power of resistance to the native race.

CHAPTER I

THE O'BRIEN HIGH KINGSHIP, 1014–1119

WITH the death of Murchertach O'Brien in 1119 ended the supremacy over Ireland founded by Brian Boru. Brian's monarchy had fallen at Clontarf, and his sons Taig and Donnchad up to 1064 were little more than kings of Cashel, that is Munster. Taig's son Turloch, the first to be called O'Brien ('grandson of Brian'), did something to revive the family tradition, and both he and his son Murchertach were regarded by the Papacy, Canterbury, the kings of England and Norway, and the princes of Wales as 'Rex Hiberniae'.[1] But after them began the strife of 'kings with opposition' (*righthe co fresabhra*) whose rivalry in the end ruined the Gaelic State.

The *Book of Rights* lays it down: 'When the king of Cashel is not king of Tara, he is king of the Southern Half.' According to this claim, O'Brien would be at least supreme over Munster, Leinster, Ossory, and Dublin. In fact the three last would resist such a claim until it could be enforced, and even in Munster there survived Eoghanacht pretenders, who regarded Brian and his race as usurpers.

RISE OF NEW ROYAL RACES

As a result of a process beginning about 900 and continuing till 1100 or so, there now emerged out of the older kingly stocks limited dynastic groups named after some hero or successful prince of the times, whose name, with 'O' (grandson) or 'Mac' (son) added, becomes the eponym of the sept.[2]

From the greatest of all these founders, Brian Boru, came the O'Brien kings of Munster and later of Thomond. From an Eoghanacht prince of 1050 came the MacCarthy kings of Desmond. From Maelsechlainn (anglicized Melaghlin), last of the Ui Néill

[1] See Ussher, *Veterum Epist. Hib. Principum Sylloge* (1632), henceforth quoted as Ussher, *Sylloge*. Also a paper by me in *J. of the Royal Soc. of Antiq. of Ireland* (1921), pp. 116–24, on 'Murchertach O'Brien, High King, and his Norman son-in-law'. (This journal is henceforth quoted as *R.S.A.I.*)

[2] The new 'O' names (or more strictly 'Ua') must be distinguished from the older 'Ui' form, implying descendants in general. Thus O'Neill implies a direct and limited family derived from Niall Glúndubh (slain in A.D. 919). The kingship of the Cinel Eoghain became narrowed down to his descendants, and kindred lines derived from the original Eoghan of A.D. 400 drop out of the succession. The word 'sept' is a convenient one, though it appears to be a corruption of the word 'sect', adopted by the English settlers to describe the Gaelic ruling families or clan-groups in general.

High kings, who died in 1022, came the O'Melaghlin kings of Meath. In Leinster MacMurrough, in Oriel O'Cervall, in Ulidia MacDunlevy (from one Donnslebhe) and in Ossory MacGillapatraic, established themselves. In Connacht, out of the original Síol Muredaigh came the O'Connors (*circa* 1030), while O'Ruairc of Brefni was founded by one Ruarc, grandson of Diarmaid, 'Tanist of Brefni', slain in 1024. In the kingdom of Aileach (or Tír Eoghain) and among the Cinel Eoghain stock, one Lochlainn, lord of Inishowen (*circa* 1020), founded the MacLochlainn line. This lasted for two centuries, but in the end their O'Neill cousins, who descended from the famous High king Niall Glúndubh, slain in 919, supplanted them. Similarly in Tír Conaill the ruling race was called O'Donnell from one Domnall of about 960, who founded the famous name that lasted till 1603. Rival branches called O'Maeldory and O'Cannanain disputed the succession, but by 1200 O'Donnell became supreme. As sprung from the younger brother Conall, the kings of Tír Conaill were nominal vassals of Tír Eoghain but did not easily admit it.[1]

THE ROYAL DEMESNES

Each of the ruling races had attached to it a large domain of 'royal' or 'mensal' land for the support of the king, his *derb-fine*, his kindred septs, his officials, and retainers. That of the Cinel Eoghain was in Inishowen and Tyrone. The demesne of O'Connor was Síol Muredaigh in the present Roscommon, Sligo, and Galway.

The patrimony of the MacMurrough kings of Leinster was the territory called Hy Kinsella (Ui Cinnselaigh) 'the land of the descendants of Cinnselach' (a fifth-century king of the province), which covered most of the present counties Wexford and Carlow and the great forest of Shillelagh in south-west Wicklow.

The Irish province-kings displayed in the century after Clontarf a considerable tendency to imitate the European monarchs of their time. They granted land-charters, built castles, and found more suitable capitals. Forsaking the ancient dúns and raths such as Croghan and Aileach, they built fortresses in the plains or along the great rivers. Especially did they turn their eyes on the seaports which the Scandinavian Ostmen had founded. Since Brian the latter had become vassals of the provincial kings. The first

[1] Eoghan and Conall, sons of Niall of the Nine Hostages, with a third brother called Enda, conquered north-west Ulster in the early fifth century. Henceforth I use the convenient form Tyrone for Tír Eoghain and Tyrconnell for Tír Conaill, though Tír Eoghain included—as well as the modern county Tyrone—south Derry and most of Armagh. The later O'Donnells are the Cinel Conaill (Kinel Konall).

Dermot, king of Leinster (1052–72), was also 'king of the Foreigners of Dublin', and in that city in 1052 entertained Earl Harold, son of Godwin, then a refugee from England. His successors were overlords also of Waterford and Wexford, and thus had three Norse towns at their disposal, but their inland or ordinary capital was at Ferns.

Kincora, near Killaloe, a *cathair* or stone-built open fortress, commanding Lough Derg, had been Brian Boru's capital, but Cashel was the ancient seat of the Munster kings. In 1101 the High king Murchertach presented the famous Rock to the Church, and the O'Briens, while still using Kincora, moved their capital to Limerick, the Ostmen of which were their vassals. So it happened with the Norse town of Cork. As the MacCarthys grew strong in the eleventh century, this Ostman stronghold on the southern sea passed into their hands and remained their capital till 1200.

The desertion of the old hill-fortresses, relics of a pagan and military past, is shown in the ease with which they could be profaned. The great stone castle of Aileach near Derry, built on a hill 600 feet high, had been the stronghold of Bronze Age kings from remote days before the Milesian conquerors Eoghan and Conall made it their capital about A.D. 400. In his great march to the north in 1101, Murchertach O'Brien demolished it apparently without any recorded resistance. The Cinel Eoghain had in fact removed themselves to the plains of Tyrone, and in 1106 appear at Tullahoge near Lough Neagh, where for centuries the O'Neills were inaugurated and near to which they built Dungannon.[1]

The capital of Connacht in the days of Queen Maeve had been Cruacha (now Rath Croghan), in Roscommon, but later the province-kings were inaugurated at Carnfree (Carn Fraoich) near Tulsk. The real capital of the O'Connors in the twelfth century was actually Tuam, and Galway, though there was no Ostman or other town there, seems to have been in their hands.[2] Thus, while the High king had no official capital as such, the local kings entrenched themselves in new and more effective centres. They even, though only in a few cases, began to imitate their feudal neighbours overseas in the art of castellation. Of those recorded in pre-Norman Ireland a certain example is that 'wonderful castle' (*caislen iongantach*), which the High king Rory O'Connor built at Tuam.[3]

[1] *Ann. Tig.* (1101, 1106).
[2] *A.F.M.* also state that in 1124 a castle (*caisteol*) was built at the mouth of the Corrib, i.e. where Galway stands.
[3] *Ann. Tig.* (1164).

THE RIVALRY OF THE KINGS

After the death of Brian, Ireland became again a heptarchy of states, namely Munster, Connacht, Leinster, Meath, Aileach, Oriel, and Ulidia, but actually only the first five counted in the struggle for supremacy.[1]

The northern Ui Néill, or Cinel Eoghain, as ruled by MacLochlainn, had moved down into the plain of central Ulster, whence they drove the Ulidians east of the Bann and Lough Neagh, took the city of Armagh from Oriel, and confined the latter kingdom to the present counties of Monaghan and Louth. Their design was to revive the ancient kingdom of Ulster; and in fact, by compelling the homage of Ulidia and Oriel, they almost accomplished the union of the whole province.

Connacht in the twelfth century was destined to produce in Turloch More O'Connor the greatest Árd Rí since Brian. His family had established its claim as the senior royal line and as chief representative of Brion, king of Connacht about 420, and of Muredach, king in 700. To the 'Síol Muiredaigh', the descendants of the latter, belonged MacDermot, O'Flanagan, and other junior septs who were O'Connor's electors and *aireacht*.

In A.D. 400 Connacht and Meath had been a united kingdom under Niall of the Nine Hostages. The connexion was broken at the battle of Ocha in 483, and thereafter Connacht continued in a line of its own. Owing, however, to the ancient union its claim to be separate was not admitted, and according to the *Book of Rights* it could not even compete for the High kingship, so that Turloch More in theory was not entitled to be Árd Rí.

In the sub-kingdom of Brefni the king of Connacht had his greatest vassal. In the time of Niall of the Nine Hostages, this High king's brother Brion had conquered from the ancient Ulster (Ulaid) the present Cavan and north Leitrim and annexed it to Connacht. Hence this tangle of lakes, mountains, and desolate heath-lands was called Brefni of the Ui Briuin (the descendants of Brion) and also the 'Rough Third' (*Garbh-trian*) of Connacht; its ruling line by 1100 was O'Ruairc.

So important was Brefni to O'Connor in the strife with Ulster that the chronicler Tighernach calls it 'the land of defence' (*ferann an im-chosnamha*), because it protected Connacht on the north-east. Its kings, the O'Ruaircs, as descendants of Brion and head of a number of septs, the 'Ui Briuin', called after him, were a

[1] The Normans, however, as we judge by Giraldus Cambrensis, imagined Ireland to be a pentarchy of Leinster, Connacht, Munster, Meath, Ulster.

proud, ambitious race, who in the period before the Normans produced a strong prince in Tighernan.

In the midlands the kingdom of Meath was very important because it contained the ancient capital Tara, its kings were of the ancient Ui Néill line, and its rich pastures made it the most desirable part of Ireland. After the death in 1022 of the High king Maelsechlainn, however, his race never flourished again, and the O'Melaghlins could hardly hold their ground against their neighbours who sought to dismember this small but fertile kingdom. Their capital was now the great rath on the shores of Lough Ennell called 'Dún na Sciath' ('fort of the shields').[1]

Munster itself, so great under Brian, now fell back to a mere competitive place. Up till 1119 the fundamental cleavage between the north and south of the province (Thomond and Desmond) was concealed, but the twelfth century was to see the great southern kingdom partitioned between O'Briens and MacCarthys. The latter, claiming to the Eoghanacht, did not forget that up to 966 they, and not Brian's race, had been kings at Cashel.[2]

The shades of the ancestors hung heavy over Gaelic Ireland, and claims derived from them were not forgotten. About A.D. 200 Cathair Mór, king of Leinster, won some vague supremacy over all Ireland. From his descendant Enna Cinnselach in the fifth century originated the royal demesnes, called Hy Kinsella (Ui Cinnselaigh) which contained ten *tuatha*, or, as the Normans called them, cantreds. In the tenth century, however, the capital of Leinster was Dinn Righ, near Leighlinbridge, or 'Naas of the kings' in Kildare, and the ruling stock was a north Leinster one called the Ui Dunlaing. Maelmora, whom Brian set up as his vassal but who fell fighting against him at Clontarf, was head of this branch. Its place was soon taken by a south Leinster line also descended from Enna. Diarmaid, of this race, who was son of one Mael na mBó ('devotee of the kine'), had a successful career, reduced Leinster and the Ostmen, and after ruling for twenty years died in battle in 1072 as 'king of Leinster, Dublin, and the Southern Half'. From his son Murchad came the MacMurrough race of kings, and it was his glory that his descendant Diarmaid II in the next century aimed to revive. Leinster was

[1] After 1014 the annals call the O'Melaghlins 'kings of Tara', since the latter was the capital of Meath, but not implying thereby the old 'kingdom of Tara', the supreme High kingship. Conor O'Melaghlin (1033-73) is the first king of the Southern Ui Néill to be so described.

[2] Ailill, king of Cashel in pagan days, had a son Eoghan Mór, *circa* A.D. 150. From his eldest son, Fiacha, came the Eoghanacht (Owenacht) line; from his younger son, Cormac Cas, came the Dalcassians.

now ruled from the south instead of from the Liffey, and Hy Kinsella with its capital Ferns was the royal domain.

But north Leinster resented Mac-Mael-na-mBó's triumph. A former monarch, Murchad, about 700, had left three sons from whom came the Ui Muiredaigh, the Ui Dunchada, and the Ui Faeláin, who ruled over three petty states in Kildare, south county Dublin, and the Annaliffey (the Vale of Liffey) when the Normans came. Their enmity to the Ferns dynasty was to prove decisive in the career of the second Diarmaid.

Of like status to Brefni was Ossory, a sub-kingdom in the heptarchy.[1] According to the *Book of Rights*, this state was a vassal of Munster, but Leinster also claimed its homage. In fact under its own dynasty, founded by one Gillapatraic in 1050, it played a vigorous part as an almost independent borderland.

But again between the High kingship and the province kingdoms lay the ancient division of the island into Mogh's (the Southern) Half, and Conn's (the Northern) Half. Whether legendary or as an explanation of some fundamental distinction between north and south, this had its practical effects, for, if the king of Cashel were not Árd Rí, he claimed, according to the *Book of Rights*, to be king over the Southern Half.

THE SCANDINAVIAN TOWNS

The chief Norse states were Dublin, Waterford, Limerick, Wexford, and Cork. After them there were strongholds or trading depots of minor importance such as Dungarvan. The greater of them were veritable sea-republics and, cut off from one another by land and communicating only by sea, they remained independent of one another under local rulers.[2]

The Ostman kingdom of Dublin was the largest and most important by far. Called in Norse 'Dyfflinarskiri' or Dublinshire, it stretched from Skerries and the river Delvin in north county Dublin to Arklow in the south, and inland to Leixlip ('Laxlaup' or 'salmon leap') and into the hill-country south of the Liffey. The modern county of Dublin was in fact Norse, and the north part, still called Fingall, was the particular 'land of the Norsemen' ('Fine Gall'). On the eminence above the river and on the south of it they had built about 900 a fortress-town to which,

[1] Ossory (Osraighe) covered the present county Kilkenny and the southern portion of Leix.

[2] See A. Walsh, *Scandinavian Relations with Ireland during the Viking Period* (1922). We have preferred to call the Scandinavian settlers Norse, as racially most of them seem to have been, though Danish is the more popular term for them.

from the *dubh linn* or 'black pool' in the stream, they gave the present name of the capital. Under Sitric Silkenbeard, 1000–42, this state reached its greatest height. This petty king, Irish on his mother's side, struck coins, installed the first Christian bishop, and founded a cathedral for the city called Christchurch or Holy Trinity. His dynasty, founded by Ivar in 870, expired soon after him, and by 1100 the ruler of Dublin was not a king but an earl (in Irish *mór-maer* or 'great steward') called Torcall or Thorkel. His son, Ragnall mac Torcaill, died in 1146, and his son again, Asgall or Hasculf, was to be the last of the line.

The second Ostman state, that of Waterford, also produced in the period after Clontarf a line of hereditary earls who, on becoming Christian, took the surname MacGillamaire from an ancestor Gillamaire ('devotee of Mary'), called later MacGilmory. Outside the town walls of Waterford lay an extensive district where Ostman farmers and fishermen dwelt, called 'Gall-tír' ('the land of the Norsemen'), now the barony of Gualtier.

Of Limerick, far to the west, the Ostmen records are more scanty. The first vikings had built about A.D. 900 a fortress on the island in the Shannon there, which the annals call 'Inis Ubhdonn', because the Norse celebrated there the pagan rites of Odin. The ruling race seems to have sprung from one Magnus or Maccus, and the citizens under Norman rule successfully claimed 'the liberties of the Ostmen and of the race of MacMaccus'.[1]

Limerick also had its contado on the mainland called by the Normans 'the cantred of the Ostmen', and the salmon fishery there, still called by a Norse name, 'the Lax Weir', was highly valued by them.

Cork also was one of those noble harbours of Ireland which the eye of the Norsemen was quick to perceive. Here, in the tenth century, arose an Ostman town governed by a *mór-maer*, and having its cantred outside the walls. Of Wexford little is known, but it had a walled capital and ships and fighting-men, as the annals record, and a rural area about it. The most thickly occupied Norse area in Ireland seems to have been the coast between Wexford and Dublin; here Saltee, Tuskar, Carnsore, Arklow, Wicklow, Dalkey, Howth, Lambay, and other names still commemorate this vigorous race, whose blood must still be considerable in the people of Leinster.

The Ostmen of Ireland were by no means absorbed into the Irish race or particularly loyal to it. But politically they had

[1] See pp. 106, 405–6. The name Ostmen, which we use for the christianized and semi-Irish settlers in Ireland after 1014, is from a Norse word meaning 'Eastman', as opposed to the Irish whom the vikings called 'Westmen'.

accepted, or been compelled to accept, a self-governing status within the native state-system. In the *Book of Rights* Brian, who was their first conqueror, had it laid down that 'the foreigners of Dublin and of Ireland in general are bound to follow the king of Cashel to battle in return for his maintaining them in their territories'. How far this was law depended on how far Brian's descendants could enforce it. But the same book recognizes that Dublin is also a tributary state of the kingdom of Leinster.

Actually in the twelfth century we find that the Ostman towns are vassals for military, naval, and tribute purposes of the province-kings, though they owe supreme allegiance like all other states to the king of Erin. Dublin, Waterford, and Wexford must serve the Leinster king; Cork must obey MacCarthy; and Limerick the O'Brien kings. Whatever naval power High king or province-king had was derived from the Scandinavian colonies. And the trading, mercantile, and productive wealth of the Ostmen was far higher than that of much larger native states. For example, in 1166 the High king Rory had to purchase the homage of Dublin with a stipend (*tuarasdal*) of four thousand cows, while only two hundred and forty were paid to the sub-kingdom of Oriel.

MURCHERTACH O'BRIEN AND THE HIGH KINGSHIP

On the death of the great Brian, king of Ireland, as the annals accept him, his diminished kingdom fell to his son Taig. The latter's time as king of Cashel was brief and he was slain by the people of Ely in 1023. To him succeeded Brian's last remaining son Donnchad, who kept an unsteady throne until 1064, when he went on pilgrimage to Rome and died there. Turloch, son of Taig, then succeeded to Munster and did something to revive his grandfather's fame. But in the 'struggle of kings with opposition' his foes were many, and in Leinster for example Diarmaid I built up the strongest power of the time. More ominous still for Irish independence, in 1066 William of Normandy conquered England and brought it into the Catholic-feudal-monarchic fold of Europe. It was a momentous event for Ireland, could she have realized it. The unprogressive Anglo-saxons had for centuries offered her no aggression, but now in Norman hands England was destined both in Church and State to bring Ireland to subjection. This consummation was however long deferred, and it is a coincidence in dating that from Hastings to the expulsion of Dermot was exactly a century of time.

Against this menace a strong native monarchy and a revived Church no longer isolated from the Continent were necessary if native Ireland were to survive. Turloch did something to face the situation. To him as 'Rex Hiberniae' came the first letters from Canterbury and an appeal from Rome urging him and the clergy of Ireland to set their house in order. He strove bravely to subdue MacLochlainn in the north and O'Connor in the west so as to make the High kingship real, but in spite of many hostings, and though the annals accept him as king of Erin, we must admit that his power as High king was a limited one. His death is recorded thus by the annals of Ulster in 1086: 'Tairrdelbach Ua Briain, king of Ireland, died in Cenn Coradh after much suffering and after long penance and after partaking of the Body and Blood of Christ, on the second of the Ides of July in the seventy-seventh year of his age.'

Turloch's son and successor Murchertach is described in the annals of Boyle as 'High king of Ireland, distinguished for wisdom and knowledge above all in his time'.[1]

It took Murchertach some fifteen years as king of Munster before he was able to assert with success the title of 'Rex Hiberniae'. We may omit the wearisome details of his long struggle with Donal MacLochlainn of Tyrone and with Rory O'Connor of Connacht, and his hostings into Meath and Ulster. At last in 1101 he carried out the 'circuit of the High king'. Backed by Mogh's Half, i.e. the levies of Munster and Leinster, he marched sunwise from Kincora into Connacht, then over the Erne at Assaroe into Ulster, demolishing Aileach on the way, then into Ulidia, along the old road of Midluachra to Tara, then back by Leinster to Kincora, thus triumphantly displaying himself as 'Árd Rí Érenn'.

MAGNUS OF NORWAY

Ireland had been much isolated from Europe since the Scandinavian raids began. But the course of events inevitably brought her into contact with Rome, Canterbury, England, and the world of the twelfth century, a changing and in many ways a progressive one. The High king had now to deal with a situation such as none of his simpler ancestors had to face.

There now appeared in British waters Magnus, grandson of Harald Hardrada, and king of Norway. The Scandinavian hold on mainland England was lost in 1066, but Magnus had come on this 'summer faring' to assert Norway's claim to the homage of the old viking colonies which stretched from Shetland to Man and Dublin, the 'Tribute lands' as they were called.

[1] He is called also Muirchertach Mór (the Great) in *Ann. Ult.* under the year 1111. 'Praeclarus scientia intellectuali istis temporibus prae omnibus' is of course the praise of a cleric, and not all Murchertach's deeds in the annals read well.

'Magnus', says the saga, 'was a man easily known. He had a red surcoat over his byrny [coat of mail], and his silky flaxen hair fell over his shoulders.' He adopted the costume of Ireland, for which he had an affection, and went barelegged, with a short kirtle and overcloak; hence he was called 'Barfod', or 'Bareleg'. On this expedition he took prisoner Laghmann, the king of Man, and when Hugh de Montgomery, earl of Shrewsbury, appeared in Anglesey with an army to know his purpose, by a lucky shot from shipboard he slew the proud Norman at the head of his knights in July 1098.[1]

Hugh's brother Robert 'de Belesme' then bought from William II the earldom of Shrewsbury and soon proved himself a typical 'bad baron', with his castles and tyrannies. On Henry I's accession he plotted to bring in as king the amiable elder brother, Robert of Normandy, for the barons, says the contemporary Ordericus, 'dreaded Henry's firm rule and preferred that of the imbecile Duke Robert who gave them licence for their evil deeds'.

Welsh princes joined in the plot, even though the 'Franks' of South Wales had in 1090 slain in battle Rhys ap Tewdwr, the native king of Dyved, and extinguished there 'the kingdom of the Britons'. After that event Robert of Belesme made his younger brother Arnulf lord of Pembroke, and in 1095 the latter appointed one Gerald of Windsor to be steward of his castle of Pembroke.[2] Gerald still further feathered his nest by marrying Nesta, daughter of the slain king Rhys. The allies next thought of Irish aid. In 1100 Gerald was sent to 'Murcard, king of Ireland' to ask the hand of one of his daughters called Lafracoth for Arnulf and to get naval aid from him, and returned successfully. It was the first sight that a Geraldine was to have of a country in which his descendants were to be so great.

The marriage took place, and at the same time Magnus, still hovering about, obtained the hand of another daughter of the High king, called Biadmynia, for his boy-son Sigurd. From the first he had shown Irish sympathies and now became an ally of Murchertach.

A feudal Celtic-Norse combination on the north-west fringe thus sought to stem the advance of the great centralized monarchy of England. But this monarchy could strike with a force and rapidity of which such enemies were incapable. Duke Robert weakly made peace with his younger brother, and Henry, turning on the Montgomery clan in 1102, drove De Belesme out of his

[1] For the sources of the Murchertach-Magnus-Belesme saga, see my paper on 'Murchertach O'Brien, High King, etc.,' in *R.S.A.I.* (1921).

[2] Gerald was younger son of Walter, son of Otho, castellan of Windsor.

earldom, though he allowed him to end his days in his native Normandy. There in due time, and after some years of exile in Ireland with his father-in-law Murchertach, his brother Arnulf joined him. The latter had by Lafracoth a daughter Alice.[1] As for Sigurd and Biadmynia, it appears the espousals came to naught.

The skilful Gerald of Windsor survived his lord and was allowed by Henry to retain his castle and lands in Pembroke. We shall return to him in time.

The end of the magnificent but futile Magnus was rapid. In 1102 he joined Murchertach in Ireland and wintered at Kincora with him. They received the joint homage of Dublin, and it is perhaps now that the Thorkel was installed who founded a line of Ostman earls there. In the next spring and summer the Norse sea-king sailed off to Ulster and spent months apparently idly meditating his return home or covering Murchertach's campaign in the north. Finally, landing to forage on the Down coast, he was cut off with his force by an Irish host and slain with the best of his captains on St. Bartholomew's Day, August 24th 1103. He was only thirty and, says Heimskringla, 'never has there been seen a nobler or more valiant man'. His young son Sigurd sailed at once for Norway and the whole expedition ended in naught. The Scandinavian power was in sooth fading fast out of the new Britain, and not for another century and a half did a Norse sea-king appear in Irish waters.

Murchertach could not expect much favour from Henry of England after favouring his feudal rebels. He wrote a letter as 'Rex Hiberniae' to Archbishop Anselm, thanking him for intervening with the King 'on behalf of my son-in-law Arnulf', but no answer is recorded.[2] But, strong in the friendship of Norway and other foreign powers, O'Brien had now his best years. In 1103 he again invaded the north to the help of Ulidia, still oppressed by Tyrone. His Árd Rí summons was answered by the forces of Munster, Leinster, Dublin, Meath, and Connacht. Marching to Armagh, like Brian he confirmed the alliance of the monarchy with the mother church of Ireland by placing a gift of eight ounces of gold on the high altar of Armagh. But his host met at Moycova near Newry a most disastrous rout at the hands of his great rival,

[1] In my paper on Murchertach O'Brien (op. cit., p. 10 here) I suggest the probability that Arnulf's daughter Alice, by Lafracoth, born about 1110, in time married Maurice, son of Gerald. It is not clear from Ordericus whether Arnulf died in Ireland or Normandy, but we certainly hear of him as in Normandy in 1118 still resisting King Henry.

[2] Ussher, *Sylloge*, op. cit., xxxv. The date of the letter must be about 1103, when Arnulf was in exile with the High king, perhaps at Kincora, and wishing to return.

Donal MacLochlainn, on August 5th 1103. There was a great slaughter of his captains, both Ostman and Gael, and the victorious MacLochlainn carried off O'Brien's royal tent and banner. Possibly Murchertach had relied on the handsome Magnus to second him but, as we saw, the Norwegian king, who was loitering in those waters, fell in an insignificant skirmish later in the same month.

After Moycova, Murchertach never recovered the glory lost to northern arms. For some years he suffered from some unnamed sickness, recovered for a while and made some show of success against his rivals, but finally after six years more as an invalid died in 1119 at Killaloe, and was buried in the cathedral church there which he (or his father) had founded.

With him passed away the Munster supremacy and his great ancestor's design of a real High kingship, to which he had contributed mental and moral rather than military ability. But his contribution to the great question of Church reform must be called one of lasting and honourable importance.

THE BEGINNINGS OF ECCLESIASTICAL REFORM, 1072–1119

For the reform and reorganization of the Irish Church we must go back some years, and connect it with the momentous event of the Norman conquest of England. William the Conqueror made out of the old Anglo-Saxon monarchy a new one, feudal in one sense, in another non-feudal, because he affirmed for good the law that the obedience of all Englishmen was due above all to the powerful State embodied in a real king. The organizing of the old stagnant Anglo-Saxon Church as part of, and controlled by, the State and romanized in practice and doctrine was the ecclesiastical side of the Norman conquest. This, with William's guarded approval, was left to the statesman-prelate, the Norman Lanfranc, archbishop of Canterbury, to carry out. In the course of a century this view of the Church was to be extended to Ireland on its Norman conquest, but meanwhile Irishmen themselves attempted a native reform.[1]

Lanfranc was an ecclesiastical imperialist. In 1072 he claimed that his primacy included Ireland as well as Britain. This claim need not have mattered had not an important section of the Irish community gladly availed of it. The Ostmen of Dublin, though

[1] The story of the Church reform has been so well written up of late that only a recapitulation of the main points need be given here. See *Life of Saint Malachy by Bernard of Clairvaux* (ed. Lawlor), introd.; Gougaud, *Christianity in Celtic Lands*; *Hist. of Ch. of Ireland* (in three vols., ed. W. Alison Phillips), vol. II, 1–50; and Kenney, *Sources of Early Irish History* (*Ecclesiastical*), chapter viii.

Christian and already having bishops of their own since 1040, were not wholly Irish, and when the Normans conquered England preferred them to their Celtic neighbours, believing them to be of their own race, as indeed the Normans were if we remember their Norse origin.

The Irish Church was a monastic one, mainly ruled by abbots dwelling in rural monasteries and Irish in speech. The Ostmen wanted theirs to be an episcopal one, but anti-Irish feeling also entered into the question among these still-Norse people who had a preference racially for Teutonic and even for Norman England. In Dublin's case the aim was to get free of the jurisdiction of Glendaloch, a remote abbey amongst the mountains, and to have a bishop of their own within their own walls. The Ostmen of Waterford and Limerick later showed the same spirit. They looked to Canterbury to confirm their local bishops, and this meant the intervention of the king of England, and raised for Ireland the question at once of religious and political independence.

As it happened, the most influential dynasty of the time favoured the claim of Canterbury. This was the O'Briens, and both Turloch and Murchertach showed themselves complaisant to Rome and the primate of England. Partly this house admitted the right of their Ostman subjects to choose their own prelates, partly they saw in a reform movement which they favoured a prop to their own power as High kings, partly they were flattered with the letters and attentions of the great See of Augustine and the still greater See of Peter.[1] The modern idea of nationality was as yet undreamed of, and in any case the Catholic Church is supernational. But there was a native party in the Irish Church, and O'Brien's complaisance with English interference was soon resented.

On the death of their first bishop, Dunan, in 1074 the clergy and people of Dublin chose one Patrick and sent him for consecration to Lanfranc. The latter received his vow of canonical obedience, consecrated him in London, and sent him home with letters commendatory to Turloch O'Brien whom he addressed as 'Rex magnificus Hiberniae'. Lanfranc took the opportunity to point out the evils and irregularities of the Irish Church, and urged him to summon a synod to set them right. We must assume that Turloch approved of all this.

Lanfranc died in 1089, and it is worth noting here that under

[1] This and other correspondence between Canterbury and Ireland is preserved in *Sylloge* (op. cit., xxix). Gregory VII's letter to Turloch O'Brien, even if a forgery, represents what the reform party wished. Lawlor (*Life of Malachy*) seems to accept it.

his influence the Anglo-saxon Margaret, wife of Malcolm III of Scotland, brought the old Church of Scotland into Roman conformity.

The gentle Anselm succeeded to Canterbury in 1093, but no less than Lanfranc did he maintain the metropolitan claims of his archsee, and the bishops of Dublin continued to be consecrated from Canterbury up till 1150. In 1096 the Ostmen of Waterford chose their first bishop, Malchus, and on a petition sent to Anselm, not merely by them but also by Murchertach O'Brien, he consecrated Malchus at Canterbury. Limerick was the next Ostman town to get a bishop of its own; this was Gillebert, in Irish Gilla Easpuig, consecrated (locally it appears) about 1107.

The significance of these elections lay in the fact that Ireland now had in Dublin, Waterford, and Limerick, three territorial dioceses based on the accepted episcopal system of the Continental church, a model for the reform of Ireland's monastic church. And it was from them or men who sympathized with what they stood for that the reforming party came. These men were in touch with Europe and the Catholic Church of the time. Malchus, bishop of Waterford (Maelisa Ó hAinmire), and Patrick, Donough, and Samuel, bishops of Dublin, had been monks at Canterbury, St. Albans, or Winchester, and Gillebert of Limerick had been a fellow-monk at Rouen with Anselm himself. Though they were Irishmen, ruling Norse cities, they were in favour of the new ideas and of a reform on Continental lines.

These were the leaders of the romanizing party whose successes appear in the twelfth century. Though they favoured Canterbury at first, it was not long until their party, rejecting the un-Irish attitude of Dublin, sought to achieve a united Church and State for their native land.

DEFECTS OF THE IRISH CHURCH

Even had the ancient native Celtic Church of Ireland needed no moral reform, its organization, woefully lacking, would have demanded attention in the age of the Hildebrandine movement. But it did grievously need moral purification along with the laity it served. The charges made against it in letters of Lanfranc and Anselm, and after them by others, may be summed up as follows.

Among the clergy these were: simony and marriage; neglect in places to perform the proper sacraments of baptism and confirmation and to enforce penance; toleration of illegitimacy and uncanonical marriages. Among the laity there were: irregular unions with women, repudiation and changing of wives, and other habits, hinted at rather than named, of pagan nature. The charges, the most severe of which were made by St. Malachy himself and other Irish bishops, may no doubt be largely explained by the dreadful upset of society due to the Scandinavian raids and partly by the survival of pagan beliefs and practices here and there throughout Ireland. After a century of reform, Pope Alexander III could still write of the *vitiorum enormitates* of the Irish, and call them *gens illa barbara inculta et divinae legis ignara.*[1] How far such charges were exaggerated by the pious zeal of reforming clerics cannot be decided.

THE COURSE OF REFORM

In short, the Church in Ireland was not doing her duty, and in the minds of the reformers could not do her duty till she was thoroughly purified, reorganized, and brought into line with the Universal Church under the discipline of Rome. She had no excuse for remaining in the rut into which Norse aggression or pagan revival had cast her, seeing that Europe itself everywhere had had to rise again out of barbarian and Moslem raids, destructive both to civilization and Christianity, and reducing vast numbers back to semi-paganism.

In the regeneration of society in religion and morals the See of Rome in the eleventh century, as was natural and right, took the lead, and the price to be paid for the reorganization of Christian society was unity and the recognition of papal authority. The Celtic churches of Ireland, Wales, Scotland, and Brittany had not, it is true, ever repudiated Catholic unity, but the connexion with headquarters was almost nil, and the monastic character of these churches and their local peculiarities constituted a form of 'ecclesiastical Home Rule', which was not heresy or schism, but clearly was not submission or conformity.[2]

This is what was now demanded, when at first the Cluniac and then the Hildebrandine reformation began to conquer Europe. Ireland was to be the last western land to succumb before this great romanizing movement, and by 1200 'Celtic particularism', seven centuries old, was a thing of the past. Backed by the

[1] Lawlor (*Life of Malachy*, pp. 160–6, and xv) sums up and explains the vices attributed to the Irish. 'Christians in name, pagans in fact' was the description of his people given by Malachy to St. Bernard, a phrase repeated by Alexander III when he conferred Ireland upon Henry II.

[2] This isolation from Rome in the case of the Irish Church is attested by the curious fact that for nearly seven centuries, from Patrick's time right up to the appointment of Bishop Gillebert in 1107, there is no record of a papal legate in this country.

prestige and blessing of the See of Peter, the Irish reformers, who were ready to 'teach all that Rome teaches', looked internally to Armagh, the titular head of the Irish Church, to become the real head, and to lead the great movement for reorganization.

Gillebert, bishop of Limerick and now papal legate, was the first leader of reform, and took it in hand about 1110 to write and address to the clergy of Ireland a tract entitled *De Statu Ecclesiae*, which, says Kenney, is 'a kind of summary of Christian doctrine and ecclesiastical law' regarded as orthodox and approved at Rome and Canterbury.[1] From the programme outlined in this, we can gather what in the eyes of the reform party was wrong with the existing Irish system. Bishops were many and limited to mere spiritual functions. They had no territorial sees or jurisdiction. The great abbots, each of whom was head not only of a famous abbey but of its *paruchia* or group of daughter-houses, were the real rulers of the Church, and had the prestige that came from being coarb (*comharba* or successor) of Brendan, Comgall, Colmcille, Ciaran, and others. They were not always in episcopal orders. Often they formed an hereditary family, all 'of founder's kin', a system that led to abuses and stagnation.

Just as there was no true diocesan episcopate, so there was, it appears, no true parochial system and, since the priesthood were mainly monks, tithe for their support was as yet unknown. While the religious life and discipline could be and certainly were taught and enforced around the monasteries, it is obvious that large tracts must have been left devoid of religious ministration and abandoned to the pagan or undisciplined state which Rome and Canterbury complained of. In order to make the Church effective to perform its moral duty, it must be organized throughout the country even to the most remote parts, and this could only be done by an episcopal church governed by a supreme archbishop and bishops subject to him, working through a parochial clergy themselves subject to the bishops, a church moreover which the laity must obey and support with glebes and tithes.

The archbishop must, after election and consecration, go to Rome to receive there the *pallium* (the collar of lamb's wool) as token that the Pope had confirmed him as metropolitan. And just as there must be unity of control, so there must be uniformity of doctrine and ritual. Ireland, declared Gillebert, was infested with 'schismatical orders'. For these must be substituted 'one Catholic and Roman office'.

The needed purification of abuses and the correction of negligence are implied or pointed out; and indeed, both by Gillebert

[1] See Lawlor, *Life of Malachy* (op. cit., pp. xxx–xxxiii).

and Rome, by foreign authorities and native reformers, notably the famous Malachy himself, the charges of simony, clerical marriage, the assumption of church offices by laymen, and the vices of the laity, form a most sweeping indictment of Ireland of the time. Doubtless the reformers could also have dwelt upon the violence of the princes with their endless feuds and wars and the lamentable absence of a strong national monarchy, such as might have enforced that order and peace which above all the Church needed in order to do its work.

If the long isolation of the Irish Church was to end and Ireland be opened up, not only to a reformed secular organization, but also to a reformed monastic one, by the entry of Roman ideas and foreign orders, the start was none too soon.[1] And it required the aid of the kings and above all of a strong supreme king, if it was to be achieved without danger to national independence.

In 1101, at a gathering of Munster clergy, the High king Murchertach handed over the Rock of Cashel as the seat for a new archbishopric for Munster. And now the alliance of High king and southern reformers was joined by the traditional head of the Irish Church, the coarb of Patrick.

For a century and a half the church of Armagh had been ruled successively by eight members of an hereditary clan, sprung from one Sinach, who held the coarbship, were often laymen and married, and retained a powerless bishop in the monastery there. Now Celsus (Cellach) of this family ended the abuse, and embraced the cause of purity and reform by uniting in himself in 1105–6 the two offices of bishop (henceforth archbishop) and coarb of Armagh.[2] Next as primate he descended into Munster, where in a local synod he erected Cashel into an archbishopric, of which Malchus of Waterford became first occupant. Gillebert as legate remained the ruling spirit, and in 1110 summoned at Rathbreasail (called also Fiadh-mic-Oengusa) the first of the national reform synods.

Here Murchertach O'Brien represented the authority and support of the State. An ecclesiastical division of the island was made which followed the old division into the Northern Half and Southern Half. There were to be thirteen dioceses in the north subject to Armagh, and twelve in the south subject to Cashel

[1] Until the Ostmen turned Christian, and up to the twelfth century, the monastic churches of Ireland were all under the Rule of Columba, Ciaran, and other native saint-founders, and the Benedictine order came in first with St. Mary's, founded in Dublin, late in the eleventh or early in the twelfth century.

[2] 'Archbishop', in the strict sense of a metropolitan, was a title up to this hardly known in Ireland. Lawlor (*Life of Malachy*, pp. xxx–xxxv, 164–6 describes the hereditary succession of the lay coarbs of Patrick, 957–1106.

(which counted as one of the twelve), Armagh to be supreme over the whole Irish Church.

Thus was an episcopal church planned for Ireland. But the working out of the plan would naturally take time, and only Limerick seems then to have had recognized boundaries. The claims of Dublin to independence under the wing of Canterbury were ignored, and the great Ostman city was subjected to the bishop of Glendaloch. The final consent of Rome was not as yet sought for these changes, to which, however, Gillebert as papal legate gave his official approval.

Thus far, and impressively enough on paper, had the reform of the Irish Church proceeded by the death of the High king Murchertach in 1119.

CHAPTER II

TURLOCH O'CONNOR AND THE PRELUDE TO THE NORMAN INVASION

THE career of Turloch More O'Connor from 1119 to 1156 shows what a man of energy and intelligence could do to make the High kingship real. A succession of such kings in one kingdom which could have established a permanent ascendancy over all the rest might have brought about a strong and united Ireland. But, unfortunately, the hereditary succession could not be attained.

Turloch (in Irish Tairrdelbach) was son of Ruaidhri (Rory) O'Connor and became king of Connacht in 1106, being then about eighteen years of age. The death of Murchertach in 1119 allowed him to aim at the High kingship, for after this O'Brien the kingdom of Cashel never revived again. Turloch had a definite purpose, to make Connacht a bastion from which to dominate Ireland and reduce or dismember the other kingdoms, so as to ensure the permanent supremacy of his own. To give away kingdoms in return for gold or cession of territory was indeed a new thing in Ireland.

Turloch was a warrior of terrific energy, who took the field year after year. His fleet from Lough Derg commanded the midlands and Munster, his fortresses at Dunleogha near Ballinasloe, Galway, and Collooney dominated Connacht on every hand, and his wicker bridges at Athlone and Athliag held the Shannon and opened the way to Meath.[1]

It was in 1118, when the O'Briens were without a competent head, that Turloch first invaded Munster with the aid of Enna, king of Leinster, Donnchad of Ossory, and Conor O'Melaghlin, 'king of Tara'.[2] In a triumphant progress, during which he camped at Killaloe, and 'hurled Kincora, both stone and wood, into the Shannon' to show his contempt for Brian's race, he divided Munster by giving Desmond to Taig MacCarthy and Thomond to the sons of Dermot O'Brien.[3] This was the cleverest and most successful of his strokes, and though he had to repeat it

[1] *A.F.M.* (1124): 'The great fleet of Turloch on Lough Derg, and the fleet of Desmond was left (surrendered) to him. He had a great camp at Athcaille from Martinmas to May. Three castles (*caisteoil*) were erected by the Connachtmen, namely Dunleogha, Gaillimh, and Cul Maeile.'

[2] This title is common in the annals for the royal line of Meath after 1022, but has not the significance of the old 'High king of Tara'.

[3] The death of the High king Murchertach is recorded in March 1119, but he had been an invalid for years. His brother Dermot died in 1118 'in Corcachmór na Mumhan'.

several times, he did in the end split up this kingdom by reviving the Eoghanacht as rivals of Brian Boru's line.

The separate kingdom of Desmond thus began, and Taig may be called its first ruler. Dying in 1123, he was succeeded by his brother Cormac, who ruled for fifteen years.[1] O'Connor had to interfere again in 1121 and again in 1127 to enforce the division. But the Dalcassians would not relinquish their claim, and in 1138 Turloch O'Brien off-slew Cormac and 'assumed the kingship of all Munster'. It was not till 1151 that the High king was again able to invade the south for one more 'settlement of Munster'. In the space of a few years, therefore, Turloch O'Connor secured the homage of enough other kingdoms to qualify as Árd Rí, and in 1120 he celebrated the Fair of Tailten, a prerogative of the High king. In the north he had no success, but the death of Domnall MacLochlainn in 1121 made clearer the way of the Connachtman.

In 1120 Turloch invaded Meath to enforce its homage, and again in 1125 hosted into this province, expelled its king, Murchad O'Melaghlin, and, say the annals of Ulster, 'placed three kings over the men of Meath'. This was 'partitioning' with a vengeance, but Murchad, who was the last king of undivided Meath, was not easily disposed of.[2]

Dublin had to render to Turloch the homage and naval aid due to a High king, and in 1126 he placed over it his son Conor. As Enna, king of Leinster, had just died, Conor was also made king of this province. There was a joint revolt in the next year, 1127, inspired by a vigorous young prince, Dermot MacMurrough, whereupon Turloch placed over Leinster and Dublin a local prince, Donal MacFaelain, lord of the Ui Faelain. His son Conor was compensated by the kingdom of Meath, but after he had reigned for a year he was slain by Ó Dubhlaich, lord of Fir Tulach, a Meathman, as 'a stranger in the sovereignty'. The High king was offending the deepest instinct of the Irish states that they must be ruled by the hereditary local line.[3]

Turloch's success, indeed, was not lasting with two of the states

[1] To Cormac we owe the beautiful 'Cormac's Chapel' at Cashel. The MacCarthy name came from Carthach, king of Eoghanacht Caisil, who died in 1045 and was succeeded by his son Donnchad MacCarthaigh.

In his *Gleanings from Irish History*, W. F. Butler maintains that the MacCarthys were upstarts and owed their good luck to the policy of Turloch O'Connor. But Munster was full of Eoghanacht branches such as O'Sullivan, O'Donoghue, and O'Mahony, and seniority is hard to decide.

[2] Murchad was father of the famous Dervorgilla who eloped with Dermot MacMurrough, and when the Normans came was remembered as the last true king of all Meath, for when Henry II gave it as an earldom to Hugh de Lacy he gave it 'as fully as Murchard Hua Melaghlin held it' (see later, p. 63).

[3] *Ann. Tig.*

IRELAND
CIRCA 1160
Miles
0 10 20 30 40 50
INIS EOGHAIN
DALRIADA
Errigal
Aileach
Coleraine
Antrim
R. Bann
R. Foyle
TIRCONAILL
KINGDOM OF AILEACH
KINGDOM
R. Finn
Sperrin Mts
Donegal
TIR EOGHAIN
OR THE NORTH
Bangor
OF
ARDA
Lough Neagh
Lough Erne
ULIDIA
R. Blackwater
L. Melvin
FIR-MANACH
Sligo
Armagh
Downpatrick
TIRAWLEY
SUB-KINGDOM
OF ORIEL
Mourne Mts
St. Donard
IRRUS
TIRERAGH
L. Allen
SUB-KINGDOM
L. Conn
R. Moy
Boyle
L. Gara
OF BREFNI
KINGDOM
MOYLURG
R. Blackwater
Tulsk
OF
L. Mask
CONNACHT
Tuam
CON-MAICNI
KINGDOM
OF MEATH
L. Owel
Drogheda
R. Boyne
L. Ree
Lough Corrib
R. Suck
L. Ennell
Athlone
Darrow
Clonmacnois
Dublin
NORSE
NORSE STATE OF DUBLIN
Galway
R. Liffey
Clonfert
OFFALY
R. Shannon
Slieve Bloom Mts
R. Barrow
Lough Derg
Wicklow Mts
Roscrea
LEIX
KINGDOM OF
Lugnaquillia
HY KINSELLA
Killaloe
THOMOND
Silvermine Mts
R. Fergus
Thurles
ORMOND
OSSORY
LEINSTER
Limerick
NORSE STATE
OF LIMERICK
Kilkenny
Mt Leinster
R. Slaney
R. Nore
Cashel
Tipperary
KINGDOM
R. Suir
Wexford
Mt Brandon
Galtee Mts
Waterford
NORSE STATE
OF WEXFORD
Corcaguiney
OF MUNSTER
DECIES
Castlemaine B.
R. Blackwater
Lismore
NORSE STATE
OF WATERFORD
L. Lene
Iveragh
Dungarvan
R. Lee
Cork
Youghal
DESMOND
NORSE STATE
OF CORK
R. Bandon
Kinsale
Berehaven
J.T. RANKIN

which he thus tried to subordinate or annex. Murchad O'Melaghlin held on more or less in Meath till his death in 1153, and in 1134 the hereditary rule of Hy Kinsella was asserted in Leinster by Dermot MacMurrough's slaying the above Donal. But in the south, Turloch's partition policy did succeed in the division of Munster into the two rival states of Desmond and Thomond.

The finest example of this was when in 1151 with a great army he marched in force into Munster and at Móin Mór shattered the opposing forces of Turloch O'Brien. 'Until the sand of the sea and the stars of heaven are numbered,' say with picturesque exaggeration the annals of Tigernach, 'no one will be able to count the sons of kings and chiefs and great lords of Munster who were slain there, so that out of the three battalions of the Munstermen that had come hither none escaped save one shattered battalion.' The High king then installed one Taig O'Brien in Thomond, and Dermot, son of Cormac MacCarthy, in Desmond.

After such a smashing defeat Turloch O'Brien could not claim to be king of all Munster, nevertheless he revived and continued to hold Thomond till his death.[1] His son, Donal More, was king of northern Munster when the Normans arrived.

The star of Turloch More, however, waned as he grew older in this endless war of 'kings with opposition'. Young and more vigorous princes appeared on the stage. Murchertach son of Niall MacLochlainn became king of Tyrone in 1136 and aimed at the High kingship. Dermot MacMurrough, because of Turloch's interference in the Leinster succession in 1127, remained anti-Connacht and pro-Ulster. Tighernan O'Ruairc, who was destined with MacMurrough to be responsible for bringing the foreigners in, appears as lord of Brefni in 1125, with his chief fort at Drumahaire. He was pro-Connacht and indeed the right-hand man of his O'Connor overlord, but as his share of the booty of war he claimed Meath. This unfortunate state suffered many dismemberments, and as late as 1152 Turloch More and Murchertach MacLochlainn united to divide it between Murchad O'Melaghlin and his son Melaghlin.

Turloch More died in 1156 in his sixty-eighth year, and though the annals of Tighernach call him 'the Augustus of the West of Europe', those of Ulster simply style him 'archking of Connacht', and those of the Four Masters call him 'king of Connacht, Meath, Brefni, Munster, and *all Ireland with opposition*'. In spite of all his efforts, it had again been shown how hard it was to make the

[1] His death seems to have occurred in 1167. He was temporarily expelled by an elder son, Murcertach, in 1165–6.

Árd Rí-ship real, and his son Rory (Rúaidhri) simply became provincial king of Connacht after him.

Some years before his death Turloch More had presided over the greatest synod yet held of the reform party in the Irish Church. This was the synod of Kells in 1152, and it recalls us to the progress made by the reform since the death of the High king Murchertach.

The earnest spirits in the Church had watched with dismay and indignation these endless and indecisive wars of kings and the violence to which they subjected the laity and the clergy. Two protests in the Ulster annals may be quoted. In 1117 Maelbrighte, abbot of Kells in Meath, and most of his monks were slaughtered by Aedh Ó Ruairc, prince of Brefni, and his men: the annalist quotes the Latin of the Psalms, 'The face of the Lord is against those who do such evil, to cut off the remembrance of them from the earth.' This did not deter the next O'Ruairc, Tighernan, in 1128 from attacking the retinue of the archbishop of Armagh, Celsus himself, some of whom he slew in the archbishop's presence, including the bearer of the sacred requisites, 'a deed foul, unheard of, and productive of ill, deserving the curse of all Ireland both cleric and lay, the like of which was never done in Ireland before'.

The guiding spirit of the first reformers had been Gillebert of Limerick. In 1139, overcome by age, he resigned his bishopric and office of papal legate and retired into seclusion. His contemporary, Malchus of Waterford and later archbishop of Cashel, remained the standby of the cause, but it now found a greater champion than any who had yet appeared. This was the sainted Malachy, whose native name was Maelmaedoc Ó Morgair.

St. Malachy, a true Ultonian, was born in Armagh in 1095. He attached himself at once to the reform cause, which the north had now taken up, and in 1119 was made by Celsus his vicar-general in the archdiocese. There he displayed both courage and energy in introducing and enforcing those reforms which his party sought, the organizing of episcopal jurisdiction, the building of stone churches, the proper rites of confirmation, confession, and marriage, liturgical music, and 'the one Roman and Catholic office'. He found a true friend in Donnchad O'Cervall, king of Oriel from 1125 to 1168, a strong prince who expanded his kingdom from the mouth of the Boyne to the mouth of the Erne, and was a friend and patron of the reforming Church. Under him, the diocese of Clogher or Louth was organized as a true example of that episcopal state which the reformers desired.

Malachy's first see was Connor, where he laboured from 1124 to 1127, and next, according to the wish of the dying Celsus in 1129, he succeeded in Armagh itself as coarb and archbishop, thus ending the possibility of the two offices being separated as before. But he soon resigned in favour of Gelasius (Gilla na Naemh), and returned to Connor, which he divided into two, making one part the bishopric of Connor, and remaining himself bishop of Down.

The task of reforming, indeed of reshaping, the ancient and venerable Church of so large an island was no easy or rapid one. Formerly bishops had been less important than abbots; now these proud coarbs, the successors of such venerated names as Columba or Ciaran, rulers each over a wide *paruchia* of dependent houses, were to be made less important than bishops. Local customs and attachments were hard to overcome in a country which was very local-minded and tolerant of old institutions and rights. How were the new episcopal and parochial clergy to be provided for in a land unaccustomed to tithes, and where new estates and glebes would need to be donated by local kings?

It was one of the objects of the reformers to free local churches and abbeys from lay taxation and public interference, but if this merely benefited the old monasteries little good seemed done.

The work of Rathbreasail had largely been on paper, and diocesan organization was slow. By 1149 there were thirty-six dioceses in place of the lesser number then decided upon.[1] The approval of Rome remained to be sought for the reforms so far laid down; still more was it necessary to impress Ireland with the fact that the great Church of Peter was behind the reformers. Therefore Malachy in 1139 set out for Rome, in order to secure for each of the new archbishops of Armagh and Cashel the pallium which was now necessary before the Papal Curia would accept an archbishop. On the way as well as on the way back he stayed with the famous St. Bernard of Clairvaux, the chief man in the Cistercian order. Bernard later wrote a biography of the Irishman, whom he greatly delighted in for his goodness and sweetness; on the other hand, Malachy gave him reports on the state of things among clergy and laity in Ireland which made the great European churchman and statesman wonder that so saintly a man could come out of 'so barbarous a nation'. It is obvious that Malachy and others like him were so eaten up with zeal for reform that the reputation of their people weighed naught with them. For example, he told Bernard that in Ireland 'there were

[1] This number was confirmed at Kells in 1172; by 1172 there were thirty-three.

many kings' but said nothing of a supreme king. The lack of a central autocrat was indeed a tragic fact for the reformers, who needed a strong monarch to back their aims, failing whom they finally consented to accept a foreign king, Henry of England, who could put the crown on the long work of reform.

At Rome, Malachy was honourably received by Innocent II and made legate in place of Gillebert, but the Pope insisted on a national synod before he would grant the pallia.

Returning to Ireland, Malachy brought with him from Clairvaux a band of Cistercian monks, and Donnchad, king of Oriel, gave them a site on the Boyne where they built the abbey of Mellifont. It was a great double event in Irish history, the first arrival of a foreign religious order and the introduction of Gothic architecture. Their first abbot was Christian Ó Conairce, the brother of Malchus, archbishop of Cashel, a determined romanizer and later a welcomer of Henry II.

The desired synod met at Inispatrick off Skerries in 1148, and Malachy was again sent to Rome, but died at Clairvaux on the way thither, no doubt worn out by his labours and austerities. It was four years before things moved to their end. Sent by Pope Eugenius III, Cardinal John Paparo, *legatus a latere*, came with the pallia, and the greatest synod yet of the Irish Church met him at Kells in March 1152, 'for the task of setting forth and purifying the Catholic faith'.[1] Many bishops and clergy with Gelasius of Armagh at their head attended. Christian, now bishop of Lismore, acted as *legatus natus* for the Pope, and among the many princes present, Turloch O'Connor, as High king, represented the lay State of Ireland.

Instead of the two pallia which Malachy had sought, Paparo brought four, and Tuam and Dublin were added to the two existing archbishoprics. On whose advice Rome had acted we cannot tell, but as Dublin was now willing to surrender its century-old independence and fall in with the Irish Church, and as the powerful Turloch O'Connor must have put in a demand for a separate archsee for his kingdom, the division of Ireland into four archbishoprics seemed good policy.

Thus was the Irish Church made one under the primacy of Armagh. Thirty-six dioceses were recognized, subject in each case to an archbishop. The unfortunate province of Meath, which had no powerful king to speak for it, was left in six petty sees,

[1] Keating's *History of Ireland* (ed. Dinneen), quoting from lost annals of Clonenagh.

and was only made into a single bishopric under the Normans.[1] On the side of moral discipline, decrees were passed against simony, usury, and immorality, and for the enforcement of tithe.

The further progress of the reform movement up to the Norman intervention may be briefly surveyed. The completed church of Mellifont was consecrated in 1157 by Archbishop Gelasius, in presence of Christian, bishop of Lismore and papal legate, and of Murchertach MacLochlainn, Donnchad O'Cervall, and other princes. Murchertach, who is styled 'Rí Érenn', gave to the new monastery a townland at Drogheda, eight-score cows, and three-score ounces of gold.[2] From this noble foundation came forth within a few years five daughter-houses and by 1200 some twenty-five.

In 1158 Gelasius summoned a synod at 'the Hill of MacTaidhg', where twenty-five bishops attended and various regulations were passed.

In 1167, an imposing synod met at Athboy under Rory O'Connor, then High king; at a synod in Clane earlier, in 1162, it had been decreed that no one should be a lector (*fer legind*) in any monastic school in Ireland who was not an alumnus of Armagh. Following this up, in 1169 the same High king Rory endowed the chief *fer legind*, or professor of sacred and secular learning, at Armagh with a yearly stipend of ten cows. This attempt to make the sacred city of Patrick also the educational centre of native Ireland unhappily came too late.

How a monastic coarb of the old school might be won over to the new episcopal system is manifested in Flavertach Ó Brolchain, 'successor of Colmcille' at Derry. In various visitations, Flavertach enforced his authority over the *paruchia* or scattered daughter houses of his order and the territories which owed dues to Colmcille. In 1158, at the Hill of MacTaidhg, the bishops conferred on him a bishop's chair in Derry, with jurisdiction over all the Columban houses in Ireland. In 1162 he began the building of a new cathedral in his city, ninety feet long, and completed it in two years, to make way for which he removed eighty houses or more. To reconcile the old coarbship over a great scattered order with the new diocesan organization, however, was hardly possible, and when this vigorous Flavertach dies in 1175 he is still only called 'successor of Colmcille' in the Ulster annals.

The work of native reform was in fact destined to be consummated with the surrender of Irish independence at Cashel in

[1] Simon de Rochford, bishop of Meath (1198–1224), turned the old sees of Meath into rural deaneries, the synod of Kells having enacted that, as the old sees were abolished, the bishops should become archpriests.

[2] *Ann. Ult.* (1157).

1172. There were two currents running together. There was a native-minded party in the Church, such as had resented Dublin's isolation, and to which the later Laurence Ó Tuathail belonged. But another party looked wholly towards Roman conformity for a solution of all ills, regarded Irish politics with indifference or disgust, and at last consented to an ecclesiastical reformation and a political sovereign from England. Christian of Lismore now represented this, which was mainly a Munster party, it would appear, though the Ulsterman Malachy had been its strongest spirit.

We would give much to know what the Irish leaders in Church and State thought of the famous papal missive which we have agreed to call the 'Bull *Laudabiliter*'. Strong, though perhaps not entirely conclusive, evidence exists to suppose that Adrian IV (Pope from 1154 to 1159) in his first or second year made a grant of Ireland to the young Henry II of England at the latter's desire. Seeing that some of her churchmen were in touch with Rome and presumably with Canterbury, and through Dublin had constant communication with the other island, it is surprising that no mention is made of this all-important document in our native records of the time. But so it is, and indeed the records, native or foreign, for this vivid period of native Church reform which survive, are disappointingly few and vague.[1]

MURCHERTACH MACLOCHLAINN, HIGH KING

The place left vacant by Turloch O'Connor was filled next by the vigorous young king of Tyrone. Indeed, the latter had been pushing Turloch into the shade for some years before his death. Murchertach asserted the right of the old Ui Néill in its northern branch to the High kingship and at least was no usurper, whereas the kings of Connacht had never had their right to the office admitted, not even in the *Book of Rights*.

Turloch More had at least set the fashion in a policy of dismembering or crushing other kingdoms so as to establish the greatness of one, and had a line of hereditary kings in any province been able to keep this up it might have finally united Ireland. But he was to be no more successful in achieving this than any other 'king with opposition'.

Naturally his friends and enemies were the reverse of those of his Connacht rival. Dermot MacMurrough had been the enemy,

[1] For the whole question of the Bull *Laudabiliter*, see pp. 36, 45, 59; Orpen, *Ireland under the Normans*, I, pp. 313–18; Norgate in *Eng. Hist. Rev.* (1893), pp. 107–52.

and Tighernan O'Ruairc the vassal and lieutenant, of O'Connor. Now MacMurrough was the new High king's friend, and Tighernan the enemy. And Turloch had left a son and heir not without vigour, Ruaidhri (Rory), who succeeded in Connacht.

In 1157 Murchertach as High king presided over the synod of Mellifont, where the abbey church was consecrated, and bestowed upon it a townland near Drogheda, called 'Finnabhair na nInghean'.[1]

Rory O'Connor did not yield his father's place without a struggle, but finally, in 1159, Murchertach gave the army of Connacht a complete overthrow at Ardee which ended the contest. Tighernan O'Ruairc, Rory's ally, had to submit and surrender Conmaicne (Longford), his share of the spoils of Meath.

MacLochlainn's great year was 1161. At Lecc-bladhma in Meath 'Diarmaid MacMurchadha and Ruaidhri Ó Conchobhair came to him. He gave all Connacht to Ruaidhri and Leinster to Diarmaid, and so was king of Erin *without opposition.* The half of Meath which was his he bestowed on Diarmaid Ó Maelsechlainn and the other (the western half) he bestowed on Ruaidhri.'[2]

Next year Murchertach crowned his triumph by marching to Dublin where the Ostmen acknowledged him. There Dermot MacMurrough met him, and with Gelasius of Armagh elevated Laurence O'Toole (Lorcan Ó Tuathail), abbot of Glendaloch, to the see of Dublin, then vacant by the death of Archbishop Grene. In this event we see the hierarchic nature of the Irish monarchic system. Murchertach, as High king, was suzerain both of Dermot and the Ostmen of Dublin, Dermot was king of Dublin as well as of Leinster, and Dublin had its own earl, Ragnall MacTorcaill.

Dermot MacMurrough shared the new High king's triumph, and for some years exhibited the spectacle of a province-king at the height of such power as was possible for a vigorous Irish dynast.

We must go back to explain how his triumph was to end in exile. Dermot was born about 1110, the son of Donnchad. On his father's death, Enna MacMurrough had ruled for a time, and after his death in 1126 Turloch More had put his own candidates on to the throne of Leinster, first his son Conor, then Donal MacFaelain. Not till 1134 does Dermot, up to that mere lord of Hy Kinsella, appear as king of his province. He was thus from early years an enemy of Connacht, and naturally of the MacFaelains

[1] An example of land-grant. See the first edition of this work, p. 40.

[2] *Ann. Tig.* add that Dermot O'Melaghlin, being deposed by the men of Meath, gave Murchertach one hundred ounces of gold for the kingship of west Meath.

and other north Leinster princes who might revive an old claim to the kingship.

Dermot was brought up by Aedh mac Criffan, abbot of the Columban house of Terryglass in Ormond, for whom the *Book of Leinster* was compiled, and a great lover of the old pagan epics. The instruction of the young prince was in the national sagas such as the *Táin Bó Cualgne*. Thus he was moulded in an heroic family tradition, which made him determined when the hour came to restore Leinster's ancient greatness, going back six centuries. When finally he got his invincible Norman *condottieri*, his only thought was with their swords to make himself High king and Leinster dominant for ever.

The game of 'kings with opposition' offered Dermot boundless scope. But in it he had to struggle with other warrior-kings, The one who resembled him most in energy, violence, ambition. and cruelty was Tighernan O'Ruairc of Brefni, and it was their ill-starred rivalry which was destined to ruin Gaelic Ireland.

By his fortunate alliance with O'Connor, Tighernan had extended his state of Brefni into Meath, and got Conmaicne (now Longford). In the north a successful prince was Donnchad O'Cervall of Oriel, who, during his reign from 1125 to 1168, extended his rule from the mouth of the Boyne to the mouth of the Erne. But over all loomed up the power of O'Connor and MacLochlainn, now the only candidates for Árd Rí-ship.

The last king of Leinster was destined to bear the reproach of his race for ages as *Diarmaid na nGall* (Dermot of the Foreigners) who 'brought the Normans o'er', though neither he nor the men of his time could have foreseen the lasting results of that. Dermot was a man of tall stature, powerful voice, manly good looks, a great warrior and leader, of unreflecting impulse, and full of capricious cruelty and restless energy. Among his private crimes stand out the rape of Dervorgilla and the shameful and puzzling episode when he sacked the sacred abbey town of Kildare and had the abbess of St. Brigid's church there shockingly treated.[1] This incident was typical of those crimes which made the churchmen despair of the regeneration of Ireland's Church and State being accomplished under such kings.

But for Dermot's political energies there is plenty of justification. It was now a case for Irish kings of being *aut Caesar aut nullus*.

[1] *Ann. L. Cé* (1132). Giraldus, *Expugnatio*, I, chs. iv and vi, gives a picture of Dermot, not flattering, but describes him as tall and largely made and a great warrior and valiant in his nation. That he was a handsome man may be inferred from Dervorgilla's infatuation for him and the 'exceeding beauty', recorded by Giraldus, of his daughter Eva.

Meath and Munster showed what happened to a weak kingdom. Dermot II decided to make Leinster great and restore the boundaries won by his ancestor of the previous century, Dermot I. This involved a threefold policy. First, the Ostman cities and states of Dublin, Waterford, and Wexford must be subordinated and the first become again a residence for the king of Leinster. They were very important with their shipping and seamen, their trade, riches, and tributes, and their communications oversea with Britain and the outside world.

Ragnall MacTorcaill was now earl or *mór-maer* of Dublin, his brother Asgall was to succeed him just before the Norman invasion. Waterford also had its earl, whose Irish patronymic was now MacGillamaire. Over both Dermot claimed to be supreme lord, but he had to enforce his claim.

The second part of Dermot's programme was to extend Leinster to the west by the reduction of Ossory, a rich and important sub-state ruled now by MacGillapatraic. Whether its homage was due to Leinster or Cashel was in dispute, but its king, Gillapatraic, had done homage to Dermot I in the previous century, and the young Dermot was bent on reviving his ancestors' claims on every hand.

On the north side, the submission of the Ostmen of Dublin would carry Dermot's arms far up towards Meath, and enable him to share in the plunder of this unfortunate kingdom.

Internally, the north Leinster rivals must be crushed, who might again, as they were by Turloch O'Connor, be set up against the Hy Kinsella dynasty. Externally Dermot took his full share in the struggle of 'kings with opposition', from which both profit and glory might come. It was a great game, and the trampings of kings and their light-armed forces could be heard over Ireland year after year.

We may recount Dermot's successes briefly. In 1134 he enforced the submission of Ossory, but its king Donnchad remained his inveterate enemy. In 1137 he besieged Waterford from sea and land, having the aid, willing or otherwise, of two hundred ships from Dublin and Wexford, and compelled the citizens to surrender.

There soon followed, in 1141, a revolt of the north Leinster chiefs. Dermot rapidly suppressed it and had the ruling lord of the Ui Faelain, of the Ui Muiredaigh, and of the Ui Dunchada blinded. In all seventeen of the principals of these royal septs were blinded. Such ferocity was put to the score against Dermot in the later crisis, and none of his subjects, save those of Hy Kinsella, felt any genuine loyalty to him. According to Giraldus, 'he was the oppressor of the nobility' and 'preferred to be feared rather than loved'. But we cannot blame him determining to be king in his own borders.

Next Dermot had to take sides in the wars of Ireland. His tradition being anti-O'Connor, he turned towards the rising star of Murchertach MacLochlainn and did him homage in Dublin in 1145.

THE RAPE OF DERVORGILLA, 1152

It was during a campaign between Turloch O'Connor and Tighernan O'Ruairc on one side, and Murchertach MacLochlainn backed by Dermot on the other, that the king of Leinster carried off O'Ruairc's beautiful wife Dervorgilla from his fort at Drumahaire. On whom the blame rested we cannot know, but the passion on Dervorgilla's side did not last long, and she soon fled back to her husband. Nevertheless O'Ruairc did not forgive or forget, and twelve years afterwards took a revenge which ruined not only Dermot and himself but Ireland along with them.[1]

The downfall of the O'Connors was Dermot's part-triumph. In 1161–2, as we saw, Murchertach MacLochlainn made a fresh settlement of Ireland in which Dermot was recognized king of Leinster and Dublin, and his brother-in-law Laurence archbishop of Dublin, the true end of Ostman independence.

These were Dermot's great years. As 'king of Leinster and the Foreigners', he had secured Dublin and Waterford. The archbishop of Dublin, Laurence O'Toole, was his brother-in-law and friend so far as a saintly man could be to such a cruel and barbarous king. His brother Murchad so far was true to him, so were his own sons Enna, Donal Kavanagh, and Conor. His father-in-law Murchertach, chief of Ui Muiredaigh, and his son-in-law Donal, chief of Ui Dunchada, lords in north Leinster, were his supporters.

Dermot's land-grants show that his sovereignty stretched from the borders of Meath to the Nore in Ossory. In Fingall we find him making a grant of the townland of Baldoyle to Edan, bishop of Louth.[2] In the south-west he confirmed the grants made by his vassal, Ó Riain, lord of Idrone, to the new Cistercian house of Jerpoint. In his deed of confirmation, Dermot *nutu Dei Rex*

[1] Dermot seems to have had a daughter by Dervorgilla, for a daughter bearing that name married Donal MacGillamocolmoc, lord of Ui Dunchada. The famous Dervorgilla herself died years after the Norman invasion in Mellifont. Tighernan O'Ruairc is called by Giraldus 'monoculus', having lost an eye, presumably in battle.

[2] See *Reg. of All Hallows* [or *All Saints*], *Dublin* (ed. R. Butler), p. 50, which has the text of the grant. Baldoyle came later to this church.

Laginensium greets all subject kings, dukes, and earls (*reges, duces, comites*) and confirms by his seal the grant of fourteen townlands which Ó Riain 'by our leave has made'.[1]

Another of his land-grants is made to the new abbey of Ferns. In this he confers on the canons of the Blessed Trinity there, certain townlands, fisheries, advowsons, and firstfruits from all his demesne lands throughout Hy Kinsella, with a certain tribute of drink called *scaith*, viz. from each brewing of mead or ale brewed in the town of Ferns a certain measure called *lagena* or gallon from him and his heirs for ever in free alms. All these shall be free and discharged of secular rent, service, or tribute to bishop, king, earl (*comes*), or any other. The election of the abbot shall be freely made by the monks, but after election and before he be created abbot by the archbishop or bishop 'he shall be presented to me or my heirs or their seneschals in recognition of our lordship (*causa dominii*) so that with our permission the bishop may ordain him'. The grant is made 'by counsel and assent of my princes and nobles' at Ferns. The witnesses are Christian, bishop of Lismore, legate, five bishops of Leinster, Laurence, abbot of Glendaloch, two lay chiefs, Florence '*regis cancellarius*', Marcus the chaplain, and others.[2]

Dermot indeed, to compensate for many crimes against God and man, was founder or benefactor of many churches. 'At Ferns he founded for monks of the order of St. Augustine the abbey of St. Mary; at Baltinglass he built the Cistercian abbey of De Valle Salutis; and the nunnery of St. Mary de Hogges of Dublin, with its dependent cells at Kilcleheen, and Athady in Carlow, owed its origin either to his policy or transient penitence.'[3] He was also the founder of All Hallows in Dublin.

This last king of Leinster lived in some state, when not on his endless hostings, at Ferns in a stone cashel amid an urban population which owed him duties and refections, and near to the abbey whose library contained the *Book of Leinster*, one of the

[1] See Bernard and Lady Constance Butler, 'Charters of Duiske', *P.R.I.A.*, (1918). Dermot's seal is not extant, but it is interesting to find his descendant, Donal Reagh MacMurrough, in 1475 renewing a grant to Duiske abbey, and having his royal seal appended, perhaps based on Dermot's own (see Curtis, 'Some Seals from the Ormond Archives', *R.S.A.I.* (June 1937), p. 76.) This fine seal is worthily reproduced there.

[2] Dugdale (op. cit.), vol. VI, pt. II, p. 1137. The date must be before 1162, while Laurence was abbot of Glendaloch. The deed is a pure replica of an Anglo-Norman charter, showing the influence of the feudal state on Ireland. Who were the seneschals? Probably chief stewards, *mór-maers*. And the *duces* and *comites* of O Riain's charter? Probably heads of *mór-tuaths* and *tuaths*. Note that Ferns had a town population, paying tributes to the king, who now makes one of these tributes over to the abbey.

[3] *Register of All Hallows*, introd., pp. i–ii.

chief glories of our manuscript literature. This massive volume contains a recension of the famous epic *Táin Bó Cualgne*, written down for Dermot's tutor, Aedh Mac Criffan of Terryglass, by Finn MacGorman, bishop of Kildare, who died in 1160.[1]

EXPULSION OF DERMOT, 1166

The sudden and dramatic fall of High king Murchertach brought Dermot his ally to the ground. The High king had given the kingship of Ulidia to Eochy, son of Donnslebhe, for gold and hostages, but deposed him in 1165. But the king of Oriel, Donnchad Ó Cervall, brought Eochy with him to Armagh and induced Murchertach to restore him, on condition of his giving hostages and surrendering the territory of Bairche (Mourne), which the High king at once bestowed on Donnchad himself.

In the next year, however, 1166, Murchertach had the unfortunate Eochy blinded while under the solemn guarantees of the archbishop of Armagh and the king of Oriel. This shocking deed made even his own vassals abandon the High king. Donnchad O'Cervall renounced allegiance and Rory O'Connor seized the occasion to win the Árd Rí-ship. Allied with O'Ruairc he entered Meath where Dermot O'Melaghlin did homage, and then marched to Dublin where the Ostmen forsook Dermot MacMurrough and accepted Rory as king. He rewarded them with a huge stipend of four thousand kine, then turned north and at Mellifont received the homage of O'Cervall. Turning south again he was joined by Dermot's rebellious vassals, MacFaelain, and other north Leinster princes. The Hy Kinsella were routed at Fidh Dorcha, and Dermot MacMurrough was compelled to bow the knee. For the moment he was left in possession of his throne while Rory made the 'circuit of the High king' into Munster and was accepted by Dermot MacCarthy and Murchertach O'Brien.

Meanwhile Donnchad O'Cervall gathered the forces of Oriel and Brefni and came upon the High king at Leitir Luin in the Fews of Armagh. There, in a petty encounter, Murchertach MacLochlainn fell, to be entombed in Armagh, the last Árd Rí of his line.

Meanwhile O'Connor, continuing the 'circuit of the High king', marched north into Tyrconnell and to Armagh, where Niall, son of the dead Murchertach, submitted to him. Content with an imposing show of homages and hostages, the new Árd Rí showed no desire for further revenge. But his grim lieutenant, Tighernan

[1] *Ann. Tig.*, under 1166, mention Dermot's *caiseoil* (stone fortress) at Ferns, and the charter to Ferns abbey calls Ferns a town (*villa*).

O'Ruairc, could not forget his private grudge. Backed by the king of Meath and a force of Dubliners he marched into Leinster, incited a general revolt, and destroyed Ferns.[1]

MacMurrough was now without friends save in his native Hy Kinsella. Instead, however, of skulking in the woods of his own kingdom, he boldly determined to seek for foreign aid to restore him. Embarking in probably an Ostman ship from the Wexford coast he sailed for Bristol, taking with him his daughter Eva (Aoife) whom Giraldus describes as 'exceedingly beautiful', and leaving his son Donal Kavanagh to maintain his cause at home.

The date was August 1st 1166, as the pathetic note of a scribe in the *Book of Leinster* tells us, adding that 'he was banished by the men of Ireland over the sea'.[2] But we do not read of any formal act of banishment by a national assembly under the Árd Rí; his expulsion was clearly the work of his inveterate enemy O'Ruairc.

Tighernan and O'Melaghlin then divided Hy Kinsella between Donnchad, king of Ossory, and Dermot's brother Murchad, called subsequently by contrast with him 'na nGaedhel' (of the Irish). He was evidently intended to be a 'tame' king of Leinster in the new arrangement.

Thus began the short reign of Rory O'Connor, last native king of Erin. In 1167 he presided over the last of the reform synods, as held under Irish kings, at Athboy in Meath. Gelasius of Armagh, Laurence of Dublin, and Cadhla of Tuam attended, so did the kings of Meath, Brefni, Ulidia, Oriel, and Dublin, but the princes of Ulster and Munster stood aloof. Thirteen thousand horsemen, we are told, thronged the roads beneath Tlachtga (the Hill of Ward) where the synod met, and 'good decrees were enacted regarding veneration for churches and clerics and for the good governance of kindreds and tribes (*treabh agus tuath*)'.

Next Rory marched north with seven kings in his train and a great hosting of all Ireland to settle Ulster. At Armagh he divided Tyrone between Niall MacLochlainn, son of the dead

[1] *Ann. Tig.* state that Tighernan's object was 'to have vengeance upon Dermot for his, O'Ruairc's, wife', and add: 'they demolished the stone house which MacMurchadha had in Ferns and banished him over sea and divided Hy Kinsella'.

[2] Quoted in O'Curry's *MS. Materials for Irish History*, p. 571. It runs in Irish: 'A Muire as mór in gnim do ringned in hErind indiu . i. hi calainn August. Diarmait mac Donnchada Mic Murchada Ri Laigen agus Gall do innarba do feraib hErend tar in muir sair. Uch uch a comdui cid do gen.'

The *Song of Dermot* makes Dermot take ship from 'a place called Corkoran', and Orpen (*Normans*, I, p. 77) locates this on the coast near Youghal, but it seems hardly credible that Dermot should then be so far from his native Hy Kinsella.

Murchertach, and his rival Aedh O'Neill. Munster and Meath suffered a similar partition. Murchertach O'Brien having fallen at the hands of his MacCarthy rival, Rory in 1168 entered the province and allotted Desmond to Dermot MacCarthy and Thomond to Donal More, son of Turloch and brother of the slain Murchertach. Next year Dermot O'Melaghlin was slain by a nephew, Donal the Bregian; Rory thereupon expelled the latter and divided Meath once more, giving the eastern half to Tighernan O'Ruairc and keeping the western half himself.[1]

Meanwhile the blinded Eochy MacDonlevy was succeeded in Ulidia by a brother Maghnus, and in Oriel the kingdom passed on the death of Donnchad O'Cervall in 1168 to Murchad of that name.

With four kingdoms thus reduced, Rory seemed to have Ireland at his feet. To celebrate his triumph, in 1168 he summoned the Aonach of Tailten, that great national assembly, part fair, part court of supreme justice, part parliament, and part festival of music and literature, which it was the special prerogative of the High king to summon.[2]

These great prehistoric assemblies in which all Ireland freely mixed and which displayed a land for a time united in one law, language, and political bond had continued to the end. Their day was now over, and the native race was soon to be shattered for centuries into isolated fragments.

Ireland, which from remote ages had under Gaelic domination enjoyed national independence and immunity and had survived the Norse attack and retained her High kings, was now if she only knew it threatened with foreign masters both in Church and State.

[1] The several divisions of Meath make a perplexing point. Turloch More O'Connor had begun the subjection of this unfortunate state. In 1144, says Orpen (*Normans*, I, p. 52), Turloch divided east Meath between Tighernan O'Ruairc and Dermot MacMurrough, but the division did not last long. In 1152 Turloch and Murchertach MacLochlainn and Dermot MacMurrough united to make a new division, Murchad O'Melaghlin getting the west and his son, Melaghlin, the east half. Tighernan O'Ruairc this time got nothing, and indeed his former gain of Conmaicne (Longford and south Leitrim) was taken from him and given to a kinsman (ibid., pp. 54–5).

For the statement about a division in 1166, given in the first edition of this work, p. 44, I cannot now find the source. But in 1169 (see p. 45) there was a division which was the last before the Normans. O'Ruairc scored, but his grasping hand taught De Lacy afterwards to take all Meath and add, or claim, as far as he could, Longford and even O'Ruairc's own land of Brefni. As the diocese of Kilmore in later times (as based on synod of Kells) ran from Drumcliff in Sligo to Kells in Meath, it would seem that Tighernan was attempting to get the whole diocese for his kingdom (*Ann. Ult.*, II, p. 500; ref. to the bishop of Brefni in 1355).

[2] *Ann. Tig.*, under 1164, say that Rory built at Tuam a wonderful castle (*caistel ingantach*) apparently on the model of the Norman towers.

The Papacy under more than a century of fearless pontiffs had secured its own freedom from lay power and the veto of the Emperor, and its own election by the College of Cardinals. It had led that reformation of the Church generally which is called the Hildebrandine Reform, and its monarchy over the Church was now generally admitted. A century before, Alexander II, an ally of the Normans of Italy, had blessed the Norman conquest of England, seeing in it the opportunity to have the stagnant Church of the Anglo–saxons reformed on the new Roman lines. Another Church, still more isolated and conservative of its old customs, needed reforming, namely that of Ireland, and though she had done much through her own reformers to set the Irish house in order, much remained to be done.

Another Alexander, the third of the name, was destined similarly to hand Ireland over to England with much the same object. But before this happened (in 1172) the English-born Pope Adrian IV had in 1154 or 1155 (if we accept the evidence) already conveyed our island to this monarch.

ADRIAN'S GRANT

The text of *Laudabiliter*, one of the most momentous documents ever emanating from the Roman Curia, may be summarized thus:[1]

'Adrian, bishop, servant of the servants of God, to our well-beloved son in Christ, the illustrious king of the English, greeting. Laudably does your Majesty contemplate spreading the glory of your name upon earth, so that, as becomes a Catholic prince, you propose to enlarge the boundaries of the Church, to proclaim the truths of the Christian religion to a rude and ignorant people, and the better to accomplish this object you seek the counsel of the Apostolic see.

'Verily as your Excellency doth acknowledge, there is no doubt that Ireland and all islands on which Christ, the sun of righteousness, has shone and which have accepted the doctrines of the Christian faith belong to the jurisdiction of the Blessed Peter and the Holy Roman Church.

'Whereas then, beloved son in Christ, you have expressed your desire to enter the island of Ireland to subject its people to law and root out from them the seeds of vice, and your willingness to pay an annual tribute to the Blessed Peter of one penny from every house and to maintain the rights of the churches of that land inviolate, we do declare our will and

[1] Orpen (*Normans*, I, pp. 294–7) gives a full translation from Giraldus' Latin original (bk. vi, ch. v, pp. 317–18). For *Laudabiliter*, see pp. 45, 59.

pleasure that with a view to enlarging the boundaries of the Church, etc., you shall enter that island and execute whatsoever may tend to the honour of God and the welfare of the land.

'Also that the people there shall receive you with honour and revere you as their Lord.

'Provided always that the rights of the churches shall remain whole and inviolate, and saving to the Blessed Peter the annual tribute of one penny from every house.'

The rest is an exhortation to carry out this moral mission worthily, both in person and by agents fitted for the task, 'that the Church may be adorned, the Christian religion take root and grow, and all things pertaining to the honour of God and the salvation of souls be so ordered that you may deserve an everlasting reward'.

Though no original has been found in the papal archives of this grant, the text of which rests on the word of Giraldus Cambrensis, that some such document was issued seems incontestable. Henry of Anjou had meditated the conquest of Ireland in his early youth; since then he had had enough to manage, and possibly would never have crossed the Irish sea had not Dermot MacMurrough been exiled. But then the document worked its potent spell. The knowledge of such an *imprimatur* from the spiritual head of Europe had obviously penetrated the minds of the Irish leaders, both clerical and lay. Nothing else can explain their amazing surrender before the English king.

The Irish bishops in the crisis give the impression of being men of childish intellects. Over-impressed with the sinfulness of the laity, despondent over the weakness of the Church and futility of the kings, they concluded that the defects and backward state of their Church and nation were a justification for subjecting their native land to a foreign king as the one destined by Heaven and the Vicar of Christ to reform otherwise hopeless abuses.

Malachy himself had filled his host, Bernard, with such stories of the barbarism and vices of his fellow-countrymen that the abbot of Clairvaux wondered that so saintly and lovable a man could come out from such a race. The bishops of the time, so Alexander III declared later, had also informed the Holy See of the *vitiorum enormitates* of their people, and Ireland certainly had to pay dearly for the pious exaggerations of her spiritual chiefs.

Certainly a great use has to be made in all this of 'the argument of silence'. Malachy's stay with Bernard of Clairvaux, the association of earlier bishops with Rouen and Canterbury, the knowledge of Ireland gained and probably communicated by the Roman legate Paparo, and letters sent by Irish prelates to Alexander III at any time after his accession in 1159, may all be reckoned as possibly providing the papal headquarters with the necessary dossier for its Irish policy, which culminated in 1172.

The cause of Irish independence was thus threatened by an alliance of Rome and England. But a third danger and one nearer at hand also menaced her from beyond the Irish sea.

THE NORMANS IN WALES

This was the Norman baronial danger. The new race in Britain, the 'Franks' (*Fraingc*) as the annals call them, had already in 1072 shown themselves in Scotland with William the Conqueror against the Gaelic king, Malcolm Canmore. The well armed and professional fighting men, formidable under a royal leader, were still more to be dreaded when under their own leaders and unscrupulously engaged in conquest of other men's lands. Having conquered the brave but untrained Anglo-saxons, the Normans were not long in turning against the more fiery and tenacious Britons of Wales, and the third step was to take them over the sea, to the conquest of the Irish Celts.

The subjection of Wales was the prelude which threatened this island with a feudal conquest before the official monarchic conquest by England could take place. Under William I and William II the new earldoms of Chester, Shrewsbury, and Gloucester and the Honour of Glamorgan had begun the hemming-in of the Welsh, and before long Pembroke became a Norman land and joined in the feudal exploitation.

THE EARLDOM OF PEMBROKE

Robert de Montgomery, called 'de Belleme' because of his fief of that name in Normandy, was earl of Shrewsbury under William Rufus. No completer specimen can be quoted of the feudal tyrant, impatient of the royal yoke, shockingly cruel and hard-hearted to enemies and weaker neighbours, and yet eloquent, courteous, warlike, energetic, indefatigable in the organization of power. Robert made his then brother Arnulf lord of Pembroke, and he made steward or constable of his castle one Gerald of Windsor. In 1103, however, Henry I skilfully banished the Montgomerys back to Normandy, but Gerald survived his lord to become ancestor of all the Geraldines of Ireland. In 1109 Henry provided Gerald with a new lord, Gilbert de Clare, founder of an illustrious family, to whom he granted 'all the land of Cardigan, *if he could win it from the Welsh*'. This was the sort of 'speculative grant', at the expense of the native race, which was to be common in Ireland.

The way for Norman mastery was prepared by the defeat and death in battle in 1090 of Rhys ap Tewdwr, king of Dyved or south Wales. But Rhys left a daughter Nesta, whose Celtic beauty was to conquer the conquerors and make her the ancestress of half the Normans in Ireland.

Norman leadership, skill, and wiliness were already established in south Wales, and this ambitious race needed only Saxon or Teutonic colonists for a foundation. Many common English flocked into the land, but the main population was found in a colony of Flemish men-at-arms, no longer needed in English wars, whom Henry I planted out in Pembroke, Cardigan, and the peninsula of Gower. The advent of these newcomers is thus quaintly recorded in the Welsh Chronicle under 1105: 'The year after that, a certain nation not recognizable as regards its origin and manner of life, and nothing being known as to where it had lain concealed in the island for years, was sent into the land of Dyved by the king. And Gerald the Steward founded the castle of little Kenarth, where he settled and fortified it with a ditch, wall, and gateway with a lock upon it.'[1]

Such was the simplicity of Norman castle-building up to that time.

The Normans of South Wales, the 'lords marchers', being given a free hand by a Crown which could not or did not wish to bridle them in their border conquests, remained for centuries the quotable example of almost independent lords, waging war with one another or the Welsh, building castles, extending their 'speculative grants', and winning and dividing the booty taken from the Britons. And this was the spirit which they carried over into Ireland and indulged there for almost five centuries. Once, however, they had conquered and could hold a country they gave it a kind of rough local peace, protected the common people, and for the most part proved 'good lords' to their own. As for their cruelties, neither Welsh nor Irish princes seem to have been any more humane.

The Normans had little race-prejudice, Gerald of Windsor

[1] *Brut y Tywysogion*, ed. Ab Ithel (*R.S.*). Rhys ap Tewdwr left a son Gruffydd (d. 1137) who kept a small territory in Carmarthen. In 1136 he led the Welsh rising in which Richard FitzGilbert, uncle of Strongbow, was slain, and had a son, the Lord Rhys, who lived till 1197. The Norse settlements in south-west Wales must not be forgotten; Swansea, Haverford, Milford, etc., commemorate their influence.

married Nesta, daughter of the slain Rhys ap Tewdwr. This was apparently about 1112, but before and after that this Welsh beauty had love-affairs with King Henry I and with Stephen, constable of Cardigan, to whom, as to Gerald, she bore several famous children.

As we have seen, Henry I had in 1109 granted to Gilbert de Clare the Welsh land of Ceredigion (Cardigan) 'if he could conquer it'. Gilbert's elder son, Richard, later earl of Hertford, was in 1136 waylaid and slain by the Welsh, but King Stephen soon after created his younger brother Gilbert Earl of Pembroke. He died in 1147 (or 1148) and his son Richard 'FitzGilbert' de Clare, the 'Strongbow' of our tradition, succeeded him. But the Welsh revival prevented his enjoying the whole of his earldom, and Henry II, who came to the throne in 1154, was very hostile to the baronage of Stephen's creation, and left as little power as he could to the Earl 'of Pembroke and Striguil' (for such was Strongbow's full title).

THE MILITARY RESOURCES OF IRELAND

What temporal resources had Ireland against the impending attack from England which the flight of Dermot MacMurrough was now to bring upon her? Our sympathy and interest may well be with the native side, especially with the churchmen who had attempted to exalt her spiritual life and bring her into touch with progressive Catholicity. But what of her lay princes who should have provided her with the political unity and military strength which alone could have saved her? Alas, they were sadly lacking in perception of this double need. In spite of a few strong kings who had upthrust themselves into a temporary greatness, such as Turloch More O'Connor, the prospect of a permanent, loyally accepted, and effective monarchy for all Ireland was still deferred. The province-monarchs alone seemed to be making something out of their local rule, and so when the invaders came the High kingship collapsed ingloriously, but several of the provincial kingdoms made a determined resistance.

By crushing rival stocks of their own blood, by limiting succession to a single surname, by welding the whole province together by force if necessary, by training armies to fight, and by annexing the lands of their weaker neighbours, the province-kings were evolving a real greatness. But this was done by militarizing a country where standing armies and regular methods of warfare had formerly been little known. Doubtless the Norse invasions had been effective in turning the Irish into a military nation with a turbulent and war-loving aristocracy, the enemies of peace and progress. Instead of, or rather alongside of, older and peaceful titles to property a new and disastrous title became common, namely conquest and occupation by the *lámh laidir* (the strong hand).

'SWORD-LAND'

From early times, since the Race of Conn first hived over Connacht, Meath, and Ulster, the abundant royal families had expanded by force and colonization. 'Royal heirs' (Turloch More O'Connor had twenty-three sons) sought to make lordships for themselves at the expense of their neighbours who, provided they submitted, were allowed to remain on as vassals or otherwise they themselves had to seek other lands. The aristocracy provided by the Gaelic system was so numerous, and they themselves so warlike and greedy of eminence, that there was no other outlet for them, and the expansion habit went on as long as it could, namely, till the sixteenth century.

MacFirbis, in his great *Book of Genealogies*, compiled *circa* 1650, says: 'For it is [i.e. was] a usual thing in the case of princes when their children and their families multiply that their clients and followers are squeezed out, wither away and are wasted.' 'Tribe extinction' by conquest or expulsion was a not uncommon fate, as we find later in the story of the MacLochlainns, part killed out by their O'Neill cousins, part relegated to obscurity.[1]

> 'The anarchical conditions (of these times) were responsible for the rise of a new title to property, "sword-land" (*tír* or *ferann claidib*), namely, land obtained by violent conquest and not by any of the older titles known to Irish law. Property of this kind, with an illegal or extra-legal origin, was held to be exempt from the ordinary rules as to descent, inheritance, and disposition. The latter did not recognize the institution of "sword-land". But instances of it occur so often in the period following the Norse invasions that the subsequent appropriation of territory was accepted with comparative placidity by the native annalists.'[2]

The MacCarthys themselves, an Eoghanacht stock whose rise was mainly due to Turloch O'Connor setting them up as a counterpoise to the O'Briens, had no reluctance in expelling or subordinating other Eoghanacht stocks in the pre-Norman times, and

[1] *Gen. Tracts*, I (*Irish Hist. MSS. Comm.* (1932), p. 26). See later, p. 129, for the MacLochlainns.

[2] Note kindly provided me by Professor Daniel Binchy, one of our leading Irish authorities on the early Irish laws.

after the Normans arrived Donal More O'Brien seized the occasion to drive the MacCarthys themselves into west Desmond. [1]

Though the prerogatives of the Irish princes have not been carefully studied, a few glimpses show us what powers such monarchs as Dermot MacMurrough had over their subjects. When in annalistic phrase 'the men of Leinster' take the field, we must suppose a levy of the freemen who owed the duty, and had the right, to bear arms. We must envisage the maintenance by the kings, small and great, of mercenaries (*ámuis*), retainers, and bodyguards, and those professional soldiers (*buannadha*) who occur too near to Norman times to be due to the invader's influence. By the right of *coinmhe* (maintenance, the 'coigny' of the Anglo-Normans) or *buannacht* (billeting), the petty king of the *tuath* could quarter his troops upon his people, and by the right of *expedicio* he could call all the freemen to arms when a state of war existed. By the right of *procuracio* he was also entitled to food tributes from every townland in his state. [2]

But when the king of the province called out the whole posse of his kingdom, all these local troops were under his command. And similarly the High king might call out the whole military force of the country, as Rory O'Connor did against Strongbow.

Certain food tributes and renders in kind seem to have been due to the province-king as well as to the local chief. The king had a regality over his whole province, but in his own demesne, which in Leinster was Hy Kinsella, he received the immediate 'maintenance' and other rights of a local Rí.

The military and other resources of an Irish province-king were thus imposing, even if the troops were amateur and most of them lightly armed. But the occasion had to be war, and his power was little if he had not the obedience and loyalty of his under-kings.

These and kindred prerogatives, retained by Irish chiefs right

[1] See later, p. 83. About the beginning of the twelfth century the Eoghanacht O'Mahonys and O'Donoghues, whose lands were in Kinelmeaky and Kinelea in south-west Cork, fell out and O'Mahony drove the O'Donoghues into Kerry, where they compensated themselves by overlaying the older O'Moriarty, who was lord of Eoghanacht Locha Léin.

[2] The grant of Baldoyle by Dermot MacMurrough above quoted (p. 31) is instructive of royal power. He grants the land with its serfs free and quit of *procuracio et expedicio* to himself and his successors in the government of Leinster and Dublin for ever. The assumption is that all his subjects owed to him directly or indirectly these duties, which, at the request of the local lords, and with their consent, he could release in the interest of an abbey or favoured person.

The fourth decree of the synod of Cashel in 1172, enjoins that 'from the lands of churches that detestable food tribute be not exacted which is levied four times a year by neighbouring princes'.

up to Tudor times, were readily adopted by the Norman lords and added to the rights which their feudal position gave them.

SCOTLAND FEUDALIZED

'Alba', as the Irish called Scotland, had been from A.D. 500 a part of the Gaelic empire of which Ireland was chief, and with the British elements it contained was almost wholly a Celtic land. Now, in the eleventh and twelfth centuries, it was for the most part lost to the Celtic tradition in Church and culture. The Lothians, or south-east, became Anglo-saxon and before long the whole south of Tweed and Forth had an influx of Norman masters such as the Bruces of Annandale, who began in 1124. The old national Church, whose first metropolis had been Iona, got a new centre at Dunkeld in 850 and a later one at St. Andrews. The Anglo-saxon Margaret, wife of Malcolm III, as queen (1070–93), romanized the Church and brought it into Continental uniformity. The Celtic period in the history of the monarchy itself came to an end in 1100 and King David (1124–53), Margaret's son, feudalized and anglicized the government, and brought in a Norman baronage.

Before long Gaelic Scotland was confined, as it remained for ages, behind the 'Highland line'. But there remained as part of the Celtic world the Isles and the adjoining coasts of Argyll and the west. Or rather, here was a Norse-Celtic world where, though Gaelic speech had conquered, the blood and temper of the mixed population was largely Scandinavian, seafaring, warlike, and adventurous.

THE HEBRIDES AND MAN

From Orkney down to Man stretched a chain of Norse-founded colonies and earldoms over which the Crown of Norway did not abandon its suzerainty till after 1263. To the Irish the Hebrides were the 'Innsi Gall', the 'Isles of the Foreigners', or Norsemen. In this magnificent archipelago arose semi-Gaelic, semi-Norse chieftains or 'kings' who spent their adventurous lives between sea and shore, castle and galley, and founded ruling families who kept the formal and feudal monarchies of Scotland and England at bay for centuries. The survival of Gaelic Ireland up to the end of the sixteenth century was largely due to the survival of Gaelic Scotland in these islands so near to the Irish coast.

About 1050 we read of one 'Suibhne of Castlesween' in Argyll, who was ancestor and name-giver of the famous MacSweeney clans. A still more outstanding name is that of Somerled (Norse for 'summer farer'), lord of Argyll, whose death occurred in 1164.

From this picturesque half-Norseman and Gaelic-speaker descended the MacDonnells, Lords of the Isles until 1499. In this island-world where Norseman faded and Celt came back, the isle of Man had a semi-Norse dynasty of its own in Godred Crovan, 1079–95, and his descendants. Somerled married a granddaughter of his and sought to unite the whole of what the sagamen called the Sudreyas (Sodor, or the Southern Isles). He and his sons at least secured the Hebrides while Man went on under petty kings.

Already the galleys of this mixed race were to be found cruising by the coasts of Ulster and Connacht, the forerunners of the gallowglasses of the thirteenth century.

CHAPTER III

THE NORMAN INVASION, 1166–1172

BRISTOL was the second-greatest of English towns and by far the most important on the west coast. It was emphatically a trading city and most of its wealth came from its commercial intercourse with Dublin. Especially did its merchants profit by the sale into Ireland of slaves and captives made in the troubled times that followed the Norman conquest of England. It was a 'royal town', and its citizens enjoyed liberties, trading and otherwise, which Henry II was soon to extend to Dublin.

Hither came Dermot MacMurrough early in August 1166. One of Bristol's leading men, Robert FitzHarding, received the distinguished refugee hospitably and lodged him in the Augustinian abbey there. Their communications were doubtless made through Dermot's 'latimer' or interpreter, Morice Regan.[1]

MacMurrough was directed to the king of England, and after a long search found Henry some time after Christmas in Guienne. There the great Angevin received him graciously and listened to his requests. In his early youth, Henry 'FitzEmpress' as he was called had contemplated the conquest of Ireland, and in 1155 the council of his barons met to discuss the matter.[2] John of Salisbury, secretary to Theobald Walter, archbishop of Canterbury, was sent to Rome and obtained from the English Pope, Adrian IV, authority for the enterprise. 'At my request,' wrote John later, 'the Pope granted Ireland to Henry as an inheritance, as his letter to this day [*circa* 1159] testifies, and he further sent by me a golden ring adorned with an emerald, for the purpose of investiture, which is still in the State archives.'[3]

[1] According to Orpen, Regan supplied the materials to some Anglo-Norman on which was based the Norman-French poem which he calls *The Song of Dermot and the Earl.* For its dating, see his edition of this poem (pp. xx–xxiv). Next after Giraldus's *Expugnatio Hibernica*, it is our chief English authority for the Conquest. For the latest view see Rev. J. F. O'Doherty: 'Song of Dermot and the Earl' in *Irish Historical Studies* (1938).

[2] Henry's mother Matilda married first the Emperor Henry V, and secondly Geoffrey of Anjou, by whom she had Henry and William. As daughter of Henry I she became queen of England in opposition to Stephen. The prestige of the empire made her title of Empress very impressive, and hence Henry II was called in England 'FitzEmpress', and by the Irish 'Mac na hImperasi'.

[3] John of Salisbury's *Metalogicus*, written *circa* 1159 (ed. Giles). It is not clear whether John meant that the emerald ring was in the papal or royal

But the Empress opposed the design, of which the so-called Bull *Laudabiliter* was the lasting fruit, and Henry dropped the matter. Probably but for the expulsion of Dermot the independence of Ireland would have survived the great Angevin.

Henry did not now pledge himself to the restoration of Dermot or the conquest of Ireland in person; what he did was to give Dermot letters patent permitting anyone 'within the bounds of our dominions' to aid and assist him in recovering Leinster. MacMurrough therefore returned to Bristol and there made contact with Richard FitzGilbert, earl of Pembroke and Striguil, the Strongbow of Irish tradition.

STRONGBOW AND DERMOT

Richard FitzGilbert was a scion of the famous family of De Clare, who claimed descent from Richard the Fearless, duke of Normandy.[1] He had been earl of Pembroke since 1148, but the Welsh were hard to subdue and he was out of favour with Henry II. The offer which Dermot now made to him of the hand of his daughter Eva (for the Earl was a widower) and the succession to Leinster after him was highly attractive, and it would seem that his own king ironically encouraged him to repair his ruined fortunes in Ireland. This alone might have stung him into defiance, but, though he was a good soldier and a man of resolution enough, he lacked the supreme audacity which would have decided him to cast off entirely from England and start off to make a kingdom for himself in Ireland.[2] The great day of the Norman race was now almost over, and FitzGilbert cannot compare with the famous names of Guiscard, Roger of Sicily, and William the Conqueror, who founded new monarchies from the Tweed to the Orontes.

archives; anyway, we hear no more of it. See p. 48 of the first edition of this work for further on the intentions of Henry *in re* Ireland.

For the Bull *Laudabiliter* see later, pp. 59, 65. It seems pretty certain that John of Salisbury, one of the most reliable historians of the middle ages, did obtain some document from the Papacy authorizing an attempt upon Ireland, which, reproduced by Giraldus, is generally called *Laudabiliter*. H. W. C. Davis, *England under Normans and Angevins* (p. 202, and appendix, pp. 531–2), discusses the authenticity of *Laudabiliter*, which Davis accepts.

[1] The senior branch, which became earls of Hereford and Gloucester, ended with Earl Gilbert, slain at Bannockburn in 1314.

[2] Giraldus, whose *Conquest of Ireland* is an epic in praise of his kinsmen the Geraldines, in clever biting language disparages the Earl, of whom he says (I, ch. xxxvii): 'He never relied on his own judgment so far as to take the initiative in ordering an attack, and he never of his own inclination staked all on mere personal valour. During an engagement, wherever his banner flew there was ever a firm rallying-point or a safe refuge for his men.' In fact, Strongbow appears as a great, if not a very great, man of his feudal kind, and his early death and leaving no son to take his place marred undoubtedly the possibilities that were in him.

Strongbow had to protest to Dermot that, while accepting his offers, he must seek the permission of his liege lord Henry, but that he might expect him in Ireland next spring. The combination of Dermot 'who brought the Normans o'er' and FitzGilbert who led the Normans in was indeed an event of lasting import for Ireland, but though it extended the Norman-French world in the end to the furthest coasts of Connacht and Munster, it came too late to found a separate Norman kingdom of Ireland. Henry was to reap the supreme profits, and it is a remarkable testimony to his masterful sway that these remote Welsh barons had to seek his approval and in the end submit the fruit of their swords to him.

Next under Earl Richard a strong family interest dominated the Norman colony of Cardigan and Pembroke, the sons and grandsons of Nesta, daughter of Rhys, by her marriage with Gerald of Windsor and her love-affairs with Henry I and Stephen, constable of Cardigan.[1] Dermot found in these men adventurers of the true Norman type, discontented with their limited fortunes and hardened in constant wars with the Welsh. The Earl permitted him to enlist them. His offer of the Ostman city of Wexford and the two cantreds of land adjacent jointly to Maurice Fitzgerald and Robert Fitzstephen met with a readier response, and they assured him that, once they had mustered a sufficient force from among their kin and such men as they could hire, they would come to his aid.

Maternally the 'Race of Nesta' were Welsh, and there was nothing of custom, speech and war among the British Celts that a century of border-life had not taught them. Paternally they were Norman-French in speech and blood, members of a restless and conquering race that for some two centuries had led the vanguard of European expansion. Ireland was a land of ancient fame with the Welsh and could not escape the attention of the Cambro-Normans, who had every reason to remember and wish to emulate their former lord, Arnulf de Montgomery, when he married the daughter of a High king and hoped to win a kingdom for himself in Ireland.[2] But where he had failed, being alone and without Norman arms, they with a numerous following might hope to succeed.

The Geraldines and their knightly neighbours had not become English, and perhaps knew little of the Teutonic speech of their Anglo-saxon and Flemish tenantry. They had only known England for a generation or two and could have no sense of English patriotism. But neither had they much reason to cling

[1] See Appendix I (A), the Pedigree of the 'Race of Nesta'.

[2] See formerly, p. 11, for Arnulf. Ordericus says of him: 'He had greatly desired through that marriage to win the kingdom of his father-in-law.'

to their lands in Wales. With true Norman restlessness and adaptability, they were ready to forsake a country where their gains had been small for one that had endless room and fiefs for all and the name of great fertility and every kind of wealth. They were, in short, well fitted to make the great jump-over and become Irish in Ireland as men of their race were becoming Scots in the Lothians or Sicilians in Palermo.

The native Welsh were a bold, hardy, and irascible people, steeped in the pride of their long history in Britain and the Arthurian legend. Musical and poetic to a degree, they were also excellent soldiers and the most expert and deadly archers of that age.[1]

Mingled with Cambro-Normans and serving them was an equally restless and military race. In 1106, says the Welsh chronicle, the *Brut*, 'a certain nation [the Flemings] of whose origin, manners, or as to where it had lain concealed in the island for many years, no one knew anything, was sent by King Henry into Dyved'. These were the Flemish mercenaries whom king and barons had employed, till, becoming a nuisance, they were quartered by Henry I in South Wales. Where they did take particular root was in the Gower peninsula of Pembroke and the hundreds of Rhos, Castlemartyn, Narberth, and Dongledy. This was the original nest from which the first conquerors of Ireland took wing.[2]

The Welsh element in the invasion of Ireland was destined to be a large one, even greater than the Flemish. Light infantry and bowmen of this race had no objection to serve the Geraldines and such gentry, who themselves had Welsh blood or kindred in them. Soon after the Conquest their names are found plentifully in Leinster; and in the next century, as tenants or professional soldiers, they followed the Normans into Munster and Connacht. Indeed in more senses than one the invasion may be called a Cambrian one.

It was with a small band of such mixed troops, commanded by Richard FitzGodebert, a Fleming from Rhos or Roche near Haverford, that Dermot finally returned to Leinster early in August 1167.[3]

[1] See Cecile O'Rahilly, *Ireland and Wales* (1924), pp. 69–83, for the Irish connexions with Wales from the Viking period to the Norman invasion.

[2] The *Brut*, under 1113, says: 'Dyved (Pembroke) was full of various nations, Flemings, French, Saxons, and the native race.' The Flemings especially settled in south Wexford under Strongbow, where they preserved a distinct dialect of English mixed with other elements till 1800 or so, and their names, Prendergast, Synott, Fleming, Roche, Bluet, Scurlock, Keating, Hackett, Cheevers, etc. are familiar in Ireland still.

[3] From this FitzGodebert descended the Roches of Cork; from his brother Richard the Roches of Wexford.

Rory O'Connor and Tighernan O'Ruairc marched against him and defeated him; he had to accept conditions of peace and was left in possession of 'the ten cantreds of Hy Kinsella', giving hostages and paying O'Ruairc an honour-price on account of Dervorgilla. But the wily king was only marking time, and on May 1st 1169 Maurice Prendergast, Hervey de Montmorency, and Robert Fitzstephen landed at Bannow Bay on the south Wexford coast with three shiploads of men.[1]

'The fleet of the Flemings came to Erin,' say the annals of Tighernach, 'they were ninety heroes dressed in mail *and the Gaels put little store by them.*'[2] Dermot and his allies took Wexford and raided Ossory; nevertheless the High king's forces drove them back into Ferns. But before long, Maurice Fitzgerald and Raymond, son of William de Carew (called 'le Gros'), arrived, and at last Earl Richard himself landed near Waterford on August 23rd 1170 with two hundred knights and a thousand men-at-arms.[3] Many of his companions were destined to win fame and rich fiefs in Ireland, such as Robert de Quency, his constable.

STRONGBOW IN IRELAND

The union of the Normans who were already there with Dermot and the Earl at once turned the tide. Waterford, which had revolted against Dermot, was attacked and taken on August 25th. Of its two Ostman earls, Ragnall and Sitric, the latter was executed, the former spared. The marriage of Strongbow and Eva MacMurrough was then celebrated in the city cathedral.

By this marriage Strongbow became heir-in-succession to Leinster at such time as Dermot should die. It was sound enough in feudal law; but in Irish law it was unknown that a man should acquire a kingdom by right of a woman, whether mother or wife. Dermot was setting aside the elective rights of his royal stock and depriving his sons and his brother of their right to succeed

[1] At a headland traditionally called Baginbun, where the earthworks thrown up by the invaders can still be traced.

[2] Giraldus's *Expugnatio Hibernica*, henceforth simply quoted as *Giraldus* (I, ch. iv) says that Fitzstephen had with him thirty men-at-arms of his own kin and retainers, sixty others clad in mail, and three hundred archers, 'the pick of Wales'.

[3] The Earl had received a guarded permission from Henry to go to Ireland and repair his ruined fortunes there. Giraldus, who constantly draws the contrast between Strongbow and his vassals the 'Sons of Nesta', makes Fitzstephen, on one occasion when hard pressed, deliver a speech boasting of the Trojan and French descent of himself and his companions, concluding, 'it may be the result of this enterprise that the five portions into which the island is divided may be reduced to one, and the dominion of the whole devolve on our posterity' (bk. I, chs. v–xi).

him.[1] But victory in the field was the immediate need, and both sides realized the importance of Dublin.

The Ostman town was small and, centred round the 'fort of Dublin' where the later castle arose, stretched down to the Liffey and eastward to the old St. Andrew's church, where it had a gate. Though small, it was the most considerable and best fortified of Irish towns. Its churches were many, its Ostman population considerable, and it was a meeting-place for traders and vikings from Britain and the Scandinavian world. It was dignified by being the residence of an archbishop, of Earl Asgall, of Donal Macgillamocolmoc, and occasionally of Dermot himself.

A map of the country for thirty miles around the city would have shown the following states:

Asgall (Giraldus calls him 'Hasculf') MacTorcaill, and his brother Hamund had a fine family demesne in north county Dublin from Swords, Kinsaley, and Portrain to Baldoyle and Howth. Here in Fingall was a strong settled population of Scandinavian farmers and fishermen. The mountain slopes to the south of the city were, as far as Bray, held by families of the same race. All along the fine coast of present Wicklow were Norse outliers, and Arklow and Wicklow had each an Ostman settlement.[2]

Among the states of northern Leinster Ó Cathasaigh, lord of the Saithni, ruled much of Fingall south to Finglas, as overlord of MacTorcaill. Such was the complexity of Irish kingship.[3]

West of the city and along the rich Vale of Liffey was the territory of the Ui Faelain, the Offelan of the conquerors. With its centre at Naas it covered north county Kildare. Its head was now Faelan MacFaelain, principal of that royal north Leinster stock which had ruled before the Hy Kinsella kings. He was one of Dermot's chief rebels at present.

South of him, and commanding the rest of county Kildare, was the sept of Ui Muiredaigh (O'Murethy). It had produced the famous archbishop Laurence, and Ó Tuathail (O'Toole) was to be its later patronymic.

On the south side of Dublin and stretching in to the Wicklow

[1] Of Dermot's legitimate sons, Connor was executed by the High king as a hostage for his father's treason. His son Enna was captured and blinded by MacGillapatraic. Donal Kavanagh, his surviving son, was, according to Giraldus, illegitimate.

[2] For MacTorcaill lands, see first edition of this work, pp. 54, 83, also Mills, 'Norman Settlement in Leinster', *R.S.A.I.* (1894). Harris's *Collectanea*, I, p. 11 (1185), now calendared in *Analecta Hibernica*, gives Prince John's grant of a carucate of land at Wicklow 'which used to belong to the Ostmen' (also given in *Chartae, Privilegia et Immunitates*, p. 5.

[3] The Saithni tribe-lands stretched from east Meath (where Dunsany commemorates them) into county Dublin, where 'O'Cadesi's land' became the barony of Balrothery West.

hills lay the land of the Ui Dunchada or Fer Cualann. The present chief, Donal, was son-in-law of Dermot. The cumbrous surname of this sept came from a Gillamocolmoc of 1050; it had extended its power, we know not how, over the river and as far as Raheny. One Donal of the stock made a permanent residence for his family in a quarter of Dublin, and his son or grandson Donal had founded the Benedictine house of St. Mary there on the north of the river. The estates of this petty king stretched from Newcastle Lyons (Liamhain) to the Dodder and the gates of Dublin, and southward to Delgany and Rathdown in Wicklow, possibly as far as Glendaloch.

A combination of these chiefs alone might have repulsed the invader; as it was, they had the High king's army now marching to the scene. Rory, who did not lack energy at this crisis, had collected an imposing array from Connacht and Oriel and the men of Brefni under the faithful O'Ruairc, and encamped on 'the Green of Dublin' to the west of the city.[1] Giraldus ascribes thirty thousand men to him, an impossible number, and five thousand five hundred to the Norman-Leinster forces, which is more credible. These were now marching against the city; the Earl, Raymond, and Milo de Cogan, one of the best of the commanders, leading the English, while Dermot and his son Donal led the Leinster forces.

The High king's army, which was mainly drawn from Ulster and Connacht, held all the passes on the west of the city by which the invaders might come. But Dermot, who knew the ground well, led his army by a forced march from Glendaloch 'by the mountain, the hard field and the open land' along the slopes of the Wicklow hills, and so evading the enemy, reached the southern side of Dublin.

Both the Irish and English accounts of the fall of Dublin are vague and puzzling. It would seen that Dermot and the Earl surrounded the city and cut its people off from the High king's army. Asgall and the chief Ostmen then sent Archbishop Laurence to negotiate a peace which might have restored Asgall to his kingdom under Dermot as before. But while Asgall was asking for time to provide hostages, Raymond and Milo de Cogan suddenly attacked and took the city, on September 21st 1170. Asgall and his chief men had time to get away by sea. Of the morality of the capture it is useless to speak. The unscrupulous Norman race was always good at a *coup de main*, and preferred a *fait accompli* to dull parleyings. Dermot too and the Earl did not mean to let

[1] The 'Green of Dublin' (*Faithche Atha Cliath*) stretched from Kilmainham to the river (Hogan's *Onomasticon Goidelicum*). *The Song of Dermot* says: 'The pride of Ireland were gathered at Clondalkin on the moor.'

the great prize of victory, Dublin, slip from their grip now that everything was at stake.[1]

The Norse foundation on the Liffey thus became the capital of the English in Ireland for more than seven centuries. Dermot and the Earl appointed De Cogan constable of the fortress, and Strongbow then returned south to Waterford, but the indefatigable Dermot marched into Meath to follow up the victory. Rory, who had kept his army together, reminded him of the former treaty by which he had kept Leinster, and bade him dismiss his foreigners and refrain from invading other men's lands. The haughty Leinsterman answered that he intended to reduce all Ireland, whereupon the High king put his son Connor and two other hostages to death.

The Irish side was now without a leader worthy of the crisis. Towards the end of 1170 the bishops under Gelasius of Armagh and Laurence of Dublin met at Armagh to consider remedies. Their chief resolution is thus given by Giraldus:

> 'It appeared to the synod that Divine vengeance had brought this judgment upon them for the sins of the people, and especially for that they had long been wont to purchase natives of England from traders, robbers, and pirates, and to reduce them to slavery, wherefore they were now themselves by reciprocal justice reduced to slavery by that very same nation. For it was the common practice of the Anglo-saxon people while their kingdom was intact to sell their children and send sons and kinsfolk to be sold in Ireland at a time when they were not suffering from poverty or famine. The synod therefore decreed that all Englishmen throughout Ireland who were in a state of bondage should be restored to freedom.'[2]

STRONGBOW AS 'KING OF LEINSTER'

The sudden death of Dermot MacMurrough at Ferns on May 1st 1171 at the age of sixty-one put a new face on the business. Richard de Clare now became, by his father-in-law's bargain with him, king of Leinster, but the position, which the Irish did not accept and Henry was not likely to approve, required more audacity and success than he was capable of.

[1] Orpen (*Normans*, I, pp. 208–13) gives a reasoned account of the fall of Dublin. See, for another view, Rev. J. F. O'Doherty's paper, 'Laurence of Dublin and the Anglo-Norman Invasion' in *Irish Ecclesiastical Record* (Nov. 1937).

[2] *Giraldus*, I, ch. xvii. William of Malmesbury (*R.S.*, III, ch. i) gives further details of this slave-trade, by which Anglo-saxon, Scottish, and other captives of war were sold to the Irish by the men of Bristol and Dublin.

Now was the moment for the High king to rally all Ireland to a supreme effort to expel the foreigners whose summoner and greatest ally had now vanished from the scene. He therefore called upon the great princes, who should at least now realize the serious prospect for the country.

Donnslebhe (Dunlevy) MacDunlevy now ruled in Ulidia, Murchad O'Cervall in Oriel, and Meath was claimed by two O'Melaghlins, Maghnus and Donal the Bregian, though she had lately been dismembered by the High king. In the north the Cinel Eoghain king, Melachlin MacLochlainn, stood haughtily aloof. In the south, Munster stood divided between Donal O'Brien and Dermot MacCarthy.

Of these province-kings, Donal More was to prove the ablest, if not the most patriotic. His rule was effective over the present counties of Clare, Limerick, and north Tipperary, and the city of Limerick was his undoubted capital. In Irish he was 'king of Thomond', in Latin he called himself 'Rex Limericensis' from his Ostman capital.

Dermot MacCarthy's kingdom of Desmond was already well defined, and stretched from Mount Brandon on the extreme west of the Corcaguiney peninsula to the headwaters of the Blackwater and along that river between the present Cork and Limerick counties to Lismore and Youghal. It had in Latin the name 'Regnum Corcagiense' and, like the 'Regnum Limericense', took this name from its capital, for by this time the Ostman city of Cork had become MacCarthy's capital.[1]

THE SIEGE OF DUBLIN, JUNE–SEPTEMBER 1171

King Henry had already before Dermot's death forbidden any more of his subjects to go to Ireland, and ordered those who were there to return. Giraldus tells us that Strongbow then sent Raymond of Carew to Aquitaine to place his Irish possessions at his feet. He admitted that it was with Henry's leave he had gone to aid Dermot 'your liegeman', and ended: 'Whatever lands I have the good fortune to acquire here, either from his patrimony or that of any other, as I owe them to your grace I shall hold them at your will and disposal.'

Any intention on De Clare's part therefore of founding a separate state beyond the Irish sea was thus renounced. Probably he doubted his power to hold his ground alone. His Geraldine lieutenants, it seems, were ready to attempt it, but were let down

[1] *Cork Arch. Soc.* (1904), p. 145. An Ostman earl (*mór-maer*) ruled in MacCarthy's name, viz. Gilbert, son of Turgar, slain in 1173 by the Normans.

by their chief. Already an overwhelming combination was forming against them, of the High king, an Irish army, and a Norse fleet, due, it is said, to Laurence O'Toole. According to the best Irish authority, Tighernach, Rory O'Connor, Tighernan O'Ruairc, and O'Cervall led the Irish host with their provincial levies; we may be sure that the north Leinster chiefs would be with them, but the English account makes the combination a far more national one.[1]

Asgall MacTorcaill had by now hired or otherwise enlisted in the cause of the recovery of his kingdom several famous vikings and a thousand or more Norsemen from Man and the Hebrides, of whom the most famous was John the Wode, or 'Mad', an adjective which implies that he was one of the old-fashioned Berserks. The general objective was that the High king should besiege Dublin from the land and the Norsemen attack it from the sea. Considering how small the Dublin garrison was and that Robert Fitzstephen was at the time cooped up in Carrick-on-Slaney by an Ostman revolt which was probably part of the plan, the prospects of the Normans in Ireland were dark indeed. The Earl himself was in the city, of which De Cogan was constable, and the investment, threatened or complete, lasted most of the summer months. But the situation, all favourable to the Ostman-Irish plan, was ruined by the premature attack of the Scandinavians. The Irish side was slow in forming the siege, the Norse too quick in attacking. In their sixty ships they brought at least a thousand men, 'born warriors', says Giraldus, 'in Danish fashion completely clad in mail; men with iron hearts as well as iron arms'. Forming up under Asgall and John the Wode, they marched against the eastern gate. De Cogan, however, attacked these formidable, axe-wielding fighters with the Norman horse in front, and another flank attack as they marched up from the Liffey also shook them. At last, after a gallant stand, they broke and fled to the ships. John, true to his viking tradition, was hewn to pieces, Asgall was taken and beheaded in his own hall. Such was the end of Norse Dublin, and again, as at Hastings, the shock of headlong Norman cavalry beat Teutonic infantry, bravely though they stood their ground.[2]

No sooner, however, had the smaller danger vanished than the greater loomed up. The High king's army and detachments

[1] *Giraldus* and *The Song of Dermot* say that the High king encamped at Castleknock (to the west of the present Phoenix Park), Donal O'Brien and Murchad MacMurrough at Kilmainham with the Leinster chiefs of north Leinster, and O'Ruairc with the kings of Oriel, Ulidia, and Meath along with O'Cathasaigh about Clontarf. The subsequent forfeitures of the Saithni, Ui Faelain, Ui Muredaigh, and Meath perhaps prove that their chiefs were at the siege and therefore technically rebels.

[2] *Giraldus*, I, ch. xxi.

hemmed the Earl up in Dublin from July to September. So hard pressed and short of supplies was the garrison that finally Strongbow sent Archbishop Laurence to Rory offering to become his man and hold Leinster of him. The High king replied that he would grant him only Dublin, Waterford, and Wexford. If this offer were declined, let him prepare for an immediate attack. The answer inevitably threw Strongbow back upon his liege lord, King Henry, to whom in fact he had already submitted. But he could also face the ordeal of battle.

At this moment of dismay, Maurice Fitzgerald revealed the true mentality of the Norman, a race landless and nationless, ready to accept or reject any allegiance, but determined to be masters of their fate. Addressing the barons, he declared for instant action. 'Is it succour from our own country we expect? Such in truth is our lot that while we are English to the Irish, we are Irish to the English. For the one island does not detest us more than the other.' There spoke men who did not mean to go home, who indeed, had no home to go to, and before many generations the clan of this Geraldine in the spirit of his words turned Irish as the Irish.

So the besieged arrayed themselves for a desperate sortie. De Cogan led the van; Raymond, Donal Kavanagh, and the Earl followed; the nucleus of the whole army being six hundred mailed men. Marching over Dubhgall's bridge and sweeping round by Finglas to the south-west, they burst in on Rory's army encamped on the Liffey and completely routed it.

Fifteen hundred of the Irish fell, the High king escaped, and his camp, with enough corn and meal to last the conquerors a year, fell into their hands. The date, according to Giraldus, was about September 1st. Tighernach says briefly: 'The earl and Milo de Cogan entered the camp of Leth Cuinn', i.e., attacked the Northern army; evidently if there were Munster and Leinster levies to the south they retreated without a blow, on hearing of Rory's defeat.

Thus fell the Irish monarchy which had existed for some seven centuries. With the defeat of his greatest effort and the following submissions to King Henry, Rory O'Connor was henceforth High king only in name.[1]

[1] The siege of Dublin is described in full detail by Orpen (*Normans*, I, pp. 222–46). He makes the order of the events to be that the High king besieges Dublin first in the late summer of 1171; his army is beaten by the Norman sally, and next, too late, Asgall and his Norse allies attack by the eastern gate. His main reliance for this order is *The Song of Dermot*. Rev. J. F. O'Doherty, in his thesis, 'Laurence of Dublin and the Anglo-Norman Invasion' (*Irish Ecclesiastical Record*, Nov. 1937) prefers the older view as based on Tighernach and Giraldus, to which he adds the saga of Earl Rognvald of Orkney. According to this, the Norse attack comes first in June, previous

In spite of the victory of Dublin, Strongbow feared that without Henry's approval and intervention he could hardly hold Leinster against the Irish forces, which must have overwhelmed him in the end.

An independent Norman kingdom was not destined for Ireland. The Geraldines and the first-comers believed that they could single-handed master the country and weld the five kingdoms into one, of which perhaps they would have made their feudal suzerain, FitzGilbert, king. They were men of no English ties, and true products of the Norman race which never doubted its capacity for any situation, however dangerous or hopeless. They at least were ready to make themselves kings in this new country, and chafed at being pursued by that royal authority in England from which they had gladly escaped. But for Strongbow, whose position as a tenant-in-chief of the Crown was a much more difficult one, this supreme audacity was impossible. Thus it befell that the centralized monarchy of England, now vested in one of her greatest kings, was able to follow the Cambro-Norman adventurers over, to rob them of the expected fruits of their enterprise, and establish here a dependent kingdom, tied for centuries to the greater kingdom.

HENRY II IN IRELAND

Henry was determined that a new realm should not rise beyond the western sea. Further, he needed a diversion from the storm raised by the murder of Archbishop Becket on December 29th 1170, over which Alexander III called on him to do public penance, and for which he was not reconciled with the Holy See till 1172.

At a council of his barons at Argentan in July, Henry obtained approval of an invasion of Ireland and, landing at Portsmouth, began his march to the Severn, while the knighthood of England by his orders assembled in Gloucestershire, and a fleet of two hundred and fifty vessels was collected at Milford Haven. On hearing of his sovereign's arrival on the Welsh borders, Strongbow sailed over and appeared before him and laid his conquests at his feet. Already at Winchester as he began his march Henry had received Murchad, Dermot's brother, and envoys of the Ostmen of Wexford, informing him that they had his 'felon' Fitzstephen safe in hand. For indeed the valiant Robert had been taken by these strange allies, who now thought to please the new conqueror at his expense.

to the siege; after its defeat the High king forms the siege, which in its turn is broken up early in September. On the whole I favour this order of the events; it must be admitted, however, that the whole story is a confused and ill-dated one.

The 'Son of the Empress', or FitzEmpress (in Irish 'Mac na hImperasi'), landed near Waterford on October 17th 1171 with five hundred knights and four thousand archers. Imposing as this army was, Henry did not intend a conquest in arms, but relied on his prestige and on Adrian's missive to bring aboul a general submission. At Waterford, to whose Ostmen he gave his favour,[1] he granted to Strongbow 'the land of Leinster' as a fief, at service of one hundred knights, but reserved to himself the towns of Dublin, Waterford, and Wexford, and the Norse kingdom of Dublin.[2]

He had not long to wait for the expected Irish submission. The south, strong in the old hostility of 'Mogh's Half' to the north, was the first to surrender. Dermot MacCarthy did homage at Waterford and received back his kingdom under tribute. Henry then marched inland to Cashel and on the way at Lismore met Christian, bishop there, whom he relied upon to win the submission of the Church at a general synod. Donal O'Brien, king of Thomond, came in, and so did the kings of the Déisi and Ossory and swore homage. During Henry's slow march to Dublin, which he reached on November 11th, or in the capital itself, the princes of north Leinster, the king of Oriel, and even, it appears, Tighernan O'Ruairc, submitted in person. As a result of their homages, O'Brien and MacCarthy were to admit royal constables for Cork and Limerick.

THE LAWS OF ENGLAND GRANTED

At Lismore, wrote Matthew Paris in the next century, Henry 'assembled a council where the laws of England were by all freely received and confirmed with all solemnity'.[3] This declaration of rights must have applied first to the Anglo-Normans who were with Henry and secondly to the princes, bishops, and other Irish who did homage to the King. From the earliest days of the Conquest the 'five royal races' (*quinque sanguines*) or kings of provinces, were entitled to justice in the Anglo-Irish courts.[4] And

[1] *Ann. Ult.*, dropping into Latin, say of this imposing visit: 'venit in Hiberniam Henricus Mac na hImperasi potentissimus rex Angliae et idem dux Normannie et Aquitanie et comes Andegav. et aliarum multarum terrarum dominus.'

Henry took the Ostmen of Waterford, who had made no resistance to him, under special protection of the Crown in a charter beginning 'Houstmanni Waterford ligei homines mei sunt' (*Carew Miscell.*, p. 466).

[2] In 1173, however, Henry restored Wicklow (which had a Norse castle or stronghold, later called Blackcastle) and Wexford to Strongbow. Strongbow then granted Wicklow to Maurice Fitzgerald.

[3] Matt. Paris: *Vita Henrici II, sub* 1172.

[4] Ball, *Legislative Systems* (appendix A) and Davies, *True Discovery* (ed. Morley, *Ireland under Elizabeth and James* (1890), p. 262), who says: 'In the

if Henry was aiming at the submission of the Irish Church, he must equally have felt bound to apply to Ireland the laws that protected the Church in England.

Fitzstephen, handed over by the Wexford men, was scolded and set free by the King for invading Ireland without leave, and the other Geraldines were rated by his royal majesty, but this was mainly show to please Irish and Ostmen who might thus look on Henry as their protector against unlicensed invaders. Before long, the 'Race of Nesta' were in possession of the fiefs promised them by Dermot and recipients of further favours from Strongbow, their head lord. Surrounded by his natural and his new vassals, Henry spent the winter on the Thing-mote of Dublin, where the Irish chiefs had made for him 'a royal palace made with admirable skill after the fashion of the land'.[1] According to the annals, every kingdom in Ireland submitted to him save Connacht, Tyrone, and Tyrconnell.

It was now that Henry gave Dublin its first civic charter. He declared it a royal city and granted it to his men of Bristol with the liberties of the same.

Provision had to be made for the government of the new realm. Hugh de Lacy, lord of Ludlow, who was with the King, was made guardian of Dublin and Justiciar or viceroy of Ireland. The resident barons would act as the council for the King's lieutenant, and later the Anglo-Irish tenaciously held that a so-called 'Statute of FitzEmpress' gave the chief officers and members of the council the right to choose the Governor of Ireland in the event of a vacancy and until the King at Westminster should make final provision.

To hold the land, Henry put garrisons into Dublin, Wexford, and Waterford. The old Scandinavian population were taken under special protection as 'the King's Ostmen'. Their land and cities had in fact been the first to be confiscated by King and barons. An ample demesne was annexed to the Crown, namely the chief Ostman cities and their territories (cantreds), the coastland from Waterford to Dungarvan, the Vale of Liffey, and other parts of Dublinshire. The tribal districts of the Ui Faelain, Ui Dunchada, Ui Muiredaigh, and the Saithni were thus taken over by the Crown or divided out among the adventurers, though something was left

third of Edward II among the Plea Rolls in Bermingham's Tower, all the five septs or bloods *qui gaudeant lege Anglicana quoad brevia portanda* are given, viz. O'Neill de Ultonia, O'Molaghlin de Midia, O'Connoghor de Connacia, O'Brien de Thotmonia et Mac Murrogh de Lagenia.'

[1] Hoveden and *Gesta Henrici*. The Thing-mote was the great mound east of the then Dublin (about the present College Green) where the Ostmen held their folk-assemblies.

to the family of Macgillamocolmoc. As these chiefs either fought against or had not steadily held for Dermot and the Earl, their later submissions did not save them from confiscation. The lands of Asgall, last Norse earl of Dublin, were also taken over, but as late as 1174 we have mention of a grant of Strongbow by which he confirmed to Hamund MacTurkil, one of this family, Kinsaley and adjacent lands held by him before the coming of the English.[1]

THE COUNCIL OF CASHEL

It now remained for the Church to complete the submission of the chiefs. During the winter of 1171–2 a council of bishops met at Cashel under Christian of Lismore, who from the death of Malachy had taken the chief place in the reform movement, and now was to make the final *rapprochement* with Rome coincide with the extinction of native Ireland.

With him were Laurence of Dublin, and the archbishops of Cashel and Tuam, while Gelasius of Armagh, too old to attend, came to Dublin later and confirmed the proceedings. This venerable representative of the old Church died in 1175.

The decrees of Cashel, confirmed by Henry, completed the work of a whole century of reform. The King was represented by Ralph, archdeacon of Llandaff, and two other English clerics, while Christian of Lismore as papal legate represented Roman authority. The constitutions, as reported by Giraldus, were passed without resistance. Four of them were concerned with due observance of marriage, baptism, wills, and masses for the faithful departed. On these matters of observance, the reformers had already pronounced. Another directed the payment of tithes of corn, cattle, and other produce at each man's parish church. Another freed church property from lay impositions and forbade local kings (*reguli*) and chiefs to exact refection and lodging from church lands or to enforce the 'detestable practice' of food tributes from church glebes. Another freed clerics from having to pay part of the fines levied on laymen for homicide, even if they were kin of the accused. These were already part of the reform programme; now it might seem that a king and a government had come which could enforce them and set the Church free from lay exactions.

But, for the distinctive character of the Church of Ireland, the most effective constitution was this: 'The divine offices shall

[1] See first edition of this work, pp. 54, 83.

be celebrated according to the forms of the Church of England.'[1] This meant that the Sarum Use in the Mass, as approved at Rome, was to be henceforth the one and only orthodox usage in Ireland.

Thus was the ecclesiastical reform, which began in 1100, completed under the aegis of the new Angevin lord. But, whereas at first Canterbury had claimed the supremacy over our ancient Church, the claim was now cancelled and she was put into immediate union with Rome as a national Church, with Armagh as the seat of the primacy among her thirty-three bishops.

The native Church through its spiritual heads thus submitted to the English king, as most of the native kings had done. It is remarkable with what unanimity the leaders, both political and clerical, of Ireland yielded at this crisis, and without making any terms for themselves individually or for their country as a whole. The bishops indeed went the whole way to oblige Henry and, if we are to believe reputable chroniclers of the next century, each of them gave him a letter with his seal attached, confirming to Henry and his heirs the kingdom of Ireland.[2] These letters the King sent to Pope Alexander III in order to obtain the papal confirmation.

That the new Angevin lord of Ireland did not now openly publish the 'Bull *Laudabiliter*' can be understood when we remember that he was estranged from the Pope over Becket's murder. Moreover, *Laudabiliter* had lapsed through non-user from 1155. Alexander III was able to make a grant of Ireland, as proceeding from himself, part of the reconciliation in 1172 with a king he could not afford to estrange. That Adrian's donation was, however, known, or at least 'in the air', we may well believe; it is hard to explain otherwise the general and voluntary surrender, both in Church and State, of native Ireland.

ALEXANDER'S GRANT OF IRELAND

As soon as Henry returned to England and was reconciled with Rome and did penance for Becket, Alexander III did in effect renew Adrian's grant.[3] Three letters of this pontiff from Tusculum in September 1172 addressed all concerned in the Conquest (the

[1] Giraldus, giving this among the other constitutions (V, bk. I, ch. xxxiv), adds: 'for it is right and just that as Ireland has received her Lord and King from England she should accept reformation from the same source'. These words are clearly his comment and not part of the decree.

[2] This is not stated by Giraldus, but it is by Roger Hoveden (III, p. 30) and in *Gesta Henrici* (I, p. 26). It does seem borne out by Alexander's statement in one of his letters from Tusculum.

[3] Henry made his peace with the Papacy over Becket's murder at Avranches in September 1172.

word then only meant 'acquisition') of Ireland. One to Christian of Lismore and the bishops speaks of the *vitiorum enormitates* of the Irish laity, as made known to Rome 'by letters patent of the bishops themselves'. The prelates are adjured to assist Henry in keeping possession of Ireland and to censure those who break their oaths of loyalty to him.

A second, to Henry, bids him continue his good work, i.e. the purifying of Ireland, 'enlarging the bounds of the Church in general', and his moral mission to its people and Church. A third, to the kings and princes of the country, commends them for receiving him as king of their own free will. In these letters the Supreme Pontiff repeats the words used by Malachy to Bernard about his own people, 'a barbarous race, Christian in name only'.[1]

Whatever may be thought of Adrian's Bull, no doubt can exist that his successor Alexander presented Ireland to Henry. In 1173 William FitzAudelin, Henry's viceroy, published his privilege and apparently repeated it on a later occasion at a synod in Waterford. At another synod, in March 1177, Cardinal Vivian as papal legate declared Henry's right to Ireland and commanded the people to give him their allegiance. From that to 1534 the kings of England, and the chiefs and clergy of Ireland had no doubt of the authenticity of the papal donation, which they attributed to Adrian.[2]

The Irish Church had submitted on cosmopolitan and religious grounds and we may call the bishops honest and disinterested, if ingenuous, men. In reformers such as Malachy and Christian, patriotism had been swallowed up by zeal for the Church Universal. But the submission of the lay princes did them less credit.

THE SUBMISSIONS OF THE CHIEFS

Each of the chiefs had his reason for this easy homaging. O'Brien was more concerned with becoming master of all Munster

[1] These letters (not in *Giraldus*) are printed in Hearn's *Black Book of the Exchequer* (1728). See also *Benedict of Peterborough* (I, 26, 28) and Roger Hoveden (II, 31). The latter and *Gesta Henrici* say that at Cashel each of the bishops present gave Henry a letter confirming to him and his heirs the kingdom of Ireland *in perpetuum*. *Giraldus* (II, ch. v) says that after Cashel the King sent to Alexander asking for a privilege. This privilege, along with the September letters, was published by the papal envoys at the synod of Waterford. Henry apparently had sent the Pope the bishops' letters after Cashel.

For a skilful and enlightening summing up of the whole evidence for *Laudabiliter* and the whole question of the papal grant, see the paper by Rev. Dr. J. F. O'Doherty in *Irish Ecclesiastical Record* (Aug. 1933). He accepts the genuineness of *Laudabiliter*.

[2] See *Giraldus* (V, 345) for the synod of Dublin.

again than saving Ireland. Dermot MacCarthy saw a way of securing Desmond for ever against his enemy of Thomond. Ossory might thus shake off the yoke of Leinster and Munster, claimants for its overlordship. Oriel and Ulidia could thus be set free from MacLochlainn. The Ostmen preferred the Angevin to Irish kings and French buccaneers, being for the most part traders and townsmen. The top kings of the time whom the race for the High kingship had prospered, such as Connacht and Tyrone, might regret, but others might welcome, a foreign intervention which secured them from subjection to their immediate neighbours. All perhaps preferred a strong king, who could protect them, to the relentless Norman buccaneers.

The extinction of one whole province-kingdom, Leinster, should have warned the other kings of a similar fate, but this and the confiscations of the Ostman towns and contados were all that had happened so far. They thought of little but their own local interests. The Árd Rí's office had been a light matter and an easy yoke. What harm to confer it upon a foreigner, 'the Son of the Empress', a European prince of dazzling greatness? In an Irish state itself 'a stranger in sovereignty' was not permitted, but he could be in the unhereditary High kingship.

When the kings at Dublin 'went into Henry's house', as the Irish ran, they thought of themselves as merely giving hostages and homage to a superior who would leave their province-kingships untouched. Henry gave his new vassals no charters for their lordships, and thus seemed to accept their position, namely as elective rulers, having demesnes and prerogatives in virtue of their office, while their subjects held under them by ancient custom.[1]

The numerous brehons and scholars of Ireland may have advised the kings that a mere state of vassalage was thus created, in which they would be left supreme over their people under the harmless suzerainty of a foreign king. But legally and in fact, as king of England Henry was supreme landlord and *dominus terrae*, from whom all titles to land and liberties depended in the ultimate, to whom estates constantly reverted or were forfeited, and under whom the lords of land had also local jurisdiction over the land and all its tenantry. Feudal monarchy and feudal lordship were in short inevitably destined to enter Ireland under the

[1] This view is borne out by Tighernach, who says, under 1170, that Henry 'received the kingship of Leinster, of the men of Meath, and of Brefni, Oriel and Ulidia'; and, under 1172, 'Henry, king of England, after taking the Southern Half of Ireland and the eastern part of the Northern Half [enough to constitute him High king in short], returned to England'.

new master. With this conception of authority, patriarchal kingship of the Gaelic type was irreconcilable. In England, moreover, every man, whether peer or peasant, was in the long run the king's liege subject, owing all his primary duties to him, and to bear arms against the king, even if your lord commanded you, was treason.

Henry had not won Ireland by the sword. 'There was scarcely any one of rank or name in the island', says Giraldus, exaggerating the numbers and the nature of their homage, 'who did not, in person or otherwise, pay to the king the homage due from a liegeman to his lord.' After reciting Henry's claims, which include the fantastic legend that Arthur of Britain had Irish kings tributary to him, this writer makes the submission appear as a legal and constitutional one, by saying that the princes of Ireland voluntarily submitted to the king of England, doing him fealty, and taking oaths of allegiance; and that such contracts, though entered into of freewill, are not free to be broken. Finally, he adds, papal authority completes and confirms Henry's title.[1]

Thus, either the Irish kings were feudal vassals in the sense that the Scottish king for a time was vassal of the English one, or else the whole Irish people by free contract had been secured in the same rights as the people of England. But, in fact, Ireland was soon to be treated as an annexed, conquered, and therefore rightless country, and this was immediately shown when Henry, before leaving Ireland, granted 'the land of Meath as fully as Murchard Hua Melachlin or any before him had held it' to Hugh de Lacy, though he had but lately received the homage of the 'men of Meath' as Tighernach tells us.[2] Though a grant by charter in formal fashion, this was a grant on a magnificent scale and of a kind which Irish law knew nothing of. It was the giving away of a kingdom, a matter of handing over nearly a million acres of the richest land in Europe to a subject, with the former rights of a native Rí and all the full new feudal regalities, all at the petty service of fifty knights. The rights of O'Melaghlin were extinguished and, before the end of Henry's reign, the precedent was successively followed in Ulidia, Oriel, Connacht, Desmond, and portions again of these.

Thus, before the great Angevin left Ireland, he created or confirmed two huge feudal principalities in this country, 'the Land of Leinster' and 'the earldom of Meath'. In De Lacy he hoped to counterbalance Strongbow and 'the Race of Nesta' who, he suspected, would consider they owed their lands not to him but

[1] *Giraldus*, I, ch. cxxxii and II, ch. vii.

[2] The charter, given at Wexford, included 'all liberties which I (the king) have or can have in Meath'. For the text see *Cal. of the Gormanston Register* (ed. Mills and McEnery), p. 177.

to their own valour and enterprise. De Lacy was in fact a man of remarkable qualities and one after Henry's own heart; dark, stoutly built, firm and steadfast in character, short in person, 'avaricious and temperate as any Frenchman', indefatigable in public and private affairs. Such was the first viceroy of Ireland, an English official rather than a feudal baron.

King Henry left Ireland on Easter Monday, April 27th 1172. In seven months he had founded the English 'lordship of Ireland', which was destined to last till Henry VIII turned it into a kingdom. But he had only founded it, and he left the unfortunate tradition that a visit to his second realm of a few months, or none at all, was enough for an English king to settle the affairs of Ireland.

CHAPTER IV

THE CONQUEST CONTINUED, 1172–1177

FOR several years after Henry's departure, though the Anglo-Irish colony had been founded, there was no government in the real sense. Strongbow and the first-comers were mainly occupied with organizing their vast fiefs, and with the Irish kings the immediate need was to protect their surviving states.

There could hardly be double lords, and the native chief had to make way for the feudal one or make good his ground. One of the most famous of the petty kings was thus removed. De Lacy arranged a meeting with Tighernan O'Ruairc at the Hill of Ward in 1172, some obscure treachery was perpetrated, and Tighernan, 'king of Brefni, Conmaicni and the greater part of Meath', was slain and his head set up over the gate of Dublin Castle.

Next Donal O'Farrell of Conmaicni was disposed of, and his state (now Longford) was annexed by De Lacy. Brefni as a single kingdom was thus broken up, but in due time reappeared as Brefni O'Ruairc, the western half, and Brefni O'Reilly, the eastern half. In the same year, 1172, Murchad MacMurrough, brother of the late king Dermot, was slain treacherously by the 'people of Fitz-Empress'. Faelan MacFaelain was dispossessed of his *mór-tuath* of Offelan. As for the ill-starred kingdom of Meath, Donal O'Melaghlin was slain by his brother Art, who continued for a time to call himself 'king of Midhe', but another of the name, Magnus, was captured and hanged by the ruthless conquerors. So everywhere the native kings or candidates were removed from the path of the feudal grantees.

In 1173 Henry again made himself felt in Ireland. He must have been surprised and mortified, after all the grand pretensions, by the resistance of the Irish and the violence of the Normans. He therefore sent over William FitzAudelin (or FitzAdelm) who published a privilege granted by Pope Alexander at a synod of Waterford. Thus it was hoped to silence Irish opposition and validate the royal claim to Ireland.[1]

This privilege, as Giraldus gives it, is a shorter document than *Laudabiliter*, of which indeed it reads like a summary. It runs thus:

[1] Orpen (*Normans*, I, p. 297) gives a translation of the privilege as well as *Laudabiliter*, and puts FitzAudelin's mission to Ireland in April 1173.

'Forasmuch as those concessions of our predecessors which are known to have been made deserve to be confirmed, We, following in the footsteps of the venerable Pope Adrian, ratify and confirm to you [Henry] the concession of the said Pope made to you concerning the lordship of the kingdom of Ireland —saving to the blessed Peter and the Holy Roman Church in Ireland as in England the annual payment of one penny from every house, to the intent that the evil customs of that country may be abolished, and that the barbarous nation, reckoned Christian only in name, may through your care assume the beauty of good morals, and that the church there hitherto disordered may be set in order and the people may henceforth through you attain the reality as well as the name of the Christian profession.'[1]

STRONGBOW AS VICEROY, 1173–1176

In August 1173 the King made Earl Richard, chief of the conquerors, 'Guardian of Ireland', and granted him Wexford and Wicklow. The advance of the Norman buccaneers was continuous, and Henry had to admit that Ireland must be for them to conquer, since there was neither a royal army nor a true government in the land to overcome and then to rule it. On every advance followed the erection of one of those elementary 'mote and bretesche' fortresses, which a few determined knights and dreaded Welsh archers could hold. Not for fifty years did the conquerors build permanent stone castles, of which the art was being perfected in England.[2]

The 'mote and bretesche' fort (hence the place-name 'Brittas' in various places) consisted of a high mound with flat summit, surrounded by a ditch or fosse, a stockade, and an outer bailey, and having on the mound itself a wooden tower for the lord and the garrison. De Lacy built one such at Trim, which made way only in 1220 for the regular stone castle which formed the keep of the massive structure that survives to-day.[3]

[1] *Giraldus*, VI, ch. vi, p. 315. The majority of authorities, however, are against the authenticity of this privilege of 1173, which certainly reads like a rehash by Giraldus of the authentic *Laudabiliter*.

[2] See Orpen (*Normans*, I, pp. 340–3), and on 'Motes and Norman Castles in Ireland' in *R.S.A.I.* (1907), p. 123. For another view on the extent and nature of Norman Motes see Westropp, ibid. (1905), pp. 313–45, 405; also H. G. Leask, 'Irish Castles, 1180–1310', in *Royal Archaeological Institute of Great Britain and Ireland* (1937).

[3] See F. M. Stenton, *English Feudalism, 1066–1166* (1932) for 'motte and bailey' castles (pp. 196–200) and *passim* for the development of the castle in England. The rapid and general encastellation of the conquered parts of Ireland was the chief cause of Norman success.

THE ATTACK UPON MUNSTER

Raymond Fitzwilliam of Carew, called 'le Gros' from a corpulence which did not prevent endless energy and ambition, had been granted by Strongbow the rich fief of Idrone in Carlow, the native inheritance of O'Ryan. But he aspired to greater fiefs still. In 1173, with the Earl's approval as viceroy, he invaded Desmond, whose king, Dermot, having recently submitted, had a good right to regard this as a breach of faith. Having plundered Lismore, part of Raymond's men sailed with the booty into Youghal harbour, but were attacked there by Dermot's vassals, the Ostmen of Cork, whose fleet was commanded by Gilbert, 'son of Turgar', the *mór-maer* of the city. But he was slain and the Normans got away in the encounter. Raymond, marching by land, encountered Dermot himself, who was coming to aid the Ostmen; he routed the king and carried off four thousand cattle from the enemy.[1]

Meanwhile Donal O'Brien had called upon Rory O'Connor and expelled the Earl's garrison from Kilkenny. Early next year, 1174, Strongbow marched to Cashel to punish him, but a force of Dubliners, summoned to the Earl's help, were held up at Thurles and cut to pieces by Donal and Conor 'Maenmoy', the High king's son. This first open victory of the Irish was followed by a widespread revolt. Strongbow was penned up in an island of the Suir by Ostmen from Waterford, and was only saved by the arrival of Raymond le Gros, who brought him safe away to Waterford, which again submitted. As reward, the Earl gave him his sister Basilia and made him his constable of Leinster, an office formerly held by Strongbow's uncle and favourite, Hervey de Montmorency. But the High king raised a most imposing army from Connacht and Ulster which the late submitting kings of Oriel, Ulidia, and Brefni joined.[2] They attacked De Lacy's fortress at Trim which Hugh Tyrel held for him; the garrison had to abandon it and the Irish destroyed it, but strangely enough retreated and did no more.

So widespread a revolt showed Henry, however, that Ireland must be won foot by foot. The Irish Church too had begun to appeal to Rome about the condition of things, and the annals of Ulster tell us that in 1175 'Conchobur son of Mac Conchaille, abbot at first of the Regular abbey of SS. Peter and Paul at Armagh and afterwards Successor of Patrick, died in Rome after arriving to confer with the Successor of Peter (*Comarba Petair*)'.

[1] Dermot meanwhile was suffering from an ungrateful son, Cormac 'Liathanach', who was in arms against him. Cormac, however, was slain in 1177.

[2] The list of the chiefs is in *The Song of Dermot* (pp. 233–41).

THE TREATY OF WINDSOR, 1175

At last Henry and the High king came to terms and a treaty was concluded at Windsor in October 1175. Archbishop Laurence was present and Rory's envoys were Cadhla (Catholicus), archbishop of Tuam, 'Cantordis', abbot of St. Brendan's church at Clonfert, and Master Laurence, 'chancellor of the king of Connacht'.[1]

The annals of Tighernach say very briefly of this treaty: 'Cadhla Ó Dubhthaigh returned out of England from the Son of the Empress, having with him *the peace of Ireland* and *the kingship of the same* over both Foreigners and Gaels to Rory O'Connor, and his kingdom to every province-king from the king of Erin, and their tributes to Rory'—an optimistic view to hold of the transaction.

The official English account is as follows:

'Henry grants to Roderick, his liege king of Connacht, as long as he faithfully serves him, that he shall be king under him, ready at his service and as his man. And that he shall hold his land well and in peace even as he held it before the Lord King entered Ireland, but paying tribute for it. And he shall have all the land and its inhabitants under him and shall bring them to account (*justiciet eos*) so that they shall pay their tribute to the King of England through him, and he shall maintain their rights. Those who now hold their kingdoms shall hold them in peace and render what they owe to the King through the king of Connacht. If he cannot bring to account rebels against him or those who will not pay tribute to the King of England, the latter's Constable shall assist him if called upon.

'He shall pay tribute of one hide for each ten animals [slain] both on his own lands and those of others—except what lands the King keeps in his demesne or the demesnes of others, viz. Dublin and Meath [*Raida* in text but obviously *Midia*] even as Murchat Ua Mailehaclin held it, Wexford and its appurtenances [apparently Strongbow's demesnes are meant] and Waterford even to Dungarvan.

'And if the Irish who have fled wish to return to the lands of the King of England's barons they may do so, paying the aforesaid tribute like the others, or rendering the ancient services which they were wont to render for their lands, and this to be at the judgment and will of their [English] lords. And if any refuse to return, and their lords require them of the king of Connacht, he shall compel them to return.

[1] Rymer's *Foedera*, I, p. 31.

'And the king of Connacht shall receive hostages from those under him and give hostages of his own to the king of England.'

The witnesses are Richard, bishop of Winchester and seven other Englishmen, and Laurence, archbishop of Dublin.

This is so remarkable a bargain that one wonders how either side supposed it could be kept. A 'condominium' was to be set up by which Rory was left as Árd Rí of the unconquered parts of Ireland, but as a tributary to Henry. Actually it could hardly have worked and did not do so. Before two years passed Henry was making formal or tacit grants of the unconquered kingdoms to his Irish adventurers.

Its one practical effect was that Rory was admitted king of Connacht, and that till the death of his brother Cathal Crovderg in 1224 this province remained an independent O'Connor kingdom, under vassalage to the English Crown.

Over the rest of the Irish states which had not been appropriated by the English Rory was left in the position of the former Árd Rí, but as Ulster had never obeyed him and O'Brien was out for his own it was hardly likely they would do so now.

The clause concerning the return of the refugees is a remarkable one. It seems to distinguish the chiefs and superior freemen who had quitted their old kingdoms petty and lands before the onslaught of the Normans, and the inferior tenants, the *daor-cheiles* and *fuidirs* of Irish law who cultivated the land or held stock from the lords at a render and who were 'at the will of their lords'. In short, the new masters, in addition to knowing all about Anglo-Norman serfdom and 'base tenures', meant to step into the places of Irish kings and gentry who controlled the services of various grades of the unfree. Whether the clause had much effect either with the free or the unfree refugee fugitives we cannot tell. But later we find all the manors of the new Norman lords in Ireland full of serfs, 'betaghs', and Irish vassals holding large tracts at rent.

Rory's conception of the position the treaty placed in which him is shown in his dealings with Donal More of Thomond. O'Brien was seizing the troubled occasion to overrun Desmond and recover the old undivided kingdom of Cashel from the MacCarthys. The High king called on the Dublin government for aid to repress him, and Raymond de Carew marched upon Limerick and captured it by a brilliant stroke in October 1175. But in the spring the news of Strongbow's death decided Raymond to evacuate the city, and Donal More held it till his death in 1194.

DEATH OF STRONGBOW

The famous Earl Richard died of an ulcer in the leg in Dublin on June 1st 1176. By his first marriage he left a daughter, who married Robert de Quency, constable of Leinster, who fell in a fight with O'Dempsey in 1172. Their daughter, marrying Philip Prendergast, conveyed Enniscorthy to him. Strongbow's legal heiress was his daughter by Eva MacMurrough, Isabella de Clare, now some five years old.[1] This child was granddaughter of a king of Leinster as well as daughter of the Earl of Pembroke, thus she was one of the greatest heiresses under the English Crown.

Strongbow was buried in Holy Trinity, now Christchurch, and for centuries his tomb was shown there, but the monument was broken by a fall of masonry in 1562 and never restored. The present so-called 'Strongbow's tomb' is not that of the first English invader of Ireland.[2]

Earl Richard's death left the government vacant, and Henry sent over William FitzAudelin again as governor, with whom were associated Fitzstephen, De Cogan, and a newcomer destined to be as famous as any of these, John de Courcy.[3] FitzAudelin was of the new official type of English, a counterbalance to the 'Race of Nesta'. He was instructed to take Strongbow's 'Land of Leinster' into the King's hands.

Maurice Fitzgerald died in September of this year, the second great invader to disappear. He left, however, a large family of sons—William, lord of Naas, Gerald, Alexander, Thomas, and Maurice, and they with their cousins, all descendants of Nesta, were destined, in spite of all, to found princely families in Ireland. FitzAudelin treated the Geraldine band coldly, refused certain rich fiefs in Wexford to Raymond and Fitzstephen, and so compelled these proud adventurers to look further afield for princely conquests.

[1] In a discussion on Strongbow's issue in the *Genealogist's Magazine* for 1933, Mr. L. Griffiths shows good reason for the belief that Earl Richard in fact left a son by Eva, called Gilbert, who, however, died at the age of twelve, some time before 1185. Isabella was heiress when she married William the Marshal in 1189.

[2] Orpen (*Normans*, I, pp. 360–1) proves that the existing 'effigy of Strongbow' has not the De Clare arms, and that the so-called figure of his boy-son alongside represents a kneeling woman rather than a youth.

[3] Orpen (II, p. 7) shows that FitzAudelin (or FitzAdelm) was not the same person as William de Burgo, 'Conqueror of Connacht', though they are often confused.

STRONGBOW'S ENFEOFFMENT OF LEINSTER

In Dublin the Earl left noble memorials of himself in Christchurch, which under him was rebuilt in Gothic, and the Hospital of St. John of Jerusalem at Kilmainham, of which the first prior was Hugh de Clahull. Outside it he built fortresses which were the sites of later stone castles, at Wexford (his chief seat in the south), Kildare (his chief seat in the north), Carlow, the majestic rock of Dunamase which commands the central plain, Kilkenny, Odogh, and Castlecomer.

His 'Land of Leinster' in extent and natural fertility made up one of the noblest fiefs now under the English Crown. It included all or most of the modern counties of Kildare, Wexford, Kilkenny, Carlow, Offaly, and Leix. After his own private demesnes had been laid out in these counties, he divided the rest, to hold of him as lord, among his original companions, the Geraldines and their kinsmen and others who had followed them over.

Offelan, as the English called Ui Faelain, was divided into three cantreds; the furthest one went to Meiler FitzHenry, the middle one with Naas to Maurice Fitzgerald, and the one nearest to Dublin to Adam de Hereford. Offaly (Ui Failghe) was granted to Robert de Bermingham.[1] The wide and noble plain of Kildare thus was taken from the native chiefs, the Ui Faelain and Ui Muiredaigh, who were treated as technical rebels. In south Kildare and towards Carlow and Leix, Walter de Ridlesford was granted a great fief in 'Omurethi' about Castledermot, where he built Kilkea Castle, and the baronies of Moone, Reban, Slievemargy, and Norragh went to Milo de Staunton, Robert de St. Michael, John de Clahull, and Robert FitzRichard respectively.[2]

In county Carlow the famous Raymond le Gros got the baronies of Idrone (O'Ryan's country) and Forth (O'Nolan's country) with land around Rathvilly and Tullow. On his death without heirs, Idrone passed to his nephew, William de Carew of Dunleckny, whose line went on for many generations. Ossory was little occupied in Strongbow's short reign, but in the north part, now in Leix, Adam de Hereford got 'half the cantred of Achebo as Dermot O'Chelli held it', and in the south Milo Fitzdavid, one of the Geraldine band, got the barony of Iverk. Griffin, a brother

[1] Meiler FitzHenry was grandson of Henry I and Nesta. His cantred afterwards became Bermingham's barony of Carbury in north-west Kildare. Offaly soon came to Gerald Fitzgerald of Naas by a Bermingham marriage, while the first Robert de Bermingham's descendants were barons of Tethmoy on the Offaly border.

[2] FitzRichard was ancestor through females of the Calf or Le Veel lords of Norragh.

of Raymond, got lands about Knocktopher, and for a few generations the FitzGriffins were barons of that place.

In county Wexford the old Ostman territory was thickly planted with commoners as well as enfeoffed with knights. The Earl kept to himself a large demesne of Wexford town and the southern parts as far as Waterford harbour. But he granted Obargy and most of the south coast to his maternal uncle Hervey de Montmorency, the *caput* of whose barony was the Great Island at Wexford, and Shelmalier (Ferann na gCenel) to Philip, son of Maurice Prendergast, who again granted the southern half of it to Robert, brother of Richard FitzGodebert, from whom descended the Roches of Wexford. Philip Prendergast, marrying the daughter and heir of Robert de Quency, got the Duffry and Enniscorthy, and Gilbert de Boreart was granted south Offelmy between Enniscorthy and the eastern coast.

This was the original feudalizing of Wexford. When Strongbow's son-in-law, the Earl Marshal, added to it, there was founded the most enduring of the original English colonies in Ireland. There was already a Scandinavian element both in Wexford town and along the coast; to this was now added a Flemish, Welsh, and Saxon population which the Norman barons planted in on the manors and petty burghs. Such familiar Anglo-Irish names as Prendergast, Sutton, Cheevers, Synnot, Hay, Rossiter, Furlong, Roche, Keating, and Hackett attest to this day the survival of this mixed Teutonic-Welsh race. At first the whole of the open country from Enniscorthy and Ferns down to Bannow and Carnsore was strongly planted. Much ground was subsequently abandoned to the Irish, but in the baronies of Forth, Bargy, and Shelmalier this sturdy colony remained 'English' and English-speaking all through medieval history.

The great country around Dublin, now a royal city, from Malahide down to Wicklow was also at Strongbow's disposal. In Fingall, the Ostman family of MacTorcaill had owned as far as Howth, Portraine, Ballybaghill, and Swords. The land of 'O'Cadesi', chief of the Saithni, extended south to Finglas and Macgillacolmoc owned Raheny. Ó Cathasaigh's land was annexed to the Crown and Strongbow gave Howth to Almeric, the first of the St. Laurences. Raheny was granted to Vivian de Curcy, and Hugh de Lacy, whose earldom of Meath was adjacent, gave Clontarf to Adam de Feypo to whom also he conveyed Santry. Hugh Tyrel was granted Castleknock. The rich coast lands, south of the city and from Bray to the Dublin mountains, were also feudalized. Walter de Ridlesford received here 'Bren and the lands of the sons of Odurchil', including Bray. The Irish district of Fercullen, now represented by the name Powerscourt, was then or later the property of a Le Poer.[1] The wild but noble mountain country now forming most of Wicklow (not a county till the reign of James I), from Delgany down to Arklow and inland to Glendaloch, Holywood, the head of Glenmalure, Glencree, the Vale of Aughrim, and the source of the Liffey, was divided between the King and the Archbishop of Dublin, who added to his Dublin lands eventually the old bishopric of Glendaloch and the abbey-lands of the same. Thus Glencree was 'royal forest', and the Archbishop's lands ran to Tallaght, Holywood, and as far as Dunlavin, all along the north slopes of the Dublin hills.[2]

STRONGBOW AND THE IRISH

Earl Richard was a man of the old adaptable and tolerant Norman stock of adventurer; in Wales he had learnt to deal with the Welsh princes and to compromise with them; in Leinster he had a title which the Irish themselves had to admit as Dermot's son-in-law, and he was bound in common honour and sense to treat well those who had aided Dermot and himself. Above all, even had he wished to expel all the native chiefs from so large a land, it could not have been achieved. Add to these considerations that the medieval man had great tolerance for other languages, customs, and races, and that linguistic nationalism was not yet conceived of, and we get the general policy of the first Norman conquerors in Ireland till England itself became nationalistic in the fourteenth century and the Statutes of Kilkenny struck a less generous note.

Strongbow therefore left large parts of his 'Land of Leinster' to the old native princes. Ferns and much of Offelmy (in the barony of Ballaghkeen) were left to Murchertach, son of Murchad and nephew of King Dermot, and here his descendants the

[1] *Circa* 1296, Eustace le Poer was lord of Powerscourt.

[2] Orpen, *Normans* (I, ch. xi) describes in masterly fashion the 'Sub-infeudation of Leinster'. See also Mills and MacEnery, 'Norman Settlement in the Vale of Dublin' (op. cit.).

The cantred of Wicklow, i.e. the territory round the Ostman stronghold on this headland, was granted by Strongbow to Maurice Fitzgerald. Though much diminished in size, the lands there remained with the barons of Naas till about 1300, when, by marriage, a De Londres acquired them.

For the grants to De Ridlesford, etc. see *Reg. All Hallows* (p. 47 and No. liii). 'Bren' would seem to be the Irish territory of Ui Briuin Cualann, from Glencree to Bray.

Ridlesford's huge grants stretched from the Barrow at Castledermot to Imaal on one side and from Donnybrook to Bray and inwards to the foot of Glencree on the other.

The royal demesnes in the Vale of Dublin were later formed into the manors of Newcastle-Lyons, Crumlin, Esker, and Saggard (Tassagard).

O'Morchoes held for centuries.[1] The faithful Donal Kavanagh retained the inland and mountainy parts of Hy Kinsella reaching into Carlow and served the Earl as 'Seneschal of his Irish of Leinster', to settle lawsuits between the town vassals, collect their tributes, and call up their military service. He was killed in an affray with O'Nolan in 1175, but his descendants held lands and office under Strongbow's heirs in Carlow till the end of the next century, and were recognized as kinsmen of the Bigods, and relatives of the sainted Laurence O'Toole.[2]

The new English conquerors and settlers contented themselves with the plains, coasts, and riverways and (of necessity indeed) left the abundant hill-country, woods, and impenetrable boglands to the native race. The policy was followed in every province: holding the best land and all the key-points, the proud Anglo-Normans believed themselves to be at once a colony, a garrison, and an aristocracy, which could easily hold down, or make continuance-terms with the rest.

Many chiefs were left in possession of at least a part of their old country, generally the wilder part, as vassals of the conquerors and responsible to them for the good conduct of their septs. Thus only half of O'Caolaidhe's cantred of Aghebo went to Adam de Hereford. Still, the significant phrase 'as O'Toole held it' or 'as O'Moriarty held it' covered numerous cases of immediate expulsion. The invader would naturally seize the chief's demesne and dún, the natural stronghold of his territory, and make it into a manorial castle, the *caput* of a barony which in time would obliterate the former tribe-area.[3]

In these ways numbers of border chiefs disappeared or were compelled to seek new grounds. The Ui Muiredaigh of south Kildare, losing the best of their patrimony, retreated into the mountain country east of Dunlavin, to become the O'Tooles. They kept the noble glen of Imaal and penetrated by the Vartry river into north Wicklow. The Ui Faeláin of north Kildare removed (by gradual stages, no doubt) into central Wicklow and became under a later patronymic the famous O'Byrne clan.[4]

[1] In north Wexford, about Gorey, a branch of MacMurroughs called Mac Daibhi Móir or MacDavy More gave the country its present popular but corrupt name, 'the Macamores'.

[2] See for an example Chapter VI, p. 110,

[3] Thus Naas, capital of the Ui Faelain, was granted by Strongbow to Maurice Fitzgerald 'with a cantred of land near Naas which Makelan (Mac-Fhaelain) held'. It became a manor-town of the Fitzgeralds. (See *Chartae, Privilegia et Immunitates*, p. 5.)

[4] The last true king of the Ui Muiredaigh was Gillacomgaill, who died in 1176. The O'Toole name had, however, been founded by 1100. The O'Byrne ancestor is obscure. *A.F.M.* under 1124 mention 'Gluniarain son of Bran, lord of East Ui Faelain, killed by Donal son of MacFhaelain,

One leading prince of north Leinster fared better than these. Donal Macgillacolmoc, brother-in-law of Strongbow, entered the ranks of the Norman barons, a unique instance for an Irish chief, and for a time retained his royal dún at Liamhain. In 1207 'Lymerhim and fifteen carucates of land and a burgage in Dublin' were confirmed to his son Dermot. In 1215, when Liamhain was made into the royal fortress of Newcastle-Lyons, 'John Deremot, nephew of Gilleholmoc' lost his lands there, most of which were taken 'for the improving of the King's manor', while the other north Dublin lands had already been taken over by Strongbow. Gradually this family, which took the patronymic FitzDermot, alienated or lost most of their lands south of Dublin, but in 1400 a John FitzDermot was still lord of the manor of Rathdown.

Of the Ostman family, which had been lords of Dublinshire for several generations, Strongbow had a natural fear. For some three or four years, Hamund, brother of Earl Asgall, was permitted to keep Kinsaley and other hereditary lands on the Fingall coast, and several members of the family survived the Conquest longer still. But they were a suspect race, which might call a Norse fleet again to their aid, and could not escape the fears and rapacity of the conquerors. A sidelight is revealed in this record: 'Laurence being then archbishop, Strongbow and Fitzstephen took Ballibaghille where dwelt one Macgoghdane, who, after four days' fighting, was captured and beheaded. The earl then gave Ballibaghille, Portraghin and Kynsali to Holy Trinity.'[1]

On the whole, Strongbow's conquest was a not ungenerous compromise between natives and newcomers. He claimed Leinster, after all, as Dermot's heir and ruled it as a 'province-king', calling out, for example, the posse of the province in 1174 against Rory O'Connor, when, says *The Song of Dermot*, 'his Irish vassals followed him' according to ancient custom.

In making his grants, Strongbow addresses 'all his friends and men, French, English, and Irish', implying that many native freeholders were left. Inevitably the conquerors took over much

royal heir of Leinster. The two Tanists of Ui Muiredaigh were also slain.' O'Donovan in a note adds that from MacFhaelain came the Mackelan name, which in the thirteenth century was replaced by O'Byrne.

O'Donovan also declares (in his edition of *Leabhar na gCeart*, pp. 205, 207) that about 1180 Walter de Ridlesford ejected the O'Tooles, who then made good their hold on Imaal at the expense of older septs. In 1202, he says again, Meiler FitzHenry and others by their pressure compelled the O'Byrnes to retreat into Wicklow.

[1] See p. 83 of the first edition of this work for an extensive note. In 1174 Henry from Woodstock confirmed Strongbow's grant to 'Hamund Maccturkyl, of Kensalich' and other adjacent lands, held by him before the arrival of the English, but in the same year Strongbow grants the land of Hamund MacTurkil to Holy Trinity, Dublin. See *Christchurch Deeds*, Nos. 1 and 44.

of the local organization and land-divisions of the older race. The units of *baile*, *tuath*, and *tricha céd* became the Anglo-Irish township, hundred and barony. For the *tricha céd* the invaders had the word 'cantred', a form of the Welsh 'cantref', or 'hundred townlands', a land-unit with which they were already familiar. Originally, it would seem, the Gaelic *tricha céd* corresponded to the *tuath*; by now it was certainly very much larger. Hence, while the invaders equated the *tuath*, which they called 'thoth' or 'theodum', with hundred and parish, the *tricha céd* corresponded, generally speaking, with the barony or cantred, though we often find two baronies formed from one *tricha céd*.[1]

Sometimes a whole *mór-tuath* was granted away, as when Earl Richard conferred Offaly on Robert de Bermingham. Offaly was shared at the time by three Irish lords, O'Connor, O'Diomusaigh, and O'Duinn, the former having the pre-eminence, but each was lord of a cantred or *tricha céd*.

The colony could in no case be a success without an Irish population to farm the land and cultivate the soil. Many of the Gaels, it is clear, remained as free tenants on the appropriated lands. The agricultural labour for the new manors was provided from the inferior tenants of the old order. The 'men' who had formerly cultivated the demesne lands of chiefs would continue to do so still. The frequent reference in Anglo-Irish records to the fixing of boundaries 'according to the custom of Ireland' refers to that system of cocultivatian and communal ownership which was universal, and communal farming groups appear constantly in the 'lands of the betaghs' in manor records. The words 'betagius', from *biatach*, 'food-provider', and 'Irishman' (*hibernicus*) were common Anglo-Irish for 'villein' till the whole system died out.

The above picture is that of the first fifty years of the Norman invasion when the natives were many, the invaders few. As the colony increased in extent and population, the treatment of the native tenants was less generous, and numerous common Englishry were introduced into the manors and small towns to displace the existing Irish.

[1] After the organization of shires was complete by 1297, the division of each county into cantreds for administrative purposes became general. J. E. Lloyd, *History of Wales*, I, p. 300, says: 'The cantref in Wales represents the smaller divisions into which the original tribe-kingdom (*gwlad*), e.g. Ceredigion, split up, the king continuing to appoint the heads of these cantrefs.' Hence the invaders of Ireland, familiar with Welsh divisions, would take the *mór-tuath* or *tricha céd* and divide it into cantreds, as they did with Offelan. (See a paper on 'The Tricha Céd', by Professor James Hogan, in *P.R.I.A.*, 1929.)

JOHN DE COURCY, 'CONQUESTOR ULTONIAE', 1177–1205

Hugh de Lacy, who like other Irish barons had served the King in France, was, now after Strongbow's death, the greatest Anglo-Irish magnate. He was appointed 'Guardian of Ireland' in May 1177 and spent the rest of his brief but active life in his adopted country.

The greatest danger for the new colony was from the warlike north, which had not even made a form of submission. At the end of 1176 Melaghlin MacLochlainn collected the men of Cinel Eoghain and Oriel and marched into Meath. There, for they realized that the Norman castles were the deadliest foe of Ireland, they took De Lacy's castle at Slane, destroyed it, and slew Richard Fleming, its warden, and the garrison of five hundred men.

The well-known divisions of the Ulster kings and the imminent need of averting the northern peril suggested the most epical exploit of the first Normans in Ireland. John de Courcy was a young Somerset knight, who had come over with FitzAudelin, and like others chafed at being an idler or mere official in Dublin. A field totally new and without competitors revealed itself in the north. Collecting a band of knights and followers, he set out on his own to conquer Ulidia, the richest and most tempting part of the Ulster province. He seems to have received no express grant from King Henry, at least none is recorded, and his whole enterprise was planned and achieved by himself and his followers. De Courcy was indeed the true Norman adventurer of the 'earlier age', to be put alongside of Raymond le Gros and Fitzstephen, and in fact achieving a greater epic than even they did. Of this epic the Anglo-Irish *chanson de geste*, the *Book of Howth*, is the chronicle.[1]

It was with some three hundred English and some native troops that de Courcy set out from Dublin, with the eagle standard of his family displayed, early in 1177. On February 1st he captured Downpatrick, the capital of Ulidia. The native king, Rury MacDunlevy, then collected a great array, and a papal legate who was then in the north, Cardinal Vivian, blessed the native cause as just.[2] In the battle which followed the Irish were routed,

[1] See the *Book of Howth*, in *Carew Miscell.* (one of the volumes of the *Cal. of Carew MSS.*). It is the earliest specimen on a large scale of literary English in Ireland.

The Song of Dermot describes King Henry before leaving Dublin as conferring 'Uluestere' upon John de Courcy 'if by force he could conquer it' (lines 2733–6), but we cannot know how far it was a serious grant, in any case it must have been a 'speculative' one.

[2] Cardinal Vivian had just come from Man, where he had married its king, Godred, to Finola, daughter of Melaghlin MacLochlainn, then ruling over Cinel Eoghain. After leaving Man, Vivian landed in Ulster to proceed to

but MacDunlevy called on Melaghlin MacLochlainn of Cinel Eoghain, his overlord, and the two kings brought a still greater army to face De Courcy once more, having with them O'Carain, archbishop of Armagh, the bishop of Down, many clerics, and the most sacred relics of Armagh to bless the host. But this great rally of the north was completely defeated on June 24th 1177, and the English slew indiscriminately the clergy as well as the laity, and captured the two bishops along with their relics, but soon released them with the affected courtesy of Norman gentlemen. Several stubborn encounters followed at Antrim, Newry, and other places, and the northerners were hard to beat, but the combination of Norman horse, archers, and mail-clad men-at-arms proved always victorious.

De Courcy's first objective had been Ulidia, and the title 'Princeps Ulidiae', which is attributed to him, would make him appear MacDunlevy's successor.[1] But ancient 'Ulaidh' had extended far west of the Bann and Lough Neagh, and such claims De Courcy was ready to revive. He aimed also at subduing Oriel and overthrowing MacLochlainn; such a threefold success would make him master of the whole province of Ulster. Another record of the time styles him 'Conquestor Ultoniae', and it is clear that both his De Lacy successor and the De Burgo earls regarded De Courcy's 'Ulster' as meaning, not merely Ulidia, but the whole historic province of Ulster or Ultonia.

After his first victories, De Courcy had no further opposition to fear and the Cinel Eoghain abandoned the Ulidians. The old kingdoms of Oriel and Ulidia were doomed to disappear under the Norman attack. Murchad O'Cervall died in 1189, a monk in Mellifont; even his patronymic came to an end, and in time the MacMahons became dominant in Monaghan or 'Irish Oriel', while Rury MacDunlevy was finally slain by the colonists in 1201. His descendants in 1272 claimed to be 'kings of the Irish of Ulster', but by 1330 they had completely disappeared among the chiefly names of Antrim and Down.[2]

Having achieved his conquest, De Courcy during the twenty-

Dublin on legatine affairs, and William of Newburgh (*Hist. Rer. Anglic.*, 1177) is responsible for the story that being at Down he encouraged the Irish to fight for their rights—no wonder, considering that the Treaty of Windsor had admitted the right of the Irish kings to their provinces. But De Courcy's victories soon reconciled the legate to the *fait accompli*, and on arriving at Dublin, at the synod which he called (March 1177), he proclaimed the right of Henry II to Ireland.

[1] Jocelin, a monk of Inch Abbey near Down, an Englishman from Furness, dedicated his *Life of St. Patrick* to John de Courcy as 'Princeps Ulidiae'.

[2] *Cal. Inquis.*, VII (7 Edw. III), 'An Inquisition on the De Burgo lands', names the Irish vassals of the Earl of Ulster, but MacDunlevy is not among them.

seven years of his rule organized it with a master hand. He founded castles at Downpatrick, Dromore, Coleraine, Newry, Dundrum, and Carlingford.[1] Carrickfergus, with the great keep ninety feet high, and the abbey, which are due to him, became a flourishing town. The Benedictines and Cistercians whom he brought in, the first to St. Patrick's priory at Down and the second from Furness to Inch abbey, a few miles away, introduced an Anglo-French civilization into the north-east. Among his lieutenants, Logan, Hacket, Savage, Russell, and others founded lasting 'old English names' in eastern Ulster. De Courcy's was the first plantation of the north, one which was French and aristocratic rather than Anglo-Saxon and industrial, and destined to disappear in part, but it has left indelible marks upon Antrim and Down.

It does not appear that De Courcy ever did formal homage for Ulster to Henry or John, though his charters admit them as his liege lords. Feeling the need of nearer allies, he married in 1180 Affrica, daughter of Godred, king of Man, and sister of Ragnall who ruled from 1187 to 1229. Godred's sister Ragnild had married the famous Somerled, lord of Argyle, and Godred himself was husband of Finola, daughter of Melaghlin MacLochlainn. De Courcy, with the Norman instinct for 'happy marriages', thus allied himself with the Norse-Gaelic world in the north, and dreamed of a feudal principality in Ulster allied with the kings of Man and the Hebrides, and the semi-Gaelic earls of the Galloway mainland.[2]

THE FIRST INVASION OF CONNACHT

As Ulster had been invaded without right, so now was Connacht. Tighernach and Giraldus describe how early in 1177 De Cogan, constable of Dublin, with forty knights and five hundred men, marched to Roscommon, where they were joined by Murchad, a son of Rory O'Connor. Guided by him, they marched through

[1] For De Courcy's imposing cylindrical keep, whose wall is eight feet thick, at 'Rath' or Dundrum in county Down and other castles see H. C. Lawlor, *History and Antiquities of Northern Ireland*. The great stone keep of Carrickfergus is attributed to him, and it appears that with him the stone castle on the English scale made its first appearance in Ireland. But the dating of such castles is uncertain and it is probable that most of his castles were of the early 'mote and bailey' type, built in several cases in stone by his successor, Hugh de Lacy. (See H. C. Lawlor on 'De Courcy's Principality of Ulster' in *Ulster Journal of Archaeology* (1938), pp. 84–9, 159–64.)

[2] The Gaelic-Norse kingdom of Man, which had a bishop of 'Sodor and Man' of its own as well as a petty king, began with Godred Crovan, *circa* 1068, and practically ended with Magnus in 1250. Edward I in 1290 annexed it to England. For De Courcy's grant of lands along the Derry coast to Duncan FitzGilbert of Galloway see later, pp. 94, 113.

the plain of Connacht to the *tochar* (causeway) of Móin Connedha (between Ballymore and Dunmore) into the high road (*slighe mór*) of Lecc Gnathail, and by Dunmore to Tuam, while their detachments burned five churches and the fort of Galway. Rory O'Connor marched to Tuam against them 'and did not allow the foreigners to lift a head till the place of battle was given them'. At last the English broke and fled back as far as Móin Connedha and to Athleague, and so out of Connacht 'not knowing how many they had lost'. The traitor Murchad fell into the hands of Rory and was blinded by his own father's orders.

In vain would we attempt either to condemn or justify such aggression. Henry had thrown the best part of a great and fertile island away to the Norman adventurers, who alone had the resources and enterprise to achieve a final conquest. Only his personal presence could have restrained them, and Ireland was the last to be considered of his many realms.

CHAPTER V

JOHN, 'DOMINUS HIBERNIAE', 1177–1199

AT the council of Oxford in May 1177, King Henry took counsel with his barons on the question of Ireland, and very weighty were the decisions that were taken.

In a synod at Dublin in March that year the legate Cardinal Vivian had proclaimed again the papal approval of Henry's conquest, and further measures on the King's part seemed called for. Prince John, now only ten years of age, was styled 'Lord of Ireland', and so was it resolved, in spite of Adrian's emerald ring and the rest, that Ireland was not to be a kingdom but a lordship, as it remained for three hundred and fifty years. A viceroy or 'procurator-general' was found for him in Hugh de Lacy, who had the earldom of Meath renewed to him at service of a hundred knights, and ruled the colony till 1185. The city of Waterford with all the province as far as Lismore 'was granted in custody as Crown lands' to Robert le Poer.

Henry then proceeded to the further enfeoffment of Ireland, and it seems clear that by now he disregarded the Treaty of Windsor, and was ready to divide Ireland among the adventurers. For Connacht alone he had any respect, and in spite of vicissitudes the O'Connor kingdom survived till 1224. As for Ulster, Henry was content to leave De Courcy to do the work there and, if he gave him no grant, he did not withdraw his confidence from him. But the whole of the great province of Munster was given away as far as royal grants could give it. Henry bestowed 'the kingdom of Cork' jointly upon Robert Fitzstephen and Milo de Cogan, two of the first Geraldine band, whose rewards so far had been much inferior to their merits. The 'kingdom' of Thomond, or Limerick, Henry granted to Philip de Braose, a knight of Brecknock in south Wales. Each 'kingdom' was to be held at the service of sixty knights, but the cities of Cork and Limerick, with the 'cantred of the Ostmen' in each case, were reserved to the Crown. The boundaries of the 'Regnum Corcagiae' were defined as from Mount Brandon in Kerry along the river (Blackwater) to 'the river at Lismore', i.e. Youghal harbour. The 'kingdom of Limerick' meant the present counties of Limerick, Clare, Tipperary, and north Kerry as Donal O'Brien then enjoyed them.

The favoured grantees, who had been at the council, left

England in November 1177 and sailed at once for Cork. There a treaty was made with Dermot MacCarthy, since the adventurers hardly felt able to remove him, and he was left in possession of twenty-four cantreds in Desmond, under terms of tribute to Fitzstephen and De Cogan. The two latter then appropriated seven cantreds around Cork, of which the four western ones went to De Cogan, and the three eastern ones went to Fitzstephen. The injustice of the grant hardly needs comment, since Dermot MacCarthy had been the first Irish king to do homage to Henry in 1171.[1]

By the grant of Limerick and Cork, Henry abrogated Rory's overlordship there as secured by the Treaty of Windsor, and abolished the rights of O'Brien and MacCarthy and of the Ostmen of Munster. Cork indeed received a Norman garrison, but was still MacCarthy's capital, just as Limerick was O'Brien's, and contained a numerous and prosperous old Scandinavian population.[2] So strong was Limerick indeed that when Fitzstephen and De Cogan attempted to put De Braose into possession of the city the attempt failed, and the allies had to retreat before O'Brien arrived. The conquest of Limerick, therefore, had to be deferred for nearly twenty years and Philip de Braose never achieved it. But if De Braose failed, Fitzstephen and De Cogan, backed by an English garrison, proceeded vigorously to divide up their seven cantreds. Robert enfeoffed Gerald, Alexander, and Maurice, sons of Maurice Fitzgerald, in the barony of Imokilly in south-east Cork.[3] He granted to his nephew, Philip de Barry, the cantred of 'Olethan' (Ui Liatháin) from near Fermoy to Midleton, which later became the barony of Barrymore, and also the two cantreds of Muskerry—Donegan and Killede, later called the two baronies of Orrery and Kilmore, which stretched from Mallow to Charleville and included Glenquin in county Limerick.

[1] The exact boundary of the two kingdoms of Cork (Desmond) and Limerick (Thomond) are vague, though roughly defined as running along the Blackwater from Mount Brandon to Lismore. It seems probable that Turloch More O'Connor first imposed them when he divided Munster. The north boundary was certainly not as to-day between counties Limerick and Cork, and Kerry was much smaller than the present county. In later times Lough Léin, the Laune, Killorglin (a Fitzgerald manor), and the Dingle peninsula were the southern boundary of Kerry. (See W. F. Butler, *Gleanings in Irish History*, *passim*. For the descent of the kingdom of Cork after Fitzstephen and De Cogan died see Orpen, *Normans*, II, pp. 48–50 and III, pp. 147–55.)

[2] See first edition of this work, p. 92.

[3] Gerald, the elder brother (d. 1203), became lord of Offaly by marriage with Eva, granddaughter of Robert de Bermingham to whom Strongbow granted Offaly.

THE DESCENT OF THE KINGDOM OF CORK

The triumphs of the two grantees, great names among the first invaders, were, however, brief. In 1182 Mac Tire, the dispossessed chief of Ui Liatháin, surprised De Cogan near Lismore and slew him. Fitzstephen died in 1185, leaving no son, and his heir was Richard de Carew, nephew or illegitimate son of Raymond le Gros. From this Richard came the Carews who held Fitzstephen's moiety of the kingdom of Cork till 1300. Then David Roche, their tenant, became direct tenant of the Crown and baron of Fermoy, while in 1336 David de Barry, by a release from Thomas de Carew, became tenant-in-chief of Olethan and Muskerry-Donegan. De Cogan apparently left only a daughter, and the De Courcys of Kinsale finally got most of his half of the *regnum*, but a branch of his family called 'the Great Cogan' held lands about Carrigaline till 1438.[1]

Dermot MacCarthy retained his lands in Muskerry on friendly terms with the invaders till his death. Nevertheless, like others of the old stock, he was doomed, and this last native king of all Desmond was slain by the English at Cuill Baghaine in 1185, leaving a son, Donal More 'na Curra', to inherit his claims.

DONAL MORE O'BRIEN

The power of O'Brien in Thomond was too well entrenched for the De Braose grant to take effect, and Donal More died in 1194, king over the present Clare, Limerick, Tipperary, and north Kerry, and having Limerick as his capital, with his royal hall on the island where the cathedral stands. As a province-king he had shown himself great. He had routed Strongbow at Thurles and stemmed the Norman tide. But his patriotism was family and provincial, and he seized the opportunity of these troubled times to restore the O'Brien kingship of Cashel. In a series of campaigns, he drove the O'Donovans of Ui Figeinte and the Ó Coilens of Ui Conaill Gabhra out of county Limerick, and the O'Sullivans and MacCarthys out of the plains of Ormond. These were all of the old Eoghanacht line. While the Norman oppression shattered the old dynasties on the east, the O'Brien onslaught ruined them from the north. The O'Donoghues had already moved westwards to Loch Léin. O'Coilen (now O'Connell or Collins) migrated into Iveragh. O'Donovan became a petty chief about Bandon; and

[1] Orpen (*Normans*, II, pp. 47–50) states that Milo de Cogan left only a daughter, Margaret. Richard de Cogan, his brother, came over after his death. From him, it seems, descended the Cogans of Cork (Cógan Mór). Caulfield in *Cork Arch. Soc.* (1904, p. 187) collects traditions of this family.

finally the great MacCarthy himself and O'Sullivan, lord of Knockgraffon, had to abandon the rich plain of Cashel and seek fresh lands and lordship on the sea coast and in the mountainy country of south-west Desmond, while Knockgraffon became a manor for Philip de Worcester.[1]

This crushing of the Eoghanacht rivals was a striking exhibition of how to make 'sword-land', a new title by conquest to the territory or service of other septs. But that an Irish king could so profit by the invasion of foreigners and the general break-up of Ireland is a proof how limited and particularist in their aims were most of the Irish kings.

Donal More was the founder or benefactor of an unusual number of abbeys. In a charter at Limerick in 1189 he confirmed to the regular canons of St. Augustine near Clare at Forgy 'the lands which I, or others with my consent, have given'. In his last year he endowed Brictius, 'bishop of Limerick', with certain lands, and elevated St. Munchin's church into a cathedral dedicated to St. Mary. He is credited with eight foundations in all, and his charter to Holy Cross, a Cistercian abbey, founded from Monaster-an-eany, itself a Cistercian house which Turloch O'Brien endowed in 1150, is extant.[2] Earlier in the century the Pope had sent to his ancestor Murchertach O'Brien a fragment of the True Cross. Donal built a beautiful fabric to house it and, under later Norman lords, Holy Cross became one of the noblest of Munster abbeys. Thus did Donal More in his munificence emulate the noble record of his house from Brian onwards as friends and patrons of religion.

THE ENFEOFFMENT OF MEATH

Under the vigorous hand and masterly skill of Hugh de Lacy, Meath was now feudalized and made English in like fashion to Leinster and Ulidia, with Drogheda as its capital.[3] His new earldom 'as Murchad O'Melaghlin held it' was in fact the old province-kingdom of Meath, a state not as large as the other 'fifths', but far more fertile and abundant in pasture-land than any of them. No less than the modern counties of Meath, Westmeath, Longford,

[1] Orpen (*Normans*, II, p. 160) quotes the authorities. Ui Figeinte equals the diocese of Limerick, and was composed of two parts, Ui Conaill Gabhra (Connello) and Ui Cairbre.

[2] For Holy Cross and Kilcooley, see Curtis, *Cal. of Ormond Deeds*, I, Nos. 4, 5; also Newport B. White, *Monastic and Episcopal Deeds*; and Murphy, *Triumphalia Sanctae Crucis*. Its Irish name was 'Ochtar Lamhan'.

[3] See Orpen (*Normans*, II, ch. xv) for the Sub-infeudation of Meath. For the earlier history of De Lacy see J. E. Morrison in *History* (October 1916) on 'Ludlow'. He and Mortimer were the two chief barons in Shropshire, and he owned over three hundred and forty hides of land in various counties at service of fifty-one knights.

and parts of Offaly and Cavan were claimed by De Lacy. Among the rich demesnes that he reserved to himself, he kept 'the lake and vill of Dissert and one knight's fee about it'. This was a significant reservation, for the earthen fort at this place was the royal seat of the O'Melaghlin kings of Meath, Dún-na-Sciath on Lough Ennel. The last of this dynasty to bear the name of king was Art, who was killed in 1185. His descendants were mere lords of 'O'Melaghlin's country', the barony of Clonlonan, stretching from Lough Ennel to the Shannon, in which country they were left undisturbed.

The Gaelic states of Meath now became baronies for De Lacy's chief men, and manors for their knights. Robert de Lacy, a cousin of the Earl, was enfeoffed in the barony of Fairbill (Fer Bile), Gocelin de Angulo in Navan, Richard le Fleming in Slane, De Muset in Lune with Athboy as his centre, De Hose in Lune with Galtrim as his centre, Hugh Tyrel in Castleknock, and De Feypo in Skreen. In western Meath, William le Petit got Magheradernon with Mullingar, Nugent got Delvin (O'Finnelan's country), Robert de Lacy was further enfeoffed in Rathwire, De Constantin in Kilbixy, and De Tuit in Granard. This last grant carried the Norman banner as far as it was destined to go in De Lacy's country, that is, into Conmaicne and Annaly, the present Longford.

Firmly established in great lordships, these baronial families survived for the most part till the battle of the Boyne. Under them arose with time a numerous secondary line of knightly tenants, Mareward, Plunkett, Cusack, Dalton, Delamare, Curtis, and others, whose names if not their estates survive to this day. Thus were formed the historic 'eighteen baronies of Meath'. The nearer Gaelic dynasties disappeared for ever. De Lacy made no attempt to turn the kings of Delbhna, Gailenga, Luighni, and other chiefs of central Meath into barons and tenants-in-chief under him. He enfeoffed the Normans thickly wherever he could, but on the borders of his vast earldom he left many of the royal septs in actual possession. Most of Longford remained O'Farrell's, and the country from Lough Ennel south to Nenagh, though in De Lacy's lordship, continued to be the territories of O'Carroll, O'Connor Faly, Mageoghegan, O'Molloy, and other ruling septs. He pushed his line as far west as Athlone; but the O'Melaghlins and others menaced it from the south, and the O'Farrells and others from the north. The Norman expansion towards the Shannon, the heart of Ireland and the most vital point, was in truth more like a spear-head than a broad shield.

Like Strongbow, De Courcy, William de Burgo, and others of

the first invaders, De Lacy realized the value of an Irish marriage to strengthen his position. In 1180, being then a widower but with two infant sons, he married Rose, the daughter of the High king. The alliance seemed a score for both parties, but it roused the suspicions of England that De Lacy was aiming at the Crown of Ireland, and earned him the hatred of Prince John. By Rose O'Connor the Earl had a son called William 'Gorm' ('dark blue'), probably because his hair was so dark as to appear blue-black, who played a prominent but not a successful part in later history.

De Lacy's castles were numerous, but of the early 'mote and bailey' type; the chief of them were at Trim, Killare, Clonard, and Kells.[1] The two last were raised on the sites of the ancient monasteries of Finnian and Columba. The old abbeys were indeed natural centres for the castles which the conquerors did not hesitate to build from the stones of the sacred buildings themselves.

Of necessity, and because it was good policy, in order to stock the new baronies and manors with cultivating tenants and artisans, De Lacy confirmed or drew into his earldom great numbers of the native race. Giraldus expresses it thus: 'He made it his first care to restore peace and order, reinstating the peasants who, after they had submitted to the conquerors, had been violently expelled from their districts, in the deserted lands, which from barren wastes now became cultivated and stocked with herds of cattle. Having thus restored confidence by his mild administration and firm adherence to treaties, his next care was to enforce submission and obedience to the laws upon the inhabitants of the towns, thus gradually bringing them into subordination.'

Here we get a picture of a new state, Norman-English in the upper and Irish in the lower strata, with the manorial demesnes and old monastic towns restocked with an Irish tenantry, and with those docile earth-tillers whom officials and observers in Tudor days were never weary of praising.[2]

But the picture alarmed the English government and especially roused the jealousy of Prince John. Giraldus adds that De Lacy's liberality and courtesy to the Irish people were such that a suspicion arose that he might throw off his allegiance and get himself accepted as king of Ireland. In 1184 he was removed from the viceregal office.

[1] For De Lacy's castles, see Orpen, *Normans*, II, ch. xiv, p. 249. The age of the true castle did not effectively begin in Ireland till 1200, and the great castle at Trim is due to Hugh's successor.

[2] 'For the churl of Ireland is a very simple and toilsome man, desiring nothing but that he may not be eaten out with cess, coyne or livery.' Tract by Sir Thomas Smith, quoted Wilson, *Beginnings of Modern Ireland*, p. 79.

A NEW TYPE OF ARCHBISHOP

On November 14th 1180 Laurence O'Toole died at Eu in Normandy, on his way from an interview with King Henry. He and six other bishops had prepared a statement on the ill-treatment of Ireland both in Church and State since 1172 for the Lateran council of 1179, but Henry saw to it that it came to nothing.[1] Laurence died full of sorrow over the wreck of his native land and the non-performance of English professions and of the papal commission. The saintly Irishman was canonized in 1225. He was succeeded by John Comyn, formerly a monk of Evesham, an experienced official of Henry's and a man of great practical talents. Comyn was the first example in Ireland of the feudalized state prelate whom England itself had only known since 1066, a man combining high spiritual office with great jurisdictions, ample lands, and rich revenues, courts both for laity and clergy, and an important position in the King's council in Ireland. Owing his office to the King, he still was a man of power under the King. Such a conception of the bishop's office, foreign to all the experience of Celtic Ireland, it took the Irish mind a long time to grasp, and longer to accept.

As a practical organizer, however, Comyn displayed the same gifts as so many of his lay contemporaries of the Anglo-Norman race then showed—incessant energy, masterful ambition, a genius for organization, and great taste in architecture and church-building. He it was who built St. Patrick's as a second cathedral for Dublin, founding it as a collegiate church. He added to the estates of the see of Dublin the lands of the bishopric and abbey of Glendaloch, and during his long episcopate of 1181–1213 the lands, manors, and towns of the archbishopric stretched from Swords in the north to Annamoe in the south, and out along the Dublin hills to Tallaght, Holywood, Rathcoole, and Dunlavin. He himself and his successors received numerous charters from the Crown of liberties and immunities which made the Archbishop one of the most privileged of subjects.

THE NORTHERN KINGS

More and more did the English, constantly reinforced by those who looked to make their fortunes here, occupy the Irish stage. How remote Connacht and Ulster seemed; the latter especially revolving on its own axis. In Tyrconnell Flavertach O'Maeldory

[1] *Giraldus* (II, ch. xxiii) says, 'Laurence, a just and worthy man, incurred the King's displeasure by asserting the privileges of his see at the Lateran council, against the King's dignity and honour, led, as was reported, by zeal for his nation. For this cause he was long delayed in England and Normandy.'

had to face a rival, Rory O'Cannanain, head of one of the Cinel Conaill stocks, whom several sons of Turloch More O'Connor, 'royal heirs', seeking for new fields to conquer, had joined. But they and Rory were beaten at the battle of Magh Diubha in 1181, where no less than five of the race of Turloch More fell. Finally Flavertach dispatched his rival at the bridge of Sligo six years later and ruled till 1197.[1]

The Cinel Eoghain were in more danger from the Normans than the remote Race of Conall. Philip de Worcester, one of the new English, had displaced the suspect De Lacy as viceroy in September 1184. Armagh was a main objective of the conquerors as the sacred capital of Ireland. In the spring of 1185 De Worcester marched with the feudal levy against the city, quartered his men there during six days of Lent, and only departed after the clergy had paid a large tribute. Doubtless the necessity of electing a new archbishop was the pretext.[2] Four years later De Courcy plundered Armagh, which as a venerable seat of native learning and the tradition of the old Irish Church never revived again.

The counterstroke was always possible, and in 1185 Melaghlin MacLochlainn invaded Meath but was slain by a colonial levy. His brother Murchertach then ruled Cinel Eoghain till 1196.

PRINCE JOHN IN IRELAND, 1185

King Henry had by now prepared a fresh expedition to Ireland, comparable in size and dignity to his own royal expedition in 1171. Prince John had been granted a generous maintenance, he had with him wise counsellors as well as young companions, and his army amounted to three hundred knights and two or three thousand men. He landed at Waterford on April 25th 1185.[3]

[1] In this 'battle of the royal heirs' at Magh Diubha, were slain Brian of Luighni (Leyney) and Maghnus, sons of Turloch More, and three sons of Aedh, another son of Turloch More. As Turloch had twenty-three sons, it is no wonder that some of them sought far fields for a patrimony. The slaughter of the above removed dangerous rivals from the path of Rory and his brother, Cathal Crovderg.

[2] Giraldus Cambrensis, in his *Topographia Hib.* (*Distinctio*, II, ch. l), says that Philip, having invaded Armagh during the holy days of Lent and wrung a large tribute from the clergy, was struck with sudden illness as he returned and barely escaped with his life. He records it as a case of divine punishment for sacrilege. It appears that the English brought back from Armagh on this occasion the famous Baculum Jesu, or Crozier of St. Patrick, which till the Reformation was in Christchurch.

The archbishopric was then vacant by the death of Conchobar Ó Conchaille. In 1185 Tomaltach O'Connor was elected.

[3] Along with him came Giraldus Cambrensis (Gerald de Barry), archdeacon of St. Davids, nephew of Maurice Fitzgerald, and brother of Robert de Barry. His *Topographia Hiberniae* and *Expugnatio Hibernica* are our fullest sources for the history and conditions of Ireland at the time of the Invasion (1166–85).

Among the young men who formed his court, three were destined to found famous families in Ireland. These were Theobald Walter, his butler, Bertram de Verdun, his seneschal, and William de Burgo, brother of Hubert de Burgo, later Justiciar of England. John was a graceless and insolent youth but he was his father's favourite son, the Benjamin of his flock. His elder brothers had either the prospect of England and Normandy or the actual possession of Aquitaine or Brittany. John was the 'Lackland' of the family. But Henry designed for him the lordship of Ireland which by a chance had come to him in 1172.[1] When the crown of the kingdom of Jerusalem, a crown going begging ever since Saladin had taken that holy city, was offered by the Patriarch Heraclius to John, his father had replied, 'I have a kingdom nearer at hand for you.' Nevertheless, in his jealousy of a new kingdom rising to the west of Britain even in an Angevin line, Henry saw to it that John was only 'Dominus Hiberniae', as he had first resolved at Oxford in 1177, and not 'Rex Hiberniae'. The emerald ring which, according to John of Salisbury, was in the royal treasury and was intended honourably to wed the Green Isle to an English lord, in reality bound her to a stranger.

The independent race of the first conquistadors was now almost gone, though only eighteen years had elapsed since the 'fleet of the Flemings' landed at Baginbun. A remarkable series of deaths prematurely removed Strongbow, Fitzstephen, De Cogan, Maurice Fitzgerald, and Raymond le Gros, all comparatively young men.[2] The way was thus cleared for a new race of colonists favoured by, and owing its lands to, the Crown. Had wisdom ruled in England, now was the chance to give Ireland a fresh start under a just, strong royal government.

Henry had sent with his son the great legist, Ranulf Glanville, Justiciar of England, who must have seen the need of a strong central government to check the greed of the colonists. But the many parchment skins which John's clerks brought with them,

[1] Thus was finally decided the title of the English kings to Ireland for three centuries and a half. John's seal bore the style 'Johannes filius Regis Anglie Dominus Hibernie'. John of Salisbury in his *Metalogicus* (IV, 42), written *circa* 1159, records that there was then in the State archives a golden ring adorned with an emerald, which Adrian IV had sent by John of Salisbury, 'by which investiture of the right to rule Ireland might be made'. Later, in 1186, Henry II had a scheme for crowning John as king of Ireland and obtained from Urban III the papal sanction and a crown of peacocks' feathers set in gold which two papal legates brought with them to Dover in December 1186. But Henry thought better of it, and diverted the legates into Normandy (*Hoveden*, II, pp. 306–7). His son Geoffrey had died in August 1186; this left Richard heir to the throne and John the only remaining son. As a possible king of England, he could not be spared.

[2] Raymond de Carew died perhaps in 1186, certainly not later than 1188.

instead of recording the submissions of Irish kings or charters to them, served for the grants to English adventurers which annulled their ancient rights.

The slow march of John was from Waterford to Lismore, Ardfinan (in both of which places he had castles begun), and Kildare to Dublin. At Waterford many petty Irish kings, eighteen it is said, came to do homage, but his own levity and the bad manners of his popinjay courtiers offended the grave and bearded Irishmen. Not a single charter to, or treaty with, a native king is recorded of all this imposing royal visit.

Finally the Prince left for England on December 27th 1185, leaving De Courcy as Justiciar. On his return he complained bitterly to his father that Hugh de Lacy, already suspect for his marriage with an Irish princess, had encouraged the Irish kings not to send either tribute or hostages. His mean soul hated De Lacy, as later he hated the manly De Courcy. Certainly his visit in this sense was a disaster. According to Giraldus, 'Our own Irishmen, who from the first coming of the Earl had been loyal, now had their lands taken away and given to Norman courtiers.'

JOHN'S LAND-GRANTS

On the other hand, the abundant enfeoffments, made by the Prince in virtue of his established position as 'Dominus' or sovereign of Ireland, greatly extended and intensified the English colony. To link up the various great fiefs was a natural policy, and the old Irish kingdom of Oriel was now Normanized and planted so as to connect Meath with Ulidia. John granted Dundalk and two baronies around it and half the barony of Ferrard in Louth to Bertram de Verdun, keeping to himself the barony of Louth. To Roger Pipard he granted Ardee in Louth, and Donaghmoyne in south Armagh, where Pipard later built a border castle. There was now planted in a numerous race of under-tenants, whose names, Gernon, Clinton, Malpas, Repentini, and others became characteristic of 'English Oriel'.

In Ormond and Thomond also the border was advanced and the interior more thickly apportioned. The extensive and fertile county of Ormond (now Tipperary) was the great prize. William de Burgo got a large grant in the north on the borders of Limerick and Tipperary, and five cantreds in south Ormond went to Philip de Worcester with Knockgraffon as his main lordship. Theobald Walter, John's honorary 'botiller', a brother of Hubert, archbishop of Canterbury, jointly with Ranulf Glanville (who was his uncle by marriage), received five and a half cantreds in north

Tipperary along with the 'burgh of Kildelo'.[1] Nenagh became the *caput* of the Butler lordship here, which covered the baronies of Owney, Arra, Ormond, Eliogarty, and the territory of Ely O'Carroll.

In these grants the former rights of Philip de Braose as lord of the Honour of Limerick were disregarded, and so were the rights of Donal O'Brien, who till his death in 1194 was still 'king of Limerick'.

The favoured Theobald Walter was also granted the manor of Arklow, and later he got from Strongbow's heir, William the Marshal, the manors of Gowran in Kilkenny and Tullow in Carlow. Naas was confirmed to William, eldest son of Maurice Fitzgerald.

DEATH OF HUGH DE LACY, 1186

Hugh de Lacy, out of office and favour with the Government, was all the more strenuous at the organizing of Meath. Among the castles with which he bridled the land, he began one at Durrow. Here stood a Columban house, one of the most venerated of ancient Celtic abbeys. To the secular-minded Norman, oblivious of Irish culture, it seemed a little thing to raise out of the stones of the sacred places fortresses for the subjection of the native race. To the latter it was at once a sacrilege and a symbol of their defeat. Two neighbouring chiefs, O'Cethernaigh and O'Braoin, found a young enthusiast ready to avenge this outrage on the body and spirit of their race. So, one day in July 1186, as De Lacy stooped to view the work of the masons at Durrow, one Gilla-gan-inathar O'Miadhaigh, who stood by, lifted an axe, smote off De Lacy's head, and running swift as a hare, sped safe away.[2]

It was perhaps less a political assassination than a protest at the sacrilege of ancient holy places, in a land where still to-day, in fear or respect of the unseen, no peasant will touch a ruined church, level an old rath, or cut down a 'lone bush', and where

[1] For this Theobald *Walter* (*not* 'FitzWalter'), whose original estates were in Amounderness in Lancashire, ancestor of the Butlers of Kilkenny, see Curtis, *Calendar of Ormond Deeds* (*passim*), and Carte's *Life of the Great Duke of Ormonde*. Also see Orpen, *Normans* (II, p. 102), for this grant. The original is no longer extant in the muniment room of Kilkenny Castle, but see *Cal. Ormond Deeds*, I, Nos. 26, 27, for a regrant to Theobald Walter by William de Braose, lord of the Honour of Limerick, in 1201. It seems doubtful (*pace* Orpen) whether 'Keldelon' or Kildelon is Killaloe; see for this Prendergast in *J. of Kilk. Arch. Soc.* (1851), pp. 390–409, on 'The Projected Plantation of Ormond under Charles I'.

[2] *Ann. Ult.* (1186) says: 'Ugo de L., destroyer and dissolver of the sanctuaries of Ireland, was killed by Ua Miadhaigh of Breghmuna by direction of the Sinnach Ua Catharnaigh in reparation to Colmcille while building a castle in his church in Durmagh in the 640th year since the church of Durmagh was founded.'

a stranger will do such things at his own peril. The Norman gentry learnt this spirit of natural piety in time; at present they shrank from no sacrilege or plunder of church lands.

If to be feudalized, Normanized, planted with Englishry, high and low, and studded with towns, manors, castles, and abbeys of foreign orders from sea to sea were a blessing for Ireland, then certainly Fate was pronouncing her veto. The premature deaths or endings in female heirs of the first conquerors make a curious story; no wonder the Irish believed it was for their sins against the native race and the native Church. Men of greater ability and ambition, or more favoured by opportunity and good fortune, were never to be found again in Ireland till the age of Elizabeth than were Strongbow, Raymond of Carew, De Cogan, Fitzstephen, Hugh de Lacy. All were cut off in their prime and succeeded by inferior men: what would have been the future of Ireland, had they, and indeed also William de Burgo and De Courcy (also the victim of baffling fortune), been allowed a long life to round off their vast estates and anglicize them, it would be vain to speculate.

Hugh de Lacy left by his first wife, Roësia of Monmouth, two sons, Walter and Hugh. As they were under age, the earldom was taken into Prince John's hands. Every such minority meant a cessation of the personal lordship so necessary then and, could it have been foreseen, a revival of the apparently extinguished native proprietors. Not till 1194 did Walter assume his father's place.

THE END OF RORY, LAST HIGH KING

Rory O'Connor was now growing old and feeble, and his son Conor Maenmoy was the young hero of the race. In 1187 he attacked and destroyed De Lacy's fortress at Killare. De Courcy, being now Justiciar, took up the challenge and invaded Connacht but, when he got as far north as Sligo, he found a combination of Conor Maenmoy, Donal O'Brien, and O'Maeldory facing him. He therefore turned back into the Curlew mountains and, unable to resist the allies as they followed him, was driven out of Connacht. The hero Conor however was himself slain in 1189. His son, Cathal Carrach, then claimed the kingship, but Cathal Crovderg ('of the Red Hand'), brother of Rory, also asserted his claim, a claim of Tanistry against lineal descent.

Rory O'Connor himself finally, after years of seclusion, ended his life in pious obscurity in 1199 in his own beautiful abbey of Cong, where a rushing pellucid stream unites the quiet waters of Lough Corrib and Lough Mask, a delightful oasis of green in a noble but barren land. There, reconciled to God and his destiny, was entombed the last native king of Ireland.

A NEW GENERATION OF CONQUERORS

De Courcy was now foremost among all the colonists. William the Marshal, an eminent baron of England, in 1189 married Isabella de Clare, Strongbow's heiress, and so became earl of Pembroke and lord of Leinster, but did not play an active part in Ireland till 1206. But a new generation of Anglo-Norman adventurers and officials arose. During the reign of Richard (the date is unknown), Prince John, now count of Mortain, granted to William de Burgo all or part of Connacht.[1] In 1197 he enfeoffed Hamo de Valognes in the two cantreds of Conello in Limerick and Hamo built a strong fortress at Askeaton. The former lord disappeared in the usual way in 1199: 'Coilen Ó Coilen, chief of Ui Conaill Gabhra, was slain by the race of Maurice Fitzgerald.'[2]

The death of Donal More O'Brien in 1194 made the Norman advance possible. Some years before his death he had given his daughter in marriage to William de Burgo, and thus William's sons by her, Richard and Walter, had the blood of Brian Boru in their veins, and were native speakers of the Irish language. Already a mixed race was in sight which could be 'English to the Irish and Irish to the English'. As the king of Thomond's son-in-law, De Burgo secured peaceful seisin of the rich lands in Limerick and Tipperary which John had granted him, and to hold them he built strong castles at Kilfeacle near Cashel, Carrigogunnel in Aescluan on the Shannon, Briginis, and other places.

Donal More was buried in St. Mary's cathedral in Limerick. This Ostman city now passed under English rule, though John in 1197 granted its citizens by charter 'the liberties of Dublin'. It was thus, and remained till Galway arose, the most westerly chartered borough in these islands. No longer did it serve the O'Briens for a capital. Indeed one notes in Donal More a recognition that his kingdom would end with his life, and that of the rich plains of Limerick and Tipperary (the famed 'Golden Vein') the Norman conquerors were the destined possessors. Of his three sons, Conor Rua, Murchertach Finn, and Donnchad Cairbrech, the

[1] It is worth while to emphasize again that William de Burgo was no connexion to William FitzAudelin (or FitzAdelm)—see Orpen, *Normans*, II, p. 195.

[2] O'Clery's *Book of Pedigrees* (see *R.S.A.I.* (1880), p. 225). The race of Maurice were interested in the settlement of Limerick, and Hamo de Valognes, who got Connello (O'Coilen's country), granted Shanid to Thomas, son of Maurice, and Croom to Thomas's brother, Gerald.

latter finally came to the front and ruled the Clare portion of Thomond from 1210 till his death in 1242.

RISE OF O'NEILL AND O'DONNELL

All the while the power of the great De Courcy was still advancing in Ulster. In 1188 his new fort at Moycova, north of Newry, gave him the command of the passes of the north, and the castle that he built at Kinsantail near Coleraine threatened Inishowen. Part of the Derry coast here he granted to Duncan, son of Gilbert, lord of Galloway.[1]

But a great leader now arose among the Cinel Eoghain. Murchertach MacLochlainn died in 1196, and Aedh O'Neill of the rival stock secured the kingdom. A rival, Conor Beg MacLochlainn, opposed him, but Egnechan O'Donnell, the new chief of Tyrconnell, saved Aedh O'Neill by sailing to his aid with a large force into Gaeth-an-Chairrgin near Portrush, and there in battle in 1201 MacLochlainn was slain.

Egnechan, who ruled Tyrconnel until his death in 1207, established, for as long as the kingdom of Tyrconnel lasted, the primacy of the O'Donnells. He himself had to fear the rivalry of the O'Maeldory branch whose last king, Flavertach, had died in 1197. Bound in a common alliance, the O'Neills and O'Donnells swept every rival out of their path, and thus the two great families of the north rose together amid the wreckage of the Norman conquest, to fall together four centuries later at Kinsale. Aedh ruled Cinel Eoghain till his death in 1230. The MacLochlainns revived once more, but finally, in 1240 at Camergi, Brian O'Neill slew Donal and ten of the MacLochlainn *derb-fine*, thus almost extinguishing the race.[2]

CATHAL CROVDERG, KING OF CONNACHT

De Courcy was no longer Justiciar, for he was deprived of office in 1192. But he was commissioned to make peace with Cathal Crovderg, in spite of the grant to De Burgo and De Burgo's support

[1] For this family, see Sir James Balfour Paul's *Scots Peerage*. Fergus, lord of Galloway (d. 1161) had two sons, Uchtred and Gilbert, and a daughter, Affreca, who married Olaf the Red, king of Man. The granddaughter of Affreca and Olaf married De Courcy. Duncan, son of Gilbert, was made earl of Carrick in Galloway by William, king of Scots, some time before 1196, and died in 1250. Roland, son of Uchtred, lord of Galloway, had two sons, Thomas, later earl of Atholl, called 'MacUchtred' by the Irish, and Alan FitzRoland, lord of Galloway. (See later, Chapter VII.)

[2] See later, p. 129. After this the MacLochlainn family survived as inconsiderable landholders in Inishowen, where their name is extant to this day.

of the other Cathal. A rude fort commanded the Shannon at Athlone and here in 1195 De Courcy recognized Crovderg as king of Connacht. To show his satisfaction, Cathal enfeoffed a Norman of Meath, Gilbert de Angulo, baron of Morgallion, who was then in his service, in the cantred of Maenmagh in Hy Many. Known as Mac Goisdelbh ('son of Gocelin' or 'Jocelin') by the Irish, this aristocratic mercenary, first of those who were to become *Hibernis ipsis Hiberniores*, founded in Connacht the race of the Costellos.

But Crovderg could not secure Connacht while Cathal Carrach lived, and at last in 1200 De Burgo, taking up the latter's cause, brought in an army from Munster and drove Crovderg into exile. But as he was the Government candidate, De Courcy and Hugh the younger De Lacy marched with him again into Connacht in 1201, but were defeated by the other Cathal and driven back over Lough Ree.

In the scramble for land and lordship, it was not long before the distinction of Gael and Gall was to disappear. Here was De Burgo, a Government favourite with a grant of Connacht in his pocket, supporting one O'Connor, who he hoped would be a tame one, while De Courcy and De Lacy in the Government's name were striving to install another O'Connor. Policy was taking the place of a Norman front and weakening the great design of a final conquest of Ireland.[1]

John was now king of England and Cathal Crovderg was his candidate for Connacht. Cathal accompanied De Courcy and De Lacy up to Dublin, and there swore obedience and was again recognized as king of Connacht. De Burgo himself had to accept the royal choice, and Cathal Carrach, deprived of his support, fell in a skirmish with his rival in 1202. The triumphant Crovderg was in the same year inaugurated king of his province with the ancient ceremonies at Carn Fraoich.

De Burgo still hoped for the lordship of Connacht, but died in the winter of 1205–6 without achieving it. As first grantee of Connacht and father of the Richard who achieved the conquest, he was called ever after in Irish tradition William 'Concur', that is 'the Conqueror'.

[1] The difficulty of 'conquering' an Irish country and the fierceness of the people (so different from the docile Anglo-saxons whom the Normans subdued so easily) were illustrated in 1202 when Cathal Crovderg and his momentary ally, William de Burgo, having quartered their mercenaries (*sersenaigh*) on all Connacht, on a rumour of De Burgo's death the *sersenaigh* were massacred in a general rising to the number of nine hundred (see Orpen and *Ann. L. Cé*).

CHAPTER VI

KING JOHN AND IRELAND, 1199–1216

JOHN, Lord of Ireland and count of Mortain, succeeded his knight-errant brother and was crowned King of England on June 2nd 1199.[1] Richard I left no issue and so, by another unlooked-for event, the whole future of Ireland was decided. Had Cœur-de-Lion left a son, John might have founded a separate Angevin dynasty in Ireland. But 'the emerald gem of the western world', which might have been the main glory of a native king, was 'set in the crown of a stranger', and became only one of the many gems that glittered in the Plantagenet diadem. The lordship of Ireland, in short, was annexed for a long future to the kingdom of England.

John at least, who deepened in character as he grew older and who might have been one of England's greatest kings had he not been capricious, cruel, and mean, always felt a responsibility for his land of Ireland, about which he knew more than most of his advisers. His policy for Ireland was a threefold one: to reduce the older baronage there; to favour the Irish chiefs for policy's sake rather than justice; and to build up a central government strong enough to override both. Had he been able to give more time to Ireland, and had he shown less of the caprice and meanness which marred his great abilities, he might have set a far more enduring mark on this country. Even as it was, we may justly call him 'the founder of Anglo-Ireland', the man who implemented the conquest begun by Strongbow, and ended the aimless feudal age that had prevailed since his father 'acquired' the land of Ireland.

It was long before King John himself came to set Ireland right, but in Meiler FitzHenry, one of the Anglo-Irish, whom he made Justiciar from 1199 to 1208, he found a servant after his own heart. Under this viceroy the vast privileges and fiefs of the first conquistadors and their heirs were brought into question, and many new grantees arrived on the stage to offset the old. Royal grants to the lords were numerous, but John took care always to reserve something for the lord of them all. There were plenty of candidates for these generous grants, for seldom in European

[1] His elder brother, Geoffrey, had left a young son, Arthur, who by strict lineal descent should have been king but was murdered by John's order in 1205.

history has a land so large as Ireland was, or one so attractive in its climate, fertility, and natural riches, been given away for the asking. The feudal, the merchant, the official, and the clerical class came over in increasing numbers; it is remarkable, however (and it proved fatal to the hope of anglicizing Ireland), that comparatively few of the industrial, cultivating, and plebeian class of the English came over. But a docile race of 'betaghs', so ill used by their former lords that a Norman lord made no difference to them, and clever native craftsmen were already there, too useful to be displaced, and forming one of the attractions of Ireland for the exploiting settlers.

THE ENFEOFFMENT OF MUNSTER

John now in January 1201 renewed to William de Braose, nephew of the former Philip, the kingdom or 'honour' of Limerick. William had to pay for it indeed; for John was ever a hard bargainer and could descend even to swindle, and the price was five thousand marks for the charter and a fixed service of sixty knights, while the King kept in his hands the city of Limerick and 'the cantred of the Ostmen there', and the gift of all bishoprics and abbeys. It was a magnificent liberty and included most of Donal More's kingdom, but the present county Clare was kept in reserve to meet O'Brien claims.

Theobald le Botiller and Philip de Worcester were thus made De Braose's tenants.[1] The Geraldines, though still minor landholders, were destined for greatness in Limerick county. Gerald, lord of Offaly, had already a grant of Croom. His younger brother Thomas already had Shanid and now got lands around Knockany.[2]

In Kerry, in 1200 John granted to the Justiciar, Meiler Fitz-Henry, 'the cantreds of Akmikerry and Offerba' and 'Eoghanacht Locha Léin' from Killarney to the sea 'as fully as Humuriardac held it'.[3]

John had set his heart on securing Munster for the English, and as the 'Regnum Corcagiae' was in his hands since the deaths of De Cogan and Fitzstephen, county Cork was at his will and pleasure. In 1207 he renewed to William de Barry the three

[1] See my *Cal. Ormond Deeds*, I, Nos. 26, 27; William de Braose renews to Theobald Walter and his heirs the former grants of 5½ cantreds (named) in Munster at service of 22½ knights.

[2] *C.D.I.*, I, No. 93. From Croom came the later war-cry of the earls of Kildare ('Crom Abu') and from Shanid that of the earls of Desmond ('Shanid Abu').

[3] Akmikerry (in Irish 'Aicme Ciarraighe') is the present barony of Trughanakmy, and Offerba (Ui Ferba) was a district along the coast northward from Tralee. 'Humuriardac' is O'Moriarty, the native chief of Eoghanacht Locha Léin, now dispossessed.

cantreds of his father Philip, gave to David Roche the cantred of Rosscarbery, and to Philip Prendergast forty knights' fees from Inishannon to Cork. A Cantitune got lands around Glanworth which later from his name was known as 'Condon's barony'. A Barrett became lord of Clochroe and Clochphilip, and founded a barony called by his name about Blarney.[1]

This vast country, robbed from O'Brien and MacCarthy and now acquired by Norman invaders, was in time destined to be grouped into two single hands, that of the Earls of Desmond and Ormond, and if we add that Waterford became half a Fitzgerald country and half remained Le Poer, we may consider Munster as one of the most French countries recorded outside France. This blood and character it was never to lose; nevertheless, large portions of it had to be left to the Gaelic race and the Gaelic speech.

O'BRIEN AND MACCARTHY STILL 'LOYAL'

In spite of these confiscations, for such these charters were though based on the King's right of grant, MacCarthys and O'Briens strove to maintain peace with Englishmen and keep such lands as they could. The treaty of 1177, still unrepealed, made Dermot MacCarthy's son king of twenty-four cantreds under tribute. It would almost seem that had MacCarthy renounced the old tradition of an Irish king and accepted a great fief of land by hereditary tenure under the Lord of Ireland, he might have become entirely a baron of the Crown as De Braose or FitzHenry was. It was hard with such a flood of Norman grantees, garrisons, and officials to kick against the pricks. For over forty years indeed, Donal More, son of Dermot of the Conquest time, and king of Desmond from 1185 to 1206, and his son again, Dermot of 'Dundrinan', king till 1230, remained loyal and undisturbed in the country west of Cork.

Intermarriages, which were not uncommon, began to unite the old race and the new, and thus the first Richard de Carew married a daughter of King Dermot of the Conquest time, and the latter's grandson, Dermot of Dundrinan, married a Petronilla Bloet. Besides, without some Irish Rí to command the allegiance of the native septs, how could the overwhelming majority of the Celts be brought to order and responsibility? The answer was: keep an Irish king going, but choose and support from the 'royal heirs' a 'tame' one who was willing to compromise. In Tudor times such a favourite of Government was called 'the Queen's O'Brien'

[1] About this time a Patrick de Courcy got lands about Kinsale and became ancestor of the barons of Kingsale, while further west along the coast to Clonakilty (the territory of Ibawn) was founded the family later called Barry Roe. The main Barry branch (Barrymore) were lords of Buttevant.

or 'the Queen's O'Neill'. If a royal clan succeeded in establishing automatic hereditary succession *versus* elective changes and Tanistry in a line the Crown could deal with, all the better, and indeed for many generations the main MacCarthy line managed to succeed son to father.

In Thomond, Donal More O'Brien was the last true king, but of his three sons the Government showed some favour to the elder, Murchertach Finn, and when John in person visited Ireland in 1210, as 'Mariadac, king of Limerick', he accompanied the English monarch on his march.

THE FALL OF DE COURCY, 1205

The policy of John was to discourage or remove the early conquerors, men of the old feudal type, and promote men more conformable to the new monarchy. Hence he vetoed De Burgo's designs upon Connacht, and resolved on the overthrow of John de Courcy.

De Courcy's northern kingdom, for which there was no patent from an English prince, was of the sort to alarm a king so jealous of his great vassals. Yet no proof exists of De Courcy's intention to shake off his English allegiance. In reality his fall was due to John's inherent suspicion of 'dangerous men', to a generous but unwise outburst against John for the murder of Arthur, and to the intrigues of Hugh de Lacy the younger, anxious to be an earl.

Walter and Hugh de Lacy had now come of age. The elder was given seisin of Meath in 1194; the latter aspired to be an earl like his brother. Sure of the royal approval, they picked a border quarrel, and when De Courcy refused to obey a summons to the Justiciar's court in 1202, Hugh marched into Ulster and defeated him at Downpatrick. De Courcy gave hostages, but would not trust himself to the doubtful mercies of John, and finally, on the last day of August 1204, the Justiciar was ordered to summon him for the last time, or confiscate his lands. As the prince of Ulidia still held out, John created Hugh de Lacy earl of Ulster on May 29th 1205, 'to hold as John de Courcy held, at service of one knight for each cantred, saving to the Crown the investiture of bishops and abbots'.

De Courcy was a magnificent hand-to-hand fighter, but his generalship deserted him now. He sailed over and collected ships and men from his brother-in-law Ragnall of Man, and besieged his own castle of Rath at Dundrum which De Lacy had taken, but was defeated beneath its walls and captured. Imprisoned for a time, and finally pardoned, De Courcy disappears from Irish history, and in England itself is heard of no more after 1219. His kinsmen and allies in Tyrone, Galloway, Man, and the Isles, and his own barons in Ulster, had all failed to save him. In the great age of the Normans he might successfully have defied so mean a king and died a prince in the Ulster he had created. But that age had gone by, and the new monarchy, strong in law, prestige, and resources, was able to cut away the ground from under the greatest of its barons.[1]

JOHN CREATES A GOVERNMENT

It was now fully time to create an Anglo-Irish capital, and build up a machinery of government for the new lordship. Henry II had done little but appoint a few officials; John built up the actual fabric of legal monarchy.

In 1204 he ordered a strong castle to be built in Dublin, suitable for the government of the country, and the defence of the city. This work was completed by 1215, and so government by 'Dublin Castle' began. To John was due the introduction of the 'Customs of England', a mixture of old common rights, feudal practice, and principles of a central law as affirmed by Henry II. Known henceforth, and adapted to local needs, as the 'Customs of Ireland', they became the precious heritage of the common freemen in the Anglo-Irish realm.[2] As British subjects carry with them to-day into every realm which is under the Crown of the Empire the common law, so the English settlers considered that they carried with them into Ireland the fast-growing 'common law' of England. But the feudal class especially considered that they brought over as their right and heritage the whole body of law and practice which governed the feudal system of land-holding.

Along with the judicial code, John introduced the legislative machinery of England. No real system of law or central or local

[1] For the patent of the earldom to Hugh de Lacy see *Gormanston Reg.*, p. 189. King John grants him 'totam terram Ultonie'. It is not clear whether 'Ultonia' was meant to cover all modern Ulster. Unlimited expansion is implied in 'a knight from every cantred'. The *Ann. L. Cé*, *sub* 1235, describe Hugh as 'Iarla Ulaidh', i.e. earl of Ulidia, not of the whole province. The Laud Annals (*Chart. St. Mary's*) *sub* 1204 describe De Courcy's fall, and say he was sentenced to perpetual imprisonment 'quia fuit rebellis Johanni Regi et noluit facere homagium et vituperavit eum de morte Arthuri legii heredis'. Probably, soon after his accession, John had demanded homage from the prince of Ulidia, who alone of the Normans of Ireland held no patent from the Crown.

[2] There are allusions in the records of Henry III's reign (1228 and 1233) to 'the laws and customs of the realm of England which the Lord King John, our father, with the common consent of all men of Ireland, ordained to be kept in that land'. The 'rights of the subject' were, from Magna Carta onward, to become the great slogan in English constitutional struggles.

administration yet existed in the new colony. We catch glimpses of some such development late in the reign of his father and of his brother, but it was left to John to introduce all that body of State law which struck at the very root of feudal exemptions.

The feature of these legal innovations, due to the genius of Henry II but all part of that revival of the State as against feudalism which marks twelfth-century Europe, was that cases involving the land-titles of the feudal class and criminal jurisdiction over common freemen were withdrawn from the baronial to the royal courts. After many protests from the feudal and privileged class the work of Henry II triumphed, and the State courts of England were open to all freemen in the thirteenth century.

This new monarchy it was John's design to apply in Ireland. Though nominally a lordship, i.e. a feudal dominion, he treated his new realm as a monarchy, exercised all royal rights there, and treated all the colonists at least as liege subjects. So he set the keynote for future kings of England, whose government claimed to be royal and sovereign even if the title was not a royal one and was based upon a papal grant. But its triumph in levelling all classes beneath the Crown was far less than it had in England, for on the one hand the Irish were not admitted to the benefits or duties of the common law, and on the other the Anglo-Irish feudal class, while claiming all the benefits of Anglo-Norman feudal law, cared little for the rights of the ordinary subject.

Quarrels over land among the knightly class in Ireland, as in England, had so far been decided in the lords' courts by trial and wager of battle. Henry II's assizes of *Mort d'Ancestre* and *Novel Disseisin* had been established to deal with them, and the advent of John made these applicable to Ireland. By letters patent in 1204, John established the system of royal writs, and extended to the colonists the English law as it then stood, in this royal edict: 'Know that we have given power to our Justiciar of Ireland that his writs run through all our land in Ireland, viz. the writ of Right and the writ of *Mort d'Ancestre*, and the term for *Mort d'Ancestre* shall be after the return of Henry our father from Ireland to England. Also the writ of *Novel Disseisin*, the term of which shall be after our first coronation at Canterbury; also the writs of Fugitives and Villeins, the term of which shall be after the taking of Dublin.'

By an edict of the same year, John extended to Ireland the jury system in criminal procedure, established by the Assize of Clarendon.[1] In 1207 he forbade any subjects to answer in any court for

[1] *C.D.I.*, No. 236 (Nov. 1204), and Betham, *Feudal Dignities*, etc., p. 229. The point of villeins was a vital one for the landed class. In England this form of property in men was safeguarded in statutes such as the Constitutions

their free holdings, or on any plea of the Crown, save before the King, his Justiciar, or their justices.

This man of demonic energy was resolved to be King in Ireland as in England, and he would never have admitted that any corner of it or man of any of its races was not in some sense under his law. His insistence upon that sacred right, the royal prerogative, is seen all through the reign. When he granted the custody of Ireland to Meiler FitzHenry in 1200, and confirmed him as Justiciar, he reserved to himself, as the imperial overlord at Westminster, all Irish pleas touching the Crown, the Mint, and the Exchange. In 1207 he established an Irish currency, the first national coinage, which bore the symbol of a harp.

It was not till his coming over in person that John established a legislative body for the colony. So far, the Justiciars had summoned the tenants-in-chief of Ireland for such immediate measures as were necessary. It was generally accepted that the King and his Great Council of barons in England could legislate directly for Ireland. His programme for Ireland was to be consummated by his visit in 1210.

THE TREATMENT OF THE NATIVE KINGS

John's treatment of the native race had statesmanship, though not of the highest kind, in it. That he could stay the course of Norman conquest or revoke land-grants was hardly to be expected. He realized, however, the value of the Irish and the Ostmen as valuable counterfoils to the Normans. It was perhaps too late to check these chartered robbers who had eaten up so much land and hungered for more. Many of the nearer chiefs had lost their richest lands to the newcomers; some had removed to other districts; some, dispossessed, hoped for restoration; others, abandoning the old kingships, thought of saving only their 'royal land', or family demesne.

To some of the lesser chiefs John showed a clemency which they could not expect from the feudal invaders. In Waterford, which was royal demesne, he granted to O'Bric, chieftain of the southern Déisí, in 1203 certain lands, making up four knights' fees, to be held of the King in chief by service of one knight. Next year, 1204, he made an agreement with Donal O'Faelain, paramount chief of the two Déisí, by which O'Faelain quit-claimed to the King the 'province of Dungarvan' which was one of the

of Clarendon. English legislation about villeins was fully extended to Ireland, e.g. the writ *de nativo habendo*, by which a lord could recover a runaway serf (see *C.D.I.*, I, p. 309).

three cantreds that this chief ruled. The other two were to be his own, one for life, one as his inheritance.[1]

A similar grant was made to the MacGillacolmoc family who were chiefs of Ui Dunchada. In 1207 John granted to Dermot, son of Donal, all the land which his father 'Gilleholmoc' held, viz. 'Lymerhim (Newcastle-Lyons), with fifteen carucates of land and a burgage in Dublin, to hold in fee by service of one knight and two otter skins per annum, saving to the king that cantred in the land of Lymerhim which the king gave to the said Dermot and his brother Roderic when he was count of Mortain'. Later, in 1215, compensation was made to 'John Dermot, nephew of Gilleholmoc', for the 'land of Limerun', taken for the improvement of the King's manor of Newcastle. But this native family, which now changed its name to FitzDermot, retained much of its domains and held till 1400 the barony of Rathdown in Wicklow.

Hard as were the bargains driven by the Crown, it is clear that the nearer chiefs, harassed by the greedy inferior colonists, were glad to surrender their wide ancient claims for a secure if smaller lordship, guaranteed by either the King or one of the greater magnates.

THE KINGDOM OF CONNACHT AND THOMOND

The Irish province-kings were in a very different position from the petty chiefs. The treaties made with them by Henry II had not been abrogated. While the colonial lords were John's *fideles*, the kings of Connacht, Limerick, Cork, and Ulster were acknowledged as such by King and Pope, and were vassals rather than subjects of the English crown.[2] Though no formal record exists admitting the 'Five Bloods' to the benefits of English law, it seems clear that they were regarded, from Henry II's time, as law-worthy and entitled to plead in the 'King's courts', or before the King's viceroy himself.

The greatest of the Irish kings, in English eyes, was Cathal Crovderg, brother of the last Árd Rí. In August 1204 Cathal entered into direct parleys with the Dublin government, and after long delay, in December 1205, the King informed the Justiciar,

[1] Orpen (*Normans*, II, p. 327) gives the O'Faelain grant. For the O'Bric grant see *C.D.I.*, I, No. 190 (Nov. 1203). According to Butler (*Hist. of Gualtier*, pp. 31–3) the places granted were in Gall-tir, i.e. the Ostman cantred on the south-west of the city of Waterford.

[2] For 'Mariadac, king of Limerick' (Murchertach O'Brien) see *C.D.I.*, I, No. 404 (1210), when he was with John. In 1220, Pope Honorius III sent a legate to Ireland as well as Scotland, the brief of appointment being superscribed: *Regibus Ultonie, Corcagie, Limerick, Conacie, Insularum, cuilibet per se* (Theiner, *Vet. Mon.*, pp. 15–16).

FitzHenry, that the king of Connacht had offered to hold a third of his kingdom as a barony, at rent of a hundred marks per annum, and to pay for the rest a tribute of three hundred marks. The King gives mandate to the Justiciar to carry out this arrangement if it is to the King's advantage.[1] No immediate treaty was signed but John continued friendly to Cathal and left him in practical possession. In 1210 at the first 'Peace of Athlone' the Justiciar De Gray made Cathal a grant, it appears, of all Connacht. But the young Richard de Burgo, coming of age in 1214, did not mean to let his claims lapse.

THE LEGAL TREATMENT OF THE NATIVE RACE

On the question of making both races equal in law, and securing to all alike the 'laws of England', John encountered a selfish interest, which was already a vested one. The Norman settlers, to whom land was useless without servile labour, and whose English followers claimed to be all freeholders, had for thirty years been enslaving the Irish who remained, or reducing to a general betaghry the various kinds of bond tenures which had existed before them. So completely did they do this that the word *hibernicus* came to be synonymous with *villanus*, *nativus*, *betagius*.[2] In cases affecting villeins, neither in England nor Ireland would the royal courts interfere, and until the fifteenth century the property of the lord in his land-serf was an unquestioned private right.

During thirty years of the Conquest great numbers also of the superior tenants of the Irish order had been violently expelled, and their lands confiscated. If the full benefits of Henry II's assizes were accorded to the native race, the courts would have to reinstate the former occupants by process of *Novel Disseisin* and *Mort d'Ancestre*. But this would undo the Conquest and alienate the established colonial faction which aimed at reducing all Ireland.

[1] *C.D.I.*, I, Nos. 224, 279. Notice the interest of the Crown, and indeed of the Irish kings, in the villein and man-power question. In August 1204 John ordered the Justiciar, 'see that the king of Connacht make villeins and fugitives from the King's (John's) two-thirds to return with their chattels and retinue. Cathal is to strengthen castles, found towns, and assess rents in these parts, and if necessary take the issues of the land and the King's rent for this purpose.'

[2] See *Cal. Justiciary Rolls*, I, p. 342. At the pleas of plaints at Kilmallock, before the Justiciar Wogan, Walter de Capella (Offyn), who had been blinded by a colonist for insulting the latter's wife, proves that though he is *hibernicus*, i.e. an Irishman, by race, he is not *hibernicus* (unfree), and so recovers heavy damages against his assailant, who pleaded that Walter as *hibernicus* had no right at law.

Therefore all that could be done was, by legitimizing the Conquest so far, to secure the native holders in their rights for the future. We have seen that according to John's writ in 1204, Henry II's assizes of *Mort d'Ancestre* and *Breve de Recto* were not to operate for pleas from before 1172, when vast confiscations were made, and the operation of *Novel Disseisin* was limited to John's own reign. The edict of 1204–5, which applied a limitation to criminal indictments, declared that no one might be impleaded for the chattels or even the life of an Irishman until after Michaelmas of that year.[1]

This limitation implied that after 1205 Irishmen might prosecute for injury to life, limb, and property, like Englishmen.

Of the other enactments, the force was that claims to landed property on the part of Irishmen must be based on ownership or tenure or ancestral possession, existing since the English invasion. No claim based on the times prior to that could hold, unless the English Crown ratified it. For the new 'Dominus Hiberniae' was in Ireland as in England *dominus terrae*, from whom all title to land flowed. Merely Irish title did not suffice; hence we find King John confirming Cathal Crovderg's grant of Maenmagh to Gilbert de Angulo in 1207.

A general Act of Oblivion was thus passed over Norman violence and fraud in the past. The question was—would the Crown or could the Crown protect the Irish from the present and future aggression? The intentions of John at least were good, and the estrangement of the races was not yet inevitable. But what was needed was a general admission to English law and liberty of the whole Irish race.

THE TREATMENT OF THE OSTMEN

If the Crown displayed an intention to take the Irish within the colony into legal protection, still more did it do so in the case of the Ostmen. This Teutonic race could blend more easily with the English settlers, they held the towns and the cantreds that were earliest occupied by the Normans, and were of indispensable value to them as merchants, sailors, pilots, and interpreters of native custom and speech. They alone knew the headlands, islands, and bays from Larne to Limerick, how to navigate the dangerous rocky seas of Ireland, and how to communicate with the inland men. Though they had not settled deeply in the interior, there were agricultural colonies of them, thousands strong, at most vital points, in north county Dublin, south Wexford, the Waterford

[1] See Betham's *Feudal Dignities*, p. 229; also Maitland, 'Introduction of English Law into Ireland' (*Eng. Hist. Rev.*, 1899).

coast, and round Cork and Limerick. A few of them had pushed up the rivers and established themselves up the Nore, the Suir, and the Liffey.

The merchants and traders among them had developed the moneylender's trade and we hear after the Conquest of several of them who were rich usurers. Though Teutonic in origin and by no means pro-Irish, it would seen that their Norse speech had almost died out save perhaps in Dublin; only thus can we explain the open way in which some of the Normans treated even the principal of them as mere Irish and exploited or destroyed them.

It was good policy as well as simple justice to take into Crown protection a race which had in a sense prepared Ireland for English invasion, and whose submission had put into English hands the keys of the island. From the first, both Henry II and John, in enfeoffing out the lands, had reserved to the Crown the Ostmen of the towns and the 'cantreds of the Ostmen' around Cork and Limerick. In particular, Henry gave to the burgesses of Waterford at their surrender a special protection as his liegemen. A branch of the old royal race there continued for over a century to claim, as Ostmen petitioners expressed it, 'English law as Henry FitzEmpress promised it'.[1]

Rulers of Limerick continued to enjoy a special 'liberty of the Ostmen', which protected them from feudal exploitations and from the jealousy of the new English burgesses. In a lawsuit of 1295, one William the Dyer of Ardfinan in Tipperary, whom some colonists had tried to reduce to Irish servitude, established his case that his father was an Ostman of the family of MacMackus of Limerick of free condition, and that his ancestors and himself had always received writs, and answered them according to the liberty of the Ostmen of Limerick.[2] For a century and more, the

[1] For Henry's charter to the Ostmen of Waterford, see A. Bugge, 'Nordisk Sprog . . . Irland' in *Aarbögr for nordisk Oldkyndighed* (1900), p. 320. The charter runs: 'Henricus rex . . . sciatis quod Hostmanni de Waterford homines mei ligei sunt'.

See *Facs. Nat.*, III, plate vii, for 'Rights of the Ostmen of Waterford', as follows: 'Pleas at Waterford before the Justiciar Wogan, 4 E. II [1310–11]. Robert le Waleys had killed John, son of Yvor MacGillemory, and admitted the fact, but pleaded that it was no felony, because John was a mere Irishman (*merus hibernicus*) and not of free blood, and offered the demand of the lord whose Irishman John was at the time of his death to pay for him as justice required. For the Crown, John le Poer replied that deceased was entitled to the law of the English in Ireland (*lex Anglicorum in Hibernia*), and alleged in support of this a charter of Henry II and a confirmation by Edward I. The latter only was produced; it confirmed a grant originally made to Gillecrist, William and John MacGillemory, who had been faithful to King Henry, of whose family John, son of Yvor, was.' Finally, the accused was sent back to prison and then released on bail.

[2] *Just. Rolls*, I, p. 59. Assize of *Novel Disseisin* at Clonmel, 1295. Three Englishmen have disseised William of a tenement in Ardfinan, and say they

city Ostmen are found holding office and serving on juries in Dublin, Limerick, and other towns. Even the landed dynasties of this race survived. The place-name Ballykilmurry in south Decies still marks the old demesne of the MacGillamaire rulers of Waterford. A descendant of the Sitric who defended the city against the Normans in 1170 held land in the county till 1230 or so.[1]

We shall have more to say of the Ostmen in dealing with the history of the Anglo-Irish towns. For the present they survived in large numbers and under the royal shield escaped the rapacity of the conquerors.

JOHN AND THE IRISH CHURCH

As far as English power went, the Irish Church now became a state church. Gone were the days when Gelasius of Armagh could journey up to Dublin modestly to accept the decrees of Cashel in 1172, having with him one cow on whose milk he supported life. The prelates of the occupied lands moved into the greater towns where the State could have its eye on them and where they lived in palaces, and petty Celtic sees were absorbed in greater ones, as Glendaloch with Dublin and Roscrea with Killaloe.[2] Bishops and abbots in their secular aspect became feudal potentates and barons under the Crown. The Normans were a race of practical piety; before long they were founding new abbeys or rebuilding old ones on twice the scale, but their abbots were intended to be English and of the English interest.

The new type of state prelate whom the Crown put into Dublin,

are not bound to answer him because he is *hibernicus et servilis conditionis*, i.e. an O'Moleyn. He answers that he is not Irish, but *Houstmannus*, viz. MacMackus and free. The jury find William's father was held for an *hibernicus*, so after his death William's mother went to Limerick and got the liberty of the Ostmen for her son. William therefore recovers seisin, and the defendants are put in mercy. The case illustrates the need for protection against the colonists and rightless position of the betaghs. *Hibernicus* here means both Irish and unfree. Maccus or Magnus, king of Man and the Isles *circa* 970, who was of the Limerick dynasty and spent part of his life there, was perhaps the MacMaccus ancestor (see *War of the Gael and Gall*, p. 271).

[1] See Power, *Place-names of Decies*, also *C.D.I.*, I, No. 2336 (1236). Mandate to the Justiciar to deliver to the King's Treasurer the demesne which 'MacChiteroc, an Irishman', held near Waterford, to make the King's profit thereout. The man thus losing his land was actually a Sitricson and an Ostman of the old royal race, but the fact that the Ostmen had become hibernicized and taken Gaelic patronymics such as MacSiocradh gave the colonists their chance to exploit them. MacSchyterok is another variant of the name.

[2] See 'Charters of Duiske', op. cit., *P.R.I.A.* After the death of Bishop O'Dullany in 1202 the new bishop, Hugh le Rous, a Cornishman, moved his seat from Aghaboe to the Earl Marshal's castle-town at Kilkenny. Simon de Rochfort, bishop of Meath (1198–1224) abolished the former Celtic sees of Trim, Kells, Skreen, and Dunshaughlin, which had survived the synod of Kells, thus making Meath one great diocese.

Meath, Down, Ossory, and Leighlin, as vacancy befell, brought a Norman party into the Church which the old Gaelic bishops feared and disliked. It was inevitable that an attempt should be made to staff the whole Church with this party, but by the end of John's reign only nine sees in the south and east had gone to Englishmen. Late in his reign, 1216, John positively directed the Justiciar not to allow Irishmen to be promoted to the chapter of a cathedral church, lest they should prevail to elect natives to bishoprics.[1]

The Irish bishops, who still were a majority, formed a Gaelic interest, which became deeply concerned for the liberties of the Irish Church, and angered at the Norman plunder of church property and the intrusion of English clerics. They accepted the English rule, but looked on it as a bargain between the English king on one hand, and the Irish nation and Church on the other, and looked to Rome, the Lord of Ireland's suzerain, to see that the king fulfilled his part. In 1202, when there was a vacancy in Armagh, a synod both of Irish and English clerics met in Dublin under the Legate John, cardinal-priest of Monte Celio, and another at Athlone, and deep resentment was evidently expressed for, on August 15th of that year, John appealed to the legate against the bishops of Clogher, Ardagh, Kells, and Clonmacnois, and others, who had resisted the King's right respecting the vacant church of Armagh. The influence of the Crown upon elections, the keeping vacant of sees and such royal dealings with the Church, were resented enough in England: in Ireland they had the further sting that John aimed at making a Norman stranger 'the Successor of Patrick'. The national stand was, however, successful, and the Irishman Echdonn held the archsee of Armagh till 1216.[2]

WILLIAM THE MARSHAL IN IRELAND, 1207–1213

For some years, William the Earl Marshal, husband of Strongbow's daughter and earl of Pembroke, took chief place on the Irish stage. This noble figure in English politics has a whole *chanson de geste* devoted to him, which tells much of his Irish doings.[3] The Earl, now a man of sixty but of unimpaired vigour,

[1] *C.D.I.*, I, Nos. 736, 739.

[2] *C.D.I.*, I, No. 168. Tomaltach O'Connor held Armagh between 1185 and 1201. On his death the question of succession arose, but it was not till 1206 that Echdonn (Eugenius) was in actual possession.

[3] *L'Histoire de Guillaume le Maréchale* (ed. Paul Meyer). It naturally takes the Marshal's and baronial side against John and FitzHenry. It seems certain that the Irish barons, like the English, were ready for a revolt against the Crown, and they actually were in touch with Philip Augustus of France in 1209. John and his viceroy, therefore, had every reason for securing all possible vantage in Ireland against a grasping and rebellious baronage. (See Davis's *England under the Normans and Angevins*, p. 361.)

had married Isabella de Clare in 1186; it was only now that, against the wish of John, he came over in February 1207 to safeguard the vast lordship of Leinster.

A fierce struggle for feudal rights *versus* royal claims now occupied the Anglo-Irish colony. FitzHenry, the Justiciar, was resuming or diminishing many fiefs of the great magnates. Among others he took over Offaly, which William the Marshal claimed, and Fercall in Meath which Walter de Lacy claimed.

The Marshal took the leadership of the barons of Ireland against the King's deputy, and was joined by Walter de Lacy, earl of Meath, and many more. But when FitzHenry seemed about to triumph, the capricious John veered round, and early in March 1208 informed the Justiciar that the Marshal and Walter de Lacy were loyal men, and De Lacy was given a new charter for Meath and the Marshal for Leinster.[1]

By the end of the year, FitzHenry ceased to be Justiciar and was succeeded by John de Gray, bishop of Norwich. The grandson of Henry I and Nesta, one of the earliest invaders of Ireland, died in 1220; he left no legitimate sons and founded no family in Ireland.[2]

The peace which William the Marshal (a man so noble that even John trusted and honoured him) made with his master in 1208 was a lasting one, and he was able to devote the years up to 1213 in organizing his lordship of Leinster. *L'Histoire de Guillaume le Maréchale* shows us the wide extent of William's earldom, and gives us the names of his knights, such as D'Erlee, D'Evreux, FitzRobert, FitzAnthony, Maillard, Huse, Porcel, many of whom founded families in Ireland. His charters reveal others who became Anglo-Irish, such as Rochfort, Archdeacon, Le Gras, De Londres, St. Leger, Dene, Keting, Chevre, and others, whose manors studded the rich plains along the Slaney, Barrow, and Nore. The founding of a numerous baronage and the manorializing of Leinster proceeded apace. At the same time, an inflow of inferior Englishry stocked the manors with a class of small freeholders, and the tillers and toilers were found among the numerous 'betaghs' or Irish *hibernici*. To the Earl Marshal indeed, rather

[1] The liberties in both cases were diminished, however. John reserved to himself the four pleas of the Crown (treasure-trove, rape, forestalling, and arson): appeals might be made to the King's court where the Earl's court failed to do justice or did injustice; crosslands, i.e. churchlands, and the higher ecclesiastical appointments were reserved to the Crown. The earls were to keep the custody of fees where the heir of a tenant-in-chief of the liberty was a minor, but the crown reserved the 'marriages' of such heirs. (See Orpen, *Normans*, II, pp. 233–4.)

[2] For the disposal of his Kerry estates, see Orpen, *Normans*, III, p. 133.

than to Strongbow, his father-in-law, is due the organizing of Leinster as a great Anglo-Norman principality.

A man of noble and civilized instincts, he was not content merely to feudalize his Irish land, but balanced it with towns, churches, monasteries, and civil institutions. The noble abbeys he founded at Dunbrody, Tintern, Duiske, and Kilkenny, the castle-town he built at Kilkenny, and the flourishing city at Rosponte or New Ross, which owed its foundation and first charter to him, all have their place in our medieval civilization.

THE EARL MARSHAL AND THE IRISH

All this organization implied an Anglo-French domination with a common Saxon substratum, and for two centuries more it was boasted by the colonists that Leinster was 'an English land'. Yet the Marshal's work was not disfigured by cruelty to the older race. Like Strongbow, he belonged to an older and more generous period, when the Norman was indifferent to race distinctions, and freely blended with peoples of other tongues and traditions. Soon, unhappily, the Norman, in becoming English, lost the fine adventurous tolerance of his race.

In Leinster, Strongbow had established a sort of *entente* with the old proprietors, and this the Earl Marshal maintained. A MacGillapatraic continued to hold lands in upper Ossory under the Earl.[1] The family of Donal Kavanagh, whom Strongbow had enfeoffed in Carlow, was left in possession and so were the other members of the MacMurrough race. O'Toole, Macgillacolmoc, and others were recognized as the Earl's kin through Eva MacMurrough and held lands under him. Those who had aided in the Conquest had the full rights of freemen.[2] As an instance we find that in 1299, at the pleas held before the Justiciar, John de Wogan, Walter O'Tothel came and showed a charter of William Marshal in the tenth year of John, enfranchizing his great-grandsire Gillepatrick O'Tothel and his issue after him with English law and with the right to serve on juries and assizes in the courts of the

[1] Donal MacGillapatraic, last king of all Ossory, died in 1185.

[2] See the Harris, *Collectanea*, I, p. 185. The King to the Justiciar: 'As Mamorch Offorthieren and Rotheric his brother have shown that they and their ancestors were always faithful, though Irishmen, in conquering the Irish on the side of the English, we command you to see that they be allowed to hold and to claim land like any Englishman.'

C.D.I., II, No. 1873 (1281), safe conduct for Art MacMurth and Caruel Alfortien, Irishmen and kinsmen of the Earl Marshal (Roger Bigod, earl of Norfolk), to visit him in England. The above Offorthieren or Alfortien is in Irish O'Foirtchern. A man of this Leinster race slew Donal Kavanagh in 1175.

King and the liberties.[1] Leinster seemed on the way to become a land of many races, living honourably side by side.

While southern and central Ireland, Gaelic a generation ago, were thus being rebuilt, the old world lived on in the north and west. No concerted drive was made to conquer Ulster west of the Bann, and Aedh O'Neill held his own against the new earl of Ulster. Tyrconnell pursued its expansion policy to the south, and in 1207 Egnechan O'Donnell, invading Fermanagh, was slain by the local array. But Aedh O'Neill renewed the alliance with Donal More, son of Egnechan. Remembering their recent blood-brotherhood, the two kings made a perpetual peace with promise of mutual aid against all adversaries whatsoever, English or Irish.[2]

KING JOHN IN IRELAND, 1210

The great fiefs of Meath, Leinster, and Ulster had been confirmed to their lords. But John repented of having permitted so much of Ireland to fall into palatine states, and a quarrel with William de Braose gave him an opportunity to resume the Honour of Limerick, as he had resumed the kingdom of Cork. De Braose owed great sums for having his charter and the payment of rents and services. John therefore ordered the debts to be levied in his Welsh estates. William stood his ground for a time, but finally fled to Ireland with his wife Maud and their children, where first William the Marshal and then Hugh de Lacy, earl of Ulster, son-in-law of De Braose, sheltered them.

This decided John to come over in person and with an overwhelming army. Feudal opposition, crushed in England, must not be allowed to look on Ireland as a safe retreat and place of defiance. His immediate purpose was to chastise De Braose and the restless Lacys, who were in touch with his enemy, King Philip of France. His general purpose was to remedy the state of things in Ireland in person and in his own way, to override the feudal liberties, to meet the claims of Gaelic kings *versus* Norman conquerors, and to give final form and energy to the Dublin government.[3]

[1] *Just. Rolls*, I, p. 271 (1299), Wogan being then Justiciar. Two Englishmen had disseised Walter of a freehold in Tancardstown, county Kildare, and replied that they ought not to answer to the court, as Walter was *hibernicus*. No verdict is recorded.

[2] *A.F.M.* (1208).

[3] See H. W. C. Davis. *England under the Normans and Angevins*, pp. 359–63) on John at this period. John had reduced Wales, brought William the Lion of Scotland into a treaty which for five years left the Scottish king in a position of dependency, and exacted the oath of fealty from all English freemen. He then turned to Ireland, where Philip of France was intriguing with the Anglo-Irish barons, with such apparent success that, according to

The indefatigable Plantagenet sailed from Pembroke with an imposing force of earls, knights, men-at-arms, and officials, carried in seven hundred vessels, and landed at Crook near Waterford on June 20th 1210. His scribes brought with them, we are told, over fifty dozen skins of parchment, sufficient to make a whole new enfeoffment of Ireland.

At Waterford John was met by Donnchad Cairbrech O'Brien, anxious for favours from so great a king. John granted him the castle and lordship of Carrigogunnell at yearly rent of sixty marks, while Donnchad's elder brother Murchertach joined John on his march and appears in the official record as 'Mariadac, king of Limerick'.[1]

While he displayed a gracious face to the Irish, John showed a stern one to his offending barons. Marching by Kilkenny and Naas, he arrived at Dublin and lodged at St. Thomas's abbey June 28th. Here Walter de Lacy's barons pleaded in vain for their lord, for John meant to root out the two brothers who held between them Meath and Ulster.

Advancing through Trim, he seized Walter's castles and at Ardbraccan was met by Cathal Crovderg, who did homage and like the king of Limerick marched with his overlord into Ulster.[2] The two Lacys had mustered an army of John's enemies but could not stand against the royal banner. John marched by Dundalk to Carlingford, and crossing the lough there in spite of some resistance from the rebels, took Dundrum ('Rath') Castle, while the Lacys fell back to Carrickfergus.

There the King, marching through Downpatrick, arrived on July 19th, and the chief stronghold of the Ulster earldom fell after a siege of nine days. There was a general surrender of De Lacy vassals from Ulster and Meath, but Walter and Hugh themselves escaped to Scotland and finally to France. William de Braose himself, the prime object of the King's wrath, also escaped and died an outlaw in France the following year. Duncan, earl of Carrick, had joined in on John's side, he captured Maud de Braose with a young son in her flight, and handed her over to

a contemporary, 'all men bore witness that never since the time of Arthur was there a king so greatly feared in England, Wales, Scotland, or Ireland'. But John was under papal excommunication from November 1209 to May 1213, and threatened by a baronial revolt and a French invasion. His treaty with the king of Scots in 1209 enabled him to make a subsidiary agreement with the earls of Carrick and Galloway, Duncan and Alan, by which he enlisted this powerful family against the Lacys and his Irish rebels.

[1] See Chap. VIII, p. 143, where John's grant to Donnchad in 1199 is quoted.

[2] It is recorded in *L'Histoire des Ducs de Normandie* that John presented the king of Connacht with a handsome war steed, whereupon Cathal, removing the heavy Norman saddle and lightly vaulting on its bare back, rode all day beside the king, to the great astonishment of the courtiers.

John.[1] His reward was a large grant out of the earldom, stretching along the Antrim coast from Larne to Glenarm.[2]

John now turned south and marched to Drogheda, making a detour as far west as Granard. On August 14th he was at Rathwire in Meath. He had dispatched Cathal O'Connor home after the siege of Carrickfergus, charging him to return with his son as a hostage, on which he should get a charter for the third of Connacht. Cathal now came to Rathwire, but without the son, displaying a natural reluctance to deliver his child to such a King, whereupon John in anger seized four of Cathal's retinue, namely MacDermot, king of Moylurg, O'Hara, king of Leyney, Find, an an officer of Cathal's household, and Torberd, his seneschal, and took them with him to England.

On August 18th John was back in Dublin, stayed there till the 24th, and sailed from thence to Fishguard. The whole campaign was a triumph of demonic energy. During it he had confiscated two earldoms and the honour of Limerick, seized some twelve chief castles of Ireland, and attested his triumph by a general exaction of hostages, and imprisoning of leading rebels.

It is clear that John did not stay long enough in Dublin on either occasion to do all the things attributed to him on this occasion. Twenty Irish chieftains are said to have done him homage at a great council held in the capital. He is said to have established sheriffs, but the oft-repeated legend that he made twelve counties in Ireland cannot be upheld.[3]

Actually the founding of an Anglo-Irish government was spread over John's reign. Yet his visit was a turning-point in the organizing of a state, where all the ills of an unbridled feudalism were

[1] The story of herself and the child being starved to death by the King's orders in Corfe Castle makes one of the grimmest records of John's cruelty. (See D'Aubigné, *King John.*)

[2] De Courcy had first begun to enfeoff these Scottish nobles on the north Ulster coast with his grant to Duncan FitzGilbert of Galloway of fiefs around Coleraine *circa* 1197.

[3] *Roger of Wendover* (*R.S.*, III, p. 233) records the submission of the Irish. *C.D.I.*, I, No. 1458, gives a writ of December 10th 1226, which says: 'When King John went to Ireland, he took with him men expert in the law, by whose counsel, at the instance of the Irish, he ordained that English laws should be in force in Ireland, and left these laws reduced to writing under his seal, at the Exchequer, Dublin.' The loss of the Patent, Close, and Charter Rolls for the year 1210 deprives us of authentic documentary details of the King's doings at this vital moment. It is impossible that John could have created twelve shires, for all Ulster, Leinster, and Meath at that time were feudal liberties, nor did the colony ever have twelve shires till at its full under Edward I. In John's time only county Dublin and perhaps Kildare and Louth could have been in any sense true counties. But of course wherever the King had any rights or revenues a sheriff was necessary.

running wild. According to the chronicler Wendover, John held a council of prelates and barons during his final stay in Dublin, where 'by common consent, the laws and customs of England were extended to Ireland'. Formerly the lordship of Ireland was without form and void. Now it had a permanent central government of its own, and in the occasional assembly of prelates and magnates, as summoned by the Justiciar, a legislating body in Irish matters. Its subjects were to enjoy the liberties which freemen in the mother country enjoyed; indeed they could be claimed by Irish and Ostmen too. Nevertheless the colony was under the final control and imperial suzerainty of the King in England, and for nearly two centuries more the Crown at Westminster could enact for Ireland by mere decree.

The viceroys John left after him, John de Gray and Henry de Londres, archbishop of Dublin up to 1215, strove to carry out his policy, to repress the feudal interest, which would have dissolved Ireland into pieces, and to exalt the central government, which alone could bind it together.

THE TREATMENT OF THE IRISH, 1210–1216

John's treatment of the Irish had been a great advance on his visit of 1185. He had dealt well with the O'Briens, and if he quarrelled with O'Connor, this was partly Cathal's fault, and was redressed by the Justiciar on John's departure. Even if Wendover's story of 'the twenty Irish kings' who came to Dublin is vague, it is clear that many of the native chiefs made a fresh homaging to their foreign overlord, and their kings accepted willingly the scarlet robes which John bestowed upon them.[1] As before, they had good reason to prefer a king, who at least was universal, to the numerous Norman conquerors who fought each for himself, and to look to a general law as against a race *semper aliena petens*, each of whom was a law to himself.

The growing difficulties of John in England made it the more necessary to have in Ireland a profitable second kingdom. A large revenue was now being drawn from the confiscated earldoms and liberties. The King, among other profitable and politic measures, ordered his episcopal viceroys to win over the Irish kings.

At Athlone, late in 1210, Cathal met the Justiciar and offered to hold Connacht of the English crown. The captured hostages were returned, and, and though the final Treaty of Athlone was

[1] *C.D.I.*, I, p. 70: scarlet robes ordered for the kings of Ireland (1211). *Lib. Mun.*, pt. IV, p. 73 (1214): order to Henry, archbishop of Dublin, Justiciar, to buy scarlet cloth (*escarlettas*) for giving robes to the kings of Ireland.

not sealed till 1215, O'Connor's offer was now accepted, and Cathal, a real diplomatist, spent Christmas amicably with De Gray.

Donnchad O'Brien was now loyal, and a tenant-in-chief of the Crown for a fine lordship in Clare and Limerick. His elder brother, 'Mariadac', was retained for some time by the English as 'king of Limerick', but was finally ousted by his junior. Donnchad Carbrech was in turn recognized by the Dublin government, and during his long reign, from about 1210 to 1242, the kingdom of Thomond, though limited in extent, was a legal and actual fact.[1]

THE ENGLISH ADVANCE, NORTH AND WEST

No such terms as the above were made with the northern kings. O'Neill and O'Donnell had declined to come in to John in 1210, and in any case the Dublin government was determined to seize the frontiers of Connacht and Ulster in readiness for a further advance west and north.

Such an advance menaced the independence of the northern kings. In 1212 Gilbert de Angulo 'mac Goisdelbh' began to build a castle at Caeluisce, to command the narrow entry from Connacht into Tyrconnell.[2] The Cinel Eoghain were to be hemmed in from the sea; and in the King's name John de Gray granted to Alan FitzRoland, earl of Galloway, a huge fief of one hundred and forty knights' fees along the coast from Derry to the Glens of Antrim, where Alan's uncle, Duncan of Carrick, already had been granted the coast as far south as Larne.

In 1214, Thomas 'MacUchtred', earl of Atholl, brother of Alan, came with ships and men to build a castle in the old monastic town of Coleraine, and shocked the native mind by throwing down 'the cemeteries and *clochans* (stone houses) and the buildings of the town, save the church, alone, to build a castle'.[3] At the same time a castle was built at Clones, to command Oriel.

Meanwhile the Justiciar De Gray had advanced to the Shannon and built at Athlone a stone castle and wooden bridge. This had long been the gateway of the O'Connors into the midlands, it now became the bulwark for the English colony of Meath. The line of

[1] The kingdom of Thomond however was now confined to the present county Clare, and to that part of north Tipperary beyond where the Butler, De Burgo, and De Worcester grants operated. The city of Limerick, however, was now lost to the O'Briens. The abolition of the De Braose lordship in 1210, of course, enabled the English government to flatter the O'Briens in a belief that this 'kingdom of Limerick' might now be restored to them.

[2] Caeluisce ('narrow water') was at the west end of lower Lough Erne, and not far from Assaroe, which was the ancient passway into Tyrconnell from Connacht over the lake where the Erne discharges in a cataract into the sea, and was one of the most vital strategic points in Ireland.

[3] *A.F.M.*

the Shannon was further secured by John de Gray's successor, Henry de Londres, who built a fortress at Clonmacnois and another at Roscrea to command upper Ormond. The usual destruction of monastic buildings, the cutting down of fruit-trees, the driving away of cattle, and the appropriation of church land in order to build and endow the fortress at Clonmacnois, one of the most holy places in Ireland, evoked indignant protests from the bishop of that see, which money compensation did little to allay.[1]

When Geoffrey de Marisco succeeded the archbishop as Justiciar early in June 1215, the frontiers of the 'English land', already covering Munster, had been pushed to the Erne, the Shannon, and Lough Foyle, and the tradition of a central authority had been founded.

IRELAND AND MAGNA CARTA

John had the Earl Marshal to thank that at his final crisis he could calculate on Irish support. When, in the summer of 1212 already excommunicated by the Pope, he had to face the rebellion of his nobles and the prospect of their bringing in the King of France, the Anglo-Irish barons proved themselves, like their descendants of 1688, 'more English than the English', and led by the noble-minded Marshal met, and swore to support the King against his foes.[2]

When John mustered his tenants-in-chief against a French landing at Barham Down, early in May 1213, the Justiciar John de Gray and the Marshal brought thither five hundred knights and many horsemen from Ireland.[3] But a week later the King submitted to the Papacy, and undertook for himself and his successors to hold England and Ireland as fiefs of the Holy See, at rent of seven hundred marks for the one and three hundred for the other, and finally, by the signing of Magna Carta, June 17th 1215, he lowered the royal banner before his feudal opponents.

A fallen man, and much in need of ready money, John showed his altered mood in Ireland by charters of pardons and restoration.

[1] *C.D.I.*, I, No. 694 and *passim*.

[2] *C.D.I.*, I, p. 73, No. 448 (Oct. 1212, according to Orpen, *Normans*, II, p. 308): from William Marshal and twenty-six principal magnates of Ireland for the rest: 'Moved with grief and astonishment, they have heard that the Pope has proposed to absolve the subjects of the King from their allegiance, because the King resisted the injury done to him regarding the matter of the Church of Canterbury. With the King they are prepared to live or die, and will to the last faithfully adhere to him.'

[3] These five hundred knights would appear to be about the whole feudal levy by stipulated knight-service of the Anglo-Irish fiefs. See p. 172 for the knight-service of Ireland, where the figures total less than five hundred.

Walter de Lacy recovered the earldom of Meath, save the royal castle of Drogheda, for a fine of five thousand marks, and many underlords of Meath and Ulster were restored, but Hugh de Lacy did not get back his earldom. Instead, John, in June 1215, made further grants to the MacUchtred family, and made over to Thomas, earl of Atholl, Coleraine and Kilsantail with ten knights' fees on both sides of the Bann.

Cathal Crovderg got the kingdom of Connacht. By a final or second treaty made at Athlone in September 1215 with the Justiciar de Marisco, O'Connor was to hold all the land of Connacht in fee, at rent of three hundred marks and saving to the English crown the castle of Athlone; he was not to be disseised without judgment of the King's court. He had to pay, however, for this charter the huge sum of five thousand marks.[1]

The custody of the counties of Waterford and Desmond (the kingdom of Cork) and of Cork city was granted at rent to Thomas FitzAnthony, the Earl Marshal's seneschal in Leinster. There was no forgiveness for De Braose, and the honour of Limerick was not restored, but Philip de Worcester got a fresh grant of his five cantreds in Ormond.[2]

John died suddenly on October 19th 1216, backed by the Pope, but still in the field against his barons, who wanted to depose him for the Dauphin. This remarkable king was the first effective foreign ruler of Ireland, and in so far as the lordship of Ireland remained a real state, bound up with the fortunes and institutions of England, he may well be called its founder.

For over forty years since Strongbow became Lord of Leinster what organizing in Church and State there had been! The English genius for organization, for doing things and getting things done, was turned on to a land that had hardly altered since the days before the Norsemen, a land in love with antiquity, and which had almost no sense of progress.

King John and his viceroys organized the State. In their fiefs, the greater lords such as Strongbow, De Lacy, De Courcy, and lesser but very tenacious lords such as Theobald Walter or Gerald Fitzgerald, down to barons of a single fief, each with the Norman-French genius then at its height, and with such a field for their energy, were all town-planning, castle-planning, abbey-planning,

[1] *C.D.I.*, I, No. 654.

[2] *C.D.I.*, I, No. 163 (July 1215): The grant included Eoghanacht Caisil (the old MacCarthy demesne), Slievardagh (Muscraidhe Cuirc), Cnoc Grafain, and covered all Tipperary south of Cashel. De Worcester's line continued in Ormond till early in Edward I's reign and then ended in an heiress.

labour-planning. In such dioceses as the Norman-French prelates could get into, the same loftiness of design and vigour of execution was displayed. Could all this energy and all this constructive and practical genius have been focused, and could a resident king or even a continuous viceroy have directed and united it as an Anglo-Norman kingdom, Fate might have been happier for Ireland.

But how was the native Gaelic race, less than fifty years dispossessed, viewing and approving all this? A majority and an irrepressible one even in most parts of the colony, their view of life was almost bound to prevail. And, however such 'royal heirs' as Cathal Crovderg or Donnchad Cairbrech might temporize with the Dublin government or Norman earls who were too strong for them, in their own minds they were still the old Gaelic Rí, living in native tradition of monarchy, and desiring nothing better than the old Gaelic life, the local independence, the continuance of the hero-age of their ancestors, hunting, fighting, feasting, dwelling in the open air. And this view of life in due time after the Conquest had failed their descendants did in fact resume; moreover they infected the Normans themselves with it.

CHAPTER VII

THE EXPANSION OF THE COLONY, 1216–1245

WHEN Henry III, a boy of nine, was crowned King of England at Gloucester on October 28th 1216, he became *ipso facto* Lord of Ireland, and a mere official intimation of his accession was all that was conveyed to the Justiciar of Ireland. The Anglo-Irish requested that either the King's younger brother Richard or the Queen-Mother might be sent to represent royalty in Ireland, but the petition was in vain. Often in future days they made a similar request, and equally in vain.[1]

A GENERAL RESTORATION

The Earl Marshal was the young king's Regent till his death in 1219; and after him Hubert de Burgh was Justiciar and chief minister till 1232; it was due to these two real statesmen that reconciliation prevailed in both countries after the Barons' war, that the Angevin heir and the Angevin monarchy were restored, and that in Ireland the work begun by John of building up a State machinery was pushed on.[2]

Reginald de Braose, son of the William of 1210, was in June 1217 restored to the honour of Limerick. But little came of it, it was an empty name, and the established tenants of Ormond and Limerick remained practically tenants-in-chief. The honour or kingdom of Cork returned to the nominal heirs, but was equally of no practical effect. Philip de Worcester and his heirs, the Butlers, and the De Burgos were the real owners of Tipperary. Equally in Limerick, Cork, and Kerry, Thomas Fitzgerald of Shanid rose steadily to the front and acquired the former grants of FitzHenry, De Marisco, De Valognes, and others who either died out or preferred England to Ireland.

Walter de Lacy had been pardoned in 1215, but did not return to his earldom of Meath till August 1220; his brother Hugh, however, was not pardoned, and when he returned in 1223 it was some time before he was restored to the earldom of Ulster.

[1] *C.D.I.*, I, No. 723; the request was in October 1216.

[2] The Earl Marshal's sons and heirs successively were: William, junior (d. 1231); Richard (slain 1234); Gilbert (d. 1241); Walter (d, 1245); and Anselm (d. Dec. 4th 1245). All by an extraordinary chance died without sons.

THE BUILDING UP OF ANGLO-IRISH GOVERNMENT

In 1219 we find a separate Irish Exchequer at work in Dublin Castle and have the name of the first real Chancellor of Ireland, John de Wortheby. In 1220 the powers of the Justiciar were defined, and later a definite salary was attached to his office.[1] Like the Justiciar of England, he was a supreme law-officer as his name implies, and head of the whole judicial and administrative machinery. The viceroy was also commander-in-chief; he called out when necessary the feudal host according to knight-service, held the King's supreme court in Dublin, presided over the Council of the barons and prelates, and perambulated the colony, holding the pleas and assizes of the Crown. In short, he was *in loco Regis*, and while the Crown appointed the great officers of State, the Justiciar named all inferior officers and the constables of the royal castles.

In 1243 Henry ordered a great hall to be built in Dublin castle 'after the manner of the hall of Canterbury', a hundred and twenty feet long by eighty wide, having glazed windows, a large rose-window, mural paintings, and marble portal.[2]

The essential unity of the Irish State was affirmed by a royal edict of 1246, in which Henry declared: 'We desire to have in our realm of Ireland only one Justiciar, Treasurer and Chancellor, under whose seal all writs shall issue, and only one Exchequer, which shall sit in Dublin.'[3]

The framework of Anglo-Irish administration, based on that of England, was already in existence, and had only to develop. In spite of the feudal liberties which the Crown had lavishly created, the common law and the county organization were under Henry III extended to most of the colony. Dublin was already a county in 1200 and, by 1260, Cork, Limerick, Oriel, Waterford, Kerry, Tipperary, and Connacht were complete shires, where itinerant justices held their eyre in the county court, and the sheriffs collected the royal dues and made their tourn.

[1] *C.D.I.*, I, No. 949 (1220): Convention between the Crown and Geoffrey de Marisco, Justiciar. The latter is to answer to the King in his Exchequer of Dublin, of escheats, wards, fines, aids, etc., of the land of Ireland. In 1226 the Justiciar is granted a fee of £580 per annum, which later (1277) was fixed at £500.

[2] See Orpen, *Normans*, III, p. 294.

[3] *C.D.I.*, I, No. 2836: An order to the Seneschal of Leinster, forbidding him to issue writs and hold assizes there, but to let the royal writs run as they did before the late Earl Marshal usurped royal liberties. Ibid., No. 985 (March 1220–1): the King to the Justiciar: 'The land of Ireland has only one justice itinerant; let two others, a cleric and a knight, be associated with that one, and so make their eyre.'

MAGNA CARTA AND THE 'RIGHTS OF THE SUBJECT'

To make the English of Ireland equal in their liberties with those of England, Magna Carta, as amended since 1215, was sent over in February 1217.[1]

In 1227 the whole process of English law, its writs of Chancery, and its legal formulae, were extended to Ireland, where the Justiciar acted in place of the King. The covering writ spoke of 'the laws and customs which are to be observed in Ireland', and these laws are to be proclaimed in every county, 'except that no one shall be impleaded for the death or chattels of an Irishman till after the fifteen days of Michaelmas this year'.[2]

In 1254 Henry granted the Lordship of Ireland to his son Lord Edward, 'so, however, that the land of Ireland shall never be separated from the Crown of England'. England and Ireland were in short united under the one hereditary crown, but the English of Ireland, enjoying 'the laws of England', had their own liberties, customs, and institutions, and their consent must be sought to measures affecting them.

But we must not exaggerate the powers or good intentions of the Anglo-Irish government. Its justiciars were seldom well chosen, and it is almost incredible that such a man as Geoffrey de Marisco (or Mareys) should have been continued in this great office for six years in 1215–21, and again in 1226–8. De Marisco, a poor knight of Somerset, who had acquired Adare and Any, was the supreme type of the baronial 'bad man', false to the Crown, and cruel and false to the Church, to the native race, and to his fellow Normans. In 1213 two Irish chiefs, Finn and Donnchad O'Dempsey, were seized treacherously, by De Marisco, taken to Dublin, bound to the horse's tail, and dragged through the streets till they died. In July 1221 the English Government itself dismissed Marisco for appropriating the whole revenues of Ireland for the past six years to his private purse. In spite of this, the Crown restored him in 1226. In 1234 he was guilty of abominable treachery towards the Earl Marshal, and was the chief agent of his death. He detained the see-lands of Cashel unjustly, robbed the see of Limerick of Kilmallock and other property, and was excommunicated by the bishop in 1235. Finally, accused of

[1] Orpen, *Normans*, III, p. 18. The Magna Carta of 1215, wrung out of John, was on the accession of the young Henry reissued, but as coming from the King's will and grace. Several of its leading clauses of 1215 were omitted. It was reissued again in 1217 and finally in 1225, in which form it was again extended to Ireland in 1320.

[2] See 'Introduction of English Law into Ireland', by Maitland, *Eng. Hist. Rev.* (1899), and Berry, *Statutes of Ireland*, I, p. 22.

plotting the King's murder, he was outlawed, and died a wanderer and an exile in 1245. Such a 'servant of the Crown' would of course have been impossible in England; in Ireland where he was responsible to no one and uncontrolled by an *absentee* king, unfortunately he *was* possible.[1]

LEGAL TREATMENT OF THE IRISH

The abiding flaw in the Anglo-Irish state was the treatment of the native race. The whole fabric of Irish civilization was now broken, and masses of the Celts had been brought under Norman feudal law. Many, if not most, of the 'betaghs' on the manors were no doubt already *fuidirs* and *daer* tenants under the old order. But it was a general practice of the Englishry, whose mind was that of a slave-owning ascendancy, to reduce whatever Irishman they could to betaghry, and *hibernicus* was taken to mean a servile tenant with no rights against his lord or other colonists, any more than the contemporary Anglo-Saxon villein had. 'Tenants, both free, i.e. English, and Irish, i.e. unfree' is a characteristic description of a manor population. The practice of expelling Irish freemen, and then pleading that they were *hibernici* and thus not entitled to hold land or tenement, to rob the Irish widows of colonists of their dowry and marriage land, to reply that the aggrieved had no right to writs of *Novel Disseisin* and the like, was common, and was complained of not only by the Irish, but by the long-hibernicized Ostmen.[2]

The noblest of the Irish in the conquered lands had to fear these wrongs as much as common artisans and free tenants of episcopal or manorial lords.

The treatment of the O'Tooles may serve as an instance. As relatives of St. Laurence, as kinsmen of Strongbow through marriage, they were among those 'faithful Irish' to whom some of their lordship was spared. They gradually lost or granted away most of their wide domains, but still kept a great tract in the hill country of Dublin and Wicklow. The Earls Marshal and the Church favoured the race. Archbishop Luke of Dublin, *circa*

[1] For De Marisco (or De Mariscis) see paper by Eric St. J. Brooks in *R.S.A.I.* (1932); also Theiner, *Monumenta*, pp. 19, 56, and *C.D.I.*, I, No. 1001. *Ann. Clon.* (1213) record O'Dempsey's death when De Marisco was 'Custos' of Ireland. Geoffrey forfeited Adare which went to Maurice, baron of Offaly.

[2] MS. transcripts of *Exchequer Memoranda* in Public Record Office, Dublin, vol. XXX, p. 89 (48–9 Ed. III): '*Consuetudines et servicia tam librorum tenentium quam hibernicorum*', on the manor of Duleek.

The *Calendar of Justiciary Rolls of Ireland* (of which only two volumes covering 1295–1307 have been published) are full of complaints and instances of the above practices.

1230, 'confirms to Meyler, son of Laurence O'Tothil, the lands which his father held freely'. These lands must have been extensive and valuable, for, on Meyler's death, an Englishman offered to pay twenty pounds per annum to have the wardship, land, and marriage of Agatha, daughter of Meyler. But in 1299 a member of this race, Walter O'Toole, had to defend himself against two Englishmen, who had dispossessed him, and who answered to the writ of attachment that he was *hibernicus*, i.e. an Irishman and a serf, and therefore they had committed no felony.[1]

Others of the chiefly races had been confirmed in their demesnes by the Crown or the first conquerors. But they were in constant danger from the rapacity of colonists and of English courtiers who procured royal grants. Thus O'Bric of the Decies had been admitted to an extensive knightly tenure in 1203. But in 1252 Henry wrote to the Justiciar FitzGeoffrey to inqure into the lands held by Cormac O'Bric and other Irishmen *in capite*, obviously with a view of dispossessing them.[2]

Many such expulsions of innocent Irishmen were managed by Dublin Castle, nor did the colonial magnates disguise their intention of annexing all the available land. Meiler FitzHenry, in endowing Conall abbey in Kildare, included in his grant ten carucates in Kerry, and all churches of his lands of Ireland 'already acquired or to be acquired' (*tam conquisitis quam conquerendis*).[3]

The province-dynasties or 'Five Bloods' were less easy to expel. Negotiations had resulted in the recognition of the O'Connor and O'Brien kingdoms. But it was by no means clear that Cathal or Donnchad was meant to hold as barons of the Crown, fulfilling all obligations and passing his inheritance to his eldest son in feudal fashion. Here was the flaw in the treatment of the Irish *reguli*; they were meant to be mere vassals by homage, holding only by life-tenure, rent, military service, and 'good conduct', the latter a phrase which could be easily interpreted to their disadvantage.[4]

Henry's government constantly needed money, and when in 1218 it demanded an aid from the English colony it directed

[1] *Reg. Alani*, II, p. 839, for grant to Meyler, and *Crede Mihi*, p. 83, for Agatha. See formerly, p. 110 for 'Walter Otothel'.

[2] *C.D.I.*, I, No. 190, and II, No. 135. The names of these Irish Crown tenants were O'Bric, MacCrane, O'Kelechan, O'Culan, MacKermikan, MacKinecan. See for these Déisí chiefs Curtis, 'Sheriffs' Accounts of County Waterford, the Honour of Dungarvan', etc., *P.R.I.A.* (1932).

[3] Dugdale, *Monasticon*, VI, pt. II, p. 139.

[4] The Irish chiefs were often addressed as vassals by the Crown. See *C.D.I.*, I, No. 1001 (July 1221), letters announcing appointment of Henry, archbishop of Dublin, as Justiciar to the magnates and to Kathel of Connacht, Odo O'Neill, king of Keneloen, Dunekan (Donnchad), and Muriardac O'Brien, Dermot Macarthi, etc.

the Justiciar to ask contributions from 'the kings of Connacht, Thomond, and the other kings of Ireland'. But this need of money exposed it to the offers of land-seekers, and Richard de Burgo, in September 1219, asked either to have the land of Connacht at once for three thousand marks, or that 'the king of Connacht shall have half the kingdom for his life, and after his death, Richard shall have the whole', and offers one thousand pounds for this. But the English government rejected this proposal, and in February 1220 a patent was issued, giving protection to Cathal, king of Connacht, his chattels, goods, men, and possessions for five years.

THE TWO RACES AND THE CHURCH

In 1216 King John had directed the Justiciar of Ireland to see that no Irishman should be promoted to a cathedral church in that country.[1] On the other hand, it seems that the native prelates equally sought to exclude men ignorant of Irish speech and sympathy, and resisted the official attempt to staff the sees with Englishmen. The intervention of Rome was sought by the Irish bishops, and the Legate James, who was sent to Scotland in 1220, received from Honorius III weighty instructions about Ireland. 'The custom introduced by King John that no Irishman should receive Church preferment' was to be abrogated. A grievance reported by the archbishop of Cashel was to be removed, namely, that when an Englishman lost anything and got six other English to swear with him that an Irishman had taken it, the latter, though of good name and guiltless, and backed by thirty or more sworn witnesses, was nevertheless compelled to restitution. To these complaints were added others about the plunder of church lands by the Normans. The legate, however, proved an accommodating person from the English side and soon quitted Ireland. Innocent IV in 1253 had to reprove again the 'damnable custom' reported by the archbishop of Cashel.[2]

THE GERALDINES IN KERRY

Ireland was now full of adventurers, engaged singly or combining in bands to push their conquests westward.[3] Among the

[1] *C.D.I.*, I, Nos. 736, 739.

[2] Theiner, *Monumenta*, pp. 15–20, 30, 56, and *Cal. Papal Reg.*, I, p. 283.

[3] Thus *Ann. L. Cé* under 1186: 'Meath was full of foreigners from the Shannon to the sea.' 'Gall' ('Foreigner', plural 'Gaill') was to be the contrast for centuries with 'Gael'. In the sixteenth and seventeenth centuries the 'old English' (*Sean-Ghaill*) were reckoned by the Irish as almost Irish compared with the 'new English' settlers. We will, however, in future use 'the English' instead of 'the Foreigners' of the annals.

most active of these were the Geraldines, a numerous band of cousins who seemed to feel that Ireland held a great destiny for them. But while their courage and enterprise were their chief assets, they were signally favoured by good fortune, by marriage alliances, and the extinction of older grantees.

In Leinster Gerald, lord of Offaly and baron of Naas and Maynooth, died in 1215 and was succeeded by his son Maurice. His brother Thomas of Shanid, dying in 1213, left two sons John and Maurice. The *points d'appui* of their vast estates were in Munster, Croom, and Shanid in Limerick and Imokilly in Cork. They were soon to gain others in Kerry, from which also to operate.

Meiler FitzHenry, whose grants in Kerry we have described,[1] was now old and, save for an illegitimate son Meiler, childless; finally he retired into Conall abbey, his own foundation, and died there in 1220. King John, whose interest in Munster was always keen, had on July 3rd 1215 granted to Thomas FitzAnthony, Seneschal of Leinster, and his heirs the custody of the counties of Desmond and Waterford and all the King's demesnes in the same and all the escheats at a rent of two hundred and fifty marks per annum. The descent of this grant was to be one of the greatest pieces of Geraldine good fortune, and John, son of Thomas of Shanid, by marrying Margery, daughter of FitzAnthony, when the latter died without sons in 1229, had the claim to it.

Now and following the retirement of Meiler FitzHenry, a great disposal of the Kerry fiefs was made. Offerba went to John de Clahull, west Corcaguiney to Robert, son of Geoffrey de Marisco, Trughanakmy (Aicme Ciarraighe) to John FitzThomas of Shanid, and Altry to his brother Maurice, while Killorglin was kept by Geoffrey de Marisco.[2] Ultimately most of these grantees were destined to vanish and the Geraldines to remain the real lords of Kerry. Altry was later called Clanmaurice, the land of the Baron of Lixnaw, and Corcaguiney with Dingle became the land of Fitzgerald, the Knight of Kerry. Tralee and Killorglin became manors of the earls of Desmond, and between the lakes of Killarney and the Shannon only O'Connor Kerry's country represented the old native independence.

THE ATTACK ON SOUTH-WEST DESMOND, 1215

The young Geraldines, who found plenty of young Cogans,

[1] See formerly, p. 97.

[2] It is not at all clear how the De Marisco grants came to the Fitzgeralds. Geoffrey de Marisco forfeited later (see formerly, p. 122), whereupon Maurice Fitzgerald got Adare, and this was probably when most of the Kerry grants to the Mariscos came to the Fitzgeralds. Robert de Marisco died by 1240, and left only a daughter, Christiana, who died childless.

Carews, and Roches to join in the fun, now seized the opportunity of a native war to build a whole chain of forts, no doubt of simple construction, around the whole Desmond coast from Baltimore to Bantry in Cork and from that around to Killorglin and Castlemaine in Kerry. The *Dublin Annals of Innisfallen* record the event thus: '1215. A great war broke out between Dermot MacCarthy of Dundrinan and his own brother Cormac Finn, the English assisting on both sides. In the course of this war the Foreigners overran all Desmond and gained much territory and power and built castles and strongholds for themselves against the Gaels.'

These 'castles of the Foreigners' are then named. A chain of them ran along the south coast of the present Cork county connecting De Courcy's lordship of Kinsale with Bantry Bay. Another ran from Dún na mBarc near Bantry to Dunkerron, Capanacush, and Ardtully at the head of Kenmare Bay, the latter being the work of Richard de Carew. Another line was formed by the building of a fort at Airloch by Gerald Roche and another at Dunlo near Killarney in FitzHenry's grant. A still stouter chain of castles ran along the river Maine to the river Laune, the sites of which were Currans, Molahiffe, Clonmellane, Castlemaine, Calanafersy, and Killorglin. This northern line was the one that was never to be lost by the English, and was probably the work of John and Maurice the sons of Thomas of Shanid. For centuries it separated Kerry proper from Desmond and marked the final mearing between the earl of Desmond's country and that of MacCarthy More.[1] We shall see later how most of these fortresses were lost to the Irish and how, a MacCarthy feud having enabled the Geraldines to get in, the revolt of Fineen of Rinn Róin drove them out.

Everything made for the later domination of the Munster Geraldines over Desmond, which under the earls of Desmond finally covered counties Limerick, Cork, most of Kerry, and west Waterford as far as Clonmel. For the present the ruling MacCarthys accepted the situation and Dermot 'of Dundrinan' retained peacefully till his death in 1230 a large territory in the south-west, and was buried in the Franciscan house in Cork which he had founded.

From the elder son of Thomas of Shanid, John 'fitz Thomas',

[1] See Orpen, *Normans*, III, ch. vi. Airloch, he says (the site is rather obscure but was to the east of the Lakes) was built by the Roches. Donal Got MacCarthy, who took Carbery from O'Mahony *circa* 1234, was slain there in 1251 by John FitzThomas in spite of Government protection, hence his sons went into rebellion.

Though the *Dublin Annals of Innisfallen* put the building of the castles under a single year 1215, it is obvious that it must have taken many years, and John and Maurice of Shanid would have been very young in that year.

came the earls of Desmond, from the younger, Maurice, came the lords of Kerry and barons of Lixnaw, whose country was called Clanmaurice.[1] John FitzThomas by a Norman wife had a son Maurice, ancestor of the earls of Desmond, and by an Irish wife, Una O'Connor Kerry, a son Maurice, ancestor of the Fitzgeralds, Knights of Kerry and lords of Dingle and Corcaguiney.[2] Another son of John, Gilbert, was ancestor of the White Knight and the FitzGibbons of Kilmallock. From another, John, came the Knights of Glin, and another junior branch were hereditary seneschals of Imokilly. From the first the Geraldines preferred Ireland to England, and sank their roots deep into every part of Leinster and Munster.

CATHAL CROVDERG AND HIS ENEMIES

The two Lacys, a discontented pair, were bent on the conquest of the midlands and the states bordering upon Meath; for one thing they had to make a principality for their half-brother William 'Gorm', son of Rose O'Connor.[3] In 1223 Hugh de Lacy returned and took up arms to recover his land of Ulster; he was vigorously aided by William 'Gorm', who hoped to win Brefni for himself, and the war filled central Ireland with confusion.

This placed Cathal Crovderg in an awkward position. True to his engagements, he wrote to King Henry as 'his most dear lord', saying that Hugh, the King's enemy and Cathal's, has returned, but Cathal remains firm in his fidelity, though he is placed in great difficulties between De Lacy and those who pretend to be faithful, and so begs for armed assistance. In a second letter Cathal repeats that he has never failed in his fidelity, and never will. He possesses a charter of Connacht from King John to himself and his heirs, and he now solicits a similar charter for his son Aedh, which would render his son and his people more zealous for the King's service. As William de Lacy, the King's enemy, holds Ui Briuin, Conmacni, and Caladh, now let Cathal have these for his son Aedh, who is ready to do homage for them.[4]

[1] Orpen, in an article in the *Eng. Hist. Rev.*, vol. XXIX (1914), pp. 302–15, refutes the old belief that the Fitzmaurices derived their claim to Lixnaw, etc. from Raymond le Gros or from a supposed marriage between Maurice and a daughter of Meiler FitzHenry.

[2] Alone in Kerry did O'Connor Kerry retain an Irish country, namely Iraght O'Connor in the north of the county, as marriage allies of the Fitzgeralds.

[3] See papers by E. J. Lloyd on 'Who was Gwenllian de Lacy?' in *Arch. Cambrensis* (July 1919). William 'Gorm' married this daughter of Llewellyn the Great but left no issue by her.

[4] The two letters are reproduced in Gilbert's *Facsimiles of Nat. MSS.*, II, plate lxxi; the letters were written soon after June 1223.

In such loyal style, Cathal O'Connor ended a career which went back to the last days of independent Ireland. The kingdom of Connacht still endured, and he had faithfully observed the treaties of the last fifty years and sought a legalized and honourable tenure under the 'Dominus Hiberniae'. His honourable perseverance in face of hostile De Burgos and De Lacys, and his confidence in the English overlord, point to the possibility that the greater chiefs of Ireland might have been turned into loyal vassals and tenants of the Crown, had that Crown been both strong and wise.

Cathal Crovderg died on May 28th 1224, being then at least seventy years of age, and was buried in his own Franciscan foundation at Athlone, leaving his kingdom to his son Aedh.

On June 19th 1224, William Marshal the younger, now earl of Pembroke, arrived as Justiciar, charged to expel the contumacious Hugh de Lacy and to protect the new O'Connor. To Aedh he granted Ui Briuin, Conmaicni, and Caladh (Brefni and the modern Longford), and marched at once against the Lacys, while Aedh attacked and destroyed De Lacy's garrison at Ardgabhla in Longford. Hugh de Lacy's knights held Trim for six weeks against the Earl Marshal, and then surrendered. William Gorm fled to the wilds of Cavan, and O'Reilly's crannoge fortress on Loch Uachtar, where he had placed his Welsh wife Gwennlian and his Irish mother, Rose O'Connor, was captured by the Marshal's troops. In Ulster, Hugh de Lacy held out for a while but surrendered in May 1225, when both the Lacys were pardoned, and Hugh was finally restored in 1227 to the earldom of Ulster.

THE NORTH STANDS ALOOF

In the remote untouched north-west, Donal More O'Donnell in several triumphant campaigns invaded Brefni, secured the homage of O'Ruairc and O'Reilly, and in 1234 slew Oengus MacGillafinnen, king of Fermanagh 'and subjected all the inhabitants of that country, so that they swore to be obedient in all things to himself and his son after him, as were the men of his own country'.[1]

In 1240 Donal More died, and his son Melaghlin succeeded him. The Cinel Conaill had sworn in 1208 to aid the O'Neills against every foe, English or Irish, and the alliance was once more put to the test. After the death in 1230 of Aedh O'Neill, 'a king who never gave pledge or hostage to Gael or Gall', a period of uncertain

[1] The subjection of the *Garbh-trian* of Connacht in 1220 and of Fermanagh in 1234 is recorded in the D (Latin) version of *Ann. Ult.*

succession set in and a Donal MacLochlainn asserted for some years the claims of his race.[1] But Melaghlin O'Donnel came to the aid of Brian, son of Niall, son of Aedh O'Neill, and a decisive battle was fought at Camergi, in 1240. The MacLochlainn power was for ever shattered and the name almost extinguished by the death in the fight of Donal himself, and ten of his *derb-fine*. Brian O'Neill took the kingship of Tyrone, and the supremacy of his race was never challenged till its overthrow by the English in 1603.

THE GRANT OF CONNACHT, 1227

In Connacht, Aedh O'Connor had succeeded to his father Cathal, with the approval of the Earl Marshal, whom he hads served against the Lacys. A curious traditional account of Aedh's short career is appended to the Gaelic tract, *The Inauguration of Cathal Crovderg*. It says that 'after the English and Irish of Ireland had risen up in 1224 against the sons of Hugh de Lacy and forced peace from them, there was then a great court (*cúirt mhór*) at Dublin and Aedh O'Connor attended it and was betrayed, till William Marshal, his bosom friend, with strong forces entered the court, rescued him and set him at liberty'. After four years (i.e. in 1228), continues the tract, Aedh was slain by one Dundon, an English carpenter, who resented his wife's bathing Aedh in the hall of Geoffrey Morris (de Marisco), the Justiciar, and was hanged for the deed by the Justiciar's orders.[2]

Aedh had wished to be as loyal as his father, but the feudal pull was against him. Richard de Burgo had his heart set upon having Connacht, and he could get at the Crown through his cousin Hubert, the Justiciar of England. The official records show that Aedh was summoned in June 1226 to the King's court at Dublin 'to surrender the land of Connacht which he ought no longer to hold on account of his own and his father's forfeiture, for, by King John's charter granted to Cathal, he only held the land as long as he faithfully served the King'. This was a most callous twisting of the terms of 1215, and a complete breach of faith. Cathal had believed that the grant of Connacht was made to him and his heirs like any barony. Aedh had certainly joined the Earl Marshal against the Lacys and fought others who were also aggressors on his borders, but so far from being a rebel he acted on the Justiciar's orders 'and faithfully

[1] See O'Neill pedigree, Appendix I: Aedh I (d. 1230) had two sons, Niall Ruadh and Aedh Meith. The latter's son Donal was slain in 1234, and finally Niall Ruadh's son Brian secured the kingship.

[2] See *Kilk. Arch. Soc.* (1852–3), and *Ann. L. Cé.*

served the King'. The Marshal was dismissed from office on June 22th 1226, and Aedh had no friends except the Earl, who expressed deep resentment against the Crown over O'Connor's treatment. Whether Aedh attended court at Dublin or not made no difference, it was easy to show that he was now in arms.[1]

In May 1227 the land of Connacht, in all twenty-five cantreds, was adjudged to Richard de Burgo, saving to the Crown five cantreds about Athlone, which were called the King's Cantreds.[2] The whole case shows how hard it was for the chiefs to maintain their position at once against the Crown and against those conquistadors who had the ear of the Crown.

De Marisco was Justiciar again in 1226. He put the resources of the State at the disposal of De Burgo and the feudal crowd and bridled Connacht with another castle at Rinnduin on Lough Ree. In February 1228 Richard de Burgo was himself made Justiciar and, uniting his public and private powers, set himself to the conquest of Connacht.

The dispossessed Aedh having been removed in the strange way related above, another and, it was hoped, a tame O'Connor was found in Felim, a younger son of Cathal Crovderg, whom De Burgo installed as king in 1230. It was convenient to keep a sort of king going, pacified with a large grant out of his former kingdom, in this case the five cantreds. But the grant to De Burgo had left so little to Felim that he naturally chafed at his vassalage and was therefore imprisoned in De Burgo's new castle at Meelick. Even the English government felt the reproach, and in August 1232 Henry wrote to De Burgo that he had been informed of his shameful treatment of Felim, and ordered his release.[3]

THE 'WAR OF KILDARE', 1234

In July 1232 that great statesman, Hubert de Burgh, was finally dismissed from his office of Justiciar by his ungrateful

[1] In 1226 the Justiciar (? Marisco) and Aedh met at Athlone and in an affray of some kind the constable of the town was slain (see Orpen, *Normans*, III, p. 169). This may have been regarded as a reason for forfeiture.

[2] For the grant to De Burgo, see *C.D.I.*, I, p. 212 and No. 1518. The King's cantreds (named in Orpen, *Normans*, p. 137) covered nearly all Roscommon and parts of Galway and Sligo. They were O'Many, Tyrmany, Moy Ai, the Three Tuaths, and Moylurg-Tirerrill as one (in Irish Ui Maine, Tir Maine, Magh Ai, Tri Tuatha, Magh Luirg, Tir Oililla). Moylurg was the country of O'Connor's most powerful vassal, MacDermot. They included the whole Síol Muiredaigh and O'Kelly's country, and were held in reserve to give or withhold, according as O'Connor 'faithfully served the King' or not. For their extent see the excellent general map of Ireland *circa* 1300 at end of Orpen, *Normans*, IV.

[3] Shirley, *Royal Letters*, I, pp. 500–3.

king, for Henry thought he could now rule alone. In Ireland the change meant the triumph of the feudal bands. Though Hubert's nephew, Richard de Burgo, ceased to be Justiciar, his place was taken by another feudal viceroy, Maurice Fitzgerald, baron of Offaly, who ruled from 1232 to 1245.

The baronial opposition to the weak Henry III in England was now curiously reflected in Ireland in the so-called 'War of Kildare'. William, the second Earl Marshal, died in 1231, and his brother Richard succeeded him. The natural leader of Henry's barons, he could not hide his disgust at the King's wretched government. After one bold protest at court against the foreigners who ruled England, Richard withdrew to his Welsh estates, allied himself with Llewellyn, made open war against the King, and finally arrived in Ireland as a proclaimed traitor in February 1234.

The grandson of Strongbow and Eva might well think himself safe in Ireland. But the royal arm was long, and Henry's foreign advisers, Peter des Roches and others, induced the feeble king to direct letters to Maurice Fitzgerald the Justiciar, the Lacys, De Marisco, and Richard de Burgo, bidding them seize the Marshal alive or dead, and promising to divide his lands among them. Geoffrey de Marisco, the particular villain of the piece, came to Richard, and urged him to draw the sword for his rights and remember his right to Ireland as heir of Strongbow. The deluded Earl openly repudiated his allegiance to Henry, and after some success, came to a conference with his secret foes on the Curragh of Kildare, on April 1st 1234. They turned it into an open encounter, in which, having but a handful of knights with him, he was struck down and died of his wounds at Kilkenny on April 16th 1234.

It was an atrocious act of treachery. But it was not an Irish affair; the murderers were all of the Norman race, and the Earl himself had declared his cause to be that 'of justice, the laws of England, and the expulsion of foreign favourites'. Thus it was but an incident of the war of Barons *versus* King over the water. Nevertheless Henry might well fear lest Strongbow's grandson should deprive him of his land of Ireland.

THE CONQUEST OF CONNACHT, 1235

In spite of a personal visit of Felim O'Connor to the English court which was honourably received, the doom of his kingdom was pronounced. The feudal array, namely the whole knight-service of Ireland, some five hundred mounted knights as called out by the Justiciar, and a still more numerous assembly of private adventurers keen for more lands, met to install De Burgo in his grant. The annals of Lough Cé name as the chiefs of the host: 'Maurice, Justice of Erin, Hugh de Lacy, Earl of Ulaidh, Walter Ridlesford, chief baron of Leinster, with whom were the English of Leinster, and John Cogan, with whom were the English of Munster.' In fact many more chiefs were there, such as Theobald Verdun, Henry Butler, Milo de Angulo, Jordan d'Exeter, and there were few of the great feudal names that did not share in this profitable official-feudal enterprise.

An irresistible machine, this host, marching from Athlone to Boyle and to Westport, traversed the plain of Connacht, crushing all opposition, and driving Felim O'Connor to seek refuge with O'Donnell. Finally he bowed to the inevitable, returned and made peace with the Justiciar, and 'the five cantreds of the King were given him free of cattle-rent and tribute'.[1]

The 'Conquest of Connacht' was one of the most triumphant and spectacular bits in all the history of Norman feudalism. Had such a force with such unanimity rolled over Desmond, Thomond, and Ulster as it did over the western province, and followed it up with such a division of the spoils, Ireland would have been normanized from sea to sea. But that was not to happen. Irresistible and terrifying as this invulnerable host of armed men and horse was in 1235, only once or twice again did it take the field in such magnificence, and before long indeed the tide of victory was to turn against the Normans themselves.[2]

THE ENFEOFFMENT OF CONNACHT

A tremendous enfeoffment followed the most successful piece of freebooting since Strongbow, and practically all the 'First Families' shared in the booty of Connacht. De Burgo and De Lacy acted like kings, and in no land-appropriation since the invasion had the Crown of England so little to say.[3] De Burgo took for himself the plain of Connacht, east of the Corrib, and Lough Mask, while retaining the lordship of the whole province. He gave five cantreds in Sligo to Hugh de Lacy, who sub-enfeoffed them to Maurice Fitzgerald. The latter also got from the Ulster earl Carbery and north Leyney, and from Jordan d'Exeter, lord of Affane in Waterford, who shared in the campaign and the booty,

[1] *Ann. L. Cé*, (1237).

[2] The host, however, that fought at Callann in 1261 and again at Athankip in 1270 (see pp. 142, 151) were impressive gatherings, and not till after the Bruce war did the Normans of Ireland lose their military pre-eminence.

[3] For the details see Orpen, *Normans*, III, ch. xxix, pp. 190–251. For the Mayo part see Knox's *History of Mayo*, and 'Anglo-Norman Occupation of Connacht', *R.S.A.I.* (1903).

the southern portion of Leyney. Thus was formed a Geraldine lordship in northern Connacht, with its centre at Sligo, where Maurice erected a castle. Hugh de Lacy also handed over to him his claims as earl of Ulster to Tyrconnell and Fermanagh. Maurice also got the manor of Lochmask in Mayo and the lands of O'Heyne in the later baronies of Dunkellin and Kiltartan in south Galway, while his son Maurice later added the cantred of Corran to the Sligo lordship.

The western portion of Sligo, Tireragh, went to Piers de Bermingham. Mayo was similarly parcelled out, and in the end thickly colonized. Sliabh Lugha, which went to Milo de Angulo, son of Philip, who was lord of Navan, became the barony of Costello, so called after his Irish name.[1] Adam de Staunton, a Leinster tenant, got the cantred of Carra and founded a family there. Gerald Prendergast of Cork secured the later baronies of Clanmorris and Kilmaine, and Jordan d'Exeter got the barony of Gallen. Piers de Bermingham also got the barony of Dunmore in county Galway, while his kinsman Meiler founded a line at Athenry and erected a Dominican friary there. John de Cogan got the lands around Clare-Galway, and Henry Butler, a kinsman of the Ormond family, got the lordship of Umhall, O'Malley's country on Clew Bay.

'THE WELSHMEN OF TIRAWLEY'

North Mayo received a plantation of unique character, which is the theme of an extant Gaelic tract of strange and curious detail.[2]

Robert de Carew of Cork had joined in the great enterprise. Being granted the cantred of Bac and Glen (now Tirawley), he sub-enfeoffed it among his Cork followers. O'Dowda, O'Hara, O'Gara of Gallen, and Sliabh Lugha, chieftains of Tireragh, and other Gaelic owners, were expelled, and a whole body of colonists settled in, the men-at-arms and lieutenants of De Burgo. Their descendants, sprung from the Barrets and their comrades, were known later to the Irish as 'the Welshmen of Tirawley', as being derived from the British followers of Strongbow and the Geraldines. Their names, given by MacFirbis, confirm the tradition, such as Barret, Howel (MacHale), Toimilin, Lynnot, Hosdy, Philbin, Merrick (Meurig, Welsh for Maurice), Walsh (Bhailseach or Breathnach).[3]

[1] See *Cal. Ormond Deeds*, I, No. 2, for 'MacGocelin'.

[2] *Tribes and Customs of Hy Fiachrach called O'Dowda's Country*, by Dubhaltach MacFirbis (ed. O'Donovan), *Irish Arch. Soc.*.

[3] Ibid. MacFirbis has preserved the tradition of the 'Welshmen of Tirawley'. The origin of the Joyces, later the dominant family in the Partry

Along with these Welshmen had come Flemish soldiery from Munster and Leinster, and so now a Fleming got Erris, the extreme north-west corner of Mayo. Other adventurers poured in—Butlers, Petits, Cusacks, Brownes (le Brun), and within a hundred years north Connacht contained at once an Irish, a Welsh, a Flemish, and a Norman population.

The De Burgos and a few of their followers established towns; thus arose Galway, Athenry, Dunmore, and Ballinrobe. Burrishoole on Clew Bay records a Norman attempt at a borough, so does Burriscarra.[1] But nothing like the urban and Anglo-Saxon organization of Leinster took place. A feudal land, a land of abundant castles, De Burgo's lordship of Connacht from the first had almost no plebeian English, nor, save for Galway and Athenry, any lasting towns. It was a colony to whom the Saxon tongue and traditions were little known; a colony too thin and aristocratic to make the land its own; hence it was the first of the conquests to turn Irish again. In medieval Connacht, and up to the seventeenth century, only in Galway was English the common speech, and the Norman lords before a century had begun to exchange French for Irish.

In this 'War of Connacht', the Norman triumph was assured by the superior military and diplomatic skill of the victors. They played on the divisions of the native kings and set *rigdomna* against *rigdomna*, enlisted native soldiery, and rapidly encastled the land. The O'Connors could make no stand, and after Cathal Crovderg his successors finally became simply chiefs of the old Síol Muiredaigh demesne.

Most of the conquerors at once entered on their new lordships. In 1234 De Burgo built a castle in Galway. In 1237, say the *Annals of Loch Cé*, 'the barons of Ireland came into Connacht and began to build castles'. The Norman control of the west seemed likely to complete the conquest of Meath, Munster, and Leinster, and leave Ulster only a breathing-space before it too succumbed. For example, Maurice Fitzgerald's lands now stretched to Lough Melvin, his claims to the Erne and the Foyle, while his lands in Galway pressed hard on what little of Thomond was left to the O'Briens.

It must be remembered, however, that the effective occupation only embraced the maritime counties, Sligo, Mayo, Galway; that

district, between Loughs Corrib and Mask, is, like their name, obscure. From one of the Barrets, Valentine or Baitin, came their irishized surname MacBhaitin or MacWattin.

[1] 'Borris' is a form of the Irish *buirgéis*, itself derived from 'burgage' or borough. In Mayo only Dunmore after 1338 survived as a small town. Henry Butler founded Burrishoole, Adam de Staunton, Burriscarra.

Roscommon in the main was left to the O'Connors and that Leitrim and Cavan, which formed old Brefni, the 'Rough Third of Connacht', remained almost untouched. The Irish still held two of the five modern counties of Connacht, though not the richest or largest.

One of the Norman-Irish adventurers, who had he lived would have got a fief in the new conquest, had already disappeared. This was William 'Gorm' de Lacy, one of the first of the mixed blood and language type which was soon to be common among our conquerors. The *Annals of Ulster* record in 1233 the death of 'William de Lacy and Charles (Serlus), son of Cathal O'Connor, slain along with many foreigners by the race of O'Reilly in Monaigh-Cranncain', no doubt in attempting to found a lordship in Brefni. His Welsh wife Gwenllian survived him and returned to Wales, but they left no issue.

THE TREATMENT OF THE O'CONNORS

Few of the Norman lords were destined to enjoy their triumphs, or use up their full energies in Ireland. The early death of the great Richard de Burgo while with the King in the Poitou campaign of the winter 1242–3 gave Felim O'Connor his chance to appeal to Henry again. He was given safe conduct in December 1243, and came to Windsor. Henry professed indignation at O'Connor's wrongs and ordered the Justiciar to reinstate him in his kingdom, but the Anglo-Irish interest was strong enough to thwart the royal command.

In need of money and men, at war with France, Scotland, and Wales, the English Crown did not disdain the help of the Irish kings, technically its vassals, and in July 1224 Henry requested 'Dovenald, king of Tircunill', 'Felim (O'Connor) son of the late king', Brian O'Neill, 'king of Kinelun', O'Brien, and other Irish chiefs, twenty-one in all, to join him in person against the king of Scots.[1]

Early next year Henry again sought Irish aid, this time against Llewellyn of Wales, and Felim, joining Maurice Fitzgerald, sailed with three thousand infantry to Henry in his camp at Conway in October 1245.

In the letter of safe-conduct for Felim, Henry spoke of his own '*proximus adventus in Hibernia*'. The royal visit was never paid, and thus was another favourable opportunity lost for the nominal lord of Ireland to come over and set right in person what he claimed to be his realm.

[1] *C.D.I.*, I, No. 1716.

The faithful Felim's only reward was, as 'son of the king of Connacht', to be left in possession of the five cantreds of 'Shilmorthy'. In 1257 the Justiciar, Alan de la Zouche, at Athlone granted him the five cantreds by royal charter; in 1262 these were reduced to four. Until his death in 1265, however, this O'Connor kept up more or less steadily the tradition begun by his grandfather Cathal Crovderg of a 'loyal king of Connacht'.

THE O'BRIEN KINGDOM

Donnchad O'Brien died in 1242, still king of Thomond. But his kingdom was now little more than the modern Clare, and Ennis, not Limerick, was his capital. Donnchad, however, called himself to the end 'Rex Tuadmonie', and grants made by his under-chiefs are confirmed by him in the old royal style. After him, however, the O'Brien monarchy descended into the same pit as the O'Connor, menaced by the greed of colonists and officials.

In 1250 the Crown granted to Conor Rua, Donnchad O'Brien's son, 'the land which his father held by charter from King John, to hold during good service' for a fine of two thousand two hundred marks. But already in 1248 Henry had granted the cantred of Tradry, between Limerick and the Fergus, at yearly rent of thirty pounds to one Robert de Muscegros, a pure newcomer. In 1253 the 'cantred of the Isles of Thomond' was granted to John FitzGeoffrey, the Justiciar, though the claim ended with his son Richard in 1297, who left no male heir. Thus the lesson was taught afresh that even the greatest of the Gaels could look for little more than a mere life-tenure of a portion of their kingdom bought at a high price, without security for their sons, and liable to be nullified by concomitant grants to English adventurers.

THE EXTINCTION OF GREAT FAMILIES, *circa* 1240

By an amazing coincidence and series of chances, a number of the greatest of the 'First Families' now came to an end, or ended in heiresses who, marrying English husbands, transferred the lordship of vast areas of Irish land to absentees. 'Tribe-extinction' was the Gaelic description of such events, for the native mind recognized no succession in females or claims through them. When we add the number of grantees who after a taste of Ireland preferred to go back to the country whence they came, we get an amazing number of lapsed claims and unused charters. All the more did the seed that fell on good ground flourish. The 'Race of Nesta', at least in the Geraldines, Barrys, Cantitunes, Carews, from the first took root vigorously, so did De Burgo. The Butler stock, though threatened with infertility for over a century, at last became fecund and Irish. So those who remained and survived and identified themselves with Ireland took up, bought, or acquired in various ways lapsed claims and derelict lordships, and the fewer they were the greater they became.

Among the lesser names of the First Conquest, De Worcester ceased to be about 1275 and the Butlers took his place in Ormond. A son of the first Walter de Ridlesford, also called Walter, who had his father's rich lordships in Kildare, Carlow, and north Wicklow, served in the Connacht campaign of 1235 and died in 1240. He left only an heiress who married Robert son of Geoffrey de Marisco, but again an heiress was left with whom it all ended. Neither Fitzstephen, Hereford, De Valogne, FitzHenry, De Marisco, nor De Braose left an enduring name behind him. The attempts to make a Scottish plantation on the Ulster coast, begun by De Courcy, also failed. The 'MacUchtred' race of Galloway, who had united the great earldoms, Atholl and Carrick, were before long extinct in the male line and their Irish grants perished with them.[1]

But the most remarkable extinction of all was in the Marshals, grandsons and heirs of Strongbow and Eva, and in the Lacys in their double line of Meath and Ulster.

THE END OF THE LACYS

Walter de Lacy, earl of Meath, died in 1241, and his brother Hugh, earl of Ulster, in 1243. Both had lived to a great age, and Walter had seen both a son and a grandson, but survived them both. Hugh's earldom escheated directly to the Crown and remained in its hands till 1254, while Walter's earldom descended to his two granddaughters, Margaret and Matilda. Meath was divided between them, and Margaret carried the western half, called the lordship of Lochsewdy, to her husband John de Verdun,

[1] See Chapter V, p. 94 for the 'MacUchtred' family; also Cokayne's *Complete Peerage* under Galloway, Atholl, and Carrick. They died out by 1256 when Neil, son of Duncan, earl of Carrick, died leaving only an heiress. She married Robert Bruce, hence the title eventually passed to the Edward Bruce who invaded Ireland in 1315. Alan FitzRoland died in 1233 leaving only heiresses, and Patrick, son of Thomas of Galloway, earl of Atholl, who was murdered in 1242 at Haddington, left no male heirs. This event led to an important Scots family being planted in Ulster. Walter Byset, the murderer, and his nephew John, flying to Antrim, were granted Rathlin Isle and lands about Glenarm by Hugh de Lacy the Earl, and became in effect lords of the Glens of Antrim in place of the MacUchtred grantees.

and Matilda eventually conveyed the eastern half, the lordship of Trim, to her French husband Geoffrey de Genville.[1]

THE END OF THE MARSHALS

The fourth and last of William the second Marshal's brothers, Earl Anselm, died in December 1245. None of them had left male heirs, and their five sisters inherited portions of Leinster or conveyed them to their husbands and heirs. Thus ended the grandsons of Strongbow and Eva MacMurrough; it was almost the extinction of a dynasty, for the great land of Leinster had been since 1172 in a single hand and had a vigorous unity in a house which commanded the allegiance of both Irish and English.

Leinster was now partitioned into five liberties. The eldest of the five heiresses, Maud, wife of Hugh Bigod, earl of Norfolk, conveyed to him the lordship of Carlow. Joan left her share, the liberty of Wexford, to William de Valence, husband of her daughter Joan, who became earl of Pembroke in 1264. Isabel, the third sister, had married Gilbert de Clare, earl of Gloucester, and their son Earl Richard now inherited the lordship of Kilkenny. Sybil, the fourth sister, had married William de Ferrers, earl of Derby, and their seven daughters now inherited her portion, Kildare. Of these seven we need only mention Agnes, wife of William de Vescy, who in 1270 got the manor and most of the lordship of Kildare. Eva, the last sister, had married William son of Reginald de Braose; of their three daughters and heiresses, Maud married Roger Mortimer of Wigmore, who thus became lord of Leix.

Each of these portions of the land of Leinster retained the former feudal liberties and each had its *caput* or central manor, where the Lord's chief court was held, presided over by his seneschal. Thus Carlow was Bigod's chief manor-town, and Dunamase that of Mortimer.

The feudal law of property and descent was one which none but the strongest of kings dare touch. But at least a John or an Edward I would have seized this remarkable occasion to reduce the regalities of these vast fiefs which covered nearly half of Ireland. But Henry III was not such a king and most of these great liberties were transmitted entire.

[1] See Orpen, *Normans*, III, pp. 286–7 and ch. xxvi, for 'The Division of Meath and Leinster'; also the *Gormanston Register* (ed. Mills and MacEnery) for De Genville and other Meath deeds. Geoffrey de Genville was second husband of Matilda de Lacy; her first, Peter de Geneva, died in 1249. Geoffrey was granted the liberty by Henry III in 1254.

CHAPTER VIII

THE FIRST IRISH RESURGENCE, 1245–1272

THE ground was already cleared for the rise of lesser men, now that the earls of Meath, Ulster, and Pembroke had passed out. Geraldines, Butlers and De Burgos were henceforth to become the chiefs of the Englishry, and in the weakness of the central government the 'great design' of completing the conquest of Ireland was taken in hand by the feudal princes. The chief of these was Maurice Fitzgerald, second Baron of Offaly, who for the moment had no De Burgo rival because Richard, son of the Richard who died in 1243, also died after a few years in 1248, and his brother Walter did not obtain seisin till 1250.

THE ATTACK ON TYRCONNELL

In 1245 Maurice ceased to be Justiciar and John FitzGeoffrey (son of the earl of Essex) took his place till 1256. Maurice in office had utilized the State revenues, the feudal levies, and the royal castles for a war upon the unconquered Irish. He induced FitzGeoffrey to continue the same policy, and a forward movement was planned, to serve at once the interests of the State and the ambitions of the Geraldines. His hereditary possessions in Leinster and Munster and his personal acquisitions in three counties of Connacht made Maurice already a potentate on a grand scale. If he could add western Ulster no baron in Ireland would equal him.

With the true eye of a strategist Maurice saw that as long as Brefni, Fermanagh, and Tyrconnell remained unconquered, the conquest of Munster and Connacht was incomplete. A double campaign was therefore planned by which Ulster was to be assailed from the Erne and the southern frontier. Already castles at Coleraine, Donaghmoyne, and Clones menaced the Cinel Eoghain; at Sligo and Caeluisce (here he built a fortress in 1252) others supported Fitzgerald's movement. In January 1247 he crossed the Erne at Ballyshannon and slew Melaghlin O'Donnell who resisted him. He then set up a 'tame' O'Cannanain, but Goffraidh, son of Donal More, slew the latter in 1248, and Maurice's first move failed.

The demands from the English overlord upon his Irish barons again and again distracted them from the conquest of Ireland.

Henry made constant appeals for men and money from the prelates and barons of Irleand. In 1253 the king of Castile threatened an invasion of Gascony, and in summoning Fitz-Geoffrey to France in May 1254, Henry 'regrets to have heard that the Irish are elated at the coming over of the Justiciar and Maurice Fitzgerald and other magnates of Ireland'.[1] But Maurice had not abandoned his claim upon the O'Donnell country, and even at his death in 1251 he bequeathed to his heirs 'the seven theods' (*tuatha*) of Tyrconnell.

THE COMPLAINTS OF THE IRISH CHURCH

The Irish Church, though timid and bent on its own wrongs, continued its constitutional protests. Early in 1255 MacFloinn, archbishop of Tuam, and the bishop of Killala, on the part of all the clergy of Ireland, laid before Henry in person certain grievances, such as 'that they and their tenants are dragged, contrary to the ancient liberties of their church, into pleas before justices in other provinces; some of the King's justices and sheriffs take bribes from one party in plaints, to the harm of clergy and laity; the clergy are vexed by frequent attachments; Irish barons prevent Irishmen faithful to the king from bequeathing their chattels', and other complaints against the attacks of the English upon Church law. Pope Alexander IV was appealed to, and while in 1250 he had condemned the custom by which English clerics were excluded from Irish churches, he now exhorted the King to do right to the Irish.

The King's answer and directions to the Justiciar and Council of Ireland to redress these wrongs fell flat like so much over-channel redress.[2]

PRINCE EDWARD, 'LORD OF IRELAND'

In 1254 Henry III granted to his son Edward, then aged fifteen, on the occasion of his marriage, the Lordship of Ireland. The grant was made to 'Lord Edward and his heirs being kings of England, so however that the land of Ireland shall never be separated from the Crown of England'.[3] The wording forbade

[1] Betham, p. 252 (Feb. 2nd, 38 Hen. III): writs are sent to the magnates and prelates, knights and freeholders of every shire, asking them for aid in the Gascon war, and a fortnight later to the freemen, citizens, and burgesses, asking them to assist the Justiciar. In July 1253 Henry received nearly four thousand pounds of Irish money.

[2] *C.D.I.*, II, pp. 54–7, 55, 74–5. The King's answer to the bishops is dated from Nottingham, July 30th 1255. For the Pope see *Cal. Papal Registers* (1198–1304), pp. 73–5, 283.

[3] *C.D.I.*, II, p. 145; and Gilbert, *Hist. and Mun. Docs.*, p. 135.

that any younger son of Edward should ever found a separate line here. It was probably Henry's intention that his heir should come in person to rule his Irish lordship. But the youth of the prince, and the baronial revolts at home, kept this one hope of royalty at his father's side, and neither as prince nor as King did Edward set foot here.

THE REVOLT OF THE MACCARTHYS

As the attack was made province by province, so resistance was made province by province. In the south-west the Geraldines were acquiring all Desmond. By 1232 Kerry was an Anglo-Irish county, numerous castles hemmed in the Irish, and John Fitz-Thomas of 'Shanid' became almost sole lord there. Desmond had been in the King's hand since the death of FitzAnthony, John's father-in-law, but finally in November 1259 FitzThomas received from Prince Edward a grant in fee of all Decies and Desmond. It is remarkable that the De Courcy and Carew claims to the titular 'kingdom of Cork' were silently ignored in his favour.

Up to the death of Dermot of Dundrinan the kings of Desmond had been on good terms with the English government. But to be subjected to an hereditary English 'lord of Desmond' was a *diminutio capitis* comparable to the subjection of O'Connor to the De Burgo 'Dominus Connacie'. However much the senior branch might accept it, a junior branch of the MacCarthys revolted against it.

THE BATTLE OF CALLANN, 1261

An intermittent succession-war between heads of the old royal race was mixed up with the war of Gael and Gall. Dermot of Dundrinan, on his death in 1230 (or 1229), was succeeded by his next brother, Cormac Finn, who *circa* 1215 had led a revolt against him, and he ruled till 1248.[1] Then a third brother, Donal Got 'the Stammerer' (also called 'Gall'), ruled till 1251 and was then slain in Airloch Castle by John FitzThomas, in spite of royal letters of protection given that year. This MacCarthy, following the expansion policy of his race which had begun when Donal More O'Brien first expelled them from the plain of Cashel, *circa* 1234, wrested Carbery in south-west Cork from O'Mahony. His sons, Finghin (Fineen) called 'of Rinn Róin', Cormac, and Donal Oge (or Maol), were before long in rebellion, partly to assert the

[1] See formerly, Chapter VII, p. 126, and Appendix I (B), Pedigree of the MacCarthys.

kingship claim derived from their father against the succession of the older stock represented by Donal Ruadh, son of Cormac Finn, and partly as native champions against the new Geraldine title. Fineen of Rinn Róin, taking the field, levelled six of the castles which the English had built around the coast from 1216 to 1230.

FitzThomas therefore called upon the Justiciar for aid and the latter, William de Dene, led the feudal army into Desmond and was joined by FitzThomas and the levy of the English of Munster. The two armies met at Callann near Kenmare on July 24th 1261, and the native race displayed against their conquerors the most determined spirit they had shown since Strongbow. Norman armour, horse, generalship, and courage were in vain. The colonial army was finally overthrown, and John FitzThomas himself and Maurice his son were slain, together with eight barons, twenty-five knights, and many more of the Englishry. Only an infant, Thomas, son of the slain Maurice, remained of the house of Shanid.[1]

Milo de Courcy, however, before the autumn was out defeated and slew the hero Finghin at Rinn Róin near Kinsale, and in the next year, 1262, the Justiciar, Richard de la Rochelle, and Walter de Burgo engaged Cormac brother of Finghin on the slopes of Mangerton. Cormac fell, but heavy losses on each side and a drawn battle attested the new spirit in the native race.

These MacCarthys had won one of the most spectacular of Irish victories, a great local triumph for them, even if they could not altogether break the English yoke in Desmond. The Norman castles built round the coast from Glandore to Killarney fell into their hands or those of their vassal chiefs.[2] The lordship of Desmond, though not withdrawn, lapsed until Edward I regranted it in 1292 to Thomas FitzMaurice 'an Ápa'. In the thirty years' interval, with no Geraldine to stay them, the MacCarthys permanently established themselves as overlords or owners in the country that stretches from Bandon round to Killarney and the Laune.

From Cormac Finn came the senior line of MacCarthy More, who finally held the whole angle from Blarney to Mallow and along the Blackwater to Castlemaine and round again to Bantry. From Donal Got's race came MacCarthy Reagh ('Riabhach') of Carbery, who held from Bantry Bay to Innishannon. The first of them ruled a kingdom of over two thousand square miles, the

[1] Thomas was later called 'an Ápa' ('of the Ape'), because a monkey is said to have saved him as an infant from fire in the castle of Tralee.

[2] Killorglin however was never taken, nor anything north of the Laune, Tralee, or Dingle.

second ruled one of six hundred, and there were in time other septs of the name.[1]

Cormac Finn's son, Donal Rua, who reigned as late as 1302 and is ancestor of MacCarthy More, maintained the compromising attitude of his ancestors ever since Dermot of the Conquest time, and was officially accepted as 'king of the Irish of Desmond'. His descendants admitted themselves vassals of the earls of Desmond, the inheritors of FitzThomas, and paid a head rent, but bore no resentment towards the great Geraldines. The race of Donal Got, however, lords of Carbery, maintained the rebel tradition begun by Finghin of Rinn Róin, and up to the end of the sixteenth century their wars with the Desmonds were said to be like 'the wars of the Guelphs and the Ghibellines'.

The important result of Callann was the check it gave to what seemed the inevitable triumph of Norman-English speech, culture, and law in the south-west corner, the conquest of which would have extinguished native Desmond. For centuries not a single English settler dare now set foot in the country of the MacCarthys and O'Sullivans, which reverted completely to Irish speech, tradition, and law.

THE O'BRIENS

Meanwhile the royal race of Thomond still preferred diplomacy and petitioning. Conor Rua ('na Siudaine') O'Brien, hard pressed by Norman grants, sent his clerk, Matthew, to Henry with generous offers of money and rent to have the land of Thomond, but the King higgled and said he must first see Donnchad Carbrech's patent of 1199. Hence it was that Conor's gallant son, Taig of Caeluisce, became a rebel.[2] Nevertheless Conor kept his petty kingdom more or less intact till his death in 1268.

THE TRIUMPHS OF TYRCONNELL, 1258–1281

The death of the great Maurice Fitzgerald of Offaly in the spring of 1257 emboldened the Cinel Conaill to appear in arms against his claim to their country. Godfrey O'Donnell took the field, levelled Caeluisce, defeated the English at Credran in Carbury, burned Sligo, and returned in triumph. But he had been badly wounded at Credran, and before he could recover, Brian O'Neill in 1258 appeared demanding from Tyrconnell the

[1] See W. F. Butler, 'Lordship of MacCarthy More', and 'Pedigree and Succession of MacCarthy More', *R.S.A.I.* (1906–7, and June 1921). 'Riabhach' (Reagh) means 'Swarthy' and the name 'Cairbreach' came from Donal Got's conquest of O'Mahony's country of Carbery in south-west Cork.

[2] For Conor Rua's offer see *C.D.I.*, II, No. 273.

ancient homage due to Cinel Eoghain. But the wounded hero, borne on a litter, routed him on the Swilly near Letterkenny, only to die of his wounds after the battle.[1]

The fortunes of Cinel Conaill, menaced by both Gael and Gall, were now dramatically restored. Donal Oge, younger brother of Godfrey, had been reared in western Scotland and married a lady of the Clann Suibhne. He now, in 1258, appeared in Tyrconell with a body of gallowglasses under command of his father-in-law, Eoin MacSuibhne. Greeted with delight by his people, the young heir boldly refused homage to O'Neill and thus broke the alliance which his race had sworn with Cinel Eoghain sixty years before. Instead, rejecting the suzerainty of both Norman and Gael, he began a career of triumph which by his death in 1281 made him 'lord of Brefni, Fermanagh, and a large part of Connacht'. This claim over these territories was never abandoned by his race till 1603.[2]

BRIAN O'NEILL AND THE BATTLE OF DOWN, 1260

The king of Tyrone and his under-kings such as O'Cahan, and the chiefs of Ulidia such as O'Flynn of Ui Tuirtre, were now subject to Lord Edward's seneschal in Ulster, and had to meet many demands for aids, rents, and fines for trespasses. It was humiliating for these warlike northerners, who of old had been 'free, non-tributary clans', and on the other hand had not been given the secure status of tenants-in-chief.[3]

The extinction of the earldom of Ulster offered a favourable moment for revolt, and Brian set to work to bring together a great

[1] Orpen (*Normans*, III, p. 273) refutes the story that Godfrey slew Maurice Fitzgerald in battle, as stated in *A.F.M.* He left his Connacht lands to his son Maurice.

[2] Rev. Paul Walsh, in his edition of the sixteenth-century Gaelic text, *Leabhar Chlainne Suibhne* ('Book of the MacSweenys'), p. xvii, gives the following pedigree: Donal Oge O'Donnell married (1) Catriona MacSuibhne, (2) a daughter of MacDomhnaill, and had sons (1) Aedh, (2) Turloch. This supplements Dr. Orpen's full 'Pedigree of Maic Somhairle' in his vol. III, p. 252. Orpen omits the MacSweeny marriage. Taig O'Connor in 1259 also married a MacSomhairle lady and received with her a band of 120 gallowglasses.

[3] *Ulster Arch. Soc. Journal* (1885), p. 155, and *Facs. Nat. MSS.*, part II, plate 73. How O'Neill and the others had fallen into vassalage to Prince Edward is not clear, probably it all began with Hugh (II) de Lacy. Brian owed 1,000 cows for trespass, and 3,092 for a fine made with the Justiciar (probably to have Cinel Eoghain), and 400 for arrears of rent of 'Keneleun'. These cows reckoned in money came to £748 2*s.* 3*d.* The O'Flynns of Ui Tuirtre (Antrim), Magennis, MacCartan, O'Kerny, and three others, owed in fines 1551 cows. The chiefs named are 'Mackanegus, Mac Kartan, O'Dungan, O'Mungan, O'Kerney, Macyanan, Macgillochan, and Tatheg MacDunleve'.

Irish confederacy. In 1258 Aedh O'Conor, son of king Felim, and Taig, son of Conor O'Brien, king of Thomond, came to O'Neill at Caeluisce on the Erne and acknowledged Brian's right to the kingdom of Ireland, and so pledged themselves to restore the old High kingship.

The Irish confederacy had soon to put itself to the test. Early in May 1260 O'Neill, along with Aedh O'Connor and his Connacht men and a number of Ulster chiefs, of whom the O'Cahans played the noblest part, marched on Downpatrick, the capital of the earldom. O'Donnell did not join them and Taig O'Brien had died the year before. The Irish host was formidable in numbers and in courage, but wearing no armour, after the native fashion, was ill fitted to meet the mailed horse and men and the archers of the Englishry.

A force drawn from the colonists of Ulster was hastily assembled under the prior of St. Thomas at Downpatrick, a knight, Roger d'Auters, and Roger le Tayllur, mayor of the city. They met the Irish kings at Drumderg outside Downpatrick, and a desperate fight was waged which ended at last in the victory of the Englishry, on May 14th 1260.

The ever growing determination of the native race was, however, displayed in the heavy losses among their leaders. Brian himself (ever afterwards called 'Brian of the Battle of Down') fell with many Ulster chiefs, and the O'Cahans paid for the post of honour by the death of their chief Maghnus and fifteen of their leading men. Aedh O'Connor survived the day, but eight chiefs of Connacht fell.[1]

Thus ended the first attempt since the Conquest to restore the Árd Rí-ship. Aedh Buidhe ('the Yellow-haired'), son of Donal, slain in 1234, took Brian's place as chief of the O'Neills and approved himself in English eyes as a 'loyal' man.

THE GALLOWGLASSES

O'Donnell came well out of a campaign which was disastrous for O'Neill. Maurice (II) Fitzgerald had left to his son Maurice his claim to 'the seven theods (*tuatha*) of Tyrconnell', but it was

[1] See *Ann. Ult.* for the losses on the Irish side. *Pipe Roll* (45 Hen. III) records the raising of the colonial forces of Louth and Down. The epic of the battle is commemorated in two bardic poems of the time, viz. one by Gillabride MacCommidhe, Brian's bard, upon his dead master, and another by Ferghal Mac an Bhaird on the O'Cahans (ed. O'Donovan in *Miscellany of the Celtic Society*).

C.D.I., II (1260), No. 661: 'The King to his son Edward, has heard how the commons of the city and county of Down have defeated Brian O'Neill who presumptuously styled himself "king of the kings of Ireland".'

an empty bequest. Before a century was out not only had the O'Donnells secured Tyrconnell but the Geraldine grants of Fermanagh and Sligo themselves passed under their lordship.[1]

Both in the north-west and the south-west angle, the Irish had now achieved a lasting victory. The battle of Callann ensured the lordship of MacCarthy More for centuries; the triumphs of Donal Oge O'Donnell led to a Tyrconnell domination in the three north-west counties. While all the rest of the native princes temporized, it was not till 1541 that Manus O'Donnell, first of the Cinel Conaill kings to do so, submitted to the king of England.

The subjection of these outlying countries was necessary to the Fitzgerald plan of a complete conquest; the failure to achieve it was the beginning of a general failure. The Irish revival became possible because of a military revival. In spite of their bravery and tenacity, an Irish army for centuries had been one of amateurs, wielding light weapons and wearing neither helmets nor mail coats. Now the stiffening of their ranks by an imported professional soldiery finally annulled the war-superiority which the Normans had held almost unquestioned since Strongbow.

The many isles and indented mountain-coasts of Argyle and the Hebrides were the home of a mixed race to which on its first appearance the Irish gave the name 'Gall-Gaedhil' ('Norse Gaels'). Speaking a dialect of Irish mixed with many Scandinavian words for ships, armour, the sea, islands, and geographic features, they added to the natural bravery of the Gael the fighting blood, the love of the open sea, the wanderlust, and the weapons of the Norseman. Men of great bulk and stature, they fought in helmets and heavy mail, with deadly axes nearly as long as themselves, and in the infantry formation of the vikings.[2]

In close touch with Norway, whose blood they shared, and nominal subjects of the Norwegian kings who were overlords of these isles, they often served him or the earls of Orkney and Shetland on sea or land, and acquired a discipline and love of war which they turned to good effect later.

The activities of De Courcy, the ambitions of the 'MacUchtred, earls', the constant state of war and unrest in the Irish-Scottish archipelago, which made fighting men and seamen necessary, gave these born fighters constant employment. There was no one on all these lonely waters and bays to prevent them from beaching their galleys anywhere along the northern or western coast and

[1] Maurice II's granddaughter, Amabilia (heir of Maurice III) finally gave her Sligo, Tyrconnell, and Fermanagh claims to her cousin John FitzThomas of Offaly, 1st Earl of Kildare.

[2] For their favourite and dreadful weapon, see a paper by G. Hayes-McCoy, 'The Gallowglass Axe', *Galway Arch. Soc.* (1937).

offering their services for pay or land to the Gaelic chiefs. They would have offered themselves just as readily to the English in Ireland, but the latter, still masters of the land as they believed, saw no need for them. The Irish chiefs, especially those of Ulster, seized the great opportunity. Known to the Irish as 'Gall-óglaich' ('foreign' or 'Norse warriors'), by the next century the gallowglasses became an essential element in native warfare, the janissaries of Gaelic Ireland, who up to the battle of Kinsale in 1602 remained the one part of an Irish army which could be trusted to stand its ground to the end.[1]

These gaelicized vikings had long since begun to haunt the Irish coasts. They were 'summer-farers' like their Norse forefathers, and after planting their crops in the Isles, went off between spring and harvest a-raiding and a-fighting.[2] The first of the gallowglass families to arrive were derived from two unconnected ancestors, Suibhne of Castlesween in Cantire and Somerled, lord of Argyll. The intercrossing began early in the thirteenth century. A daughter of Turloch O'Connor, Benmidhe, married Maelmuire MacSuibhne and had two sons, Suibhne and Murchad. The latter, in raiding the western coast, was finally in 1267 captured by Donal O'Connor, son of Manus, and handed over to Walter, earl of Ulster, who had him put to death. It was his nephew, Eoin son of Suibhne, who accompanied Donal Oge O'Donnell, his son-in-law, to Tyrconnell in 1258

THE CLANN SUIBHNE

Eoin's reward was in Irish land. Donal Oge granted him the peninsula of Fanad, of which the reigning Ó Breslin was ruthlessly

[1] See *Leabhar Chlainne Suibhne*, op. cit., for the MacSweeny clan, and Eoin MacNeill, 'Chapters of Hebridean History', *The Scottish Review* (1916), pp. 254–76. Eoin MacSuibhne was first of his race to settle in Tyrconnell, by invitation of Donal Oge O'Donnell his son-in-law, where he drove out the O'Breslins in 1261, and became chief of Fanad, from whence in time the MacSweeneys branched into the three stocks of MacSuibhne Fanad, Bannagh, and Doe. The Lord Deputy St. Leger says thus in a dispatch to Henry VIII in 1543 (*State Papers*, III, 444): 'They, the Irish, have but one sort of footemen which be harnessed in mayle and bassinettes, having every man of them his weapon called a sparre moche like the axe of the Towre, and they be named gallowglasse, and for the most part their boys have for them three dartes apiece, which dartes they throwe or [ere] they come to the handstripe. These sort of men be those that do not lightly abandon the field, but byde the brunt to the death.'

A recent book (1937) by G. Hayes-McCoy, entitled *Scottish Mercenary Forces in 16th-century Ireland*, contains some good pages on the gallowglasses of the thirteenth and fourteenth centuries.

[2] The famous chieftain's name, Somhairle (Irish), Sorley (Anglo-Irish), Somerled, comes from 'Sumarlidi', in Norse 'the summer farer'. MacNeill, *Phases*, op. cit., p. 329, traces the earliest appearance of 'Mac Somhairlidh' and the gallowglasses.

dispossessed. Before long a second territory, 'na Trí Tuatha', of which Ó Baoighill was former chief, was conveyed to Eoin's race, who were called MacSuibhne na dTuath (in English 'of Doe'). Later again another scion of Clann Suibhne got Ó Baoighill's country of Banagh from an O'Donnell and founded a third branch in south-west Tyrconnell. In time the MacSweeney gallowglasses were found in the service of Connacht and other southern chiefs.[1]

THE CLANN DONNELL

Somerled of Argyll was the hero-founder of the Clann Somhairle and the romantic names of Clandonnell, Clanranald, and the Lords of the Isles. Of his two sons, Dugall and Ragnall, the latter was ancestor of the MacDonnells who got their patronymic from Domnall son of Ragnall. From Domnall's brother Ruairi came the MacRory name, and from later branches came the MacAlisters and MacSheehys. Domnall again was father of Angus More who died in 1294; he may be regarded as the first 'Lord of the Isles'.

The MacDonnells established themselves as O'Neill's captains or constables of gallowglasses, but naturally not until the earldom of Ulster was overthrown.[2] These were the Tyrone Clandonnells. But in Oriel hereditary gallowglass families who were not of Clann Donnell entered into permanent service with MacMahon and other local chiefs. These were the MacCabes, related to MacLeod of Arran, and even some of the latter name, at the present day disguised locally as McGlade.

The gallowglass forces were naturally at first not large. A chief

[1] See *Leabhar Chlainne Suibhne*, op. cit., for MacSweeney history. *Ann. Ult.* (1251): Gillacrist Ua Breslin, chief of Fanad, and his kinsmen slain by Cellach Ua Baoighill. Ibid. (1281): Maelruana Ua Baoighill, chief of the Three Territories (toisech na dTrí Tuath) was slain. Doe Castle was the key of this lordship. The modern name 'Doe' is derived from 'na dTuath' and has only a fanciful connexion with 'na dTuagh', of the Battle-axes.

[2] See Pedigree of Clann Somhairle in Orpen: *Normans*, III, p. 252, and another in Hayes-McCoy, *Scottish Mercenaries in Ireland* (appendix). As regards the Tyrone gallowglass branch of Clanndonnell, *Ann. Ult.* (1365) give the death of Somhairle, son of Eoin Dubh MacDomhnaill, 'constable of the Province of Ulster'. Ibid. (1368): Alexander Oge MacDonnell, lord of the Galloglasses, died. There seems some doubt as to the year in which Angus More died and it may be 1300 (so Hayes-McCoy).

In the published maps of the Escheated Counties of Ulster (1609), copied at the Ordnance Survey Office, Southampton, a district called 'Clankarnie', between the Cusker and Callan rivers (now the in barony of Upper and part of Lower Fews) is marked: 'this contrie the O'Neales have used to give unto the captains of their galloglass for their entertainment and bonaght [maintenance]'. South of this, in the Lower Fews, is marked 'Ever Buye McDonnell the galloglasse his countre'.

MacSuibhne or MacDonnell would be O'Donnell or O'Neill's 'marshal' or 'constable'; his officers or gentleman-rankers would be young men or veterans of his or kindred names; in time, however, the ranks would be swelled with enlisted privates of Hebridean stock now planted in Ireland and become numerous. Fighting on foot and in close-knit 'battles', these formidable axemen were to fight dozens of deadly intertribal encounters in Ireland between 1260 and 1603.

KING HAAKON OF NORWAY AND THE LORDSHIP OF THE ISLES

Disappointed in the hope of a native Árd Rí, certain leaders of the native race, probably in Ulster, bethought them of a foreign saviour, of a race long familiar to them. In 1263 Haakon, king of Norway, was lying with his fleet off the Hebrides, which Alexander III aimed at annexing to Scotland. While there, messages came to him from Ireland that the Irish offered to come under his power, and that they needed much that he should free them from the thraldom which the English had laid on them, 'for that they then held the best towns along the sea'. Later, as Haakon lay in the Clyde, the envoys he had sent to Ireland to discuss terms returned to say that the Irish would keep his host all the winter, if he would free them from the English. But before the matter went further Haakon, landing with an army, suffered a repulse at the hands of the Scots at Largs, and died soon after in the Orkneys in December 1263.[1] Before sailing away, he sold his claims on the Hebrides to the king of Scots. Henceforth no viking fleet ever appeared in Irish or Scottish waters, and the long connexion of Ireland with Scandinavia ceased. The Norwegian suzerainty over the Sudreyas came to an end with Haakon, and the Clan Donnell, descendants of Somerled, before long ruled this island-kingdom as Lords of the Isles till 1500, in mere nominal vassalage to the king of the Scots.

This second failure to procure either a native or foreign Árd Rí threw the Irish back again upon local resistance, and save for an occasional flourish or the menace of a powerful combination, no Irish king for three centuries took on himself to revive the monarchy of Tara.

[1] *Hakonarsaga* (ed. Dasent), *R.S.* *Ann. Ult.* (1263) say that at the time of his death 'Ebdon', king of Norway, was coming to Ireland. The remark of the Irish, 'that they [the Irish] then held the best towns along the sea', seems to mean that as the earldom of Ulster was in abeyance, and the Clan Sorley, etc. had easy sailing to and fro with the northern coast, the Irish controlled the ports where Haakon might land.

THE DE BURGO EARLDOM OF ULSTER, 1264–1333

In 1264 Prince Edward, as Lord of Ireland, regranted the earldom of Ulster to Walter de Burgo, who was already lord of Connacht.[1] Under this family the northern earldom was to become the greatest lordship in Ireland and the bulwark of the whole colony. The feudal class that De Burgo represented was now narrowing down to a few names holding vast estates. He himself had almost two provinces of Ireland in his hand. The feebleness of royal authority in Ireland enabled his class to extend their lordships, increase their independence, and make war at will upon one another. Englishmen of little rank and of no account filled the office of viceroy from 1256 to 1267. For a year after the battle of Lewes on May 14th 1264, the King and his son Edward were captives of De Montfort and his baronial party. The masterless barons of Ireland filled the interval with their irrational feuds. Angered by the grant of Ulster to De Burgo, who was his rival in Connacht and now became his overlord in Ulster, Maurice (III) Fitzgerald made war upon him, and when the Justiciar, De la Rochelle, interfered, seized him at a conference at Castledermot, and for a time kept the King's representative prisoner. Aedh O'Connor and O'Donnell served the occasion to reunite their gallowglass forces to level the Geraldine strongholds of Sligo and Banada, and to harass the Welsh settlers of Mayo. Aedh Bui O'Neill, who was married to one of the Anglo-Irish, Eleanor de Angulo, openly assumed the title of 'king of all the Irish of Ireland'.[2]

THE BATTLE OF ATHANKIP, 1270

Felim O'Connor had not openly declared himself when his son Aedh joined O'Neill in 1260, but both had reason to fear the vengeance of the English. In spite of an appeal by Felim to King Henry against Walter de Burgo, the latter launched an army against the O'Connors in 1262. After a war of general devastation, father and son submitted, and four of the king's cantreds, Moy Ai, Trí Tuatha, Tir Many, and Moylurg, were left to Felim at rent for a fine of five thousand marks. Henceforth Aedh was the real king, and the aged Felim died in 1265. His effigied tomb in the

[1] *C.D.I.*, II, No. 860 (1520 and 1548). Orpen (*Normans*, II, p. 266) refutes the legend that De Burgo got Ulster through marriage with a daughter of Hugh de Lacy. No such marriage can be traced, and Walter's wife was Avelina, daughter of John FitzGeoffrey.

[2] *C.D.I.*, I, No. 1840. It is dated conjecturally 1230, but obviously refers to this Aedh, and not the earlier Aedh, who died 1230. Orpen (*Normans*, III, p. 285) says that Eleanor was daughter of Milo 'MacCostello'.

Dominican friary at Roscommon and his silver seal, still extant, show Felim to us as the new type of Irish leader, chief rather than king, adapting himself to Norman custom, and in war and diplomacy not much inferior to the conquerors.[1]

His son and successor, however, was not a compromiser, and soon proved himself a hero of the Gael.

Robert d'Ufford, Justiciar in 1267, at last threw some energy into affairs, rebuilt Sligo, and began a new castle at Roscommon. In 1270 he joined all his forces to those of Walter de Burgo, 'they had all the foreigners of Erin with them', say the annals, and the joint army marched through Roscommon to Carrick-on-Shannon against the O'Connors, only to meet at the ford of Athankip a disastrous defeat. Aedh, who had with him Turloch O'Brien, made such a sudden onslaught 'that in an instant nine of the chiefest of the English were killed', the Normans were defeated, and in their flight abandoned a hundred war-horses with their mail-coverings and saddles, and a hundred suits of mail of their riders. In the fighting Walter de Burgo after showing great courage only saved himself by flight, but his brother, William Oge, did not survive the battle.

Of the battle of Athankip the Ulster annals say: 'no greater defeat had been given to the English in Ireland up to that time.' We may suppose that here for the first time Aedh's band of gallowglasses proved they could face and repulse Norman horse.[2]

While De Burgo and the viceroy escaped with difficulty from the field, Aedh united with O'Donnell to level Roscommon, Sligo, and others of those castles which the Irish feared more than armies. In the next year Walter de Burgo died in his castle of Galway. He was only forty-two years of age, and his son and heir Richard was a minor who did not succeed till 1280. Fate left few of the Normans in Ireland time to complete their designs or to leave vigorous adult sons behind them. Aedh O'Connor himself died in 1274, still 'Rex Connacie', an Irish hero who had triumphed over the foreigners as decisively at Athankip as Finghin MacCarthy had at Callann.

The neighbouring province, Meath, had been agitated by this De Burgo war, and in 1264 Art, son of Cormac, son of Art O'Melaghlin, hereditary claimant to the kingship, defeated the

[1] *C.D.I.*, II, p. 114 and No. 713, and 35, *Rep. D.K.*, p. 44. For his seal see end of this chapter. The striking gallowglass figures on Felim's tomb are of a later date (see article by Lord Walter Fitzgerald, 'The Effigy of Felim O'Connor', *R.S.A.I.* (1900), p. 366).

[2] For the battle see *Ann. Clon.*, *Ann. Ult.* and Clyn's *Annals*. In 1259 Alan, son of Rory the grandson of Somerled, brought one hundred and sixty gallowglasses to Aedh when the latter married his niece.

English on the Brosna and 'burned all the castles and street-towns of the foreigners in Delvin MacCoghlan, Brawnie and Calrie and banished the Englishmen out of them'.[1] Such revolts in time were to lose most of west Meath to the colonists.

LOYAL KINGS AND 'SWORD-LAND' IN ULSTER

It is a possible theme that the Irish princes, when subjection really seemed inevitable, preferred the distant English Crown, which often addressed them as local kings (*reguli*), to the Norman adventurers at hand, who strove either to dispossess them or reduce them to dishonourable vassalage. So it was shown in Ulster now. The death of De Burgo and the minority of his son gave the chiefs a chance once more to approach that suzerain whom they felt it no dishonour to obey, while as 'free clans' of royal blood they resented subjection to mesne lords. In 1272, Henry III's Justiciar, De Audeley, reported that O'Neill, MacMahon, O'Cahan, and other Irish chiefs have come into the King's peace, and that he has presented them with scarlet robes, ermine furs, and saddles. This was just before Edward I's accession, and the kings continued their loyal submission into his reign. In 1272 FitzWarin, the new Seneschal of Ulster, fell out with Henry de Mandeville, formerly Seneschal (in 1270), who had to be put down by force. The mayor of Carrickfergus having charged Aedh Bui O'Neill and others with abetting him and his party, these chiefs wrote to the new King that in fact they had aided the Seneschal against the rebels, and prayed Edward not to listen to charges made against them in the Council and elsewhere, but to confide in his Seneschal, whom they will obey.[2]

Though such a loyal address was no doubt welcome, in fact a

[1] For Leinster and central Ireland the best authorities are *Ann. Clon.* and Clyn and Dowling's *Annals*.

[2] *C.D.I.*, II, p. 148, account of De Audeley, formerly Justiciar of Ireland, from 1270 to 1272; ibid., Nos. 952–3. The chiefs who wrote to Edward were Aedh O'Neill, 'king of Kinel Owen', Cumidhe O'Cahan, 'king of Keinaght (Ciannacht)', MacDunlevy, 'king of the Irish of Ulidia', O'Flynn, 'king of Ui Tuirtre', O'Hanlon, 'king of Oriel (*recte* Orior)', MacGilmori, 'king of Anderken', and MacCartan, 'king of Onelich'.

The King's Seneschal was of course ruling Ulster in the minority of the heir Richard de Burgo.

Orpen (*Normans*, III, p. 285) quotes a deed of 1269 by which 'Odo Onel Rex Kenelean' admits that he bound himself in 1260 to Walter de Burgo, earl of Ulster, in three thousand five hundred cows to be paid in three following terms, and also to deliver four hostages

Aedh was also related by marriage to the Earl. His wife was Eleanor, daughter of Milo de Angulo (MacCostello) by a daughter of Hugh Earl of Ulster. Earl Walter himself was son of Egidia Lacy, daughter of Walter Earl of Meath, who married Richard de Burgo, conqueror of Connacht. The marriage of Aedh and Eleanor is recorded in *Ann. Ult.* (1263).

new Ulster was being created and, in the opportunity given by Norman invasion and the fluctuations in the earldom, native chiefs were as ready as the invaders to seize on sept-lands not their own *vi et armis* and to hold them by the law of 'sword-land'.

O'DOHERTY, O'CAHAN, O'FLYNN, MACDUNLEVY

The great peninsula of Inishowen, so vital for whosoever would command Ulster, was the patrimony of an old race, O'Gormledhaigh or O'Gormley. But the name of O'Dochartaigh (O'Doherty) was destined to supersede it. This was a sept of the Cinel Conaill and, since 'branch-expanding' (*craobh-sgaoileadh*) was the practice of royal princes, it was encouraged by the O'Donnells, who were themselves arrivists, to migrate into Inishowen and possess it. About 1197 we hear of an O'Doherty in Inishowen. The MacUchtred family had designs on this country, but their lapse and that of the Lacy earldom prevented any forward move there. In various battles O'Gormley was beaten out, but it was not till after the overthrow of the Ulster earldom in the fourteenth century that O'Doherty became secure lord, and in the period 1280 to 1333 there seemed every prospect of a Norman occupation of Inishowen. The O'Neills had long since quitted this original home of their first founder, 'the island of Eoghan', for the plains of Tyrone in 'Eoghan's land'.

Another striking dispossession was that by which the O'Cahans became and remained till 1603 lords of Ciannacht or 'Oireacht Ui Cathain' in the present county Derry. This Cinel Eoghain sept was also encouraged by the O'Neills, especially by Brian of 'Down', to plant themselves in upon the ancient royal race of O'Connor of Glengevin.[1]

Again the beating out and the planting in took time, but these O'Connors were at last reduced to insignificance, and we read in the annals of Ulster under 1213 of Fergal, first O'Cahan king of Ciannacht, a territory which is now the barony of Keenaght in county Derry.[2] No wonder the O'Cahans fought manfully at Down beside O'Neill: their fortunes were bound up in their patron's.

O'Flynn was the hereditary chief of the Tuirtre, a royal Ulidian stock who ruled over Moy Linny, a territory stretching from Belfast

[1] The centre of this was Dungiven, O'Cahan's chief seat for centuries.

[2] See p. 152, where O'Cahan in 1272 styles himself 'Rex Keenaght'. He was favoured indeed by the English. See Orpen, *Normans*, III, p. 285, who quotes a deed by which Dermot O'Cahan, king of Fernecrewe, surrenders to Earl Richard in 1278 the land of Glenoconcahen which he held immediately of Earl Walter.

Lough to the Bann and containing also the district of Loughlinsholin west of Lough Neagh which bordered on Keenaght.[1] Among the first to feel the Norman impact, they had to bow the knee and strive to retain their kingship by compliance with kings, earls, and royal seneschals. Hence in the loyal address of 1272 O'Flynn is 'king of Ui Tuirtre'. Their final fate was deferred till after 1333, and it came then not from the English but at Gaelic hands. The later expansion of the Clann Aodha Buidhe O'Neills overlaid or extinguished the old Gaelic dynasties of central Ulidia, and in 1386 the death is recorded of Thomas, the last reigning O'Flynn.[2]

A greater name still, that of MacDunlevy, which since 1100 had provided the kings of Ulidia, was destined to a similar disappearance. De Courcy and De Lacy had proved themselves not unkind lords to the Irish of Antrim and Down, and in 1259 and again in 1272 a whole roll of Gaelic vassals appear as loyal vassals still displaying their old titles.[3] But for some reason, perhaps because he was too dangerous as hereditary Ultonian king, MacDunlevy, who is in the roll of loyal vassals of the earldom in 1272, is not in that of 1333, and thereafter the name disappears from eastern Ulster, and indeed from the landed septs of Ireland.[4]

In view of these local gains of 'sword-land' and war of Gael on Gael, we shall not attribute too much weight to a general patriotism which then hardly existed. The general attempt of 1260 was a gallant, but hardly more than a gallant, event. The winning and enforcement of local lordship by both Norman and Celt was the order of the day. Naturally those who were already in possession strove to defend their own, but found no more generous treatment from Gaelic than from Norman aggressor. Personal relations were after all what counted most to the medieval man and especially to the Irish Celt. To the ordinary man what mattered was to have a lord. Accept him as lord and he might in time become a good lord. This argument was what in due time established the Normans themselves in Ireland.

Thus in 1272 ended in a drawn fight the first armed resurgence of the Gaelic race since the Invasion, fought out mainly in local battles. Their chiefs, forsaking the old order, now began to have their castles and their hired troops and to make treaties and

[1] Loughinsholin is 'Loch Innse Ui Fhloinn', 'the lake of O'Flynn's island'.

[2] *Ann. Ult.* (1359): Murchertach, son of Thomas O'Flynn, heir of the Tuirtre, slain in treachery by Aedh, son of Brian, son of Aedh Bui.

[3] See pp. 144, 152.

[4] See pp. 167, 210, for the De Burgo Inquisition of 1333.

marriage alliances with the Norman barons, on whom they modelled themselves. They had learned the art of diplomacy, and used heraldic seals and devices of their own.[1] But though they styled themselves 'Rex' and 'Dux', they were in fact much less sovereign than Cathal Crovderg or Donnchad O'Brien had been in their province-kingdoms, and found it hard to maintain themselves even in their demesne lands.

In spite of a few feeble injunctions and concessions, the long reign of Henry III had failed to put the chiefs in a secure position under the Crown and to bring the Irish under one equal law with the colonists. Henry, dying in November 1272, left these and other problems of his Land of Ireland still unsolved to his son Edward.

[1] See E. C. R. Armstrong, 'When Heraldry was adopted by the Irish Chiefs', *R.S.A.I.* (1913), also *Ulster Arch. Soc.* (1853), p. 225, and Petrie in *Irish Penny Journal* (1840–1), p. 35, who gives seals of seven kings, including Felim O'Connor (d. 1265). Donal MacCarthy, king of Desmond (d. 1303), Brian Rua O'Brien, and Brian 'Rex Kenel Eoghain' had seals which still exist. See for additions to this question Curtis, 'Some Seals out of the Ormond Archives', *R.S.A.I.* (1936–7).

CHAPTER IX

THE ENGLISH LORDSHIP AT ITS HEIGHT

1272–1310

THE reign of the first Edward in England gave monarchy a decisive triumph over feudalism. In Ireland the same end was pursued, but only to show that the feudal magnates were the true lords of Ireland.

We must imagine the Lordship or State of Ireland as centred in Dublin and acting still with unquestioned authority and considerable vigour in a half-arc all around it, but with its writs unable to run effectively in the great liberties of Leinster, Desmond, Meath, and Ulster. In a greater half-arc around it are the lords of these liberties and great fiefs, bent more on their separate greatness than on the greatness of the State, ruling over a great class of English underlords and tenants by feudal law, and dealing at will with a still greater population of Irish. Outside again is an Irish world still ruled by 'kings' who, though they had for the time sought terms with the King or with the Anglo-Norman magnates, looked forward to remoulding their ancient kingships.

THE CHIEF ANGLO-IRISH

The greatest of these, Richard de Burgo, known to history as the 'Red Earl', was yet a boy, but when he came of age in 1280 he inherited Connacht and Ulster, and a wide territory in Limerick and north Tipperary, ringed round the lordship of Castleconnell. The Red Earl was the true type of the Norman of Ireland as history was moulding it, already half-Irish and understanding Irish, bent on building up and rounding off his great lordships, and sparing no means, whether of force, craft, or princely concession, to bring under him the Gaels and the Englishry of two whole provinces. The De Burgos and their descendants the Mortimers, descended as they were from Brian Boru on one side and one of the First Conquerors on the other, were held as long as they lasted to be 'chief of the English of Ireland'. But a young Geraldine was to become almost as important as the Red Earl. John FitzThomas of Kildare was a mere scion of the great race of Offaly and Naas, and grandson of the famous Maurice who died in 1257 after great efforts in Connacht and Tyrconnel. But beginning junior and of little estate, by the time the young Thomas came to full manhood he came into possession of all the Geraldine inheritance in Leinster and Connacht, along with Croom and Adare in Limerick. Gerald, 4th Baron of Offaly (whom Clyn calls 'capitaneus Geraldinorum'), dying without heirs in 1287 passed the inheritance to John. One cousin, Juliana, wife of John de Cogan, bequeathed him her lands, and so did another, Amabilia, her Connacht inheritance and the claims on Tyrconnell and Fermanagh. By 1293, as the result of a remarkable falling-in, the young FitzThomas became lord of all, and finally ended as earl of Kildare.[1]

The head of the Munster Geraldines, Thomas Fitzmaurice 'an Ápa', did not come of age till 1282, but his kinsmen Maurice, lord of Kerry, and Gilbert, son of John of Callann, held the huge family estates together.[2] Nothing could better illustrate the mingled feudal and Irish tenures and the vast mixture of towns, manors, castles and fiefs, typical of the age, than the inquisition made on Thomas's lordship of Desmond in 1282 and at his early death in 1298, in Kerry, Cork, Limerick, and Waterford.[3]

THE BUTLER LANDS

Similar inquisitions *post mortem* attest the steady growth of another family which had so far played little public part in the colony but was destined to rival both Geraldines and De Burgos.[4] The first Theobald Walter, 'Butler of Ireland', who died in 1206, owned the northern half of Tipperary.[5] Here his 'caput baronie' was Nenagh, where he built the great castle donjon which still survives. At first the hold on Ormond along the Devil's Bit mountains ('Bearnán Éile') seemed secure; for the native lords, the O'Kennedys, were at present submissive. But in Ely O'Carroll the hold was precarious from the first and the settlers few.

In Leinster Theobald Walter got Arklow from Prince John, a noble manor reaching up to Aughrim, and later Tullophelim (Tullow) in Carlow, which was held of the Earl Marshal. In addition he, or his son the second Theobald, got Bray in Wicklow and the manor of Gowran in county Kilkenny. Close by this

[1] See Appendix I (A), the Pedigree of the Fitzgerald Barons of Offaly.
[2] See 'Unpublished Geraldine Documents', *R.S.A.I.* (1876), and Appendix I (A), the Desmond Pedigree.
[3] See first edition of this book, pp. 169–70.
[4] For Butler properties see *Cal. Ormond Deeds*, I, II, *passim*, and *Red Book of Ormond* (ed. White). Also *C.D.I.*, II, No. 1912 and IV, Nos. 551, 727. For the history of the office of Butler of Ireland see later, p. 257.
[5] For the Butler descent see Pedigree, Appendix I (A). From Theobald I (d. 1206) to Theobald V (d. 1299) is so rapid a succession that Carte (*Life of the Great Duke of Ormonde*) suspected that Theobald III and IV must be the same, but it seems impossible to decide.

latter, Polestown (the modern Paulstown) was to give its name to a famous branch of the family in the fifteenth century.[1]

Theobald IV, who first adopted the surname 'Le Boteiller', added in county Dublin the manors of Turvey and Corduff, and Cloncurry in Kildare. The main strength of the family was however to lie in Kilkenny and Tipperary. Theobald III, marrying Margery, daughter of Richard de Burgo, received with her the manor of Ardmayle near Cashel and extended the family power towards the Suir, where Carrickmagriffin (Carrick-on-Suir) and the land about Clonmel became theirs.

Even claims in Connacht came to them when Philip de la Rochelle conveyed to Theobald IV lands about Aughrim in O'Kelly's country of Hy Many. They were in fact no gain, and the O'Kellys held on to their patrimony, yet in the sixteenth century the earl of Ormond got his old claims there allowed by Elizabeth.[2]

In such ways, marriage, buying out of English absentees, inheritance, and the like, did those Normans who preferred Ireland, in this lucky time for them and before the Irish revival, become in English law owners on a vast scale of Irish soil.

The remarkable dying out of original grantees favoured the Butlers, as it favoured the Geraldines in Kerry and Limerick. By the grant of John in 1185 Philip de Worcester had been enfeoffed in five cantreds in south Tipperary. When his grandson Ralph died in 1275 without heirs male and the property was dispersed, the Butlers profited and expanded into south Tipperary. Originally De Braose, lord of the honour of Limerick, had been the overlord of both, but when in Henry II's reign this lordship, though renewed in 1216, lapsed by non-user, the Butlers became immediate tenants of the Crown in Ormond. In Kilkenny, where they had Gowran and other estates, they were, after the extinction of the Marshal earls, tenants of the earl of Gloucester, titular lord of the liberty, but in fact they steadily became the great people in this county. On the death of Theobald V in 1299 his brother Edmund succeeded to the family estates, receiving seisin in 1300, and with him the Butlers, formerly a race that seemed likely to expire, struck deep roots and ascended into the highest ranks of the Anglo-Irish.[3] Among the acquisitions which he like his predecessors made a notable one is that of the barony of Iverk in Ossory, which in 1315 Roger FitzDavid, last of the Geraldine lords of this noble fief, made over to Edmund.

[1] For the Butler manor of Arklow see L. Price in *R.S.A.I.* (1936), and for Nenagh see Gleeson, 'The Castle of Nenagh', ibid., pp. 247–70.

[2] For the Connacht lands see Curtis: 'Original Documents relating to the Butler Lordship of Achill etc'. in *Galway Arch. Soc.* (1934–5).

[3] For Edmund, later created earl of Carrick, see Round, 'Earldom of Ormond' in Foster's *Coll. Genealogica* (1881–4).

THE EARLDOM OF MEATH

The great De Lacy principality in Meath had now fallen into two. The lordship of Trim, the richer and more colonized part, had been ruled by Geoffrey de Genville since 1254 when Henry III granted to him the liberty. This French knight held Trim for over fifty years till 1307, but save for the continued organizing of his lordship played no active part in Irish affairs.

The other half of Meath, the liberty or lordship of Lochsewdy or west Meath, was now held by Theobald de Verdun.[1] It was supposed to contain the present Westmeath (save Rathwire) and Longford, but in fact, less thickly feudalized than east Meath, most of it was falling back to the O'Melaghlins, Mageoghegans, O'Farrells, and other native septs.

EDWARD I'S POLICY FOR IRELAND

From the State point of view, the policy of the new Lord of Ireland should have been to create a government in Dublin whose orders would be obeyed throughout the island; to bridle or abolish the liberties; and to end the race-war by giving the Gaelic chiefs legal status under the Crown, and confirming to the Irish '*inter anglicos*' the benefits of royal law.

That Edward understood these necessities and after a fashion aimed at this policy seems clear. This legal-minded King had beyond the Severn a situation very like that of Ireland, and when by the Statute of Rhuddlan in 1284 he imposed English law on the annexed principality of Wales, leaving to the Welsh many of their own Celtic customs, he made a settlement which was no bad model for his island lordship.[2]

But his policy in Ireland wavered badly. Few of his English viceroys dared defy the baronial interest, and even when they put the King's orders into effect and took over feudal liberties, Edward often withdrew his orders. Nothing but a royal visit could have

[1] He died in 1309, his son Theobald II on July 27th 1316; thus the male line expired. Of his four daughters and coheiresses Joan married Sir Thomas Furnival and so transmitted claims in Westmeath to the famous Sir John Talbot (see p. 292).

[2] Edward, however, a thorough Englishman and unifier, had no sympathy for Celtic codes of law. His Ordinance for the governance of Scotland (then annexed) in 1305 says: 'it is ordained that the usages of the Scots (Gaels) and Brets [Britons] be forbidden henceforth, so that they shall be used no longer.' Instead, his Lieutenant there is to collect the [feudal and Anglian] laws of King David etc. and send them enrolled to London where the King with English and Scots barons shall make them to be proclaimed. (See his opinion on the Irish laws, p. 161.)

effected a general reform, and such a visit was not paid. Anglo-Irish feudalism remained in effect in the saddle.

Edward also made some attempt to enfranchise the older race, but well-meaning fiats were powerless against the rooted determination of the Anglo-Irish—without whose assent nothing could be done—to keep the Irish and their lands as the preserve of the conquerors.

From 1272 to 1276 Edward was represented successively in Ireland by two Anglo-Irish justiciars, viz. Maurice, third Baron of Offaly, and Geoffrey de Genville, lord of Trim.

LEINSTER UNDER THE BIGODS

As long as the Marshals maintained the Land of Leinster, its Irish population had accepted their rule, and even under such absentees as the Bigod lords of Carlow peace had continued. But Strongbow's earlier tradition faded, and the newer tradition was less favourable to those Irish who had been Strongbow's allies or had sworn homage to him and his heirs. Moreover, the division of Leinster among absentee aliens evoked the memory of those Gaelic lordships whose heirs still existed and in a broken fashion maintained their kingship.[1]

The natural leaders of the Leinster Irish were the descendants of Dermot. So far, Donal Kavanagh's heirs had been tenants and officers of the Marshals in Carlow, but when the direct heirs of Strongbow and Eva expired, the tradition that a MacMurrough was the true king of Leinster was bound to revive.

About the year 1280 we find Art 'MacMurgh' in receipt of an annual fee from his kinsman, Roger Bigod, lord of Carlow, while his brother, Murchertach or 'Moriardagh', enjoys a smaller fee.[2] An imposing number of native chiefs looked to the Kavanaghs as their lawful head. Such were the MacDamores of Wexford, the O'Nolans and O'Ryans of Carlow, and the O'Byrnes and O'Tooles

[1] Even the English government at this time and onwards admitted O'Connor etc. as at least 'Princeps' or 'Dux hiberniensium Connacie' etc. A 'king of the Irish' of a province could be safely admitted, but not over the English of a province.

[2] Inquisition on Bigod's lands (1279–94) in *Just. Rolls*, II, p. 346: Art received £13 per annum, Murchertach £1 13*s*. 4*d*. per annum. The *Laud Annals* in *Chart. St. Mary's*, II, p. 318, call 'Morydagh' chief in 1275, and the O'Clery *Pedigrees* make him the elder. Bigod's seneschal must have favoured Art and made him 'Seneschal of the Irish' like his ancestor, Donal Kavanagh. The ruling Bigod, earl of Norfolk, was now Roger II (1270–1306). An interesting roll survives of his Carlow lordship illustrating his rents and rights and its organization under his officers (see Orpen, *Normans*, IV, pp. 264–7). In 1245 the office of Earl Marshal passed to the Bigod family.

of Wicklow. O'Byrne represented the Ui Faelain, driven from Kildare into the Wicklow mountains, while O'Toole, now located about Imaal, represented the Ui Muiredaig. They had removed into what in law were the lands of the King and the see of Dublin, but before long they boldly claimed them as their own, and O'Toole called himself lord of Imaal.

Beyond the Liffey, O'Connor of Offaly, O'Dempsey of Clanmalier, O'Dunn of Iregan, and O'More of Leix had formerly obeyed MacMurrough and were ready to do so again, though for the time the English colonies along these rivers had severed them from their old suzerain.

ENGLISH LAW AND LIBERTY

But many of the Irish still looked to the Crown for redress. A new reign kindled hope, and the 'Community of the Irish' made a general request for English liberties through Edward's Justiciar, the Englishman, Robert d'Ufford, who was appointed in June 1276, accompanying it with an offer of eight thousand marks. Edward let the question hang fire, hoping to receive a higher sum and a contingent of infantry from the Irish, but in 1279 informed D'Ufford that it seemed meet to him and the Council of England that such a grant of English laws should be made, because the Irish laws were 'detestable to God and so diverse from all law as not worthy to be called laws at all'. He then bade his Deputy summon the peers, prelates, and others of Ireland to consider whether the laws of England might be extended as desired. There the matter ended, for the Anglo-Irish oligarchy apparently would not have it, and Edward, who brooked resistance ill in England, stomached it from his Irish barons, and practically shelved the question for his reign.[1]

Instead of a general and generous enfranchisement a peddling subterfuge was adopted, and grants of English liberty, purchased with money, were made to familes and individuals, especially to those Irish, free or bond, who dwelt *inter anglicos*. The records contain numbers of such acts of denization, but the unrecorded numbers were apparently great, if we can believe that Edward made three thousand pounds in a short period over such transactions. It is probable that by this method considerable numbers

[1] Edward indeed made in 1290 a 'favourable statement' as to emancipation (see note, p. 162), but what was wanted was a general State edict or act to that effect. Orpen (*Normans*, IV, p. 22) argues that the request of the Irish was only a local one made by the Irish of Wicklow. A request, however, made by the 'Community of Ireland' and backed by so large a sum, and so seriously considered by the King, must surely have been made by a much larger section of the Irish, possibly all Munster and Leinster, if not agents acting for all Ireland. The request is given in *C.D.I.*, No. 1409.

of the richer Irish in the 'English land' redeemed themselves from 'Irish servitude', and that after a generation or two the freed Irish were numerous in the east and south.[1]

THE O'BYRNES OF GLENMALURE

Meanwhile the mountain fastness of Glenmalure became the stronghold of the O'Byrnes and other Leinster rebels. In 1274 the first of many expeditions against it, led by the Prior of the Hospitallers, was overthrown there, and a second attempt in 1276 under the Justiciar, Geoffrey de Genville, who contributed two thousand men from Meath alone, was also repulsed in this narrow and dangerous defile, which remained the stronghold of the O'Byrnes for centuries.

THE LEINSTER RESURGENCE

The O'Byrnes were willing vassals of the MacMurroughs and were now, it would seem, working in concert with them. Yet the latter were still willing to trust to the Bigods whom they still esteemed as of the blood of Strongbow and Eva, and because they all had St. Laurence O'Toole in the family.

In 1281 Earl Roger got a safe-conduct from the Crown for 'Art MacMurch and Caruel Alfortien, Irishmen and kinsmen of the Earl', to come to him in England. But Art got no further on his journey than Arklow, early in 1282, when the English of that port, hostile to all Irish chiefs, murdered him, to the indignation of Bigod, who protested strongly to the King.[2] Naturally such a deed alienated these 'kinsmen of the Earl'.

The Leinster war flickered for many years, till in 1295 Sir

[1] See grants to Hugh Kent and Robert de Bree (*C.D.I.*, III, p. 525 and No. 924). In the case of the former, *circa* 1290, 'King Edward in his Great Council at London declared that all who demanded this grant of English laws should have them.' *C.D.I.*, III, p. 290 (1290) makes the statement that the King gained three thousand pounds in one day by issue of charters of liberty; probably this means that an accumulated sum from several years was sent to him representing thousands of such enfranchisements. But it was easier to decree than to make the colonists observe, and in 1321 (*Cal. Pat. Rolls* (1321), p. 563) a royal patent reaffirmed to such Irishmen the English law of life and limb which the colonists refused to them. For such charters of liberty. see Curtis, 'Rental of Manor of Lisronagh', *P.R.I.A.* (1936), and later, pp. 206, 420.

[2] *Laud Annals*, p. 318; *Ann. Clon.* (1276); *C.D.I.*, II, p. 267 and Nos. 1873 and 1919. Possibly Murchertach was with his brother Art at Arklow. 'Interfectus est [*sic*] Moritagh et Arte MacMurgh frater ejus apud Arklowe in Vig. S. Marie Magdalene, 1282' (*Laud Annals*). *Ann. Ult.* (1282) say: 'Muirchertach MacMurchadha, king of Leinster, and his brother Art were slain by the Foreigners.' Bigod's complaint to King Edward, however, only names Art as having been killed at Arklow.

Thomas FitzMaurice of Desmond, 'Custos' of Ireland, entered into terms with the insurgents, and 'Mauritius mac Muryarthi MacMurchoth (i.e. Murchad son of Murchertach) with all his nation and following' was received into the King's peace.[1]

The Irish resurgence in Leinster was accompanied by a strong tide of race-recovery.

The King, the lords of Leinster, and the archbishop of Dublin had annexed the whole coast and hinterland from Wexford to the Liffey, and the forest and the highlands of Dublin and Wicklow were 'chase and vert' for the Crown and its tenants-in-chief. Families such as Hereford, Ridlesford, FitzGriffin, and FitzRhys had been richly enfeoffed in these borderlands. Now the recovery of the Irish deprived the Crown of its forest-land. The O'Tooles took the place of FitzRhys in the highlands of Imaal. The Borearts and others vanished and left to O'Murchada the lands of Ui Feilme with which Strongbow had enfeoffed them.

The striking disappearance of the original families has already been emphasized. Thus Griffin, brother of Raymond le Gros, had been enfeoffed by him with lands in the barony of Forth in Carlow. But by 1250 the family had ended in an heiress Clarice, who dispersed the family lands among her three husbands. So the noble grants of Walter de Ridlesford, after the second of the name who died about 1240, ended in an heiress. By 1300 the lands of the three Hereford brothers, who had divided north-east Kildare between them in the Conquest, had all gone to Rochforts, Stauntons, and others, husbands of the heiresses.

It was the same fate which had overtaken the Marshals, Lacys, and other families of the highest rank. And so the colonial families had to recede to their estates along the Liffey and the river valleys, but even there their names dwindled, and many of them ceased to exist by the time of the Tudors.[2]

Strategically the effect of this resurgence was to bring most of the coast from Bray to Wexford into Irish hands, and on the other side of the mountains to threaten the capital and the colonies of

[1] *Cal. Just. Rolls*, I, p. 61.

[2] For the above see *Reg. St. Thomas*, pp. 102, 366; *Chart. St. Mary's*, I, pp. 29, 108; *C.D.I.*, III, p. 294; *Crede Mihi*, liv and p. 51.

The archbishop of Dublin had Glendaloch and much country east of it, defended by his fortress at Castlekevin, near Annamoe, and also had Coillach, a hill-tract between the sources of Liffey and Dodder. The Crown had the old Irish district called Ui Cellaigh (Okelly) to the south of Tallaght stretching across the entrance of Glenasmole, Obrun (Ui Briuin Chualann), and Othec, stretching between them from modern Shankill south to Newcastle McKinegan where there was a royal castle (Hogan, *Onomasticon*). Both were naturally great losers by the Irish revival.

the Liffey, and the Barrow which commands the passes into Munster.

THOMOND AND 'THE TRIUMPHS OF TURLOCH'

Successive grants to De Muscegros and other Anglo-Normans had by now threatened the O'Brien kings with extinction. After the death of Conor Rua in 1268, Brian Rua, his remaining son (for the elder, Taig 'of Caeluisce', was dead), held only two cantreds in Corcomrua under the English Crown. Finally, in January 1276, King Edward conferred on Thomas de Clare, a brother of Gilbert, 9th Earl of Gloucester, 'the whole land of Thomond' with the usual liberties at service of ten knights. Robert de Muscegros was bought out and retired to England, while the O'Briens were adjudged, as guilty of treason, to have no right to the land.[1] We are told nothing as to what O'Brien had done to deserve this confiscation. The grant was followed by a spectacular clash between feudal law and Irish patriarchal chieftainship.[2]

De Clare had the true Norman vigour and ruthlessness, and a succession-dispute between Brian Rua and his nephew, Turloch, son of Taig 'of Caeluisce', served his turn. Hard pressed, Brian sent to De Clare in Cork offering to surrender to him all the land between Quin and Limerick. Arriving at once, Thomas threw up a castle at Bunratty, but his foe Turloch was not less active, and, calling in Irish auxiliaries from Galway, overthrew Brian in battle and slew his Norman ally, Patrick FitzMaurice, brother-in-law of De Clare (1277). Brian fled to Bunratty, only to be blamed for Patrick's death, and in spite of De Clare's most solemn oaths of alliance, he was by order of the latter barbarously done to death. It was one of the atrocities specially detailed to the Pope in 1317.

Appeased by De Clare's apologies for the murder, Donnchad, Brian's son, was induced to adhere to the Norman side, and the civil war, so profitable to De Clare, went on.

Richard de Burgo, on coming into the possession of his estates,

[1] *C.D.I.*, II, No. 1194, and p. 528 (September 1284): 'the King having given to Thomas de Clare the lands, etc., which belonged to O'Brien, an Irishman, which had escheated to the King by O'Brien's forfeiture, etc.'

[2] The story of the forty years' war in Clare is told in a remarkable prose saga, *Caithréim Toirdelbhaigh* ('The Triumphs of Turloch'), written by Sean MacCraith soon after 1364. The opening of the *Caithréim* is a remarkable insight into what an Irish literary man, safe under his own king, could think of the Norman Conquest: 'The government of Ireland having in the year 1172 come into foreigners' hands and regal dignity being divorced from all and singular, the clans of Milesian blood, Donnchad Cairbreach O'Brien became chief in his father's stead over Thomond. He, being the first to drop the royal style and title that had ever been his forefathers' wont and use, was inaugurated O'Brien.' (Standish Hayes O'Grady's translation, published by the Irish Texts Society.)

now intervened to protect Turloch O'Brien, and it was clear that the sharp division of Irish and English was fading away. Finally Donnchad was slain in battle, and the premature death of Thomas de Clare in 1287 left Turloch O'Brien supreme in most of Thomond. De Clare had shown great organizing skill, but his time had been too brief, and the tender age of his heir, Gilbert, who was but seven, left the whole work unachieved.[1] In 1287 Turloch's lieutenant, Cumidhe MacNamara, took and burned De Clare's castle at Quin, and the 'Brian-descended Turloch' died victorious in 1306. For some thirty years, however, Clare was still reckoned a feudal barony and a county, and it was not till 1318 that a final O'Brien triumph was achieved.[2]

THE REGRANT OF DESMOND, 1292

Donal Rua MacCarthy, son of Cormac Finn, was now chief of the Irish of Desmond. In 1285 he visited Edward in person, to complain of the encroachments of the Geraldines. But when in 1292 Edward granted to Thomas Fitzmaurice 'the land of Decies and Desmond with the homages and the custody of Dungarvan castle and the homages, rents and services of both Irish and English', MacCarthy made no such protest as that of Callann. By some sort of agreement with Fitzmaurice, Donal was left in possession of the south-western parts of Desmond. It is clear that the new lord of Desmond was content with a head rent and suzerainty over the MacCarthys, and that in Kerry he regarded only the land north of Killorglin and the Laune including Corcaguiney as English and feudal land.

Donal Rua died in 1302, and was succeeded by his son, Donal Oge. The silver seal of the latter shows this Irish prince on horse with sword in hand, and the inscription '*sigillum Dovenaldi og fili Dovenaldi Roch Macarthi*'.[3]

THE RED EARL AND THE O'CONNORS

Aedh O'Connor 'of Athankip' died childless in 1274. A period of dispute in the succession followed him, and no less than six

[1] Gilbert died in 1308 and was succeeded by his brother Richard.

[2] For De Clare's lands see *Cal. Inquis.*, II (16 Edw. I), No. 696.

[3] *C.D.I.*, II, p. 564 (1284): 'Donal Rufus, lord of the Irish of Desmond, vehemently desiring to be subjected to the King's domination, sends to the King Brother Walter of Kilkenny, reader of the Dominicans of Cashel.' May 1282, letters of protection are given to Donal, coming to the King of England. The seal of his son is described in a note to O'Donovan's *A.F.M.* (1302), p. 478. For the grant of Desmond in 1292 see *C.D.I.*, II, p. 424 and III, No. 817, and *Just. Rolls*, I, p. 153.

kings ruled or claimed to rule between 1274 and 1293, when Aedh of the line of Cathal Crovderg succeeded till 1309, and this line never lost the kingship thereafter. The branch, however, which was sprung from Brian of Luighni (Leyney), a brother of the High king Rory, established itself in Sligo. For forty years the real king of Connacht was Richard Earl of Ulster. Only two and a half cantreds of Shilmorthy were now O'Connor's, held under the English Crown, and De Burgo's castles of Galway, Meelick, Ballymote, and Ath-an-chorainn dominated the Corrib, Lough Derg, and the Shannon.[1]

THE ULSTER CHIEFS AND THE DE BURGO EARLDOM

Native Ulster had now fallen into two groups, dominated by the Cinel Eoghain and the Cinel Conaill. The alliance between the two was dropped and an agelong rivalry for greatness set in. Donal Oge O'Donnell pursued his expansion policy and, invading Tyrone in 1281, was defeated and slain by Aedh O'Neill and his English allies in a battle at Disert-dá-crich near Dungannon, where along with him fell nineteen chiefs, his vassals, whose names support the claim of the Ulster annals when they call Donal 'lord of Fermanagh and Oriel, a great part of the Gael of Connacht, and all Breffni'.

Little did these dignities affect the English, to whom O'Donnell was merely an 'Irish felon'. His body was mutilated, and a colonist carried his head to Dublin for the sake of reward.[2] Donal Oge was succeeded by his son Turloch and then by Aedh, his eldest son by Catriona MacSuibhne, who ruled from 1295 till his death in 1333. He continued his father's victories on the south, and the Maguire chiefs, who now appear in Fermanagh, began and continued as vassals of O'Donnell.[3]

Aedh Bui O'Neill and his urrighs, or 'under-kings', were now apparently at peace with the Crown and with the Earl. The Irish lords of Oriel and central Ulster now and for many years are found

[1] For the Earl's Connacht and Ulster lands and the nature of his rule as illustrated by the inquisitions on the death of his grandson in 1333, see *Cal. Inquis.* (7 Edw. III), pp. 371 *seq.*, and Knox, 'Anglo-Norman Occupation of Connacht', *R.S.A.I.* (1902–3).

[2] *C.D.I.*, II, No. 2049: Stephen, bishop of Waterford, Justiciar, orders to be paid to Thomas de Mandeville what is due to him for the head of O'Donnell, which Thomas caused to be borne to the Exchequer.

[3] *Ann. Ult.* (1302): 'Died Donn Maguidhir, king of Firmanach, viz. the first king of Firmanach of the sons of Maguidhir.' *Meguidhir Fermanach* (ed. Dinneen) shows that at this date the Maguires were mere acting lords for the O'Donnells in Fermanagh.

holding their lordships and lands by military service of the Earl.[1]

In 1283 Aedh O'Neill himself was slain in battle by MacMahon of Oriel and O'Reilly of Brefni in attempting to subject them. Donal, son of Brian 'of the Battle of Down', then put forward his claim against Brian, son of Aedh Bui, whom the Earl supported, but finally in 1295 Donal slew his rival at Craebh Telcha, and from this to 1318 was the sole O'Neill.

This fight, one of the most eventful of Irish clan-battles in its causes and results, deserves further comment. In 1270 Henry de Mandeville was the Earl's seneschal in Ulster. He was of a family originally estated in Louth and Meath, one of whom is found as a tenant-in-chief in Ulster under Hugh de Lacy in 1221. This Henry had the custody of the castle of Coleraine and other places, and in the absence and on the death of Earl Walter appropriated to himself the bailiwick of Tweskard, a district reaching from Ballymoney up to Ballycastle which later was called the 'Route'.[2] When the Crown appointed a new seneschal, Fitzwarin, a feud arose in which Henry was slain. Richard the 'Red Earl', on coming of age, appointed Thomas de Mandeville (another of the family, called 'MacMartin' by the Irish) seneschal in place of Fitzwarin. Thomas was backed up by the O'Cahans and other Irish chiefs, and in 1281 at the battle of Disert-dá-crich fought with Aedh Bui O'Neill against Donal Oge O'Donnell, whose head he sent to Dublin. On the death of Aedh Bui in battle, the Mandevilles supported his race and finally, with the aid of Byset (called MacEoin by the Irish), in 1290 set up his son Brian.

But after five years this nominee of the Earl and the English of Ulster, was defeated and slain at Craebh Telcha. The Englishry had supported him, and in the battle one Stephen Mandeville fought along with other Normans on his side. But though Donal O'Neill triumphed, his rivals of the Clann Aedha Buidhe were allowed by the Earl, and perhaps encouraged by the victor, to seek a new lordship for themselves east of the Bann.[3]

Though the 'Red Earl' had in 1295 to accept an O'Neill not to his liking, he had the leading chiefs of central and southern Ulster

[1] Orpen, *Normans*, III, p. 284, and 'Earldom of Ulster' in *R.S.A.I.* (1913–15). The De Burgo inquisitions of 1333 show O'Neill, O'Cahan, MacMahon, O'Hanlon, Maguire, and other Ulster chiefs holding by military service of the Earl probably by a long-standing arrangement. (See later, p. 210.)

[2] Tweskard is in Irish 'Tuaisceart', i.e. 'the northern part'. See Curtis, 'Sheriff's Accounts of Tweskard etc', *P.R.I.A.* (1932); also paper by the same on 'The Mandeville-MacQuillan Lords of the Route', ibid. (1938).

[3] For the founding of their state, Clandeboy, see later, pp. 221, 239.

bound to military service or *bonnacht* under him.[1] Whatever happened in the interior, with a sound strategic eye he devoted his energies to extending his Ulster lordship from Coleraine along the whole north coast. The castle of Northburgh, which he built in 1305 in north-east Innishowen, commanded that great peninsula which had never yet been conquered. From the bishop of Derry he secured Fahan and Inch on the eastern shore of Lough Swilly, and in 1311 Edward II granted him the city of Derry itself, so that the whole coast of Ulster from Carlingford round to Fanad was legally his. And in 1299 FitzThomas of Kildare had released to him his claims on Tyrconnell.

THE DUBLIN GOVERNMENT

In this war for the Conquest of Ireland, whole or piecemeal, almost all had been done by the feudal conquistadors and almost nothing by the Crown. But the latter still commanded the general allegiance of the colonists, even the most privileged, and we must turn back to Dublin and the State.

From 1276 to 1312 a long-sustained attempt was made to bring the Land of Ireland under the Crown, or at least as far as the whole occupied area went, and a series of English-born or English-minded viceroys were sent to repair the damage done by Irish justiciars, to organize the King's land and the King's revenues, to diminish the feudal liberties, and make this realm a valuable appanage of the ever needy English Crown.

The first three of these, who ruled from 1276 to 1290, were Robert d'Ufford, Stephen de Fulburn, bishop of Waterford, and John de Sanford, archbishop of Dublin.

In the six years from Michaelmas 1278 to September 1284, over thirty thousand pounds came in to the Irish Exchequer, no mean sum considering how much of Ireland was Gaelic or in liberties.[2]

A large part of this revenue came from the *magna custuma* on wool, wool-fells, and hides. The magnates of England assembled in Parliament in 1275 made a perpetual grant of these export duties, and Edward then induced twelve absentee Irish magnates to sign a recognizance that they had in the English parliament granted the same for their Irish estates. In sending this cool document over, Edward requested his Justiciar to get the assent of the prelates, earls, barons, commons, and merchants of Ireland. Whether any voice was raised in opposition we know not, but at

[1] See later, p. 210, for the inquisitions of 1333.

[2] *C.D.I.*, II, p. 526. The actual sum was £31,253 odd, the highest year being 1282–3, when £6,642 odd came in.

all events the magnates of Ireland, without summoning the rest, made the *custuma* a perpetual grant from Ireland also.

EDWARD'S LAWS EXTENDED TO IRELAND

In legislation, the King acted as if mere royal decree made applicable to Ireland the statutes passed by his English parliament. His writ of 1285 ordered the Statutes of Gloucester, Mortmain, and Westminster to be proclaimed in Ireland.[1] The *Quo Warranto* inquiry which flowed from the Statute of Gloucester was Edward's most effective weapon in England against feudal franchises, regalities, and liberties, and for the emancipation of freemen from manorial jurisdictions.

Edward's governors made a gallant attempt to achieve a like result in Ireland, and had they been backed consistently, the Lordship of Ireland might have escaped its final fate of feudal disintegration. But Edward wavered, fearing to lose Ireland altogether through the resentment of that baronage, absentee or resident, to whom Ireland had been handed for a prey. Thus when in 1282 Fulburn held his court in Bigod's land of Carlow on the ground that the four pleas of the Crown belonged there to the King, the Earl Marshal's protest moved Edward to order his viceroy to do nothing against the Earl's liberties.[2]

John de Sanford, archbishop of Dublin, who governed from 1288 to 1290, had been trained as an itinerant justice. A contemporary record outlines for us the journeys and activities of this episcopal viceroy, now while the medieval lordship of Ireland was at its height.

On the death of Fulborn in July 1288, the Irish Council elected Archbishop Sanford as 'Custos', and in May 1290 they sent a justification and eulogy of his conduct to the King.[3] His first action, they said, had been to survey the King's castles in Connacht and then in September at Kildare to summon the whole service of Ireland, assigning to the seneschals of Kildare, Wexford, Carlow, and Kilkenny each his part of the marches to defend against the Irish. He then went into Desmond and brought Donal 'Roche' MacCarthy to peace, his eyre reaching as far as Cork, Buttevant, and Limerick. The service being ended, he spent nearly six hundred pounds in putting troops into Rheban and other holds,

[1] Berry, *Statutes*, I, pp. 47–77. The Statute of Winchester was sent over in 1307.

[2] *C.D.I.*, II, No. 1919.

[3] *C.D.I.*, III, No. 599 (1288–90). The election of a temporary governor was in accord with the 'Statute of FitzEmpress'.

and created five itinerant justices for county Tipperary, and instructed them on their duties. Then early in 1289 he made another tourn in Ormond and Desmond, and then into Meath and Connacht to inspect the royal castles and raise a force against O'Melaghlin. There he kept the field with one hundred horsemen and four thousand five hundred vassals together with the king of Connacht for twenty-two days. He travelled on this service from Drogheda, through Meath, to Randown, Roscommon, Tuam, and Dunmore, and so back to Maynooth. Again in June and July he made an *iter* round by Limerick, Kilmallock, Buttevant, and Callan. Then in September he led forces against the Irish of Offaly and Leix from Baltinglas and brought them to peace. He held two parliaments in Dublin in that winter and spring, and in May 1290 went against the Irish who had attacked Athlone. He then prepared to survey the state of Ireland, and the deeds of the ministers, so that justice might be done to all, and the King's dignity everywhere maintained. Throughout his eyre he proclaimed that all who complained of the King's ministers or others in Ireland should be before him on certain days. He journeyed from Dublin to Drogheda, Kells, Mullingar, and so to Connacht, to Roscommon and Tuam, and back by Nenagh and Thurles to Tipperary, Limerick, Cork, Waterford, and Ferns, and 'so rectified the King's peace that Ireland thereafter was at peace'. Not often till Tudor times was a viceroy to 'ride' the Anglo-Irish colony again with such honesty, vigour, and efficiency as this, and to cover so much of Ireland.

TWO GREAT QUARRELS

On September 12th, Archbishop Sanford was ordered to give up his office to William de Vescy. Vescy, through his Marshal mother, was lord of Kildare, and set himself to restore this liberty. At once the jealousy of the Anglo-Irish for returning absentees was shown. John FitzThomas especially, whose barony of Naas was held of the honour of Kildare, felt his practical possession of that wide and fertile land threatened by the return of his nominal overlord, one of those 'Englishmen by birth' who easily roused the hostility of the 'English by blood'.

FitzThomas, the future earl of Kildare, had inherited one by one the Connacht and Sligo lands of his race, and the manors of Adare, Croom, and Grene in Limerick; and by the death of his kinsman Gerald, in 1287, became 5th Baron of Offaly and head of the Leinster Geraldines. The De Burgos and the two Geraldines had in fact become 'kings of provinces' after the Irish fashion, and that by direct act of the Crown. As such, boundary disputes and feuds were inevitable between them. Thus FitzThomas's lordship of Sligo was right in the path of that double lordship of Connacht and Ulster which the Red Earl was welding together, and a long and bitter feud between the two went on till 1299. Then, after full investigation by the Crown, the Justiciar, de Wogan, summoned FitzThomas as prime offender before him at Athboy, and the chief of the Geraldines only atoned by surrendering his lands of Lochmask and Sligo, and his claims on Fermanagh and Tyrconnell, to Earl Richard, for compensation in Leinster or Munster.[1]

Eliminated from the north-west, FitzThomas turned his energies to Leinster and to the overthrow of De Vescy. Some violent words attributed to this feudal viceroy at a parliament of Irish barons were made by FitzThomas the basis of a charge of treason against him. According to FitzThomas, De Vescy had accused the King of acting with perfidy and cruelty to Simon de Montfort's party at Kenilworth during the Barons' war of 1265, and had said moreover that the people of Ireland were the most miserable he knew, for, if they willed, they could be great lords and well maintain the lands and franchises of Ireland, notwithstanding the King, 'who is the most perverse and dastardly knight of his realm'. Summoned to Westminster along with his accuser, De Vescy denied the words and offered combat to FitzThomas, who, however, did not appear. The King, however, in 1294 removed De Vescy from the justiciarship and deprived him of Kildare. On De Vescy's death in 1297 a portion of his estates was granted to Walcran de Wellesley, a tenant of the dead man, but finally in 1316 the whole county was made into an earldom for FitzThomas, who was in fact the real owner.[2]

A GREAT STATE VICEROY

All through medieval Irish history the royal government in Ireland was to oscillate between the Anglo-Irish feudal viceroy and the English State viceroy. Of the former type De Vescy is a good example, and no words can better express than his do the feudal view that barons of Ireland owed little to the King and (more curious still) that they owned Ireland. Of the other, the official type of viceroy, no better example is found in our medieval history until Poynings came than Sir John Wogan, who arrived as Justiciar in December 1295. Never again till Tudor times was

[1] *C.D.I.*, IV, Nos. 268, 835; *Just. Rolls*, I, pp. 131, 234, etc.
[2] *C.D.I.*, IV, Nos. 137, 147, 365.

the State apparently so strong as under him in military and financial resources.[1]

Wogan was the greatest viceroy that had yet come to Ireland, and the length of his rule alone marks him out from the usual fleeting representatives of England. He governed the country directly for twelve years till 1307, and again from 1308 to 1312. A man after Edward's own heart, he was indefatigable in his duties, dowered with a practical genius for law and policy, and devoted to the interests of the State. A true Englishman, and a born official, he strove to enforce that centralism by consent which was Edward's great aim in England. The formation of an Anglo-Irish parliament between 1297 and 1310 was his great achievement.

A task which needed infinite tact was that of reconciling the Irish magnates and binding them again to their English sovereign. Both had one object, that of making the Anglo-Irish colony a fruitful source of men, money and supplies for Edward's wars. The consent of the Anglo-Irish was to be sought and their local institutions confirmed and developed; an appeal to which they responded generously.

The *Justiciary Rolls* show Wogan holding the royal pleas throughout Munster and Meath, and as far as Roscommon in Connacht and Ardfert in Kerry. Everywhere he set his face against those liberties and regalities which hampered the power of the State and diminished the 'King's land'. In 1297 at De Vescy's death, he took Kildare into the King's hand, and it was made shireland along with Meath in the parliament of that year. In 1301 the liberty of Wexford was also resumed, but Edward directed it to be restored to Joan de Valence. In 1306 the lordship of Carlow was taken into the King's hand at the death of Roger, the last of the Bigods, but when Edward's second son, Thomas of Brotherton, had the earldom of Norfolk revived in his favour, this Irish lordship went to him and his heirs.

Hampered by his master on one side and Anglo-Irish resistance on the other, Wogan, nevertheless, took many spoils from Irish feudalism, and greatly enlarged the shireland and the demesne of the Crown.[2]

[1] Wogan was great-grandson of Gwgan, one of the royal Welsh race of Brecknock. His son Thomas got a grant of the manor of Rathcoffy in Kildare in 1317 and founded the Irish Wogans.

The total feudal array or knight-service in 1284 was 427 and a fraction. See Bateson in *E.H.R.* (1903), p. 497, *Irish Exchequer Memoranda* (MS., Corpus Christi College, Oxford). Though it was the core of an imposing host, the figures show on what easy terms the Crown had granted Ireland out to the tenants-in-chief.

[2] See *Just. Rolls*, I, pp. 102, 203, 316. In 1302 Ralf Pipard, baron of Ardee, surrendered Donaghmoyne, Ardee, and other estates to the King (*C.D.I.*, V,

Wogan, more than any medieval viceroy, was most fitted to procure the general emancipation of the Irish, but he made no public declaration on the point, in deference to Anglo-Irish feeling, though it often came before him. In a case in 1297 an Englishman had seized the messuage of one Philip Benet, deceased, on the ground that he was a royal betagh (*hibernicus Regis*), whereupon Philip's son Adam declared that his father had been English and had Irish law forced on him by the seneschal of Kildare who then ejected him from his carucate of land. Wogan gave judgment against Adam on the ground that an Irishman (*hibernicus*) had no hereditary right to the land. But the King on appeal declared Adam to be a freeman and confirmed him in English law.

Wogan was technically right if *hibernicus* is taken in the villein sense, not in the racial; in another case, that of Walter Offyn, the verdict was to his credit, and it was during his viceroyalty that the 'rights of the Ostmen of Waterford' were affirmed.[1]

Never again was the medieval lordship of Ireland to exercise such wide control. The whole apparatus of government as then understood in England existed, if only in embryo, in Dublin, and its orders ran through half of Ireland. Sheriffs in ten counties put these orders into effect by issuing directions to the sergeants of cantreds, the units of the Anglo-Irish shires. The office of coroner was already in existence, guardians or justices of the peace were soon to be organized as in England.

THE ANGLO-IRISH PARLIAMENT

At war with Welsh, Scots, and French, Edward needed all the help he could get from Ireland, and in 1295 instructed Wogan to raise ten thousand men there. So great a demand had to be submitted to a full colonial assembly and in 1297 Wogan summoned to Dublin a more representative body than had ever yet come together. The terms of his summons are given thus:

> 'The Justiciar, by common council of the King in this land, in order to establish peace more firmly, ordained and decreed a general parliament for this day. And orders were given to archbishops, bishops, abbots and priors, whose presence was necessary for this purpose, also to earls, barons, and other

Nos. 149, 167). Pipard could not defend these outposts against the Irish, and Oriel soon came to be distinguished as 'Irish Oriel' (Monaghan of the MacMahons) and 'English Oriel', i.e. Louth.

[1] *Just. Rolls*, I, pp. 123, 271) and *Mem. de Parliamento* (*R.S.*), p. 246. For the case of Offyn see earlier, p. 104, also that of Walter O'Tothel, p. 110. An *hibernicus Regis* was a serf on the royal demesne. For the rights of the Ostmen of Waterford see earlier, p. 106.

optimates, viz. to each individually. Also orders were given to the sheriffs of Dublin, Louth, Kildare, Waterford, Tipperary, Cork, Limerick, Kerry, and Roscommon, and likewise to the seneschals of the liberties of Meath, Wexford, Carlow, Kilkenny, and Ulster, that each of them personally in his full county court, or in the full court of his liberty, by assent of the county or liberty, should cause to be elected two of the better men of the shire or liberty in order to be here, having full power of the whole community, and that each sheriff and seneschal shall be here in his own person.'

So was begun the representative parliament of the English in Ireland, but in limited fashion, and not taking its final shape till the next century, in 1372.[1]

This one of 1297 showed the loyal, middle-class, anti-Gaelic, and anti-feudal spirit which under the direction of the viceroy and Council so many of its successors were to show. One of its acts declared that colonists who do not wish to be treated as Irish must refrain from wearing Irish garb and the long locks of the Irish, otherwise they will be taken for Irish and treated as such—a significant phrase.

Another act against absentees, another forbidding the keeping of kerns, another ordering every holder of twenty plowlands to keep horse and armour for the defence of the State, showed the same spirit. In a similar mood, this parliament directed that Ulster, Kildare, and Meath should henceforth be reckoned as counties, a step which greatly increased the area of common law at the expense of the feudal liberties.[2] The famous phrase 'the degenerate English' is for the first time used as a description of the remoter Anglo-Irish who were already becoming hibernicized.

In 1300, however, this great viceroy, pressed hard by his royal

[1] We do not hear of any Irish chiefs being summoned among these 'optimates'. Yet they did attend the Justiciars and come to local councils, e.g. in 1302 Genville, lord of Trim, summoned 126 nobles to discuss the expedition to Scotland, of whom two, Aedh O'Connor and Donal O'Neill, were Irish (*Lib. Mun.*, I, pt. IV, p. 160). Since the first edition of this book (1924) much has been written and many new views advanced on the origins of Parliament in England. For the Irish one see M. V. Clarke, 'Irish Parliaments in the reign of Edward II' (*Trans. Royal Hist. Soc.*, 1926), and 'Viceroyalty of William of Windsor', *P.R.I.A.* (1932); also Richardson and Sayles, 'Irish Parliaments of Edward I', *P.R.I.A.* (1929).

[2] For an account of the parliament of 1297 see *Miscell. Irish Archaeological Soc.* (1846), based on a Latin record in the *Black Book of Christchurch*; also Berry, *Statutes of Ireland*, I, pp. 195–213. In Act xi 'degenerate English' is applied to the Norman-English of the Marches.

Though Meath was made a shire with Kells as capital town, it must be noted that Trim also remained a liberty as far as the rights and title of the Genville family and next heirs are concerned.

master for Irish aid, reverted to the older method of getting money votes or passing local measures in local or county assemblies. He first issued writs for a parliament at Easter in Dublin, but before it met he went to Drogheda and induced the mayor and commons there to make a local grant. Parliament itself meeting without spokesmen for the towns, the magnates and knights excused themselves from paying the subsidy, and said to Wogan: 'Go through the counties making your own bargain, and we will prevail on the commons of the same to consent and will ourselves contribute.'

Armed with this *carte blanche*, the Justiciar proceeded to Trim and thence through Munster, raising £2,361 6*s*. 8*d*. in all from the counties, liberties, church-lands, and towns of Ireland.[1] But the moral was obvious that the towns and merchant classes should be consulted in a general, not a particular, assembly. Wogan, in short, had interested the English of Ireland in politics and they soon realized the value to themselves and the dignity of them.

So in February 1310 was held at Kilkenny a more advanced parliament. Wogan called together eighty-eight magnates, summoned each by writ, two knights of each shire, and two members from each of certain towns, 'having full power on behalf of the said communities to parley, treat, and ordain with the Justiciar, the council and the nobles of the land, upon certain matters'.[2]

The tone of this assembly and others under Edward II followed that anti-Irish and anti-feudal note which was struck in 1297. The parliament of 1310 enacted that 'no mere Irishman (*nullus merus hibernicus*) shall be received into a religious order among the English in the land of peace in any part of Ireland'. The phrase 'mere Irishman' (i.e. pure-blooded, or native Irishman) was to become as famous as 'degenerate English'.[3] In 1323 we find the commons opposing the four earls and demanding that the grandees shall apprehend all felons of their surnames and adherence before parliament shall next meet.

THE SCOTTISH WAR

Wogan had now successfully enlisted the Anglo-Irish for the Crown. The full resources of Ireland in men, money, and ships

[1] *Just. Rolls*, I, p. 304; cf. Appendix III on the Towns. As an instance of local agreements, on February 2nd (38 Hen. III), writs were sent to the magnates and prelates, knights and freeholders of every county, asking for aid in the Gascon war, and a fortnight later to the freemen, citizens, and burgesses asking them to assist the Justiciar. In July 1253 Henry received four thousand pounds of Irish money.

[2] The writs for this parliament are the earliest extant for Irish parliaments. The published Statutes begin also with this date (Berry, *Statutes of Ireland*).

[3] But see for the prompt annulment of this statute, p. 180; and Macinerney, *History of the Irish Dominicans*, p. 563.

were used against the Scots, whose war of independence was led first by Wallace and then by Robert Bruce. Reconciled by Wogan, the earl of Ulster, Theobald Butler, and John FitzThomas joined Edward at Roxboro in May 1296, with over three thousand well-appointed horse, archers, and men-at-arms. In 1301 Wogan was ordered to come with all the lieges of Ireland, and royal letters for aid were sent to a hundred and eighty Irish magnates, including O'Connor, O'Neill, O'Brien, MacCarthy, and seventeen other Gaelic princes. From 1302 to 1306 De Burgo and FitzThomas did constant good service in Scotland. At the same time huge supplies for the armies which fought to extinguish the nationality of Scotland were constantly demanded from Ireland, and providing them became one of Wogan's chief cares.[1]

But this draining of Anglo-Irish wealth was a fatal error. The revenues were unprofitably consumed in a wicked and wasteful war. The Anglo-Irish baronage, though they owed foreign service, and though part of it was paid for, contracted crushing debts in the service of the Crown. The demands of the Crown diverted them from their lordships and uncompleted conquest. Moreover, the Scottish war of independence had its reverberation among the Irish Celts, and ere long the Anglo-Irish were bitterly to regret having joined in the war against Scottish rights.

WOGAN'S LAST YEARS

The reign of Edward I ended on July 1st 1307. Wogan had filled twelve years of that reign with a gallant attempt to make Ireland a second realm for his master. He had for the time reconciled the Norman-Irish with one another and with the Crown, brought the semi-independent towns into the general unity, given the colony something of the dignity of a nation, and enlarged the area of the common law.

There still seemed to be a chance that all the elements of a real monarchy might be drawn finally into one, the nobles made obedient, and the island anglicized in speech, law, and institutions from sea to sea. But the reign of the contemptible Edward II was to quench these prospects.

Indeed the great Edward I had displayed little in Ireland of the realm-making and legislating qualities he showed in England. He might well have secured an official and general recognition of 'English law and liberty' for the Irish; this was not possible for

[1] *C.D.I.*, IV, pp. 19, 358, for the summons to magnates. For Irish troops in Scotland see Stevenson, *Docs. illustr. History of Scotland*, II, p. 124, and *C.D.I.*, I, p. 151. For the numerous demands in kind see Gilbert's *Hist. and Mun. Docs.*, *passim* from 1280 to 1315.

all Ireland perhaps, but it *was* possible for the native race in all the occupied areas. His attitude towards the remaining Gaelic *reguli* was less definite and conciliatory than his father's had been. Perhaps he is hardly to be blamed for renewing to Thomas Fitz-Maurice in 1292 the grant in fee of Desmond made in 1259, since that was an hereditary grant. But in conveying to Thomas de Clare the land of Thomond he was certainly unjust to the O'Briens, who from 1194 to 1276 had displayed a remarkable tradition of compliance towards English rule. The hope, indeed, was now fast fading that the greater Irish might be made hereditary tenants under the Crown in such a way that they might finally have blended in the ranks of the Anglo-Irish tenants-in-chief. The Gaelic revival was now at hand, and the chiefs themselves when they had the open choice preferred to rebuild their old kingships in local autonomy.

In fact also those Anglo-Norman 'First Families' who believed they had conquered, and ought to rule, Ireland and had only a conditional loyalty to England, were left as great as ever, and steadily became less English, while the failure to bring the Irish under the law was evident. In his latter years Wogan had to unfurl the royal banner against English rebels on the one hand and Irish enemies on the other, and of the two the English rebels were the more dangerous to the State. In June 1308 the confederated clans of Wicklow burned the border fortress of Castlekevin, and Wogan, marching against them, was overthrown near Glenmalure with heavy loss. Four years after, in 1312, marching with the royal service against Robert de Verdun, a rebellious baron, Wogan was again 'miserably overthrown'. Such were the difficulties of the strongest of viceroys even when the English lordship was at its height.

CHAPTER X

EDWARD II AND EDWARD BRUCE, 1307–1327

SIR JOHN DE WOGAN continued as Justiciar of Ireland for the five years of the new reign in which one of England's greatest kings was succeeded by one of her worst. His rule indeed was interrupted for one year, June 1308 to July 1309, when Piers Gaveston came over as the King's Lieutenant.[1] This worthless minion of the new King certainly enlivened Dublin for a year with a gay court, but did nothing else that was memorable, and after him Wogan ruled till 1312.[2] His main task was to enlist the Anglo-Irish nobles in the war against Robert Bruce, whom his party had crowned King of Scots at Scone in 1306. These levies were commanded by the Red Earl of Ulster, but he must have felt little enthusiasm for the war, seeing that his daughter Elizabeth had in 1302 married Robert Bruce himself.

Never again were the Anglo-Irish magnates to be at once so powerful, numerous, and loyal. The power of the Red Earl in three provinces was almost kingly. In Kildare the senior line of the Geraldines was represented by the vigorous John FitzThomas, who made Maynooth the seat of his race and united in himself all the branches of his family. His kinsman Maurice FitzThomas succeeded his father as lord of Desmond and Decies in 1299. Edmund Butler, who inherited from his brother Theobald in 1299, proved himself to be the first prominent, capable, and long-lived man of his race, which since its founder had shown a tendency to die out. In the liberty of Trim the aged De Genville still was lord and in the Lochsewdy half of Meath in 1309 Theobald (II) de Verdun succeeded his father, the first Theobald.

ROGER MORTIMER AND THE ABSENTEES

The young Roger Mortimer, lord of Wigmore in Montgomery, who arrived in Ireland in 1308, though a newcomer, was by law heir to a great Irish heritage. He was married to Joan, granddaughter and heiress of Geoffrey de Genville, and the latter, retiring in his old age into a monastery, left the lordship of Trim

[1] 'King's (or Lord) Lieutenant' (*locum tenens Regis*), of which this seems the first instance, was a title implying higher and more emergency powers than that of Justiciar.

[2] It was Wogan who carried out the Irish part of the suppression of the Templars. (See Wood, 'The Templars in Ireland', *P.R.I.A.*, 1906–7.)

to Roger *iure uxoris suae*. The latter's grandfather, also Roger, had married Maud de Braose, one of the heiresses of Leinster; this lady, dying in 1301, had left to her grandson, the present Roger, the lordship of Leix.

The return of so great an absentee, heir to two lordships according to the feudal law of property, was regarded with jealous eyes by the established Anglo-Irish families, just as the creation of De Clare as lord of Thomond found no favour with the existing lords.

THE ANGLO–IRISH AND MALE SUCCESSION

It now became a standing fear with the 'Conquest Families' that at any moment men whom they regarded as foreigners would return to claim Irish lordships which they did little but draw rents from, or which neighbouring lords had quietly appropriated. There was also a second grievance in the feudal law by which Anglo-Irish heiresses could carry their fiefs to English and absentee husbands, even though brothers, nephews, and kinsmen of the late lord survived. To this the Normans in Ireland opposed the custom of tail male. The Gaelic law barred women from lordship, and did not admit claims through females; according to an Irish maxim, 'a land without a lord is a dead land'. The Norman-Irish soon adopted the native tradition of purely male succession, so convenient for them and essential to the warlike conditions of Ireland. Any baron of Ireland might leave only a daughter, but there were seldom wanting collateral males of the family to defy the English law by which a whole lordship could pass away from the men of a race who boasted that they had originally conquered it with the sword.

Thus, when Meath was divided in 1241 between the daughters of Earl Walter, the transaction was resented by the junior branch of the Lacys of Rathwire, who descended from Robert, a brother of the first Hugh de Lacy. They thought Meath should have been theirs, and did so again in 1308 when Roger Mortimer and Theobald de Verdun divided the earldom once more.

Even the claims of the latter were resisted by a junior branch of the surname, though De Verdun himself was one of the original Anglo-Irish. The junior and more Irish stocks of great feudal families were beginning to resent the head lordships even of their own race, and any great lord who of necessity had to keep up his English and official side had to keep in mind 'those Irish country cousins' who before long in many cases proved fatal to the senior stock.

This defiance of feudal law by kinsmen, where it could be safely done, was to become a common practice, and to spread to the highest families. It led of necessity to a form of Irish chieftainship, for all the near male kinsmen of a lord would be regarded as capable of succeeding him if necessary, and thus would resemble the *rigdomnas* of Irish law, while the reigning lord would be the *capitaneus nacionis suae.*

THE RACE WAR

The occupation of the Anglo-Irish colony with the Scottish war undoubtedly aided the native resurgence. Though this lacked cohesion and direction, it is clear that a widespread revolt was preparing among the native race. The spirit of the race war had entered into the Church itself. Already in 1297 the bishops of Armagh and Down had been accused of refusing to receive clerics of English blood. The native bishops and abbots resented the influx of men alien in language and sympathy, and the native people resented the appointment of foreign prelates who were little better than officials. On the other hand, the English party feared the irishizing of the Church that would follow upon the influx of natives into the higher offices and of native monks into abbeys in the English land.

The attitude of some of the mendicant orders was particularly bold, and in 1299 the bishop of Kildare had to fulminate against certain friars 'who in the Irish language spread the seeds of rebellion'.[1] The remedy seemed to be the exclusion of Irishmen from the English abbeys, and in February 1310 the parliament at Kilkenny enacted that no 'mere Irishman' should be received into any religious house among the English. But Wogan revoked this unchristian act in May that year at the request of Walter Jorz (or Joyce), archbishop of Armagh, and some magnates, and by order of the King.[2]

The fault, however, was not all on the English side, and the oldest and chief Cistercian abbey in Ireland reflected the racial feud. In 1297 Edward I commanded the abbot of Mellifont to see that half of the monks in houses under him should be of English race. In 1306 he had the temporalities of the abbey seized on the ground that the brothers were mere Irish. In 1322 complaint was made that the monks would only admit those who swore that they were not of English race. The heads of the order in England had to condemn such a damnable division wherever practised, and to warn the Cistercian abbots of Ireland,

[1] *C.D.I.*, IV, No. 2035. [2] See for this excluding act, p. 175.

of whom grievous complaints had been made, that they should indifferently admit persons of all nations.[1]

THE WAR IN THE MARCHES

The borderlands between Irish and English, abundant in great woods, boglands, and mountains, which were called 'the Marches', were a constant battleground between the unyielding chiefs and the warlike Normans. One of the most active of the latter was Piers de Bermingham, baron of Tethmoy in Kildare, and one of his most notorious exploits was the treacherous murder of the O'Connors of Offaly, old neighbours and enemies. He invited the chief of this sept with his headmen to celebrate the feast of Holy Trinity with him at his castle of Carrick in Carbery, and there he had his unarmed and unsuspecting guests massacred on June 13th 1305. Murchertach, the O'Connor Faly, two of his brothers, and twenty-nine of his chief men were murdered and their heads sent to Dublin, where the government richly rewarded Sir Piers.[2] That such a slaughter failed to extinguish the O'Connor dynasty illustrates one of the insuperable difficulties of a complete conquest. Such a clearance might have extinguished the Butlers or other limited feudal stock, but as long as an Irish king had a full complement of 'royal heirs', a complete failure in the succession was next to impossible.

A great Irish confederacy answered such deeds as this. In 1305 Ballymore, Athy, and other strongholds of the English on the Barrow and the south marches of Dublin were burned, and 'great war arose, and Irishmen came to help the Irish of Leinster from all parts of Ireland'. Then in 1311, 'a great army assembled out of Leinster to expulse and drive away the Berns and Toles out of Glandelor (Glenmalure) and other strong places, and Sir Edmund Butler in Lent following did overcome O'Brene in Glendelore and force him to yield'.[3]

THE BRUCE INVASION, 1315–1318

The wise statesman Wogan left the Irish stage in August 1312, and after him everything worked towards a great catastrophe for the lordship of Ireland. His last public service was an expedition

[1] Macinerney, *Hist. of the Irish Dominicans*, pp. 563–75 *passim*.

[2] See *Clyn*, *Book of Howth*, *Laud Annals*, and *A.F.M.* *Just. Rolls*, II, p. 82: it is agreed by the Justiciar Wogan, and the whole Council in presence of the earl of Ulster that Piers have one hundred pounds for decapitation of the O'Connors.

[3] *Laud Annals*, pp. 333–42 *passim*, and *Book of Howth*.

against Robert de Verdun of Louth, who was in arms over the division of Meath. Wogan was defeated and the episode was most significant. Inured to war and nursed in the spirit of feuds, the Anglo-Irish of the *petite noblesse* did not hesitate to oppose the army of the State under the King's viceroy himself and inflict a shameful defeat upon him.

Feudal and personal aims were stamped over all the actions of that colonial nobility which ruled Ireland, and the test of their loyalty to the Crown and to one another was now to come. The forces of Anglo-Ireland were summoned to Scotland once more, in March 1314, but in vain. Bannockburn was fought on June 24th; and the Scots next carried the war into Ireland.

Among the proud nobles who fell on Edward's side in the battle that set Scotland free for three centuries was a great Irish absentee and titular lord, Gilbert de Clare, earl of Gloucester and lord of Kilkenny.[1] Again heiresses, his three sisters, divided a great inheritance which went to their husbands, Hugh le Despenser, Hugh d'Audeley, and Roger d'Amory. The absentee lordship of Kilkenny still further disintegrated, and before eighty years a resident Irish magnate, James Butler, already earl of Ormond, was to become proprietor also of this great land of Ossory.

The young Edward Bruce had played a great part in the war of independence, and Robert looked round to find a crown for this brother, whose warlike and aspiring character might be dangerous if pent up at home.

A wide field for intrigue lay open in Ireland and Wales. The Bruces knew something of Ireland, for Robert was son-in-law of the earl of Ulster, and had in the winter of 1306–7 sought refuge in Rathlin, where the Clan Sorley of Kintyre and John Byset of the Glens protected him, and the Earl must have connived. Robert, moreover, had inherited the earldom of Carrick from his mother, the granddaughter of Duncan 'MacUchtred'. This title he now passed on to Edward, and the latter had thus a favourable ground from which to invade Ulster, and ancestral claims along the Antrim coast.

The Irish chiefs had heard with joy the triumphs of the Scots. Their *literati* could easily show that the Bruces on the female side went back through the old Scottish kings to Fergus MacErc and the Milesian kings of Erin and Alban. Within living memory at the coronation of Alexander III at Scone in 1249 a Highlandman,

[1] With this Gilbert, who died *sine prole*, ended the great house and name of De Clare which claimed descent from an illegitimate son of Richard the Fearless, duke of Normandy, and of which Strongbow had been a junior scion. The family of De Clare in Thomond ended in 1321.

as was customary, recited a Gaelic pedigree of the king going back to 'Ibar (Eibhir) the first of the Scots'. Scotland was a land of many races, Normans, Angles, Picts, Gaels, and Britons of Strathclyde. The *lingua Scotica* still meant the common Gaelic of both countries; this was the language of all northern and western Scotland, and the Anglian dialect of English, though destined to triumph as 'broad Scots', was as yet confined to the south-east.[1]

Familiar already with the mixed racial features of their own country, the Bruces were prepared for a similar task in Ireland. In the campaign which ended at Bannockburn the heads of the Clann Somhairle had been gallant allies, and the Irish looked on these 'Lords of the Isles' as heroes of their own race.

The enterprise of the Bruces was not undertaken, we may believe, without an Irish invitation. Donal O'Neill, now king of Tyrone, was an enemy of the earl of Ulster, and son of the 'Brian of Down' who in 1260 had attempted to revive the High kingship. He was now ready to surrender his hereditary claim to the kingdom of Ireland to the Norman-Gaelic brother of the king of Scots. In fact, Edward Bruce was a feudal-minded person with merely a Milesian strain in him, as had many of the claimants to the Scottish throne; he spoke French and probably English but it is doubtful if any of his speech was Gaelic, and the Gaelic note in his campaign was a piece of propaganda.

But it was good propaganda, even if it only carried war into the enemy's country for a few years, and the Bruces in fact planned a general revolt of the Celtic race everywhere against the English.[2] The feuds and discontents of the Anglo-Irish offered further opportunities. In Meath the Lacys of Rathwire were in arms against the Mortimer claim, and the earl of Ulster had taken up their cause and knighted their two chiefs, Walter and Hugh, at Trim in 1308. Emboldened by this powerful patronage, they

[1] For the diffusion of Gaelic in Scotland see R. S. Rait, *Relations between England and Scotland, 500–1707*. Barbour's *Bruce* (written in 1375) is the beginning of the Scottish contribution to English literature; he wrote it, as he says, in 'Inglis'. Fordun (d. *circa* 1394) in his Latin work, *Scotichronicon*, divides the Scots as speaking either the *lingua Scotica* or the *lingua Teutonica*, the latter being English. It is he who describes the *Scotus montanus* as retailing Alexander's descent *Scoticis verbis*.

[2] Harris, *Collect.*, I, p. 395 (1310): the King's letters 'pro adhaerentibus Roberti de Brus in Anglia, Hibernia et Wallia arrestandis', speaks of Bruce's adherents in Man. According to Powell, *History of Wales*, pp. 311–12, Sir Gruffydd Llwyd urged the union of the 'Albanian Scots' with the Britons against the Saxons, and Edward Bruce, then in Ireland, agreed to invade Wales on condition he should have such lordship over the Welsh 'as your prince [the last Llewellyn] formerly most fully used to exercise'. Gruffydd revolted, but was defeated by an English army and imprisoned in Rhuddlan castle.

claimed all Meath, and went so far as to besiege the younger Theobald de Verdun in Athlone castle in 1309 and take him prisoner. The junior Verduns seized on Ardee and the lordship of Louth, the inheritance of the elder Theobald, at his death in 1309, and went even further than the Lacys by defeating the viceroy Wogan himself in 1312. When the Scottish invasion occurred, the Lacys were in fact refugees from Meath, whence Sir John Bermingham, of the Athenry family, had by Government orders expelled them, but a whole army of themselves and their adherents was in the field.

In Ulster the grievances of the Bysets provided the Bruces with another ally who could secure the Antrim landing-place for them. A Scottish victory promised not only the recovery of their kingdom for Irish chiefs but also Meath for the Lacys, Louth for the junior Verduns, and the lordship of the Glens for the Bysets.[1]

When it became evident that an invasion of Ireland was afoot, Edward II sent as a special envoy to Ireland, John Hotham, later bishop of Ely, to discuss the affairs of the realm with the magnates. In March 1315 he appointed Edmund Butler as Justiciar, and addressed general letters of credence to the prelates, nobles, and commons of Ireland, and particular ones to twenty-two Gaelic chiefs and sixty-three bishops, abbots, lords, and town magistrates, enjoining on them to hear and assist the Justiciar, and his fellow-officers. But the decisive interval had been ill spent, and the storm now burst on an unprepared State.

THE BRUCE INVASION

On May 25th 1315 Edward Bruce landed in Larne harbour (then called Olderfleet) with six thousand fighting-men. With him were the earl of Moray and many other Scots nobles, the Clann Somhairle chiefs, and Sir John Byset. It was a well

[1] For the earlier Bysets see earlier, p. 137. Walter Byset, a Scotsman of Galloway, had been enfeoffed by Hugh de Lacy, earl of Ulster, in Rathlin and lands about Glenarm. When John Byset died in 1260 without heirs male his land by law went to heiresses, but his collateral kinsmen held on to the lands, became known as MacEoin, and were lords there till 1400, when their heiress, Margery, married John MacDonnell of the Isles. As for Lacys and Verduns: in July 1312 Wogan was 'miserably overthrown' by Robert and Nicholas de Verdun and their accomplices (*Laud Annals*). The death of Theobald the elder in 1309 had roused the hopes of his Irish cousins, who seized Ardee and the lordship of Louth, and in 1312 defeated a force of colonists who had the Justiciar's commission, near Ardee. (See for the case of the Verduns and Lacys, 1312–17, *Chart. St. Mary's*, II, app. ii and iii.) According to their enemy Mortimer, the Lacys were the villains of the piece; they themselves denied any real complicity with Edward Bruce, but clearly they and the Verduns had, since 1308, resisted by arms the legal transference of Irish property to the heirs-at-law.

mixed Norman-Scottish-Gaelic force, typical of the whole adventure.

Before long a large part of Ireland was for the Scots, or stood neutral, prepared for their triumph. 'There adhered to them,' says Clyn, 'while they were in Ireland, almost all the Irish of the land, and few kept their faith and loyalty.'[1]

According to a complaint made later by Edward II to the Pope, 'the prelates of the Irish race do not cease to provoke against us the spirit of the people', and many of the native friars and secular clergy openly incited the Irish to renounce allegiance to England.[2]

Bruce's first triumph was an easy one over the local levies of the Ulster colonists under Mandeville and Logan, whereupon Donal O'Neill, O'Cathain, and four other Ulster chiefs renounced their allegiance to the Earl and joined the Scots. The invading army was one of tried veterans, no colonial force could stand against them, and time and time again did the mail-clad Scots roll over the light armies of the colony. Their Irish allies with their mobility and knowledge of the country made excellent auxiliaries, though the Scots chronicler accuses some of them of treachery, and of waiting to see which of the combatants was like to prevail.

On the other side the feuds and divisions of the colonial magnates fatally weakened their cause, and the English government sent no troops over till the end of 1316.

Dundalk was the first considerable town to fall to Bruce on June 29th 1315, but Carrickfergus, though closely besieged, held out against him for over a year.

The earl of Ulster was now in Connacht, from whence he raised a large army and marched against Bruce. The Scots fell

[1] That Clyn does not exaggerate is shown by the fact that Dermot MacCarthy of Desmond had to be pardoned after the Bruce invasion, and it is clear that Ulster, Thomond, Connacht, Meath, and Leinster joined in the revolt. The Scottish side of the Bruce episode is told in Barbour's *Bruce* (ed. Skeat) and Fordun's *Scotichronicon* (ed. Hearne). For the native Irish side see *Ann. L. Cé*, *Ann. Ult.*, etc., but contemporary Irish evidence is scanty. The *Cath Fhochairte* ('Battle of Faughart'), ed. and trans. by H. Morris in *Louth Arch. Soc.*, vol. I, represents a modernized form of an old Gaelic account of the invasion. (See H. Wood, 'Letter of Fineen MacCarthy', *P.R.I.A.*, in which the extent of the Irish federation to bring in Bruce is newly discussed.)

[2] In August 1316 King Edward wrote to the general of the Friars Minor in Ireland complaining that some friars were stirring up the lay Irish to rebellion. In April 1317 John XXII wrote to the archbishops of Dublin and Cashel that friars of the mendicant orders and many rectors, etc. of parish churches in Ireland labour to rouse the Irish people to renounce fealty and impugn the royal rights (*Foedera*, III, p. 295, and *Facs. Nat. MSS.*, III, plate xii). In the same year the Pope excommunicated Edward Bruce and all his adherents in Ireland, 'and all friars minor who preach rebellion' (*Foedera*, II, p. 643, and *Cal. Pap. Reg.* (1305–42), pp. 127–38 and *passim*).

back and fought their first great battle at Connor in Antrim on September 10th 1315. The Red Earl was totally defeated but escaped from the fight, while his cousin William 'Liath' (the Grey), son of William Oge, was taken and sent captive to Scotland.

Edward then invaded Meath, where Roger Mortimer, now present in his lordship of Trim, gave him battle, but was defeated at Kells, early in December, owing, it is said, to the treachery of Walter and Hugh de Lacy. The two last now openly joined Bruce, guided him into the midlands, and brought over to his standard no less than seventy of the chief gentry of Meath and four Gaelic chiefs, of whom O'Melaghlin represented the ancient kings of that province.

After spending Christmas at Lochsewdy, Bruce then invaded Kildare, and at Sketherys, near Ardscull, overthrew the royal forces under Edmund Butler and John FitzThomas on January 26th 1316. But to secure the north was his first essential, and he retired to Carrickfergus. The siege of this place became a test of strength. The Dublin government sent fifteen shiploads of men to it, and the garrison of the citadel, though their commander, Thomas de Mandeville, fell, beat off the determined attack of the Scots on Easter Eve, April 10th.

At least Edward Bruce had made good his claim to the monarchy of Ireland. The Ulster princes urged him to take the crown; Donal O'Neill renounced in his favour his ancient hereditary right; and Edward was crowned King of Ireland in the open air on the hill of Knocknemelan near Dundalk, on May Day, 1316, in the presence of many Irish allies.[1]

TWO EARLDOMS CREATED

The consternation among the Irish magnates was naturally great. Each of them boasted he alone could raise an army 'sufficient in itself to subdue the Scots', but they could in fact neither win nor unite. Yet the feeble government of Edward II threw the saving of the State upon them. In February 1316 Hotham brought the ten chief magnates together in Dublin, and made them swear 'in life and death to hold with the king of England, to make peace in the land, and destroy the Scots'. If the other magnates would not swear to this, they were to be held enemies of the King. The greatest of them all, Richard, earl of Ulster, was absent, but after the fall of Carrickfergus in September

[1] *Ann. L. Cé*: 'The Gaedhil of Ireland proclaimed him king of Erin.' The northern Irishmen gave substantial help, and when the two Bruces marched against Dublin in the early spring of 1317 they had with them the Irish 'army of Ulster'.

1316 the nobles met again to swear to die for their lord the king of England, and this time De Burgo was with them.

To encourage their loyalty, Edmund Butler was created earl of Carrick in September 1315, and in April 1316 John FitzThomas was made earl of Kildare, an honour which he did not long enjoy, for he died in September of that year.[1] In July 1316 Theobald (II) de Verdun died and, though his brother Milo continued the main line of the family, the lordship of Lochsewdy lapsed with Theobald, who left only an heiress.[2]

Meanwhile an almost universal rising of the native people swept the country. A confederacy of O'Tooles, O'Byrnes, and the hibernicized Harolds and Archbolds, raided the Wicklow coast from Arklow to Bray. In the north-west, Aedh O'Donnell seized the opportunity to level De Burgo's castle of Sligo and enforce his supremacy there. Rory, son of Donal O'Connor, surrendered to O'Donnell the lordship of Carbery in Sligo, which had been Fitzgerald and then De Burgo property. O'Donnell now installed this O'Connor, sprung from Brian of Leyney, as his vassal in Carbery, and his family became known as O'Connor Sligo.

THE BATTLE OF ATHENRY

Edward Bruce's immediate plan was to encourage the native kings to throw off the English yoke and recover with his aid their former kingdoms. For this plan, Connacht seemed to offer the best prospect.

The house of Cathal Crovderg had kept the kingship till 1309, when Aedh son of Eoghan, who had ruled since 1293, died. But ever since Aedh of Athankip a *derb-fine* war had rent the royal race asunder. Aedh mac Eoghain was slain by his rival Aedh the Brefnian, who represented the line of Murchertach Muimhneach, brother of Cathal Crovderg. He ruled a year and then was slain by Seonac Mac Uidhilin, commander of his bodyguard, who under his Norman name was a Mandeville of Antrim, taking to the profession of a mercenary soldier. The Brefnian's brother Rory then claimed the kingship, but Aedh, son of Eoghan, had left two sons, Felim and Turloch, and the elder of these, a youth

[1] Horace Round in *Dict. Nat. Biog.* says the patent failed to make Edmund's issue earls of Carrick; later, however, his son James, marrying in 1327 Eleanor de Bohun, granddaughter of Edward I, became hereditary earl of Ormond.

[2] Namely Joan (d. 1334), who married Thomas, Lord Furnival. Their daughter and heiress, Joan Furnival, married Thomas de Neville, and their daughter and heiress, Maud Neville, married John Talbot, the famous earl of Shrewsbury, who thus had a claim to Westmeath.

of twenty, was in 1310 elected king by the MacDermot of Moylurg, hereditary 'kingmaker' of Connacht.

When Richard de Burgo marched northwards on the campaign which ended at Connor, the young Felim accompanied the lord of Connacht, but before the battle Bruce sent secret messages to O'Connor, offering him, if he would desert the Earl, the undivided sovereignty of Connacht. Felim no longer waited for the battle, but returned home, excusing himself to De Burgo on the ground that his interests there were in danger from his rival Rory. But the crafty Bruce had also communicated with Rory, urging him to attack the Englishry of Connacht but to spare Felim. Thus encouraged, Rory devastated Athlone and other strongholds of the English, and was inaugurated in due fashion at Carn Fraoich.

When Earl Richard got back to Connacht, he found Rory in full possession, and the annals of Loch Cé describe how the Earl entertained at once four disinherited chieftains, Felim O'Connor, Murchertach O'Brien, Maelruana MacDermot, captain of Felim's host, and Gilbert O'Kelly of Hy Many. 'But he could do nothing for them, for during this year he was himself a wanderer through Erin, without sway of power.'

Early next year, Felim summoned his adherents and finally met his rival Rory at Móin-coinnedha and slew him in battle there in March 1316. He then 'assumed the sovereignty of Connacht from Assaroe to Slieve Aughty', and aspired to banish the English out of the whole province. But they were still the master race, and William 'Liath' de Burgo, returning ransomed from Scotland, mustered the Berminghams of Athenry and all the available Englishry of Connacht and Meath. On the other hand, a great native army flocked to O'Connor's banner, and Donnchad O'Brien, O'Melaghlin of Meath, O'Ruairc of Brefni, Maghnus, son of Donal O'Connor, Tanist of Connacht, and Taig O'Kelly of Hy Many, with many other lords of the centre and west, came together in aid of Felim.

The two armies met close by Richard de Bermingham's town of Athenry, Felim commanding the one side, and William de Burgo and Bermingham the other, on August 10th 1316. After enduring a whole day the terrible losses inflicted by the English archery and horse, the Irish were totally defeated, but the conquerors themselves acknowledged that never since the Conquest had a native army fought so long and so well. The young Felim, 'king of Connacht, and heir to the sovereignty of Erin, from whom the Gaels expected more than from any man of his time', was slain with his standard-bearer, O'Devlin, beneath the royal banner.

Taig O'Kelly and fifty-six other chiefs also fell in the front of the battle, and the losses among the native ranks bore terrible witness to their stubborn courage.[1]

The victors, it is said, walled Athenry out of the profits of the arms and armour taken from the bodies of the fallen enemy; evidently then the Irish were no longer the 'naked men' of former battles.

So was quenched the greatest hope for a century of restoring a Gaelic kingdom. The defeat and death of Felim at once restored De Burgo's lordship; the Earl set up a tame chief, Cathal, son of Donal, and the O'Connor 'kingdom of Connacht' was henceforth but an empty name.

THE TWO BRUCES IN IRELAND, 1317

Carrickfergus finally fell to the Scots in September 1316 and Robert Bruce arrived to aid the new king of Ireland. In January 1317 the two brothers, with a huge army which included the Ulster Irish, invaded the midlands, marching to Slane and burning and devastating in the true way of medieval war, so that their ravages, combined with the poor harvests of those years, soon brought about a famine and pestilence, which disheartened even their allies.

From Slane the two kings marched on Dublin, and for a time English rule seemed lost. But the citizens of Dublin by their unaided efforts saved the State. The earl of Ulster, though commander-in-chief, had sought refuge in the city from the march of the Scots, and was suspected of wishing to surrender the city. The mayor, Robert Nottingham, therefore boldly arrested him and imprisoned him in the castle on February 21st 1317. Already the Scots were at Castleknock, four miles west of Dublin, and Edward Bruce, who had no artillery to reduce so strong a town and castle, halted in the hope that the Earl or other partisans would deliver the capital to him. But the citizens organized their own defence, burned Thomas Street, and throwing down St. Saviour's church used its stones to extend the city wall on the north. By accident the fire spread and set much of the suburbs on fire. The sight of the town ablaze impressed the

[1] The best Irish accounts of the battle are in *Ann. L. Cé* and *Ann. Clon.* The best Anglo-Irish account is *Laud Annals* (p. 351), which say that 'four Irish kings rose against the English', and that about eleven thousand of the Irish were slain. The figures are incredible; it is probable that in the published text an original 1,100 has been made into an 11,000.

The *Ann. Ult.* record that along with Taig O'Kelly were slain 'twenty-eight of the Clann Cellaigh who had a right to the kingship'. If correct, this was an amazing wipe-out of a royal *derb-fine*.

Scots with the resolution of the townsmen, and when Bruce realized that Dublin was impregnable and that the Earl was a captive he turned west to Leixlip on February 24th and abandoned the hope of taking the capital. Guided once more by the Lacys, and in a long march through Callan to Limerick and Castleconnell and back through Cashel to Kells in Ossory, the two Bruces made terrible ravages in the rich central plain and burned numbers of small towns.

The earl of Ulster was only released from the hands of the citizens by a royal order and the intervention of the peers, and after swearing to seek redress against them by legal means. Finally, on June 24th, he was released in the presence of the magnates, having first sworn to answer to the law and shun the enemies of the King, both Scots and Irish. He was further relieved of the command of the royal forces, and retired, a deeply humiliated man, to his estates. It must always remain a matter of conjecture to what extent Earl Richard favoured the Bruce cause in Ireland.

MORTIMER LORD LIEUTENANT

At last the English government sent a man and an army. Roger Mortimer had been appointed to the supreme rank of Lieutenant in November 1316. As a concession to the Irish, he was instructed to admit the native race to the full use of English laws. Twenty large ships were collected at Haverford to transport 'the great multitude of soldiers, both horse and foot', who were to accompany him, and finally he arrived at Youghal on April 7th 1317.[1]

Mortimer hastened to join the army which Thomas, the new earl of Kildare, had collected at Kilkenny, and faced with such odds Edward Bruce (for Robert had returned to Scotland) fell back into Meath and finally retreated into Ulster. Mortimer did not follow him but drove the Lacys and their adherents, who had been proclaimed in Dublin, out of Meath. They found safe refuge

[1] *Cal. Pat. Rolls* (1313–7) for Mortimer's instructions. He granted some individual or sept-charters, e.g. to O'Madden (see later, p. 196). On the question of the Irish and the English law, Betham (*Dignities*, I, p. 283) records a petition of the English of Ireland to the King and Council of England, that 'they had a law by which an Englishman found guilty of a capital offence (e.g., of theft above 12*d.*) should suffer death, but if an Irishman was convicted of such, the judge had discretion to condemn him to execution or allow him to be ransomed. Now the justices permit all Irishmen to ransom themselves for money, e.g., for slaying an Englishman £100, for theft 20*s.*, etc., and evildoers become bold and audacious.' The King therefore issued a writ to the Justiciar directing a parliament to be held once a year and no pardons to be issued for slaying an Englishman or for arson save by consent of the faithful lieges in parliament, and then £100 shall be paid to the King.

for a time with Bruce, but Walter's son John was taken and starved to death in Trim castle.

THE REMONSTRANCE TO POPE JOHN XXII

Meanwhile the native princes who had espoused the cause of Bruce made their case and their motives known to the world in the Remonstrance which they addressed to the Avignon Pope, John XXII. The latter, who had embraced Edward II's cause against the Bruces, had sent two cardinal nuncios to England in the latter half of 1317 with a mandate to Bruce and his adherents to refrain from invading the king of England's lands in England, Wales, and Ireland, and it was probably then, and to these, that the Ulster Irish addressed this statement of their case.[1]

The Remonstrance is evidently the work of some scholar or lawyer, perhaps a Scot, accustomed to diplomatic forms, coached in native tradition and actual conditions, and competent to frame a telling indictment. Possibly Bruce had urged upon his Irish supporters the necessity of stating their wrongs and their case in a document which would come not only to the Holy Father himself, but also to the court of England, their enemy, and the chanceries of Europe, so making their cause an international one. There was the further significance that the Pope was, by Henry II's agreement with Rome, the suzerain of Edward II as Lord of Ireland.

The Remonstrance is addressed to the Pope 'by his attached children, Donaldus Oneyl, 'Rex Ultoniae', true heir by hereditary right of all Ireland, as well as the kings (*reguli*), nobles, and Irish people in general of the same realm'. Donal, speaking in royal style in the first person, proclaims the high antiquity of the Irish monarchy and the independence of the Irish realm down to Laeri ('Legarius', supposed to be the first Christian Árd Rí) from whom 'I, Donal, derive in direct line my origin'.

It then continues as follows:

> 'After Laeri, native kings ruled Ireland till Pope Adrian, on false representations and blinded by English prejudices, handed

[1] The text of the Remonstrance is found only in Fordun's *Scotichronicon* (ed. Hearne), III, p. 908–26. It is translated in King's *History of the Catholic Church in Ireland*, p. 1136. The exact date of its composition is uncertain, but as it was finally dispatched to Rome through the papal nuncios Luke and Gaucelin, the date of transmission would seem to be after May 1317, for the commission of these nuncios was made out at Avignon in that month, and they spent the latter half of the year in England and most of 1318 seeking in vain to bring Robert Bruce to terms with Edward II.

the dominion of Ireland *de facto* over to Henry II though he had no right *de iure* to do so. Through the oppressions of the English we have been driven to the woods and the rocks, and fifty thousand of both races have perished by the sword alone in virtue of Adrian's Bull. The English kings moreover have violated the very Bull and narrowed the bounds of the Church, yet our bishops are so slavishly timid that they never venture to appeal to your Holiness. The Irish have been depraved, not improved, by intercourse with the English who have deprived them of their ancient written laws and introduced other infamous ones such as that no Irishman may sue an Englishman: no man of this race is punished for the murder of an Irishman, even the most eminent: an Irishwoman, no matter how noble, who marries an Englishman is deprived at his death of her dowry: on the death of an Irishman the English seize his property, thus reducing to bondage the blood which flowed in freedom from of old.

'Further, an iniquitous statute has of late been passed at Kilkenny forbidding Irishmen to be received into monasteries in English land, and this by counsel of certain bishops, the principal being the archbishop of Armagh, a person of small discretion and no knowledge.

'The English of Ireland, "the middle nation", differ so widely in their principles of morality from those of England and all other nations that they may be called a nation of the most extreme degree of perfidy. Lay and cleric, they assert that it is no more sin to kill an Irishman than it is to kill a dog. All the land that they occupy in Ireland they occupy by usurpation. By their scheming they have alienated us from the king of England, hindering us from holding our lands as voluntary tenants under the Crown. Aliens from us in language, circumstance, and actions, all hope of maintaining peace with them is out of the question. We have made long attempts to obtain legal equality; for example two years ago several of our nobles addressed the King through John de Hotham, now bishop of Ely, describing our wrongs and offering to hold our lands directly of the King (according to Adrian's Bull, of which we send your Holiness a copy) or that he should with consent of both parties divide the land between us, but we have had no answer from him or his Council. Therefore, if we are driven to fight against both him and our enemies here, we cannot be accused of disloyalty or perjury, inasmuch as neither we nor our ancestors ever did homage or fealty to him and his ancestors. All this we verify by testimony of twelve bishops.

'Finally, despairing of justice, we have called in Edward Bruce, a descendant of some of the most noble of our ancestors, and by letters patent have granted to him our whole right and—for the establishing of justice and equity in the land, which have failed hitherto for want of a proper supreme authority—have constituted him our Lord and King by unanimous consent. May it please your Holiness, then, to sanction our proceedings, forbidding the king of England and our adversaries here from molesting us further, or at least enforce from him and them the due requirements of justice.'[1]

This appeal to the Papacy came too late in history. It was not the age of a Hildebrand or Innocent III, even if those pontiffs cared to use their strength for Ireland. The Papacy was now in exile at Avignon, under the influence of France; it was feeble and opportunist, and at the moment was trying to persuade the victor Robert Bruce to come to terms with the contemptible Edward II. It is hardly likely that John XXII would declare that the latter had forfeited Ireland unless Edward Bruce with the aid of O'Neill and the native race could succeed first in firmly establishing the independence of Ireland under a new Scottish king.

His response to the Remonstrance was in fact a tepid and disappointing one. On the one hand he excommunicated friars, mendicant and others, who preached rebellion, and issued a further Bull against the adherents of Edward Bruce; on the other he informed King Edward of the complaint of the Irish and urged him to carry out the necessary reforms in accordance with Adrian's Bull.[2]

Mortimer now subdued the Wicklow septs and then marched to the Shannon, where Turloch O'Connor, brother of Felim of Athenry, as 'Princeps Hibernicorum Connacie' submitted to him in March 1318. In return the Lord Lieutenant by treaty granted to him 'the lands of Shilmorthy and the King's lands of Fethys and Tirmany, saving the lands of Englishmen or those granted in

[1] The above is only a lengthy summary of the document omitting many acts of English oppression as stated. For the facts about the 'iniquitous statute of Kilkenny' referred to, see p. 180.

[2] *Reg. Papal Letters*, II, pp. 148, 422, 436, 440, and 3 Kal. Jun. 1318: To the King: the Pope has received the letters addressed by the Irish magnates and people to Cardinals Gaucelin and Luke, papal nuncios, touching the donation of Ireland made by Adrian to King Henry, complaining of their wrongs under that king and his successors. The Pope urges the King to consult with his Council touching correction of the said grievances, and sends him the letters of the Irish together with the case containing the said donation. Cardinal Gaucelin and Luke are ordered to assist the King in carrying out the necessary reforms.

burgage, all at the accustomed rent, on good behaviour'.[1] The legal conveyance of the long-disputed five cantreds, their ancient demesne, to the O'Connors was a small but solid triumph for the royal race. For the moment it was a gain to the Government because it detached the O'Connors from Bruce. But it meant a withdrawal from the Shannon frontier, a policy which, followed by other withdrawals, in the end abandoned the greater part of Ireland to the old race.

THE BATTLE OF DYSERT O'DEA

In Thomond the fight of Clann Turloch against the combination of Clann Brian Rua and De Clare still continued. Murchertach O'Brien succeeded his father Turloch 'of the Triumphs' who died in 1306, and in August 1317 his young brother Dermot slew Donnchad, chief of Clann Brian Rua, in a battle at Corcomroe.

Richard de Clare then invaded Thomond from his strong castle of Bunratty along with the next heir of the Clann Brian Rua, Brian Bán, but at Dysert O'Dea was attacked first by Felim O'Connor of Corcomroe and Connor O'Dea, and then overwhelmed by Murchertach O'Brien himself, coming to the aid of his vassals, on May 10th 1318. According to the vivid account in the *Cathréim*, the Normans proved worthy of their old military repute. 'So stubborn was the hand-to-hand encounter that neither noble nor commander of the English left the field, but the greater part of them fell where they stood.' Brian Bán, however, cut his way out, crossed the Shannon, and survived to found a branch of the royal race in Duithche Arra which was called MacBrien of Arra. Richard de Clare himself was killed, and when the news reached Bunratty that he had fallen and that O'Brien was at hand, his wife and the garrison 'with one consent, betook themselves to their fast galleys and sailed up away the Shannon, taking with them the choice of the town's wealth and valuables and after setting it on fire. From which time to this, never one of their breed has come back to look at it.'

Not often had an Irish chronicler the good luck to record and

[1] *Rot. Canc. Hib. Cal.*, p. 23. 'Shilmorthy' is Síol Muiredaigh, the patrimony of O'Connors, and the Fethys ('Fedha' or Faes) was a wooded district on the west side of the Shannon from the southern extremity of Lough Derg to Clonmacnois. Tirmany was part of Hy Many. Turloch only ruled for a year, then was ousted by Cathal O'Connor of the Sligo branch who ruled till 1324, then Turloch slew him and reigned more or less steadily till 1345. Thus the race of Cathal Crovderg remained in final possession. We have no evidence that the O'Connors henceforth ever paid the stipulated rent to the Government in Ireland.

My statement on page 243 of the first edition of this work that it was to Cathal that Mortimer made the grant seems unfounded.

glory in such a Gaelic victory. Thomond, which had been dominated by the Anglo-Irish since 1240, was now cleared of them at one stroke and till 1540 it remained a purely Irish country, the kingship of O'Brien. De Clare left an infant son Thomas, who died while under age in 1321, and so the feudal grant of the lordship of Thomond expired. The loss of Thomond, the surrender of Roscommon to the O'Connors, and the failure to subject Tyrconnell and the MacCarthys were all part of the great failure to complete the Conquest of Ireland.

DEFEAT AND DEATH OF EDWARD BRUCE

Mortimer was recalled in May 1318 and Alexander Bykenore, archbishop of Dublin, became Justiciar. The famine had abated, the harvest was early and abundant, and suddenly the Bruce enterprise came to an end.

A colonial army, led by John de Bermingham, whom the Irish Council had appointed commander, now marched north against Bruce, who kept the field near Dundalk. None of the magnates were there, but Roland Joyce, archbishop of Armagh, blessed the army, which was mainly drawn from the gentry and militia of Meath, Drogheda, and the towns, who, unlike the magnates, dared to face the Scottish lion. Robert Bruce had promised to join his brother, and Edward might have deferred the battle, but he was the knight-errant to the end, and with his three thousand Scots and Irish allies encountered the far greater colonial array. At the hill of Faughart near Dundalk, on October 14th 1318, the Scots met their first and last defeat. Edward Bruce was slain in the thick of the fight by John Maupas, a burgess of Drogheda, whose dead body was found above him after the fight; Alan Steward was slain in single combat by John de Bermingham; two-thirds of the Scots fell; the Lacys escaped from the battle and got away to Scotland; and the head of Edward Bruce was sent to Edward of England.[1]

There is nothing to show what Bruce's designs for the ruling of Ireland were, save that he would have rewarded the Lacys and such supporters, and given Ireland a Scottish aristocracy instead of an English one. Had he been less of a soldier and more of a statesman, had he mastered Ireland bit by bit, taken the large towns, spared Ireland his devastating and useless marches, and relied more on the aid and sage counsel of his brother, he might

[1] The *Ann. Ult.* add that MacRory, king of Innse Gall (Hebrides) and MacDonnell, king of Argyle, were slain on the Scots side. These two seem to have been Angus Oge MacDonnell, son of Angus More (d. 1310), and Lochlan MacRory.

from a secure base in Ulster and backed by his Irish allies have conquered all Ireland from the disunited magnates and the feeble English government. But already before his death the fires of the Irish insurrection were burning low; famine and slaughter had exhausted the land, and the epitaphs of the native annalists indicate a disillusionment with Bruce which had probably set in before his death. Some of their flimsy comments we may discount as being written after the event. But the Norman-French nobility had been long enough in Ireland to make many of the Irish wonder whether it was worth while exchanging them for new Scottish rulers. This view is expressed in a contemporary Gaelic tract, written to prove that O'Madden had a superior claim to Hy Many against the O'Kellys. It praises De Burgo who had secured the O'Maddens in half of this territory, and blames the Ulster and Connacht chiefs for wanting to call in 'Scottish foreigners less noble than our own foreigners, in imitation of the Eoghanachs (the O'Neills)'.[1]

THE O'MADDEN TRACT

Mortimer had been charged in 1316 to admit the Irish to the law, and among the individual charters of English liberty which he issued one given at the instance of the earl of Ulster granted English law to Eoghan O'Madden of Hy Many, his brothers, and their heirs. The Earl also made a personal treaty with this chief, and divided Hy Many between him and O'Kelly. The tract describes the purpose of this treaty thus: 'one-third of the province (of Connacht) to be under O'Madden, no English steward to preside over his Gaels, and he and his free septs to have equal nobility of blood with his lord the Earl, contrary to the former decisions of these English lords who declared that the Gael was bond (*daer*), while the Saxon was noble (*saer*).'[2]

This curious local tract then goes on to eulogize 'our own foreigners', that is the Anglo-Irish who, like the De Burgos, had been in Ireland for a century and a half and knew the Irish and their language, and in some cases had royal Irish blood in them, thus: 'In his (Eoghan's) time arrived foreigners less noble than our own, for the old chiefs of Erin prospered under those princely

[1] *Tribes and Customs of Hy Many* (ed. O'Donovan).

[2] *Tribes and Customs of Hy Many*, op. cit. The claim about one-third of the province is certainly an exaggeration; what the O'Maddens received was the south-east of Hy Many ('Síol Anmchadha'). The O'Kellys, however, though they had lost so many of their chief men at Athenry and were now being punished by the Earl, were the true lords of Hy Many, and in spite of this flourish soon put the O'Maddens into a minor position in this country. (See *Rot. Canc. Hib. Cal.*, pp. 26–8, for charters of denization including O'Madden.)

Irish lords who were our chief rulers and who had given up their foreignness for a pure mind, their surliness for good manners, their stubbornness for sweet mildness, and their perverseness for hospitality. Hence it was unjust in our nobles to side with foreigners who were less noble than they, in imitation of the O'Neills, who first dealt treacherously by their own lords on this occasion, so that at this crisis Erin became one trembling sod of commotion, save for the territory of Eoghan O'Madden, who took care not to violate his truth by acting treacherously towards his lord without reason.'[1]

The moral is that while the 'Lord of Ireland' was far away the great Norman lords were near, and if they would admit the free blood and petty kingships of the Gaels and treat them as equals with the baronage, the Irish would ask no more. The Crown was hardly thought of in these remote lands, and Ireland was soon to be a land of a ruling aristocracy, each lord in his own 'country', who, even when they fought, understood one another. Local independence rather than centralized unity was what the Gaels were of old accustomed to, and even the feudal conquerors were going that way too.

THE AFTERMATH OF THE BRUCE INVASION

So ended the most decisive three years in Irish history since Strongbow arrived. The Anglo-Irish lords and the king of England deserved on every count to lose Ireland. A chance victory restored it to them, won by the townsmen and the local colonists. But even then the opportunity was lost to issue a general charter of liberties based on the Remonstrance, in favour of the whole aggrieved native race. And yet in the half-hearted and indirect way which the Anglo-Irish state had always pursued, the lesson was taken to heart.

Mortimer was made Lieutenant again in March 1319 and, probably on his advice as knowledgeable about Ireland, concessions were made both to the native and the Anglo-Irish race.

In 1321 a fresh royal edict guaranteed to all Irishmen 'both within and without the liberties' who were already admitted, or should be admitted, to English law, the right to the English law of life and limb.[2] This was not a general enfranchisement, but

[1] *Rot. Pat. Canc. Hib.*, p. 28, June 14th 1320: Eoghan O'Madden, two brothers and a nephew and their heirs, at instance of the earl of Ulster, whose *hibernici* they are, are granted the use of English laws.

[2] *Cal. Pat. Rolls* (1317–21), p. 563: January 20th 1321, from Westminster by the King on petition of Council: 'Mandate for five years to the Justiciar that all Irishmen who have been or shall be admitted to English law shall use the said law of life and limb and shall be treated after the custom of the

from this time individual grants of English liberty are common and, in addition to the State, the great lords took it on themselves or were permitted to enfranchise their Irish tenants or vassals.[1] The Norman-Irish thus did locally what the Lord of Ireland failed to do as a whole, and made personal terms with the neighbouring chiefs.

To reassure the Anglo-Irish, who claimed all the rights of Englishmen as the law then stood, Edward II also in 1320 extended Magna Carta once more to Ireland.[2] It had in England become traditional for each new King at accession to confirm this great Charter, but its benefits were deferred in the case of Ireland where the Crown regarded itself as despotic.

The native alliance in favour of Bruce fell to pieces after Faughart, and Donal O'Neill, expelled from Tyrone by the Red Earl, died in obscurity in 1325. A rival O'Connor, Cathal, kept the kingship from 1318 to 1324 but was then slain by Turloch, brother of Felim of Athenry, who ruled till 1345, and established for good the right of Cathal Crovderg's line. Dermot MacCarthy, 'prince of the Irish of Desmond', and others received special pardons.

The Gaelic triumph was not a general one, and neither did a native Árd Rí nor a new Scottish king emerge from these wars, but the local gains were many and serious for the English. Thomond went over for good to O'Brien; Tyrconnell, Sligo, and Fermanagh to O'Donnell. The Bruces and their Irish allies had ruined irrevocably large tracts of colonial land and many small midland towns and manors, and into this old inheritance the native chiefs now entered.

The rebellion of the Anglo-Irish was easier to punish than that of the Irish. Walter de Lacy died in Scotland in 1324, his brother Hugh returned with a pardon in 1331, and, after long legal protests against the verdict of treason pronounced against them by

English *saving to the King and other lords their right to the goods and chattels of the "natives" who are called "betaghs" and who are admitted to the said law, and their issue.* Both in the time of the late King and of the present King many complaints were made that, *because Irishmen admitted to English law did not enjoy the said law of life and limb*, the King's peace in that land had often been broken, and in the Parliament at Westminster at Michaelmas last a remedy for this state was petitioned for.' The words italicized show the difficulty of full emancipation in the way of denizened Irish and Irish villeins, and the opposition of the colonists. Yet the edict was of general scope applying to both liberty and shireland, and showed an honest intention to meet the bitter charge of the Remonstrance, that killing an Irishman was neither a sin nor a crime.

[1] In 1328 the earl of Kildare was given special power to receive his Irish tenants into English law (Orpen, *Normans*, IV, p. 24).

[2] Berry, *Statutes*, I, pp. 281 and 375.

Mortimer, the family retained a portion of their land in Meath.[1] The rebel Robert de Verdun had been slain in the course of the war, but some of his line continued to hold lands in Oriel, while Milo de Verdun, brother of the Theobald who had died in 1316, remained head of the family, and was ancestor of the Verduns of Clonmore in Louth. The Bysets retained their lordship in the Glens.

Great ruin had fallen upon the colony, but beyond compensating Dublin and Drogheda for their losses, Edward allowed Anglo-Ireland to right itself with time. Among the prominent royalists, John de Bermingham, victor of Faughart, was made Earl of Louth.[2] Richard de Burgo had played a curious, and as some thought, a treasonable part, but he was allowed to retire to his estates and devote himself to rebuilding his lordship in Ulster and Connacht.

Roger Mortimer held office again from March 1319 to July 1321, but the colony needed a greater statesman than he was. He held a parliament in 1320 which forbade the great to quarter their men 'on abbeys and honest folk', and where he proclaimed the royal concession that the army of Ireland might not be summoned by the Justiciar without consent of the magnates. But the pacification of Ireland and the restoration of central authority needed more force and ability than the Government could command, and in fact the Anglo-Irish nobles were now the great barrier between the Crown and the common folk, English and Irish.

Every magnate aspired to have armies of his own who by preference should be Irishmen, and thus we read that in 1314, 'Edmund Butler (lord of Carrick) gave coyne to the kerns of Dermot mac Turloch O'Brien on the English farmers (*gall-bhrughaibh*) of his country'.[3] The English free tenants would not endure these quarterings, but Irish tenants would; hence the lords soon preferred to stock their lands with Irish tenants, and thus decayed that English or French-speaking population which in the first flush of the Conquest seemed likely to make in Ireland a second England.

The militarizing of the native race now proceeded apace. The annals and such tracts as *The Triumphs of Turloch* reveal to us

[1] For the forfeitures of the Lacys and others and grants in reward by the King, see *Rot. Pat. Canc. Hib. Cal.*, pp. 23, 25, 26, 28, and for the whole Lacy and Verdun case *Chart. St. Mary's Abbey*, II, app., pp. 407–23.

[2] Dr. Orpen was of the belief that John de Bermingham, victor at Faughart, was a son of Sir Piers, lord of Tethmoy, but I incline to the older view that he was of the Athenry branch of the family (see p. 204).

[3] *Dublin Annals of Innisfallen.*

the Irish chiefs and nobles going into battle in armour and helmets. They were beginning to build castles in imitation of the English, and we read of Eoghan O'Madden, the Red Earl's protégé, that he built at Magh-bhealaigh 'a strong castle of stone and timber'. They were able before long to take over many a Norman castle of Butler or De Burgo. They quartered on their tenants professional light troops (*buanadha*) and kerns (*ceithearna*), or hired those heavy-armed professionals, the gallowglasses. The Norman-Irish also enlisted such troops, and with them fought out their wars with one another or the Irish. Thus steadily most of Ireland became a land of war, and 'the land of peace' diminished.

A UNIVERSITY FOR DUBLIN

Still, the Anglo-Irish government was given another fifty years to show whether it was capable or not of its great task, and for the moment the prospects in Ireland were still fair. An attempt had already been made to give the colony a culture-centre. In 1312 Pope Clement V—at the request of John de Leche, archbishop of Dublin, who had represented that 'in Dublin there are some doctors and bachelors of theology who give lectures, but there is no *studium generale*'—ordained, if the suffragans of Dublin should consent, that there should be in the city a *universitas* with power to give doctors' degrees.

In 1320, under the new Archbishop Alexander de Bykenore (1317–49), four masters were made, of whom William Rodiard, dean of St. Patrick's, was appointed first chancellor of the university. In 1321 Bykenore issued an 'ordinance for the University of Dublin', and reserved for himself the right to appoint secular or regular readers in theology. Bykenore afterwards fell into disgrace as a partisan of Queen Isabella, and the infant university languished, but at any time under Edward III it might well have come into full flower as a centre of culture and civilization among the colonists, as a means for the diffusing of European thought, and as the most effective agent for anglicizing the native race.[1]

In the field of letters John Clyn, a Franciscan friar of Kilkenny, whom James, earl of Ormond, made warden of his Franciscan foundation at Carrick-on-Suir in 1336, wrote in Latin the annals of Ireland, which are of first-hand value from 1315 to 1349, when he died, probably of the pestilence which he describes in a vivid passage. Clyn alone of the Latin annalists of Anglo-Ireland

[1] See *Grace's Annals* (1320) and notes; also Mason, *History of St. Patrick's*, app. vii, and Harris's edition of Ware's *Antiquities*, p. 243.

deserves the name of historian, but the annals which are attributed to St. Mary's abbey, Dublin, and which begin in 1162, are full and first-hand records of the period from 1300 to their close in 1370.[1]

In politics no great change was possible while England was torn with civil dissensions and Ireland with feuds. The English parties thought only of Ireland as a pawn in the game, and when Sir John Darcy came over as Justiciar from 1324 till 1327, and announced certain concessions, such as that Ireland should enjoy free trade with England and Wales, the object was to win the Anglo-Irish for the King against Isabella and Mortimer.

The greatest figure among the Anglo-Irish left the stage of which he had been chief figure since 1280 when at the parliament of Kilkenny in 1326 Richard de Burgo gave a great feast to peers and commons. The Red Earl then retired to die at the end of July in his own abbey at Athassel, leaving as his heir his grandson William (called by the Irish 'Donn', the brown-haired), a boy of fourteen. Edmund Butler, earl of Carrick, had died in 1321, leaving also a young son James.

At the end of 1326 the miserable Edward II succumbed before his enemies, was deposed in January 1327, and soon after was murdered. The Mortimer faction appointed Thomas, earl of Kildare, Justiciar, and in February the young Edward III began his reign as King of England and Lord of Ireland.

[1] Clyn's *Annals* (ed. Butler) in *Irish Arch. Soc.* (1849), and the (so-called) *Laud Annals* in *Chart. St. Mary's*, II (R.S.).

CHAPTER XI

THE REBELLIOUS ANGLO-IRISH, 1327–1360

EDWARD III, destined to be medieval England's great soldier-king, was hardly fifteen years of age when he succeeded to the throne which he was to occupy for over fifty years. The government therefore for three years passed into the hands of the faction which had deposed his father, and Roger Mortimer, Earl of March, ruled along with his paramour, the Queen-Mother Isabella. But in 1330 the young King asserted himself and overthrew Mortimer, who in November of that year was hanged as a common malefactor at Tyburn, while Isabella was imprisoned for life. The Mortimer estates in Wales and Ireland were forfeited and not restored till 1354, when the attainder was reversed in favour of Roger, grandson of the executed man, who thus became 2nd Earl of March and Lord of Trim and Leix.

In the three years 1327–30, the great Anglo-Irish who had favoured Mortimer were left to govern Ireland, and two of them were further ennobled.

THE PALATINE EARLDOMS OF ORMOND AND DESMOND

At the parliament of Shrewsbury in Michaelmas 1328, where Mortimer was made Earl of March, James Butler was rewarded with the earldom of Ormond. As he had married Eleanor Bohun, a granddaughter of Edward I, his heirs were regarded as 'cousins' of the Crown, having many rich manors in England. Henceforth they took up that leadership of the English interest in Ireland which became the tradition of their race. In the grants of the earldom only the four Pleas of the Crown (rape, arson, forestalling, and treasure-trove) were reserved to the King. Twenty years later, in 1347, Ormond was made a palatine liberty for James, the 2nd Earl, with Nenagh as its capital manor.

In August 1329 Maurice, head of the Munster Geraldines, was created Earl of Desmond. Kerry was similarly in that year made a palatine liberty for him. Meanwhile among the other magnates, William 'Donn' de Burgo, the new Earl of Ulster, was now but a boy of fifteen. Thomas, 2nd Earl of Kildare, died in 1328; after his son Richard, who died in 1331, his second son Maurice became 4th Earl.

The fortunes of the First Families were to a large extent built upon the ruins of the absentees. In 1306 the Bigods of Norfolk, lords of Carlow, were extinct. So were the De Clares, earls of Gloucester and lords of Kilkenny, in 1314 with the death of Earl Gilbert at Bannockburn, when his three sisters divided the inheritance.[1]

So when Aymer de Valence, Earl of Pembroke and Lord of Wexford, died in 1324 without heirs, his sister conveyed these titles to her husband, John Lord Hastings. When their descendant, John Lord Hastings, died without heirs in 1389, the Greys of Ruthyn took the title Lord of Wexford. These English claimants drew rents from Ireland, but otherwise might as well not have existed, and Butlers, Geraldines, MacMurroughs and other Norman and Gaelic residents took their places. Thus did the once-united and English 'land of Leinster' fall to pieces.

The Irish lords now began to grumble over those absentees, 'the English by birth', who drew money out of the country and never came near it, and so let the Irish enemy in; while secretly they hated the idea of their return, built their vast lordships from the ruins, and encouraged the Gaelic chiefs to resume part of their old territories. The lesser Englishry in Parliament sincerely wished the return of the absentees as a fresh buttress of the threatened Anglo-Norman civilization and State of Ireland, and urged the Crown to turn the dead liberties into common-law land. But a strong baronial interest both in Ireland and England opposed all resumption. The King was in the hands of his nobles; and the growth of local lordship and immunity from the beginning of Edward III to the end of the Wars of the Roses became the leading feature of society in both countries.

In Ireland the Crown was weaker than in England, and the feuds of the magnates, personal or territorial, filled all the first years of the reign, as they had filled the latter years of Edward I's reign. One of them was disastrous for the borders of the colony.

THE MURDER OF THE EARL OF LOUTH

The Englishry of Oriel (the Verduns, Gernons, Clintons, Cusacks, and others) resented having John de Bermingham, the new Earl

[1] The earldom of Norfolk with the title of Earl Marshal and the Irish titles was in fact revived in 1312 and 1316 for Thomas Brotherton, younger son of Edward I, and finally the liberty of Carlow came in Richard II's time to Thomas Mowbray, Earl of Nottingham, whose mother Elizabeth was granddaughter of this Thomas. Of the inheritors of the Kilkenny lordship we need only note the family of Despenser. Eleanor, Earl Gilbert's sister, married Hugh Despenser, and their great-grandson Hugh was made Earl of Gloucester by Richard II. Margaret, a second sister, married Hugh de Audeley (made Earl of Gloucester in 1337), who conveyed to Ralph, Baron of Stafford, his Irish lands acquired by this marriage.

of Louth, imposed upon them. They chafed under the strong hand of the conqueror of Bruce; and there were more intimate grievances, for the Earl had taken a girl of the Verduns against her father's will, and would not let an illegitimate daughter of his marry another Verdun 'who loved her as his life'. Finally the colonists of this region took arms, declaring, as the annalist says, 'nolumus hunc regnare super nos'; and in a pitched battle at Balibragan (Bragganstown) in Louth, on June 10th 1329, the Earl was slain with eight other Berminghams and two hundred soldiers of the Pale. He left no son and the earldom passed away with him.[1]

'This slaughter', says the *Book of Howth*, 'was a great hindrance to the north of Ireland, for this was the only key and wall thereof, for if the Earl had continued in prosperity, Ulster had been civiller than Leinster.'

It was something new and portentous that Anglo-Irish rebels should extinguish one of the great feudal lordships, but the way had been pointed out by the Lacys and Verduns in the previous reign. The secondary families, now thoroughly rooted in Ireland, were already forming patriarchal septs after the Gaelic fashion. Clyn and Grace frequently mention the 'naciones et cognomina' of the 'Geraldini', 'Poerini', 'Rupenses', 'Ketyngs', 'cum aliis nacionibus' of the time. Meanwhile the natural attraction of Irish culture was asserting itself with all, for the Earl of Louth had with him at Balibragan his Irish harper, who perished along with his master and earns a striking epitaph from Friar Clyn.[2]

THE IRISH RESURGENCE

The Englishman, John Darcy, who ruled as Justiciar from 1329 to 1331, found the colonial fortunes at a low ebb.[3] The armed resources of the State were so small that Desmond was allowed to raise an army by quartering Irish mercenaries upon his English tenantry. All along the borders the resurgence of the Irish was displayed. In 1325 John de Bermingham and Thomas le Botiller had to lead an army against O'Carroll, 'who in this year scarcely left a house, castle, or town in Ely O'Carroll among the English

[1] In the annals quoted (Grace) the Earl is represented as being brother of Richard de B., Lord of Athenry.

[2] 'Cam [*recte* Maelruanaidh 'Caech', 'the half-blind'] O'Carwyll, famous tympanist and harper, in his art a phoenix, who, if he was not the first inventor of the art of string music, was of all who preceded him and of all his contemporaries teacher, master, and director.'

[3] Sir John Darcy married Joan, daughter of Richard, 'Red Earl' of Ulster, widow of the 2nd Earl of Kildare; a son of his, William, got Irish property and founded the Darcys of Platten in Meath.

and lovers of peace which he did not destroy by fire'. Some of the more irishized English of Ely, says Clyn, even aided Brian Bán O'Brien when in the same year he ravaged Ossory, 'and slew the faithful Englishry in the defence of their property'.

In 1327, Grace in his annals tells us, 'the men of Leinster made them a king, Donal, son of Art MacMurgh'. This was the first open inauguration of a king of Leinster since Dermot, and a significant event in the Irish revival. But Donal, who 'wished to flaunt his banner within two miles of Dublin and then to traverse all Ireland', soon after was captured and imprisoned in Dublin castle.[1] He escaped however a year later, and continued to lead the war of the Leinster Irish against the English.

EDWARD III'S 'REFORMS FOR IRELAND'

In May 1331 Sir Anthony Lucy arrived as Justiciar, bringing with him a number of ordinances lately passed at a parliament in Westminster in March of that year.

His Irish advisers urged the young King and his council to take the whole Lordship of Ireland into review, to bring the Irish under the law either by peaceful concession or armed force, to strike a blow at those First Families who dominated Anglo-Ireland, to strengthen the royal administration, to compel the absentees to return, and thus save the threatened English colony from extinction. On the point of revenue alone it could be shown that the larger part of the colony yielded nothing. These weighty considerations having been placed before the English parliament, it adopted the King's proposals for emancipating the Irish, compelling the absentees to return, resuming the liberties granted by Mortimer, and forbidding the keeping of Irish soldiery save in the Marches. To crown all, the English Estates begged the King to visit Ireland in person.[2]

Of Lucy's ordinances three were of capital importance. The first of them declared that the Irish and the English were to be under the same law, excepting the 'servitude of the betaghs', who were to remain subject to their lords in the same way as the villeins were in England.

We cannot say that this edict of emancipation took general effect, or that it was ratified by any Anglo-Irish parliament. Yet it was pleaded in the courts of the colony, and a little later a grant of English law and liberty was made to two important chiefs and their 'iraghts' or chief vassals, namely, Donal

[1] *Laud Annals* (1327), *Clyn* (1325), *Grace* (1331).
[2] *Foedera*, II, p. 812, and *Lib. Mun.*, I, pt. IV, p. 11.

MacCarthy of Carbery and Dermot O'Dwyer of Kilnamanagh of Ormond.[1]

Lucy's second ordinance was nothing less than a declaration of war upon the Anglo-Irish magnates.

On the ground that everything done under Mortimer was a usurpation, the King proclaimed an Act of Resumption, revoking all grants made in Ireland during his minority, as due to certain evil counsellors (such as Mortimer). Thomas of Brotherton, Earl of Norfolk, and twenty other absentee Irish landlords were ordered to dwell upon, or at least to put garrisons into, their Irish lands. Lastly, 'according to the request of the people of Ireland and by advice of Parliament', the King announced his intention of coming over in person, and troops and transports were prepared.[2]

This programme for Ireland was at once opposed by the Norman baronage, whose power it proposed to break. An Anglo-Irish 'Patriot Party' formed itself, and we hear the first utterance of the spirit that was behind Swift and Grattan. The Patriots of the fourteenth century, like those of the eighteenth, resented English domination from overseas, were bent on keeping the government and power of Ireland in their own hands and, while averse to a general enfranchisement of the Gaelic population which might lead to a reversal of the Conquest on which their land-titles rested, were ready to make their own terms as overlords with the Irish and admit them to a guarded equality. Ready to obey the King or any Prince of the Blood coming in person, they hated those officials, 'English by birth', against whom they proudly styled themselves 'English by blood', and especially resented the authority of English viceroys, who stayed but a short time, oppressed the land with exactions, and did no good, or, worse, appropriated to themselves the subsidies voted by Parliament for the needs of the State. The question of the absentees touched their self-interest on a tender spot. The absence of titular lords had enabled the Irish to recover much ground, but the Anglo-Irish themselves profited; yet they had no wish for the claimants to return and form a new 'English interest' hateful to the

[1] *Exch. Mem.*, vol. XVIII, p. 603 (7 Edw. III): the two chiefs take an oath of fealty and promise to be answerable to the King's court and to his officers.

In a lawsuit of 4 Edw. III where a colonist had robbed an Irishman and pleaded that he need not answer to an *hibernicus* the Irishman replied *quod Dominus Rex statuit in parliamento suo quod omnes hibernici ad pacem Domini Regis existentes sint ad communem legem*, etc., and won his case. Betham, *Dignities*, I, p. 292. See also Harris, *Collect.* II,, p. 10 (1328): King to the Justiciar Darcy—'on behalf of some Irishmen who ask that all Irishmen who wish it may have English law, let this request go before the next Parliament'.

[2] *Foedera*, II, p. 285. Elaborate preparations were made for Edward to come over, but finally were cancelled in the English parliament in December 1332.

descendants of the conquerors, who had never been English in the racial sense and were becoming steadily Irish.

But the Act of Resumption was an immediate menace. The new earldoms of Ormond and Desmond were threatened among other royal grants; who then could be safe? Lucy lost no time in putting it into effect; among other proceedings he had an inquisition made into the descent of the kingdom of Cork, by the findings of which it was made to appear that Fitzstephen had left no legal heirs of his moiety of that kingdom, so that half of the land of Desmond (the Earl's particular domain) was ordered to be resumed into the King's hand.[1]

Moreover, the Crown had refrained from reissuing Magna Carta for Ireland, though this precious charter had been renewed for England, as was now considered necessary at least once for every new sovereign, and it seemed a deliberate act, preventing the Anglo-Irish from claiming the right not to be disturbed in their properties, rights, liberty, and persons save by 'the judgment of their peers and the law of the land'. The resistance of the 'Patriot Party' was therefore one of legality against arbitrary power.

From the Crown's point of view the lordship of Ireland must now be won or lost. To win it, the native race must be conciliated, the liberties must be diminished, the shire-land increased, and the government be made as efficient as that of England. The State's income was steadily falling, only the Leinster counties could be relied on to provide revenue, and whereas early in Edward I's reign Anglo-Ireland easily yielded £6,000 from all sources, in 1335 less than half of this was raised. The magnates evaded payment of their feudal dues, the towns the payment of their fines—all the colonists alike took the line that the Crown had thrown upon them the defence of Ireland and of themselves and nothing more could be asked.[2]

The lordship of Ireland had begun as a despotism and now, after the beginnings of a representative parliament had been made, the idea of a direct despotism exercised from Westminster by a viceroy recurred. The attempt after a long struggle proved a failure and had to end in the affirmation of parliamentary institution for the English colony and the publication of Magna Carta.

The winning of Ireland meant a royal army, and save for the garrisons of the King's castles, there was none. Owing to the grants of huge fiefs on almost nominal terms, the total array

[1] Orpen (*Normans*, IV, p. 236) shows that the finding was unjust. (See for the descent of the kingdom of Cork granted in 1177 to Fitzstephen and De Cogan, pp. 83, 117, 125.)

[2] In 1334–5 the ordinary revenue yielded £2,766 (*Exch. Mem.*, xviii, p. 2). In 1291 it had been some £4,300.

which the Justiciar could call forth by royal knight-service was far from imposing. When the Justiciar unfurled the royal standard not many more than four hundred military tenants were bound to attend him or pay the scutage commutation.[1] Certainly if the magnates were agreeable they could bring to his banner thousands of armed tenants, both Irish and English, but it was these very lords with their armies whom the Crown must break if it meant to have a real monarchy.

Backed by the second line of baronage, Poers, Purcells, and the like, the Anglo-Norman earls and lords of Ireland by now formed themselves into a thickset hedge which no English king could break down, though many a royal deputy attempted it. By a tacit and local, but universally practised, understanding with the native race, the descendants of the conquistadors became all the more unbreakable.

The struggle was indeed becoming with every generation less and less one of race. The great Anglo-Irish had minstrels of their own and loved native music and poetry. The Irish chiefs with their gallowglasses and *buanadha* ('bonnaughts'), their castles and armour, were now a foe to be respected, and the differences of speech and custom became merely those between men whose first speech was Gaelic, and those who knew it along with French and English. Since the Crown had failed to meet the Irish demand stated in the Remonstrance of 1317 for an equal division of land between Normans and Gaels, it was left for the former to throw open their vast lordships to the Irish, and by treaties of vassalage to recognize Gaelic chieftains as heads of territories and of the populations which obeyed them.

But however Irish in sympathy, habit, or speech they might become, the great Anglo-Irish did not repudiate the nominal supremacy of the English Crown or their status as tenants under that Crown. For the present they were willing to perform the duties of that status, and though kings after Gaelic fashion to their Irish tenants, they were still earls and barons to their English ones. It is clear that the actual heads of the First Families were far more English than the younger and more resident members. Thus William, the 'Brown Earl' of Ulster, had an English mother,

[1] See Bateson, *E.H.R.* (1903), p. 497, on 'Irish Exchequer Memoranda' (MS. Corpus Christi College): The total knight-service of the colony in 1284 is given as 427 and a fraction. In 1330, when the Justiciar Darcy called on the Earl of Desmond for military help, the Earl, it is said, brought up ten thousand men, but these must have been for the most part Irish, and Brian Ban O'Brien led part of them (Orpen, *Normans*, IV, p. 230). There were of course also the militia levies of the 'obedient counties', for the Statute of Winchester, extended to Ireland in 1307, imposed military service on all the colonist population.

Elizabeth of Gloucester, and was wedded to Maud of Lancaster, the King's cousin, but he had De Burgo cousins in Connacht who had never seen England and were all but Irish.

THE VICEROY HANGS A GREAT LORD

Sir Anthony Lucy, a mere knight, had a dangerous task to perform. His first step was pacific: he summoned the magnates to reconcile their feuds, and on March 21st 1331 'the Earl of Desmond and Sir William de Bermingham made peace with the Justiciar, and swore fealty and peace with the King and the people for ever'. This William, who was a great noble and brother of the dead Earl of Louth, had been Desmond's chief supporter in the feuds of 1328–9, and was regarded by the Governor as one of the worst of the feudal lawbreakers.[1] Lucy then summoned Parliament to Dublin for July 1st, but Desmond and his supporters refused to attend; later, however, when it was summoned to Kilkenny, they came and were pardoned in the King's name. But Lucy meant to strike down these mighty subjects; and his officers arrested Desmond, Sir William de Bermingham, his son Walter, and many other prominent Anglo-Irish. William was hanged in Dublin on June 11th, in spite of the charter of peace granted him, an event which shocked the whole colony. 'He was a noble knight, the noblest and best of thousand of knights in the art of war. Alas and alas, who can refrain from tears in speaking of his death?' is the epitaph of the Anglo-Irish annals, which henceforth are for the English lords of Ireland against the English Justiciars and 'the English by birth'.[2]

But faced with so general an indignation from the Anglo-Irish, the English government for the time dared not proceed further. The Act of Resumption was dropped for the time, Edward recalled Lucy in November 1332, and sent Darcy back again with a general pardon. Desmond was released to play later again the part of a Patriot leader, and not to be finally pardoned by the Crown till 1355.

THE MURDER OF THE YOUNG EARL OF ULSTER

Meanwhile disastrous events in the west and north were shaping the fate of the colony. William, the young Earl of Ulster, was opposed by refractory English tenants and his own Irish cousins. Walter, son of William 'Liath' de Burgo and his Irish wife, Finola

[1] For these wearisome feuds, see Orpen, *Normans*, III, pp. 219–27. Orpen regards William as a younger brother of the Earl of Louth, and therefore of the Tethmoy line, but (see p. 209) it is not certain that the Earl was of the Tethmoy family.

[2] *Laud Annals, sub* 1332.

O'Brien, having defeated Turloch O'Connor in 1330, aspired to play a great part in Ulster and Connacht.[1] The Earl had him taken and thrust into Northburgh castle in Inishowen, where he was done to death in 1332. Now, Walter had a sister, Gyle, wife of Sir Richard Mandeville, one of the Earl's greatest tenants in Ulster, and at her instigation, Robert, son of Martin Mandeville, and other of the colonists of Antrim murdered the young Earl, then only twenty-one years of age, at the ford of Carrickfergus, June 6th 1333.[2]

The Justiciar, Darcy, sailed to Carrickfergus and dire vengeance was wrought on the murderers, but the irreparable evil was done. Maud of Lancaster at once took ship for England with the Earl's infant child, Elizabeth, through whose marriage later with Lionel of Clarence the earldom of Ulster and the vast lordship of the De Burgos passed by English law to a royal absentee.

No such blow had yet befallen the Anglo-Irish colony. The whole De Burgo lordship, which had reduced the proudest of the Irish to vassalage and had been the shield and rampart of the English interest in the north and the west, fell at one stroke. Released from a yoke which they alone could never have broken, the O'Neills and O'Donnells were able to subject eastern and southern Ulster on the one hand, and De Burgo's lordship of Sligo on the other. Within fifty years practically the whole province went back to the Irish order.[3]

[1] He was the eldest son of William 'Liath' (see Pedigree of De Burgo in Appendix) who was son of William Oge, brother of Earl Walter, slain at Athankip in 1270. The Walter murdered in 1333 seems to have aspired to make Inishowen his particular domain. The *Ann. Conn.* say: 'Walter son of Sir William Burc was captured by the Brown Earl and taken to the new castle of Inishowen, and he died of hunger in the prison of that castle.'

[2] See *Clyn*, *Laud Annals*, Grace's *Annals*, etc. The late Miss Maude V. Clarke thought the murder took place in the 'Earl's meadow', still so called, near Carrickfergus. *Clyn* says: 'In the same year (1333) on June 6th William de B. Earl of Ulster, etc., was treacherously killed by his armour-bearers (knights) whom he trusted. The authors of this crime were John de Logan, Robert son of Richard Mandeville, and Robert son of Martin Mandeville. This evil was due, it is said, to a woman, Gyle de Burgo, wife of Richard de Mandeville, because the Earl had imprisoned Walter her brother, and others.'

[3] The De Burgo possessions are detailed in *Cal. Inquis.*, VII (7 Edw. III). For the Connacht estates see Knox, 'Occupation of Connacht by the Anglo-Normans after 1237', *R.S.A.I.* (1902–3), and for the Ulster and Meath estates Orpen, 'Earldom of Ulster, etc.', *R.S.A.I.* (1913–15, 1921). The Earl ruled Connacht from his great court at Loughrea; it is especially interesting to find that the cantred of Síol Anmchadha is under 'O'Madan, the Irish king of that country by the Earl's grant'; (see formerly, Chapter X, p. 197). In Ulster the entry 'services of the sergeantries of the Irish' shows eleven Irish chiefs holding of the Earl by military service, viz. Henry and Odo O'Neill, Rory Maguire, two MacMahons, O'Hanlon, MacCartan, O'Cahan, O'Floinn, and two MacGilmores. The total service imposed as a condition of tenure on these is three hundred and forty-five foot-men or 'satellites', or else commutation at £1 per man.

The maritime power of the earls had circled the north coast. Now save for Coleraine, to which the English clung desperately for another fifty years, the sea was thrown open, the northern chiefs could draw from the Scottish Isles unlimited gallowglasses, and so was knitted again the old Gaelic world of Erin and Alba, severed for a time by the Anglo-Norman wedge driven in it by De Courcy and his successors in eastern Ulster.[1]

THE TRIUMPH OF THE BURKES

In Connacht, the triumph was that of the rebellious Norman-Irish. The dead Earl's kinsmen were resolved that no absentee should succeed by marriage and by English law to the great heritage of their race. William 'Liath' had left other sons besides Walter, of whom the two elder were William (in Irish Uillec or Ulick, a diminutive) and Edmund. The latter was still in Scotland, whither he had accompanied his father when William 'Liath' was taken captive by Bruce at Connor, and hence he was called 'Albanach' by the Irish. Returning to Ireland in 1335 to share in the De Burgo partitionment, Edmund showed how little the Norman-Irish cared for feudal baronies compared with building up a Gaelic kingship in the hearts of the native race. 'Twenty years did that Edmund remain in Alba,' says the Gaelic history of the later Burkes, 'when, by the death of the Brown Earl, son of the English countess, tribe-extinction came upon the Burkes, and Edmund returned and landed in Umhall O'Maille (the Owles of Mayo), and his chief poet and ambassador to the Connachtmen was Donn O'Breslin, and Edmund took to wife Saiv, daughter of O'Maille.'[2]

Thus strangely had the aspect of the Norman conquerors of Connacht changed, and Edmund, half-Irish by his mother, with an Irish wife, an Irish brehon, and Scottish gallowglasses in his train, would hardly have been recognized by the William de Burgo of 1200. Yet these were the appeals which won the Irish heart, and before his death in 1375 Edmund was master of Mayo, and

[1] Clyn says of the murdered Earl, 'He was of most subtle intelligence and a lover of the State and of peace' (*reipublice et pacis amator*); a good distinction between such English and official-minded magnates as he stood for and their local-minded hibernicized cousins.

[2] We have for these events and later Burke history the evidence of the Gaelic and Latin historical tract called *Historia et Genealogia Familiae de Burgo* (T.C.D., F.4.13). Burke, a form of De Burgo or De Bourg or De Burgh (in Irish 'A Burc' or 'De Burc'), now becomes the surname of the family (for this tract, ed. by Tomás Ó Raghaille, see *Galway Arch. Soc.*, XIII, No. 182, pp. 50–60).

founded there the race of MacWilliam 'Ichtarach', or the 'Lower Burke'.[1]

At the same time his brother, William or Ulick, seized upon the De Burgo lordship on the broad plains of Galway. From him came MacWilliam 'Uachtarach', or the 'Upper Burke', and the earls of Clanrickard, who remained also till 1396 lords of the city of Galway. In Munster Edmund 'na Féasóige' ('the Bearded'), a son of the Red Earl, was already in possession of the Burgo lands in Tipperary and Limerick, a country later called Clanwilliam; he was the ancestor of the Burkes of Castleconnell.[2]

The three Burkes had thus defied the feudal law of inheritance. The English Crown, guardian of the heiress's right, would give the established Burkes no legal sanction for their lands, and when the descendants of Lionel and Elizabeth became kings of England the MacWilliams of Connacht were regarded as pure usurpers. Hence it was that of all the Norman conquerors the De Burgos became the earliest case of *Hibernis ipsis Hiberniores.*

Thus did the western province lose even the official Anglo-Norman veneer it had. An Irish revival followed the feudal one. While Edmund Albanach fought with Edmund na Féasóige, who claimed the Burke chieftainry, till in 1338 he took him and had him drowned in Lough Mask, Turloch O'Connor, brother of Felim of Athenry, assumed the sway of Connacht again and, say the Irish annals, 'Leyney and Corran of Sligo were wrested from the English and the hereditary native chiefs resumed their captainships.' These two baronies had belonged successively to the Fitzgeralds and to De Burgo, but now that Donal O'Connor held Carbery and Sligo town, the whole lordship became Irish again. As overlord in the north-west, O'Donnell took the place of De Burgo, whose claims to Fermanagh and the seven theods of Tyrconnell lapsed, and Aedh O'Donnell, who died in 1333 after a reign of fifty years in his fort of Assaroe, is called 'lord of Tyrconnell, Cinel Moen, Inishowen, Fermanagh, and Brefni'.

Such an Irish or Norman-Irish revival might seem a remote thing to the colonists of Leinster and Meath, but this 'land of peace' itself was the scene of a widespread race-revival. The MacMurroughs and their vassals overran the inland parts of Leinster, and uniting in a general confederacy threatened the towns that had been planted like garrisons along the Liffey, the Nore, and the line of the Barrow. In the heart of Ireland, the O'Melaghlins,

[1] The division of the Burkes into the 'Upper' and the 'Lower MacWilliam' did not take place till 1401 (see later, Chapter XIV, p. 281).

[2] See Pedigree of the De Burgo and Burke family in Appendix. It seems probable, though not entirely certain, that Edmund was younger than Ulick.

O'Molloys, Mageoghegans, and others, formed a midland confederacy to destroy the colonial settlements. Longford, most of Westmeath, all Leix and Offaly, and the northern parts of Tipperary and Kilkenny were thus lost. Not only had the plan of a thorough conquest of all Ireland failed, but the occupied belts were growing smaller and more isolated, and the whole Anglo-Irish State was being battered to pieces.

THE IRISH RESURGENCE

The native victories were won by single chiefs or confederacies of chiefs in hundreds of local battles. No all-Ireland aim or truly national chief is recorded. But of local heroes there were many, who rebuilt the lost lordships of their ancestors before the Conquest. One such is Lysagh (Laoiseach) O'More, who in 1342 made himself lord of Leix, where the Mortimers were titular possessors. Friar Clyn says of him: 'He stirred up to war all the Irish of Munster and Leinster by persuasion, promises, and gifts, and expelled nearly all the English from their lands by force, for in one evening he burned eight castles of the Englishry, and destroyed the noble castle of Dunamase belonging to Roger Mortimer, and usurped to himself the lordship of the country. From a slave he became a lord, from a subject a prince.'[1]

Another such hero was Taig O'Carroll who fell in battle in 1346: 'He slew or expelled from Ely the nations of the Brets, Milbornes, and other English, and occupied their lands and castles.'

An inquisition held in 1337 on the death of the 1st Earl of Ormond shows strikingly how the English line was recoiling in Ormond, which had been widely enfeoffed early in the Conquest.[2] At Nenagh there was a castle with five towers, and the chief manor contained seven and a half theods (*tuatha*), and ninety carucates in demesne, free tenures, and lands let to farmers. But the Irish had thrown off the Butler yoke in the northern parts, and the petty towns were decaying; for example, 'the burgesses at Balyhaghil used to render per annum to the lord eight marks, but now they render only twenty shillings in time of peace, and nothing in time of war because of the Irish'. As to the Irish vassals, 'the heirs of John and Donohyr [(?) Conohyr] O'Kenedy and Conol O'Kenedy used to hold ten carucates (some one thousand two hundred acres at least) at rent and royal service, now they pay nothing, for they are at war: and so it is with the heirs of O'Mathy [O'Meagher], O'Hogan and Macgyltin'.

The line of O'Kennedy, formerly 'Rí Ur-Mhumhain', had for a

[1] Clyn (1336, 1342, 1346). [2] *Cal. Inquis.*, VII, p. 117.

century and a half remained quiescent under the Norman grantees. As late as 1336 Roderick (Rory), son of Alan (Amhlaidh) O'Kennedy, enters into a treaty with the Earl of Ormond by which the latter is admitted to be direct overlord, O'Kennedy and the men of his nation are to make suit at the court of Nenagh, and Rory is to retain fourteen carucates (at least one thousand six hundred and eighty acres of arable land) in Clonmolyn and Moyanargyth. But in 1347 Donal O'Kennedy raided Ormond and drove out Berminghams, Cantwells, Cogans, and other settlers and burned the town of Nenagh, but failed to take the castle. The Butler line was threatened, nevertheless the earls did not lose Nenagh for good till 1377.[1]

As for the key-fortresses, Sligo was now the seat of a separate O'Connor line, sprung from Brian of Leyney; Roscommon fell to Turloch, brother of Felim of Athenry; Ballymote, a noble stronghold built in the best style by the Red Earl, passed to MacDonagh; and save for Athlone, which was never altogether lost, the Shannon frontier had to be abandoned. De Clare's castle at Bunratty was destroyed by Murchertach O'Brien in 1332. Similarly in the extreme north De Burgo's fortress of Northburgh in Inishowen fell to O'Doherty, who became lord of Inishowen, under a double vassalage to O'Neill and O'Donnell.[2] In 1331 the two castles of Arklow and Ferns were taken 'by stratagem' by the Leinster Irish, but the former was recovered by the Justiciar next year.

THE CONSTITUTIONAL REVOLT OF THE ANGLO-IRISH

By 1333 the young King abandoned the thought of coming to Ireland in person and turned his warlike genius first against the Scots and next against the French. It was a fatal decision for the English interest in Ireland. The colony was at the crisis of its fate, but a royal army might yet complete the conquest of the Gaels.

[1] See *Cal. Ormond Deeds*, I, Nos. 682, 683, and Gleeson, 'Castle of Nenagh', op. cit. Clyn *sub* 1347 says that 'Donaldus filius Philippi O'Kenedy' headed a combination of Munster, Connacht, Meath, and Leinster in this raid, made at Christmas 1347–8, but at the end of March 1348 he was taken and later executed at Thurles.

[2] *Ann. Ult.* (1342): 'Donal O'Doherty, arch-chief of Ard Midhair, died and there was little wanting from his having the lordship of Inis Eoghain and the cantred of Tír Enna.'

Hogan ('The Irish Law of Kingship', *P.R.I.A.*, 1932) says that Ua Dochartaigh, king of Cinel Conaill, by 1197 gained control of Inis Eoghain and Magh Itha (the latter is roughly the barony of Raphoe and much the same as Cinel Moen), which were incorporated in Tyrconnell 1180–1209, thus excluding the Cinel Eoghain from the region west of the rivers Foyle, Mourne, and Derg, but the O'Neills continued for centuries to claim the tribute of Inis Eoghain and Magh Itha and had a continuous feud over it with the O'Donnells.

Darcy ruled the colony from 1333 to 1337, and the Anglo-Irish at the King's request sent an army under Desmond and Ormond over in 1335 to help in imposing Edward Balliol as king upon the Scots, and voted a generous subsidy of two shillings per plowland from 'all the land of peace', a tithe from the clergy, and an aid according to their means from the towns; all of which, however, was a love grant 'not to be drawn into a precedent or custom'.[1]

In spite, however, of Anglo-Irish help against the Scots, the firm policy of Lucy and Darcy was continued, and in May 1338 Thomas de Cherleton, 'Custos' of Ireland, was instructed to dismiss incompetent officials; to put into effect an ordinance of the King and Council in England that none but Englishmen born should hold legal offices; and to make strict inquiry into all grants of lands and liberties made by the King or his father.

Finally, the long-smouldering resentment of the Anglo-Irish burst into flame, when in March 1341 the Justiciar Sir John Darcy (son of the former viceroy of this name) named as his deputy Sir John Morice, a plain English knight, on whose advice King Edward had relied for this whole Irish policy. One of the edicts which Morice was instructed to enforce ordered that all officers within the land of Ireland, who had estates or were married in the country, should be replaced by Englishmen whose estates were altogether in England, 'by whom we think to be better served than by Irishmen, or by Englishmen married and having property in Ireland'. It was assumed that such new officials would be welcomed as being more honest and impartial, more efficient, and less easily intimidated. But England, then as often afterwards, was to find itself baffled between the apparent loyalty and the secret disloyalty of her own colonists. In face of what seemed like a proscription of 'the English by blood', the Patriot Party re-formed itself under Desmond, and so great was the general indignation that the Latin annals of Ireland, which are all for the Anglo-Irish side, say of this year 1341, 'the Land of Ireland at this moment stood at the point of breaking for ever from the hands of the King of England'.

DESMOND'S PATRIOT PARLIAMENT, 1341

When Morice, after dismissing the old officialdom, summoned Parliament to Dublin for October 1341, Desmond and Kildare, scornful of the mere knight who came in the place of a king, appealed to the whole colony, and summoned a rival parliament to Kilkenny in November, where nobles, clerics, and burgesses

[1] Clyn (1335), and *Lib. Mun.*, I, pt. IV, p. 12: one hundred and seventy leading Anglo-Irish were summoned, and fourteen Irish chiefs.

united as one. 'Never', say the Anglo-Irish annals, 'was there so notable a division between the English by birth and the English by blood.' Desmond's parliament resolved to appeal to the King in person, and sent to him by two envoys a long and searching indictment of the Irish government past and present.[1] They could not endure, they said, that the realm of Ireland should be ruled by the King's ministers as it had wont to be. A third of Ireland was now lost to the Irish, and of late the castles of Athlone, Roscommon, Rindown, and Bunratty had fallen. The cause lay in the neglect and corruption of the King's ministers, as did the decay of the revenue. These officials continually override the rights and laws of Irish subjects. Cases are frequently cited to English courts which could be settled in Ireland. Lands are ruined by neglect of the absentees, who never come to defend them, but draw all the rents they can out of them. 'Scots, Gascons and Welsh have often levied war against the Crown, but your loyal English of Ireland have ever been true lieges, and, please God, will always be so.' Yet in return 'needy men have been sent from England to govern without knowledge of Ireland and, having little or nothing of their own, they practise extortion to the great destruction of your liege people.' The Act of Resumption was an injustice, for, according to Magna Carta, no man can be deprived of his freehold without due process of law. How is it, they conclude, that 'a realm of war can be governed by one unskilful in war; how is it that an officer under the Crown that entered Ireland poor can in one year grow to greater wealth than men of great patrimony can in many years; how does it come about that, seeing they are all called lords of their own, the Lord of them all is not one penny the richer of them?'[2]

This first remonstrance of the Anglo-Irish against domination from England struck a note that was often to be heard in later centuries. The Patriots of the fourteenth, like those of the eighteenth, century were loyal to the Crown, but hostile to English ministries; they were strong in protest but feeble in suggestion; they were preoccupied with their class interest, that of an ascendancy bent on the domination of Ireland; and they said nothing about the native race whose emancipation they alone could achieve.

For the moment the protest was successful and the King, deeply engaged in war with France, forbade Morice to proceed further,

[1] See Berry, *Statutes*, I, pp. 333–63, for this petition.

[2] In 1323 Edward II had issued an ordinance for the State of Ireland; among the points of which was that his Justiciar and officers in Ireland should not purchase lands within the limits of their jurisdiction; the above is a complaint of non-observance of this measure (Berry, *Statutes*, I, p. 293).

and in a reply to the petition on April 14th 1343, repealed the statute which excluded the Irish-born from office.

DUFFORD AND A 'STRONG POLICY'

But after an interval Sir Ralph Dufford, a pure Englishman, was sent over to attempt the reformation of Ireland once more, and landed at Dublin on July 13th 1344, accompanied by his wife, Maud of Lancaster, widow of the late Earl of Ulster, and an army of knights and archers. He proclaimed a general pardon for the Anglo-Irish, and turned his arms against the Ulster chiefs who had usurped the lands of the earldom, deposing Henry O'Neill in Tyrone and setting up in his place Aedh, son of Donal O'Neill.

The new Justiciar was commissioned to inquire into lands given to various lords in Ireland, and soon showed himself high-handed and severe to the 'middle nation', whom his wife detested as the murderers of her first husband. 'This justiciar was an invader of the rights of the clergy and laymen, both rich and poor; the defrauder of many; a robber of goods under the colour of good; never observing the law of the Church nor that of the State; inflicting many evils on the native-born, the poor only excepted, in which things he was led by the counsel of his wife,' say the Anglo-Irish annals, reflecting the colonial sentiment which has so often thwarted English viceroys when grimly bent on crushing the great men of Ireland.

Finally, when Dufford summoned parliament to Dublin on June 7th 1345, Desmond again refused, and called his supporters to Callan, to which he marched with thousands of men. But when the viceroy prohibited the assembly, Desmond's supporters wavered, for loyalty was still a tradition, and the magnates were not yet ready to defy the Crown. His presumption in summoning a parliament, the King's prerogative, could not be forgotten; he was outlawed and his earldom forfeited. Kildare was arrested in Dublin, and Dufford with a colonial army and with the royal banner unfurled marched at the end of June into Munster against the Earl, though the peers refused their assent. No confederacy of Anglo-Irish could as yet match, or perhaps did not yet dare to defy, the forces of the Crown. Desmond's castle of Askeaton fell before the vigorous Justiciar; and Castleisland in Kerry, where the Earl's captains made their last rally, was taken. Here Dufford had the defenders, John Coterel, the Earl's seneschal, Eustace le Poer, and William le Grant, hanged, drawn, and quartered. The first was accused of 'exercising, maintaining, and inventing many foreign, oppressive, and intolerable laws', which apparently were those Irish practices of coyne, livery, and the like, which were so odious to the lesser English, the Irish parliament, and the Dublin government.[1]

Dufford now returned to Dublin, where a prolonged assize dealt severely with the adherents of the Anglo-Irish rebellion. But this able viceroy died on April 9th 1346, to the general joy of the Anglo-Irish, whom Edward placated by appointing as Justiciar Sir Walter de Bermingham, son of the William who had been executed in 1332. The Crown had too much on hand in France, and the Anglo-Irish had a viceroy of their own from 1346 to 1349. A general pardon was proclaimed in May 1346, and though Desmond was exempted from it, he was allowed to lay his case before the King, and along with Kildare was taken into favour and served with Edward at the siege of Calais.[2] In effect his vast earldom, with that of Ormond, was saved by the Act of Resumption being finally dropped.

THE BLACK DEATH, 1348

Nevertheless it was a time of gloom for the Anglo-Irish colony which, having begun well in the first century of the Conquest, had ceased to be recruited as it ought with fresh blood from England, either in its higher or lower ranks. Its population, already no match for the fertile native majority, was now further reduced by the plague called the Black Death, which, according to Clyn, killed fourteen thousand people in Dublin alone from the beginning of August to Christmas 1348 (no doubt greatly exaggerated, still, the figures express a terrible mortality) and finally, it would seem, ended the life of the annalist himself.

It can hardly be doubted that the ravages of this disease wrought far more deadly losses among the Anglo-Irish packed in their little towns and manors than among the Gaels, a scattered and open-air race, and that it assisted along with the race-war in increasing the balance of population for good in favour of the old native population.

'LOYAL' AGAINST 'REBEL' ANGLO-IRISH

While the Irish resurgence continued, and in a single week at Easter 1346, the central chiefs, O'More, O'Connor, and O'Dempsey,

[1] See Clyn, *sub* 1344–5, but the extant records for these events are lamentably scanty.

[2] It must not be forgotten, in treating of Anglo-Irish baronial resistance, that Edward III had much trouble also in England with his parliaments and nobles, a common friction in medieval reigns.

'took three great castles, Lea, Kilmehyde, and Balylethan' and 'all the Irish of Leinster as one man set themselves to war against the English and the lovers of peace', the semi-hibernicized Poers, Tobins (whose original name had been 'De Sancto Albano' or 'De Saint Aubyn'), and other 'naciones et cognomina' of the Old English, did almost as much damage to the 'obedient English' as did the Irish. The old spirit that insisted on male succession in imitation of chieftainship, and refused to let heiresses of the blood convey the family lands away to strangers and absentees, of which the Burkes had shown the greatest example, constantly showed itself. Thus when Sir Walter Bermingham, the Justiciar, died in 1350, without sons, his patrimony went to sisters, one of whom married a Lancashire knight, Sir Robert Preston, founder of the Gormanston family. She brought to him *inter alia* the barony of Carbery in Kildare, but junior Berminghams resisted this feudal claim, and during the process turned Irish, and became enemies of the State. Among the Irish they took the patronymic of Mac Fheorais ('son of Piers', in Irish 'Feoras').

But on the other hand local barons fought gallantly either for the State or the earls who were their suzerains. For example, Fulc de la Frene, lord of Listerling in county Kilkenny, is especially praised by Clyn. In 1333 there was war between the famous Leysagh O'More and Fulc, 'who maintained the cause of the Englishry of Ossory', 'for the same O'More united all the Irish of Munster and Leinster for war, and only Scanlan Macgilpatrick and Henry O'Ryan took the side of the English and of peace'. In 1347 the gallant Fulc went with Maurice, Earl of Kildare, by the King's summons to France, and served at the siege of Calais. In 1348 Fulc, returning and 'having the care and custody of the lands of the Earl of Ormond, then in England, put a strong guard into Nenagh, and restored to their homes and lands the banished lieges, and forced the Irish to rebuild the walls they had destroyed, and, by great payments of cows and hostages, to buy themselves back into their former obedience'.[1]

In addition to the losses in these small pitched battles against the Irish, the colonists lost castle after castle to them. The Gaels had not been a castle-building race and it was not till after the Bruce invasion that we find them erecting stone-roofed castles for themselves and wearing armour in battle. Nevertheless, what between their overwhelming numbers, their attacks at every

[1] Donal O'Kennedy had in 1347 wrought all this damage around Nenagh. Fulc was head of an important Anglo-Irish family, De Fraxineto in Latin, De la Freyne in French, in modern form Freney or Frene, who were lords of Listerling, Clone, and other places in county Kilkenny (see *Cal. Ormond Deeds, passim* for frequent references).

point, their employment of the redoubtable *gall-óglaich* and other mercenaries, the tide of military pre-eminence definitely turned against the Normans of Ireland in the fourteenth century. Their castles fell in great numbers to the triumphant Celts, whose chiefs needed not to build fortresses for themselves when they could take over the magnificent structures raised by the feudal invaders. These great strongholds of the conquerors had been numerous in the first century and more of the Invasion; their epoch as castles of the State and garrisons for all who obeyed it now came to an end, and castle-building after the Irish resurgence was revived on another basis.[1]

Like the Gaels, the Normans of Ireland, whom the Government called 'the March English', ceased to unite in a general plan, and, becoming each a lord in his own country, became less formidable as a mass. But even in holding their own against Gaelic neighbours, now almost as redoubtable, their ancient pride of blood, courage in battle, genius for the art of war, adherence to superior armour and weapons, continued to distinguish them, and the 'Old English' of Ireland remained to the end a masterly and much admired race among the bards and chroniclers.

THE GOVERNMENT'S WAR EFFORTS

Little as the Norman-Irish did to assist the State, vigorous governors made constant efforts to save and defend the English land, and all through the reign small but efficient armies of light horse (hoblers), men-at-arms, and archers followed the Justiciar against the 'Irish enemy', and in the year 1344–5 Dufford spent some £3,576 on a paid colonial army.[2]

The recovery of Connacht and Ulster was the immediate charge of the justiciars. The heiress Elizabeth was betrothed in 1341 to Edward's second son, Lionel of Clarence, and in 1347 this young prince was created Earl of Ulster. But both the earldom and the lordship of Connacht were empty names. In Ulster one after another Lacys and De Burgos had gone, and the O'Neills and their Irish vassals remained. The royal race of Tyrone had now divided into two branches, of which the senior, under Aedh More, son of Donal of the Remonstrance, king of Tyrone from 1344 to 1364, generally bore among the English the title of

[1] Mr. Harold J. Leask, 'Irish Castles, 1180 to 1310', *Royal Arch. Institute* (1937), points out that the first age of castle-building in Ireland is 1180 to, say, 1320. A fresh age of construction began in the fifteenth century, but this time the castles are for the local and private purposes of the semi-irishized Norman lords.

[2] *Exch. Mem.*, XXIII, p. 420; XXIV, p. 185; and XXVI, pp. 132–52.

'O'Neill the Great'. The second branch, which took its rise from Aedh Bui, king from 1260 to 1283, being expelled by the senior line, now sought their fortunes in the vacant earldom east of the Bann, where in the next fifty years they founded the principality of Clandeboy ('Clann Aedha Buidhe') a state which by 1550 covered most of the country between the Glens of Antrim, Strangford Lough, and Lough Neagh.[1] But along the coasts of Antrim and Down many powerful families of the Englishry survived, such as Byset or MacEoin of the Glens, and the Savages and Russells whom De Courcy planted in Down; and these families, though they became mainly Irish in speech and habit, clung to their feudal titles and English tenures.

A GREAT VICEROY

A memorable English justiciar was now found in Sir Thomas Rokeby, who arrived in December 1349 and ruled till August 1355. A large part of his duty was to war on the insurgent Irish with troops paid by subsidies from the colony, and Rokeby fought a vigorous campaign against Dermot O'Brien who became king of Thomond in 1343, and whom he reduced to temporary submission. Against another Dermot, the MacCarthy who had overrun Muskerry, he also waged a spirited campaign.[2]

He also made attempts to bring the chiefs to honourable submission. Already in 1333 English law had been granted to MacCarthy and O'Dwyer. In 1346 Dufford granted English law and liberty to 'Maurice', son of Maccon MacConmara, O'Brien's chief man. Finding it impossible to combat the clan organization which the outlying English were adopting, the Dublin government decided to work through this system and, by recognizing the Irish or Norman chief as 'head of his nation' (*capitaneus nacionis suae*), to make him a stable agent and guarantee for order and peace, while the chief himself would welcome an external sanction for his office from the Lord of Ireland, whose light yoke the Gaelic lords were not unwilling to accept.

'CAPTAINS OF THEIR NATIONS'

This was especially necessary on the Leinster marches, and in 1350 three border chiefs, English and Irish, submitted to Rokeby. Seán O'Byrne, 'captain-elect of his nation', took oath in presence

[1] See later, pp. 238–40, for a more detailed account of the rise of Clandeboy other lordships in east Ulster.
[2] See later, pp. 223, 229.

of the Justiciar to observe the King's peace, and should any of his progeny or following commit felony or robbery on the King's faithful people, the chief should hold them to account till called upon to surrender them to the King's justice.

Similar terms made with two 'degenerate' English or Ostman families, the Harolds and Archbolds of the Dublin marches, and Rokeby confirmed the title of *capitaneus* to Walter Harold and Matthew Archbold, who had been chosen chiefs by the leading men of their name. The recognition of clan chieftainries henceforth was a common practice, and was continued even by Henry VIII and Elizabeth. But while the Tudor monarchy was powerful enough to make the terms obeyed the Plantagenet lordship was not. Rokeby in effect had to legalize Brehon custom and the adoption of Irish chieftainship by the 'degenerate English', and to allow Gaelic and Norman 'captains and lords of countries' to stand between the common people and the State.[1]

MAGNA CARTA CONFIRMED, 1351

The struggle of Justiciar *versus* Barons was now ended by the triumph of Desmond's opposition. The King ordered to be published in 1351 a body of ordinances, twenty-five in number, which had been passed in a parliament at Kilkenny in October the former year, held before Rokeby. They were all 'for the honour of God and of Holy Church, the good government of our said land of Ireland, the peace of its people, and the better keeping the laws and chastising evildoers'. The first article granted 'that Holy Church be free and have all her franchises without infringement, and that all the articles contained in the Great Charter of the King be in all points held firm and established'.

Magna Carta had been regranted for Ireland by Edward II in 1320; it had to wait thirty years before his son confirmed it. But it ended the King *versus* Baronage question in Ireland. The famous clause: 'no freeman shall be taken or imprisoned, disseised, outlawed, or exiled, or in any other wise destroyed, nor will we pass upon him nor send upon him but by the lawful judgment of his peers or by the law of the land', protected Desmond, Ormond, and the great grantees of 1327–30 against arbitrary dispossession. Their Anglo-Irish peers would certainly not have dispossessed

[1] *Exch. Mem.*, vol. XVII, p. 603; Harris *Collect.*, II, p. 203; and my article in *E.H.R.* (Jan. 1910), 'The Clan System among English Settlers in Ireland'. Among those who present Walter Harold as captain are six of that name, two Howels, one Archbold, one Lawles. The lands of these families (which included 'Harold's country') stretched all the way from Saggard to Kilruddery, Bray, and Dalkey.

them. The provocative Act of Resumption therefore of 1331 fell to the ground.

In July 1355 Rokeby retired from office and died the next year in Kilkea Castle, earning the epitaph of a plain and honest minister of the Anglo-Irish commons; who, according to Grace's annals, 'chastised the Irish well and paid honestly for all the victuals he took', and said, 'I prefer to eat and drink out of wooden vessels and to pay gold and silver for my food, clothing, and soldiery.'

Such well-meaning English viceroys must have been sore puzzled with the complexity of their task in Ireland, so large a country and with such variegated elements, to deal with which they had been given so few resources. While a few Wicklow chiefs, who from their hills could look down on Dublin castle, might fear it, fifty miles away chiefs were resuming their old kingships or carving out others as if the State did not exist. In Hy Many, for example, the O'Kellys were celebrating their release from the yoke of the Crown, the De Burgo earls, and the Butler claimants, and William O'Kelly's feast to all the poets of Ireland in 1351 was justly celebrated by the latter.[1]

In order to understand medieval Irish history and be fair in our judgments, it is essential to face the fact that, generally speaking, Irish chiefs regarded the circumstances of English conquest and rule *pro* and *contra* according as these circumstances favoured them as individuals or their septs as local kings. Lordships were now being formed on every hand, partly by revival of old kingships such as that of O'More, the triumph of one claimant over another as O'Kelly over O'Madden, and the invasion of lands left derelict by the Anglo-Normans, such as that of Inishowen by O'Doherty, of central Antrim by O'Neill of Clandeboy, of Butler's lands on Lough Derg by Clann Brian Rua. One of the most striking cases of the last is the triumph of Dermot MacCarthy, a scion of the Desmond race, who, though often warred upon by the English before his death in 1368, founded a third MacCarthy race, lords of Muskerry, in western Cork.[2] Geography, which had made Ireland so varied a country of mountains, boglands, forests, fought for the natives; and the small, heavily armed forces of the justiciars could do little against the light-armed, swift-footed

[1] See the poem (52 quatrains) '*Filidh Éreann go haointeach*' ('the Poets of Ireland came to one house') ed. in *Eriú*, V, pp. 50–67. It is by the famous bardic poet Goffraidh Fióinn Ó'Daláigh, who died in 1387. The readiness of his caste to serve both Gael and Gall is illustrated in that he was at first poet to the Earl of Desmond, then later to MacCarthy More.

[2] For this Dermot see Butler, 'Pedigree and Succession of MacCarthy More', *R.S.A.I.* (June 1921), pp. 32–48. He was brother of the reigning king Donal Oge (d. 1391), and founded the Muskerry branch of the MacCarthys.

natives, who could turn to fight as suited them in the woods and the wilds.

MAURICE, EARL OF DESMOND

After serving as Justiciar for a few months, the Earl of Desmond, now pardoned and reconciled to the State, died in Dublin on January 25th 1356, and was interred at Tralee.

The career of Maurice FitzThomas is memorable for that Anglo-Irish movement which he formed and led, not against the English Crown but against the domination of English-born officials and the ruling of Ireland from Westminster. He is the first of the 'Patriot leaders' in the long history of Anglo-Ireland. The ill governance of Ireland certainly justified an Irish Bruce and a war of independence, but Desmond and his followers could not shake off the spirit of the 'middle nation', the colonial race, which, though Irish to the English, was English to the Irish. Like later Geraldines, the Earl might dream of a separate Crown, but in fact he was wanting in the iron resolution which alone could have made a native lord the monarch of Ireland. His sympathies were with native culture, but not with native independence. In 1339 he suppressed a native rising in Kerry and, as his own kinsman, Maurice, lord of Kerry, had aided the Irish, he took him and had him starved to death in prison. Hence the Anglo-Irish annals praise him as 'a just man in his office, for he would hang his own kinsmen for their evil deeds as well as strangers, and well chastised the Irish'. Among the Irish, who loved a great man to be at once a stern warrior and a man of sympathy, the Earl was regarded as the chief example of those 'princely English lords who gave up their foreignness for a pure mind and their harshness for good manners, their stubbornness for sweet mildness, and their perverseness for hospitality', and to whom all was forgiven for their love of Irish speech, letters, bards, and chroniclers.[1] Thus did the Geraldines, who never were English in England, after a short period, turn Irish in Ireland, and prove by their versatility the legend of their mixture of Florentine, British, and Gaelic blood.

[1] See the O'Madden tract, op. cit., p. 196.

Davies, *Discovery of the True Reasons, etc.* (op. cit., p. 307) writes of this Earl: 'This much then we may observe that this Maurice FitzThomas was the first English lord that imposed coigny and livery upon the King's subjects, and the first that raised his estate to immoderate greatness by that wicked extortion and oppression; that he was the first that rejected the English laws and government and drew others away by his example to do the like; that he was the first peer of Parliament that refused to come to the Parliament when summoned by the King's authority; that he was the first that made a division and distinction between the English of blood and the English of birth.'

TRIUMPH OF THE ANGLO–IRISH

The constitutional party had for the time succeeded. From 1356 to 1361 the Government was mainly in Anglo-Irish hands, and Maurice of Kildare and James of Ormond ruled the colony either as justiciars or deputies. A whole body of edicts, summed up in an *Ordinacio facta pro statu terrae Hiberniae*, having been passed by the King and Council of England, was sent over in 1357 with the object of reforming administrative abuses, appeasing the wounded feelings of 'the English by blood', recognizing their rights to be ruled with their own consent, and to share in the same legal rights as the English-born.[1]

To remedy the general lack of governance, officials were to make yearly account and be supervised by commissions of the Justiciar and other high officials, and magnates of the locality concerned. The evils of purveyance were to be mitigated. 'The affairs of our Land of Ireland shall be referred to our Council here, but shall be determined in our Parliament there (i.e. in Ireland).' 'All Englishmen born in Ireland as well as those born in England shall be taken to be true Englishmen bound by the same laws, rights and customs', such rights to be *secundum legem et consuetudinem terrae Hiberniae.*

More efficiency and force was needed to impose these edicts than the State possessed, but they had the effect of assuring the loyal English of the nearer counties that a government after their own heart ruled in Dublin. A royal edict of March 1360 excluded the native Irish from holding office in the Church, the towns, or the State among the Englishry. It enacted that 'no pure-blooded Irishman of Irish nation (*nullus mere hibernicus de nacione hibernicana*) should be made mayor, bailiff, or other official in any place subject to the King, or hold canonries, ecclesiastical benefices, or livings among the English'. 'Yet,' it continues, 'at the request of Irish clerks living among the English, We have commanded that Irishmen of this sort, of whose loyalty our judges are assured, shall not in any way be molested.' A clear distinction was made by the Crown between the outer Irish living under their chiefs and the clanless Irish.

On certain elements at least the Government could still trust. The towns were the true strongholds of the English interest, and numerous charters of self-government, fresh liberties, and murage grants enabled the burghers to wall their towns and entrench themselves like petty republics. There was a strong pro-English element in the Church; many of the bishops were Anglo-Irish and

[1] Berry, *Statutes*, I, pp. 408–21.

occasionally of pure English blood, the orders were divided, and even among the Franciscans there was a minority which did not in the Irish tongue preach up the native cause as a strong element had done in the Bruce invasion. The rural colonists in the nearer areas, who had no great lords over them, looked to the State and had a strong anti-Irish spirit. The 'Pale' as it came to be called in the next century, or 'obedient shires', was still large and covered the lands from Dundalk to Bray, and ran inland over most of Meath. The Government could, had it collected its forces, have proved more than a match for any single body of opposition, and indeed had recently shown it in the suppression of Desmond's armed resistance.

There were still the materials for an anglicized Ireland, though the greatest of all, a university, was lacking. In 1358 the Irish Council forwarded to the King a petition from the clerics and scholars of Ireland, who pointed out the lack of facilities for learning in the country, and the perils of crossing the sea, and desired to study in Dublin the civil and canon law, with other sacred sciences. The King in reply took under his special protection 'all scholars, masters and clerics coming to the said city from all parts whatsoever'. But this wide invitation needed the backing of generous donors, and found them not. There was some small endowment, and a few students continued to frequent the scanty *domus scholarum*, but that was the end of all projects for a medieval University of Dublin.[1]

[1] Harris, *Collect.*, III, p. 27. In the Church history of the time the famous name is Richard FitzRalph, archbishop of Armagh 1346–60. See several studies on him by Rev. Aubrey Gwynn in *Studies* (1933–7).

CHAPTER XII

THE STATUTES OF KILKENNY AND THE GAELIC REVIVAL

Lionel of Clarence, the second son of Edward III, was in 1361 in his twenty-third year, and a most princely youth, tall, strong, and handsome. In right of his wife Elizabeth de Burgo he was Earl of Ulster and Lord of Connacht, once a splendid lordship, but now fallen for the most part into the hands of O'Neills, O'Connors, and rebellious Burkes.

In March 1361 Edward announced that his son was about to proceed to Ireland, and sixty-four absentees were summoned to Westminster for Easter, to give counsel, to provide troops, and to come in person or proxy with him. The preamble, as addressed to Humfrey, Earl of Northampton, Constable of England, ran thus: 'Because our land of Ireland—by the attacks of Irish enemies, and through the impotence of our lieges there, and because the magnates of our land of England, having lands there, take the profits thereof but do not defend them—is now subjected to such devastation and destruction that, unless God avert and succour the same, it will be plunged soon into total ruin, We have therefore, for the salvation of the said land, ordained that our dear son Lionel shall proceed hither with all dispatch and with a great army.'

Among the absentees named were Ralph, Earl of Stafford, and Edward le Despenser, joint heirs of the liberty of Kilkenny; Margaret Countess of Norfolk, heir of Carlow; the Countess of March, mother of Edmund Mortimer; and Agnes de Valence, wife of John Hastings and Lady of Wexford. Between them these claimants nominally owned four lordships of Leinster and the county of Meath.[1]

Lionel was appointed Lieutenant on July 11th 1361, and proclamation was made that all Crown lands occupied by the Irish and all domains of non-residents were to be granted to English subjects who would dwell upon them. Finally he sailed from Liverpool and landed in Dublin on the 15th of September, having with him 1,500 men, knights, esquires, hoblers, and archers, under command of the Earl of Stafford.

[1] Rymer's *Foedera*, III, pt. ii, pp. 609 *et seq.* Trim and Leix had been restored in 1355 to Roger (II) de Mortimer. Thomas of Brotherton, Earl of Norfolk and Lord of Carlow, died in 1338; his granddaughter Elizabeth married John Mowbray, and their son, Thomas Mowbray, was created Earl of Nottingham in 1383, Earl Marshal in 1386, and Duke of Norfolk in 1397.

The advent of a royal viceroy revived the fears of the Anglo-Irish nobility. It was obvious that what was chiefly intended was the recovery of Leinster, where not only had the Irish reconquered the Crown and archbishop's lands of Wicklow and overrun north Wexford, but the resident Butlers, Geraldines, and others had appropriated most of the vacant lordships of Kilkenny and Carlow.

Lionel had come to break the wings of the Anglo-Irish, whom the Crown still suspected and feared. Hence, when he set out on a campaign against the O'Byrnes, he forbade any of Irish birth to approach his pure English camp; but the result was that a hundred of his men were cut off, either by treachery or through neglect of advice from the Anglo-Irish, who were better versed in the tactics necessary to Ireland. 'Seeing this,' say the *Laud Annals*, 'he collected all the people, both of England and Ireland (i.e. both Anglo-Irish and English-born), in one, and prospered well and made many wars everywhere with the Irish.'

Lionel remained here for five years, save for eight months' absence in England in 1364. We know little of his campaigns save that he led armies into Desmond and against the Leinster clans. Froissart tells us how MacMurrough dared to face the King's son in open field. 'One of their kings, Arthur Maquemaire, king of Leinster, fought with Duke Lionel near the city of Leinster; in the battle many were slain and taken on both sides, but the king of Leinster escaped.' The Irish annals record that in 1362 'Art MacMurchadha, king of Leinster, and Domnall Riabhach, heir of Leinster, were made prisoner treacherously by the son of the King of England and died in prison'.[1] But they left a famous avenger, Art Oge, Domnall's younger brother.

Having cleared the line of the Barrow, Lionel rewalled Carlow and refortified the castles of Dublin, Trim, and Athlone. In Ulster he had a seneschal, and a constable at Greencastle, but little profit came of it, and beyond Carrickfergus most of the earldom was practically lost. Aedh O'Neill it appears did formal homage to him as Earl; Mahon O'Brien, king of Thomond, and his son Brian, later king, also did homage. The lordship of Connacht was far gone, but Lionel deprived William, son of Raymond de Burgo, of the custody of his wife's lands there, and appointed a treasurer of his own, who, apparently, had little success in enforcing rents and services.[2]

[1] *A.F.M. sub* 1362. For Froissart see later. What the 'city of Leinster' was we cannot tell. For Lionel's officers in Connacht and Ulster see *Cal. Reg. Sweteman* (ed. Lawlor), *P.R.I.A.* (1911), pp. 259, 283. The latter mentions an indenture of peace made between the Duke and O'Neill.

[2] See my *Richard II in Ireland*, pp. 40, 136. Brian O'Brien in submitting in 1395 declares that he and his father had submitted to Lionel.

Some interesting legal records of this time throw light on the efforts made by such viceroys as Lionel and Rokeby to recover the English land for the colonists, efforts attended with little lasting success.[1]

'At pleas of juries and assizes held in Cork before Gerald FitzMaurice (3rd Earl of Desmond) on March 13th 1368, a jury was summoned as to whether Richard Oge Barrett and five other Barretts unlawfully disseised Geoffrey, son of Richard Cogan, of his free tenements in Ballyhiche, Corkcally, Moyal, and Anhoe, namely sixty carucates of land, wood, etc. (in all 8,320 acres).

'Richard Oge Barrett came and said that the King granted him for good service all the lands *a filo aque de Lee* (the mid-channel of the Lee) to the mid-channel of the water of Avonmore in the cantred of Muscrymytan,[2] and all lands and tenements from the Lee in the north to the river Bride in the south, and from Inchiaill and Moraghcolagh in Dundrynan and Bruyn, which have long been wasted by the Irish of the parts of Munster, enemies of the King, and which were perambulated by the King's lieutenant (Lionel) with a great army and by great war acquired—to have and to hold to Richard and his heirs by rent of one rose.'

The King's grant above was attested by Lionel, September 20th 1366:

'Inquisition by a jury who say Geoffrey Cogan was seised of said tenements in Anhoe, etc., and he and his tenants in burgage there, in spite of MacDermot and his accomplices, in the time of Thomas de Rokeby held the land and laboured it, at the time when the King's grant to Barrett was made.[3] In Corrys, which is a hamlet of Anhoe, two tenants called Coll held one messuage, and five and a half carucates of Geoffrey by service of five marks per annum. These tenements were ruined by MacDermot so that the English could make no profit thereof, until Thomas de Rokeby, the Justiciar, drove out MacDermot from Balyhithe and Marestown, and proclaimed that all Englishmen should return to the devastated lands within forty days

[1] *Exch. Mem.*, vol. XVIII, pp. 62, 77, and XXIX, pp. 151–85.

[2] Avonmore is the Blackwater. Muscrymytan is *Muscraighe Mitine* in north-west Cork, and corresponds to the barony of Muskerry West *alias* Muscraighe Ui Fhloinn, the deanery of Musgrylin from Dripsey to Ballyvourney.

[3] For Dermot MacCarthy, 'MacDermot' as the English called him, see formerly, pp. 221, 223.

and reside, or forfeit. Geoffrey did so, therefore he is to recover the land [Richard Barrett's plea being that Geoffrey had not resided].'

A similar assize follows between Richard Oge and the above five Barretts and John Lumbard as regards a free tenement in Manokyth, Glascortan, Cnocnemarw, Oldecastell, and Faigh near Mayoly, viz. twenty messuages, twenty-four carucates of land, forty acres of wood, and one thousand acres of pasture, etc. The same King's grant is recited with the same boundaries, save Dundrynan and Bruyn. The lands were recovered by Duke Lionel with a great army, and the grant tested by him at Kilkenny on September 20th 1366. Lumbard answers that the lands were not waste at the time of the grant but inhabited by himself and his men, and shows a grant by Edward III of the castle of Gynes and the said lands (thirty carucates) by reason of forfeiture of the said Dermot MacDermot taken into the King's hands, and let to him because of non-residence of English at forty shillings per annum. He had done good service, and when war began he collected all the free tenants of the cantred of MacKill and Olethnum with horse and arms for guard. This grant was tested by Rokeby at Cork, February 1st 1353, and confirmed at Westminster on June 11th 1356. The ordinance compelling the English to return to dwell on their lands within fifteen days is again quoted. Therefore an assize of *Novel Disseisin* is called against the Barretts and John Lumbard recovers seisin.

In another such case, the said Geoffrey, son of Richard Cogan, puts himself against the same Barretts as regards the manors of Ballycarty and Ballydoudan. After the expulsion and death of MacDermot and proclamation as above, Geoffrey let the manor of Balycarty to one Fynyn MacCarthy, to have and to hold at the will of Geoffrey, paying a certain rent, and after that to one Donghan yCorry and Donghah Roth MacCarthy, at will and at rent. Then yCorry went into rebellion and Geoffrey granted it to Donal MacTayg who held it till the Barrets invaded Geoffrey to occupy the lands. Barretts make the same plea of non-residence, but the case is left undecided.

Lionel's successes, however, were not lasting; his troops were few and the absentees were slow to come over, so that in February 1362 the King had to order those who lingered 'to proceed with troops to Ireland, where my dear son and his companions stand in imminent peril'.

It is significant of the decay of the colony that the parliamentary subsidy had to be reduced, and a royal proclamation forgave the earls, prelates, barons, magnates, and commons of Ireland, both lay and cleric, all their debts and accounts, reliefs, escheats, fines, etc. up to October 1362. The state to which the revenue had fallen is shown in 1360 when the gross receipts for the year reached only some £2,140, and the expenses were some £1,945.

In 1363 Lionel's wife Elizabeth died, leaving an only child, Philippa, who later married Edmund Mortimer, Earl of March.

By now the royal viceroy, who was created Duke of Clarence in November 1362, was already wearying of his unattractive office, and in particular of the dissensions between the English of Ireland and 'the English by birth', which made it necessary in June 1364 for him to order 'that none of the English, born in England or Ireland, shall make any dissension, reproach, or debate among themselves on pain of fine and punishment'.

Anglo-Ireland was already divided into the two elements of 'the March lords' or 'degenerate English' and the still loyal people of the towns and the 'obedient shires'. It was on these latter that Lionel had leaned, and it was their spirit, anti-Gaelic and anti-feudal, which triumphed in the parliament of Kilkenny which Lionel summoned to meet him on February 18th 1366.[1]

THE STATUTES OF KILKENNY, 1366

Though many magnates were present, the shire and town deputies probably formed a majority; the Council would reinforce them, and it is to these elements that we must attribute the English spirit of the enactments. The preamble of the thirty-five enactments ran as follows:

> 'Whereas at the conquest of the land of Ireland and for a long time afterwards, the English of the said land used the English language, mode of riding, and apparel, and were governed, both they and their subjects called "betaghs", according to the English law—now many English of the said land, forsaking the English language, manners, mode of riding, laws, and usages, live and govern themselves according to the manners, fashion, and language of the Irish enemies, and also have made divers marriages and alliances between themselves and the Irish enemies, whereby the said land and the liege people thereof, the English language, the allegiance due to our

[1] The original roll of this parliament is lost, but a transcript exists in Lambeth Library, which was published and edited by Hardiman in 'Tracts Relating to Ireland' (*Irish Arch. Soc.*). This is also printed in Berry, *Statutes*, I, pp. 430. The language is Anglo-French.

Lord the King, and the English laws are put into subjection and decayed, and the Irish enemies exalted and raised up contrary to reason.'

To prevent all this and to recall the English lieges of the King to obedience and the law, certain enactments are passed. The English lieges are forbidden to make alliances by marriage, concubinage, gossipred, or fostering with the Irish. They must use the common law and in their lawsuits are forbidden to use 'March law' or 'Brehon law' (*lei de Marche ni de Breon*), 'which rightly ought not to be called law, being bad custom'. Nor shall they sell to any Irish in time of peace or war, horses or armour, or any manner of victuals in time of war. They may not entertain or make gifts to Irish minstrels, rymers or story-tellers. All Englishmen, and Irish dwelling among them, must use English surnames, speak English, and follow English customs. If any Englishman, or Irishman dwelling among the English, use Irish speech, he shall be attainted and his lands go to his lord till he undertake to adopt and use English.

Irishmen 'of the nations of the Irish' are excluded from cathedrals, benefices, and religious houses. The Irish of 'the marches' may not pasture on the lands of the English or of the Irish at peace.

In order to make joint resistance to the Irish, parleys and treaties with them must be in common by legal permission. There is to be but one peace and one war throughout the whole of the King's land of Ireland. The English must not break peace legally made between English and Irish.

In every county four of the most substantial men are to be made Guardians of the Peace, with power to assess the inhabitants, to provide horsemen, hoblers, and foot, and review them from month to month. Kerns and hired soldiers may only be maintained on the marches. Every chieftain of English lineage (*chieftayne de linadge Engleis*) shall arrest and detain malefactors of his own lineage, adherence, or retinue, till delivered by the law. The colonists are to forsake hurleys and quoits and learn the use of the bow 'and other gentile games which pertain to arms'.

The 'English' or 'obedient' land is reckoned as the counties and liberties of Louth, Meath, Trim, Dublin, Kildare, Carlow, Kilkenny, Wexford, Waterford, and Tipperary. Finally, excommunication is declared against those who shall contravene these statutes; and the archbishops of Dublin, Cashel, and Tuam, and the bishops of the joint diocese of Lismore and Waterford, of Killaloe, Ossory, Leighlin, and Cloyne, 'being present in the said parliament, did in parliament fulminate sentence of excommunication against all who should so contravene them'.

The evident purpose of the Kilkenny statutes was not to declare war upon the Irish race as such, but, at the cost of abandoning a large part of the 'English land' to the Irish and to the 'chieftains of English lineage', to preserve the remainder for the English speech, race, and law. Inside this 'land of peace' all Irish inhabitants were to be forced into English speech and custom, so that they should not impair that purity of English tradition which the statutes aimed at securing for ever. Such Irishmen could without difficulty secure or buy 'English liberty'. The Irish living outside the chosen land were not entirely rejected, as we see by later kings and viceroys taking their homage and granting them charters of denization, but the statutes were so interpreted that even the 'Five Bloods' lost after 1366 that unwritten privilege of English liberty which up to then in theory they had enjoyed.[1]

No general edict of admittance to English liberty was included among the Statutes of Kilkenny, and the reason seems clear. By this time the Irish themselves had ceased to make the general demand for it which they had made several times between 1270 and 1320. Betaghry was dying out in the English land, and the former serfs were slipping into common freedom. Great numbers of the Irish living *inter anglicos* had been emancipated by individual charters of freedom, for which there was a fixed charge and formula. The outer Irish who had preserved the old order in the west, or on the borders of the Englishry, had by now either won complete independence, or else the earls and great lords made indentures and treaties with them by which the chief, in return for certain services, ruled his own people undisturbed. Abandoning all thought of reviving the High kingship and of a general expulsion of the foreigners, the Gaelic chiefs were content to share with these Normans who had become so Celtic the lordship and spoils of Ireland.

That the Statutes of Kilkenny were essential to their peace and freedom became the *idée fixe* of the common Englishry of Ireland. Like Magna Carta, they were confirmed again and again, and the

[1] We find the Justiciar De Windsor in 1375 making a grant of English law to Molrony O'Griffa, 'capitaneus nacionis suae', Molrony his son and Neil and Dermicius his brothers, *qui fideles ligei Domini Regis devenerunt et ad fidem et pacem Regis se ac homines et servientes suos bene et fideliter confirmarunt*, at Clonmel, by request of the Earl of Desmond. Harris, *Collect.*, II, p. 203, and *Exch. Mem.*, XVIII, p. 603. Yet the famous Art MacMurrough was not admitted to the barony of Norragh inherited by his Anglo-Irish wife (see later, p. 265).

last time was at Poynings' parliament in 1495. But by that time it was clear how futile they had been, for the act against the use of the Irish language by the English had to be regarded as null, and no longer capable of being enforced among the bilingual people of the 'obedient shires'.[1] The acts against fosterage and alliances were soon set at naught by collusion of the Anglo-Irish and the Crown itself. The successor of Lionel as viceroy, Gerald, Earl of Desmond, in 1388 got the royal licence to have his son James fostered with Connor O'Brien. The English had failed to plant their own culture, and it was inevitable that they should yield to the flowing tide of Irish speech, music, and minstrelsy. Ten years after the Statutes of Kilkenny, we find the Irish parliament enacting that 'Donal O'Moghane, Irish minstrel, may dwell among the English and be in their houses'.[2]

Lionel's task was now finished, and he left Ireland for good on November 7th 1366. A splendid second marriage was arranged for this handsome young widower with Violante, niece of the Visconti lord of Milan. It was celebrated with great pomp at Milan, May 27th 1368, but after five months of feasting and extravagance, Lionel was taken ill, and died on October 6th that year, leaving no child by his Italian bride.

The greatest effort made, if not in armed force, at least with the splendour and authority of a royal prince since Edward II's reign, thus ended. Lionel left his earldom of Ulster and lordship of Connacht as derelict as before, and the absentee lords of Kilkenny, Carlow, Wexford, Leix left their Irish lands to the practical possessors, native or Norman. An Anglo-Irish reaction followed his tired effort, and Gerald, 3rd Earl of Desmond, ruled the colony from 1367 to 1369. The natural head of the Patriot Party, and known to the Irish as 'Gerald the Poet' because he composed in Irish verse, he became in later days the hero of both races.[3]

THE EFFECT OF THE STATUTES

The Statutes of Kilkenny form the Great Divide in medieval Irish history. After a long attempt to conquer the whole island

[1] *Statutes of Irish Parliament* (1786): cap. 8 of Poynings' parliament (1495) reconfirms the Statutes of Kilkenny—'*those that will that every subject shall ride in a saddle and those that speak of the language of the Irish, alone excepted*'.

[2] Harris, *Collect.*, III, p. 220 and *Pat. Rolls* (*England*) 49 Edw. III. For licence to Desmond see *Rot. Canc. Hib.*, p. 139. The foster-father was Connor, brother of Brian, king of Thomond, 1369–99. For the Statutes see Appendix IV on 'Legal Treatment of the Irish'.

[3] *A.F.M.* (1398) say that Gerald 'excelled all the English and many of the Irish in knowledge of the Irish language, poetry, and history'. Several of his poems, of great merit and interest, have been of late years discovered in the MS. *Book of Fermoy*. (See pp. 237, 280.)

and after various efforts to bring the Irish within the law, the design was abandoned and the Government decided to keep what it could of the country. The Irish *inter anglicos* were to be treated as subjects with citizen rights provided they would conform to English law and adopt English surnames. Actually, as things worked out, the mass of Irishmen living within the colonial land, 'the Pale' which was still large, was so great that anglicization was impossible, and in fact the Irish language and Irish names spread steadily among the colonists up to 1600 instead of the opposite process.

Further, the English and old Norman stock throughout the island, no matter how 'degenerate' and hibernicized, had their rights as liege and natural subjects of the King preserved, and never in subsequent times lost their rights of citizenship. Though often treated as 'English rebels', they could always seek pardon and return to their natural allegiance. To be able to prove an 'ancient British origin' or descent from 'the blood of the First Conquest' was sufficient to entitle a man to full legal rights of property and civic equality.

But to be proved of 'Irish and Irish nation' entailed, even for those who might have peacefully lived among the English, denial of civil rights and equality with their colonial neighbours. Numerous cases can be given of this right up to Tudor times. Only an official grant of English law and liberty freeing the recipient from 'the yoke of Irish servitude' could ensure just treatment, and admittance to the rights of trading, marrying, fostering, and taking church offices among the Englishry.[1]

Of the Irish who did not live among the English, or were able to defy their jurisdiction and live the old sept-life under their own chiefs, we may say that, in the spirit of the ancient Romans dealing with the Italian tribes whom they conquered, but knew better how to deal with than did the Anglo-Irish, they were refused the threefold rights of *ius connubii, ius suffragii, ius commerciandi*, that is, they were legally forbidden to trade, marry, and enjoy citizen rights with the colonial race. In short, they were put outside the law.

The Statutes of Kilkenny amounted indeed to a real outlawry of the 'mere Irish' in so far as they refused to become English in speech, law, dress, custom, and name. Until the abolition of these statutes in Chichester's parliament of 1613–15, it was always possible in law to deny the right of 'an Irishman of Irish nation' to freehold land, property, trade, or office. And equally, penalties

[1] See Appendix IV on 'Legal Treatment of the Irish', and for specimens of charters of liberty.

for fraternizing with the Irish in the forbidden matters entailed severe penalties on any of 'the old English' marrying Irish wives or adopting Irish ways and language.

In fact, however, the law was so feeble, the population it had legislated against so large, the pull against the statutes so strong, that they remained largely a dead letter, to be enforced only when possible. For all that, by making the Irish at best only vassals and never 'lieges', it created a division between the two races which added fuel to their feuds and prevented their peaceful blending for over two centuries.

To the majority of Irish chiefs, however, the enactment of such laws seems to have mattered as little as the condition of Hindu peasants under the British Raj formerly did to the native princes of India. The flowing tide of success was with the Gaelic chiefs; more and more of the land was falling back to them. Bent as they were on the recovery of their old lordships, they could not foresee that in the sixteenth and early seventeenth centuries their very title to these lands would be straightway denied in Anglo-Irish courts of justice, or by juries charged to find a title for the Crown or for Anglo-Irish noblemen such as Ormond who still kept title-deeds inoperative since the thirteenth century.

On their part the Gaelic dynasts never willingly abandoned any of their family claims, and the following fragment of lost annals shows the tenacity with which such claims were handed down.[1] After reciting O'Reilly's right to his country of Brefni, the modern Cavan, it concludes:

> 'Know everyone who shall read this that this is the length and breadth of the country that the Nugents and Plunketts took from the territory of the Clann Mahon in spite of O'Reilly and the race of Calvach, son of Felim, who had the possession and overlordship of the country, with its rent to O'Reilly and to the Lord of Clann Mahon, namely from *Béal-atha-fiodha-an-atha* to *Gearra-chinn-Coraidh* and from *Béal-atha-na-mBó* to *Béal-atha-na-gCeannaidheadh*; and whoever shall succeed in adding this country to the Brefni again he has right and justice to it, and it is above *Ceann-Bhaile-Ghabhair* that *Gearra-chinn-coraidh* is, near *Loch Leighin.*'

TRIUMPH OF THE 'IRISH ENEMIES'

'Irish enemies' became the official designation of the border chiefs who made war upon the Pale. In several fields it was now

[1] From a fragmentary 'Register of the O'Reillys (1161–1583)' in Trinity College, Dublin (23 F. 12). Three of the place-names appear to be Ballannaganny, Gerrakincorra, Ballygore.

shown how formidable they had become. Brian O'Brien, king of Thomond, overthrew Earl Gerald, 'with all the English of Desmond' in battle at Monasteraneany near Croom, and took prisoner the Earl, 'whose army was cut off with incredible slaughter' on July 19th 1370. Brian then pushed on and captured the mainland part of the city of Limerick; the citizens capitulated; and O'Brien set Sheeda Oge Macnamara as warden over them. Macnamara was soon slain in an immediate rally of the burghers, but O'Brien retired with the spoils of the fifth-richest city in Ireland.[1]

The triumphs of native lords in Muskerry, Inishowen, Keenaght, and elsewhere have been noted. The details of the petty battles and raids in which they wore out the Englishry fill the annals, both Latin and Gaelic, but defy description in any one general picture. It is certain that their advance, suspended for a time by the impressive arrival of an English prince, was continued after his departure.

THE WAY CONNACHT WENT

While Ulster for the most part fell to native chiefs, the Lordship of Connacht passed completely out of legal hands. O'Dowd, O'Connor Sligo, O'Malley, O'Shaughnessy, and others recovered or occupied great tracts, and shared with the degenerate English the inheritance of De Burgo. Thus in 1340 MacDermot, chief of Moylurg and Airteach in north-west Roscommon, 'extended his sway over Sliabh Lugha (Costello's country) by the strong hand', and in 1371 O'Dowd of Mayo 'recovered Tireragh from the English and divided it between his kinsmen'. The Burkes were now lords, in fact if not in law, of all Mayo and county Galway. Sir Edmund Albanach, the greatest man in Connacht, was technically a usurper and rebel, and is described as such in a Chancery inquisition *post mortem* on the death of Lionel in 1368. This *inter alia* says: 'The Duke held of the King in chief in right of his wife by the courtesy of England the manors of Loughrea, Tobryd, Tyloghoban, Loghmaske, Sligo, Galway, and Portumna in Connacht by service of twenty knights' fees when scutage befalls, and they were worth when the said Duke was in Ireland £200 per annum but now nothing, because they are occupied by Edmund de Burgo, knight, and other rebels of the King, both English and Irish, nor

[1] *Laud Annals* (1370). *Ann. L. Cé* and *A.F.M.* say 1369. The King's lieutenant, De Windsor, had to ransom Desmond from O'Brien and it was while he was captive that the Earl composed the Irish poems referred to above. Brian, who was son of Mahon, received from this exploit the name 'Brian Catha-an-Aonaigh'.

has any minister of the King dared to go thither to execute his office.'[1]

But the O'Connors, though the line of Cathal Crovderg had by now ended the competition against them of Clann Murcertach and the race of Brian of Leyney, became themselves fatally divided between the branches of O'Connor Roe and O'Connor Don.[2] In 1384, on the death of Rory, son of Turloch O'Connor, 'two kings were made in his place, namely, Turloch Ruadh, son of Aedh, son of Felim, was made king by MacDermot and Clann Murcertach and other chieftains of Síol Muiredaigh, and Turloch Oge, son of Aedh, son of Turloch, was made king by O'Kelly, Clanrickard and Clann Donough, etc.; so that common war grew up in all Connacht and that they made many ills, plunderings and evils on account of it'.[3]

THE WAY ULSTER WENT

We have seen how before 1300 Irish lordships such as O'Cahan's began to be founded on the north Ulster coast.[4] Nevertheless still by 1333 the chief Irish, including even O'Neill of Tyrone, in central and southern Ulster, were military vassals under De Burgo and might well have continued so had not the earldom fallen with a crash in 1333. This event was the first to clear the way to a complete Gaelic recovery, the second was the failure of Lionel of Clarence to recover De Burgo's lordships. The north coast as far east as Coleraine went over to O'Donnell, O'Doherty, and O'Cahan. There, however, the town of Coleraine held out, and an irishized Norman family, De Mandeville, which took an Irish patronymic MacQuillan (Mac Uidhilin), became lords of the Route, a country in north Antrim, stretching between the Bann and the Bush rivers to Ballycastle, along the course of the former almost down to Ballymena, and inland to the Glens, with Ballymoney as capital and Dunluce as chief castle.[5]

[1] 'Occupation of Connacht by the Anglo-Irish', by T. Knox, *R.S.A.I.* (1903).

[2] See O'Connor Pedigree, Appendix I (B).

[3] *Ann. L. Cé.* The division continued; the old Shilmorthy demesne was cut in two, and subsequent other laments attest what a fatal blow it was to the unity and power of the O'Connors. A third branch, as we have seen, was that of O'Connor Sligo which lasted well into the seventeenth century.

[4] The founder of the O'Cahan greatness, as it lasted till 1600, seems to have been Cú-mhuidhe Ó Cathain who died in 1385. His beautifully canopied tomb is still to be seen in Dungiven church, county Derry; a specimen of the new type of medieval chief, on the altar tomb his effigy is in full armour, on the sides are figures of gallowglasses. He is known in local tradition as 'Cooey na Gall' (i.e. of the Foreigners; probably because he adopted English armour and ways).

[5] 'Rúta meic Uighilin' is first mentioned in *Ann. Ult.* (1357). For the history of this family see my article, 'The MacQuillan-Mandeville Lords of the Route', *P.R.I.A.* (1937).

The history of this family (whose Gaelic name comes from one Hugo or Hugolin of about 1270) is one of the earliest and most striking examples of the degeneracy of the Norman stock into Irishism, and the forsaking of their feudal allegiance to the Crown in order to become lords in Irish fashion of a compact country of their own.

Henry de Mandeville, a chief tenant of the Earl, having been seneschal in 1270, made himself dominant in the Tweskard (Tuaisceart), the district which afterwards formed the Route. Thomas de Mandeville, also seneschal in 1280, called 'Mac Martin' by the Irish, embraced the claim of Aedh Bui O'Neill and his son Brian to the kingship of Tyrone right up to 1295, when, however, at the battle of Craebh Telcha the main stock, led by Donal son of Brian O'Neill, slew Brian and so ended the rivalry of his line.[1] The permanent O'Neill capital in Tyrone now became Dungannon, where Donal, who reigned till 1325, built a castle.

Nevertheless with the aid of the Mandevilles, the connivance of the Earl, and the acquiescence of 'O'Neill the Great', glad to be rid of a dangerous rival, the Clann Aedha Buidhe were able to cross the Bann and make a new state for themselves in Antrim and Down. The murder of the 'Brown Earl' in 1333 was the work —an unforgivable one in the eyes of the law—of the Mandevilles; while some of them remained loyal, the murderers or their connivers naturally became outlaws. But since the times favoured defiance, the rebel Mandevilles defiantly held on to the country they were dominant in, and made it into a lordship which lasted intact till 1586.

Taking early to the mercenary profession, a natural one for unemployed Normans, scions of the Mandevilles were found serving the O'Connors and claiming to be hereditary 'constable of the Bonnacht of Ulster', under the Earl or his successors, Lionel and the Mortimers.[2] Their great founder, however, when the time (*circa* 1400) came to establish great Norman-Irish 'countries' over all Ireland, was Sinicin Mór (Jenkin More) who ruled for the remarkable period of 1389 to 1449. Henceforth the MacQuillans were indistinguishable in language, government, and habit from surrounding Irish chiefs, save that they were known to be of English feudal descent, that they preserved better armour and superior war-tactics, and, however rebel, were still of 'the King's allegiance'.

[1] Nevertheless, on the death of Donal O'Neill in 1325, Henry, grandson of Aedh Bui, succeeded to the kingship of Cinel Eoghain until 1344; he was then expelled by Aedh of the senior line, who ruled till 1364. Henry was the last of his branch to assert this claim.

[2] 'Slemni (Stephen) MacUighilin, constable of Ulster' died in 1368 (*A.F.M.*).

Aided by such 'degenerate English' the Clann Aedha Buidhe took the determined step of invading the very lands of the earldom, east of the Bann and Lough Neagh, where alone the feudal settlers had been deeply planted. There is little evidence how the descendants of Aedh Bui (Brian, Henry, Murcertach, etc.) achieved this expansion (a clear case of 'sword-land') but it was done at the expense of the old resident chiefs, the MacDunlevys, O'Flynns, and others. In 1359 Murcertach, son of Thomas O'Flynn, was slain by Murcertach, head of the Clann Aedha Buidhe; henceforth the kings of Ui Tuirtre passed into insignificance, and the race of MacDunlevy, former kings of the province, after 1333 pass out of Ulidian records altogether.

In the end Clandeboy, the second-greatest O'Neill state, though other branchings occurred later, reached from the ford of Belfast to Glenravel in Antrim and south to the borders of Lecale, Kilwarlin, and Kinelarty; on the west it included Kilultagh on the south-east side of Lough Neagh, and beyond the Bann included Coill Ichtarach in south-east Derry in the old O'Flynn country of Loughinsholin.

Meanwhile in the Glens of Antrim the Bysets remained lords. On the death of John Byset in 1260 his claims passed to daughters, but, after the usual Anglo-Irish fashion, junior males ignored this and continued to rule the Glens as MacEoin (son of John). Within a few decades, however, they were to be supplanted by MacDonnell lords.[1]

Further south, in the Ards and along Strangford Lough, the Savages, who claimed to be hereditary seneschals of the earls in county Down, continued in similar hibernicized fashion. In fertile Lecale in south-east Down, however, a strong English colony managed to survive of De Courcy's and De Lacy's time, namely Russells, Swords, Fitzsimons, etc. Up to the middle of the fifteenth century indeed it would appear that the coastal English of Ulster were still a numerous, puissant, and united colony.

THE REVIVAL OF THE LEINSTER IRISH

The revival of the old MacMurrough kingship of Leinster and of its vassal 'urrighs' in the fourteenth century coincided with the revival of the province-dynasties elsewhere. The extinction of the families of Bigod, De Valence and De Clare, in the period 1306–24, left the great liberties of Leinster derelict or in absentee hands, and aided the descendants of Donal Kavanagh to claim

[1] See p. 184. The 'Glynns' is the older and probably more correct name of the 'Nine Glens of Antrim'.

again the ancestral kingdom, whereas for long in Carlow they had merely been officers of the Bigods, 'as Irishmen and kinsmen of Roger the Earl Marshal', for their native vassals, and had themselves been tenants of a portion of Hy Kinsella.[1]

We have seen how in 1324 Donal MacMurrough, son of Art, was openly elected 'king of the Leinstermen'. This proud chief had family grievances to avenge, for his grandfather Art and his grand-uncle, the reigning chief Murcertach, had been slain treacherously in Arklow in 1282 by the English of that town, and later, in 1305, 'Moryerdagh More McMorgh,' 'Murght and Douenald Oge' and Henry, all of that surname, were treacherously slain by some of the English of Ferns.[2]

Donal's assumption of the royal title led to nothing for the moment; he was indeed captured and imprisoned, but escaped from Dublin Castle to lead the Leinster septs again till he was slain in 1347. Art More, of the senior line, king after him, displayed the ever-growing boldness of the race. But he too, daring to face Duke Lionel in the open field, was, say the Four Masters, captured along with his son Donal Riabhach in 1361 and died in prison. The casualties among this insurgent race were indeed many; Dermot 'Lamh-dearg' (Red-hand), king from 1361 to 1368, was captured by the 'Black Knight' (as the annals mysteriously call some colonial leader), and in 1369 was 'drawn to death' in Dublin; Gerald Caemhanach, 'makings of a king of Leinster', was also slain by this 'Black Knight', and Donnchad, king of Leinster, was in 1375 slain by Geoffrey de Valle near Carlow.[3] But the son of Art More, Art Oge, was destined to revive the old Leinster kingship on a scale not unworthy of pre-Norman days.

Beyond the Barrow the old vassals of Leinster, O'More of Leix, O'Dempsey of Clanmalier, O'Connor of Offaly, all revived singly or in alliance their ancient lordships. East of the Barrow the O'Byrnes were steadily building up a lordship that in the end stretched from Delgany to Arklow and inland to the head of the Vartry river, to the recesses of Glenmalure, and to Aughrim, where it touched on MacMurrough's territory of Shillelagh. In

[1] *Cal. Just. Rolls*, II, p. 347 (1307): inquisition on lands of Roger le Bigod: 'Donald MacMurworth held for term of his life two carucates in Fynnagh (Fynnore in county Carlow).'

[2] *Cal. Just. Rolls* II, p. 143, where the date of the first murder is given as July 21st 1282; see ibid., p. 466 for that of 1305. It is uncertain whether these MacMurroughs were prominent men of the royal race.

[3] See the Pedigree of MacMurrough in Appendix I (B). *Ann. Ult. sub* 1375 say: 'Donnchad Caemanach Mac Murchada, archking of Leinster, was killed treacherously by the English; and there came not from Brian Boruma downwards a man that destroyed more of the Foreigners than he.'

north and west Wicklow the O'Tooles had expanded from Imaal to Glencree, and in 1376 'Aedh Ua Tuathail, king of Ui Mail, was slain by the English'. North Wexford passed into native hands again; and so in the end from Enniscorthy and Ferns up to Bearna-na-gaoithe at Delgany all the country went back to the old race. It was made clear how fatally the Normans had erred in taking over only the richer lands for settlement, and in leaving vast tracts of the hinterland to the Irish, from which in due time they emerged triumphantly.

BUYING OFF THE CHIEFS

But indeed the bewildered and rapidly disintegrating colony was assailed on every side, and the standing duty of the King's lieutenant was to repel, conquer, or conciliate the aggressive chiefs and their confederates.

The Council of Ireland reported to the King in 1371 that 'O'Brien, Macnamara, and nearly all the Irish of Munster, Leinster, and Connacht, and many English, have risen and are confederated to make a universal conquest of all Ireland'. The Government stooped to buy off chiefs who threatened the capital itself, and the famous black-rents began as a way of staving off the ruin of the Anglo-Irish state. In 1372 the Earl of Kildare, then viceroy, and the Council offered Donnchad MacMurrough twenty marks as a reward for 'the safe keeping of the royal roads between Carlow and Kilkenny', and the triumphant chief gave his receipt from his seat at Fynnor as 'Donat Kevenagh called MacMurgh'.[1]

The policy of recognizing important men as 'captains of their nations' and to use then against one another, could be continued, and in 1377 the Earl of Ormond was empowered to offer certain payments to Turloch O'Brien 'constitutus per Curiam Hiberniae capitaneus nacionis suae', for which the latter claimed repayment later in 1380, when he demanded also payment for troops maintained by him against 'MacMurgh, styling himself King of Leinster'.[2]

[1] *Rot. Canc. Hib.*, pp. 85, 87. See *Exch. Mem.*, XXX, pp. 342 and 233, (1372) 'an English cloak worth 71*s*. given to Donat McMurgh now in our peace and obedience'. Fynnor would seem to be Kilfenora (Cell-fhinnabhrach) near Kellistown in county Carlow. This Donat is apparenty Dónnchad Riabhach (slain by the English in 1375).

[2] *Exch. Mem.*, XXXIII, p. 13 (3 Rd. II). Turloch, who died in 1398, was asserting the claim of Tanistry against his nephew Brian who became king of Thomond in 1369, Brian being son of Turloch's elder brother Mahon, king of Thomond Turloch was, however, driven out by Brian, and the Earl of Desmond gave him land in the Comeraghs in county Waterford.

For the black-rents see paper by D. B. Quinn, 'Irish Parliamentary Subsidies', *P.R.I.A.* (1935).

'MURROGH EN RANNAGH'

But the most terrifying, confederate, destructive, and long-remembered onslaught upon the colonial settlements was that of Murchadh 'na Raithnighe' ('of the Fern') O'Brien. In 1377 the Irish parliament itself had to buy off out of a depleted Exchequer this 'Irish enemy', and the transaction marks the lowest point yet reached in dignity by the Norman conquerors of Ireland. The Close Rolls record how, at the parliament of Tristeldermot in Lent 1377, the Justiciar, James Earl of Ormond, the Chancellor, and other officers, with the Council and the prelates, magnates, nobles, and commons of Ireland, considered among other things, 'how Murgh O'Brien—who, with a great force of Irish of Munster, is now in the parts of Leinster in aid of the Irish of the same, and meditates making war on the King's lieges there—might best be put back from Leinster'. It was agreed that the said Murgh should have a hundred marks on condition of withdrawing without delay from Leinster—for performing which he took his corporal oath on the Holy Gospels before the said Justiciar, Chancellor, etc.; whereupon the clergy, magnates, and commons of the counties of Dublin, Kildare, Kilkenny, and Wexford freely granted the said hundred marks save nine—'but, as the said Murgh would not depart unless full satisfaction were made, it was agreed that the said nine marks be paid to the said Murgh out of the Treasury of our Lord the King'.[1]

Such invasions must have seemed to the bewildered colonists like what the raids of Teutonic tribes on the march were to the quaking Romans of the decaying Empire. Luckily for the threatened colony, the Irish chiefs, though they might take towns (and never again was a place so great as Limerick taken), could be bought off by black-rents and other inducements, and, as they were all battle-leaders, they fell prematurely and frequently in those battles which they waged with the loyal Englishry.

[1] Berry, *Statutes*, I, p. 473. 'Murgh' O'Brien was Murchadh 'na Raithnighe', son of Brian Bán and head of the dispossed Clann Brian Rua which had located itself east of Lough Derg in Aradh and were latter called Mac Ui Bhriain or MacBrien of Ara. The exaggerated traditions of Murchadh's great raid were still vivid in Munster in Spenser's day, for he says in his *View of the State of Ireland* that 'Murrogh en Rannagh' ('Morrice of the Fern') made himself master of Clare, and next overran all Munster and Connacht and clean wiped out many great towns such as Inchiquin, Killaloe, Thurles, Mourne, Buttevant, of some of which there is now no memory or sign remaining; after which with a mighty army he marched forth into Leinster, and soon after created himself King, and was called King of Ireland'.

TANISTRY AND LINEAL SUCCESSION

The practice of Tanistry (*tanaiseacht* or 'second in succession') now generally adopted, in imitation it would seem of English primogeniture, did much to strengthen the Gaelic ruling races. Succession-wars, which had been so often raised by *rigdomnas* ('royal heirs'), and members of a given *derb-fine*, did not cease even now, but at least a chief's rivals were fewer, and limited to those nearer kinsmen who were eligible to succeed by tanistry, whether brother, son, or uncle.[1]

Before the Invasion it would seem as if direct lineal descent in Irish kingship was establishing itself, and after the Norman occupation the struggle to narrow down the succession claims and secure descent in limited families and from father to son had much success. The line of Turloch More O'Connor established itself in Connacht, the MacCarthy descent showed considerable tendency to primogeniture, and among the O'Neills, after the MacLochlainns were ousted, the line of Brian 'of the Battle of Down' got a lead which it never lost. But in Connacht the struggle of royal heirs of several lines after 1270 grew bewildering, and finally the division after 1384 into O'Connor Don and O'Connor Roe, becoming fixed, ruined this great family. In spite of several successful assertions of the lineal and father-to-son succession, as among the O'Neills, the clash of shifting and elective as against hereditary automatic kingship continued to agitate and to fatally weaken the Gaelic dynasties till the Elizabethan period.

As the Normans had now abandoned the idea of a final conquest, so the Gaels had abandoned the idea of a final deliverance. They were, in fact, all through the fourteenth and fifteenth centuries unable to uproot the great Norman families of Ireland. The class that did perish before them was the small gentry, small townsmen, and the free tenantry whom the absentee lords and the Crown of England left shamefully neglected. Such of these as did not disappear had to turn Irish themselves finally out of self-preservation, unless they found shelter under the great earls.

[1] The best treatment and illustration of all this is to be found in Professor James Hogan's masterly and exhaustive paper, 'The Irish Law of Kingship', *P.R.I.A.* (1932).

See MacNeill, *Phases*, p. 295, on the question. The Tanist or 'next successor' was legally appointed during the chief's lifetime. It is a question at what date Tanistry began, or rather became generally accepted. MacNeill thinks the fourteenth century, but there seems evidence for a much earlier date. In *A.F.M.* under 1024 we read of Ruarc, grandson of Diarmaid, Tanist of Brefni.

It was enough for the Gaelic chiefs to ruin the towns, drive out the border colonies, and plant their people back again in districts long feudalized. The greater ones might style themselves 'Rex Lagenie' or 'Rex Ultonie', etc., and occasionally one of them, invading English land, was urged by his bard to proclaim himself Árd Rí at Tara, but even such a vain ceremony on the famous but abandoned hill was never achieved, and the hero would turn back content with black-rent from the colonists, and a scarlet cloak, a fee, and the empty title 'chief of his nation' from the Dublin government.

But though the military triumph of the Irish was incomplete, the revival of Gaelic tradition, language, and habit was universal: it captured the palatine lands and finally even the Pale itself.

DECAY OF ANGLO-IRISH CULTURE

Left without a university or educational system, never reinforced by fresh blood from England, the once-promising Anglo-Norman civilization of Ireland steadily decayed.

The heart had indeed gone out of the English colony. When the historians cease the end of a state is at hand. Clyn ends in 1348 and the *Laud Annals* in 1370; the fruits of Anglo-Irish literature in either French or in the new English had been few; and now the 'English land' could inspire neither historian nor poet. The once wide-laid veneer of Anglo-Norman civilization was indeed wearing thin.[1]

In the decay of their own culture the Anglo-Irish naturally turned to the wells of native culture, though their own Statutes of Kilkenny forbade them to drink thereof. In the clash of the two civilizations, it was the Irish world alone which moved. The native princes, though content politically with their local lordships, united to rebuild the common culture of the race, of which they were the natural patrons. Numerous entries in the annals now suggest a revival in the fields of medicine, law, poetry, history, and imaginative literature, a revival which contrasts strongly with the silence of the two former centuries.

As an instance of this revived spirit, Niall More O'Neill built in 1381 'a house for the entertainment of the *literati* of Erin' at Emain Macha near Armagh, the most famous traditional site in Ulster, once capital of King Concobar, in the time of the *Táin Bó*, which had been abandoned for many centuries.[2]

[1] For the decay of the English language, etc. see my 'Spoken Languages of Medieval Ireland', in *Studies* (1919).

[2] *A.F.M.*, curiously corroborated in *Sweteman's Register* (calendared by

THE RISE OF ART MACMURROUGH KAVANAGH, 1376

The Leinster colony, the main stronghold of Anglo-Ireland since the Ulster earldom fell, was threatened now by the rise of the greatest hero that had appeared among the native race of that province since Strongbow. This was the chief that was known to the Irish as Art MacMurchadha Caemhanach.

We have already traced the revived MacMurrough dynasty from the extinction of the Bigods, legal lords of Carlow, in 1306. Donnchad, king of Leinster, was slain in 1375. His younger brother, second son of Art More, then succeeded; this was Art Oge ('Art the younger') himself, destined in a long reign of forty-three years (1375–1418) to restore the kingdom of his ancestor Dermot in its later medieval shape.

It was the standing policy of the Anglo-Irish to play one chief off against another. A less-known Art, son of a former chief Dermot, described as 'Arth filius Dermicii McMorgh de Kenseley', was summoned to a parliament at Dublin under the Earl of Ormond in January 1377, and undertook in the name of his 'nation and adherence' to take the King's side against the insurgent Irish of Leinster, and was taken into service for a year at a fee of forty marks. But the rising star of the other Art indicated him as the man to make terms with. Art Oge, described by the Government as 'Art Kevenagh, pretended captain of the Irish of Leinster', immediately after his inauguration in 1375 had taken the field with a great army, and now demanded the fee paid to his predecessor Donnchad in 1372. As the Government hesitated to pay, he ravaged far and wide in the counties of Wexford, Carlow, Kildare, and Kilkenny. The Justiciar and Council therefore gave way, and later in 1377 paid the retaining fee which, at the rate of eighty marks per annum, was duly paid out of the Exchequer to the MacMurrough chiefs up to the early sixteenth century.[1] Art Oge was inaugurated in 1375, being then about twenty years of age, in the traditional site of Cnoc-an-bhogha near Ferns, O'Nolan proclaiming him king as was customary.

A bardic poem to celebrate the occasion was written by Eoghan MacCraith, and the significance of the poem is greater than its merits as poetry, for it signalizes the return in this great province of Irish culture which had disappeared from Leinster since the

Lawlor), *P.R.I.A.* (1911), under date August 1374: Niall O'Neill is charged with threatening to make his manor-residence (*manerium*) at 'Hewynnae near Armagh, which is the Archbishop's land'. Hewynnae clearly represents 'an Eamhain', now called the Navan Ring.

[1] *Rot. Canc. Hib.*, p. 100 b. (See under Poynings' Acts, p. 354.)

days of Strongbow.[1] We shall resume in its place Art Oge's career as the greatest of the King's 'Irish enemies' in the reign of Richard II.

[1] *MS. Royal Irish Ac.* (23, F. 16). MacCraith speaks of Leinster as 'the golden province' (*ni leas-ainm Laighnidh an Óir*) from its gold deposits, and by a play on words calls himself 'the Gilder' (*an tÓrthoir*).

Quiggin, 'Prolegomena to the Study of the Irish Bards', in *Proc. Brit. Acad.* (1911–12), p. 105, states that there is no bardic poetry in Leinster from the Conquest 1172 to the time of Art Oge, for whom this inauguration ode was written.

CHAPTER XIII

THE FAILURE OF THE 'FIRST CONQUEST', 1366–1399

AFTER Lionel's departure Gerald, Earl of Desmond, ruled the colony for two years. Then a fresh attempt was made to strengthen and restore the Anglo-Irish state. England was now in a state of bankruptcy, discontent, and division because of the growing failure of the war in France and the imbecility of the ageing King. Money and troops on a sufficient scale could not be spared for Ireland, which was in danger of being lost; but a determined viceroy pledged to strong measures could still be found.

WILLIAM OF WINDSOR, VICEROY 1369–1376

In June 1369 Sir William de Windsor, one of Lionel's knights, arrived as King's lieutenant with almost sovereign powers and a salary of a thousand marks per annum. He had to cope with 'the Irish enemies', to restore the efficiency of the Government, to consider the relations of the Anglo-Irish to the mother-country, and above all to make them pay for their own defence, and if possible contribute to England's war in France. Once again, as often again, a 'strong man' attempted with a policy of 'Thorough' to make England's dominion of Ireland both pay for herself and contribute to English needs. Unsuccessful in its main objects, De Windsor's viceroyalty marks a significant epoch in medieval Irish history.[1]

De Windsor began by treating separately with the citizens of Dublin and Drogheda, the prelates, and the knights of the shire for Louth and Meath and procuring money grants from them. Again at Kilkenny, in Hilary term 1371, the prelates, peers, and commons of Parliament were forced into granting three thousand pounds 'of their own pure and spontaneous will'. Finally De Windsor summoned a parliament to Balduagh in Trinity of the same year, and in this poor village the chapel where the assembly met was so small and lodging so difficult that the commons, 'worn out with the tedious stay', granted a further two thousand pounds so as to be able to depart.[2] These sums were professedly

[1] See a notable article on him by Maude V. Clarke in *P.R.I.A.* (1932), based upon new contemporary material in the Bodleian, and the *Chancery Rolls*.

[2] Miss Clarke, rejecting the former identification of this place as Baldoyle near Dublin, places it at Ballyduagh, four miles south-east of Cashel.

for the defence of the 'English land', but the amounts and the method revived the already sentient patriotism of the Anglo-Irish.

The complaints against this dictatorship were so strong that the King in October forbade the levy of all 'such undue tallages'. De Windsor was next recalled in the spring of 1372, and an embassy sent over from the Irish parliament accused him before the King's Council in September 1373 of making separate agreements with the counties, towns, and estates, and exacting arbitrary taxes and tallages. In spite of this, the King restored De Windsor as 'Governor and Keeper of Ireland' in September 1373, and order was given for collection of the disputed subsidies.

He returned in April 1374 and there was peace for a year. In October 1375 he summoned a fresh parliament at Kilkenny and asked for a willing subsidy; this was refused, and the continuous resistance of the Anglo-Irish, led by Milo Sweetman, archbishop of Armagh, prompted a fresh riposte. De Windsor produced royal letters under the Privy Seal commanding sixty representatives of the Irish parliament to appear before the Council of England, to treat with the latter on the affairs of Ireland in February 1376.[1] The sixty were to be elected, two from each county as representing nobles and commons, two clerics from each diocese, and two members from each corporate town. The Anglo-Irish sensed a design against their parliamentary institutions, and in the Irish parliament the archbishop of Armagh answered for the clergy that 'we are not bound according to the liberties, rights, laws and customs of the Church and land of Ireland to elect any of our clergy and send them to England for the purpose of holding parliaments or councils in England'. Finally the whole body of nobles and commons of Ireland declared 'unanimously and with one voice' that, 'according to the rights and liberties enjoyed from the time of the Conquest and before', they were not bound to send such representatives, and though they now elected such, they reserved the right of assenting to any subsidies made in their name. Moreover, their present compliance was not hereafter to be taken in prejudice of the rights, laws, and customs which they had enjoyed from the time of the Conquest and before.

Nevertheless the Irish parliament was bent upon the punishment of De Windsor and his chief officials. Articles of indictment were brought over by their delegates, and as a result of the charges contained, the Chancellor, Treasurer, chief and second Barons of the Exchequer, two judges, and several lesser officials of the

[1] The English parliament itself was summoned for February but was postponed and did not assemble till April 29th; this was the famous Good Parliament of 1376, which was dissolved on July 10th the same year.

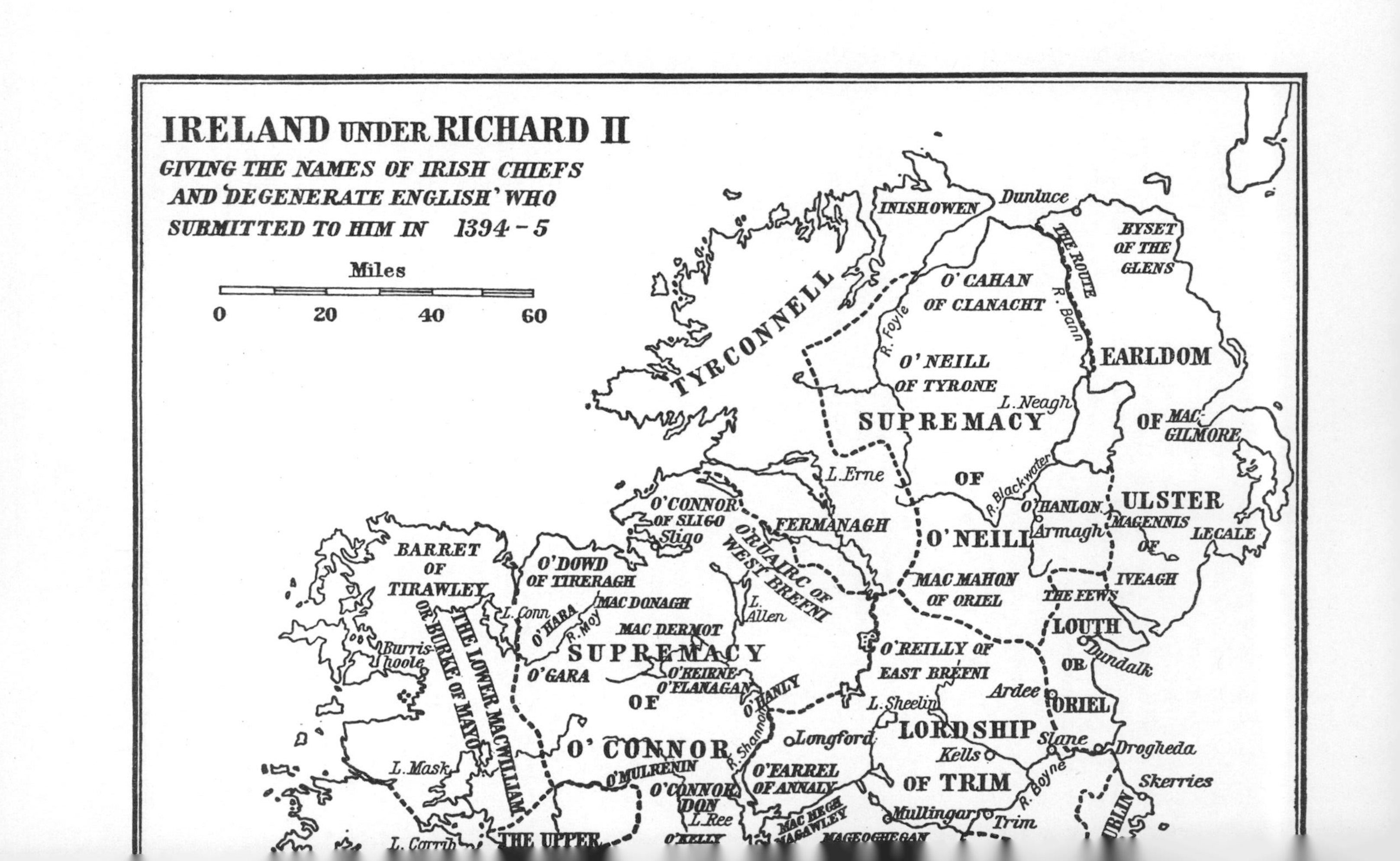
IRELAND UNDER RICHARD II
GIVING THE NAMES OF IRISH CHIEFS AND 'DEGENERATE ENGLISH' WHO SUBMITTED TO HIM IN 1394-5
Miles
0
20
40
60
TYRCONNELL
INISHOWEN
Dunluce
THE ROUTE
BYSET OF THE GLENS
O'CAHAN OF CLANACHT
R. Foyle
R. Bann
O'NEILL OF TYRONE
EARLDOM
L. Neagh
SUPREMACY
OF
O'NEILL
OF MAC GILMORE
R. Blackwater
L. Erne
O'CONNOR OF SLIGO
Sligo
FERMANAGH
O'RUAIRC OF WEST BREFNI
O'HANLON
Armagh
ULSTER
MAGENNIS OF IVEAGH
LECALE
BARRET OF TIRAWLEY
O'DOWD OF TIRERAGH
MAC MAHON OF ORIEL
THE FEWS
L. Conn
O'HARA
R. Moy
MAC DONAGH
L. Allen
LOUTH
MAC DERMOT
SUPREMACY
O'REILLY OF EAST BREFNI
Burrishoole
O'GARA
O'HEIRNE
O'FLANAGAN
OR
Dundalk
THE LOWER MACWILLIAM
OR BURKE OF MAYO
OF
O'HANLY
L. Sheelin
Ardee
ORIEL
R. Shannon
Longford
LORDSHIP
Slane
Drogheda
O'CONNOR
Kells
L. Mask
O'MULRENIN
O'FARREL OF ANNALY
OF TRIM
Skerries
O'CONNOR DON
R. Boyne
L. Ree
MAC HEGH MAGAWLEY
Mullingar
Trim
L. Corrib
THE UPPER
O'KELLY
MAGEOGHEGAN

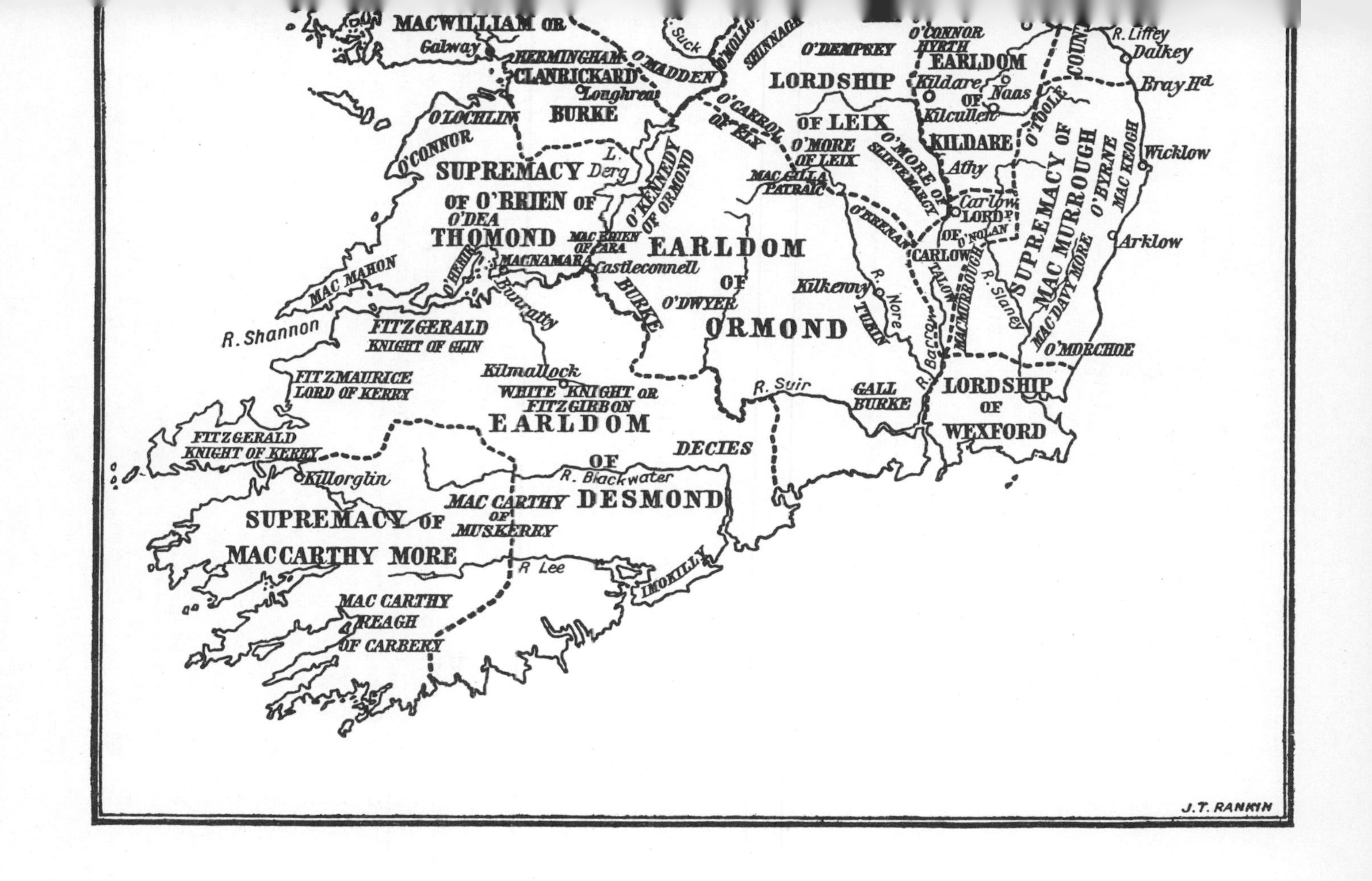

MACWILLIAM OR
Galway
HERMINGHAM
CLANRICKARD
O'MADDEN
Loughrea
BURKE
O'LOCHLIN
O'CONNOR
SUPREMACY
OF O'BRIEN OF
O'DEA
THOMOND
L. Derg
O'KENNEDY OF ORMOND
MAC BRIEN OF ARA
MACNAMARA
Castleconnell
MAC MAHON
Bunratty
BURKE
R. Shannon
FITZGERALD
KNIGHT OF GLIN
Kilmallock
FITZMAURICE
LORD OF KERRY
WHITE KNIGHT OR
FITZGIBBON
EARLDOM
FITZGERALD
KNIGHT OF KERRY
Killorglin
OF
DESMOND
R. Blackwater
DECIES
MAC CARTHY
OF
MUSKERRY
SUPREMACY OF
MACCARTHY MORE
R Lee
IMOKILLY
MAC CARTHY
REAGH
OF CARBERY
Suck
O'MOLLOY
SHINNAGH
O'DEMPSEY
LORDSHIP
OF LEIX
O'CARROL
OF ELY
O'MORE
OF LEIX
MAC GILLA
PATRAIC
O'MORE OF
SLIEVEMARGY
EARLDOM
OF
ORMOND
O'DWYER
Kilkenny
R. Nore
TULKIN
O'BRENAN
R. Suir
GALL
BURKE
O'CONNOR
HYRTH
EARLDOM
Kildare
OF
Naas
Kilcullen
KILDARE
Athy
Carlow
LORD P.
OF O'NOLAN
CARLOW
TALOW
MACMURROUGH
R. Barrow
R. Slaney
LORDSHIP
OF
WEXFORD
O'TOOLE
SUPREMACY OF
MAC MURROUGH
O'BYRNE
MAC KEOGH
MAC DAVY MORE
O'MORCHOE
R. Liffey
Dalkey
Bray Hd
Wicklow
Arklow
J.T. RANKIN

Dublin government were dismissed between July 18th and August 12th. Attempts were made in combination with the Black Prince's party (in which Edmund Mortimer was prominent) in the Good Parliament to bring the viceroy himself to account, but it failed, and De Windsor was merely superseded in office on July 24th by the Earl of Ormond. Never in fact through its whole existence was the Irish parliament to develop the power to dismiss or punish by impeachment or otherwise the King's lieutenant.

THE MEDIEVAL IRISH PARLIAMENT

In spite of the failure of his immediate objects, De Windsor's period of office is epoch-making. 'He is the true founder of the Irish parliament', who trained it in spirit and procedure by holding no less than eight parliaments and two Great Councils in less than five years.

The Irish parliament, of which Wogan had indeed laid the foundations in the reign of Edward I, was now, in the reign of the third Edward, formed into a shape which lasted till the Reformation parliament of Ireland in 1536. 'The doctrine of taxation with the consent of elected representatives given in parliament was accepted. Two clerical proctors from each diocese were finally added to the commons. The obligation imposed on lay magnates to attend parliament became exclusively a matter of tenure. The issue of writs of summons was restricted to earls and barons.'[1]

To these sapient conclusions may be added that the Irish medieval parliament remained a single body, not developing as the English one did into two houses, that its full numbers, when prelates, peers, commons, councillors and chief ministers were all assembled, was seldom more than 120, that it never developed the self-assertion of the English legislature which frequently called ministers to account by impeachment or attainder, and in short was, and remained, a much more embryonic and Government-controlled body. From the first the native Irish had no representation in the Irish parliament, and indeed, as the area from which its members came grew more limited, the less Gaelic were its constituents. Its official language was Latin or French; its language of debate was at first French and then English; the speech

[1] So Miss Clarke, op. cit., who gives an excellent summary of the methods and sources of State taxation in medieval Ireland. She adds that each of the changes which she summarizes as above 'brought the Irish parliament nearer to the Parliament described in the *Modus Tenendi Parliamentum*, the Irish version of which first appears early in the fifteenth century' (on the *Modus* she wrote a later masterly article, 'The Irish Modus', now printed in her volume, *Medieval Representation and Consent*). (See later, p. 292.)

of the native race was not heard within its walls, and the Parliament of Ireland was in essence a colonial assembly. Nevertheless, according to the accepted theory of the *plena potestas* and the fiction that the King and his Parliament of Ireland bound all Ireland, such statutes as those of Kilkenny were taken to be, and in fact were, binding over the whole island and upon the native race also as far and when they could be enforced.

James, 2nd Earl of Ormond, succeeded De Windsor as Justiciar from 1376 to 1379, at the old salary of five hundred pounds, for the English government, bankrupt at home, thought only of getting an Irish viceroy cheap. Few Englishmen would serve on the unattractive service of Ireland for such a pittance, but a native nobleman could treat the highest office of State as a mere appendage to his great hereditary dignities. But there was a danger concealed in this, as the next century showed.

MORTIMER, 'LORD OF THE ENGLISH OF IRELAND'

The Home Rule patriotism of the Anglo-Irish, which Desmond had headed in 1331–41, had scored once more over a centralizing viceroy. In the struggle for constitutional rights the Anglo-Irish followed the mother country, and could now boast of a parliament and government of their own. That their lives and lands were in danger from the Irish enemy, against whom they refused to vote war-supplies, seemed of little importance to them beside their legal and constitutional liberties.

The constant desire of the English in Ireland was to be ruled direct by some Prince of the Blood (if the King himself could not come over), or at least some great personage of the nobility. If he were of their own stock all the more desirable. They now had in the young Edmund Mortimer all that they desired, and in 1372, in the midst of the De Windsor crisis, a Great Council in Dublin had petitioned that he should assume the Irish government in person. This Edmund (II), 3rd Earl of March, great-grandson of Roger, 1st Earl of March, was in 1372 twenty-one years of age, married to Lionel's daughter Philippa, and in her right Earl of Ulster. In his own right he was Lord of Trim and Leix; if the possession had been actual he owned more than half of Ireland, but most of his claims were paper ones, those of an absentee on a colossal scale.[1]

But Ireland still remained to be recovered, and if great names

[1] For his lordship of Trim see Wood, 'The Muniments of Edmund de Mortimer', *P.R.I.A.* (1932), which traces the descent of the Lacy earldom of Meath. In 1355 the liberty of Meath and other Irish lands were restored to Roger, father of Edmund, by reversal of the attainder of 1330. The liberty

have a magical appeal Edmund Mortimer had such a name, which in fact illuminated his descendants for the Anglo-Irish until the Wars of the Roses were over. As husband of a royal princess who combined the names of De Lacy and De Burgo, and as the greatest Irish landlord, his pre-eminence among the Anglo-Irish was admitted by all, while the Gaels themselves honoured a prince whom they looked on as chief among the 'Old English' of Ireland.

RICHARD II AND IRELAND

Edward III died on June 21st 1377, and his grandson Richard, a boy of ten, took his place. Since William of Windsor, the Earl of Kildare, the Earl of Ormond, and other short-lived justiciars had ruled Ireland. But on October 22nd 1379 Edmund Mortimer was appointed King's lieutenant, a fine young man only twenty-eight. By the terms of his commission, he was to have all the revenues of Ireland, and in addition twenty thousand marks from the English Exchequer to be spread over his three years of office, a significant admission that Ireland could not provide in state for its viceking.[1]

Landing at Howth in May 1380 with a considerable army Mortimer marched northwards, and at Coleraine built a fortified bridge over the Bann and recovered this old outpost of the north. There the Ulster chiefs, once vassals of the De Burgo earls, came in and did homage in old Irish fashion. 'The nobles of the Gael', say the annals of Ulster, 'came into his house headed by the heir of the king of Ireland, namely Niall (More) O'Neill. But Art Magennis, king of Iveagh, was taken prisoner by treachery in the house of Mortimer and the Gaels of Ireland took fear of him from that out, so that they and the English of Ireland avoided him.'

Mortimer then invaded Tyrone and thence marched to the Shannon, where he recovered the royal castle of Athlone, and, continuing into the midlands, made war on the 'rebel English' and forced O'More of Leix to admit that he was his hereditary vassal for his lands there. Finally entering Munster, the Earl reached Cork by way of Kilmallock, but died suddenly on December 26th 1381 from the effects of crossing a river in midwinter, and was buried in the Dominican house of Cork.

His infant son Roger, now eight years of age, was left heir to

of Trim was greater than its name implies, for in 1330 that of Westmeath or Lochsewdy was merged in the liberty of Trim, which then covered all Meath with claims upon Westmeath. In effect the liberty of Trim was the old earldom of Meath.

[1] Ramsay, *Genesis of Lancaster* (*1369–99*), II, pp. 298–9: Edmund as Lieutenant between October 22nd 1379 and December 1381 received from the English Exchequer £4,444 6*s.* 8*d.*

the Mortimer lands, and later, in 1385, as grandson of Lionel Duke of Clarence, was declared heir to the throne next after his cousin King Richard.

Under a new Lieutenant, Philip de Courtenay (1383–6), the Irish parliament, in 1385, petitioned that, in view of the great power of Irish enemies, English rebels, and enemies of Scotland and Spain, the King himself or the greatest and most trustworthy lord of England should be sent over.

Robert de Vere, Earl of Oxford, now had 'all the heart of the king', and in October 1386 Richard made him Duke of Ireland with almost complete royal rights. But the King's uncles and barons would not endure any minion of the King, and in 1387, after the battle of Radcot Bridge, De Vere was an exile in the Low Countries and had never seen the realm of Ireland.

When Richard was in Ireland, in a letter he sent to the Regent in England he described the people as divided into three kinds: 'the wild Irish, our enemies; the Irish rebels; and the obedient English.' By the second he meant the hibernicized Norman-English, and by the third, the English of the towns and the Pale.

It was the second class which stood in the way of a thorough conquest and anglicizing of Ireland, for their lands 'in the marches of war' resisted royal writs, refused royal subsidies, and evaded reliefs, homages, and feudal duties. They interposed between the Dublin government and the Irish who had recovered so much of Ireland; for the Irish could not be subdued or brought under the Crown without the co-operation of the March lords, and so far from helping, they had often stood between warlike justiciars and the Irish confederacies. Without the consent and aid of this 'middle nation' Ireland could not be reconquered. But, so far from turning to English allegaince, this great class, the race of 'the First Conquest', which held a third of Ireland, was becoming with every generation more and more Irish in habit, speech, custom, and sympathy.

The Normans in England, who had been more or less French till 1360, then turned English and spoke the new English of Chaucer. In Ireland the Normans, who had spoken French until 1360, turned first out of necessity and then with real affection to the ancient speech and unbroken tradition of the Gaelic majority.[1] This was the contrast between the King's two realms.

[1] Irish was now a companion language to French, and sometimes English, with the Normans of Ireland. Thus the Exchequer Roll which records the submissions of the Irish chiefs in 1395 states that the Earl of Ormond spoke both languages (Irish and English) fluently: 'qui bina idiomata vulgariter loquitur'. (See later, p. 270.)

THE BUTLER GREATNESS

Yet the three earls of Kildare, Desmond, and Ormond for the present continued the loyal or semi-loyal tradition of English law, speech, and government in which a century before all the colonial aristocracy were united. Most loyal in English allegiance, most faithful to the English tradition, were the Butler earls of Ormond. It was at this time that the Butlers, though they lost upper Ormond to the Irish, were generously compensated in the south and east.[1] In 1391 Sir Hugh le Despenser, the younger brother of Thomas who was created Earl of Gloucester in 1397, sold to James, 3rd Earl of Ormond, his inheritance of the castle and manor of Kilkenny, with Callan and many other fiefs in that county. In 1392, at the request of the Earl of Stafford, the King also granted to Ormond the custody of Stafford's portion of the liberty of Kilkenny. Thus did the Butlers complete their lordship in Ossory, and make the noble castle of Kilkenny the permanent home of their race and Kilkenny city the centre of an Anglo-Irish principality which was never lost to the English or their speech and culture.[2]

The Earl of Ormond was now the greatest of the resident nobles of Ireland, even if Mortimer was the greatest titular one, and was the most trusted by the Government. We find James (II) in September 1358 made 'chief Guardian of the Peace for the whole of Munster, to deal with those of English and Irish nations who are confederated to destroy the faithful people of Munster and usurp their lordships by conquest'. This was in contrast with the Desmond Earl who, as leader of a Patriot Party, was asking England to keep her hands off Ireland and let the Anglo-Irish rule things. This James was also appointed Justiciar in July 1376; such marks of confidence were to be frequent with the loyal Butlers.

THE PRISAGE OF WINES

On the death of this James in 1382 the Escheator's accounts name among his vast possessions, titles, and perquisites 'the

[1] In the great raid of Murchadh 'na Raithnighe' O'Brien in 1377 Nenagh castle seems to have been taken, and remained in the hands of MacBrien of Arra, his race, till the time of Piers Roe Butler, Earl of Ormond, in 1533; while the O'Kennedys recovered most of the present baronies of Upper and Lower Ormond.

[2] For the transaction see *Cal. Ormond Deeds*, II, pp. 213–22 (1391–3). It transferred in effect most of county Kilkenny to the Earl of Ormond. Hugh le Despenser was descended from Eleanor, sister of Gilbert de Clare, Earl of Gloucester and Lord of Kilkenny (*o.s.p.* 1314). Henceforth after 1399 the earldom of Gloucester was in abeyance.

liberties and regalities of county Tipperary' of which, now that Nenagh was lost or insecure through the O'Kennedy revival, Clonmel or Crompstown in south Tipperary became the palatine capital. He also had 'the prise wines of all the ports and places near the sea, as well cities and towns as other places, in all the realm of Ireland, excepting the prisage of Cork and half that of Waterford'—a valuable hereditary perquisite going back to the time when his first ancestor in Ireland landed as Prince John's honorary Butler.[1]

TREATIES OF EARLS AND IRISH CHIEFS

The warfare of two centuries had shown that the rights of the old native chiefs could not be extinguished. The Crown had failed to establish them in a secure and general tenure-in-chief, but instead the great Norman lords entered into local treaties with them. They on their part, once it was admitted that they were free of blood and equal in noble status to the 'Foreigners of Erin', did not refuse to make bargains in which they admitted the overlordship of the nobler of these foreigners. Examples are numerous. In 1356 James, Earl of Ormond, 'principal of his nation in Ormond', 'and his people and liegemen' entered into an agreement with Rory O'Kennedy, his nominal vassal, and Mahon O'Kennedy, and their nation and subjects, by which, though the O'Kennedys and their nation pledge themselves to be obedient and respondent to the Earl, it is on honourable terms.[2]

In 1359 the Earl, being then Justiciar, made a treaty with Murtough O'Brenan, lord of Idogh, the hilly district around Castlecomer in Kilkenny. By this agreement, made at Kilkenny, O'Brenan swore to serve the Earl against Irish foes or English rebels, and himself keep the peace, receiving from the Earl five marks of silver yearly. By a later similar treaty in 1400 Geoffrey O'Brenan for himself and his heirs became the liegeman and tenant of the Earl at six marks rent per annum, and bound himself to

[1] For the above Butler references see *Rot. Pat. Canc. Hib.*, 73; Carte, *Life of the Great Duke of Ormond* and vols. I, II, III of *Cal. Ormond Deeds.* The butlership did not in fact become fixed or hereditary in the Ormond family till the fourteenth century but was finally granted by the Crown for good in 1355. The rate was then one tun from each cargo of nine tuns and upwards to twenty and two tuns or their value (40*s.* each) from a cargo of twenty upwards. The prisage of wines remained in the Ormond family till the nineteenth century. For further details on this subject and the nature of the palatine powers see the above *Cal. Ormond Deeds* in the several volumes, e.g., vol. I, No. 693, II, No. 32, III, Nos. 252, 261, 316, 342, 348.

[2] *Cal. Ormond Deeds*, II, Nos. 34, 35. One of the earliest examples of such treaties is between Ralph Pipard, lord of Ardee, and Enegus MacMahon in Oriel *circa* 1290, see *Cal. Ormond Deeds*, I, pp. 106–7 and II, p. 14.

pay double fines (*keyn et ard keyn*; in Irish *cáin* and *árd-cáin*) if he or his men should make transgression on the Earl's tenants; the Earl pledging himself on his part to make amends for the trespasses of his own men.[1]

Such written treaties, charters, and indentures are found also among the Gaelic princes. Thus by written understandings O'Neill and O'Donnell strove to arrange that standing dispute over the vassalage of O'Doherty, lord of Inishowen, the suzerainty of Fermanagh, and the homage of O'Donnell himself for Tyrconnell and Cinel Moen (the plain of eastern Tyrconnell), all of which O'Neill claimed as being in race senior to the Cinel Conaill, and because Inishowen and Cinel Moen had been centuries ago the homeland of the Cinel Eoghain. The whole body of claim was a standing cause of feud, but peaceful and legal ways were sought, as we see by various entries in the annals.[2]

The new relations of Gaelic chiefs with the old hated 'middle nation' were also based on fosterage and marriage. So far, the heads of the two Geraldines and of the Butlers had married English or Anglo-Irish wives, but they gave their daughters liberally to Irish chiefs. Thus Joan, daughter of Maurice, 4th Earl of Kildare, married Donal Cairbreach, the head of the MacCarthys, and their son Taig succeeded to the Irish kingship of Desmond. Joan, daughter of the 2nd Earl of Ormond, married Taig, chief of the O'Carrolls of Ely. Examples of such marriages, contrary to the Statutes of Kilkenny, became numerous and soon led to any given chief being 'both Gael and Gall' when his bard wished to praise him as being of the mixed blood. But to give daughters to Irish vassals or neighbours was one thing; the heads of the leading families till 1450 or later continued to take wives of English blood; the junior Burkes in doing so from William Oge onwards had been exceptional.

ABSENTEE ACTS, 1368, 1380

If the lordship of Ireland were not to become wholly Irish or so Irish that the loyal English there should be a mere remnant driven to extremity by the Gaels and the hibernicized English, the balance of the pure English blood must be restored. A fresh plantation was not yet thought of or needed more money, thought,

[1] *Kilk. Arch. Soc.* (1849–51), p. 237: 'King's Council in Ireland' (*R.S.*), p. 52; *Cal. Ormond Deeds*, II, pp. 246–7.

[2] *Ann. Ult.* In 1514 Aedh O'Donnell and Art O'Neill made peace on the bridge of Ardstraw and *new charters* were granted by O'Neill along with *confirmation of the old ones* for Inishowen, Cinel Moen, and Fermanagh.

and determination than the feeble Government of Ireland had at command.[1] But if the great absentee proprietors could be compelled to return to hold and populate, or at least to garrison, their vast lands, and if the exodus of 'mere English' out of the 'land of peace' could be stopped, the balance might be swung aright. Therefore in 1368 in an ordinance made by the King and Council in England 'concerning the Land of Ireland', based upon the deliberations of a parliament held in Dublin in May of that year as to the grievous state of the country, it was ordered that all those in England of whatsoever rank who had lands in Ireland should reside upon them in person with their families and men-at-arms, or at least send men-at-arms to defend such lands, before next Easter. In default of performing which, they should be deprived of such lands, lordships, possessions, and inheritances. In the English parliament itself at Guildford it was enacted that absentees should return to Ireland before Easter 1369 or forfeit their estates.[2]

In 1380 a second, more stringent, and final Act of Absentees was passed. By enactment of an English parliament the King provided that all who have lands, rents, benefices, offices, etc. should go and reside there before the Nativity of St. John next and guard and defend their lands there, and all who have castles and fortresses there should restore and guard them. Moreover, that if any such were absent of necessity they should send men to defend such lands and castles or forfeit two-thirds of the profits of their lands, rents, benefices, offices, etc.—saving those who are in the King's service or students in the universities.

There is no evidence that this sweeping Act was firmly applied, or that it led to any considerable return of the absentees or substantially checked the exodus of the Anglo-Irish which was already well set in. Lordships, offices, rents, etc. indeed had frequently two-thirds of their profits sequestrated to the profit of the Exchequer in future. Seneschals continued, however, to be appointed for absentee lords of liberties.[3]

THE DERELICT LORDSHIPS

The absentee lordships and the lapsed grants and conquests of the earlier period were now part of the Irish problem which faced the young King of England. What was to be done about them? Partly the legal proprietors, such as Mortimer, wished to be restored; in other cases such as Westmeath the original heirs were

[1] See pp. 267, 288, for proposed plantations.
[2] Berry, *Statutes*, I, pp. 470–1.
[3] Berry, *Statutes*, I, pp. 470–6; and Gilbert, *Viceroys of Ireland*, p. 230.

extinct, but in all cases the Irish and native-born Normans were in possession.

Roger Mortimer, the King's right-hand man and, if he should die childless, the heir to England, desired keenly to be restored to his Irish lordships, a vast inheritance but needing a large army and much beside to win it back in any real sense.

In Ulster MacQuillan of the Route, Byset or MacEoin of the Glens, Savage of the Ards, and a few other feudal families in Lecale, with the towns of Downpatrick and Carrickfergus, were practically all that was left of De Courcy's plantation. The Clandeboy O'Neill was in possession of the inland parts of Antrim and Down; O'Neill of Tyrone ruled all central Ulster; and Turloch 'an Fína' O'Donnell, who reigned in Tyrconnell from 1380 to 1422, was paramount over Fermanagh and Sligo.

Niall More, son of Aedh, had been chief of Tyrone since 1365; his eldest son, Niall Oge, was now acting for him. The father had submitted to Edmund Mortimer in 1380 and might well do so to another Earl of Ulster as his overlord.

The gallowglass clans of MacSweeney in Tyrconnell, of the Clann Domnnaill or MacDonnells in Tyrone, and, in other parts of central Ulster, the kindreds of the latter, MacDugall, MacRory, and MacSheehy were now well established. About 1350 another family of these hereditary fighting men, the MacCabes from Lewis, also came in, and enlisted under the chieftains of Brefni and Oriel.

THE MACDONNELLS OF THE GLENS

A new element was now to appear in Ulster, that of the Scots of Antrim, a contrast to the older-established gallowglasses who were now becoming Irish. John or Eoin 'of Isla' MacDonnell, head of the Clann Somhairle, was confirmed as 'Lord of the Isles' in 1372 by Robert II of Scotland, whose daughter he married: he died in 1387 as 'king of the Innsi Gall (the Hebrides)', so the annals of Ulster call him. His two sons Donal 'of Harlaw' and John or Eoin quarrelled about the inheritance, and Donal drove John out of Scotland to take refuge with O'Neill.[1] Meanwhile in the Glens of Antrim, in 1383, John Byset (or in Irish MacEoin) had been slain by the Savages. He left no sons, and the vigorous John MacDonnell cast greedy eyes upon this vacant lordship.

[1] It does not seem certain which of the brothers was the elder. Hill (*MacDonnells of Antrim*) makes John, whose mother was a MacRory, the elder; Donal, as grandson of Robert II, was apparently favoured by the Government. From John (d. 1425), whose son was Donal Ballach, descend the earls of Antrim.

Finally he secured it by marrying Margery, heiress of the Byset, and so founded the MacDonnell lordship of the Glens of Antrim, while junior members of the MacEoin race remained in insignificance. Henceforth northern Antrim was an open colony for the Hebridean Scots who, as well as hiring themselves out as soldiers, made good farmers and populated the land.

John MacDonnell, as we shall see, when Richard II came aspired to be taken into the service of the King or Mortimer as constable 'of the Irish' or 'Bonnacht of Ulster', but already this was a title in a branch of Clan Sorley which was settled in Ulster.[1]

THE LORDSHIP OF CONNACHT

By the law of feudal descent the De Burgo inheritance in Connacht was also Mortimer's, but his remote Irish cousins, the race of Edmund Albanach and Ulick, were in actual possession. In the strict legal sense these Burkes were intruders upon the Mortimer lordship, but events showed how strongly they were entrenched there.[2]

On the death of Edmund, Earl of March, in 1381 the Crown became guardian of the Mortimer estates, and in 1385 the Dublin government appointed one Thomas O'Casey to be seneschal of Galway city and receiver of the King's rents in Connacht, with power to hold courts, levy the royal rents, and appoint officers. But the Burke party resisted this attempt to restore royal authority, and in 1388 Galway revolted under the lead of Henry Blake and others, who delivered the keys to William (Ulick), son of Richard Burke, and transferred to him the allegiance due to the King.

The King's justices, Milo bishop of Clonmacnois and Thomas Hill, were sent to investigate the case at Ballinrobe in 1390, when Blake and others were indicted for treason in joining William Burke 'the King's enemy', but it is significant of the ceasing of royal law beyond the Shannon that the sheriff, Walter de Bermingham, lord of Athenry, refused the bishop escort, and the latter had to give the son of O'Kelly, chief of Hy Many, ten pounds in silver for his safe-conduct. The King's justices could no longer make their eyre safely in the former counties of Roscommon and Connacht. The facts had to be accepted, and the Burkes were pardoned and left in possession. As a token of pardon and

[1] See *Ann. Ult.* (1368): Sorley son of John, constable of the province of Ulster, died.

[2] Edmund Albanach de Burgo died in 1375, and his son Thomas was now in his stead. Ulick having died in 1353, his son Richard Oge followed him, and died in 1387. His son again, Ulick 'an Fina' ('of the Wine') succeeded him as the Upper MacWilliam, and died in 1423.

favour, Sir Thomas de Burgo was appointed sheriff of Connacht. Later, however, Galway city was won back to allegiance by a fresh charter, making it a royal instead of a 'lord's' town, with a corporate body under an elected sovereign in January 1396.[1]

THE LORDSHIPS OF MEATH AND TRIM

In these also Mortimer needed to be restored by strong measures, though the eastern part of Meath between the sea and Mullingar was still comparatively an 'English land', of which the portion west to Trim was never entirely lost to the Anglo-Norman tradition. Mortimer was 'lord of Trim', and at the lapse of the heirs of the Lochsewdy or Westmeath half of the old earldom its liberties and lands had been in 1330 annexed to Trim. But, on the west or Shannon side great tracts were Irish lordships under chiefs of whom Mageoghegan of Keneliagh (Cinel Fiachach) was the most powerful, though O'Melaghlin of Clonlonan was 'hereditary king of Midhe'. And at the same time De Lacy's original 'barons of Meath' were, like all their kind in Ireland, forming compact blocks of territory for themselves, such as the Nugents of Delvin and the Tyrells of Fertullach.

In another Mortimer inheritance, that of Leix, the O'Mores had for some forty years now reasserted their ancestral lordship and ousted the English settlers.

'THE LAND OF LEINSTER' AND ART MACMURROUGH

Of the five liberties of Leinster, Wexford, which had passed successively from Marshals to De Valence and then to Hastings, now in 1390 by the usual descent of feudal property was the property of Reginald de Grey, lord of Ruthyn. As regards Carlow, the Bigod claim had now passed to Thomas Mowbray, who in 1383 was created Earl of Nottingham and later Earl Marshal. In 1394 the lordship of Carlow was granted to him. Kilkenny, as we have seen, was in 1391 conveyed to the Earl of Ormond; and similarly in Kildare a native magnate, the Earl of Kildare, had acquired the liberty. Leix was Mortimer's inheritance. If Mowbray, Hastings, and Mortimer could have their Irish lands restored in full and replanted or even given military colonists, the 'land of Leinster' might become as before an 'English land'. But Art MacMurrough Kavanagh, chief of the King's 'Irish enemies', stood in the way.

[1] Hardiman, *History of Galway*, pp. 160–1; and *King's Council in Ireland* (ed. Graves), *R.S.*, p. 230. For the text of Blake's pardon with some notes see Curtis, 'Pardon of Henry Blake, 1390', in *Galway Arch. Soc.*, XVI, iii, iv.

PALATINE LIBERTIES

Well had it been for its own interest if the Crown had divided the vacant lordships between the occupying Normans and Gaelic chiefs, or even had it revoked all dead absentee claims and proceeded to a fresh conquest and real plantation of the island. But it would never allow the rights of its feudal peers to suffer even if they never came near Ireland. It would of course have needed a strong monarch to carry out such an unpopular measure, and no monarch strong enough was found till Henry VIII with his Act of Absentees.

A large element, official and anti-feudal, urgently recommended the abolition of such liberties, and their reduction to shire and common-law land. The King's Council in Ireland in 1352 protested against allowing liberties, whenever they came into the King's hands by forfeiture, to be so lightly restored by directions from England 'to the King's manifest loss'. In 1399 it again complained that the counties of Meath, Ulster, Wexford, Tipperary, and Cork, which have been given as palatine liberties, yield no revenue to the Crown, which also gets nothing from counties Carlow, Kilkenny, Waterford, Kerry, Limerick, Connacht, and Roscommon.[1]

The Crown in fact did nothing to check this growth, which left it no real sovereignty or effective revenue in its Irish lordship, and till the reign of Elizabeth the area of feudal Ireland grew steadily at the expense of the rest of Ireland, whether Gaelic or 'obedient to the law'.

ART MACMURROUGH IN IDRONE AND NORRAGH

Up to a time which the young chief might well remember, his family had held no more than inland portions of the wooded and mountain tracts of Hy Kinsella. But now by year after year of warfare against the Leinster colonies he was recovering most of the ancient royal demesne with the level and fertile plain of Carlow. The records of the time show him constantly taking the field with his vassals O'Nolan, O'Ryan, and other Irish enemies, and, 'openly at war', raiding in a great circle around him the counties of Kilkenny, Carlow, and Kildare.

Black-rents had become a tradition which was to last till Tudor days, and MacMurrough's fee was a charge on the dwindling Exchequer, but these did not stop the overrunning of the 'land

[1] *Cal. Close Rolls, England,* (26 Edw. III); and *King's Council in Ireland,* pp. 261–9.

of peace'.[1] But in the course of his wars MacMurrough made a lasting acquisition, namely the former feudal lordship of Idrone in county Carlow. This splendid barony, stretching fifteen miles along the Barrow and eastward of it six or seven miles, had at first been granted to Raymond le Gros de Carew; he had granted it to a nephew, since when the Carews of Dunleckny had continued to rule there. But when about 1380 a Carew died without direct male heirs, Art MacMurrough seized on the barony and held on to it. O'Ryan was the pre-Norman lord and aided Art in the Conquest, but Idrone became in fact a MacMurrough lordship, a good example of 'sword-land' achieved at the expense both of Gael and Gall. Nevertheless O'Ryan got back more than the Norman lords had allowed him: similarly MacMurrough's chief vassal O'Nolan recovered his ancient title to Forth O'Nolan (Fotharta Ui Nualláin) in Carlow.[2]

To add to his triumphs, the king of Leinster got a claim to the rich and important barony of Norragh in county Kildare by his marriage with Elizabeth de Veel, heiress of the fief.[3]

The story of Norragh makes a curious one. The barony was granted by Strongbow to Robert FitzRichard, from whom in due time it descended about 1320 to the family of Le or De Veel (in English 'Calfe', in Latin 'de Vitulis'), of whom a Sir Robert was the last. The barony was held in chief by knight-service of the earldom of Kildare. Sir Robert dying without heirs male in 1378, his daughter Elizabeth became sole heiress.[4] After marrying Sir John Staunton, by whom she had daughters, she gave her hand in marriage to Art MacMurrough some time about 1390. But both the Government and the gentry of the Pale were determined

[1] A similar event was seen in the northern border of Anglo-Ireland. There the Dundalk-to-Mullingar line, which protected the colony of Meath and Louth, was threatened by the MacMahons of Monaghan, entrenched in the vacant earldom of Louth, and by the O'Reillys of Cavan, who had to be bought off by the county of Meath in 1392, by permission of the Council, with a sum of eighty-four marks.

[2] The extinction of the Carews is an obscure event but is well attested. *Rot. Canc. Hib.*, p. 86b, records the death (1374) of Leonard de Carew, 'who held of the King in chief'. Later Carews occur indeed, but it seems clear they lost Idrone. *Pat. and Close Rolls of Chancery, Ireland* (Hen. VIII–Eliz.), p. 519, give the original Inquisition of 18 Ric. II on the extinction of the Carews. For Sir Peter Carew's recovery under Elizabeth and the treatment of the then MacMurrough holders see my *History of Ireland*, pp. 190–1. For O'Ryans as underlords of Idrone see later, p. 312; and p. 357, first edition of this work.

[3] The whole question is treated in my article, 'The Barons of Norragh', in *R.S.A.I.* (1935).

[4] In the first edition of this work, p. 301, I state that Elizabeth was a daughter of Maurice Fitzgerald, Earl of Kildare, but in my paper on 'The Barons of Norragh' I give reasons for rejecting this old legend (p. 90). It rests apparently on D'Arcy M'Gee's romantic *Life of Art MacMurrough*; he professed to find it in Lynch, *Feudal Dignities*, pp. 297–8, but it is not there.

that so valuable a fief, right in the heart of 'the English land', should not pass to 'an Irish enemy' in the teeth of the Statutes of Kilkenny. In January 1391 Elizabeth's lands were seized 'as an adherent of MacMurrough, one of the King's chief enemies in Ireland'. She joined her Irish husband, and Art took the field more devastatingly than ever. In 1392 'MacMorugh, O'Bryn, O'Tothul, O'More, and other Irish enemies of our Lord the King of the parts of Leinster assembled a great host and came to the town of Carlow, which town, together with the other part of the county Carlow and a great part of the county Kildare, they gave to fire and flame'. In the next year Castledermot was so hard pressed by MacMurrough that it had to buy him off with eighty-four marks, the levying of which was authorized by the Council.[1]

But the story of Art's campaigns, which no spectacular large-scale battles illuminate, but which were effective in taking the heart out of the Leinster colonies, need not be continued. It was a style of war in which the mobile Irish on their own terrain had the permanent advantage of the mail-clad Englishry, who would have preferred stand-up encounters.

RICHARD II IN IRELAND, 1394–1395

In July 1392 James, 3rd Earl of Ormond, was appointed Justiciar, and ruled till the King's coming. Son of the second Earl who died in 1382, Ormond was popular with the Irish, he spoke their language fluently, and was brother-in-law of one of their great chiefs, Taig O'Carroll. In 1392 the Anglo-Irish requested the personal coming of the King, and Roger Mortimer urged the recovery of his Irish lands. The young King himself badly needed the prestige of some great military or diplomatic triumph. Of all urgent affairs of state, those of Anglo-Ireland cried most loudly for cure, and Richard, a true Renaissance prince, sensitive and artistic, seems to have felt deeply the reproach of Ireland and the decay of his lordship there.

Later, a private grief, the death of his wife Anne of Bohemia in June 1394, made him seek distraction, and an English parliament at Winchester, anxious to see the prestige of England restored somewhere oversea, voted a generous subsidy for the recovery of Ireland.

The English government had been kept well informed of the state of Ireland, and luckily the proceedings of the Irish Privy Council for the two years before Richard's arrival have come down to us. They enable us, with other evidence, to draw a

[1] *King's Council in Ireland*, pp. 41, 129.

detailed picture of the problems which Richard had to face in Ireland.[1]

Richard arrived from Haverford at Waterford on October 2nd 1394 with a great army, and having with him several great peers, namely, Roger Mortimer, Earl of Ulster, Thomas Mowbray, Earl of Nottingham, inheritor of Carlow, John Holland, Earl of Huntingdon, and Edward of Albemarle, the King's cousin, Earl of Rutland and recently created Earl of Cork.[2] With them Richard hoped to swell the ranks of the Irish peerage.

Well advised from the Irish side, Richard had come to make terms with the Irish princes, and in a letter to O'Neill, dispatched before his voyage, had promised to do right and justice to every man. But first he had to march upon Dublin and make an imposing display before the Leinster rebels.

Art MacMurrough refused to be intimidated, and burnt New Ross before the King, but Richard, marching up by Kilkenny along the Barrow, sent Ormond and the Earl Marshal inland to attack the Leinster chief in the woods and wilds under Mount Leinster where he had his forest-fortress of Garbh-coill. Finally the King reached Dublin early in November, and stayed there at the castle till the end of January 1395. There, while still treating MacMurrough as the great rebel, he evolved a general plan for the pacification and recovery of Ireland.

This plan had four distinct objects:

(*a*) The Irish chiefs, except for MacMurrough and his Leinster vassals, were to surrender the lands they had 'usurped' from the English and to swear a double allegiance, one to the King as liege lord, and another to the Norman earls, to whom they owed simple homage as their suzerains. In return they were to be confirmed in their 'Irish lands', that is, in those territories which they had always held from the time of the Conquest.

(*b*) The 'rebel English' were to be pardoned and induced to return to their due allegiance.

(*c*) A definitely 'English land' was to be created in eastern Ireland, east of a line drawn from Dundalk to the Boyne and down the Barrow to Waterford. In this English 'Pale' grants

[1] *A Roll of the Proceedings of the King's Council in Ireland, 1392–3* (ed. Graves), *R.S.* (with appendixes from other sources). This provides a most valuable and almost unique account of the state of the English Lordship of Ireland in these times (1392–9) and again in 1440.

[2] See my volume *Richard II in Ireland and Submissions of the Irish Chiefs* (1927) *passim* for the whole visit. Froissart attributes to Richard an army of 30,000 archers and 4,000 men-at-arms, an incredible number. For more on this point see p. 26 of my *Richard II in Ireland.* Richard's army on his expedition into Scotland in 1385 totalled 4,730 men-at-arms and 7,653 archers; it is hardly likely he conveyed as many by sea to Ireland.

were to be made to new Englishmen with the intention of a fresh colonization there.

(*d*) In order to carry out the latter plan the warlike Art MacMurrough and his 'urrighs' must be compelled to quit the lands of Leinster.

To his uncle the Duke of York, then Regent in England, Richard wrote thus: 'There are in the land of Ireland three kinds of people; the wild Irish, our enemies; the Irish rebels; and the obedient English (*irrois savages, nos enemis; irrois rebelz; et Englois obeissantz*). To us and our Council it appears that the Irish rebels have rebelled because of the injustice and wrongs practised upon them for which they have no redress, and unless they are wisely treated and given hope of grace, they will most likely ally themselves with our enemies.'

Richard was sympathetic towards these 'degenerate English', but in fact it was precisely the 'Irish rebels' or hibernicized English who were the true danger to the State.[1]

Richard now determined to do what no King or viceroy had done since the Conquest, and admit the kings and primary chiefs of the Irish to full legal status under the Crown. In token of his grace, he substituted for the leopard flag of England the arms of Edward the Conqueror, a saint much venerated by the Irish. Thus, says Froissart, did 'four of the princypall kynges and moste puyssaunt after the maner of the countrey come to the obeysaunce of the Kynge of Englande by love and fayreness, and not by batayle nor constraynte.'

THE SUBMISSIONS OF THE IRISH

There followed a remarkable series of submissions, attested by legal instruments, by which the kings of provinces and some fifty of their 'urrighs' submitted and did homage. Richard renounced all idea of a conquest, and the Irish, under their natural leader O'Neill and induced by Archbishop Colton of Armagh, Maurice O'Kelly, archbishop of Tuam, and the earls of

[1] Richard, by the injustices done to 'Irish rebels', probably referred *inter alia* to the passing of estates by marriage to English claimants which had led many families to turn Irish and become enemies of the State. A 'message' sent to England by the Guardian and Council of Ireland at the end of 1399 said that 'the English septs (*les nacions Englois*) who are rebels in all parts of the country, such as the Butlers, Poers, Geraldines, Berminghams, Daltons Baretts, and Dillons, are not amenable to the law, and though they wish to be called gentlemen are in truth nothing but sturdy robbers' (*King's Council*, op. cit., p. 255). I quote Froissart in Lord Berners's translation (*Tudor Translations*, vol. VI). The wording 'Irish rebels' of course implies that the 'degenerate English', though in revolt, were still subjects; not so the '*irrois savages, nos enemis*'.

Ormond and Desmond, decided to make a national act of submission, such as their ancestors had formerly sought in vain, to the English Lord of Ireland.[1] It is clear that Niall More induced the general submission of the Irish, as we find by his letters to Richard. 'I have ever recognized your lordship,' he wrote to the King, 'and do ever recognize it.' Also, in a letter to Archbishop Colton, 'We would not have your lordship ignorant that, according to your sage counsel, we made to come to us all the great men among the Irish of Ulster, to consult and deliberate with them about my going to the King's court (in Dublin), and there are with me envoys from O'Brien, O'Connor, MacCarthy, and many more of the southern Irish, urging us strongly not to go to the King, but we preferred your counsel far above that of others,' etc.[2]

During the first four months of 1395 Richard received the Irish princes in person at Drogheda, Dublin, Waterford, and Kilkenny. The submissions were made province by province, and the royal bloods ('principes Hibernicorum Ultonie', etc.) were treated as suzerains over their 'urrighs'. The King as Lord of Ireland, and Mortimer as Earl of Ulster, received the homage of the northern chiefs, save Turloch O'Donnell, who stood aloof, as did his vassal Maguire.

Niall Oge was now acting chief of Tyrone, his father Niall More being infirm. At the end of 1394 Niall senior wrote to 'his most excellent lord Richard, King of England and France, and Lord of Ireland,' styling himself 'your most humble liege subject, Nellanus Oneyll, Prince of the Irish of Ulster', and going on:

> 'When I heard of your arrival in your land of Ireland I rejoiced greatly, and still rejoice, hoping to obtain redress for many wrongs done to me and mine by the March English. And if in anything I have offended against your Majesty's subjects, I did not do so as renouncing your lordship, for I have always recognized the same, and do so now. And had I got justice from your ministers for the wrongs done to me, I should never have exacted satisfaction, as I have done. But

[1] The following pages are based on a careful study and abstract of *Exch. K. R. Mem. Roll* (18 Rd. II) in *P.R.O.L.*, a roll of seventeen membranes of public deeds, etc. beginning 'de instrumentis publicis indenturis et aliis munimentis tangent, terram de Hib. ad Scacc. per episcopum Johannem Sarum Thes. Anglie liberat. irrotulatis', i.e. the submissions and various letters of the chiefs to Richard. Since the first edition of this work appeared (1923), I have published the full texts of these submissions and letters of Irish chiefs to Richard II in *Richard II in Ireland* (1927), to which I refer the reader for the introduction, the texts and translation, a map of Ireland at the time, and notes on the submitting chiefs and lords.

[2] See my *Richard II in Ireland*, pp. 210–16, 223–4.

I am ready to make requital, begging you to receive me into grace and to be a helmet and shield of justice between me and my lord the Earl of Ulster, in case he exact from me more than he has a right to. And I am prepared to render to the Earl all rights which are justly his.'

Then, on January 20th 1395, in the Dominican house at Drogheda, in the presence of the King, Niall senior presented letters patent in Latin from his son, which ran thus:

'I, Niall O'Neill junior, captain of my nation, have ordained in my place my beloved father, Niall senior, giving him power in my name to appear before the illustrious prince, my lord Richard, king of England and Lord of Ireland, and before my lord Roger de Mortimer, Earl of March and Ulster, and to treat of peace with them for me and my nation and subjects, and to surrender whatever lands, liberties, services, and customs I unjustly possess or allow others to possess, and especially the Bonnaght of the Irish of Ulster. Further giving him power to offer amends for all wrongs whatsoever which I have done to the King, Earl, or their lands and subjects, and to make any indentures of peace whatsoever, and seal them with my or his seal. Also giving him power to offer myself, my country, and all my goods as satisfaction for such; also to make bond of allegiance, homage, and fealty by such solemn oath as shall be thought fitting in order to obtain peace of the said King and Earl. In witness whereof I have put my seal to these presents. Given at Maddoyn, the fifth of January.'

On March 16th 1395 Niall Oge, as 'captain of his nation', did homage and took the oath of obedience to Richard in the Dominican convent at Drogheda. Niall admitted himself Richard's liegeman, and swore to obey the King and his deputies, and come to parliaments when summoned by the King or his deputies.

The rest of the Irish kings followed the lead of Niall Oge; their submissions all like his being in Irish, rendered into English by interpreters, and recorded in Latin. Those of Ulster, who looked on O'Neill of Tyrone as their native king, on the Earl as their overlord, and on the King as lord paramount, were Magennis, O'Cahan, O'Hanlon, MacMahon, MacGilmore, MacCabe, a gallowglass captain, and John MacDonnell 'chief of his nation, and constable of the Irish of Ulster'.[1]

[1] For John MacDonnell (who styled himself in a letter to Richard 'captain of his nation and constable of the Irish of Ulster') see pp. 150, 175 of *Richard II*

From Meath and south Ulster O'Melaghlin, Mageoghegan, O'Molloy, O'Farrell of Annaly, O'Reilly of Cavan, and others also came in and submitted at Drogheda.

Brian O'Brien, 'Princeps Tothomonie', had written to Richard early in February, offering to submit, and affirming that 'among all the English and Irish of your land of Ireland I have acquired no lands or possessions by conquest, but only such as your predecessors, kings of England, granted to my ancestors, together with your arms and standards and other liberties; and whatever complaints English or Irish have against me in this matter, I submit to be judged in the presence of your Majesty. Moreover we are most clearly your vassals, and when Prince Lionel came to Ireland my father and I were before all in fealty and honour to him.'

On March 1st Brian did homage to the King in a room of St. Thomas's abbey, Dublin, his interpreter being the Earl of Ormond, 'in lingua hibernica bene eruditus'.

Turloch O'Connor Don, who claimed to be the true king of Connacht, delayed submission till he feared that Turloch O'Connor Roe would find favour with the King, and then wrote on April 3rd from Roscommon as 'Teotricus O'Chonchowyr, Major Hibernicorum Chonachie dictus, vester semper humilis obediens subditus', stating that the greater part of the Irish of all Connacht were subject to him. Finally he appeared on April 20th, in the church of the Friars Minor at Waterford, and did homage on bended knee to the King, along with Brian O'Brien and his son Dermot, who now renewed their submission. Turloch's oath bound him 'to be faithful in all things, and to come to the Lord Richard, King of England and Lord of Ireland, and to his heirs, and to their parliament and Council whensoever they should summon him, and to do all that a good and faithful liegeman ought, and is bound, to do to his natural liege lord'.

At this imposing ceremony, which was attended by the archbishop of Dublin, five bishops, and three earls, after homage had been rendered, the bishops of Kilfenora and Kilmacduagh, both Irishmen, attested that O'Connor had power to do liege homage for these nations: O'Hara, O'Gara, MacDermot, O'Madden, O'Ruairc, O'Kelly, O'Dowda, and four other chiefs of Síol Muiredaigh. Also that O'Brien had power to speak for these: Macnamara, MacMahon, O'Connor, O'Lochlin, O'Hechir, and O'Dea. Of these, Taig O'Kelly and Taig Macnamara submitted at Kilkenny. The chiefs of upper Ormond submitted as vassals of the

in Ireland. His object, to be made 'the King's captain and constable throughout all your land of Ireland with as many armed men as you wish me to have with your royal Majesty', was a tall order, not granted.

Earl of Ormond. Turloch O'Brien, son of 'Murchadh na Raithnighe', Taig O'Carroll, king of Ely, two O'Dwyers, and three O'Kennedys submitted at Kilkenny on April 25th.[1]

'Tatheus Makarthy, Princeps Hibernicorum Dessemonie', namely Taig MacCarthy More (Major), as he styles himself, also wrote to Richard in a letter dated February 13th from Ballaghath thus: 'I submit myself and all my goods to your domination. My ancestors and I from the time of the Conquest have been faithful to you and your ancestors. I will attempt nothing against your Majesty, nor will I retain any lands save those I hold from you and from my Lord the Earl of Desmond.' At Kilkenny on April 6th Taig did homage to the King, undertaking like others to attend parliaments when summoned. Two other MacCarthys of Carbery and Muskerry also did homage.

So far the terms had been honourable to the Irish. They were in effect promised or secured in the 'Irish lands' they already held.

THE TERMS WITH MACMURROUGH

But a different note was struck in those made with the Leinster chiefs from whom the King and the absentees designed to recover the old inheritance of the Marshals. The natural chief of these was Art MacMurrough who was recognized as prince of, and answerable for, the 'urrighs' of the province.

> 'An identure made the 7th day of January [1395], in a field near Tyllagh [Tullow], between Thomas, Earl of Nottingham and Marshal of England, and Arthur MacMurrough, liege of the said Lord King, for himself and his men. He promises to surrender all lands, castles, etc. unjustly held, and swears for himself and all his subjects to keep fealty to the King, his successors, and deputies. Also by the first Sunday of Lent he will quit the whole land of Leinster with all the armed men of his nation and following, retaining all his movable property, and shall have, both he and his men, wages from the King to go and conquer other lands occupied by rebels against the King. And Arthur and his men shall have and hold such lands as they may conquer of the King and his successors as his true lieges and subjects, and enjoy them for ever in hereditary right. Also

[1] Three O'Kennedys submitted, Philip, Odo (Aedh), Thomas. After Brian O'Kennedy, king of Ormond, who died in 1371, the family split into O'Kennedy Donn and O'Kennedy Finn; an instance of the process by which the great lordships won or recovered by the Irish again split up between branches of the ruling race.

the King shall provide for Arthur eighty marks a year for ever together with the heritage of his wife in the barony of Norragh.'[1]

By the same indenture were pledged Art's 'urrighs' in Leinster, O'Byrne, O'More, O'Nolan, O'Dunn, MacDavy More, and others of Hy Kinsella; they are to abandon Leinster at the date fixed and be at the King's pay till they conquer fresh lands.

These oaths were pledged on the Holy Scriptures and the cross, and the Earl affixed his seal on one hand and MacMurrough and O'Byrne on the other.

Finally, 'in a field at Balygory on February 16th, Gerald O'Bryn, Donal O'Nolan, Malachy O'More, Murgh O'Connor, and other chiefs of Leinster did homage to the Earl Marshal, and thereupon Arthur Mac Mourgh, captain of his nation, seated on his black horse, did liege homage under the same form as the rest, and bound himself, if he should not observe the conditions already entered into with the Earl, to forfeit to the Papal Camera twenty thousand marks.'[2]

Successively and at various places—Dublin castle, Carlow, Leighlin, and Tristeldermot—there submitted to the King or the Earl Marshal, MacGillapatraic, O'Toole, O'Brenan, O'Dempsey, O'Nolan, and the captains of Leix and Offaly, viz. Malachy O'More and Murchadh O'Connor Faly.

THE 'REBEL IRISH'

The response of those 'degenerate English' whom Richard had styled 'Irish rebels' was nothing like the general and generous one of the native Irish. But two Barretts from Mayo, Walter de Bermingham of Athenry, William or Ulick de Burgo of Clanrickard, Maurice Fitzgerald of Kilmallock, and Adam, son of Richard 'Syn Tobyn' (Tobin or 'De Sancto Albano'), with a few others submitted and were received back to grace.[3]

[1] Richard's patent for Norragh is referred to in *Rot. Canc. Hib.*, p. 156, under 1400, when it was confirmed by Henry IV. The 'armed men', etc. are in the text 'omnes homines armati bellatores seu guerrantes de comitiva familia seu nacione ejusdem Arthuri'. As in the transplantation to Connacht under Cromwell, the fighting aristocracy were to migrate and the peaceful labouring Irish to remain.

[2] According to my friend Mr. Edward O'Toole of Rathvilly ('Where is Balygory?', in the *Kildare Arch. Soc.* for 1931), the site of this place is now Bawnogephlure in the parish of Grangeford in the county Carlow. Grangeford lies on the road from Carlow to Tullow. It seems a very appropriate meeting-place.

[3] *A.F.M.* say, 'Thomas MacWilliam Burke (the other MacWilliam) went into the King's house and received the lordship of the English of Connacht', but the submissions do not mention him.

THE KING DEPARTS

Finally 'on the first of May, in the King's ship called *Le Trinitie* in the port of Waterford, came Terrelagh O'Concor Don de Conacia, William de Borgo, and Walter Bermygam, who formerly, as was said, were rebels against the said King, who came on board and were created knights by the King'. During the negotiations also, Richard invited O'Connor, O'Neill, O'Brien, and MacMurrough to Dublin, entertained them nobly, and on Lady Day made them knights in Christchurch cathedral. The ceremony is described by Froissart from the relation of one Henry Christede, a squire of the King, whom Froissart afterwards met at Eltham.[1] This Christede told the chronicler that he spoke French, English, and Irish, for from his youth he had been brought up in Ireland and had spent many years among the Irish. At last, when riding to war against the Irish with his master the Earl of Ormond, his horse took fright and carried him among the Irish, of whom one, by a great feat of agility, jumped on the back of his horse, held him fast and carried him to his house 'which was strong and, in a town surrounded with wood, palisades, and still water called Herpelipen'. With his captor, who was a very handsome man, called Bren Costerec, Christede lived for seven years, married Costerec's daughter and had two girls, 'till Art MacMurrough, king of Leinster, raised war against Lionel, Duke of Clarence, and, as the English prevailed, my father-in-law was taken, but was released on condition he would free me, which at first he would not do, because of his love for me, his daughter and our children, but finally accepted on condition he might keep one of my daughters. So I returned to England with my wife and the other daughter and dwelt at Bristol. My two children are married; the one in Ireland has five children and the one with me has six; and the Irish language is as familiar to me as English, for I have always spoken it to my wife and introduce it as much as I can among my grandchildren.'[2]

At the royal banquet in Dublin castle, it was Christede and the Earl of Ormond who interpreted for the four Irish kings to

[1] Jean Froissart, *Chroniques* (ed. Kervyn de Lettenhove). I quote from Berners's translation (*Tudor Translations*). Froissart says that Richard gave the Irish kings 'un bel hostel' in Dublin and knighted them on Lady Day (a Thursday) in 'the cathedral of Dublin', which may have been Christchurch or St. Patrick's. Of the submissions he says with point: 'The honour was great but the profit small.'

[2] For this picturesque story from Froissart see the first edition of this work, p. 313. The O'Connor Don *versus* O'Connor Roe question is a difficulty, for which see my *Richard II in Ireland*. As to whether both submitted we cannot be sure; but anyway O'Connor Don was finally received and knighted on Richard's ship as above.

King Richard, and induced them to accept knighthood after feudal fashion, though they answered proudly that it was their custom for every chief's son to take arms at seven years of age. The haughtiness of the Norman towards his inferiors was foreign to these elected chiefs; they sat at table in neighbourly fashion with minstrels, servants, and retainers, and ate and drank with them. Attached to their Irish raiment, these kings accepted with reluctance from Christede the linen breeches and gowns of silk, furred with minever, which were necessary for the ceremony of knighting. When the ceremony was over, they departed, having asserted in a dignified aloofness the tenacious traditions of their race.

So the King of England sailed from Ireland on May 15th 1395, after eight months' stay in Ireland. Before he went, he made several extensive grants in Leinster with the intention of a new plantation or at least a new landlordry. For example, to his admiral John de Beaumont on April 28th 1395 at Waterford he granted all the lands, services, and knights' fees 'between the Slaney in the south part and the Blackwater at Arklow on the north and from the sea on the east to the borders of Kildare and Carlow on the west, excepting the lands of the Earl of Ormond'.[1]

RESULTS OF THE SUBMISSIONS

With the exception of the Leinster chiefs, the settlement had been a triumph for the Gaelic chiefs, almost amounting to that solution which the authors of the Remonstrance had proposed, of dividing Ireland between them and 'the middle nation'. They established their argument that they had always held their proper lands from the English Crown. Whatever they had usurped they would surrender, and MacCarthy, O'Kennedy, and O'Neill respectively admitted the Earls of Desmond, Ormond and Ulster, as mesne lords between them and the Lord of Ireland. After such binding instruments, and if they were observed, no doubt could exist that they had received legal status for their lands and captaincies.

But the settlement with MacMurrough and his 'urrighs' makes one wonder how the English king could impose, or the Leinster chiefs undertake, such sweeping conditions. If Richard's parchment deeds could have effected it, the whole of Leinster, including Offaly and Leix, remote places which even the Norman conquerors at their best could neither conquer nor inhabit, would know the 'captains of nations' and their swordsmen no more; Leinster would thus easily become once again an 'English land'.

[1] See my *Richard II*, op. cit., p. 44, and my paper, 'Janico Dartas, Richard II's Gascon Squire', in *R.S.A.I.* (1933).

But where would Art Oge lead his Irish captains and where were the lands of 'rebels' whom they could dispossess? We cannot suppose that the Leinster chiefs seriously meditated leaving the fair hills of their hereditary province to adventure among O'Briens, O'Neills, Geraldines, and Burkes, races not less warlike than themselves.

Whatever may have been intended, actually Richard's high hopes came to little. The Irish princes welcomed the additional prestige of a title from the Crown, and were flattered when bards addressed them as 'knights of England's king'. But the Anglo-Irish parliament, with its French and English speech, its feudal peers and bourgeois commons, was not an assembly where they would have felt at home, nor as yet would they have been safe there.

Art and his 'urrighs' took no step towards vacating Leinster, and the lordships of Carlow and Wexford, like the earldom of Ulster, for the most part remained Irish with but an English fringe, the nominal tenants of an absentee lord. It is doubtful if the English land in Ireland was increased to any extent worth speaking of by the Submissions.

ROGER MORTIMER, VICEROY

On Richard's departure, the Earl of March was left as the one hope of the colony. He was created King's lieutenant in April 1396 and held the office till his death. Leinster was still the test of power. Here Art MacMurrough still held Norragh, but he and the Irish of Leinster refused to depart according to their engagements. Mortimer therefore, backed by Ormond, made war on the intransigent septs. An Irish army under O'Byrne and MacDavy was in the field, and the Earl of March engaged them in battle at Kellistown near Carlow. But his forces were overwhelmed, and Earl Roger, who wore only the linen dress of an Irish chief, was slain on June 10th 1398. The name of Mortimer, to which Ireland had been so fatal, finally devolved on a young son Edmund, and a daughter Anne.[1]

Thus in an obscure Irish battle died the heir to the throne of England, and the unfortunate King's right-hand man against his baronial enemies. Filled with fury and despair, Richard declared MacMurrough's land of Norragh forfeit and bestowed it on his

[1] According to the Monk of Evesham's *Hist. vitae et regni Ric. II* (ed. Hearne) (1729), when the Earl of March was killed, his body was torn in pieces. See also *Adam of Usk*, pp. 165–72, for Mortimer's wearing Irish dress, etc. Why he discarded armour is strange. Mr. Edward O'Toole, who has done so much to salvage local tradition, in the *Kildare Arch. Soc.* (July 1933), pp. 268–71, records finds of skeletons, possibly going back to this battle.

half-brother Thomas Holland, Duke of Surrey. The latter was appointed Lieutenant, and landed at Dublin on October 7th 1398. His task was to prepare the way for a second coming of the King.

RICHARD'S SECOND VISIT TO IRELAND

Still under the spell of the Irish enigma, Richard made the fatal decision to return thither, to avenge Mortimer and vindicate the royal majesty against the Irish.

A fresh army was raised and Richard, leaving his uncle the Duke of York again as Regent, landed at Waterford on June 1st 1399, accompanied by the Dukes of Exeter and Albemarle and the Earl of Gloucester.[1]

From Kilkenny the whole army marched against MacMurrough, suffering terribly in the trackless hill country on the borders of Carlow and Wexford. Art could not be drawn to battle, so finally the King sent the Earl of Gloucester to meet the Leinster king, who, rejecting all ideas of pardon and submission, declared: 'I am rightful king of Ireland, and it is unjust to deprive me of what is my land by conquest.'[2]

The meeting between Gloucester and MacMurrough with his three thousand men, in some unnamed glen in Leinster, as graphically told by Creton, and pictured in his text, gives us one of the few personal pictures we have of a medieval Irish king. Art is described as a fine large handsome man, of stern, indomitable mien. His horse, which had cost him the price of four hundred cows, had neither saddle nor housing, and rushed down the hill faster than any deer or hare. Facing the Irish king, who was dressed and mounted as his ancestor Dermot had been, the illumination shows the serried ranks of Gloucester's mail-clad English knights, the heroes of fourteenth-century Europe, but useless in Irish war.[3] MacMurrough demanded peace without

[1] The Duke of Exeter was John Holland, formerly Earl of Huntingdon, created so in 1397. The Earl of Gloucester was Thomas le Despenser, created so in 1397.

[2] *Ann. L. Cé* (1398: *recte* 1399) say: 'King Richard came to Ireland, and MacMurrough, king of Leinster, was much weakened. MacMurrough went on a hosting, and the English of Leinster and Meath overtook him, and a great many of the Saxons fell and many of MacMurrough's hired kerns and four chiefs of Leinster.'

[3] The illuminations to Jean Creton's contemporary French poem, 'Histoire du Roi d'Angleterre Richard' (ed. J. Webb in *Archaeologia*, XX), have several times been reproduced, as in Green's *Short History* (illustrated edn. 1898).

MacMurrough is pictured with high conical cap covering the nape of the neck, particoloured cloak, long coat and undercoat all of gay yellow, crimson, and blue. He is charging on horseback. (*Harleian MS. Brit. Mus.* 1319, printed in *Archaeologia*, 1824.)

reservation, and when Richard, who had reached Dublin on July 1st, heard this he paled with anger, offered a hundred marks for Art alive or dead, swore he would burn him out of his woods, and marched fruitlessly back to Waterford. There the news of Derby's landing at Ravenspur reached him, and the last of the Plantagenets sailed for Milford Haven on August 13th 1399, to meet his tragic doom of deposition and death in England.

So Art Kavanagh, having first wrought the death of Mortimer, now, by delaying Richard in the wilds of Leinster, let in usurping Bolingbroke, and wrecked the unity of England for a hundred years.

We may say that after Richard the English lordship of Ireland in any real sense ceased to exist. Never again till Tudor times was such an attempt possible. Henceforward a Gaelic and Norman aristocracy divided the land, and only a few towns and eastern shires stood for that 'land of peace' which a century before had embraced the greater part of Ireland.

CHAPTER XIV

IRELAND, FEUDAL AND GAELIC, 1399–1447

THE great plan of the last Plantagenet thus failed, and the usurpation of the House of Lancaster, which brought about a new England, allowed a new Ireland to emerge.

Richard had designed enough of a new peerage in his Lordship of Ireland to stiffen the old and make a new English interest, but in the event neither Mortimer, Mowbray, Albemarle, nor Grey succeeded in restoring the old lordships or planting garrisons or colonies in Ulster, Desmond, or Leinster. His plan of a Pale east of the Boyne and the Barrow in which, after MacMurrough and his chiefs had marched out, new grantees such as Beaumont should make their grants effective, also came to nothing, and neither the old Irish nor the settled 'Old English' population received any new blood.[1]

It is equally notable that Richard, who tired of Ireland before he made a job of it, convened no parliament, though he had announced his intention of the same to ratify the measures he took and the submissions of Irish chiefs.[2] It might have occurred that now was the moment for a general admission of the Irish to 'English law and liberty' and a repeal or revision of the Statutes of Kilkenny. But nothing such was done, and the 'mere Irish' remained outside the law till the accession of James I. The fault of the great failure cannot be altogether ascribed to the English side. The chiefs, who were now in the full tide of their local triumphs both against the peaceful colonists and the Norman 'chieftains of lineage', had little wish to make terms or need to accept them from the English king and the Anglo-Irish feudal lords, and it cannot be said that they made any efforts to fulfil the terms of the submissions, to come to Councils in Dublin, and vacate the conquered 'lands of the English'.

It is doubtful in fact whether the English land, language, and law gained a single foot of recovery against the Irish revival as the result of the submissions. The 'obedient English' were so

[1] Yet the grants remained valid in law. *The Lismore Papers* (ed. Grosart), I, p. 141, record in 1609 the petition of the undertakers of county Wexford (Kinselaghes' country) to have De Beaumont's grant renewed; it covered no less than thirty thousand acres. See also *Cal. State Papers, England, James I* (1613), p. 439.

[2] Walsingham, *Historia Anglicana* (*R.S.*), II, p. 215, says that after Christmas 1394 Richard held a parliament in Dublin, but there appears to be no official record of one.

convinced of the failure that in 1421 the Irish parliament requested the King ('inasmuch as the great chieftains of the Irish nation, MacMurrough, O'Brien, O'Connor and others, who did become liegemen to King Richard for themselves and their kindred for ever, are now at war and have broken their oaths and become open rebels') to seek power from the Pope to proclaim a crusade against them.[1] This request, directed against a Christian people, could not of course be entertained.

Nevertheless, however little the Irish leaders of the time thought or foresaw, the greatest general admission of English sovereignty since Henry II had been made, and the greater part of the chiefs of Gaelic Ireland had recognized the King of England as Lord of Ireland and, in most cases, the Earls of Ulster, Desmond, Ormond, etc. as their feudal suzerains. The deed could not be ignored, and when in 1541 Henry VIII got an Irish parliament to proclaim him King of Ireland the submissions of 1395 were one of the chief historic arguments advanced.

THE 'LANCASTRIAN AGE'

The Lancastrian period marks a new age for both England and Ireland. For England, after further brilliant but useless victories, came the end of her imperialistic adventures in France, dearly paid for at home by the wreck of internal unity, the decay of governance, the growth of local lordship, and all those evils which culminated in the great succession-struggle called the Wars of the Roses.

For the King's nominal lordship of Ireland, we have a not dissimilar picture, an ever dwindling 'English land', the native chiefs in possession again of half the island, and in the rest, the Anglo-Irish lords reproducing that particularism which was the general feature of Europe at that age, and showing as little reverence for legal monarchy as their peers did in northern and western England.

The new England that had lost France lost also the linguistic connexion. The English of Chaucer became by 1400 the official and national language of England, and the worn-out French of the court and nobility was put away.[2]

But in Ireland neither English nor French had struck deep root. Never officially recognized, it was Irish which became the almost universal speech of Ireland in the two centuries from 1350

[1] *Rot. Parl.*, IV, pp. 198–9.

[2] 'On petition of Parliament in 1362 King Edward III enacted that "as the French language is much unknown in the realm, all pleas shall be pleaded before the King's justices or in the courts and places of other lords in English and enrolled in Latin".' Adams and Stephens, *English Constit. Docs.*, p. 128.

to 1550.[1] An antiquated English indeed survived in the towns and a few rural areas, and the heads of the Irish government began to correspond with England in the new English. The language of statutes, charters, and official records remained French or Latin till Poynings' Acts of 1495. But the Anglo-French which their ancestors had brought to Ireland dwindled away among the nobility, who came more and more to use the language of their Irish tenants and allies.

The new Lancastrian England had at first little time, and later little heart, to adventure on a reconquest of Ireland. While the revived French wars were on, from 1415 to 1447, she had few troops to spare, and if she sent generals trained in France over as viceroys it was with small array and to hold the lines rather than to win the battle.

'GEARÓID IARLA'

Gerald, 3rd Earl of Desmond, who died in 1398, after forty years of rule, illustrates how far by now the Anglo-Normans had become Irish. His affection for the native race was displayed when he procured permission for a Macnamara, one of 'the mere Irish', to go to Oxford to study, or again when he got royal licence for his son James to be fostered with Conor O'Brien.[2]

We find in Earl Gerald that sensitive temperament which, whether it came from their fabled Italian, or their actual Irish and Cambrian blood, recurred constantly among the Geraldines, and made them the most loved and longest lamented of the 'Old English'. The Earl's Irish verse was admiringly preserved in Irish manuscripts, and made him in tradition one of Ireland's poets. His epitaph in the annals of Clonmacnois: 'he was a nobleman of wonderful bounty, cheerfulness in conversation, easie of access, charitable in his deeds, a witty and ingenious composer of Irish poetry, a learned and profound chronicler, and in fine one of the English nobility that had Irish learning and the professors thereof in greatest reverence of all the English of Ireland', makes him a man after the heart of those Gaelic *literati* who so powerfully controlled Irish opinion.[3]

[1] For the decay of English in Ireland see my article, 'Spoken Languages of Medieval Ireland', *Studies* (1919). The *Cal. of Ormond Deeds*, vols. III and IV, illustrates the prevalence and use of English and Irish side by side in the fifteenth century.

[2] Harris, *Collect.*, III, p. 209: De Windsor, by intervention of Desmond and 'at request of our dear and faithful son Conmar Mac Conmarre chief of his nation', grants permission to Matthew Mac Conmarre, cleric of the diocese of Killaloe, to go to England and study in the schools of Oxford and elsewhere: given at Limerick, 1375.

[3] The Earl's Irish verses are found in the *Book of Fermoy* and in the *Dean of Lismore's Book*—the latter a Scottish Gaelic compilation of 1512.

The folk imagination also took hold on Gerald and made of this princely and generous personality a race-hero alike of the Gael and the Gall. Like Arthur among the Britons, it was believed for centuries that 'Gearóid Iarla', who was but asleep, would rise again on an enchanted steed from beneath the waters of Lough Gur to save Ireland in her extremity.

Gerald's son, John, was drowned in the Suir soon after, in 1400, leaving a young son Thomas; and between the youth of Thomas and the Irish upbringing of James, younger son of Gerald, was enacted afterwards a strange drama.

THE LOSS OF NORTH AND WEST

Connacht was now the practical lordship of the two Burkes; legally they were usurpers, and though a young Edmund Mortimer under age in England had Ulster, Connacht, Leix, and Trim in his cartularies, the western land was in effect gone for good to the two branches of the junior De Burgos. It was now (1401) that the definite distinction and separation of the 'Upper (Uachtarach)' and the 'Lower (Ichtarach)' MacWilliam, or the two Burkes of Clanrickard and Mayo, took place, which lasted till the former became Earl of Clanrickard and the latter Viscount Mayo. The *Annals of Loch Cé* say under 1401: 'Thomas, son of Edmund Albanach Macwilliam à Burc, lord of the Foreigners of Connacht died. Two Macwilliams were then made, viz. Ulick (Uillec) son of Richard Oge and Walter son of Thomas, *but he (the latter) submitted to Macwilliam of Clanrickard on account of seniority.*' The words in italic seem to prove that Edmund Albanach, though much more prominent than his brother Ulick (William), was in fact junior to him.

In Ulster, 'O'Neill the Great of Tyrone' (Niall Oge till 1403 and then his nephew Donal till 1432) was effectively both lord and overlord and counted as his 'urrighs' Magennis of Iveagh, O'Cahan of Derry, MacMahon of Monaghan, and others (but this supremacy varied according as he could enforce it), whose 'bonnacht' or military service, anciently due to the Earl of Ulster, he now claimed.

The landed Englishry were turning into Irish chiefs in outward appearance, but the Savages, MacQuillans, Russells, Whites of Dufferin, and others retained enough of their origin to be known as men of the First Conquest. Among them, Savage of the Ards claimed an hereditary seneschalship of Ulster for the absentee Earl; and a rare voice from the northern colony survives from this time when its head sent to the Government an address praising the seneschal Janico Savage for his noble defence of the people of Down against Irish, Scots, and Breton raiders.[1]

So the south Ulster border, a vital point, 'the Gap of the North', was lost, and communication with the northern colony had to be by sea. In 1302 Ralf Pipard had surrendered his lands about Donaghmoyne to the Crown, and how to get a defender for this marchland at the foot of the Ulster hills became a problem. Twice under Edward III, Donaghmoyne was let to Anglo-Irishmen, charged to build a castle there and settle English tenants. But finally the Lieutenant, Thomas of Lancaster, let it with the lordship of Farney in south Monaghan to the local chief, MacMahon.[2]

THE MIDLANDS AND LEINSTER

Of the derelict and absentee lordships, John Talbot, later Earl of Shrewsbury, now claimed the manor of Lochsewdy through his wife, but in fact the lordship of Westmeath had gone derelict. De Lacy's baronage, Tuits, Petits, Tyrrels, Daltons, Herberts, Dillons and such still held their ground tenaciously there, save for the south-west corner along the Shannon, but they were now 'nations', almost oblivious of English law and feudal duty.

Substantially the nearer parts of Meath and Leinster were now all that was left of the true 'English land', the absentees had ceased to count, and in Leinster the titular Lords of Carlow and Wexford were but empty names. When Richard, only son of Thomas le Despenser, Earl of Gloucester, died in infancy in 1414, the Earl of Ormond became complete master of the Kilkenny liberty.

ANGLO-IRISH 'LORDS OF COUNTRIES'

Compelled by the pressure of Gaelic foes to consolidate themselves, and indeed animated with the same desire to be petty kings in a kingless country, the 'Old English' everywhere at this time devoted their energies to welding together composite blocks of territory around them, conquering what they could without and within, subjecting Gaelic chiefs and Anglo-Irish tenants to admit their sovereign power. Hence on every hand, 'Roche's

[1] See O'Laverty, *Diocese of Down and Connor*, V, p. 342. In my first edition I date the above address at 1410, but, as the bishop of Down and Connor signs, it must be some time after 1442, when the two dioceses were united. The other signatories are the prior and archdeacon of Down, the abbots of Inch and Greyabbey, the community of the city of Down, the towns of Ardglas and Kilclief, and George Russell, baron.

[2] See later, p. 287.

country', 'Grace's country', 'the country of Barrymore and Barry Oge', and the like.

Yet, for all the going over to Irish ways and the lapse from English loyalties, the State found occasional sturdy servants such as the Ormond earls and a few Englishmen who came over ready to make their home here. Such a one was Janico Dartas, Richard II's 'Gascon squire', truly an honest official and brave soldier even if he did feather his nest well in his adopted country, where he served the Crown from 1394 to 1426.[1] A few more men like him backed by some thousands of the disbanded archers and men-at-arms whom England no longer needed for the French wars would doubtless have restored the lordship, but no such plan was thought of by the feeble Government of Ireland.

EXODUS OF THE ANGLO-IRISH

The State could still in 1400 count upon the towns, many of the nobility, and most of the gentry and common Englishry of the nearer counties to which before the end of the century the name of 'the Pale' was given.

It was to retain and reinforce this 'English land' that the martial viceroys of the next half-century came. But the race-recovery of the Irish and the hibernicizing and feudalizing of the 'Old English' made Anglo-Ireland even less substantial than it appeared to be in extent. No laws for the defence of the Pale nor Absentee Acts could check the flight which set in to England, or into the towns, of the labourers who could not endure a land of war, of priests who would not dwell among the Gaelic-speaking people, and of English freeholders whose places the lords preferred to fill with Irish tenants. By the exodus of the lesser Englishry the rural population became Irish again, for as farmers the Irish were willing to bear heavier burdens than the colonists, and as fighting men they suited better the traditions of local war. In vain did statutes strive to check this many-sided emigration, and it would be hard to estimate which did more to ruin the colony, the flight of the freeholders and cultivators, or the departure of the learned. Lest the supply of lawyers, scholars, and theologians should perish, and as Anglo-Ireland had no university, the Government granted licences to spend a term of years at Oxford,

[1] See for this interesting adventurer my paper on 'Janico Dartas, Richard II's Gascon Squire', in *R.S.A.I.* (1933), pp. 182–205. Like De Beaumont (see formerly, p. 274), Dartas had received from Richard a handsome grant in Leinster, namely in the marches of county Dublin. In his case he *did* join the ranks of the Anglo-Irish aristocracy and, though the established septs prevented his grant being made good in county Dublin, he founded a family with handsome estates in Meath.

Cambridge, or Paris, but always with a fear, often justified, that the absenting one would never return. It is noticeable that the flight of ecclesiastics was mainly from Wexford, Waterford, Kilkenny, and Louth, counties where the alternatives for the Englishry were to turn Irish or emigrate. In spite of all penalties, there was a constant departure without return, and the English blood decayed rapidly in the 'obedient shires' themselves. Against such a tide all reissues of the Kilkenny statutes or other such attempts to keep an all-English land were futile.[1]

'COIGN AND LIVERY'

The Anglo-Irish lords themselves fostered the Irish revival, largely because they found the prerogatives of Irish kingship more lucrative and suited to native tradition than their feudal ones. Their growing lordships naturally shaped themselves in native tradition, and hence arose all those exactions, 'coign, livery, mart, bonnaght, kernty', and such, which the English tenants would emigrate rather than endure. 'Coign and livery' together meant the exacting of pay and provender for horse and man, and the quartering of troops on one's tenants. 'Coign' (Irish *coinmhedh*, 'maintenance') by itself was the right of Irish local kings to be maintained, as they travelled, by the people of their country. It went far back into pre-Norman times.[2]

To maintain the chief's mercenaries and provide him with food-dues were acknowledged obligations that lay on the chief's whole 'country', for he had but a private demesne apart from these prerogative rights. The English lords, already possessed of vast feudal rights, sought to add to them the prerogatives of Gaelic chiefs. The Earl of Desmond, the Burkes of Connacht, and other great lords already had such rights over their Irish, and henceforth extended them over their English tenants. The necessities of State gave colour to practices so hateful to Tudor reformers in later days, for the revenues were so small that the

[1] See *Exch. Mem.*, vol. XXIV *passim* for numerous cases of flight of ecclesiastics, and Government permission to go to English universities to study. The sheriff is often ordered to distrain two-thirds of the property of obstinate absentees, according to statutes. Many native Irish got leave to go to English universities. See *Ann. Ult.* (1382): Matthew Ua Eoghain 'the Great Master', archdeacon of Devenish on Lough Erne, who spent fourteen years continuously at Oxford reading and lecturing (*ag denumh leighinn*).

[2] See formerly for 'maintenance' (p. 42). A case of exemption from 'coign' is given in *Facs. Nat. MSS.*, II, plate. lxi (*circa* 1160), from the *Book of Kells*: the church of Ardbreccan is exempted by deed of the High king and the king of Loeghaire in Meath from a tribute due to the latter, viz. one night's *coinmhedh* every quarter of a year.

King's lieutenants themselves resorted to coign and livery in order to maintain the State army. The officers of State were found, in default of an honest revenue, quartering their troops on the English of the Pale. In 1404 the Irish parliament, in granting a carucage of half a mark on the plowland, made a condition that coign and livery should not be exacted, and in 1410, that 'no Lieutenant or Justiciar shall put coign or livery upon the people'. But they had finally to connive at this convenient if hated method of providing for the defence of the Pale. The great men followed suit. Before long 'March lords' had their hired kerns or standing gallowglasses; their heads became 'captains of nations'; and the quartering and enforced payment of these troops at the expense of the tenantry, English and Irish, became universal, except in the small area where the Government could check such practices.

The weakness or absence of royal government in both countries led to the same phenonenon in England and Ireland, the rise of lordship. In the former country, 'livery and maintenance', 'lack of governance', the expulsion of men from their estates by powerful neighbours, the waging of local feuds everywhere, and the overriding of State justice were evils growing more marked when the feeble reign of Henry VI (1422–61) marked the decline of Lancastrian monarchy.[1]

THE IRISH KINGS TAKE LESSER TITLES

The style of 'King' ('Rí') had for long centuries been used by the great dynasts, and it is convenient to continue speaking of them as 'kings' and their territories as kingdoms. Limited though they were in size, still they were sovereign in themselves save where they obeyed some province-king. But from Richard II's time the title of 'king' is generally abandoned, and those who made so general a submission to him evidently thought it henceforth ill befitting to style themselves kings. We therefore find that MacCarthy in future is content with the title of MacCarthy More and abandons the name of 'king of Desmond'. The royal race of Connacht was now so divided that for O'Connor Don or O'Connor Roe to use the ancient style 'king of Connacht' would be absurd. In the case of O'Brien, their epic would indicate that

[1] 'The Earl of Devon and Lord Bonville carried on a quarrel of such ferocity from 1440 to 1455 that the law was unable to stem the torrent of murders, robberies and devastations that resulted. The Earl of Devon alone was said to be followed by eight hundred horsemen and four thousand foot' (quoted in Bennett's *The Pastons and their England*, p. 191).

from 1200 the name of 'king of Thomond' was abandoned for 'the O'Brien'.[1]

Even in the case of O'Neill, admitted to be the greatest of them all, we find the title 'king of Ulster' displaced by one less ambitious.[2] Only in the case of the MacMurroughs, who were on the pay-roll of the Dublin Exchequer, did family pride maintain the ancient title of 'king of Leinster' up to Henry VIII's reign. The annalists indeed and other traditional writers continue to use the empty names of 'king of Ulster', etc. But those who had come in to Richard II as admitted 'princes of the Irish of Ulster', etc., could hardly after that resume the old royal titles. Henceforth in fact O'Neill is 'the O'Neill', O'Donnell 'the O'Donnell', etc., as in all our Irish tradition.

OWEN GLENDOWER AND ART MACMURROUGH

Embarrassed as it was at home, Henry IV's government had yet to turn its eyes towards Ireland. For one thing, the great rising of Owen Glendower in 1400 in Wales seemed like stirring the troubled waters of Celtic Ireland too. This great Welshman tried to bring malcontent Ireland into a league of Welsh, Scots, and French against England. In November 1401 he sent messengers with letters in Latin to the 'lords of Ireland' urging them to send him aid against 'our and your deadly foes, the Saxons'; and though we do not know who these were, it is probable that Art MacMurrough, whose armies held the field within a short sail of Wales, was among them. But the messengers were captured ere they got oversea, and executed without pity, and Glendower, though he held out till 1416, never afterwards sought or found help from Ireland.[3]

In effect, the formidable Art had been mollified for a time by a regrant from Henry of the late King's patent of January 1395, securing to him the yearly fee of eighty marks and the heritage of his wife in Norragh. This was done at the request of Sir John Stanley, who came over as Lieutenant in March 1400, and wrote that MacMurrough was 'the most dreaded enemy of the English in Leinster'. But the Leinster chief did not keep the barony of

[1] The Irish tract, *Triumphs of Turloch* (see formerly, p. 164) says of Donnchad Cairbreach (1210–42) 'he the first, when he dropped the royal style and title that had ever been the wont of his ancestors, was inaugurated O'Brien'.

[2] A note by the eighteenth-century scholar, Charles O'Connor, in the *MacFirbis Pedigrees* (in Irish) says (on what authority we cannot tell): 'the first person who was ever called O'Neill was Niall Oge son of Niall More' (d. 1403).

[3] *Chronicle of Adam of Usk* (ed. Thompson), pp. 72–3. Welsh authorities assert that Glendower had been in Ireland with King Richard, whose fortunes he shared to the last.

Norragh for long; it was granted in 1402 to Janico Dartas, and finally after the death of Elizabeth Calfe in 1445 passed into the hands of the Wellesley family. Art seems to have parted from his Anglo-Irish wife about 1400 and not to have had any sons by her; certainly his heirs never claimed Norragh again. But he continued to make war upon the English for many years yet.

THOMAS OF LANCASTER, KING'S LIEUTENANT

To satisfy the demands of the Anglo-Irish for a Prince of the Blood, the King's second son, Thomas of Lancaster, was made King's lieutenant in July 1401, and held this office nominally till 1413.

A mere boy of fourteen, the Prince arrived in Ireland on November 13th 1401. His chief support was in the gallant burghers of Dublin, who, under their mayor Drake and carrying the timeworn black flag of their city, marched out against O'Byrne and slew near five hundred of his men near Bray.[1]

But the advent of the 'King's son' had a magic spell upon the Irish chiefs, and in December 1401 Murchad O'Connor Faly, Donal O'Byrne, and two Ulster chiefs, Eoghan O'Reilly and Eochy MacMahon, submitted on honourable terms. MacMahon, having by indenture bound himself to be in future the King's faithful liegeman against all his enemies and rebels, Lancaster granted to him the land and lordship of Farney in south Monaghan, the castle of Louth alone excepted, for life at yearly rent of ten pounds. Thus the whole lordship of the Pipards went to an Irish chief by English law, and the south Ulster frontier was abandoned.[2]

On November 8th 1403, Lancaster left Ireland, and his deputy, Sir Stephen Lescrop, and James, 4th Earl of Ormond, who succeeded his father in 1405, ruled the English colony. Uniting with the Earl's illegitimate brother, Thomas le Bottiler, prior of Kilmainham, called 'Bacagh' or 'Lame', they won a smashing victory at Callan on September 14th 1407, when Taig O'Carroll, the Earl's

[1] Marlburrough's *Chronicle* (*Ancient Irish Histories*, 1809). Henceforth Lieutenants, paid in part from the English Exchequer, generally supersede the older Justiciars paid at the inadequate sum of £500 per annum. In 1425 the fee of Lord Talbot was fixed at £1,000, the old one being inadequate. (Harris, *Collect.* IV, pp. 288–90.)

[2] *Rot. Canc. Hib.*, p. 165: 'Indenture by which Aghy McMahon has promised that for ever in future he will be a faithful liege and with all his power will be prepared against enemies and rebels of the King; whereupon the Lieutenant granted him for term of life the land and lordship of Farney, saving only the castle, at £10 per annum' (December 13th 1401). Finally in May 1425, James Earl of Ormond, King's lieutenant, granted the whole territory at rent to Bernard MacMahon, captain of his nation, and Rory and Magnus his brothers, which ended the matter (Shirley's *Farney*, pp. 17–19).

brother-in-law, fell on the Irish side. Taig was an ardent patron of the Gaelic revival, and is commemorated as 'a man of great account and fame with the professors of poetry and music of Ireland and Scotland'.[1]

Again on August 2nd 1408, Prince Thomas returned charged to make war on MacMurrough, enforce the Absentee Acts, and bring two families from every parish in England to replant Ireland. But it was too late for such a programme. Lancaster's servants having come to blows with those of Gerald, Earl of Kildare, when the latter had come to kiss hands, the Prince imprisoned Kildare in Dublin castle and only released him for a fine of three hundred marks. The pride of 'the English by blood' was roused. Lancaster was tired of all his baffling duties and departed for good in June 1409. Made Duke of Clarence in 1412, his fate was to fall at Beaugé in 1421, in one of those wars of France which the princes preferred above the dull statesman's task of saving the Lordship of Ireland.

WAR UPON THE BARDS

With the brilliant but short-lived soldier-king, Henry V (1413–22), a martial English patriotism measured itself against French, Scots, Welsh, and Irish. To Englishmen, generally, the non-English parts of these realms were proper subjects for scorn or fear, and it must be allowed that what the English heard and saw of the raids and ravages of Scots, Welsh, and Irish on the hard-pressed Anglo-saxon race everywhere justified the sturdy Englishism which was still traditional in Shakespeare's day.[2]

PARLIAMENTARIANISM IN IRELAND

Lancastrian constitutionalism, based on the Revolution of 1399 which overthrew Richard II and his absolutism, was now imitated by the Anglo-Irish. Like that of England, it was in no sense democratic but based on the aristocracy and gentry, the Church

[1] *Ann. Clon.* (1407). James, the 4th Earl of Ormond (1405–52), was called the 'White Earl'.

[2] Celtic bards, as inciters of Celtic resistance, were especially obnoxious to the English. In 1403 a statute forbade the bards to follow their vocations in north Wales. This was in the mind of Sir John Stanley who came over as King's lieutenant in October 1413. *A.F.M.* say: 'He was a man who gave neither mercy nor protection to clerics, laity, or men of science (i.e. the poets), but subjected as many as he could to cold, hardship and famine. He plundered Ó Huiginn at Uisneach in Meath.' But when Stanley died on June 18th 1414, the poets flattered themselves they had berhymed him to death, for 'Niall Ó Huiginn made satires on him and he only lived five weeks after them'. In 1415 Talbot, Lord Furnival, apparently in revenge for this, 'despoiled many of the poets of Ireland', including the famous O'Dalys (see later, p. 292).

and the upper middle-class who sought to control the Government through Parliament. The Anglo-Irish secured the principle without much of the advantage, and it coincided with an ever-growing spirit of colonial or 'Old English' patriotism which had arisen in the previous century. The smaller the Pale grew the greater was the Home Rule which it enjoyed. But to their surprise the Anglo-Irish found that the pronounced English nationalism of Westminster was likely to confound them with the native Irish whom they regarded as the common foe.

ANTI-IRISH STATUTES

The Dublin parliament of 1410, held under Thomas le Botiller, prior of Kilmainham, in its petitions summed up the grievances and prejudices of the English colony. The exacting of coign and livery by lieutenants and others was declared treason.[1] Parliament was not to be adjourned or discontinued without cause shown. Mariners must not convey labourers or servants beyond sea. No Irishman adhering to the enemy might pass beyond sea by colour of going to the schools of Oxford, Cambridge, or elsewhere, and no one should have letters of denization unless he gave security not to adhere to any Irish enemy. To the second of these the King replied: 'Let the form of adjournment be after the manner of England.' Magna Carta was once more renewed.

England was now much concerned with her labour problem, which had been going on since the Statute of Labourers in 1349 had attempted to solve it, and how to rid the land of aliens and vagrants, Irish and otherwise. In May 1413 a parliament at Westminster enacted that 'Irishmen and Irish clerks, beggars, shall depart out of England, save graduates, sergeants, apprentices at law, religious, and merchants born in Ireland, for quiet and peace within this realm of England and for the increase and filling of the realm of Ireland'.

In 1380 an Irish parliament had enacted that 'men of Irish nation and enemies of the King' should not obtain Church promotion. In 1416 the Parliament of England confirmed this, 'because men of Irish nation, being prelates, abbots, or priors, bring Irish servants to parliament, and these find out the secrets of the English'.

IRISHMEN AT OXFORD, ETC.

Ireland having no university or schools of canon and civil law of her own, her Anglo-Irish and native students frequented the

[1] For 'coign and livery' see pp. 42, 199, 305, 353; and Gilbert's *Viceroys of Ireland*, pp. 564–5, on 'cess', 'coign', 'purveyors', etc.

two English universities and Inns of Court at Westminster.[1] But they aroused English hostility, and got mixed up with the Lollard and other troubles then affecting the university towns. Many of them no doubt were undesirables and not serious students, and anyway England was in an ungenerous mood on all questions of vagrancy, unemployment, and Welsh, Scots, and Irish intruders. Therefore, following on the Act of 1413, an English parliament in 1422 passed this law:

> 'Forasmuch as divers manslaughters and other felonies have been done of late in divers counties of England as Oxford, Bucks, Wilts, and Berks, as well by divers persons resorting to the town of Oxford as by others dwelling there under jurisdiction of the University—of whom some are lieges of our lord the King born in Ireland, the others are not lieges at all but enemies to him and his kingdom called "wylde Irishmen", and their malice and misdeeds continue from day to day to the great slander of the said University which is the fountain and mother of our Christian faith—therefore it is enacted that all people born in Ireland shall depart out of the realm within a month after proclamation, saving graduates in the schools, men beneficed in Ireland, men of the law, merchants, religious and burgesses of Ireland, Irishwomen married to Englishmen and Irishmen to Englishwomen. Irishmen graduates are not to have hall or hostel of their own but to abide among English scholars under principality of others. Irish scholars shall only be entered into Oxford or Cambridge by letters under seal of the Lieutenant or Justiciar of Ireland, brought to the Chancellor of England, otherwise they shall be treated as rebels.'[2]

The results of this exclusion policy were disastrous. Badly did the colony need men trained in law, letters, and the sciences. The project of a Dublin university had failed. The Anglo-French culture of Ireland had run dry, and if it was to be saved must be saved from the mother-country. Even for the mere machinery of administration, Anglo-Ireland needed a supply of sons trained in

[1] For the Irish at Oxford see *Munimenta Academica* (*R.S.*); Rashdall, *Universities in the Middle Ages*; Maxwell-Lyte, *History of the University of Oxford*; Wood's *Annals*.

[2] See Berry, *Statutes*, I, p. 560–1, and *Rot. Parl.*, IV, pp. 13 and 190. It followed a protest made in an Irish parliament in 1421 against the treatment of the Irish at Oxford, etc.

A further English Act in 1423 made it necessary for all Irishmen dwelling in England to carry as in the Act of 1422 letters testimonial which must be presented to the chancellors of those universities, justices of the peace, and mayors and bailiffs of towns.

English theory and practice. True, the measures seemed to hit only the 'Irish enemy', against whom the Anglo-Irish were ready to legislate, but they hit the Anglo-Irish too, who, even when they spoke their antiquated English, were looked on as aliens in England. The English had legislated sweepingly and ungenerously on a matter vitally affecting Ireland. In defiance the English of Ireland asserted their colonial nationhood and became more and more Irish as the century went on.

Many were the subsequent complaints about the exclusion of the Irish-born from Oxford and the English schools; they were a part of the parliamentary disputes of the Patriot and Unionist parties in Ireland.[1] The excluding statutes remained on the statute-book on the English side but it would appear that after 1442 they were allowed to fall into abeyance, until in the next century Henry VIII himself founded Inns of Law in Dublin itself.

IRELAND AT THE COUNCIL OF CONSTANCE

Henry, the victor of Agincourt, had little care for his lordship here. Yet on a spectacular occasion at this time, the name of the kingdom of Ireland was proudly uttered among the kings and bishops of Europe. At the General Council of Constance for reform of the Church in 1415, over which the Emperor Sigismund presided, was debated a point on which the Cardinal of Cambrai had written learnedly but with French bias, namely whether the envoys of France had precedence over those of England, 'a mere German province'. But the English ambassador gained his point thus: 'Europe was from of old divided into four empires or *regna*, that of Rome, that of Constantinople, that of Ireland, and that of Spain; but as that of Ireland has been by Adrian's Bull translated to England, it is manifest that the King of England and his kingdom are among the more eminent and ancient kings and kingdoms of Europe, which prerogative the kingdom of France is not said to obtain.'

JOHN TALBOT, VICEROY, 1414–1419

Again a great viceroy was found in John Talbot, Lord Furnival, who landed at Dalkey on November 10th 1414, as King's lieutenant for six years with a yearly salary of four thousand marks paid from the English Exchequer. This 'ancient fox and politique captain' as Hall calls him, made later Earl of Shrewsbury, was now thirty-six years of age, and was the born soldier to the end till he fell at Castillon forty years later.

[1] See later, p. 300; especially the concession of 1442.

A man of action, he set himself to crush the 'degenerate English' and to clear the frontiers of the English land, and carried the royal banner far into Meath, Ossory, and Munster, so severely handling Irish and Normans in his expeditions that the annals of Ulster say, 'from the time of Herod there came not anyone so wicked'.[1]

But most of Talbot's energies went into a long feud with the Anglo-Irish. He was a returned absentee on a large scale, his wife Maud Neville, who was descended from Theobald (II) de Verdun, being claimant to part of the Verdun lordship of Westmeath, and himself by descent from De Valence a claimant to the honour of Wexford.[2] Returned absentees were never popular, and the Earl of Ormond headed a Patriot Party which asserted against this domineering viceroy the rule of Ireland by the Irish. During Talbot's absence in England in 1417, the Patriots held a parliament at Trim, where Cranley, archbishop of Dublin, indicted the King's lieutenant for various oppressions and unpaid debts. Returning to Ireland, Talbot on June 26th 1418 arrested the Earl of Kildare, Christopher Preston of Gormanston, and other magnates at Slane for plotting with the prior of Kilmainham against him. In Preston's possession was found a copy of that *Modus Tenendi Parliamentum* on which was based Lancastrian constitutionalism. Whatever he thought of Anglo-Irish opposition, Talbot could not refuse them what his royal master accepted for England, and therefore had the Great Seal affixed to this document.[3]

But a warrior viceroy, the enemy of great lords, was ever the hero of the lesser folk, and meanwhile an assembly of some hundred of the obedient English wrote to the King in June 1417 praising Talbot for his vigorous action against English rebels and Irish enemies.

> 'He marched against O'More, MacMahon, O'Reilly, O'Farrell, O'Connor, and O'Hanlon, who all made peace by indenture. In Ulster he cut a great pass through woods two leagues or more: and O'Neill, the Great, O'Neill-Boy, Magennis, Maguire, and O'Donnell sent to have peace. Morice Keating, chief of his nation, traitor and rebel, yielded himself and peace was

[1] *A.F.M.* (1415): 'He plundered Leix, Oriel, and Mic na mBrethnach (the Walshes of Kilkenny), hanged Thomas Caech of the Geraldines' blood, and plundered the O'Dalys, poets of Meath.' His oppression of the latter was doubtless due to his claim upon Westmeath.

[2] See Pedigree, Appendix I (A). Reginald Lord Grey de Ruthyn having died in 1440, Talbot's claim by descent to Wexford was allowed by the Crown.

[3] For the *Modus*, its significance, and Irish counterpart, see a chapter in Miss M. V. Clarke's *Mediaeval Representation*.

granted him. Further he repaired Athy bridge and built a tower there against Leix. Also he delivered the young Earl of Desmond from prison.'[1]

ART OGE AT PEACE WITH THE ENGLISH

Meanwhile Art Kavanagh MacMurrough had waged a sporadic war against the English along with his two sons, Donnchad and Gerald. But Art was growing old, and in a deed of July 1417 (or 1421), through his deputy John Doun, abbot of Duiske, he admitted himself to be liegeman and subject of the King, who accepted his submission and received his son, Gerald Kavanagh, into protection, and granted him safe-conduct to come and go through all Ireland and the King's dominions by land and sea with all his retinue.[2]

Early in 1418 Art died in his own fortress.[3] To this striking personage must be ascribed the restoration of the MacMurrough kingship of Leinster, and the ruin of the English colony in its earliest conquest. He was undoubtedly a great province-king, making vast conquests by 'sword-land' but we cannot attribute to him any all-Ireland aim or even constant repudiation of English lordship.

His son and successor Donnchad began his reign badly. In May 1419, 'Donatus More Cavenagh MacMurchard, chief captain of all the Leinstermen, whom they had named king of Leinster, was taken and sent to England, where for seven years he was laid in the Tower, till afterwards he was sent back to Ireland on certain terms.'[4]

[1] Ellis, *Original Letters Illustrative of English History* (2nd Series), I, pp. 56–63.

[2] Harris, *Collect.*, IV, p. 206.

[3] *Ann. Ult.* Where this was we cannot be sure; it was probably Ferns, which the MacMurroughs had now recovered, but 'Garbh-choill' in Idrone had been his residence earlier. This is near Bagenalstown, county Carlow, now called Garryhill; in 1585 Murtogh Kavanagh 'of the Garquil' was head of the senior branch of the MacMurroughs.

[4] Thady Dowling's *Annals* (ed. Richard Butler), *Irish Arch. Soc.* (1849). Dowling was Chancellor of Leighlin (d. 1628).

The Exchequer fee of eighty marks per annum going back to 1372 seems to have been continued to Art throughout all his life. It was also continued to his son, and was an Exchequer charge right up to 1532. The date of the safe-conduct (which I give in my first edition as 1417), and of Art's death in 1418, I admit are puzzling. Harris (quoted) gives Henry V's safe-conduct grant as given at Southampton in July in the ninth year of his reign. This is 1421. *A.F.M.* say that Art died 'of poison as some assert given him by a woman' at New Ross on the seventh day after Christmas 1417 (i.e. 1418). Dowling states that 'Donatus More' (his son) was captured in 1419. If he was then 'chief captain of the Leinstermen and king of Leinster', his father Art Oge could not have been alive, unless he had resigned in favour of his son. *Ann.*

With this last triumph Talbot departed in July 1419, leaving his brother Richard, archbishop of Dublin, and Chancellor of Ireland in 1423, to uphold the 'English interest'. Richard lived till 1449, and all that time waged a long feud with James of Ormond, who headed the 'English of Ireland' till his death in 1452.

THE EARLS OF ORMOND AND DESMOND

James, fourth of his line, called the 'White Earl' of Ormond, was a gallant knight who had won his spurs in France, and a man of education and refined culture, whose castle-seat at Kilkenny was the centre of a flourishing Anglo-Irish culture. He was a great lover of history, antiquity and heraldry, and left some of his English lands to endow the College of Heralds. His secretary, James Yonge, dedicated to him his English translation of the *Secretum Secretorum,* which treats of prudence, justice, fortitude, temperance, chivalry, the King's title to Ireland, and other themes.[1]

Even more 'Old English' than Ormond was James, 6th Earl of Desmond, a remarkable character, who now appears among the great lords of Ireland, and whose name takes us back to 1400.

Sir John, 4th Earl, son of Gerald the Poet, had been drowned in 1400 and left a son Thomas, then fourteen years old. For over ten years Thomas followed his father in the Desmond earldom, and then was expelled under circumstances very difficult to verify. Legend relates that the young Earl fell into unknightly and un-English ways, wrote Irish verse, and married Catherine MacCormack, the beautiful daughter of a common Irish tenant. James, that younger son of 'Gearóid Iarla' who had been fostered among the O'Briens, therefore seized the opportunity welcome to an ambitious mind, and ousted his nephew from the earldom.

The English records here give us little help. According to them, Thomas is undisputed Earl till 1413, and his rival is only James 'de Dessemond'. On August 14th 1413 we find Thomas in England about to proceed to Ireland along with Ormond 'for the defence of the same', with a hundred men-at-arms and four hundred and sixty archers between them. According to the annals of the

Ult. also give Art's death as 1417: this would be in New Style 1418. I incline to think that Harris copied 5 Hen. V wrongly as 9 Hen. V, and that 1417 is correct.

Dowling makes Art, 'ferax rebellis cuius potentiae omnes Lagenienses resistere non potuerunt', surrender to the royal grace in 1420, but this chronicler's dating is very defective.

[1] Yonge says that English was the Earl's 'modyr tongue'. For this writer see St. John D. Seymour, *Anglo-Irish Literature, 1200–1582*, pp. 135–44; also Kingsford, *Prejudice and Promise in 15th-century England*, p. 40.

Four Masters, in 1411 Thomas was expelled by his own kinsman, James, son of Gerald. Possibly the forces of 1413 were intended to recover his right as well as succour Ireland; these annals put it in their own way under 1414, 'the Earl of Desmond came to Ireland with many Englishmen to devastate Munster'. Evidently James was too strong for him and took the young Earl prisoner; for the letter of the Irish assembly praising Talbot, which we have quoted above, says that Talbot 'bore greate labours and costes about the deliverance of the Earle of Dessemond who was falsely and deceitfully taken and detayned in prison by his unkle to the great distruction of all the contry of Mounstre until now that he is delivered by the said leiftenant'.[1]

But though set free, Thomas could not recover his ground, and went off to England, then to France, where finally he died and was buried at Paris on August 10th 1420, the King of England attending his funeral at the house of the Friars Preachers there.[2]

As Earl Thomas left no sons, James was left without a rival in the earldom, which he ruled till 1462. The English Crown had lost all control, and had to accept what was in effect a pure usurpation, or even an Anglo-Norman assertion of Tanist-right. It is hard to believe that any Irish sympathies which Thomas may have shown gave James anything but an excuse, for James himself was Irish-fostered and almost certainly spoke Irish. But while the Normans thought it no dishonour to marry a princess of the Five Bloods, a plebeian Gaelic marriage was an offence to the proudest of the 'Old English', and possibly Catherine MacCormack lost her husband the loyalty of his Englishry and the respect of his Irish, and thus enabled James to depose an unworthy nephew.[3]

Thus did another province go over to the Norman-Irish order, though not so completely as Connacht. The alliance of the great earls and the age of aristocratic Home Rule had begun. Ormond, arriving at Waterford as King's lieutenant on April 4th 1420, allied himself with James, procured him recognition from the Crown, and in December 1420 appointed him 'Guardian of the Peace' in counties Waterford, Cork, Limerick, and the Cross of

[1] See Ellis, *Letters*, op. cit.

[2] See for the whole matter *Rot. Canc. Hib.*, pp. 186, 204, *et passim*, and the chronicles of Marlburrough, Dowling, Holinshed, Hall; also Vicary Gibbs, *Cokayne's Complete Peerage*.

[3] In any case by marrying an Irishwoman Thomas offended against the Statutes of Kilkenny, but as the Government supported him, this objection could not matter. It seems a sheer case of expulsion, Irish only in the sense that James asserted himself as the better man, more fitted to be *capitaneus Geraldinorum* and 'chief and principal of his nation'. But the whole story is obscure and puzzling.

Kerry, and, on January 31st 1422, governor of the baronies and lordships of Inchiquin and Imokilly and the town of Youghal for life, with half the rents and profits of the same. When, in 1422, Ormond called on James to aid him against Calvach O'Connor Faly and Meiler Bermingham, 'then designing to make a final conquest of Meath', Desmond came with five thousand horse and foot, and was paid by a State subsidy and rewarded with the constableship of the castle of Limerick and fifty pounds annual rental out of the city.[1]

ORMOND AS VICEROY

The rule of Ormond as Lieutenant, 1420–2, was shaken with the great feud of the Talbots and the 'English interest' against Ormond and the Home Rule Party. Parliament was the arena of their battles. In 1421 the archbishop of Cashel, Richard O'Hedigan, and FitzJohn, bishop of Cork, were accused by the bishops of Lismore and Cloyne of having Irish hearts. O'Hedigan 'made much of the Irish, loved none of the English, gave no benefices to them, and went about to make himself king of Munster'. O'Hedigan was an enthusiast for the Gaelic side. As for the 'English interest', they strove to put the anti-Irish statutes into force. The Talbot party made charges against Ormond, accusing him of treason, of setting the laws at naught, and favouring the Irish enemy, as for example, allowing Calvach O'Connor Faly to impose black-rent. The Patriot Party again in April 1421 sent a declaration of 'the community of the land of Ireland' to the King, attacking Talbot for his late monstrous oppressions, and praising Ormond as the model viceroy, 'who had abolished a bad, most heinous and intolerable custom, called coigne'. They begged for the King to come in person, and made many and bitter complaints. 'English lieges, born in Ireland of good and gentle families, are no longer received at the English Inns of Courts. Landholders, artificers, and labourers are leaving the land in great numbers, being laden with charges and wars; money should be coined in Ireland as in England; the land is destroyed by Irish enemies and English rebels; if the King himself come not, the land is lost.' But the King they addressed was a dying man, and on August 31st 1422 the hero of Agincourt made way for his infant son Henry. When Talbot raised these matters in the English Council, Henry V's brother, John, Duke of Bedford, now Regent of England, dismissed them with others as 'dissensions, commotions, lawsuits, scandals, and intolerable evils' with which

[1] Gibbs, *Cokayne's Complete Peerage.*

unfortunate England was now ridden and was to be more so as the reign of Henry VI went on.[1]

Ormond was Lieutenant and made vigorous wars against the Irish. His most famous fight was at the Red Moor of Athy in 1420 when he slew 'many of the kin and the terrible army of O'More', and the sun, naïvely state the Anglo-Irish chroniclers, stood still for the space of three hours till the English destroyed the Irish.

THE LAST MORTIMER

Edmund, Earl of March and Ulster, son of the Roger Mortimer slain in 1398, was now a man of thirty, and would have been a very great personage had not his unaspiring nature made him a man without a party, for many thought him, as grandson of Lionel of Clarence, a truer heir to the Throne than the infant Henry himself. But in Ireland his name alone bore weight; he was 'the Lord of the English of Ireland' and a more royal personage than any man of England could be. In February 1424, Mortimer arrived as Lieutenant with a maintenance of five thousand marks per annum. No one was so fitted to reconcile all Ireland, and when Edmund held the court of his liberty at Trim, the great men of the north came in. Eoghan O'Neill, son of Niall Oge, Neachtan, son of Turloch O'Donnell, Brian O'Neill of Clandeboy, MacDonnell of the Glens, and MacQuillan did homage to him as Earl of Ulster.[2] But Edmund died suddenly of plague, on January 19th 1425, and thus was extinguished the all but royal name of Mortimer.

SUBMISSIONS OF IRISH CHIEFS, 1425

The Irish Council, acting under the 'Statute of FitzEmpress',[3] at once appointed Talbot as Justiciar, he being then in Ireland, and he marched west to complete the submission of the chiefs. According to the annals of the Four Masters, 'the English of Meath captured Eoghan O'Neill, Mac-I-Neill-Buidhe (the Clandeboy O'Neill), Neachtan O'Donnell, MacQuillan, and MacDonnell'. This is the common charge; probably the chiefs had not yet dispersed after their submission at Trim. Anyway the leading chiefs were brought to Dublin, and there or elsewhere entered into indentures of fealty. Talbot surrendered his office to Ormond,

[1] Berry, *Statutes*, I, pp. 563–83; *Rot. Parl.*, IV, pp. 198–9.

[2] Nechtan O'Donnell was acting as proxy for his brother Niall Garbh, their father Turloch having retired into Assaroe abbey in 1422 and died 1423.

[3] For this so-called statute see Berry, *Statutes*, I, p. 586; the appointment of Kildare in 1461 and 1471; also p. 381 in the first edition of this work.

and he as King's lieutenant (from April 1425 to July 1427) received the final submissions of the chiefs on terms similar to 1395.

At Dundalk on July 23rd 1425, Eoghan O'Neill 'not impelled by fear or force but freely, spontaneously, and of his own pure will' admitted himself liegeman of the King, and tenant, subject, and true man of Richard, Duke of York, the then heir of Edmund, Earl of March. O'Neill was confirmed in all 'the Irish lands' which he then held, to hold them immediately of the Duke. All lands held by him and his adherents and subjects which they have occupied before the date of the present indenture are confirmed to them. O'Neill pledges himself to surrender the rest of the Duke's lands and those of the Englishry, and to render to Richard when he shall come of age the 'bonnacht' (military and allied services) which his ancestors owed to the earls of Ulster, to ride with him against all enemies, to forswear the black-rent levied on the English, and to restrain his people from injuring the King's lieges.[1]

Brian MacMahon of Monaghan and his two brothers, Dermot O'Toole, Donogh O'Byrne, and Calvach O'Connor Faly made similar terms. MacMahon had the barony of Farney confirmed to him. Calvach O'Connor at Dundalk on the same day as O'Neill renewed terms made by him at Trim on March 27 with Talbot. He also promised to restore 'all English lands' and surrender 'the tribute called black-rent' upon Meath, to give a thousand marks for peace, and to come to the Justiciar when called upon.

O'Byrne swore to protect the loyal English of the lordship of Wexford, and recognized the right of the archbishop of Dublin to have jurisdiction and collect his rents among O'Byrne's subjects.[2]

THE MACMURROUGH MENACE

When Ormond retired from office at the end of July 1427, Sir John de Grey and Richard Talbot, archbishop of Dublin, successively ruled till 1431. The menace of the Leinster Irish at this time is depicted in a letter addressed by Swayne, archbishop of Armagh, to the English government, protesting because Grey had come with so few troops. Grey had brought back to Ireland the

[1] O'Neill's submission is printed in vol. I, v of the *Irish Record Commission* (1810–15), p. 54. Richard, Duke of York, born in 1411, was son of Richard Duke of Cambridge and of Ann, sister of Edmund Mortimer who died in 1425. As such he was heir to all the Mortimer titles in Ireland. Eoghan O'Neill was not chief at the time, for his cousin Donal Mac Énrí ruled from 1403 to 1432, but Eoghan was evidently Tanist and playing up to the Government to support him as against his cousin Donal.

[2] For the text and significance of the treaty see my paper in *Hermathena* (1931) on 'The Bonnacht of Ulster'.

prisoner Donnchad MacMurrough, son of Art Oge, and released him 'on certain terms', but all the same, Donnchad was in arms the next year and, says Swayne, 'The kyngys enmys of the south partis, seeing that he [Grey] had fewe men with hym, all of oon consent they went to war and Makmorth was their captaine, and he haide with hyme as men seyde eight battayls of fotmen arrayede of the gyse of this countre, that is owery man an acton, habirchon, pischane and basnete, and in every battayle they commonly have men two hundred; and this Makmorth with his men came into the Englishe countre to a towne callede Connall, and there they brent the ouses of offsye of the abbey [all] but the grete churche of the same and the cloyster, and brent that day many other townes.' Next, he continues, MacMurrough raided Kildare, forced Wexford county to pay him two hundred and forty marks ransom, took Tristeldermot, a walled town, and captured its lord Sir Thomas Wogan, till at last the King's lieutenant had to pay MacMurrough the eighty marks yearly his father had.

The archbishop also wrote at this time to Ormond: 'In good faith the Englisch grounde that ys obeying to the kyngis laue in this lande I suppos is not so moche of quantite as on schir in Englonde.' The purveyors of chief governors exact 'horsmete and manmete', and pay in tallies, rarely honoured, so that 'there is owing in this lande by lieutenants within these past fewe years £20,000 and more. And the housbonde pepill for the mischefe and governance aforesaide be gone out of the londe within fewe yeris into Englonde and oder countreys, so that in good faith as I suppos there is more gone out of the londe of the kynges lege pepyll than be in it.'[1]

The Acts of the Irish parliament at the time have a monotonous sameness. In 1428 it is enacted that labourers and servingmen leaving Ireland without licence shall be arrested. None may sell corn, iron, salt, or other victuals to the Irish enemy without leave. In 1430 the penalties of treason are affirmed against those who practise coign and livery or marriages, fosterage, and gossipred with the Irish enemy. It is forbidden to entertain or let land in the Marches to 'Irish rymers and others, outlaws and felons, who come with their creaghts (*keryaghtes*) into the land of peace called the Maghery'.

In 1428 Parliament complains to the King that clerks, merchants and other honest men of Ireland, going to Chester, Coventry,

[1] *Reg. of Archbishop Swayne*: transcript in T.C.D., I, pp. 419–21. Acton, habirchon, pischane and basnet are respectively body-armour, sleeveless coat of plate or chain mail, gorget, and light helmet. The Irish who in the first century of the Invasion used to come 'naked' to the battle were now clearly a race of armoured men. For 'coign', etc. see formerly, pp. 284, 289.

Oxford, and London have been robbed and beaten, and men of Ireland hindered from going to Inns of Court in England.[1]

In 1431 it is forbidden to merchants and other lieges to frequent Irish fairs and markets and buy or sell there divers merchandises, 'whereout the enemy take great customs and benefits to the depression of our boroughs and trading towns'.[2]

In matters of state, a parliament in 1430 complained that lieutenants were changed too often: 'therefore we beseech the King that while we stand well such change be not made hereafter for fear of losing this land as it hath been of late'. 'Complaints against governors should be examined by Parliament or Council of Ireland and the result certified under the Great Seal of the same.' Against this demand of the Home Rule Party that the King's ministers in Ireland should be made responsible to the legislature of Ireland, the pro-English party petitioned the King never to abandon his power to change viceroys and to examine into their conduct. As for Parliament doing this, the truth would never be discovered, 'for the nobles and great men fill it with their nominees, who little regard the weal of the King or his subjects'.

A further complaint of Parliament in 1430 that 'nearly all the loyal counties are Irish or rebellious' was emphasized by a royal hosting of Eoghan O'Neill, who, in spite of his submission in 1425, ravaged the plain of Louth, put Dundalk under black-rent, then marched into Meath and gave 'stipends' to Calvach O'Connor, O'Molloy, O'Madden, Mageoghegan, and O'Melaghlin, who thus in Irish fashion became his men. Moreover, 'there came the Baron of Delvin, the Plunkets, the Herberts and the English of the west of Meath in general to meet that Eoghan to submit to and honour him, in respect of their own lands'.

That De Lacy's barons should thus acknowledge an Irish king was unprecedented. But Meath was full of walled towns, castles, and colonies of the Englishry, and for all their hostings and black-rents, the Irish chiefs never subdued a country of which the control would have carried them up to the gates of Dublin.

In 1432, his rival Donal Bog O'Neill having been slain by the O'Cahans, this Eoghan was inaugurated king 'on the flagstone of the kings at Tullahoge by the will of God and men, bishops and

[1] See *Facs. Nat. MSS.*, III, plate xxxix. *Rot. Canc. Hib.*, p. 263 (1442): Thomas Chace, Chancellor of Ireland, 'sent by the Council to ask that lieges of Ireland may travel to England and stay there to study the law, brought back a full and effectual answer under the Great Seal of England'.

[2] See Berry, *Statutes*, II, p. 11–43, for these enactments. The 'Maghery' now for the first time mentioned was the plain (*machaire*) of the Midlands, the Pale. The creaghts (*caoruigheacht* in Irish) were the flocks and herds of migratory Irish.

sages'. In September 1434, along with Niall Garbh O'Donnell, he descended to levy black-rent on Dundalk, but the viceroy, Sir Thomas Stanley, attacked them, and Niall spent the rest of his days in captivity in Dublin, London, and the Isle of Man, Stanley's lordship.

During this viceroyalty, in 1435 the Council at Dublin reported thus to the English government:

> 'In the nether parts of Meath, Dublin, Kildare, and Louth, there is scarcely left out of the subjection of enemies and rebels thirty miles in length and twenty in breadth as a man may safely ride or go to answer to the King's writs.[1] County Carlow was within these thirty years one of the keys of the land between Dublin and the outer parts. It is now inhabited with enemies and rebels; of 140 castles defensible therein only two now are left, namely Carlow and Tullow. The counties of Kilkenny, Wexford, Waterford, Cork, Limerick, Tipperary, and Kerry are destroyed, and the lieges dwelling there are too few to victual the cities of Waterford, Cork, Limerick, and the walled towns of those counties. So with the provinces of Armagh and Tuam —all are lost save for Galway, Athenry, and the castles of Carrickfergus and Ardglas. For thirty years no lieutenant or other governor has gone thither save for a sudden hosting. We pray that the lieutenant may receive homages in Ireland. Our seas are scourged by Spaniards, Bretons, and Scots. The Admiral of England should visit our coasts. Ireland should be under the same peace and truce with England by special word. Let the King's lieutenant, that now is, come with sufficience of goods and men, or else some other great man of the King's blood.'[2]

But the bankrupt England over which the young Henry was king, engaged in a losing war with France, had no men or money to spare for Ireland.

ORMOND *versus* THE TALBOT PARTY

An undistinguished Leo or Lionel, Lord Welles, was Lieutenant from 1438 to 1442; then the Earl of Ormond, having been Deputy in 1441, became Lieutenant from that to 1444. A fresh attempt was made against the Earl, who was the acknowledged leader of the Anglo-Irish. Archbishop Talbot and Richard Wogan, the Chancellor, induced the parliament of Martinmas 1441 to transmit

[1] This was roughly what the Pale had become by 1494 as recognized in Poynings' Acts.

[2] Gilbert's *Viceroys*, pp. 330–3. Stanley was at the time absent in England.

charges against him by Giles Thorndon, Treasurer of Ireland, of which the tenor was as follows:

> 'The Earl is old and unwieldy and cannot even defend his own lands. He has made Irish grooms and pages knights of the shire to as to support him in parliament, and allowed temporal and spiritual lords to absent themselves from the same. He has never been absolved from charges of treason brought against him by the Earl of March and Lord Talbot. The discords between him and Lord Talbot and his brother are so great that no suit touching the other can have due process in Ireland. The substance of the gentles and commons of Ireland, at Lord Welles's departure, desired that the Earl snould in no wise be his deputy. Let the King therefore discharge him, and send a lord of the birth of your noble realm of England whom your people in Ireland will obey, for men of England keep better justice in Ireland and execute your laws and favour more your common people and have ever done so, more than ever did any man of Ireland or is ever like to do.'

Ormond having been appointed Lieutenant in February 1442, the charges, returned under Privy Seal, were tried before the Irish Council at Trim on June 5th 1442.[1]

The Home Rule aristocracy was too strong for Talbot's Unionist faction. The Council repudiated the charges and denied that the Martinmas parliament ever desired them to be drawn up. Wogan, having fled to Wales, wrote thence to the King pleading that the charges were truly drawn up and that the acts at Trim clearing Ormond were enrolled by the Clerk of the Rolls 'for drede of his life of the seide erle', and pleaded ignorance, because of 'his newe comyng into yower seide lande of Ireland' of the custom by which in the Irish parliament one man could appear as proxy for two lords spiritual or for two shires or two towns. Wogan was deprived of the Great Seal and Ormond bestowed it on Sir Richard Fitz-Eustace. Although summoned to London, the Earl returned in triumph, still the King's lieutenant.[2]

In August 1445 he procured for his ally, James, Earl of Desmond, royal licence 'to appear in parliaments and Great Councils by proxy, whenever he cannot attend in person, and to acquire

[1] *King's Council in Ireland* (*R.S.*), appendix, p. 304, and *Carew Miscell.*, pp. 391–4. As the envoys of the Talbot party addressed the demand for 'a lord of the birth etc.' from England, the text says 'for men of this land (i.e. England) keep' etc., and speak of Ireland as 'that land'.

[2] For further details of this tedious quarrel, see my *Cal. Ormond Deeds*, III, pp. 140–55: 'Documents relating to the Earl of Ormond's government' (1441–4).

lands and rents held in chief of the King by any tenure whatsoever—the King having learned of his (Desmond's) great labours in preserving and keeping the King's title in the counties of Waterford, Cork, Limerick and Kerry from the King's Irish enemies and rebels'.[1]

In 1444 the King summoned Ormond to appear before the English Cabinet. The Earl thereupon assembled a Great Council at Drogheda where his conduct was eulogized by Sir James Aleyn, the speaker of the Commons, by the bishop of Cork and his clergy, and Lords Barry, Roche, and other vassals of Desmond. The game old Earl then crossed to London to fight his chief accuser, Thomas Fitzgerald, prior of Kilmainham, but the King forbade the combat.

THE HOME RULE TRIUMPH

Although the Talbot party was reinstated for a time during the years 1444–7 with the Archbishop as Justiciar, and then Furnival, made Earl of Shrewsbury in 1442, as Lieutenant, the Anglo-Irish nobles henceforth ruled Ireland, dominated Parliament, divided offices of state among them, and took into their hands the prerogatives of the absentee monarchy. From this time the dislike of the common Englishry for the 'great chieftains of lineage' disappeared, and the mass of the Anglo-Irish accepted, or dared not oppose, the leadership of the great earls who, with an aristocracy behind them in which the Gaelic chiefs played no small part, built up a rampart of native rule which till 1534 no English government was able to break. This race which, said Sir John Davies, 'did ever, both English and Irish, desire to be governed by great persons', found them, not in English viceroys, but in Butlers, Geraldines, and Burkes.

The legislature of this Home Rule oligarchy was a very restricted representation, both in area and numbers. A Great Council was a favourite substitute for a true parliament and to a *Magnum Concilium* in June 1444 at Drogheda, Ormond summoned, 'by prive seale as the custume of the land is', the archbishops of Armagh and Dublin, the bishops of Kildare and Meath, twenty-seven abbots and priors, four archdeacons and one dean, the baron of Slane and four other Meath baronies, the sovereigns of Kells, and the provosts of Athboy, Navan, Trim, and Naas, ninety-seven knights and gentry from counties Dublin, Kildare, Louth, and the Cross and liberty of Meath, and the mayors and bailiffs of Dublin and Drogheda; a total of some hundred and twenty-five,

[1] *Cal. Pat. Rolls, Eng.* (1441–6), p. 358.

apart from the Council.[1] The true electing area had by now shrunk to the shires of Leinster and Meath, and the Irish parliament resembled rather a large county court than a national assembly. Yet in law no Parliament was regarded as complete unless all the English land was summoned, and thus Poynings' parliament of Drogheda in 1495 declared void the proceedings of a previous assembly of 1494, held under Lord Preston, because only the four shires were summoned.

At the same time the shrinkage of feudal dues, rents from royal demesnes, customs, and other sources of revenue, was continuous. In 1441 Thorndon informed the English government: 'the King hath no custom of any manner of merchandise in Ireland save only hides, wool and fells', and, 'the charges of the Justiciar of Ireland and his officers this year exceed the revenues by £1,456'. About 1442 the total revenue for four years came to £5,380 or some £1,340 per annum, and in 1420 Ormond with difficulty procured from Parliament a subsidy of a thousand marks. Later, in 1480, Edward IV directed Kildare not to demand more than 1,200 marks as a subsidy in any one year 'as hath been accustomed'.[2]

THE DESMOND EARLDOM

In extent and power the lands of the March lords and palatine earls grew as fast as the 'obedient shires' decayed. Under James of Desmond most of Munster formed in effect a small kingdom. None of the Old English had yet so completely subjected English and Irish, vassals, towns and tenants under one seigniory. The MacCarthys, O'Sullivans, and other Irish lords owed military service and head-rents to the Earl.[3] Norman and Gael bound themselves to vassalage. Thus, in 1421, an indenture between Earl James and Patrick Fitzmaurice, 'captain of his nation', Lord of Kerry, made at Castleisland, binds Patrick, his heirs, and his people to answer the Earl at his assizes for all assessments, burdens, and levies whatsoever as all other tenants and subjects of the Earl in Kerry are bound, namely upon a cantred and a half. If any contention arise between the two parties or between Patrick and the sons of Gerald 'MacMorys' or the sons of Richard 'MacMorys', the Earl shall decide, and if Patrick shall not pay the said burdens then he binds himself and his lands in the sum of

[1] *King's Council*, op. cit., pp. 305–8. The documents show that the language of debate in the Irish parliament was standard fifteenth-century English.

[2] *Carew Miscell.*, pp. 393–4.

[3] See Butler, 'Lordship of MacCarthy More', *R.S.A.I.* (1906–7). *Carew Miscell.*, vol. I, p. 416: Carbery (in Elizabeth's reign) was held by MacCarthy Reagh of the Earl for sixty-seven beeves yearly.

three hundred pounds. The Earl promises him protection and security; he shall not be taken or attacked coming to assizes; all offices of his, accustomed from of old, are confirmed to him. The Earl guarantees him his 'slanyaght'. The witnesses are all Anglo-Irish, but the whole transaction attests how far in independence and Gaelic custom the Earl and the once feudal Englishry had gone.[1]

Others of the Barrys, Roches, Barretts are found thus subordinating or parting with their lands to the Earl. In 1421 Robert, son of Geoffrey Cogan, 'captain of his nation', granted to Earl James all his possessions in county Cork, viz. fifteen manors in the barony of Ciarraighe Cuirce, including Shandon, with the services of the free tenants, etc.[2] As Cogan's land included the castle of Carrigaline which commanded Cork harbour, the Earl commanded the chief ports of Munster, namely Limerick, Tralee, Youghal, and Cork. Already master of counties Limerick, Kerry and Cork, half of Waterford, the Decies, was his also.[3]

Earl James was a great builder and restorer of castles, such as Askeaton, Imokilly, and Newcastle Connello with its noble hall called by the people, as long as Irish was spoken, the 'Halla More'. Their splendid ruins with those of many an abbey attest the civilization of Desmond under this great lord.

'IRISH EXACTIONS'

The compilation of elaborate rentals had already begun among the great Anglo-Irish families; but for the whole summary of Desmond rights and revenues we must go to the inquisitions of 1583 when half the earldom with a million Irish acres was confiscated to the Crown.[4] Many of the Irish exactions for which his

[1] Harris, *Coll.*, IV, p. 217. 'Slanyaght' is Irish *slanuigheacht*, and equates with Anglo-saxon *mund*, i.e. personal protection and guarantee. (See also Gibbs, *Cokayne's Complete Peerage*, under 'Desmond'.)

[2] *Carew Miscell.*, p. 362: inspeximus of Cogan grant at Cork by the Official-general of court of spiritual causes of diocese of Limerick (June 1421). Caulfield (*Cork Arch. Soc.*, 1867–8), asserts that in 1438 Desmond got Carrigaline from Myles the Great Cogan, who died without male heir, leaving, however, one or two nephews. The grant of 1445 already referred to (p. 302) enabled Earl James to acquire such lands and rents in Desmond as by original tenure were held of the Crown.

[3] This noble country of the Déisí (now the baronies of Decies within and without Drum) Earl James granted to his younger son Gerald, who founded a long line of Fitzgeralds of the Decies.

[4] See first edition of this work, pp. 351–3. 'Rental of Connello' (given in Begley's *Diocese of Limerick*, pp. 323–33) drawn up about 1452, was compiled for this Earl and covers his lands in Limerick. Since the above was written the Desmond Inquisitions preserved in the Public Record Office, Dublin, have perished in the ruin of the Four Courts in 1922. The earliest example of a family rental of this kind is *The Red Book of Ormond*, drawn up in the fourteenth century; it has now been published, edited by Newport B. White (*Irish Manuscripts Commission*, 1932).

son Earl Thomas later suffered death were obviously imposed by James. The Elizabethan inquisitions record that the late Earl had on his Irish, and sometimes on his English tenants, 'shragh, marte, sowth, repaste, gillycon, kernety, sorrowen, koonebeg, coyne and livery'.

All this later aspect was due to this usurping James, the first of the 'Old English' to combine a power derived from feudal grants, Brehon custom, and acquisition of Crown rights, and to rule a whole province as a palatine earl, to reign over an Irish population like a Gaelic king, and in Dublin to take his place among the peers of the State.[1] The original 'kingdom of Cork' had in fact become his.

Fostered among the Irish, Earl James favoured the native race and the native order. To his foster-brother Brian, son of Conor O'Brien, he made over the wardenship of Carrigogunnell, and enfeoffed him in an area of county Limerick afterwards called 'Pobal Bhriain', now the barony of Pubblebrien, with Carrigogunnell as its capital.[2]

About 1420 Earl James brought in MacSheehy to be his captain of gallowglasses; and his household poet or 'dán-maker' was an O'Daly, of a famous hereditary bardic family. Married to a daughter of Clanrickard, a stock already more than half Gaelic, he had the Burke alliance as well as the O'Briens. On the other hand, no open accusation, after his usurpation, could be made by the Government against James, for in person or proxy he attended parliament, preserved Munster for the Englishry, and went no further in his nationalism than to support Ormond and the Home Rule Party.

THE GERALDINES AND FLORENCE

The fame of the Geraldines now circulated in the Italian cities, and especially in Florence, from which according to tradition, Otho of Windsor, the first of the race, had come. In 1413 an Irish bishop and a priest, Maurice Fitzgerald of Ardfert diocese,

[1] *Carew Miscell.*, p. 394. Holinshed's *Chronicle* says: 'James Earl of Desmond being suffered and not controlled, during the government of Richard Duke of York his godsib and of Thomas Earl of Kildare his kinsman, did put upon the King's subjects within the counties of Cork, Kerry, Limerick and Waterford the Irish impositions of quinio (coign) and liverie, cartings, carriages, lodgings, cosherings, bonnaght and such like; which customs are the very breeders, maintainers and upholders of all Irish enormities.'

[2] *Ann. MacFirbis sub* 1450; *A.F.M.* (1502): 'death of Donnchad O'Brien, lord of the country from Adare to Limerick, and from Baile Nua to Mainistir-an-enaigh, also lord of Aherlow.' The former district represents 'Pobal Bhriain' or the lordship of Carrigogunnell, and Donnchad was grandson of Conor O'Brien, the Earl's foster-father.

had visited the Gherardini of Florence, reminding them of a distant kinship. And now Earl James, lord of the noblest harbours of Munster, was all the more worth courting. In 1440 Leonardo Bruni, Secretary of State to the Signory of Florence, wrote to the Earl in the name of the Republic: 'If it is true that your progenitors were of Florentine stock and of the right noble and ancient stock of the Gherardini, one of the greatest families in our State, we have ample reason to congratulate ourselves not only that our people have acquired possessions in Apulia, Greece, and Hungary, but also that our Florentines, through you, bear sway even in Hibernia, the most remote island in the world. We therefore send to you Giovanni Betti di Gherardini, a noble youth, who his father wished should become better acquainted with you and his kinsmen of your stock.'[1] We hear no more of Giovanni, but the connexion with Florence became for the Fitzgeralds a family legend refreshed from time to time by letters of Desmond or Kildare to the Signory, while Florentine traders gladly availed themselves of the trade with Munster, where Desmond was real king.

TALBOT AGAIN VICEROY

In 1446 Talbot, now Earl of Shrewsbury, was appointed Lieutenant again, and in 1447 was created Earl of Waterford and Baron with regalian rights over the whole coast from Youghal to Waterford city, this being ancient Crown demesne. But the 'Old English' saw to it that this 'new Englishman' got little profit therefrom. Against the 'degenerate English' Talbot had fought for thirty years, and at a parliament under him at Trim in January 1447 it was enacted that all who would be taken for English must abandon the Irish *crombeul* or moustache, and shave both lips, 'for there is no diversity of habit between English marchers and Irish enemies'.

Shrewsbury retired in 1447 and saw Ireland no more. A gallant soldier, Talbot could scatter Irish armies and bring rebels to heel, but he had not the constructive genius which his office needed. Nevertheless he is interesting as the last of the old viceroys up to Henry VIII's time, who strove by warring down the great lords, English and Irish, to keep England's colony in Ireland true to the English tradition.

[1] For Italian trade with Ireland in these centuries see Westropp, 'Early Italian Maps of Ireland', *P.R.I.A* (1913). For the Florentine letters see Gilbert's *Viceroys*, pp. 334–6, and Bryan, *Great Earl of Kildare*, pp. 268–74.

RICHARD, DUKE OF YORK

No great man in Ireland, native or English-born, could compete with the next Lieutenant of the King. Richard, Duke of York, was in 1447 a man of some thirty-seven years of age. As heir to his uncle Mortimer, he was Earl of March and Ulster and Lord of Trim and Connacht. The native Irish saw in him the true heir of Lacy and De Burgo, and a descendant of Brian the Great. As for the 'English of Ireland', here was one before whom all could bow, that Prince of the King's Blood whom they had often asked for, indeed one who a large part of England thought had a better right to the throne than the feeble Henry himself. Richard, appointed King's lieutenant in December 1447 for a term of ten years, did not actually arrive till July 1449. When he came into what the Lancastrians hoped was an honourable exile for the most dangerous man in England, he saw in Ireland a fine jumping-off ground for his party. Hence the facile charm with which he won Irish hearts to the White Rose of York; hence the indifference with which he abandoned Ireland to its Home Rule earls.

CHAPTER XV

ARISTOCRATIC HOME RULE, 1449–1477

ENGLAND was by now heading towards the Wars of the Roses, and as Ireland for the greater part embraced the cause of the 'White Rose of York', a survey of events in the greater country is necessary here.

Richard of York was the man who enlisted the Anglo-Irish in this struggle. Born in 1411, there came to be centred in this boy from several sides the duchy of York and the earldoms of Cambridge and Rutland, and finally of March. The last came to him at the age of fourteen when his maternal uncle Edmund Mortimer died without children. Along with the Mortimer estates in England and Wales there came to the young Richard the earldom of Ulster and the lordships of Trim, Leix, and Connacht, which made him Ireland's greatest absentee proprietor.

He was thus a landlord on a vast scale (but England was full of such and their divisions were leading up to a desperate civil war), but it was his claim to the throne which made Richard especially important in all eyes. As heir to Lionel of Clarence, he was, if descent through females was allowed, a more rightful heir to the Crown than the feeble Henry himself. The young Prince, however, for a long time caused no anxiety, attached himself in his young manhood to Humfrey Duke of Gloucester, and served gallantly in France.

The loss of the French conquests from 1435 onwards split the English government into two parties, that of Gloucester leading a war-faction determined not to make peace with France, and that of Edmund Beaufort, Duke of Somerset, and William de la Pole, Earl of Suffolk, which favoured making terms while there was time. In 1444 Suffolk procured a French wife, Margaret of Anjou, for Henry VI, ceding Maine and Anjou in return. The war-party could not forgive this, especially as Margaret proved a strong-minded woman who completely ruled the simple king, and identified herself with the Beaufort party. Finally, in February 1447, Gloucester, their chief enemy, was done away with mysteriously at Bury. But, as Humfrey had been next heir to the childless king his nephew, and left no children himself, York became the next in succession if the royal marriage were unfruitful, and the leader of the anti-Suffolk party. As a fine soldier, a handsome and attractive man, the brother-in-law of Richard

Neville, Earl of Salisbury, and having other noble connexions, Richard was a far more dangerous man than Gloucester. The Cabinet, therefore, decided to get him out of the way by sending him in virtual exile to Ireland, of which he was appointed Lieutenant on December 9th 1447 for a term of ten years. The pretext was that Ireland was in rebellion, and that a vigorous governor, especially one with such Irish connexions as York had, was needed. But Richard was a skilful politician; he resolved to use these Irish connexions so as to win Ireland over to his side in what threatened to be an inevitable struggle in England.[1]

Not till two years later, however, did York leave 'the disordered commonwealth of England' for the Irish Lordship, and Ireland meanwhile remained in the hands of her native nobility.

THE THREE EARLS

Ormond, Desmond, and Kildare were successively to have a supremacy over the Anglo-Irish which lasted for a century. In the house of Kildare this became hereditary for three generations. But at present the Leinster branch of the famous Geraldines was out of the running, and indeed in danger of extinction.

Gerald, son of Maurice, was 5th Earl from 1390 to 1432.[2] His daughter Joan, wife of James, 4th Earl of Ormond, was his heir-at-law, and Ormond in her right claimed handsome Geraldine estates. Gerald's brother John may be reckoned 6th Earl, but was already old and was apparently dead by 1434. His son John, called 'Cam' ('crooked' or 'crippled'), was not recognized as Earl by the Crown and the succession remained in doubt until 1456, whe Thomas, son of John 'Cam', was recognized as 7th Earl.

James, 6th Earl of Desmond, ruled his vast earldom till 1462, little concerned with Dublin affairs, but his son and heir Thomas was already a prominent and splendid nobleman.

As for Ormond, the 'White Earl' survived till old age in 1452. His eldest son James began an English connexion which proved fatal to the main branch by marrying Eleanor, sister of Edmund Beaufort, Duke of Somerset. He was in 1449 created Earl of

[1] See my paper, 'The Viceroyalty of Richard, Duke of York', *R.S.A.I*, (December 1932), which contains some unpublished material.

[2] For the obscure question of the Kildare succession see Vicary Gibbs, *Cokayne's Complete Peerage*, under 'Kildare'. My *Cal. Ormond Deeds*, III, pp. 65, 72, 83, 86, 120, 383, throws some new light on the problem. James, 4th Earl of Ormond, had no children by Joan Fitzgerald, who was his first wife, but the Butlers continued to claim border manors such as Rathmore and Maynooth, which was part of the later Geraldine-Butler feud in Kildare.

Wiltshire, and threw in his lot with the Lancastrian party. Meanwhile at home a branch of the Butlers, of Polestown (or Paulstown) in county Kilkenny, was vigorously expanding under Edmund 'MacRichard', son of Richard, a younger son of the 3rd Earl; a typical race of 'Irish' cousins who, beginning with Richard, married Irish wives in defiance of the Statutes of Kilkenny and patronized Irish culture. A younger brother of Richard of Polestown, James 'Gallda', base in blood, had also founded the Butlers of Caher. Thus did the branchings (in Irish *craobh-scaoileadh*) of the established Normans cover the land.

GAELIC AND NORMAN 'LORDS OF COUNTRIES'

Having fought the race-war to a standstill, reared in mutual toleration by marriage, fosterage, and the use of Irish speech, the 'Old English' and Gaelic lords were now united in a common ambition to dominate each his own country. The recovery of the Gaelic chiefs was especially marked. By their indentures with King Richard and with Lancastrian viceroys, most of them had accepted the position of vassals of the State and secured, as they thought, not only their ancestral demesnes but even the lands recovered from the colonists. While they admitted the pre-eminence of Butlers, Burkes, and Geraldines, they had attained full equality with the lesser baronage of the Englishry.

In the case of the MacMurroughs, Donnchad, son of Art Oge, had been in 1428 confirmed in the eighty marks yearly paid to his father, and in 1440 was, in consideration of reforming himself and other Irish of Leinster, taken into grace by the Lieutenant, Lord Welles.[1] He was succeeded by his nephew Donal Reagh ('Riabhach', 'the swarthy') son of Gerald, who reigned till 1476. About 1460, Saiv, daughter of this Donal Reagh, married Sir James Butler, son of Edmund MacRichard Butler, an event which made allies of the two families. The revived MacMurrough power reached its height under Donal Reagh, who dwelt at Enniscorthy castle, once the seat of the Prendergasts. His style was royal, 'MacMurchada rex Lagenie', and as late as 1522 his son Gerald Kavanagh called himself 'king of Leinster and leader of the Leinstermen'.[2]

This great Donal Reagh founded a Franciscan house at Enniscorthy, and in 1475 granted to the Cistercian abbey of Duiske eightpence per annum from each plowland tilled of all his lands,

[1] *Rot. Canc. Hib.*, pp. 246, 261b. Donatus is called 'sue nacionis capitaneus'; is paid a fee of forty marks.

[2] Dowling's *Annals*, *sub* 1522; Hogan, *Description of Ireland* (a MS. of Elizabeth's reign), p. 54.

binding to continue the same his heirs descending in the lordship in male descent.[1]

The history of this famous abbey testifies how the Irish resurgence had covered the land. Dedicated to St. Saviour, it was founded in 1204 by the elder William Marshal and retained till the close of the fourteenth century that English character which an early grant or, Adam fitz Sinnott, a Fleming, meant it to have when in 1204 he made certain lands over to it on condition that he and his heirs might for ever appoint a monk to the abbey who should be English (*de lingua Anglica*). Then, in the fifteenth century the abbey and its daughters go over to the Irish tongue. In 1424 Henry O'Ryan, lord of Idrone, confirms to the daughter house at Killenny a grant of lands made by his ancestor Dermot, lord of Idrone, about 1164, and confirmed by Dermot, king of Leinster at the time. In 1417, John Dound, abbot of Duiske, had been Art Oge's deputy in his act of submission to King Henry. Now, in 1475, Dermot MacMurrough's descendant, Donal Reagh, signing himself 'Dominus totius Lagenie', makes this grant to Duiske, which he seals as 'king of Leinster', and of the nine witnesses named, of whom two are his sons Cathal and Gerald, all are Irish.

O'NEILL OF TYRONE

In 1432 Donal, son of Henry Aimhreidh, having been slain by O'Cahan, Eoghan his nephew, son of Niall Oge, succeeded. 'He went to Tullahoge and was crowned on the flagstone of the kings by the will of God and men, bishops and ollavs'. Eoghan had submitted to Ormond in 1425 but showed little regard for the treaty then made, and more than once triumphantly raided the Pale. His reign from 1432 to 1455 was that of a vigorous warrior and conqueror, of great moment in the history of the Cinel Eoghain. Like many of the Gaelic and Norman lords of the time he was 'a great ancestor', and his sons Aedh, Art, and Felim founded sub-states under him. The greatest conquest was the Fews, an extensive mountain country in south Armagh, which for long was the gateway of the north. Its Anglo-Irish proprietor, Pellew or Pedelewe, had to retreat before this invasion into Louth, and Aedh founded the line of 'O'Neill of the Fews', or 'Sliocht Aedha' ('Race of Aedh'), which lasted till Cromwell's time.

The O'Neills had for a century striven hard to establish direct lineal succession in one stock. Eoghan also associated his son

[1] 'Charters of Duiske' (or Graigenamanagh), ed. Dr. Bernard and Lady Constance Butler, *P.R.I.A.* (1918), pp. 5, 139, 149. Donal's handsome seal is reproduced by me in *R.S.A.I.* (1937), pp. 75–6; the inscription runs: SIGILLUM DONALL MEICMURRACHADA REGIS LAGENIE.

Henry with him in the kingship, and as a result the line of Brian 'of Down' ruled practically without a breach from 1344 to 1493. Hence the various agreements and submissions made with English kings, viceroys, archbishops of Armagh, and earls of Ulster: they were an imposing demonstration of support for the hereditary line as against rivals of 'Sliocht Airt', 'Sliocht Felim', and other such kinsmen.[1]

The constable of Eoghan's armed forces was Turloch MacDonnell, head of a now hereditary race of gallowglasses in Tyrone. Ulster was an armed camp, and the petty wars of the Gaelic chiefs, among whom MacQuillan counted, were constant and universal, as the annals reveal. The great external rival of O'Neill was O'Donnell, lord of Tyrconnell, and overlord of Fermanagh and Sligo. Niall Garbh of this race succeeded his father Turloch 'an Fina' ('of the Wine', who ruled from 1392 to 1423), but in 1434 in raiding Meath he was captured by the Lieutenant, Stanley, and spent the rest of his life captive. His brother Nechtan took his place, and had to face O'Neill's ancestral claim to the overlordship of Inishowen and the Strabane country. In 1439 Eoghan and Henry defeated Nechtan, who came to them at Castlefinn in 1442, 'and made peace with O'Neill and surrendered to him the castle and all Cinel Moen and the tribute of Inis Eoghain'.

Having made a treaty of submission to the young Richard of York in 1425, Eoghan, as we shall see later, renewed it through his son Henry with the same Duke in 1449.

In July 1455 Henry took the place of his father and was made king at Tullahoge by O'Cahan, Maguire, MacMahon, all the O'Neill clans, and the 'successor of Patrick', viz. John Mey, archbishop of Armagh. This inauguration was followed by confirmation at the hands of the Archbishop at Armagh on August 4th 1455. It is recorded thus in the archbishop's register:

> 'Eugenius O'Neill, captain of his nation, having lately resigned because of the failure of his bodily powers, and Henry his first-born having been elected captain and principal of his nation—the latter came before our lord the Primate in his hall in the monastery of SS. Peter and Paul, saying and seeking that his election should be confirmed and instituted by the Lord Primate as his temporal lord. The said Primate, believing him to be a good man and likely to be of good to the Church and people of Ulster, held, approved, and confirmed him as O'Neill and

[1] For the O'Neills and their pedigree see Prof. Hogan's masterly paper, 'The Irish Law of Kingship', in *P.R.I.A.* (1932); also my paper, 'The Bonnacht of Ulster', in *Hermathena* (1931).

captain and principal of his nation before all then present, cleric and lay, in great multitude.'[1]

Such a blending of ancient Irish law and Christian benediction had not been done with an O'Neill for centuries, and it was part of the great attempt to establish primogeniture among the O'Neills, and to fix a succession stricter than elective chieftainships and the practice of Tanistry. Henry had already in 1449, in his father's name, renewed with Richard, Duke of York and viceroy the treaty of 1425. He ruled the Cinel Eoghain from 1455 to 1489 and achieved great importance and glory. In 1463 King Edward sent him, as greatest of the Ulster Irish who owed traditional allegiance to the Earl of Ulster, a present of scarlet cloth and a collar of gold of the King's livery. Finally, in 1480 the marriage of his son Conn to Eleanor, daughter of the 7th Earl of Kildare, united in honourable alliance the two greatest names, Norman and Gaelic, in Ireland.

O'DONNELLS AND IRISH 'SWORDSMEN'

The pedigree of the chiefs of Tyrconnell at this time shows us that Turloch 'of the Wine' had six sons, of whom Niall Garbh again had seven, and Niall's brother Nechtan had six. What was there for these numerous *rigdomnas* to do, being of noble blood, but to be 'swordsmen' or 'idlemen' as the Tudor English called such fighting gentlemen? They took no part in foreign wars and seldom or never left their native country. All that was left, if such a one could not be 'king' or 'Tanist' in his time, was to seek some new lordship or rather overlordship such as MacMurroughs and O'Neills were then making at the expense of Gael and Gall. But most of them perished prematurely in the feuds, the fightings, and the forays which they considered their *raison d'être*, the seniors of their own stock being delighted to diminish the numbers of dangerous rivals by fair means or foul. Still, the number of fighting aristocrats was so great that it took the Tudor sovereigns a whole century before the swordsmen and their world were brought to an end.

Nechtan O'Donnell was slain in 1452 by his nephews Donal and Aedh Rua, sons of Niall Garbh, who, as Connalian patriots, resented his subjection to Tyrone. Eoghan O'Neill then intervened and put in Rory son of Nechtan, keeping as before Cinel Moen, Castlefinn, and the tributes of Inishowen. But Rory was soon dispatched by Donal, and he again by Henry O'Neill. After

[1] Mey's *Register* (copy in T.C.D.), pp. 400, 402.

several years of turmoil, at last Aedh Rua in 1461 overthrew O'Neill's candidate Turloch Cairbre, whom he maimed so as to incapacitate for kingship, and himself began a long rule which lasted till 1505 and to the great age of seventy-eight. For over a century the O'Donnells, like the O'Neills, successfully asserted direct lineal succession in the kingship.

Like Henry O'Neill, Aedh Rua marked a new type of Irish chief, establishing the succession in his son, communicating freely with the earls of the south, visiting the Scottish royal court and, while still calling himself 'king of Tyrconnell', proving himself that modern type of 'Irish lord' with whom the Tudors had to deal, a type quite as warlike as their ancestors and far better equipped for war, but more subtle and tenacious, and boldly claiming their place in the Ireland of their day.

THE WEST

In 1464 died Taig O'Connor, son of Turloch, 'half-king of Connacht', after whom there was no king of Connacht, only O'Connor Don and O'Connor Roe. The Clanrickard Burke was now the true king of the west, and had become a kind of hereditary seneschal for the King and the heirs of Mortimer in Connacht. At Magh-cronn in 1467, a grand intertribal battle, in which eight-score gallowglasses fell, Ulick Ruadh, the 'Upper MacWilliam', affirmed his supremacy over Richard, the 'Lower MacWilliam', with whom he was often at war, O'Connor Don being his ally, and O'Connor Roe ally of the Mayo Burke. His wife was Slaine, daughter of Conor O'Brien, and he 'rested in a good old age' in 1485.

RICHARD OF YORK, VICEROY, 1447–1460

Richard, Duke of York and King's lieutenant, finally landed at Howth on July 6th 1449, 'with great pomp and glory', accompanied by his beauteous wife Cecily Neville, 'the Rose of Raby', and a considerable army. He was received, say the annals of the Four Masters, 'with great honour, and the earls of Ireland went into his house, as did also the Irish adjacent to Meath, and gave him as many beeves for the use of his kitchen as it pleased him to demand'.

Richard began by calling out the 'royal service' of the colony to reinforce his own troops and set forth by Trim into his earldom of Ulster. Before August 15th Magennis, MacMahon, O'Reilly, MacQuillan came in to him with three thousand troops between them. Turning south again, he invaded Wicklow and there Brian

O'Byrne submitted at Symondeswood (now Kiltimon), swore allegiance, promised tribute, and undertook to let the law run in his country, to wear English apparel, and to learn English himself and his children. It was one of those naïve formal treaties, an early specimen, which became common in Tudor times, which the submitting chiefs either did not mean or were unable to keep. The fact is that modern Wicklow was practically all O'Byrne or O'Toole country, the colonists gone out of it, and the whole coast void of English settlers and English ships.

The submissions that followed were on a scale seldom witnessed since the English came to Ireland. The midland and other south Ulster chiefs made gifts of kine amounting to 3,620. A long roll of lords, from Meath, Munster, Ulster, both Norman and Gaelic, came in before Michaelmas, and it became the thing to march in imposingly with troops and visit this gallant deputy of the King, who the Irish thought was himself every inch a king. Naïvely says a contemporary document: 'All these beth (be) kynges, dukes, erlys, and barones that beth come in to my lord of Yorke byfore Mighlemes A.D. 1449 *anno regni Henrici sexti xxviii* and beth sworn trew legemen to ye Kyng of England and his heyrs male and to my lord of York and to his heyrs male and leid hostages and beth ibound by endenture and with the myght of Jesus or twelmonth come to an end ye wildest Yrishman in Yrland shall be swore English.'[1]

But the most impressive treaty of all was made with Richard's greatest Irish vassal in Ulster. Archbishop Mey of Armagh (though by now the primates of all Ireland resided at Termonfeckin in Louth *inter anglicos* and received little rent and exercised little authority in the parts of their archdiocese which were *inter hibernicos*) brought O'Neill into submission to himself and the hereditary Earl of Ulster. On August 27th 1449, at Drogheda, Henry O'Neill, eldest son of Eoghan, acting for his aged father, made by indenture terms with the Duke similar to those of 1425.

O'Neill declared himself, his father, brothers, etc. to be the men of the Duke as Earl of Ulster and pledged himself and them to restore to him all such manors, castles, and lordships of his as were formerly possessed by Walter and Richard, Earls of Ulster, and which Eoghan, Henry, their sons, etc. have occupied. Also to surrender the ancient 'bonnacht' or military service due from the Irish chiefs of Ulster to the De Burgo earls. If the Duke or his heirs or their deputies shall be at war with any Englishman or

[1] See my paper, 'Viceroyalty of Richard, Duke of York', in *P.R.I.A.* (1932), in which I give unpublished documents as to Richard's stay in Ireland from Titus B.xi, vol. I (*Cotton MSS., Brit. Mus.*).

Irishman in his country of Ulster, Henry and his heirs will support them with a force of five hundred horsemen well armed and five hundred foot with lances, axes, and bows. He and they will surrender all lands usurped from the Englishry, especially the Fews, the heritage of Sir John Pedelewe junior. Also they will render all temporalities, rents, and tithes due to the Archbishop and other bishops and ecclesiastics. Finally, Henry undertakes for the homage and fealty of himself, his father, sons, and brothers to pay six hundred fat beeves to the Duke.[1]

Probably little of this treaty was carried out. The Duke no doubt got his fat beeves, which were plentiful enough in Ireland, and the Archbishop for a time recovered authority and rents in his northern diocese. Henry gave some military service to the Duke, for later in a parliament of 1481 his 'loyal service' was publicly recognized. But there is no evidence that Pedelewes or any other English tenants entered again into occupation of lands which the Irish had recovered or that the 'Bonnacht of Ulster' was exercised in future by the Earl or his deputies. O'Neill had assumed the military vassalage of the Ulster chiefs, and with him it remained in so far as he could enforce it.

What the treaty did was to bind O'Neill once more to an *entente* with English authority which was profitable to him against his rivals, and which indeed put the chiefs of Tyrone for a whole century on the Government side.

But most of the treaties and complimentary visits of Irish chiefs gave Richard little comfort; secretly, for he was a good Englishman at heart, he must have longed to lead an English-Irish army against these flighty vassals. But among the Anglo-Irish his cause was taken more seriously, and when in October 1449 a son George, afterwards Duke of Clarence, was born to his wife and himself there was great enthusiasm; the Earls of Ormond and Desmond stood sponsors at the font; and ever afterwards Clarence and in time his unfortunate son, Edward of Warwick, were regarded in Ireland as 'one of ourselves'.

The Duke opened his first parliament in Dublin on October 18th 1449. It was filled with complaints of coign and 'cuddies' and other grievances suffered by 'the poor husbandmen and tenants of Ireland', and the quarterings made upon them by the 'captains of the Marches'.

About the same time the English of the city and county of Cork addressed a memorial to York's young son, Edmund, Earl of Rutland, who bore the title of Earl of Cork, and to the viceroy and lords of the Council in Dublin, to the effect that ruin was

[1] See my paper on 'The Bonnacht of Ulster' in *Hermathena* (1932).

impending in Munster on account of the dissensions of the English lords, the Carews, Barnewalls, De Courcys, Arundels, etc.[1] These had fallen 'at variance amongst themselves; the weakest took Irishmen to their aid and so vanquished the enemies; but at last the Irish were stronger than they and drove them all away and have now the whole country, but that the Lords Roche, Barry, and Courcy do remain with the best part of their ancestors' possessions'. Wherefore the townsmen of Cork, Kinsale, and Youghal prayed that after parliament the Duke and Council would come to Cork and bind the English lords on pain of loss of land, life, and goods not to make war upon each other; that two good justices should be sent to set the general lawlessness in order, as also 'some captain with twenty Englishmen, that may be captains over us all; and we will rise with him when need is to redress these enormities all at our cost, and if you do not we are all cast away, and then farewell Munster for ever'. The petition, however, was in vain.

In Richard's next parliament, held in April 1450 at Drogheda, the commons elected a Speaker, John Chever, 'to show and declare in the said parliament for them all manner of business which they have to declare, and to answer for them in matters moved or to be moved. But if it happen that the said Speaker show or say anything to the displeasure of the most high and puissant Prince, Richard, or of the prelates, lords, and peers from ignorance or otherwise, without assent or by assent of the said Commons, let it be not recorded or reported.'

But in spite of this loyal note, Richard's heart was not in Ireland, where he neither had the money or force wherewith to recover the 'English land', nor could he get the rents due from his English estates. He spent the winter in Trim, in the castle of his Lacy ancestors, and his arms are still to be seen, those of Mortimer and York, above the doorway of the old church in that town.

But in September 1450 he departed for England, where events were moving fast in the direction of war. In the spring Suffolk had been impeached, banished by the King, and murdered by a mob as he sought to escape from the country. Next, in June, 'Jack Cade' as he was called, but whose real name seems to have been John Mortimer and thus a kinsman of York, raised a fruitless rebellion in favour of the Duke's party.

As Deputy, York left behind him Sir James Ormond, son and heir of James, the 4th Earl. A number of short-period deputies

[1] Gilbert's *Viceroys*, pp. 356–7. This undated petition may have been as late as 1460 when the young Edmund, Earl of Rutland and Cork (born in 1443), was nominally Chancellor of Ireland under his father, the Duke. But it may have been addressed earlier to him as Earl of Cork.

filled the office of viceroy until Richard himself received a fresh commission as Lieutenant in December 1454.

BUTLERS AND GERALDINES

The 'White Earl of Ormond' ended his long life in August 1452 at Ardee, still in harness against his Irish enemies, 'the best captain of the English nation that ever was in Ireland', say the MacFirbis annals. He was the last of his great line to serve Ireland, for his son James, 5th Earl, was destined to perish in the Wars of the Roses and his brothers to become absentees. The supremacy among the Anglo-Irish after 1452 passed to an Earl of Desmond, and, after him, to the house of Kildare.

The White Earl's brother, Richard of Polestown, illustrates how the cadets of the Conquest families became Irish. No senior Butler had ever yet married Irish, but this Richard wedded an O'Reilly, and their son Edmund MacRichard also married an Irishwoman, Catherine O'Carroll. Edmund's son James, after a love-affair with Saiv Kavanagh, daughter of Donal Reagh MacMurrough, finally married her, and had by her two sons, Esmond and Theobald, 'born in affiance of the two before espousals' and a third 'born after espousals', who was therefore held legitimate, called Peter or Piers the Red ('Ruadh' or 'Roe'). Piers was destined after a long and active life to end up as Earl of Ormond and Ossory and begin a new line of Ormond earls.[1]

The disputes of Butler, Kildare, and Desmond over borderlands in Leinster and in Munster were aggravated by the numbers of their cadets, inordinately proud of their name, much in need of fiefs, and able to call on Gaelic allies. The fatal feud of Ormond and Kildare, which went on nigh a hundred years and ended in the ruin of the latter race, had already begun.

A memorial from county Kildare to 'the mighty prince and right gracious lord Richard, duke of York' in June 1454 stated that 'the land of Ireland was never at the point finally to be destroyed since the conquest of this land as it is now', and complained of the 'misrule and governance of divers gentlemen of the county and liberty of Meath and the counties of Kildare and Uriel', and of 'a variance betwixt therle of Wiltshire, Lieutenant of this lande, and Thomas FitzMorice of the Geraldynes for the titles of the maners of Maynooth and Rathmore in county Kildare which hath cased more destruction in the said county of Kildare

[1] For this eventful and interesting marriage in defiance of the Statutes of Kilkenny see the documents in *Cal. Ormond Deeds*, III (under 'Butler, Sabina', in the index).

and Liberty of Meath than was done by Irish enemies and English rebels of longe tyme befor.'

The memorial ends dramatically: 'the destruction of Kildare will be the destruction of Dublin, and the destruction of Dublin will be the destruction of Ireland'.

A hundred years later, the fruits of all this were still visible. The gentry and freeholders of county Tipperary wrote to Henry VIII in 1542:

> 'This country was well governed till the White Earl going to England left his kinsmen to govern, who then fell out and became murderers and manslayers of one another. After that Earl's death, his sons being in high favour in England neglected their inheritance, and so the quarrels revived by marriages and confederacies with the Irish, maintained by the Earl of Desmond, which brought the land to destruction till about 28 years ago [1515], after decease of Thomas Earl of Ormond who abode all his life in England. Sir Piers then recovered much of his power and Sir James was brought to obedience but Sir Esmond Botiller continued by usurped power to charge complainants with coyne, livery, coddies, coysers, hounds, hounts, stokekepers, masons, etc., and so does Sir Thomas, son of Esmond, namely coddies at Christmas and Easter, or certain sums in lieu, kepers of hounds and stoods, coyne and livery for horsemen, horses and horsekepers, also exactions for wine at Christmas, maintaining garrisons and castles, with aid towards marriage of every one of his daughters, a sheep of every flock, and a cow of every sixty kine; also he levieth on every colp or carrue of land in the cantred of Clonmel a bushel of oats called summer oats, also a retinue of kernetye perpetually on the same cantred, which retinue was never granted to the Earls of Ormond except for ministrations of justice and executing of Seneschals' processes.'[1]

While York was absent in England, an attempt was made to unseat him here, and in May 1453 James Earl of Ormond and Wiltshire got a grant of the Lieutenantship from the Somerset government in England. This new Earl stood for the Lancastrian side in Ireland; though it was in a minority, his house and the towns and country it controlled stood firm for the Red Rose right up to the Tudor age.

[1] For these two documents see Gilbert, *Facs. of Nat. MSS.*, III, plates xli and lxxv; Ellis, *Original Letters illustrative of English History* (2nd series), vol. I; and *Cal. Ormond Deeds*, IV, pp. 209–15. Sir Esmond mentioned in the text was of the Caher branch of Butlers.

Meanwhile on October 10th 1453 Queen Margaret bore a son, Edward, and this unexpected event knocked Richard of York out of the succession. He kept the peace, however, and was twice made Protector of England in 1454 and 1455 during the imbecility of King Henry. But on May 22nd 1455 took place the first battle of the Wars of the Roses at St. Albans, in which Edmund, Duke of Somerset, was slain.

Again York in 1454 was renewed as Lieutenant of Ireland for a term of years, but in 1455 he made Thomas, Earl of Kildare, his deputy, who directed the Irish government for four years and a half and held four parliaments in his name, for by now this assembly met once every year. But outside Dublin local independence and local anarchy prevailed, and the petty Parliament and the Anglo-Irish aristocracy could or would do nothing effective to restore the royal power and save the Pale from destruction. They were lords in their own counties, and as for Parliament, they dominated it in order that it should serve their interests and secure them the offices of state.

In England there was a sham 'Love-day' staged in London when Parliament met on Lady Day in 1458, and the Duke of York and the Queen walked in procession hand-in-hand. But the lords who were there 'never came together again after that time to Parliament or Council unless it were in field, with spear and shield'.

Finally the gage of battle was thrown down. But fortune favoured the Crown, and at the 'Rout of Ludlow' (October 12th 1459) the Yorkist forces were scattered. York made for Ireland; his son Edward, Earl of March, and his nephew, Richard of Warwick, made for Calais. These were at once the two refuges and jumping-off places reserved by the Yorkists for their cause in England. Especially did the Duke see in Ireland a safe stronghold, and in order to keep it he was ready to conciliate Irish ideas.

The English parliament, at Coventry in November, attainted him, Salisbury, Warwick, his sons, and their chief adherents, so that legally all his offices, including that of Lord Lieutenant of Ireland, ceased. But this was nothing to the Irish magnates and the Home Rule Party. They now had a 'king of their own' and meant to make use of him. When Richard landed in Ireland on a November day in 1459, he was welcomed 'like a Messiah', and the enthusiasm of Dublin can only be imagined. He summoned Parliament to Drogheda on February 7th 1460, and it gave almost sovereign power to this superseded viceroy. They ratified his appointment as Lieutenant for the term indicated in the letters patent of March 1457, and gave his person as much honour and safeguard as if he were King himself, for to him as the royal deputy 'such reverence, obedience, and fear ought to be given as to our sovereign Lord, whose estate is thereby honoured, feared, and obeyed'. To plot against the Lieutenant was therefore as if to plot against the King. 'If any person imagine, compass, excite or provoke his destruction or death or to that intent confederate or assent with Irish enemies he shall be and stand attainted of high treason.'[1]

The 'English nation in Ireland' now proceeded to assert its legislative independence in these words: 'The land of Ireland is and at all times has been corporate of itself by the ancient laws and customs used in the same, freed of the burden of any special law of the realm of England, save only such laws as by the lords spiritual and temporal and the commons of the said land shall have been in Great Council or Parliament there held admitted, accepted, affirmed, and proclaimed.'

Ireland had also her own Great Seal 'of ancient custom, privilege, and franchise', wherefore it was enacted that no person or persons in Ireland were to be 'by any command given or made under any other seal than the said Seal of the same land compelled to answer to any appeal or any other matter out of the said land'.

It was further enacted that appeals of treason were to be determined before the Constable and Marshal of Ireland in Ireland. Thus not only were writs under the Greal Seal of England excluded, but the practice of having Irish subjects called into England to answer appeals of treason, often done 'of great malice', was to be stopped as derogatory of Irish liberty. For 'it has not been seen or heard that any person or persons inhabiting or resident in any other Christian land so corporate of itself ought to obey any mandate within the said land given or made under any other than the proper Seal of the same'.

Thus did Ireland assert a complete separateness from England except for the personal link of the Crown.[2] Richard accepted these declarations, for, whatever misgivings he may have had as an Englishman and as a possible English King, they certainly suited his purpose for the moment. He had enlisted on his side

[1] Berry, *Statutes*, II, pp. 639–801. The language is Anglo-French.

[2] Irish nationalism in the modern sense cannot be looked for in the acts or words of this Parliament; as compare the following: 'inasmuch as the Duchy of Normandy and the Duchy of Guienne, when they were under the obedience of the said realm of England, were nevertheless separated from the laws and statutes of the same and had also coins distinct from the coin of the said realm of England, so the land of Ireland, though it be under the obedience of the said realm, is nevertheless separate from all laws and statutes thereof, etc.' (Berry, *Statutes*, pp. 663–5.)

the Irish magnates and made Ireland a stronghold for the Yorkist faction.

Of the sixty-three other measures of the parliament of Drogheda, several are noteworthy. One enjoins that each subject having twenty pounds yearly shall keep in his house 'one archer mounted and arrayed defensively with bow and arrows fit for war according to the English fashion, to be ready at all times upon warning for the defence of the said land in manner and form as heretofore has been accustomed, so long as the most high, puissant prince the Duke of York remains in the said land. For the defence of the English nation of this land from the danger and malice of the Irish enemies rests and depends on English bows, which to the said enemies give the greatest resistance and terror of any weapon of war used in the said land, now very nearly destitute of any great number of the said bows, which are not in these days employed in exercise of the occupation of archery.'

Another, that Ireland ought to have her own coinage, was part of the demand for internal independence. Mints were ordered to be set up at the castles of Dublin and Trim, and three varieties of coin were to be struck, viz. a silver 'Ireland' valued at a penny sterling, with a lion on one side and a crown on the other, and the name Ireland written round the lion; a 'Patrick', valued at one-eighth of the 'Ireland', having a demi-crown with the name on one side and a cross on the reverse; and a groat, valued at four-pence, bearing a cross and a crown and the name of the place where struck.

Richard made his young son Edmund, Duke of Rutland and Earl of Cork, Chancellor of Ireland and showed every sign of putting the Yorkists into power there. The English government could not hope to dislodge him with attainders and writs, and they had not the resources to proceed against him with force. While he was thus entrenched in Ireland, his nephew Warwick was in Calais, whence he sailed with a fleet of twenty-six ships in the spring of 1460 to confer with York at Waterford, and an invasion of England was planned. Warwick returned to Calais and from thence landed in Kent. Marching north, he defeated the Lancastrians and took the King prisoner at Northampton on July 10th 1460. No sooner did the news of this victory reach York than he appointed the Earl of Kildare his Deputy and left for England accompanied by numbers of devoted followers from Ireland. He made a triumphal entry into London, with trumpeters and clarions, his Duchess by his side, his sword borne before him, and on his banners the whole arms of England displayed, as if he meant to assume the royal estate and power. The throne of

England was now almost within his grasp. Parliament reluctantly admitted his claim on October 25th, but it was stipulated that Henry should reign for the rest of his life with York as his chief minister, heir, and successor.

The Duke did not live long to enjoy his triumph. On December 31st 1460 he was killed outside his own castle of Wakefield, having rashly offered battle with his small force to a great Lancastrian one collected by Queen Margaret, for he scorned 'to be held within walls by a scolding woman'.

After the barbarous fashion of these wars, his young son Edmund, Duke of Rutland and Earl of Cork, was murdered after the battle. The heads of both were placed over the gate of York, and Richard's was in derision crowned with a paper crown. Thus perished the hero of almost all Ireland, with many of his Irish tenants around him to the last.[1] But at least he had won almost all Ireland to the cause of the White Rose for some forty years to come.

The military genius, however, was on the Yorkist side, which had two brilliant young leaders in York's eldest son Edward and Richard Neville, 'the Kingmaker', Earl of Warwick, his cousin. Edward, marching rapidly up from Wales to London, was crowned King of England by his partisans on March 4th 1461, and secured his throne by the victory of Towton Field on March 29th. James, Earl of Ormond, was taken in the fight and executed later after the wholesale fashion of these fights; for the Wars of the Roses were a 'barons' war' on a national scale. Luckily for England they were the last of such.

While England was full of fratricidal hatreds and of paid retainers, wearing the badges and uniforms of their noble employers, Ireland too was full of armed men, the kerns, gallowglasses, and armed tenants of the great lords, and the war-cries and slogans of the chief families were heard on many a field and at many a gathering.[2]

[1] An extract from *Record, Turr, Lond.*, given in Carew, *Miscell*, p. 478, puts the final loss of Ulster down to York: 'In fine during his government there, he so gained the hearts of the Irish nobility that divers of them, especially those of Ulster, Clandeboye, the Glins and the Ardes, which at that time were better inhabited with English nobility than any part of Munster or Connacht, came over with him against Henry VI to wit famous battles, as to Blorheth, Barnet, Northampton, and lastly to Wakefield, where they not only lost their lives with him but also left their country so naked of defence that the Irish cast up their old captain O'Neale, relyed themselves with their ancient neighbours the Scots and repossessed themselves of amost the whole country, which is the utter ruin of Ulster.' The statement, however, is a general one, and no historical research has yet been directed to the part played by Anglo-Irish fighting men in the Wars of the Roses from 1455 to 1485.

[2] Such as 'Crom Abu' of the Kildare Fitzgeralds, 'Shanid Abu' of the Desmond ones, 'O'Donnell Abu' of the Tyrconnell chiefs.

THE ATTAINDER OF THE BUTLERS

Acts of attainder in Parliament were the usual sequel of such a military and political triumph. The Butlers were now on the losing side. Edward IV's parliament of Westminster in November 1461 passed a sweeping Act of attainder against the chief Lancastrians, such as Henry, Duke of Somerset; and John and Thomas, the brothers of James of Ormond and Wiltshire, were included in it, for the Ormond house had great possessions in England. The Irish parliament, now also Yorkist, followed suit, and on October 15th 1462 attainted John of Ormond and Thomas his brother, together with their cousins, Edmund 'FitzRichard', Piers, son of James Butler, and eight others 'who had adhered to the King's enemies'.[1] But Edward IV, an easy-going man apart from wars, almost at once by royal grace allowed Sir John to enjoy the profits of his lands in England and Ireland, for he had a great admiration for John, of whom he said that he was 'the goodliest knight I ever beheld and the finest gentleman in christendom'.

THE MORTIMER POSSESSIONS COME TO THE CROWN

With Edward IV the whole Mortimer heritage in Ireland and Wales merged in the Crown. Though not of much value to the absentee monarch at this time, the 'King's title', now acquired to Ulster, Connacht, Trim, and Leix was to be made a great deal of in the Tudor period. It was not without significance for Irish loyalty to the Crown that there was now a king on the throne who was the heir of Lacys, De Burgos, Mortimers, and, through an early De Burgo marriage, having the blood of Brian Boru in his veins. As Edward IV is ancestor of all subsequent Kings of England, this Irish and Anglo-Irish descent has not been without practical as well as romantic effect.

Edward, however, owed so much to Ireland that he had to leave it to the Home Rule lords who were professedly Yorkist. Under him this peerage was reinforced by new creations of men who had served York well, such as Sir Robert Barnewall, Sir Roland FitzEustace, Sir Robert Bold, and Sir Robert Preston, who became respectively Barons of Trimleston, Portlester, Ratoath, and Viscount Gormanston.

Thomas, Earl of Kildare, acted as Justiciar till March 1462. The King's brother, George Duke of Clarence, was then made

[1] Berry, *Statutes*, III, pp. 25–9. For the history of these attainders see also *Cal. Ormond Deeds*, III, pp. 190–3, 216, 220, 228.

Lieutenant, but did not come over, and left the government to Irish deputies.

A LANCASTRIAN RISING, 1462

Thomas, son of James, Earl of Desmond, succeeded his father in the earldom in August 1462. He had at once to unite with the Earl of Kildare against a Lancastrian or rather Butler insurrection led by Sir John of Ormond. The titular Earl, attainted in England, sailed for Ireland to make another bid for fortune there. In 1462 Waterford, Kilkenny, New Ross, and other towns declared for him. Edmund MacRichard and the junior Butlers of Kilkenny and Tipperary rose, and an army of five thousand men took the field for him in Meath led by John de Bermingham of Carbery and others of the 'Old English', reinforced by O'Connor Faly. Thomas Earl of Desmond raised twenty thousand men at his own cost, wasted the Ormond country for seventeen days, reduced the Meath rising, and at Pilltown or Baile-an-phoill near Carrick-on-Suir defeated Ormond himself so completely that 'for certain it might not be known how great a number was slain, and Sir John himself was discomfited and put to flight'. In Ireland the feud was to be not so much between York and Lancaster but, as here, between Geraldines and Butlers and their mutual adherents.

In this battle Edmund MacRichard, who was a famous warrior, commanding a thousand horsemen with helmets, had four hundred men slain and himself taken, and as part of his ransom paid over to the victor, Desmond, two great manuscript books in Irish out of his library, the *Book of Carrick* and a copy of the ancient *Psalter of Cashel,* made for him at his castle of Rath-an-photaire in 1454, and dedicated 'with a blessing on the soul of the archbishop of Cashel, Richard O'Hedigan, for it was by him the owner of this book was educated'.

The battle of Pilltown practically finished the Butler-Lancastrian rising, though it simmered on to the next year. Earl John left Ireland for good, spent most of his life in England and abroad, and died in 1478. While in Ireland in 1462 he appointed Edmund MacRichard his 'deputy in the earldom and principal governor of his lands and lordships in Ireland'. Edmund died in June 1464, but the deputyship to the absentee Earl was continued to his son and heir, James, and after his death in 1487 to his son again, Piers Roe.

The attainder of the Irish Butlers was reversed in Irish parliaments of 1465 and 1468, and so was the attainder of Earl John himself and his brother Thomas by act of a Dublin parliament in

July 1475. Maynooth and Rathmore, fruitful causes of feud between Ormond and Kildare, were by this latter act declared to be ancient inheritance of the Fitzgeralds.[1] In England the attainder was reversed in 1485 by Henry VII. But the senior line of 'Le Botiller' saw Ireland no more. Earl John died abroad in 1478, leaving only an illegitimate son by Reynalda O'Brien, who afterwards played some part in Ireland as James 'Dubh'. Earl Thomas his successor lived in England quietly till his death in 1515.

The Polestown Butlers therefore became the real heads and protectors of the great Butler lordship in Ireland. James, son of Edmund MacRichard, had by Saiv or 'Sabina' Kavanagh three children, Esmond, Theobald, and Piers Rua. These two former were legitimated by Parliament in 1467 as being born 'in affiance between the two before espousals', and a royal patent freed Saiv and her issue by James, begotten or to be begotten, 'from all Irish servitude', and enabled her and them to enjoy English laws 'in the same manner as Englishmen within the said lands', with power to acquire and purchase lands, and answer and be answered at the King's courts. Piers, however, born about 1467, in due wedlock, regarded his elder brothers as illegitimate and himself as his father's lawful heir.[2]

THOMAS OF DESMOND, LORD DEPUTY

For the present, however, the feuds of the great ones were not pronounced, and in Thomas, Earl of Kildare, and Thomas, Earl of Desmond, were found two civilized and reasonable men with some regard for their office and the State as well as their regalities. This Kildare had been finally recognized as 7th Earl in 1456; he firmly allied himself with the other and (for the present) greater Geraldine, as joint leaders of a Patriot and Home Rule Party. In April 1463 Desmond was appointed Deputy for the Duke of Clarence, now Lieutenant, and in January next year Kildare was made Chancellor.[3] At Desmond's first parliament late in 1463 the Earl of Kildare, for his services against John of Ormond, was *inter alia* granted the custody of the lordships and lands of Carlow and Ross and the seigniory of Dungarvan for a term of sixty years. These derelict lordships lay like No Man's Land between Irish chiefs and 'degenerate English'; the best fate for them was to fall into the hands of one or other of the great magnates. Whatever

[1] *Cal. Ormond Deeds*, III, No. 213. [2] Ibid., III, Nos. 230, 231.

[3] The title of Deputy now becomes common, for Ireland was nominally ruled from this time into Henry VIII's reign by Lord Lieutenants of the Blood Royal who never or seldom came over.

Kildare did with a lordship so far off as the Shrewsbury inheritance of Dungarvan, it is certain that in the case of Carlow he used the grant to add a large part of this border country to his own one of Kildare.

The result of Richard of York's enlisting of Ireland on his side and then the triumph of his house, pledged as it was to friendship to Ireland, was to put the Home Rule aristocracy into the saddle for fifty years. It is now that we find the Council appointing a chief governor at a sudden vacancy according to their treasured 'Statute of FitzEmpress'; the Deputies, who were practically Lieutenants, appointing their own substitutes, naming the chief officers such as the Chancellor; and the chief officers holding for life, in defiance of the Crown's prerogative of appointment.[1]

THE LIEGE PEOPLE

The common Englishry of Ireland in 'the obedient shires' must not be omitted from the picture. They were to be the main ground on which 'strong' English viceroys felt they could safely stand now when the 'great of lineage' were hostile or unhelpful. But the area of this 'land of peace' was diminishing steadily, and before long only the four counties of Dublin, Meath, Louth, and Kildare could be counted in what came to be known as the Pale. Yet, when the towns great and small, and outlying but loyal areas, such as south Wexford and Lecale in Down, and the adjacent parts of the great towns and the English part of the Church are reckoned, England could still, if her own monarchy revived, count on a great support in this lordship.

To take the military strength alone, in addition to the 'royal or scutage service' (commuted knight-service), the manhood of the Pale could be called out against 'English rebels' or 'Irish enemies' according to the Statutes of Kilkenny and Edward I's Statute of Winchester.[2]

[1] The most striking case of long tenure is that of Roland FitzEustace Lord Portlester, who was Treasurer practically from 1454 to 1492. In 1483 Robert St. Lawrence, Lord Howth, was appointed by Kildare Chancellor for life with power to name a deputy (*Lib. Mun.*, I, pt. IV, p. 99). An Act of 2 Richard III allowed the chief officers of state to hold for life.

[2] See *Rot. Canc. Hib.*, 209b: Commission to Bartholomew Verdun and three other *custodes pacis* in county Louth for assessing and arraying men of said county to horse and arms, namely archers, hoblers (light horse), horsemen, and foot and taking musters of them in their twenties, hundreds, and thousands, and leading them to the Marches against rebels and enemies, according to the Statutes of Winchester and Kilkenny, etc. (Given at Trim, March 11th 1417.) In 1421 royal service proclaimed at two pounds the service for county Louth (Harris, *Collect.*, IV, and other instances pp. 112, 139, 225).

DESMOND'S ACTS

Desmond's first parliament, held in the winter of 1463–4, passed a statute which admitted the futility of one part of the Statutes of Kilkenny: 'Whereas the profit of every city and town in the land depends principally on the resort of Irish people bringing merchandise thereinto, the people of Cork, Waterford, Limerick, and Youghal may trade with the Irish, in spite of all statutes contrary.' Yet in the spirit of another part of them, by his next parliament in 1465 (in which the attainder of Edmund Butler, lord of Dunboyne, was reversed, and the sovereign and inhabitants of the town of Kilkenny with others were pardoned for their part in the rising of 1462) the Irish among the English of Meath, Louth, Dublin, and Kildare were ordered to take English surnames of towns, trades, colours, such as Sutton, Trim, Chester, White, Smith, Carpenter, etc., to dress as English, and be sworn as lieges within a year.[1] To terrorize evildoers, 'Old English' or Irish, another act was passed allowing any liege man 'without fear of impeachment' to slay any thief or thieves going in or out to steal, especially in the land of Meath, having with them no faithful man of good name and fame in English apparel.[2]

THE COLLEGE OF YOUGHAL

That Desmond was a cultured and civilized man is shown in his care for education and religion. At this parliament of 1465, then sitting at Drogheda during October and November, it was enacted that 'inasmuch as the land of Ireland has no university within it, which if it had would promote as much the increase of knowledge and good governance as avoidance of riot and misgovernance, it is ordered that there shall be a university at Drogheda where may be made bachelors, masters and doctors in all sciences and faculties as at Oxford'.[3] This design of a *studium generale* for Ireland was inspired as much by the prevalent nationalist sentiment as by wounded feeling over the exclusion of Irishmen from English universities. Unfortunately it came to nothing. But Earl Thomas himself founded in his town of Youghal on December 27th 1464 a noble collegiate church. Called by him the Church of the Blessed Virgin at Youghal, its community consisted at first of a warden, eight fellows, and eight singing-men, living in collegiate manner and

[1] This seems to be the first legal recognition of these counties as 'the Pale', in which alone now, what between 'Marcher English' and 'Irish enemies', the English language, habit, and loyalty could be expected or enforced.

[2] Berry, *Statutes*, III, pp. 41–265 and 272–369.

[3] Ibid., p. 369.

having a common table. Endowed by the Earl with lands, etc. yielding six hundred pounds per annum, the foundation was later confirmed by Thomas's son James and by Papal Bull in 1468 and 1494. It survived and flourished long after its founder, but after the ruin of the Desmond house in 1583 fell a prey to the fortune-seekers, and finally under James I came to that most successful of the Munster 'Adventurers', Boyle, Earl of Cork.[1]

Meanwhile the Earl of Desmond's dealings with the 'Irish enemy' and the constant extension of his Irish lordship were rousing suspicion and fear in the Council room of England.

Desmond's vast palatinate was in truth a small kingdom which had few equals even among the great earldoms of England. And it was in one aspect an Irish kingdom, for its Gaelic vassals and tenants were more numerous than its Englishry. Son of the O'Brien-fostered James and of a Burke lady, it is certain that Thomas spoke Irish and had Irish sympathies. When he held Parliament in Dublin in 1464, MacWilliam of Clanrickard his cousin, Aedh Rua O'Donnell, and 'many of the English and Irish' attended him there, and the unusual sight was seen of Irish chiefs with their gallowglasses walking the streets of the capital—a token that Norman and Gaelic chiefs were now joint lords of Ireland, whose ancient enmity was steadily relaxing. Thomas had allowed the race of Conor O'Brien to keep the lordship of Carrigogunnell and Pobal Bhriain in Limerick, founded under his father Earl James, which stretched to within a few miles of Limerick city. In 1466 Taig, son of Turloch O'Brien, king of Thomond since 1459, retaliating because the Earl had sheltered this rival branch, invaded the earldom, 'and', say the MacFirbis annals in their quaint English form, 'we heard not of such an host with any of his name or ancestors since Brian Boru; so that the Irish of Desmond and Iarmond all obeyed him; also he bribed the Old Irish of Leinster so that they were working his coming; but he retired to his house after he had conquered all the country of Clanwilliam, and the county of Lymerick, it being made sure to him from the Earle in lieu of granting peace to the said Earle and to his country, and the townsmen of Lymerick gave sixty marks yearly to him for him, but he afterwards died of a fever in his

[1] For the project of a university and for Youghal College, see Dalton's *History of Drogheda*, pp. 150 and 157, and Smith's *Hist. of County and City of Cork*, p. 55. Twenty years later a similar college was founded at Galway, known as St. Nicholas's (in 1484), for a warden, fellow, and choristers. Again in 1518, St. Mary's college, Maynooth, was founded by Garret Oge, Earl of Kildare, as a collegiate church on similar lines, 'to pray for the prosperity of the Kings of England, for the good estate of the Earl of Kildare, his wife, and their kindred, while living, and for their souls after their death'.

own house'.[1] Such were the terrifying triumphs of native chiefs at this time, and the O'Briens of Thomond kept till the next century that black-rent upon Limerick city to which the Earl had consented.

Such 'overmighty subjects' as Desmond the English monarchy sooner or later was bound to challenge both in England and Ireland. In Earl Thomas it was an especial offence that he was more Irish than any Patriot leader had yet been. The Irish exactions of coign, livery, etc., begun by his father and continued by him, were of all offences the most heinous—a surrender of the citadel to the 'Irish enemy', like the shameful buying off of Taig O'Brien.[2] Later, Sir Roland FitzEustace, Treasurer of Ireland, was accused of having incited the Earl to take the throne of Ireland, and whether the idea ever entered Desmond's head or not, it is certain that for over seventy years, it was a constant fear in England that some 'Irish wyrling' would take it on him to assume the sovereignty of Ireland.

By one of the most dramatic surprises in our history, the pride of the greatest nobleman in Ireland was suddenly quenched in his own blood.

Sir John Tibetot or 'Tiptoft', Earl of Worcester, was 'the most learned nobleman in England'. An art lover and true child of the Renaissance, he was educated at Balliol college; went on pilgrimage or tour to Jerusalem; and while sojourning at Rome delivered a Latin oration which moved to tears the great Aeneas Sylvius himself. Tibetot translated *Tullius his Book of Friendship*, and Caxton published it in 1481 with a lament for the noble Earl, cut off in early manhood in these bloody wars of York and Lancaster. But, as if to show how culture and party ferocity could animate the same breast, Tibetot as Constable of England had adjudged to savage execution by the 'law of Padua', which he had studied to good effect in Italy, so many noble victims of the Yorkist triumph that he earned the name of 'the Butcher'.

This was the man who came over to strike down the greatest of the Anglo-Irish, and that with a sudden ruthlessness not witnessed again till the time of the Tudors.

THE EXECUTION OF DESMOND

Appointed Lieutenant of Ireland in 1467 and displacing Desmond, Worcester was given a free hand to conciliate the Irish

[1] See *A.F.M.* (1464, 1466, and 1502). We find the county Limerick under Henry VII paying forty pounds a year in black-rent to O'Brien.

[2] Dowling says *sub* 1462 that Thomas 'burdened the counties of Waterford, Cork, Limerick, and Kerry with Irish impositions, and some say it was on account of these outrages and exactions against the King's peace and the laws of Ireland that he was decapitated'.

Butlers, and to make a demonstration of English power, even if it meant striking a blow at those who had embraced the Yorkist cause. Tibetot reserved this demonstration for an Irish parliament held at Drogheda at the end of 1467 and lasting till November 1468. Here the sovereignty of Edward as Lord of Ireland in virtue of Adrian's Bull was reasserted and the bishops were ordered to enjoin general obedience to him as such. The attainder of Sir James Butler of Polestown was reversed and his children by his Irish wife Saiv Kavanagh were by Act of Parliament legitimized. The liberty of Meath was restored, to be under a seneschal as before with the same powers as in former times. A great Act of Resumption was passed, but with so many exceptions in favour of church, towns, and individuals as to be of little effect.[1] Among the minor acts it is interesting to note how the anti-Irish statutes of 1366 still were of force. Robert FitzEustace, constable of Ballymore castle for the archbishop of Dublin, having made one Laurence O'Bogan sub-constable in his place there ('*an Irishman and of Irish nation on the side both of father and mother, who by nature of blood betrays the secrets of Englishmen and not having his charter of liberty*') Parliament ordains that Robert shall put in a guard of Englishmen and no Irishmen.

But the real thunderbolt was the attainder launched against Desmond and Kildare. This drastic measure was suddenly passed (or forced through by personal pressure of Worcester himself) against the heroes of Anglo-Ireland, and at the instance of Sherwood, bishop of Meath, the Earls of Desmond and Kildare and Sir Edward Plunket were, on February 4th 1468, attainted and their lands forfeited 'for horrible treasons and felonies as well in alliance, fosterage, and alterage with the Irish enemies of the King, as in giving to them horses, harnesses and arms'. Before he could escape or appeal, Desmond was taken and beheaded at Drogheda on February 14th 1468. Kildare, however, escaped to England and procured the reversal of his attainder at this very parliament of Drogheda later in the year, binding himself 'to do faithful service and bring the Irishmen of Leinster to peace to the best of his power'.

The judicial murder of Earl Thomas struck both Irish and Anglo-Irish with horror. 'Slain by the swords of the wicked, or shall I say rather made a martyr in Christ', is one epitaph upon

[1] Yet, like so much else of Tiptoft's Drogheda parliament, it anticipated the more famous and lasting one of Poynings' parliament of Drogheda in 1494–5. Its eighty-four Acts cover no less than pp. 29–649 in Berry, *Statutes*, III.

him, while the MacFirbis annals praise him as a native hero, 'bountiful in bestowing good gifts on both laity and clergy and on all the learned, both antiquaries, poets and *aesdanas* (bards) of all Ireland'.[1]

The dead man's son James, whose earldom it was impossible to confiscate, at once rose in arms, ravaged the King's land of Meath, and swore that he and his would never attend Parliament or Great Council again, or enter walled town of the King's allegiance, except at their own pleasure; a 'privilege' only renounced by his successor in 1540. This 8th Earl went even more Irish than his father, for he later married Margaret, daughter of Taig O'Brien who had made the great raid of 1466. For the English interest it was certainly a disastrous step to drive the greatest of the Old English of Munster over to Irishry, and in doing so to lose south-west Ireland to the loyal English tradition.

The idea of a reconquest of Ireland was bound to present itself to the next strong king that England should produce. Edward's father had acted on the maxim, 'he who would England win must with Ireland first begin'; the Tudor kings of England were to turn the lesson the other way round, and, from a united England, conquer a still feudal and Yorkist Ireland.

But an established strong monarchy did not come for another generation yet. Worcester who, had his forces been equal to his resolution, had it in him to be at once a Talbot and a Poynings, returned to England at the end of 1468. His master Edward for a time was overthrown by a combination of Warwick, Clarence, and Queen Margaret; and, though after six months' exile he recovered his throne and slew Warwick at the battle of Barnet in 1471, Tiptoft was captured early in the rising and beheaded on Tower Hill. Edward's traitor brother, George Duke of Clarence, was forgiven, but later, in 1478, impeached and secretly done to death. He left two infant children, Edward, Earl of Warwick, whom the Irish under Henry VII considered the true heir to the throne, and a daughter Margaret, afterwards Countess of Salisbury.

THE KILDARE SUPREMACY BEGINS, 1470

The restored Edward attempted nothing more against Ireland. Clarence became nominal Lieutenant till his execution, but

[1] See Gilbert's *Viceroys*, p. 386, for Holinshed's story that Desmond's execution was due to the resentment of Elizabeth, queen of Edward IV, because Desmond had advised Edward not to marry her. I agree with Orpen (*Eng. Hist. Rev.* (1915), p. 342) that there is nothing in the story and that Desmond's real offence lay in his adoption of Irish custom.

Thomas, Earl of Kildare, acted as his Deputy most of the time. When the governorship suddenly fell vacant by Worcester's execution in 1470, the Irish parliament, acting on the Statute of FitzEmpress, named Kildare as Justiciar, adding: 'this election—the land being without a governor by avoidance of the Earl of Worcester—is declared by authority of Parliament to be good and effectual in law, and by the same authority is ratified and approved'.

Henceforth the house of Kildare became more and more the ruler of Ireland. As the Irish parliament was the body through which the Kildare earls clothed their doings with legality, let us survey the proceedings of this assembly in the ten years from 1470 to 1480. It was a parliament now representing little but a few towns of Leinster and Munster, the commons of four shires, viz. Dublin, Meath, Kildare, and Louth, and such bishops and 'lords of parliament' as still performed their parliamentary duties. It had much of the outward appearance of its English prototype; immunity from arrest, a Speaker, recognition that laws were made at the request of the Commons. By the Declaration of Right in 1460 the Irish parliament had claimed to be supreme over the internal affairs of Ireland, and accordingly, when in 1468 the Irish House ratified an English Act of Richard II concerning rape, it laid down the principle asserted in 1460, that English Acts could only bind Ireland when accepted by the Irish legislature, by adding: 'From henceforth the said act and all other statutes and acts made by authority of Parliament within the realm of England, concerning all manner of rapes, are ratified, confirmed, and adjudged by authority of this parliament, from the said sixth day of March.'

If avoidance of taxation be a token of freedom, the freedom of England's colony was now almost perfect. Owing to the Irish reconquest, rents and profits from feudal tenures ceased to count for much in the revenue. The parliamentary carucage which occasionally supplemented the State resources fell so greatly in amount that in 1480 the Deputy Kildare was instructed by King Edward not to demand more than one subsidy in the year and this not to exceed twelve hundred marks 'as hath been accustomed'. In short, a parliamentary tax of eight hundred pounds per annum was as much as could be got to supplement the standing income from customs, Crown lands, feudal dues, absentee fines, rents, and profits of justice.

To maintain the dignity of their chosen viceroy, the Irish parliament in 1472 granted Kildare a retinue of eighty archers, increased in 1474 to a hundred and sixty-three spears. Much more impressive was the Guild of St. George, established in March 1474, by act of Parliament for the defence of the Pale. A force of two hundred fully equipped men, namely one hundred and twenty mounted archers, forty horse, and forty pages, paid out of the customs, was to be commanded by the Deputy and twelve of the most honourable persons of the four Pale counties, who should elect a captain every year in Dublin on St. George's Day. As the next Earl, Gerald, when he was confirmed Deputy in 1481, was further granted a retinue of forty spears by the King's orders, and as the Guild of St. George was really a force maintained for this native viceroy, who was its captain, it meant that an imposing guard of nearly five hundred of the best troops in Ireland rode ever at his command, as many as the King of England had. True the salary granted him in this same year, six hundred pounds, was but small, but then he had the profits of the whole lordship of Ireland.[1]

The nature of enactments in these parliaments of the colony can be seen in those summoned in the years 1472 to 1475.[2] In that held under Kildare early in 1473, it was enacted that the Deputy may appoint to offices of State. At Dublin in July 1475, before Sherwood, bishop of Meath, the attainder of John, Earl of Ormond, was reversed. In the parliament of 1472, Collon in Louth is described as 'on the frontier of the marches of Uriel, and is the key of that part of the country'. In 1475, Siddan in Meath, 'which is the key of the country there, and is surrounded by lords who take coign and livery and leave English conduct', has confirmed to it the liberties granted to it *circa* 1290 by Philip Telyng, and may impose customs for murage as it has never been walled.

In 1472 bitter complaint is made that 'the writs of the king nor the law of the king nor his court is not used betwixt the people of the king of Ulster'—so justices may inquire by juries of men of the next county just as if they were in Ulster. 'All Ulster is lost save for Carrickfergus and Ardglass.'

This picture of the loss of the northern frontiers brings us back to the Gaelic lords of the north.

Aedh Rua O'Donnell had in 1464, as we saw, marched into Dublin as an adherent of Thomas, Earl of Desmond. In 1469, having got Richard, son of Thomas, the Mayo or Lower Burke, to submit to him, he marched against Ulick of Clanrickard.

[1] Gilbert's *Viceroys*, pp. 592–9, for the instructions of the King in 1480, and p. 600 the viceregal indenture between the King and the Earl of Kildare in 1481.

[2] Tomás O'Muirgheasa of the Public Record Office of Ireland kindly allowed me to see a most valuable table of contents which he made of the statutes beginning 12–13 Edw. IV, the originals of which have perished in the Four Courts. (Transcripts are now (1938) on the point of publication, and those of 1470–85 have been utilized by Donough Bryan in his *Great Earl of Kildare*.)

Conor O'Brien of Thomond came to the help of Clanrickard, who had married Conor's daughter Slaine, but they were defeated at Glanog. Next year O'Donnell took Sligo Castle from Donal O'Connor, the reigning chief there, and got submission and tribute from lower Connacht, while O'Connor had also to surrender two precious books, which had been a long time in his family, viz. the *Lebhor na hUidhre* and the *Lebhor Gearr.*[1] Thus did O'Donnell affirm his former paramount lordship in the north-west.

It was this long-lived Aedh Rua, king of Tyrconnell till 1505, who built Donegal Castle and in 1474 the fine abbey of the Franciscans there, and made this his 'manor of Donegal', just as Dungannon with its castle was now O'Neill's seat.

[1] The entry in *A.F.M.* on this is (1470): 'The castle of Sligo was taken after a long siege by Red Hugh O'Donnell from Donal, son of Eoghan O'Connor. On this occasion he obtained all his demand by way of reparation, beside tokens of submission and the tribute of lower Connacht and he recovered the *Leabhar Gearr*, the *Leabhar na hUidhre*, and the chairs of Donal Oge, which had been carried thither in the time of John, son of Conor, son of Hugh, son of Donal Oge O'Donnell.' An entry in the *Lebhor na hUidhre* asks, 'a prayer here for Aedh Ruadh who forcibly recovered this book from the Connachtmen and the *Leabhar Gearr* after they had been taken away from us from the time of Cathal Oge O'Connor to the time of Rory son of Brian O'Connor and ten lords ruled over Carbury (Sligo) between them'. (O'Curry, *MS. Materials*, pp. 183–4.) The *Lebhor* (*Leabhar*) *na hUidhre* or 'Book of the Dun Cow', compiled about 1100, contains a version of the great Conchobar epics.

CHAPTER XVI

THE GREAT EARL OF KILDARE, 1477–1513

THOMAS, 7TH EARL OF KILDARE, died in March 25th 1477, and Gerald his son succeeded, being then about twenty-one years of age. 'The Great Earl', 'Garret More' as he was called by both Irish and Anglo-Irish, was to be with some vicissitudes the real ruler, the all-but king, of Ireland till his death in 1513.

Gerald succeeded to a huge family inheritance in Kildare, a palatinate in fact if not in name which, as we see by the family rentals, had spread or was to spread over the Irish and English of counties Kildare, Carlow, Wicklow, and in the neighbouring Leix and Offaly.[1] His father had ruled Ireland for long enough years to found a tradition that the house of Kildare was the dominant one among the Anglo-Irish, a tradition aided or made permanent by the fact that the Earl of Desmond had gone Irish and ceased to aspire to this leadership, and that the main line of the Butlers was permanently absentee and gone English. Kildare also was nearer the seat of government than either of them had been; a prince as he was on the Curragh of Kildare and at Maynooth, an easy ride up to the capital enabled him to dominate Dublin and win the affections of its people. At this epoch favourable to him and Home Rule, the English power in Ireland was at its lowest ebb, and 'the blood of the First Conquest', as was said later, 'in a manner worn out'.

His position was in a sense made for the Great Earl, in whom was summed up the semi-nationalism of England's first colony, the culmination of the feudal and chiefly independence which had come to the Normans of Ireland through the permanent absence of a monarchy able to bridle them. Though the main Leinster Fitzgeralds had never married Irish since first they got Kildare, they had begun with Welsh blood, and for centuries had been subjected to Irish influences to which their fluid and sympathetic temperament responded easily. In Gerald we have the first representative man of the mixed race, the typical Anglo-Irishman with the blended humour and adaptiveness of the new stock, its readiness in action and wit in speech, mixed in his case with an apparent levity and even buffoonery well fitted to delude the

[1] For the *Red Book of 1503* and the *Rental of 1518* see pp. xv–xvi of Donough Bryan, *Great Earl of Kildare* (1933). The standard work on the Kildare Fitzgeralds is *The Earls of Kildare*, by the Marquess of Kildare (1858) with *Addenda* (1862 and 1872).

more serious English of oversea but which did not take in himself or his people.

Garret More, the first 'Uncrowned King of Ireland', thus had the character equal to his opportunities, and without him Irish history would indeed have taken a different course. All this inherited power of his and dominance among the Anglo-Irish who came to adore his house, he enhanced and fortified on every hand by marriage alliances both with the Gaelic and the English chiefs of his country. He himself was married to Alison, daughter of Roland FitzEustace, Treasurer for long years of Ireland. His brothers Thomas of Laccagh and James were to prove valiant warriors and right-hand men of his. Of the six daughters whom he had by Alison, one, Margaret, married later Sir Piers Roe, head of the Butlers; another, Elizabeth, married Christopher Fleming, Baron of Slane; another, Eleanor, much later married Donal Mac Carthy Reagh; Eustasia or Anastasia married Ulick Burke of Clanrickard; Alice married Conn Bacach O'Neill; and the last, Joan, married Maelruana O'Carroll of Ely. By his second marriage with an English wife, Elizabeth St. John, the Earl had five other sons, all of whom by an extraordinary ill fate perished with their nephew Silken Thomas at Tyburn in 1537, after the failure of his rising.

Thus bound up with the lords of the Pale, the Great Earl was intermarried with the Irish. The marriage of his sister Eleanor in 1480 with Conn, eldest son of Henry O'Neill, Lord of Tyrone, united the two greatest houses, English and Irish, in Ireland. The marriage defied the Statutes of Kilkenny, but an Act of Parliament in 1480 covered the flaw, and made Conn and his issue by Eleanor of free estate and condition in law.[1]

The ruling Aedh Rua O'Donnell, though there was no marriage alliance, entered into a military alliance with Garret which remained unbroken till his death.

Backed by such resources, Kildare, a convinced but cautious Yorkist, contrived to rule Ireland in the name of Edward IV and Richard III, then, getting the better of Henry VII, to rule Ireland in the name of the Tudor king, and to establish a sovereignty which, continued by his son, was only ruined by the folly of his grandson Silken Thomas in 1534.

[1] The Act of 20 Edw. IV states: 'In consideration of loyal service done by Henry O'Neill, captain of his nation, and by his son Conn, lately married to Elianor daughter of Thomas late Earl of Kildare, it is enacted that the said Conn be of free estate and condition in law as the King's liegeman, and that he and his issue engendered by the said Elianor be adjudged English and of English condition, and may plead and be impleaded as the King's liegeman in all courts as if he had been the King's subject.' Quoted in Hardiman's *Statutes of Kilkenny*, p. 52. (*Tracts rel. to Ireland II*, Irish Arch. Soc.)

Immediately at the beginning of his power, Garret More had to face, and dared to defy, the Crown of England. The Irish Council elected him Justiciar in succession to his father. But Clarence, nominal Lieutenant, having been attainted and done to death in February 1478, Edward by Privy Seal deprived Kildare of his office and sent Henry, Lord Grey, over instead. But Home Rule had gone too far; FitzEustace, the Chancellor, would not surrender the Great Seal, nor Keating, prior of Kilmainham and constable of Dublin castle, admit Grey, while Kildare on his own responsibility called a parliament to Naas which protested against his dismissal by mere Privy Seal, voted a subsidy in support of his government, and gave him power to adjourn and prorogue Parliament at pleasure.[1] Grey had to yield, and by royal command had a new Great Seal made. Further a parliament summoned by him at Trim enacted that in future (according to the Statute of Fitz-Empress) the election of a temporary Justiciar in a vacancy should be by majority of the Council and by consent of Parliament till the King's pleasure was known.

Although royal infants were successively named Lieutenant by the Crown, in fact Kildare ruled Ireland till the fall of the House of York, and Edward confirmed him as Deputy in May 1482.

Meanwhile, in 1487, John 6th Earl of Ormond died and his brother Thomas succeeded, but his continued absence till his death in 1515, and the marriage of his only child Margaret to Sir William Boleyn, completed the disappearance of the senior Butlers from Ireland. As no Irish lordship could exist without a visible head, the Butlers of Polestown took the place of the senior line, though the Caher line was very active in building up a semi-Gaelic, semi-feudal lordship in Tipperary.[2] Sir James, son of Edmund MacRichard, acted as deputy for the Earl in succession to his father from 1477 to his death in April 1487. In his will he left to his son Piers Roe, 'the custody and defence of the lands of my lord the Earl of Ormond as it was given to me'.[3]

This was a sort of Tanistship, as it were, among the Anglo-Irish. The Polestown Butlers hoped that if the absentee earls died without male issue the Ormond titles and properties would revert to them. Meanwhile Sir James and Piers Roe after him had the practical possession of the huge inheritance of the race in counties Tipperary and Kilkenny. Piers Roe, who came to full age about 1487, proved to be a remarkable man, full of vigour, ambition, and wiliness, and lasted to the remarkable age for those times of

[1] The proceedings of this 'pretended parliament' were annulled in November 1478.

[2] See formerly, p. 320, for the plaint of the Englishry of Tipperary in 1542.

[3] *Cal. Ormond Deeds*, III, Nos. 228, 298 and *passim* for all this period.

seventy-two. He too had a hard part to play. He might be regarded as a Lancastrian, and his family sympathies had been this way; certainly when the Tudors came in he was for them. But it was largely a mask. Piers and the Butlers, a realist race, the House of Argyle of Ireland, were generally with whatever was the strong and legitimate government. Their real quarrel was with the Geraldines of Kildare and Desmond on either side; to build up a house-power was the ambition of all these men.

At first, however, Sir Piers and Garret More were apparently friends. Piers married the Great Earl's daughter, Margaret; was glad of his aid and her determined character against all enemies; and it was not till after 1500 that he came out against Kildare.

THE BUTLER-FITZGERALD FACTIONS

These Butlers had Irish connexions no less powerful than those of Kildare and Desmond. Piers Roe was grandson of Catherine O'Carroll, wife of Edmund MacRichard and daughter of that Maelruana O'Carroll whose sister Margaret, wife of Calvach O'Connor Faly, had earned the encomiums of all the learned of Ireland for her princely entertainment of them in 1433.[1] The father of Maelruana O'Carroll, Taig, slain in 1407, had married Joan daughter of the 2nd Earl of Ormond. Calvach O'Connor Faly, who was thus allied by marriage to the Butlers, after building up a formidable power in Offaly, died in 1458. Piers himself was grandson of Donal Reagh MacMurrough Kavanagh, king of Leinster, who died in 1476. Donal was succeeded by his sons Art Bui and Gerald and, as Sir Piers Butler was their nephew, the MacMurroughs were now closely connected with this great Norman house.

By the end of the century there was a regular Butler-Fitzgerald division into two parties, which not only affected Leinster and Munster but Ireland generally, and is notable in the various records, annals, and official accounts. Indeed the Ormond *versus* Kildare alinement persisted up to Elizabeth's reign. O'Neill and O'Donnell were steady in the Kildare attachment, MacMurrough and O'Carroll on the Butler side.[2]

[1] For the feast given twice in one year by this noble woman to 'the learned families of Ireland' and 'the aesdána (bardic poets)' to the number of 2,700, see under 1451 in *Ann. MacFirbis*, op. cit., p. 227, referring to the year 1433 (*Ann. Ult.*).

[2] Campion's *History* relates that, when the Earl of Kildare was sent for to England in 1527, Sir Piers Roe 'came to Dublin with an army of Irishmen, having captains over them, O'Connor (Faly), O'More and O'Carroll, and at St. Mary's abbey was chosen Deputy by the King's council'.

GALLOWGLASSES IN THE PALE

Great as were Irish chiefs and Norman lords, there was no lack of fighting spirit in the Pale, and English bow and spear could still prevail against the light Irish array. So that when O'Reilly of Cavan with two thousand men ravaged Louth in 1470, John Bole, archbishop of Armagh, and the mayor of Drogheda collected five hundred archers and two hundred poleaxe men, who were joined at Ardee by Sir Robert Taaf with seventy horse, which little force of near eight hundred men the archbishop blessed; then they marched to Corbally near Malpas bridge and there put O'Reilly to rout and slew four hundred of his men.[1]

By coign, livery, and the like the Irish lords now commanded whole armies of men. Garret More was the first great man who openly dared to impose Irish 'cuttings and cessings' upon the Pale. 'The first coin of gallowglasses called *coin bon* that was cessed within these fifty years in these quarters that Gerald, father to Gerald late Earl of Kildare, cessed in the county of Kildare was one Barret having but twenty-four sparrs (axes), who came to him being exiled out of Connacht. The said gallowglasses so increased in the time of Gerald his father that in his time they came to one hundred and twenty sparrs.'[2]

With such small but effective armies of 'bonnaughts', kerns, and gallowglass did chiefs and lords alike fight their deadliest battles. But no other single lord or alliance of such could rival in armed array Garret More, who was at once a palatine earl, a Gaelic Rí, and viceroy for the Crown. As such he interfered in the many wars of Ireland in a way no English viceroy had done for two centuries, and while this undoubtedly spread a Geraldine hegemony over all the island it did also enforce a central authority and rough kind of order.

In Tyrone the Earl naturally supported Conn More, his brother-in-law, against his rivals till in 1483 Henry, now aged, resigned his place to his son Conn, and this brother-in-law of Garret was enkinged at Tullahoge, 'by will of his father and of all Tyrone'.

RICHARD III AND IRELAND

The end of the short-lived Yorkist régime was now at hand. Edward IV died on April 9th 1483, and his eldest son, a youth of

[1] Dalton's *Drogheda*, II, p. 160, quoting from a lost 'Register of the Mayors of Drogheda'.

[2] Report of Justice Luttrell in 1537: given in Richey's *Lectures*, II, p. 29. *Coin bon* was *coinmhe bona* or 'fundamental coign' as distinguished from excess coign', which would be called *coinmhe bairr*.

twelve, by law succeeded to the throne as Edward V. But his uncle Richard, Duke of Gloucester, seized both him and his brother, Richard, Duke of York, and the two unfortunate 'Princes of the Tower' disappeared soon afterwards. On July 6th 1483 Richard was crowned King of England. The short reign of the last Yorkist allowed Home Rule in Ireland to reach its zenith. The King's only son Edward, who died next year, was named Lieutenant, but Kildare was confirmed as his Deputy and continued also in office under the next Lieutenant, John de la Pole, Earl of Lincoln, nephew of Richard and now heir to the Crown.

An Irish parliament in 1485 enacted that the existing Chancellor, Treasurer, Chief Baron of the Exchequer, the Clerk of the Rolls, and the King's Sergeant should hold for life, and together with the peers, might, according to the Statute of FitzEmpress elect a Chief Governor in time of vacancy. It was a significant declaration of Ireland's right to approve of her own president.

The rule of Kildare showed a mixture of self-interest and statecraft. In 1481 Parliament empowered him to appoint receivers over two-thirds of all manors, rents, etc. of persistent absentees, and appropriate them to the defence of the land. Further, he was empowered to take possession of the vacant lands in Kildare and Carlow 'namely, from Calveston to Carlow castle and thence to Leighlin bridge which the Earl had recovered from the Irish'—the absentee proprietors to forfeit all right if they did not make good their claim within six years. The result was that the Earl added greatly to his Kildare lordship in Wicklow, Carlow, and the marches of Dublin, and enclosed and appropriated land in every direction.[1]

To defend Carlow the Earl built a castle at Tristledermot 'as a true means of causing the waste lands of Carlow to be inhabited by the English subjects'. But the pretence of a 'pure English land' was wearing very thin. Castledermot, Carlow, Leighlin, Bray, Trim, Collon, and Siddan were the outposts of the Pale, but in 1515, it was reported to the King 'all the English folk of the said four counties be of Irish habit, language and condition, except the cities and walled towns'.

King Richard in his difficulties felt the need to woo Irish hearts as his father had done. In 1484 a royal commissioner, Thomas Barret, bishop of Annaghdown, appeared in Ireland with letters from the King to Kildare, Lords Barry and Roche of Munster, the

[1] See Gilbert's *Viceroys*, p. 409–10 for Act of 1485; and Bryan's *Great Earl of Kildare*, pp. 60, 61, for the 1481 Act. The additions thus made in Carlow remained in the family till the attainder of 1534.

Baron of Delvin and others in Meath, and Lords Bermingham, Barret and others of Connacht. Kildare was told that the King desired to recover his earldom of Ulster, but that he could the more aid in this, 'because the Great O'Neill, who now has and occupies the most part thereof, has married the Earl's sister, and for the sake of this marriage the King's grace will incline to accept O'Neill into favour, as his brother King Edward before had his father and gave him his livery'.

The Burkes were not included in the letters addressed to the great men of the west, for they were treated as usurpers on the lordship of Connacht. Indeed in the charter which Richard gave to Galway city in December 1484, Clanrickard's sovereignty over the city was abolished, and the citizens were empowered to elect annually a mayor and two bailiffs to rule over them.[1]

To conciliate James, Earl of Desmond, still sore over his father's execution, was also part of the bishop's mission. Royal letters, 'to be showed to the King's cousin, the Earl of Desmond, and all other nobles and gentles of the land of Ireland', thanked Desmond for the manifold services and kindnesses done by the Earl's father to Richard of York, condemned the extortionate slaying of the late Earl, promised all possible satisfaction in law, and tendered to the Earl an oath of allegiance. The Earl is to be shown the King's pleasure that he shall not enter into marriage with any blood without the advice and knowledge of his Grace, who will provide him with a wife of noble blood. The King desires also that the Earl shall renounce the wearing and usage of the Irish array and sends him by the hands of the bishop a gown of cloth of gold, two doublets of velvet and crimson satin, hose, bonnets, and other apparel, and the King's livery, namely a collar of gold with the White Boar of Warwick pendant from a collar of roses and suns.'[2]

THE TUDOR MONARCHY

But on August 21st 1485, in the battle of Bosworth, the last Plantagenet 'died like a king', and Henry Tudor, Duke of Richmond, assumed the Crown of England. With Henry VII began a new age. England was weary of being a dynastic slaughter-house and accepted this unexpected victor with his dubious claim. The last 'barons' war' had been in effect fought out. In England

[1] See Ellis, *Letters Illustrative of Eng. Hist.*, I, pp. 122–4, for the bishop of Enachdun's mission. For the charter to Galway see Hardiman, *Galway*, p. 69.

[2] Ellis, *Letters*, op. cit., I, pp. 122–4. Desmond was probably then contemplating marriage with Margaret O'Brien, contrary to the Kilkenny Statutes and alarming to those who dreaded the irishizing of the great lords.

the true medieval baron was dead or all but dead (for the Star Chamber had yet to suppress 'livery and maintenance') in the Wars of the Roses or by the headsman's axe.[1]

In Ireland, the 'New Monarchy', centralized, official, and efficient, did not operate for fifty years yet. The medieval age went on, and the romance of the White Rose died hard among a tradition-loving race who thought everything of pedigree. Moreover, the old personal devotion to the House of York went on, 'for Richard, Duke of York, being sent to Ireland, had won such favour among that people as that they could never be separated from him and his lineage'.[2]

Garret of Kildare now had to consider the results for him and Ireland of the victory of Bosworth. Like most of the Anglo-Irish he could not believe that it would endure, for was there not much truer royal blood alive than Henry's—such as John, Earl of Lincoln, Edward of Warwick, son of George Duke of Clarence—perhaps even the Princes of the Tower?

Henry for many years had too much on hand in England. He displaced Lincoln, the existing Lieutenant, by his uncle Jasper Duke of Bedford, but continued Kildare as Deputy, and Garret remained the all-but-king of Ireland till 1492. It was obvious policy for Kildare to conciliate the Irish Butlers whom the new dynasty would obviously favour. He therefore effected a marriage between his daughter Margaret and Sir Piers Roe. Margaret, 'the Great Countess' as she was called for her noble spirit and masculine gifts, lived to 1542 and saw the tragic ruin of her own house. Henry, as was natural, allowed the attainder of the pro-Lancastrian Butlers to be reversed at the petition of Earl Thomas in an English parliament of November 1485. For the present at least the two rival houses had peace.

THE CHIEFS OF NORTH AND SOUTH

Since the middle of the century the O'Donnells had fought a continuous war with Clanrickard, of which the battle of Glanog in 1469 had been the chief incident. Ulick 'MacWilliam Uachtair' of Clanrickard dying in 1485, his son Ulick succeeded, and as he

[1] Henry, Duke of Richmond (the only surviving Lancastrian scion), was son of a Welsh gentleman Edmund Tudor and his wife Margaret Beaufort, daughter of John Beaufort, Duke of Somerset, grandson of John of Gaunt (son of Edward III) by his wife Katherine Swinford. As King, however, Henry by marrying Edward IV's daughter Elizabeth united the Houses of York and Lancaster, and thus gained the Irish estates of York. Though his accession was regarded as a Lancastrian restoration, in fact Henry continued the Yorkist principle of a 'constitutional despotism'.

[2] Stow, *General Chronicle of England* (published 1631).

was grandson of Conor O'Brien, who ruled Thomond till 1496, he had the continued O'Brien support. This was the great quarrel in the west as that of Butler and Geraldine was in the south.

THE FIRST GUNS IN IRELAND

Garret More, as the greatest man in Ireland, interfered in the petty as well as the grand feuds, and the annals record his endless hostings in which he supported his own candidates for chieftainship or strengthened one sept against another. The use of light guns, now for the first time seen in Ireland, gave him a striking force few could equal, as when in 1488, he broke down Balrath castle with 'ordnance' on its lord Mageoghegan.[1]

In June 1489 died Henry O'Neill. His son Conn More ruled till January 1493, when his own brother Henry slew him and ruled till 1498. Then succeeded another brother, Donal, till 1509, then Art, son of Aedh 'of the Fews' till 1513, then Conn More's son Art Oge till 1519, when finally Conn 'Bacach' (the Lame), youngest son of Conn More and Eleanor Fitzgerald, was inaugurated king. In the end in 1541 this representative of the ancient High kings accepted Henry VIII as King of Ireland and was made Earl of Tyrone.

Until the accession of the sons of Conn More this was a period of weakness for the royal race of Tyrone; and Tyrconnell under the vigorous Aedh Rua was the strongest state in the north. The O'Neill history since 1344 had been a determined effort to establish lineal succession, and this definitely triumphed from Eoghan (1432–55) to 1493, when each king associated his son and successor with him in the kingship. It was achieved by the aid and recognition of the English government, the primate of Armagh, the titular Earl of Ulster, and Gerald of Kildare. Had each of the great dynasties followed the same policy with the same success and the Crown turned them into tenants-in-chief like the Anglo-Irish earls, their fate and that of Ireland would indeed have been different and perhaps more fortunate. When Henry VIII attempted this it was too late. But with the death of Conn More the old principle of the succession of collaterals, of Tanists and *rigdomnas* with subsequent succession-disputes, returned again.

[1] Guns are first mentioned in Ireland in *A.F.M.* under 1488. As for muskets, in 1489 'a great rarity was sent to the Earl of Kildare, namely six hand-guns (muskets) out of Germany which his guard, during the time that they stood century, bore before his habitation in the Great Hall at the entrance into his house at Thomas Court' (Ware's *Annals*, quoted by Bryan, op. cit., p. 144). The Earl's Dublin house was called 'The Carbrie', close by Skinners' Row.

LAMBERT SIMNEL, 'EDWARD VI'

For some twelve years Anglo-Ireland was the stage for two successive attempts against the new Tudor monarchy. Affection for the House of York was one part of it; attachment to Home Rule under the House of Kildare which the Yorkist line encouraged was an even greater part.[1]

Early in 1487 a priest of Oxford, Richard Simons, brought to Dublin a boy of ten years or so ('a comely youth well favoured and not without some extraordinary dignity and grace of aspect,' says Polydore Vergil), who, he claimed, was Edward, Earl of Warwick.[2] Historians have generally decided that the boy was really Lambert, a son of Thomas Simnel of Oxford, and that he was but a stalking-horse for a plot intended to put on the throne of England either John, Earl of Lincoln, or the real Edward of Warwick, then in the Tower. The lords of Ireland decided that the lad was Warwick, and pledged their support to him at a meeting in Dublin attended by Del Palacio, archbishop of Armagh, Fitzsimons, archbishop of Dublin, the bishops of Meath, Cloyne, and Kildare, Earl Garret himself, Desmond, and other peers.

The Earl of Lincoln now betook himself to the court of Flanders, where Margaret, sister of Edward IV and widow of Charles the Bold, Duke of Burgundy, stood by the White Rose with all her woman's heart. She hired two thousand German *lansknechts* under a famous captain, Martin Swart, who landed in Dublin on May 5th 1487, along with the Earl of Lincoln. It was spread about in Dublin that the prisoner in the Tower whom Henry had recently paraded through the streets of London as the true Warwick wes 'a boy whom the King had schooled to take the Earl of Warwick's name, to blind the eyes of simple folk and to defeat the lawful inheritour of the good Duke of Clarence, their countryman and protectour during his life'. The Irish were thus

[1] Since the first edition of this present work appeared the whole formerly obscure period of Henry VII in Ireland has been enlightened by Miss Agnes Conway's *Henry VII's Relations with Scotland and Ireland* (*1485–98*) and by Donough Bryan's *Great Earl of Kildare*.

[2] Warwick was son of George, Duke of Clarence, by Isabel daughter of the famous Warwick the Kingmaker. Born in 1475, he was in 1485 placed by the new King, Henry VII, in the Tower as a possible Yorkist heir, where he spent the rest of his life till executed in 1499.

John de la Pole was the son of John, 2nd Duke of Suffolk, by Elizabeth, sister of Edward IV. Richard III had made him his heir to the throne. Slain at Stoke in 1487, he left two brothers, Edmund and Richard. Edmund (Earl of Suffolk) was handed over by Spain to Henry VII and executed early in his reign by Henry VIII. Richard was slain at the battle of Pavia in imperial service in 1525. On the death of this exile, who was called the 'White Rose', the family ended and the Yorkist cause may be regarded as substantially ended, though some descendents remained.

persuaded that here was the true Warwick, son of their Dublin-born Clarence.

On May 24th 1487 the lad whom almost all Ireland believed to be the true Prince was crowned King Edward VI of England—'and he was surely an honourable boy to look upon'—with a golden circlet taken from a statue of the Blessed Virgin at St. Mary del Dam.[1] But it was 'a coronet, not a crown'.

The Home Rule lords thus had got a king of their own liking. A government was instituted 'which dyde kepe courtes, parliaments and made styles and processes in the ladde's name'. Only Waterford stood out boldly for King Henry and was besieged for six weeks in July and August by Sir Maurice, brother of the Earl of Desmond. The Butlers, and the Butler towns, Kilkenny, Callan, Clonmel, and Fethard, upon a message from Thomas, Earl of Ormond, took up arms for Henry. The Yorkist cause, though dominant in Ireland, had, moreover, to stand the test of battle in England.

Early in June the combined army landed at Furness and at Stoke near Newark on June 16th 1487 the ordered valour of the Germans and the desperate courage of the Irish were combined in vain. The leaders, Swart, Lincoln, Thomas Fitzgerald of Laccagh, brother of Kildare, and Edward Plunket died along with their men after a battle in which, says the *Book of Howth*, 'they fought very valiant on both sides, for that Allmaynes [i.e. because the Germans] wear very good and apt soildoures and so wear their captens. The Irishmen did as well as anie naked (unarmoured) men would do, and at length they wear slaine about 4,000 and more.'[2]

The end of the poor 'ladde', captured in the battle, was to be a scullion in Henry's kitchen. It was impossible to punish his Irish supporters and, finally, after the Pope issued a Bull in January the next year against the Irish bishops who had crowned Lambert, the King forgave Kildare and left him in the Deputyship. As for the true Warwick, he remained prisoner in the Tower of London.

Meanwhile, in December 1487, James, Earl of Desmond, was murdered by instigation of his brother Sir John, and was succeeded by his next brother Maurice 'Bacach' (the Lame), who reigned till 1520.

[1] It is to be noted that he was not crowned as separate King of Ireland but as succeeding to both realms as true heir to Edward V, the unfortunate son of Edward IV. Possibly his Irish adherents hoped to abolish the inferior title 'Lord of Ireland' and have him 'King of Ireland' as well as King of England.

[2] *Book of Howth*, pp. 473–4, which has a most picturesque account in English of all these times and the Great Earl's doings.

EDGECOMB'S MISSION

Henry now sent over a commissioner, Sir Richard Edgecomb, to bring the Irish lords to their allegiance. Arriving at Kinsale with five hundred men on June 27th 1488, Edgecomb took the allegiance of Lords Courcy and Barry, and so by Waterford came to Dublin where he lodged at St. Saviour's on July 5th. Kildare, scorning a mere knight, did not arrive till July 12th, and taking up his quarters at St. Thomas's, for nine days along with the assembled lords stood firm against the oath of fealty which Edgecomb proffered them, by which their lands should be forfeit should they again rebel, 'whereat they declared with one voice they would sooner turn Irish every one'. Finally, however, on July 21st, the lords spiritual and temporal, assembled at St. Thomas's abbey, swore allegiance, whereupon a full pardon was proclaimed under the Great Seal to Kildare and the forty or more chief supporters of Simnel. On July 30th Edgecomb sailed for England.[1]

PERKIN WARBECK AND IRELAND

In the late autumn of 1491 there arrived at Cork in a trading ship from Lisbon a handsome youth of seventeen under care of a Devonshire man, John Taylor, formerly a servant of King Edward. According to Margaret of Burgundy, Charles VIII of France, the Emperor Maximilian, and James IV of Scotland—for the Yorkist ring was now wider than ever—the youth was Richard, King Edward's second son, who had escaped from the Tower. To Henry's supporters he was Perkin Warbeck or Osbeck of Tournai, an impostor.

The Irish accepted him as Prince Richard, and again a large party declared for the supposed Yorkist heir, led by John Waters, mayor of Cork, Maurice, Earl of Desmond, Lords Barry, Roche, and Courcy, the White Knight and the Knights of Glin and Kerry, David Creagh, archbishop of Cashel, and the bishops of Waterford and Cork-Cloyne. This time Munster was the seat of the movement and Desmond the leader, with Kildare playing a cautious part. This, however, was a less dramatic and brief episode than Simnel's.

After a short stay, Warbeck departed from Ireland for France and Flanders, where Maximilian recognized him as King of England, and did not return to Ireland till 1495.

Henry now realized the Irish danger. He could not take a

[1] The chief of those pardoned were Kildare, Portlester, Lords Slane, Gormanston, Howth, Dunsany, and the prelates of Meath, Kildare, Dublin. Nearly all are Anglo-Irish. (Harris, *Coll.*, IV, pp. 389–90.) Edgecomb's *Voyage* (MS. in T.C.D.) is printed in Harris, *Hibernica*, pt. I.

second Yorkist plot as lightly as the first. In June 1492 he removed Kildare from office and made FitzSimons, archbishop of Dublin, Deputy. In the same month he also sent over as 'the King's Governor and Treasurer of his land of Ireland', and later as constable of Limerick Castle, one Sir James Butler, called 'Dubh' (the Black), an illegitimate son of the late John, Earl of Ormond, by Reynalda O'Brien. The present Earl, Thomas, appointed this nephew of his guardian of his Irish lands and James was charged with working up the Butler and royalist cause in Ireland. Sir Piers, who had the hereditary deputyship of the Earls, naturally resented this newcomer, and swung over to Garret More, while Roland Lord Portlester, Kildare's father-in-law, was angered by his removal from the treasurership which he had held on and off for forty years. Sir James, however, showed great courage and tenacity in the Tudor cause, brought in Kavanagh and O'Brien allies against Sir Piers and the Geraldines, and planned to become the next Earl of Ormond.[1]

Bitterly piqued, Kildare turned to aid 'the French lad', and seems to have plotted bringing in the King of Scots. In pursuance of the plot, his ally Aedh Rua O'Donnell in July 1495 'went to the house of the king of Scotland and they formed a compact and league to assist one another mutually in their need'. Scottish State accounts record a visit of 'the Great O'Donnell' to James at Edinburgh, and the Scottish king hesitated whether to invade England or Ulster in the Yorkist cause.[2]

But nothing came of the compact, and immediately on his return from Scotland in August we find Aedh engaged in assisting his son Conn against O'Connor Sligo who, backed by Ulick of Clanrickard, was in revolt against O'Donnell suzerainty.

POYNINGS IN IRELAND

There now arrived at Howth on October 13th 1494, as Deputy to Prince Henry, a governor whose advent gave the later headline to the Tudor Reconquest. The new type of servant to the new type of king, Sir Edward Poynings had the will, if not the power, to crush 'the overmighty subjects' of Ireland. But with his petty force of a thousand men, he could only do what he did, namely, annul the Home Rule triumphs of the century.[3]

[1] The parentage of this Sir James 'Dubh' is well established in *Cal. Ormond Deeds*, vol. III, pp. 275, 279, 287, 292. It is not easy to see why Earl Thomas dispossessed Piers Roe after the Polestown branch had been trusted for so long.

[2] Tytler, *Hist. of Scotland*, IV, ch. iii., and *A.F.M.* (1495).

[3] Though small, it was an effectively trained army, consisting of men-at-arms, archers on foot and on horse, horsemen, and gunners (see Conway, op. cit., 'Army Accounts', pp. 192–8).

To replace the Anglo-Irish, Poynings brought with him one Englishman for Chancellor, another for Treasurer, and others as the two Chief Justices of Common Pleas and King's Bench, and Chief Baron of the Exchequer. The two first were Henry Deane, bishop of Bangor, and Sir Hugh Conway; while William Hatteclyffe came as subtreasurer and financial expert to go into the whole question of Irish revenue and royal rights.[1]

Poynings' first step was to impress the northern chiefs who held the King's earldom of Ulster by a campaign against the northern chiefs, O'Hanlon and Magennis, Kildare being with him and gravely suspect, and so back along the Barrow where Sir James Fitzgerald, Garret's brother, defied the Deputy and held the castle of Carlow against him till forced to surrender.

POYNINGS' PARLIAMENT

The next step was to bring down the arch-Yorkist himself. A parliament was summoned to Drogheda on December 1st 1494, and its first proceeding was on that day to attaint Earl Garret 'for treason and rebellion, taking coign and livery in the English shires, inciting Irish enemies and English rebels to war against the King and his Deputy, and agreeing with the King of Scots to send an army into Ireland to aid him and Desmond to the destruction of the Deputy and all true subjects'.[2]

It certainly was a packed house which thus could impeach the greatest man in Ireland. After some resistance, the Earl was arrested in Dublin on February 27th 1495, and on March 5th was sent to England and lodged in the Tower.

Poynings' commission was to reduce the Lordship of Ireland to 'whole and perfect obedience', and to suppress those who practised on 'the innocent and true English subjects, great and divers robberies, murders, burnings, and the universal intolerable and damnable extortions of coign, livery and pay'. For this purpose, the King went back to the rights he had in 1327, when the First Conquest began to fail. An act of this obsequious parliament revoked every royal grant made during a hundred and sixty-eight years and passed a sweeping Act of Resumption. But so many exemptions were added that it would have had little effect; in any case it was not put into force.

[1] Agnes Conway, *Henry VII's Relations*, op. cit., pp. 160–98, gives in most valuable appendixes Hattecliffe's (MS.) Accounts.

[2] The Acts of this famous 'Poynings' parliament' (forty-nine in all, great and small) have been for the first time fully reproduced in Conway, op. cit., pp. 202–19, which has a chapter by me (pp. 118–43) on 'The Acts of the Drogheda Parliament'.

So far as sovereignty could be restored by Acts of Parliament it was now done. The Crown resumed the judgment of treason and rebellion, the command of the royal castles (now shrunk to seven), the choice of officials, and the control of the legislative body.[1] The Chancellor, Treasurer and other chief officers, who by custom and an Act of 1485 had formerly held for life, were henceforth to hold only at the King's will and pleasure. The Act of the Drogheda parliament of 1460 'that no writ of treason under the Great or Privy Seal, nor letters missive out of England shall be of effect in the land of Ireland' was repealed—'which said pretensed and unlawful prescription was approved, ratified and confirmed by authority of parliament late holden within the said land, before Richard, Duke of York, being then in rebellion and pretending himself Lieutenant of the land of Ireland'. Henceforth such English writs are to be of force. The proceedings of the Government during the stay of Simnel in Dublin were all declared null and void.

To break the power which the Anglo-Irish had assumed of appointing the chief governor in an emergency, the Statute of FitzEmpress was annulled, and it was enacted that in future the Treasurer should fill up the office in a vacancy till the royal pleasure was known.[2] The Guild of St. George, which gave Kildare a royal bodyguard, was dissolved.

But the most memorable, famous, and lasting act of this parliament was that known hereafter as 'Poynings' Law'. Headed 'no parliament to be holden in this land till the acts be certified into England', it enacts that no parliament shall be held in Ireland 'till the Lieutenant and Council of Ireland shall first certify the King under the Great Seal of Ireland of such causes, acts, etc. as them seemeth should pass. Then the King and his (English) council, after affirming such causes and acts good and expedient

[1] Cap. 14 says English-born men are to be constables of Dublin, Trim, Leixlip, Athlone, Greencastle, Carlingford, and Carrickfergus castles. No less than four Acts were directed against the notorious Sir James Keating, prior of Kilmainham, and his predecessor Sir Thomas Talbot, who were accused of alienating and squandering the possessions of the Order of St. John of Jerusalem in Ireland. Sir James was a leading supporter of Kildare. He became Grand Prior in 1461, and was a scandalous character who could not however be expelled till Poynings' parliament dealt with him. He died in obscurity, and an Act of this parliament directed that all subsequent priors should be English-born.

[2] But this Act again was explained and revised in an 'Act for the election of the Lord Justice' in a parliament of 1497 (see *Cal. Ormond Deeds*, III, pp. 276–7). By this, on a sudden vacancy, the Chancellor or Keeper of the Great Seal shall assemble the King's counsellors dwelling within the shires of Dublin, Meath, Louth, Kildare (and six other counties) and proceed to 'elect such a Governor, etc., to be either English-born or English of blood and surname'.

for the said lands, shall send his licence thereupon, as well in affirmation of the said causes and acts as to summon the said parliament under his Great Seal of England. That done, a parliament shall be holden after the form and effect afore rehearsed—any parliament to be holden hereafter contrary to these forms to be void and of no effect'.

Another Act in the legislative sphere declares that 'all statutes concerning the public weal, made within the realm of England as well in the time of our Lord the King as in the time of his progenitors, Kings of England, be by authority of this present parliament, deemed good and effectual in law and be accepted and used within this land of Ireland'.[1]

Thus was wiped out fifty years of Home Rule and of colonial nationhood, in which 'the mighty men' of Ireland had made Dublin the capital of an Anglo-Irish state. The Act generally quoted afterwards as 'Poynings' Law' rendered it impossible for a native Deputy to make a parliament his creature and to get laws passed at his own discretion or for his own interest, and equally prevented the Irish parliament from offering a native earl, a Yorkist claimant, a Scottish or French king, the Crown of Ireland. If the then King of England could secure a line of English viceroys, then a double authority, beyond Ireland's control, would decide what laws might be passed for Ireland, namely, the King in his Council of Westminster and the Crown-appointed Deputy and Council of Ireland.

But it was not intended that the Parliament of England had power to bind Ireland. The Tudors did not intend to share the throne with Parliament either in England or in Ireland. Holding their imperial crown of God alone, they regarded their Lordship of Ireland as annexed to that imperial crown, but otherwise a sister and equal of the Realm of England. The 'acts concerning the public weal' (such as the Act of Treasons 1352) made in England formerly were extended to Ireland by ratification of the present Irish parliament. But the whole wording implied that any future Act of the English legislature to be effective in Ireland must be ratified here, and that, for purposes of internal law, taxation, and government the Parliament of Ireland was, within the land of Ireland and subject to the royal veto, supreme.

Poynings' work was completed and crowned by Henry VIII when he assumed the Crown of Ireland in 1541, and it is to the

[1] These two Acts are numbered 9 and 39 in the restored original enactments given by Conway (op. cit.) but as 4 and 22 in the published *Statutes at Large (Ireland)* of 1786.

two first Tudors that we owe the Kingdom of Ireland with its full machinery of government as it existed till the Union.

ACTS AGAINST 'COIGN AND LIVERY', ETC.

Other acts strove to recall the 'English of Ireland' to English law, speech, and loyalty. The great war-cries, so often heard in battles of Butlers, Burkes, and Geraldines, such as 'Crom Abu' and 'Butler Abu', were forbidden. No one should take money or amends, according to Brehon law, for the death or murder of his friend or kinsman other than the King's laws allow.

The Statutes of Kilkenny (1366) were re-enacted but, as a commentary on their futility (for by now even the four shires spoke Irish), it was added—'those that will (i.e. command) that every subject ride in a saddle and those that speak of the Irish language alone excepted'. A strong Act was directed against 'coign and livery' as practised by subjects, but the next Act provides for Poynings' army to be quartered and maintained by the people in such time as there is war or invasion of the Pale; this itself was a form of coign and livery and became the usual device for maintaining the State army.

The Pale having dwindled to the nearer parts of counties Meath, Louth, Dublin, and Kildare, in an Act for 'ditches to be made about the English Pale', it was ordered that the inhabitants there, from the Annaliffey to 'the mountain of Kildare', and from the Liffey again to Trim and so to Meath and Louth, should make and build a double ditch of six feet high above ground on the part 'which mereth next unto Irishmen'. The real object was to prevent reivers driving cattle out of the Pale, since cattle could not easily pass over such a stockade at night, when robbers were most abroad.[1] But even this line receded before long.

A political tract of 1515 gives Dundalk, Derver, Ardee, Siddan, Kells, Dangan, Kilcock, Clane, Naas, Kilcullen, Ballymore-Eustace, Rathmore, Rathcoole, Tallaght, and Dalkey as the then frontier towns of the Pale, which actually dwindled even after 1495.[2]

Thus a territory only fifty miles long by thirty broad now represented 'the land of law' and the old 'English land' which in 1366 had embraced at least ten shires. And though it was said

[1] The 'mountain of Kildare' seems to be the highest point in that county, Grange Hill (744 feet). For more about the boundaries of the Pale (in Irish 'The Maghery' or Plain) see first edition of this book, p. 402; also D'Alton, *History of County Dublin* (1838), p. 34; Gilbert's *Cal. Ancient Records of Dublin*, I, p. 33; and Conway, op. cit., pp. 42, 90, 127, 139, 215.

[2] Quoted by Philip Wilson, *Beginnings of Modern Ireland*, p. 43.

to 'mere upon Irishmen', actually, though MacMahons in the north and O'Byrnes in the south menaced it, almost everywhere the 'March English' were the immediate foes of its peace. Most of Kildare's land lay outside it; on the Meath side Nugents, Petits, Berminghams, and others of De Lacy's men were gone Irish; and south of Dublin the hill country but a few miles away was held by Harolds, Walshes, and Archbolds who did not obey the common law, with O'Tooles and O'Byrnes behind them.

Parliament ended, Poynings stayed in Ireland till January 1496, maintaining a small but trained army wherewith to enforce obedience and the homagings of chiefs and, through Hatteclyffe, inquiring into the shrunken finances of the lordship of Ireland, for 'his Grace intends to have a resumption of his whole revenues since the last year of Edward the second's reign'. This inquiry showed that the subsidy which the seventeen baronies of the old earldom of Meath formerly paid, on its two hundred and thirty-six carucates of geldable land (viz. some 33,000 acres of cultivated land) came with a clerical grant to £457 odd, that Dublin county, taxed on a hundred and fifty-four carucates, should pay £454 odd; that Kildare and Louth were the only two other counties which would meet the demands of the State; and that the total parliamentary subsidy on the laity and clergy of the Pale reached at best only £1,293 13*s.* 4*d.*[1]

A shameful feature for royal pride were the small but galling fees or black-rents paid to Irish chiefs out of the State exchequer or by the 'innocent and true English subjects'[2]

THE END OF WARBECK

In July 1495 Warbeck landed at Cork and with eleven ships besieged Waterford while Maurice of Desmond blockaded it by land. From July 23rd to August 4th the *urbs intacta* held out, till Poynings arrived from Dublin, when Warbeck threw up the game and sailed for Scotland where James gave him his own cousin, Lady Catherine Gordon, to wife.

Meanwhile King Henry found that only Kildare could govern

[1] Gilbert's *Viceroys*, app., p. 610, gives the accounts of Poynings' force, commanded by Captain Garth, for which Poynings' parliament voted a benevolence of £454.

[2] Among the customary black-rents paid by the rural colonists or towns to Irish chiefs at this time we find Lecale paying to the Clandeboy O'Neill £20 per annum, county Louth to O'Neill of Tyrone £40; Meath and Kildare to O'Connor Faly £80; Kilkenny and Tipperary to O'Carroll £40; county Limerick to O'Brien £40; while MacMurrough got £53 from the Exchequer and £40 from county Wexford (see Davies, *Discovery*). For fees paid by Poynings to MacMurrough see Conway, op. cit., pp. 96, 173, 178. He received £26 13*s.* 4*d.* in 1495 and in 1496 £53 6*s.* 8*d.*

Ireland. The Earl's attainder was annulled and he was released from the Tower and restored to the Deputyship on August 6th 1496. Further, as his first wife had lately died, Henry gave in marriage to the Earl, as a great compliment and bond of loyalty, an English wife, his own cousin Elizabeth St. John.

On August 26th 1496 a general pardon was issued to Warbeck's supporters, from Kildare and Desmond down, and so with a contemptuous tolerance ('they will crown apes next') Henry perforce took into grace and restored to power that Irish noblesse which still hoped to see the true House of England restored.[1]

Again in July 1497 Warbeck with his wife and infant children arrived at Cork, but the troubled waters would stir no more, and embarking for England his enterprise came there to a miserable end. Surrendering to the royal grace, he was at last, in November 1499, executed at Tyburn with John Waters and, five days later, the unfortunate Edward of Warwick was beheaded, 'the winding ivy slaying the true vine of royalty'. Yorkist hopes in Ireland had henceforth to feed on other sprigs of the Plantagenet blood.

A NEW AGE

But the time for 'great chieftains of lineage' was nearly over and Garret More had to perceive that a new age was come. Even in Scotland the Crown dared to lop off the noblest heads, and in 1499 the annals of Ulster record with horror the deed that was done by the King of Scots, 'namely, John More MacDonnell, king of the Hebrides, and John Cathanach his son and two other sons, were hanged on one gallows a month before Lammas'. If the weak James of Scotland could thus ignominiously extinguish the MacDonnell 'kings of Innsi Gall', the Lords of the Isles, whose blood and title went back four centuries to the great Somerled, there could be no doubt that a King of England could, if bent upon it, overthrow a Percy in Northumbria, a Kildare in Leinster, or an O'Neill in Ulster.

Poynings, however, had only touched the fringe of that Norman-Gaelic Ireland which it took the Tudor monarchy a whole century to reduce to English law and obedience. Till the revolt of Silken

[1] For their names see *Lib. Mun.*, I, pt. IV, p. 101: *perdonatio pro hibernicis.* The famous and picturesque story of King Henry's interview with Kildare, released from the Tower, in which the Bishop of Meath, attacking Garret More, said 'all Ireland cannot rule yonder gentleman', and the King, who had a pretty dry wit, replied, 'Then he is meet to rule all Ireland, seeing that all Ireland cannot rule him', comes from the *Book of Howth.* In the same interview Garret, when charged with burning the cathedral of Cashel, answered, 'I would never have done it had I not been told that the archbishop was within', and this in the presence of the archbishop himself.

Thomas in 1534 nothing essentially was changed: then Leinster fell to the Crown; but till 1576 Munster, till 1585 Connacht, till 1603 Ulster, were in governance, law, speech practically feudal-Gaelic as in 1494. What had been gained was the bridling of the Irish parliament, the ending of the Yorkist danger, a lightening of the aristocratic yoke, and the encouragement of that long-stifled voice of the 'true English commons' who looked to the Crown against Irish enemies and English rebels.

Actually Poynings' Acts aided Kildare rather than otherwise, an unexpected effect, for while formerly he had played the role of a rebel or semi-rebel at the head of a sovereign Parliament which might have gone too far for him, he was now left master of Ireland with King Henry's full approval, commanding the whole revenues such as they were, while a bridled parliament, fully at his control under Poynings' Law, left him free to pursue his private designs.

KILDARE'S LATER PERIOD

And so for the seventeen years that remained to him Garret More, in a new but thorough fashion, continued to dominate both English and Irish. With subtle skill he kept Butlers and Geraldines at peace, and backed Piers Roe against Sir James Dubh till Piers slew this able but unsupported adventurer in an encounter between Dunmore and Kilkenny on July 17th 1497.

Garret's hostings into Desmond, Connacht, and Ulster year after year were constant and imposing. But they led to no great piece of statecraft, such as the submission of the greater Irish chiefs to English law or the repeal of the Kilkenny anti-Irish statutes.[1] Kildare was indeed what the Irish thought a true Rí and the 'Old English' a great lord, splendid, imposing, and affluent, ever visible in hall to his subjects and in the field to his enemies, a patron, too, of those bards and shanachies whom both Irish and English now delighted to honour. Doubtless he still secretly hoped for a Yorkist triumph which would have been all to the

[1] It might have been expected of Henry VII, who was a real statesman, that he would have seized the occasion of his new monarchy to emancipate the Irish and get the Kilkenny statutes repealed. He did not do so, however, and they remained on the statute book till James I. But he did empower commissioners 'to admit to the King's grace all such of the natives of Ireland as be willing to submit themselves'. By particular grant Henry in 1488 emancipated Florence MacCarthy and Cormac MacTaig (MacCarthy), granting them and their issue freedom 'from the state of Irish servitude, and extending to them the laws and privileges of Englishmen.' In 1489 he sent to these two MacCarthys a gift of scarlet cloth. (Campbell, *Materials for the Reign of Henry VII*, II, pp. 309, 496.) A copy of the charter of emancipation to this Cormac MacTaig, lord of Muskerry, is given also in *Cal. Ormond Deeds*, III, pp. 263–5.

interest of Ireland as he knew it and himself. Further he hardly dared to go, and the Yorkist hope grew thin.

In the north a fine clan-battle was fought at Glasdrummond near Dungannon on June 28th 1493, where Donal, the reigning O'Neill, was defeated, and Raghnall MacDonnell, constable of gallowglasses, with his three sons and five others of his name, Scots who well earned their pay, were slain. Henry, his brother, held the kingdom till on July 21st 1498 he fell in a fight with Turloch and Conn, sons of Conn More and nephews of the Earl of Kildare. On Henry's death, Donal was reinstated by Garret More, who joined with Aedh Rua O'Donnell, the sons of Conn More, 'and very many of the Gaels of the south', and at the end of October took the castle of Dungannon from Henry's men with a new weapon, those great guns, which were finally to prove the ruin alike of Norman and Gaelic chiefs.[1]

THE O'DONNELLS

The year 1497 was a remarkable one for the royal race of Tyrconnell and shows how, save for an occasional contact, the Gaelic world of north and south revolved in its own orbit with little thought or fear of the Government at Dublin or at Westminster. Aedh Rua had in 1480 made Egnechan son of Nechtan his Tanist in order to meet his succession-claim. But this was resented by his own sons, and the eldest of these, Conn, in March 1497, slew Egnechan in battle. Aedh Rua resented this and resigned the chieftainship, whereupon Conn was made the O'Donnell. But in September the same year Conn, invading Connacht against Taig MacDermot of Moylurg, suffered a great defeat and 'the *Cathach* of Colmcille was wrested from them and its steward slain'.[2] Then in October Henry Oge, the O'Neill, invaded Tyrconnell and Conn was slain in battle and over eight-score with him. In this time of defeat and dismay, the aged Aedh Rua emerged from retirement, resumed the chieftainship,

[1] Big guns were used first in Ireland at the siege of Waterford in 1495 by Poynings, with impressive effect as we may conjecture. In this siege of Dungannon, Kildare was using 'the King's ordnance' for what could hardly be called the King's business; it was often charged against him and his son Garret Oge after him.

[2] The *Cathach* (the Battler) was the most precious and ancient relic of the O'Donnells; so called because it was carried into battle to secure victory for them, and borne thrice round the host by a priest MacRabhartaigh, who was the hereditary custodian. It is a silver case within which, in a wooden box, was a copy of the Psalter, supposed to have been written by Columba himself, who was of the race of the northern Ui Néill from whom the O'Donnells descended and was their patron saint (see Murphy, *Life of Red Hugh O'Donnell*, p. clvii). It is now in the National Museum, Dublin.

and redeemed the honour of Tyrconnell against O'Neills and all others. Two years later (1499) he accompanied Garret More in a great hosting (*sluaigead mór*) into Connacht, in which the Earl with his guns took four castles, Athleague, Tulsk, Roscommon, and Castlereagh. Taig MacDermot having died and his brother Cormac succeeding him, O'Donnell forced this inferior chief to submit and to restore the *Cathach*, a relic which the O'Donnells valued more than any mere victory.

During these years, King Henry left Kildare almost a free hand. In 1503 Garret was summoned to London whither he sailed on April 30th, and returned in the autumn with great honour. In February next year his son Gerald or Garret Oge was appointed Treasurer of Ireland.

His landed possessions steadily grew, and it must have been no small concern to the official mind in England, anti-noble as it was, to hear how three single earldoms now owned most of southern Ireland. On the death of his father-in-law Roland FitzEustace, Lord Portlester, in 1496, Garret acquired the manors of Ardglass and Strangford in county Down, and the valuable fishing port at the former remained long a Geraldine property.

THE BATTLE OF KNOCKTOE

The activities of the Earl and the confederacy-wars of the Irish and Norman chiefs culminated at last in the most spectacular battle that had been fought in Ireland since Strongbow. Ulick the Clanrickard Burke, who was married to Kildare's daughter, Eustasia, had ill-treated her, he had taken three castles from Melaghlin O'Kelly of Hy Many, who went to Garret to complain; he had also occupied Galway town; and anyway he was the lifelong foe of O'Donnell, Kildare's ally and friend. Therefore in 1504 both sides mustered for a fight which brought in half of Ireland under one banner or the other. The Earl was backed by Aedh Rua O'Donnell, O'Connor Roe, MacDermot, Art, son of Aedh O'Neill, O'Reilly, O'Kelly, the Mayo Burke, most of the lords of the Pale, and O'Connor Faly. To Clanrickard rallied Turloch, son of Taig O'Brien, and the septs of Thomond, O'Carroll, and O'Kennedy of Ormond. The two armies met at Cnoc Tuagh, now Knocktoe, eight miles east of Galway on August 19th 1504, and never since the Conquest had Irish armies presented so formidable an array or fought so desperately. The gallowglasses who were now the core of Irish armies bore the whole brunt: of Clanrickard's nine battalions of these fighting men only one thin battalion escaped alive, and the battle went completely against

Clanrickard and his allies of the south and west. According to the *Book of Howth*, the old hatred for Irish divided even the victors, and Lord Gormanston said to Earl Garret after the slaughter: 'We have for the most part killed our enemies, and if we do the like with the Irishmen that are with us, it were a good deed.'[1] Returning in triumph to Dublin with his son, who had fought very bravely if rashly, Garret dispatched the archbishop of Dublin to give the King an account of the battle. Henry no doubt smiled dryly over this remote Irish victory, but rewarded the Earl by making him a Knight of the Garter.

Stirring as a battle though it is, Knocktoe was only the grand explosion of feuds which had gone on for half a century among the western lords. It was in the eyes of the Gaelic annalists a war of province against province such as earlier history had often recorded, a triumph of Lagenia and Ultonia over the Connachtmen and the Momonians. To Kildare in his more English mind it was the crushing of a great rival, who was a rebel rather against the Geraldine hegemony than against the English king. It is certain that with the prestige of his name and with such forces as he mustered against his fellow English and Irish at Knocktoe, Garret More could have swept England's petty forces out of Ireland and made himself a King. But he was not of the Bruces and the nation-makers of history. To be actual Lord of Ireland, while a Henry had the name, was enough for this subtle and self-ambitious man, and the 'Old English' of whom he was the archetype preferred their 'middle nation' autonomy under an absentee monarchy to all that independence could offer.

In July 1505 died Aedh Rua O'Donnell after a reign of forty-four years and in his seventy-eighth year. He is described as 'lord of Connacht from the mountain down (i.e. from Boyle northwards to the Erne), and the rent of Inishowen and the "Bonnacht" of Cinel Moen were due to him'. The O'Donnell kingship over Tyrconnell, Sligo, and Fermanagh, which lasted all through the next century (the last old Gaelic kingship to survive), and its equality with Tyrone was undoubtedly the work of this man. His son, Aedh Oge, was proclaimed O'Donnell after him at Kilmacrenan in August 1505. This young Hugh was even more of a modern man than his father, a steady ally of the Great Earl and even a Yorkist, active in the conspiracies of Garret's later years. This new type of 'Irish lord' went on pilgrimage to Rome in 1510, and received great favours from the Pope, and visited

[1] See *Ann. Ult.*, *A.F.M.* (1504), and *Book of Howth*. If as is generally stated a 'battle' of gallowglasses was 200, then the core of Clanrickard's army consisted of 1800 *gall-óglaich*.

Henry VIII's court, for he spent four months in London in going and four in returning from Rome, and was knighted by Henry in February 1511. The Ulster annals record impressively that he was able, 'in the midst of his age and power, in despite of every one', to leave Tyrconnell for a year and a half.[1]

THE GREAT EARL'S LATTER YEARS

Kildare had some nine years yet of life and fame after Knocktoe. The accession of Henry VIII in April 1509 made no difference to the real king of Ireland, for the young Henry was too full of exuberant youth and a desire to shine in tourney and war with the princes of Europe to care who ruled Ireland.

The Great Earl's latter years were filled with marches into Munster, Connacht, and the midlands, succouring his allies and enforcing a rough justice among English and Irish. In 1510, along with Aedh Oge O'Donnell and the English and Gaels of the Pale, he made a hosting into Munster and took the castle of Pailis upon MacCarthy More. There he was joined by Maurice, Earl of Desmond, and MacCarthy Reagh and 'the English of Munster'. The united host marched against Turloch, son of Taig, king of Thomond, and his supporters, but, after plundering his country, they were worsted by O'Brien at Móin na mBrathar in county Limerick. Here, says Ware in his annals, 'there was a sore fight with great loss to either side, but on the Earl's side the greater loss, his army being laden with spoils and spent with long marchings. Night ended the battle. The next day the Deputy by the advice of his officers (the armies keeping their ranks) withdrew and without any other loss returned home.' O'Donnell distinguished himself by his cool leadership, bringing off the rear of the Earl's army.[2]

Móin na mBrathar thus failed to be another Knocktoe for the Great Earl. But the vast armies he could raise, reminiscent of the hostings of the High kings of the times before the Normans, while they attest his dominance among Gael and Gall, make one wonder again that with such support he did not end the feeble hold that England then had upon Ireland, and not waste it in the mutual and profitless slaughter of Irish and English, who by now were becoming a race of one blood.

This perhaps is attributing and antedating modern nationalistic ideas to Garret More, such as Irish leaders knew nothing of till

[1] *Ann. Ult.*, and *A.F.M.* (1510–11). Hall's *Chronicle* states that 'a great man or lord of Ireland called O'Donnell' was knighted by Henry VIII on February 13th 1511 (see Ellis, *Letters*, op. cit., 1st Series, I, p. 186).

[2] *Ann. Ult.* (1510) and Ware's *Annals*.

Hugh O'Neill. The Great Earl was rather a fifteenth-century man, a splendid nobleman, a warrior rather than a great general, with few ideas of statecraft or Machiavellian politics, and with his energies bent upon personal 'wars of magnificence' rather than solid achievements. As such, Garret More was a great success and must have thought his days well spent. As actual ruler of Ireland, an aristocratic Yorkist 'Lord of Ireland' would have suited him and the Irish nobles best. As it was, he squared the official unromantic Tudor monarchy and kept Ireland in the old mould. Henry on the other hand, with many cares on hand, had a right to be grateful to one who kept Ireland quiet as far as he was concerned and did not openly reject the English overlordship.

THE BUTLERS

Sir Piers Roe Butler was Anglo-Ireland's greatest man after Garret More. By 1505 he had won back the friendship and favour of Thomas, Earl of Ormond, and was acknowledged by him as deputy and protector of the Butler interests in Ireland, seneschal of the liberty of Tipperary, and governor of the Earl's lordships in Kilkenny and Tipperary. In fact, if not in title, Piers was the dominant personality in south-east Ireland.

On the death of Earl Thomas of the senior line without sons in 1515, Piers might well expect the earldom and he openly took the title, but it was not till 1528 that the reluctant Henry VIII admitted him as Earl of Ossory and in 1537 as Earl of Ormond also. For the claims of Earl Thomas had passed to the heirs of his daughter Margaret, who married Sir William Boleyn.

The feud of the Butlers and Geraldines ('the Guelphs and Ghibellines of Ireland') was kept low in the time of the Great Earl, whose daughter was wedded to Piers Roe; and, moreover, the power and authority of the Kildare in his double aspect of Deputy and hero of Anglo-Ireland was too great for any single man to traverse. It was in the time of the next Earl of Kildare, Garret Oge, and his son Silken Thomas, that Piers saw, and was a prime mover in, the overthrow of the rival house, assisted by the Boleyn house which Henry VIII favoured. The Great Earl and his son played on a dangerous string, that of Yorkist-England and pro-Ireland, the Butlers on a safe one, Tudor-loyal and pro-English.[1]

After many hostings, Garret More found his death on campaign and in a petty fight with the O'Mores of Leix, and died of his wounds on September 3rd 1513. By a strange coincidence, he

[1] For Sir Piers and above references, see *Cal. Ormond Deeds*, III, pp. 309–10, 312, 321, and IV, preface *et passim*.

owed his death while still only fifty-four to a shot from one of those muskets which he had introduced into Ireland.

It was a great and critical moment in the history of the Three Kingdoms, and once again England's luck prevailed. James IV of Scotland had planned to attack Henry VIII through Ireland. O'Donnell had been at his court and, could Garret More have kept the field, it is possible that Ireland might have had a Scottish sovereign again as in 1315, or a Yorkist king. But, just as James decided to invade England, the greatest man in Ireland died. On September 9th the King of Scots with all his chivalry was slain at Flodden, and Kildare's ally, Aedh O'Donnell, could only write to Henry from his manor of Donegal, and explain that he had had no sinister designs in visiting the Scottish king.[1] It was the last wave of the Yorkist sentiment of Ireland; nevertheless, as long as Richard de la Pole lived, this sentiment was never dead.

The vast estates and lordships, the lands in demesne and domain, the castles, especially the noble pile at Maynooth, the rents and rights over burgesses and English tenants, and the 'duties upon Irishmen' as far afield as Hy Many, which the Earl had inherited or acquired and handed down to his son, are abundantly detailed in the Fitzgerald rentals.[2] The civilization attested by his and his son's library at Maynooth of English and French books, with the furniture, plate, and splendid garments which became the spoil of the victors after Maynooth was taken by Skeffington in 1535, has often been described in print.[3]

Garret More, whose family inherited and retained his popularity in the Pale and among the Irish till their overthrow and long afterwards, so much so as to displace the Yorkist house in their affections, was not only 'the Chief' in Ireland, our first 'Uncrowned King', but the Irishman most known abroad, who renewed with Florence the correspondence which the Signory had begun with James, Earl of Desmond, long before.[4]

The Anglo-Irish chronicler, Stanyhurst, who wrote while his memory was still green, wrote his epitaph thus: 'A warrior incomparable, a man hardly able to rule himself when moved to anger,

[1] Ellis, *Letters*, op. cit., pp. 224–5. Under 1513 *Ann. Ult.* say: 'O'Donnell went with a small force to Scotland at invitation by letters of the King . . . and after spending a quarter of the year there with the King, and having changed the King's intent to go to Ireland, he came home safe to his own house.'

[2] 'Rentals of the Earls of Kildare', in *Kilkenny Arch. Soc. Journal* (1858–9 and 1862–3), ed. H. F. Hore; also calendared in *Hist. MSS. Comm.*, 9th *Report*, pt. II, xxxvii (1883).

[3] For example, in Donough Bryan's *Great Earl*, op. cit., pp. 268–74.

[4] Ibid., pp. 252–3.

yet not so sharp as short, being easily displeased and sooner appeased, a good Justicier, but towards the nobles that he fancied not somewhat headlong and unruly.'

Such were the personal characteristics that made Garret More the hero of the mixed race, who combined their virtues and defects in such measure as to make him the unchallenged leader of Ireland for his whole lifetime.

CONCLUSION

IRELAND IN 1170 AND IN 1500

THE death of 'The Great Earl of Kildare' does not end a period but rather falls in its heyday, for the Geraldine 'all-but-kingship' of Ireland was to last over twenty years after him. Dividing lines are notoriously hard to draw in history. This is particularly so in Irish history, and in fact the fall of the house of Kildare in 1534 was only a prelude to the Reconquest of Ireland which it took the whole Tudor age to accomplish. The ruin of the house of Desmond had to be brought about in 1583, and that of the house of O'Neill in 1603, before the Conquest of Ireland, feudal and chiefly, Gaelic and 'Old English', was finally achieved.

THE TUDOR RECONQUEST

The sixteenth century, on which we have only entered, thus put a forced end to the Ireland of which our pages have described the building up. Had religion not entered into the question, and if Henry VIII had not made the great breach with the Papacy, which, after an interim, his daughter Elizabeth made permanent, Irish history would have taken a very different direction. But it might have been a direction fatal to the old Gaelic and pre-Norman ethos of Ireland, which has been the emotional and ancestral force behind the creation of modern Irish nationalism. 'The blood of the First Conquest has in a manner failed', was the official Tudor comment upon our country as official eyes surveyed her then. The remedy was a new English conquest, at first by power and persuasion, then by force, very far from acceptable to the Irish, the Norman-Irish landed class, and the originally English townsmen who were by then becoming a blended people.

The new Conquest took from 1534 to 1690 to accomplish. Curiously enough the greatest, though not perhaps the most manly opponents of it (for the Gaels, especially the Ulster ones, made the best fight), were the 'English by blood' of the First Conquest. English in a sense though they were when they came over with Strongbow, they were racially and in speech French and in no sense Anglo-saxon. The development of the mixed Anglo-French nation of England which took place in the thirteenth and fourteenth centuries did not touch or include them. To put it briefly, they did not accept the English legend, and, while the epigram 'more Irish than the Irish' is an obvious exaggeration as applied to them, they did in essentials feel, and in many cases completely accept, the 'Irish legend', the ancestral tradition formed long before them, which got into their blood after five centuries of native living in Ireland.

Nevertheless had the Tudor monarchy remained Catholic of the papal allegiance, it seems fair to affirm that the 'Old English' of Ireland, proud of their Conquest descent and for the most part inclined to be loyal, would have willingly joined the Government forces in completing that final Conquest of Ireland which their ancestors of the thirteenth century failed to accomplish. Old charters of Butlers, Geraldines, and the like would have been produced, and the Gaelic proprietors of old nominal Norman lands would have been ousted. The State and 'the loyal lieges' would have co-operated against the 'Old Irish', who even at their most submissive had never been complete 'liege subjects' under the common law, but only vassals, ready to render homage provided their Gaelic lordships were left to them.

But, as it happened, the 'Second Conquest' had to be a Protestant as well as a modern-English one, for Elizabeth and James decided that the 'Old English' Catholics of Ireland could not be trusted or tolerated. Thus the Reconquest of the sixteenth century had to be achieved at the expense of both the 'Gael and the Gall' of earlier times, and in the end the descendants of the English conquerors or immigrants of the period 1170–1250 have become as completely members of the new Irish nation of to-day as the 'Old Irish' themselves.

Our story therefore might well be prolonged into 1534–7, when the Kildare supremacy and the Home Rule period which began in 1460 ended in the rising of Silken Thomas, son of Garret Oge, Earl of Kildare. When—after the surrender of this unfortunate young man, enticed into rebellion by *agents provocateurs* of the pro-English faction in the Council and the hereditary enemy, Piers Roe, Earl of Ossory—he and five uncles of his were hung like common criminals at Tyburn, the tardy, but in the long run inevitable, Tudor reconquest began, and the Anglo-Irish nation of which we have shown the growth and self-assertion was effaced by a monarchy which would tolerate no opposition and had no sympathy with, or wish to understand, Irish or Anglo-Irish national distinctiveness. Had a Yorkist monarchy, aristocratic, tolerant, medieval-minded, Catholic, of perceptible Irish blood and connexion, persisted, things would have been very different. But that is as much as to say that the Middle Ages should have persisted;

and at least in these islands a new centralized and bureaucratic monarchy began in 1485 which finally by 1603 had subdued and embraced the whole British Isles.

We must therefore leave the story of later events to others and attempt a picture of Ireland *circa* 1500 in contrast of the picture presented in our opening pages.[1]

THE IRELAND OF 1170 AND OF 1500

The Ireland which Strongbow entered in 1170, though in many ways isolated from Europe, had already felt the pressure of those great forces which were remaking twelfth-century Europe—the reform in the Church, the development of State monarchy, and less calculable changes in the field of art and thought. Then suddenly broke in the Cambro-Normans, and next, in the breach made by their swords, entered the Angevin empire of England. Henceforth for good or evil there was a new Ireland, and though the Celtic revival in some ways restored the old order, its real day was over, and by 1500 the Gaelic princes themselves ceased to look back to the monarchy of Tara.

THE RENAISSANCE IN IRELAND

For into the Ireland of 1500 were already entering the forces of the new, the Renaissance, Europe. In the brief spell of 1450 to 1530, when Ireland was ruled by a native aristocracy, she progressed in art and literature, in the amenities and luxuries of life.

We have shown what a flaw in the Anglo-Irish state was the absence of a university. Yet it seemed as if the great lords of this time meant to put the land of Ireland on an honourable level with other lands. The project of a *studium generale* for the colony at Drogheda, broached at Desmond's parliament of 1465, unhappily came to nothing. But even Bykenore's foundation of a university at Dublin in 1320, though it had a transitory and vague existence, did in a sense continue to exist, and might well have anticipated Elizabeth's university. Archbishop Alen's *Register* records that at a provincial synod held at Christchurch cathedral in 1494 under Archbishop Walter Fitzsimons, certain sums were voted by the suffragan sees of Dublin for the support of lectures in the university for a term of seven years, the total annually from five sees being

[1] See Bagwell, *Ireland under the Tudors*, vol. I; Philip Wilson, *Beginnings of Modern Ireland*; but the early Tudor period in Ireland undoubtedly awaits far more scholarly investigations from every aspect than it has yet (1938) received.

some £27, a trifling endowment certainly, but which must have kept a certain life in the *domus scholarum* of the capital.[1]

It was the great earls who were now the head and hope of Irish culture. Garret More aspired to found a collegiate church as notable as that of his cousin Desmond at Youghal. Before his death he assigned certain lands to endow a college at Maynooth, and in 1515, at Garret Oge's request, Henry VIII granted leave to found a 'perpetual college' consisting of six chaplains, of whom one was to be master, and two clerks to celebrate masses for the souls of the founder and his ancestors; the eight to form a college of the Blessed Virgin, and to be a corporate body for ever. The archbishop of Dublin confirmed the foundation, and Earl Garret Oge built a beautiful chapel and endowed the college which flourished for some twenty years, but was dissolved and surrendered to the Crown in 1541.

To these foundations we may add Kilkenny school, founded by Sir Piers Roe Butler, Earl of Ormond, early in this century; a school which had a famous history and produced many famous men.[2]

Anglo-French civilization, which died out in so much of the colony, continued to flourish around Kilkenny, the capital of the Ormond earls. It is probable that from early times the Butlers spoke Irish, and the 3rd Earl was interpreter for Irish kings in 1395. But they were the most English of the 'First Families'. Piers Roe, though his grandsire Edmund MacRichard was an enthusiast for Gaelic things and his mother was a princely Kavanagh, loved the English tradition, and with his grammar school at Kilkenny welcomed the Tudor peace as an opportunity to bring in foreign refinements. His Fitzgerald wife, Margaret, the 'great Countess', was the inspirer of this warlike earl. Together they introduced Flemish weavers of carpets and tapestry into Kilkenny; unhappily later troubles did not allow the colony to survive.[3]

The Kildare earls, though more pro-Ireland than the Butlers, and less Gaelic than the Desmonds, showed a generous sympathy

[1] *Reg. Alani* (original in Diocesan Office, Dublin), fol. 105b. The document states that at the said provincial council it was ordained that the 'generalis universitas Dublinie' should be regulated and, for the sustenance and support of lecturers, and in order that lectures might be continued there in certain faculties, it was granted for a term of seven years, that the archbishop, his chapters and clergy should pay annually £10, the bishop of Ossory etc. £5, Ferns £5, Leighlin and Kildare five marks each.

[2] *Facs. Nat. MSS.*, III, plate xviii, and Corcoran, *State Policy in Irish Education*, p. 45.

[3] See *Facs. Nat. MSS.*, III, plates lxxi–lxxiii; Ledwich, *Hist. of Kilkenny*; and Healy, *Hist. of Kilkenny*, I, p. 376 etc. For literary cultivation at Kilkenny see Rev. St. J. Seymour, *Anglo-Irish Literature, 1200–1582*.

for the three cultures of Ireland, and the three spoken languages on which they rested, namely Irish, French, and English. The 9th Earl's library at Maynooth contained 112 parchment books, a very considerable collection for those times, many of which had belonged to Garret More. Of these, 34 were Latin, 36 French, 20 Irish, and 22 English.[1]

LORDSHIP IN IRELAND

We have dealt with the effects of the continued absence of the Crown. One of the greatest of these was the growth on a vast scale of lordship expressed in land-power and man-power. Ravenously did the first conquerors fall upon the vast spoils of Ireland, and since the Crown neither came with a new plantation, nor compelled the absentees to return, nor created new peers to reinforce Anglo-Irish magnates, the result was that by 1500 three families alone, Butlers and two Fitzgeralds, divided between them all Ireland south of the Boyne and Limerick.

Ireland by 1484 had completely fallen into the hands of a warlike noblesse, 'the great of lineage'. England itself showed the same picture. The greater part of England and Wales, on the north and west, was then a medley of palatinates, baronies, and liberties, ruled by feudal and March law.[2]

The reduction of these to common law was the first task of the new monarchy. The reduction of Irish feudalism and chieftainship seemed a similar task, just as essential to law and order. But in Ireland, once the Reformation began, the feudal lords were able to call to their defence national and religious passion, and the suppression of these great liberties became a war against Irish speech, custom, popular feeling, and Catholic sentiment.

THE GAELIC REVIVAL

Another result of the absenteeism of the Crown was the general revival of Irish speech, law, land-tenure, and social order. The Norman-English-Welsh who effected the temporary conquest of two-thirds of the island, few in themselves and never reinforced by fresh colonies, were destined to become a semi-Gaelic aristocracy

[1] O'Grady, *Cat. Irish MSS. in Brit. Mus.*, p. 154. *Facs. Nat. MSS.*, III, plate lxiii.

[2] The warlike armament of Ireland both Norman and Gaelic in the early Tudor period is illustrated in a paper by L. Price in *R.S.A.I.* (1932): 'The Armed Forces of the Irish Chiefs in the Early 16th Century' (from a MS. in the British Museum), in which a contemporary estimate attributes to the Irish chiefs permanent forces of 21,000 in all, viz. 2,460 gallowglasses, 3,345 horse and 15,704 kerns.

ruling over the mass of Gaelic humanity which swamped the Englishry. Inevitably, after the moment passes in the thirteenth century when Ireland might have been made a second England, the dominant English turned Irish as surely as the Franks in the Holy Land turned into Orientals.

But the colonists did not lose all pride in their Englishry. Right up to the fall of the House of Kildare, the 'Old English' prided themselves on a sort of colonial or 'middle nation' patriotism, not unlike the eighteenth-century patriotism of Swift, Grattan, and Flood. They might well have rejected England as Scotland did under the Bruces, but, high as their resentment rose and great as their Home Rule independence grew, they never openly broke with the legal authority at Westminster. But, under cover of an 'Old English' nationalism, the Anglo-Irish developed a great if unpolitical affection for native things. Some of their Gaelic aspects were of necessity. Thus, while everywhere they retained English feudal tenures, rules of land-succession and inheritance, and much manorial jurisdiction and custom, they took over, as something too deeply rooted and indeed too suited to the country to be displaced, the old Gaelic communal organization. The 'betagh' system indeed practically disappeared, even as villeinage did in England, but the old Irish rural economy, the renting of stock and land on short leases, survived, and indeed displaced English innovations.[1]

As with land, so with Brehon law. The Anglo-Irish adopted it, partly of necessity, partly because their subjects had an invincible attachment to it, partly because the profits were so great, and besides, their own origins dated back to a time when feudal, Celtic, and Germanic law had nothing repugnant for one another. Everywhere in the sixteenth century the Tudor officials found the 'degenerate English' using Brehon law. Even Sir Piers Roe had an Irish brehon over his country, one 'Rory MacLaughire'.[2]

That form of patriarchal union which we call for want of a better word the clan system, had by now asserted itself among all the 'Old English', even in the towns and the Pale. Under the circumstances of Ireland it was an inevitable development. Thus in 1543 we find several Burkes, chiefs of five small septs of that name, accepting the arbitration of the Deputy, St. Leger, the Earl of Clanrickard, the archbishop of Tuam, the bishop of

[1] For an outline of this development, see my paper, 'Rental of the Manor of Lisronagh, etc.' in *P.R.I.A.* (1936).

[2] MacLaughire's true name was Ruaidhri Mac Fhlannchadha; see O'Rahilly, 'Irish Poets, etc. in English Official Documents', *P.R.I.A.* (1922). In 1562 it is stated: 'many lords even within the English counties do take *cains* (money-atonements), etc. by Brehon law and keep brehons' (*Cal. Carew MSS.*, I, p. 343).

Clonfert, and a famous brehon, Boethius MacEgan, over a townland in dispute between them and Galway city. The award being duly given was signed at St. Francis' monastery in Galway by the arbitrators, and Boethius signs and agrees in Irish. So, in the deeds and wills of the Blake family of Athenry we find strict entail on the male line, alienation to strangers of family property barred, females excluded from inheritance. This family becomes a clan making laws for itself, and a Latin deed of as late as 1527 says: 'a woman ought not and cannot be heir according to the custom and ordinance of the Blake nation'.[1]

But it was in language above all that the 'Old English' became one with the native people. French died out; and English became limited to the towns, to the southern part of Wexford where Strongbow's colony preserved till the nineteenth century a curious composite speech mainly derived from Somerset and the south-west of England, and to Fingall with the eastern portions of the Pale reaching from Ardee to Dublin. The rulers of Anglo-Ireland, such as the Ormond and Kildare earls and the gentry of the Pale, certainly adopted and spoke English, but in the sixteenth century, among the Burkes and Desmonds, it was an accomplishment to be remarked upon. When Henry VIII appointed Roland de Burgo, grandson of Ulick, Lord Clanrickard, bishop of Clonfert in 1541, Roland could neither understand nor speak English. A little earlier it was reported as something unexpected among the Munster nobility, that Sir John of Desmond, son of Earl Thomas executed at Drogheda, 'could speak very good English', and so could his nephew James, 12th Earl, though his mother was a MacCarthy, and 'wore his hair and cap English fashion'.[2]

The affection of the 'Old English' for the native tongue and culture was scarcely less now than that of the native chiefs themselves. And this affection, which at first had been a necessity, soon became a passion, as the Tudor Reconquest degenerated into a crusade against not only the old-time liberties of Gaelic and Norman lords, but against the language, lore, culture, and faith of most Irishmen. The Irish language then became the symbol of a patriotism which now England's first colonists had no less embraced than the 'Old Irish' themselves.

In 1600 a spy unnamed wrote to Cecil: 'There is great danger to the English Pale from the Irish house at Douay, of which Christopher Cusack is chief. Sixty young gentlemen are here, eldest sons

[1] *Blake Records*, I, Nos. 65, 84, 102–3. MacEgan is described as 'arbiter secularis', which just expresses what the Irish brehon was.

[2] For Roland see *Haliday MSS. in Hist. MSS. Comm.*: 15*th Rep.*, pt. III, p. 226; *Cokayne's Complete Peerage* (ed. Gibbs) under 'Desmond' (report of Captain ap Parry to Cromwell in 1535).

of the principal gentry of the Pale, namely Plunkett, Barnewall, Rochefort, and many merchants' sons of Dublin and Drogheda; they pray for Tyrone and speak all Irish, and it is to be feared that these offspring of the colonies of the English conquest may become in language and disposition fermented with the ancient hatred of Irish to English.'[1]

'Old Irish' and 'Old English' was in the sixteenth century the recognized distinction between the two races of Ireland. The latter were dominant only in the smaller part of the country, in Leinster, Meath, Munster, and in parts of Connacht and Leinster; but these were the richer and more fertile parts of the island. The 'degenerate English' had never been deprived of their legal rights, while the mass of the Irish, living under Brehon law, remained till 1613 excluded from the common law. To be of 'the Blood of the Conquest' was the boast of all who could assert it; a traditional dislike of Irish enemies was maintained, as we find in Lord Gormanston's remark after Knocktoe; and sometimes Anglo-Irishmen by their wills sought to confine the benefits to their own 'English nations'.[2]

Every effort on the part of the State was made, and had long been made, to prevent feudal land passing into Irish hands. But the distinction between the races was fast becoming a distinction without a difference. To Tudor Englishmen there was little to distinguish the once-Norman colonist in speech, dress, and habit from the Gael, and even when he spoke English it was of a kind so isolated and pre-Chaucerian as scarce to be understood.

As for blood, few of the 'Old English' were without a Gaelic strain, and many a Gaelic chief had wedded an earl's daughter or had an Englishwoman for mother. The great chief of Tyrone, Shane O'Neill, is often taken for the typical Irish Celt, yet in fact his grandmother was a Fitzgerald. Certainly the Fitzgeralds of Kildare had always married Anglo-Norman wives, and Silken Thomas had an Anglo-Irish grandmother and a pure English mother. But as for the Geraldines of Desmond, four earls between 1470 and 1540 married Irish, and two had Irish mothers.

GAELIC CHIEFTAINSHIP

So tenacious was the Irish tradition that most of the Gaelic stock still lived in the thoughts of five centuries gone. Till

[1] *State Papers, Domestic* (1598–1601), p. 496.

[2] Alen's *Reg.*, op. cit., fol. 133: will of N. Aleyn, dean of St. Patrick's, Dublin, *circa* 1547—a house to be built for eleven paupers who shall be good Catholics of English descent, and chiefly of the nations of the Barrets, Begges, Hillis, Dyllons and Rodiers.

Elizabeth's reign their chiefs fought battles over quarrels older than the Conquest. In 1543 the Deputy St. Leger and the Council intervened between Conn O'Neill and Manus O'Donnell as to which of them was rightly suzerain of Inishowen, lord of Cinel Moen, and overlord of Maguire, O'Ruairc, and MacMahon; and further whether O'Donnell himself did not owe homage to Tyrone. The viceroy and council contemptuously reported that these claims were based on 'certain parchments and old tracts (*libelli*) composed by vain poets and *ploratores* of Irish history, hired for small reward and blinded by affection for their lords'. But they awarded Inishowen to O'Donnell with a head rent to O'Neill, declared O'Donnell independent, and forbade both to exact tribute, 'bonnacht' or service outside their own territories.[1]

The Gaelic 'king' was still in theory at least an elective patriarchal president. The Irish 'country' was still divided into the lord's demesne land; the lands of the freeholders, such as near kinsmen, brehons, poets, gallowglass chiefs; and 'chargeable land' which provided the lord with tributes, services, and quarters for his fighting forces. Sometimes the demesne was small, as five thousand acres in Maguire's country of Fermanagh; sometimes large, as thirty-seven plowlands out of the ninety-three which made up Ely O'Carroll; or seven and a half quarters (27,000 acres) which O'Sullivan More in 1568 had out of the total of fifteen quarters which made up his country.[2]

For all that, things were moving towards a more modern, feudal, and State chieftain, an hereditary landlord after the European fashion. Thus, when Sir Cormac MacTaig MacCarthy of Muskerry made his will in 1583, he placated both the State and vested clan interests by leaving the lordship to three Tanists in succession, his brother and two nephews, then to his son Cormac Oge and his heirs male, so that Irish Tanistry should then expire.[3]

Far greater, too, than in 1100 was the chief's personal power in men and revenues, in private property, in war strength, in the so-called Irish 'cuttings and cessings', such as we have described touching the 'Old English' lords. Thus while O'Sullivan More in 1586 had half the country for demesne, the rest going in shares to the Tanist, to the next in claim to the Tanist, and then to the nearest of the royal kin, yet he had in his own hands four quarters of private or chiefly land belonging to his lordship of Dunboy.

[1] *Cal. Carew MSS.*, I, p. 204.
[2] See for the best study of this question, W. F. Butler, *Gleanings from Irish History*.
[3] *Cork Arch. Soc.* (1892), p. 193.

GAELIC LITERATURE

Out of such a traditional world and race came that Gaelic literature which, in its imaginative, scholarly expression kept the Gaelic race of 1500 in direct touch with the Ireland of a thousand years before, and enables us to read our history back to the most remote pagan age.

To the modern mind the dry annals tell little of most Irish chiefs to boast of, yet when we read that the *Book of Ballymote* was written for MacDonagh, lord of a great country in Sligo and Roscommon, about 1390, we find that this vellum book of five hundred folios contains among other things the *Leabhar Gabhála* or story of the first pre-Celtic conquests of Ireland, the history of Niall of the Nine Hostages, the *Book of Rights*, a translation into Irish of Nennius' *Historia Brittonum.*

The Irish preoccupation with antiquity may have been a fault in the Gaelic aristocracy, making them incapable of that compromise with the modern world of the Tudors which alone could have saved them. But in literature as in all else, the native race of 1500 was taking the impress of a new, a Renaissance Europe.

Not a single Gaelic chief took his oath of submission to King Richard in 1395 in any other language than Irish. But at the end of the following century, the learned class of the Irish were studying English, French, and Spanish. The *Book of Lismore,* compiled *circa* 1500 for Fineen MacCarthy Reagh, contains a translation of the book of Marco Polo. One Fineen O'Mahony about 1475 translated *Maundeville's Travels* from English, and Irish versions of *Turpin's Chronicle,* the *Adventures of Guy of Warwick,* the *Triumphs of Charlemagne,* etc. show that Ireland had a window towards Europe.

But the type *par excellence* of the new Gaelic lord is found in Manus O'Donnell, son of Aedh Oge. This Manus, who became chief in 1537, was first wedded to Joan, sister of Conn Bacach O'Neill and granddaughter of Thomas, 7th Earl of Kildare. His second wife was Eleanor Fitzgerald, daughter of the great Earl of Kildare. Both Manus's father and grandsire had visited the courts of England, Dublin, Scotland, and Rome, and when the Deputy St. Leger met Manus in 1540 at Cavan, he was greeted, as he records, by an elegant gentleman, magnificently dressed in crimson velvet, whose chaplain was 'a right sober young man, well learned and brought up in France', and who undertook to accept Henry as King of Ireland, asking in return a title worthy of his rank.

But English or annalistic records would not give us the true civilization of a personage such as Manus. For him was compiled in 1532, and he himself did much of the editing, a voluminous *Life of Colmcille*,[1] the patron saint and legended hero of Tyrconnell. Manus was further a charming poet in the native tongue, and of the love verse which has come down to us, four poems of his, one of which is addressed to that 'daughter of the Earl' whom he wedded, are among the most charming.[2]

THE BLENDED RACE

There seemed many reasons therefore why both the English and the Irish of Ireland should be honourably reconciled with one another under that hereditary Lord of Ireland, whose claim both had many a time admitted.

In spite of their adherence to 'the laws of Cormac MacArt', which, wrote the Four Masters in 1616, 'have bound the Irish to this day', it is probable that the chiefs, won over by royal peerages, might have won over their people to accept the kingdom of Ireland. Henry did 'by sober waies, politique drifts, and amiable perswasions' indeed induce them in 1541 to confer on him the Crown of Ireland, 'as united and knit to the Crown of England', and to accept in return the earldoms of Tyrone, Thomond, Clanrickard, the baronies of Upper Ossory and the like, in which they were to rule almost undisturbed. Such was the purpose of numerous 'Surrender and Regrant' treaties by which Irish chiefs and Norman lords were to hold their countries direct from the Crown.

As the Irish had in Henry 'FitzEmpress' accepted a foreign Árd Rí, so in Henry VIII they accepted a King of Ireland who was a foreigner indeed, but also a great-grandson of the beloved Richard of York, in whose veins flowed the blood of Mortimers, De Burgos, Lacys, and O'Briens. To win over the Norman and Celtic lords to that loftier dignity of King which he took instead of the old Rome-given lordship was a master stroke. And had Henry Tudor seized the moment to bring all the Irish into the law, to allow government of the native-born, to care as much for raising the poor as for bribing the rich; had he and his successors dealt tenderly with the language and race-traditions of the people, admitted the papal allegiance as compatible with loyalty, and touched the national pride by a separate coronation and frequent visits of the Crown in person, the Kingdom of Ireland, revived after four centuries, might well have rooted itself in the hearts of the fast-blending people of Ireland.

[1] *Betha Colaim Chille*, published by A. O'Kelleher.
[2] *Dánta gradha*, edited T. F. O'Rahilly (1916).

This, however, was left undone, and in any case Henry's policy was an interim one, based on reluctance to spend money on a real Conquest of Ireland, which his successors discarded in favour of a more complete reduction. It must be admitted that, the Tudor monarchy being what it was and its claims so imperial, the difficulties were great of disarming so warlike a country and reducing so great and privileged a nobility. Had all that been done even by great royal armies and all been reduced by the common master, less resentment and ruin would have followed. The reduction by sporadic exhibitions of force, the encouragement of Elizabethan adventurers to conquer on their own like the Normans before them, the religious oppression, and the harsh measures of confiscation followed by unjust plantations, were, it must be admitted, the worst kind of Reconquest policy that could have been adopted. But they were effective at least in bringing to an end the medieval Ireland that we have traced so far in these pages.

APPENDIX I

PEDIGREES OF CHIEF FAMILIES IN THIS PERIOD

(A) NORMAN LORDS

(B) GAELIC CHIEFS

THE following pedigrees contain only the chief or important names, and the ruling chiefs or heads of families are in capitals. Abbreviations are:

anc. = ancestor.
a quo = from whom descend.
d. = daughter of.
d. = died of natural or other causes.
d. *ante* = died before.
illeg. = illegitimate.
iure uxoris suae = in right of his wife.
K. = King, in case of a Gaelic ruler.
m. = married.
ob. patre vivente = died during father's lifetime.
o.s.p. = *obiit sine prole*, died without children.
succ. = succeeded.
ex. = executed.
cr. = created.
sl. = slain.

A date such as 1230–48 indicates the period of rule.

(A) PEDIGREES OF CHIEF NORMAN LORDS

THE "RACE OF NESTA"

RHYS AP TEWDWR

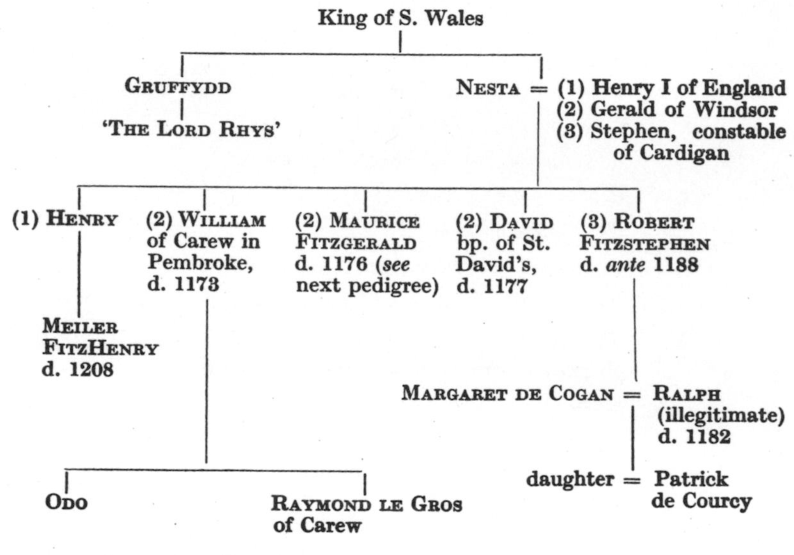

PEDIGREE OF THE FIRST FITZGERALDS

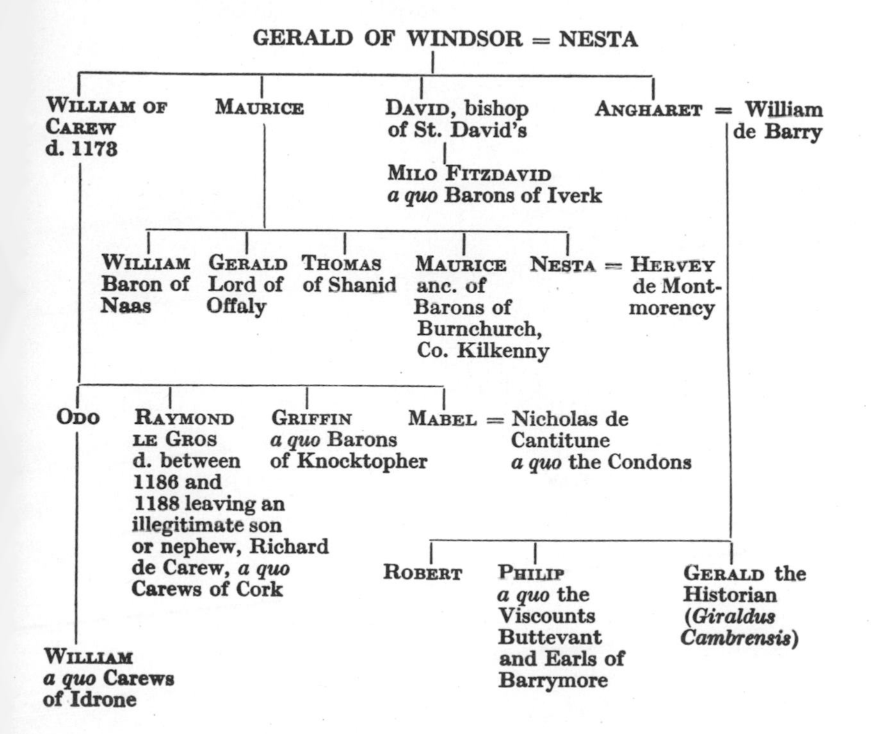

THE FITZGERALD BARONS OF OFFALY

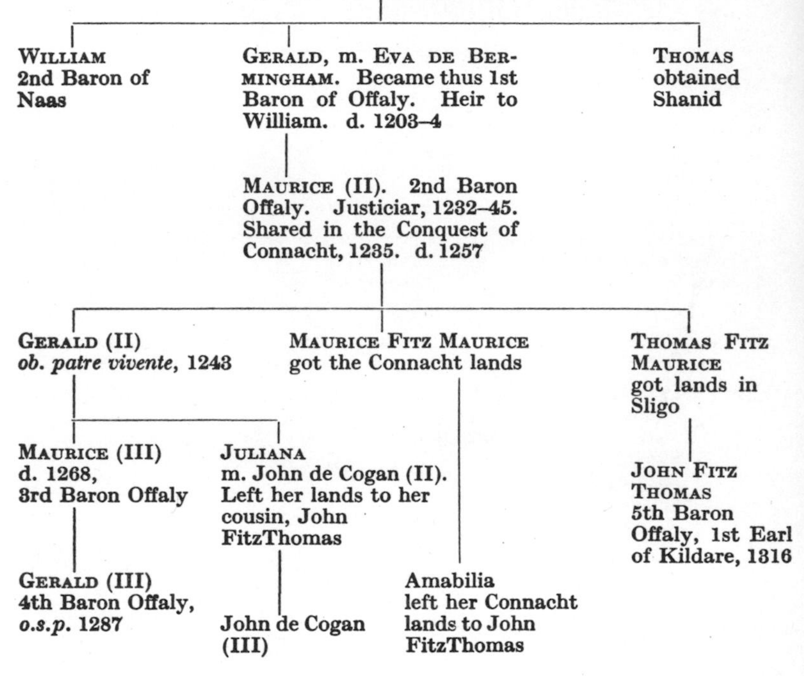

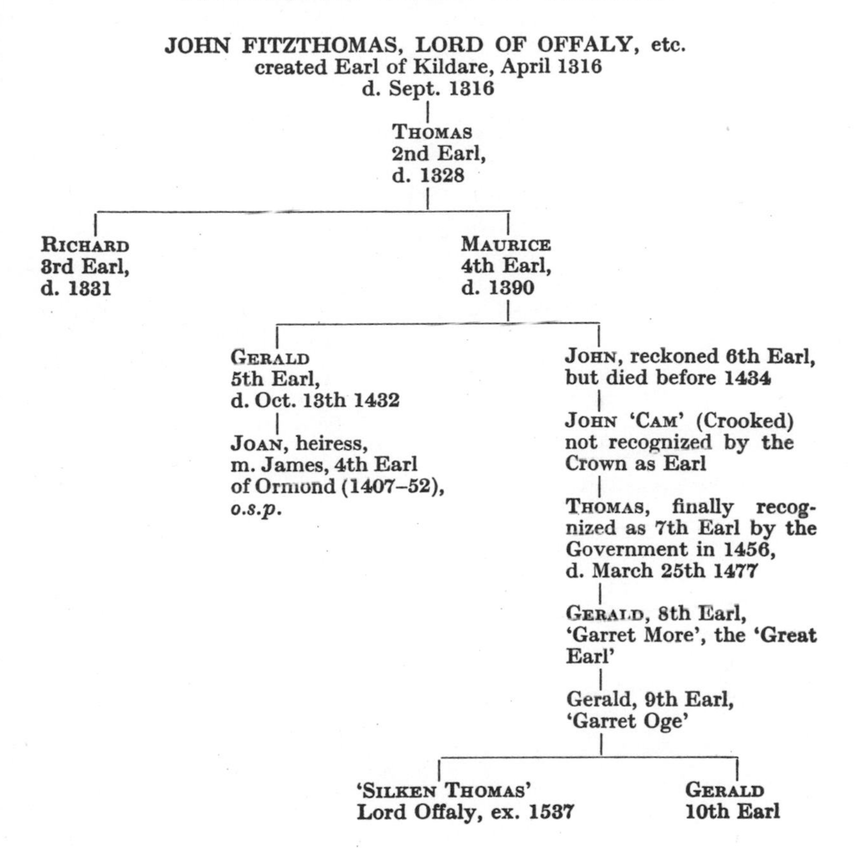
FITZGERALD EARLS OF KILDARE
JOHN FITZTHOMAS, LORD OF OFFALY, etc.
created Earl of Kildare, April 1316
d. Sept. 1316
THOMAS
2nd Earl,
d. 1328
RICHARD
3rd Earl,
d. 1331
MAURICE
4th Earl,
d. 1390
GERALD
5th Earl,
d. Oct. 13th 1432
JOAN, heiress,
m. James, 4th Earl
of Ormond (1407–52),
o.s.p.
JOHN, reckoned 6th Earl,
but died before 1434
JOHN 'CAM' (Crooked)
not recognized by the
Crown as Earl
THOMAS, finally recognized as 7th Earl by the
Government in 1456,
d. March 25th 1477
GERALD, 8th Earl,
'Garret More', the 'Great
Earl'
Gerald, 9th Earl,
'Garret Oge'
'SILKEN THOMAS'
Lord Offaly, ex. 1537
GERALD
10th Earl

THE GERALDINES OF MUNSTER

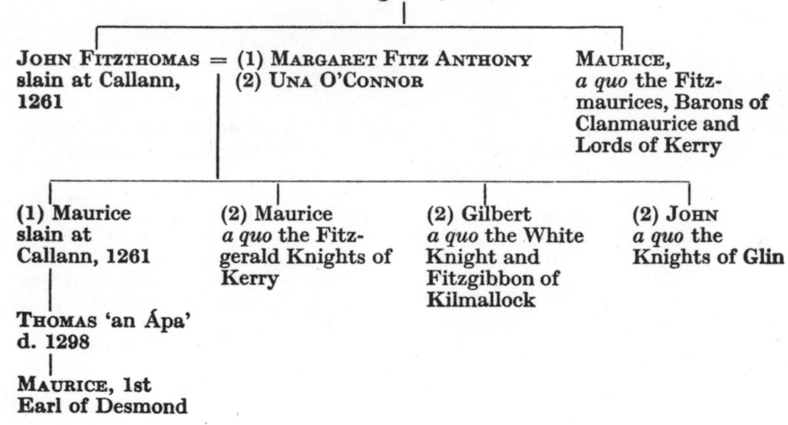

FITZGERALD EARLS OF DESMOND

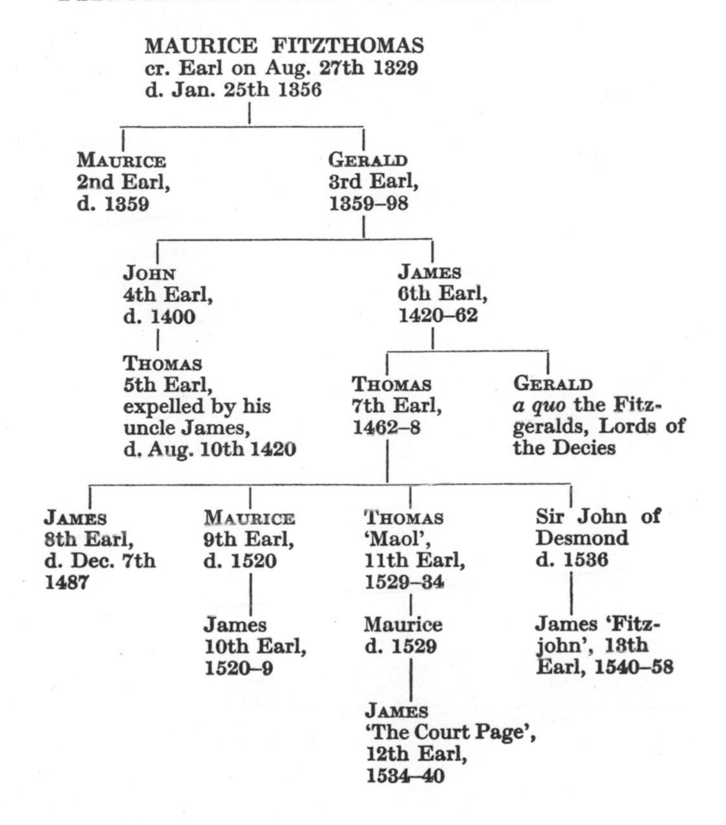

STRONGBOW AND THE MARSHALS

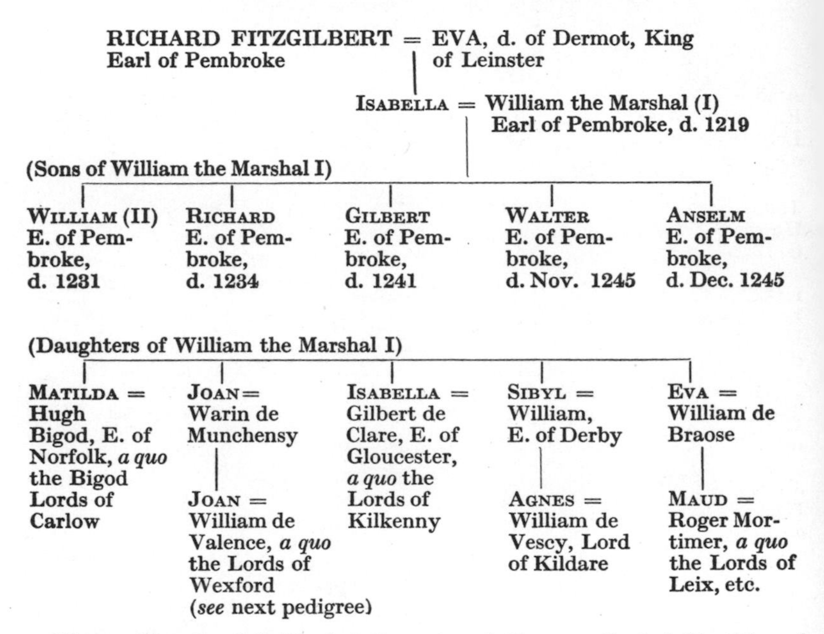

NOTE.—For the full Marshal descent and the complicated 'Partition of Leinster' *see* Orpen, *Normans*, III, pp. 49–75, 94–8.

THE LORDS OF WEXFORD

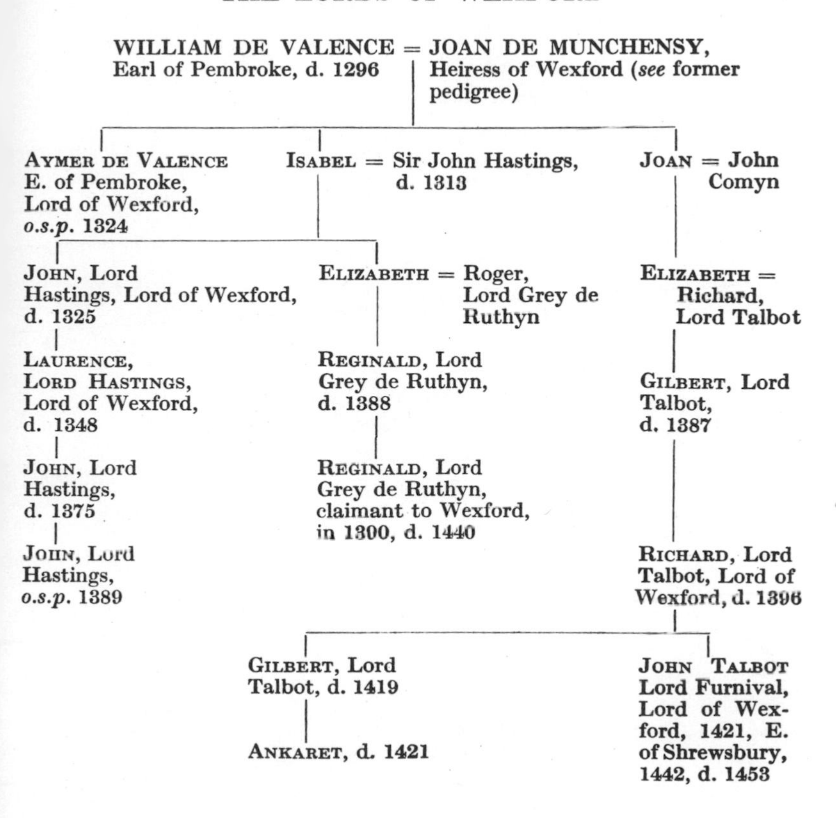

THE DE LACY DESCENT

(For the full pedigree see Orpen, *Normans*, III, Appendix.)

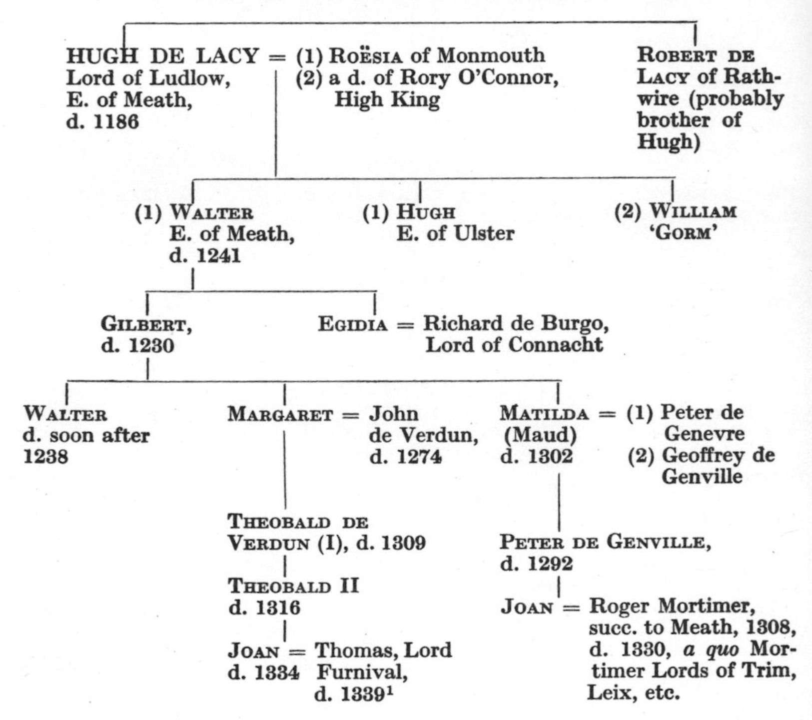

[1] Their granddaughter Joan m. Thomas de Neville, and their daughter Maud Neville m. John Talbot, Lord Furnival, Earl of Shrewsbury.

THE DE BURGO FAMILY

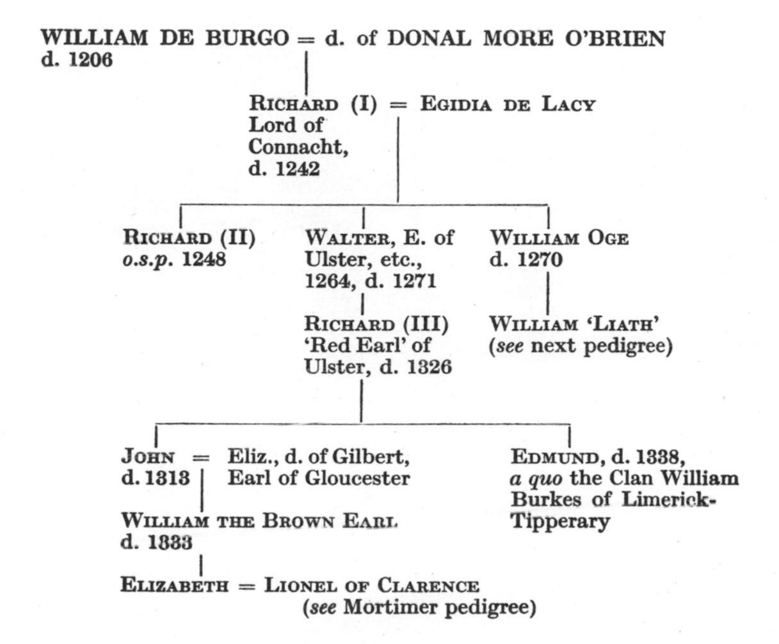

THE MACWILLIAM BURKES OF CLANRICKARD AND MAYO

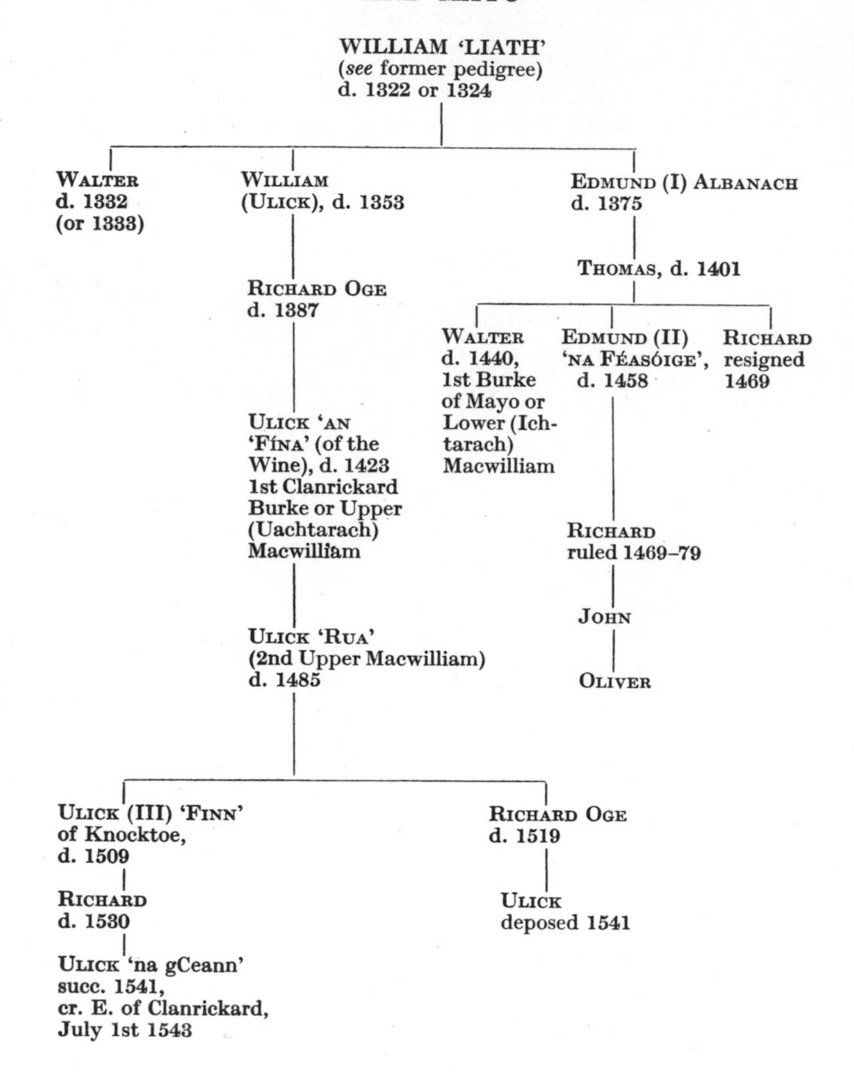

THE BUTLER EARLS OF ORMOND

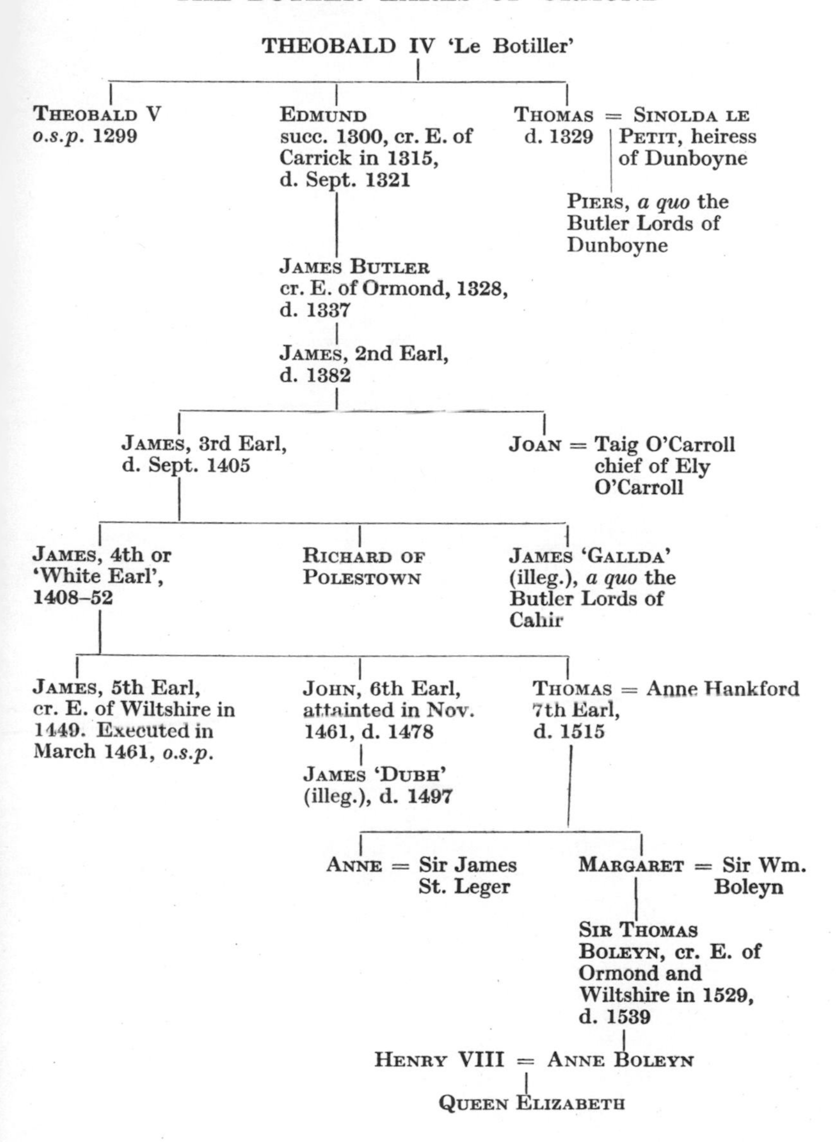

THE POLESTOWN BUTLERS

JAMES, 4th Earl of Ormond

RICHARD OF POLESTOWN (*see* former pedigree)

EDMUND MACRICHARD made guardian of the Earl's Irish estates, d. 1464

SIR JAMES remained guardian of the Earl's Irish estates, d. 1487 = SABINA, d. of Donal Reagh MacMurrough Kavanagh, K. of Leinster

SIR PIERS ROE born 1467, cr. E. of Ossory in Feb. 1528 and E. of Ormond by a new creation, 1538, d. 1539

DESCENT OF MORTIMER
EARLS OF ULSTER AND LORDS OF TRIM

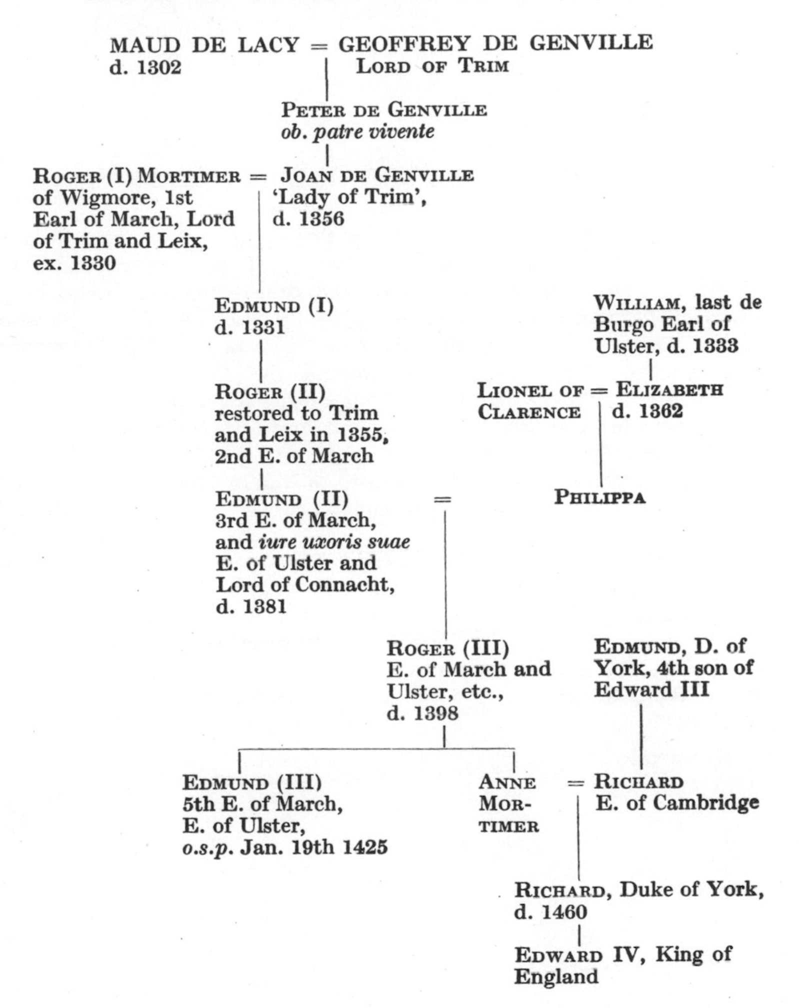

(B) PEDIGREES OF GAELIC CHIEFS

NOTE.—The native Irish pedigrees are by no means certain and published pedigrees are often contradictory. I have endeavoured to get them correct in the main lines and been generously helped by several modern authorities, such as Mr. Philip Grierson, of Gonville and Caius College, who is preparing the chief Irish medieval pedigrees for a forthcoming supplementary volume of the *Cambridge Mediaeval History*; Mr. A. Martin Freeman, who is editing the unpublished *Annals of Connacht* for the Irish MSS. Commission; and the late and much regretted Mr. W. F. Butler, a chief authority on the MacCarthy and Butler pedigrees. On the latter name, as well as the Fitzgeralds and MacMurroughs, my *Catalogue of Ormond Deeds* (4 vols.) throw much new light.

The four volumes of Orpen's *Ireland under the Normans* contain valuable pedigrees of the descendants of Nesta (vol. I); of the Fitzgeralds of Desmond and Fitzmaurices of Kerry to 1350; the MacCarthys (to 1325), the Carews of Cork, the Clann Somhairle, the Lacys (vol. III); and in vol. IV, the O'Connors of Connacht, 1119–1345; the Barons of Offaly; the O'Briens; and the House of De Burgo, all, however, ending about 1380.

THE MACCARTHY KINGS OF DESMOND

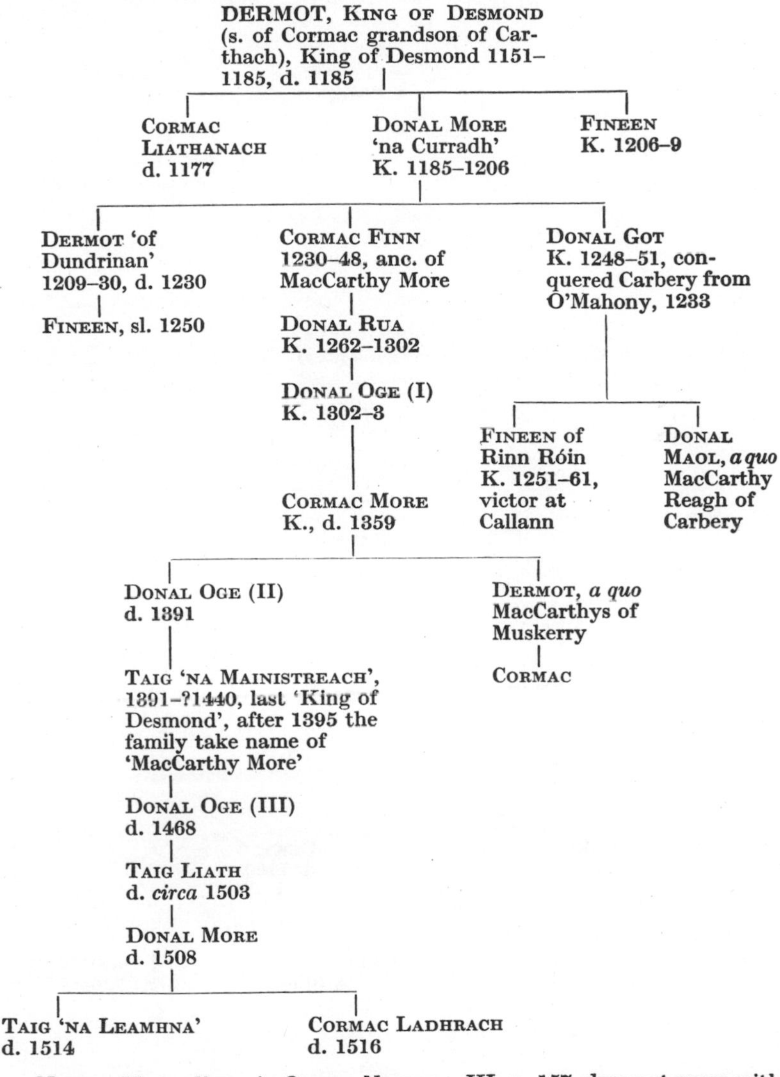

NOTE.—The pedigree in Orpen, *Normans*, III, p. 157, does not agree with W. F. Butler's 'Succession and Pedigree of MacCarthy More' in *R.S.A.I.* (1921), but as the latter was a chief authority on the pedigree I follow him.

THE MACLOCHLAINN KINGS OF CINEL EOGHAIN

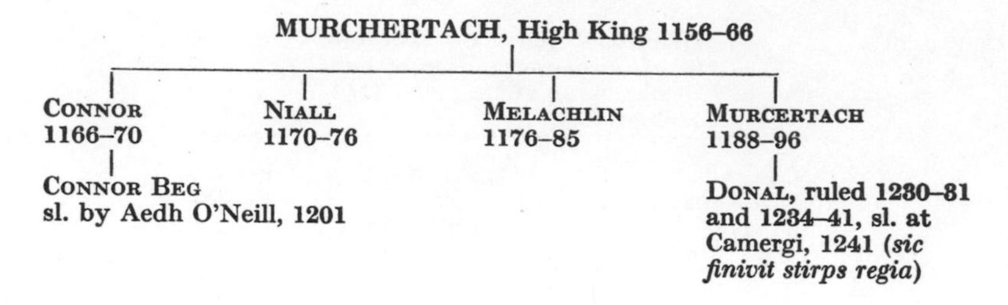

THE MACMURROUGH KINGS OF LEINSTER TO 1376

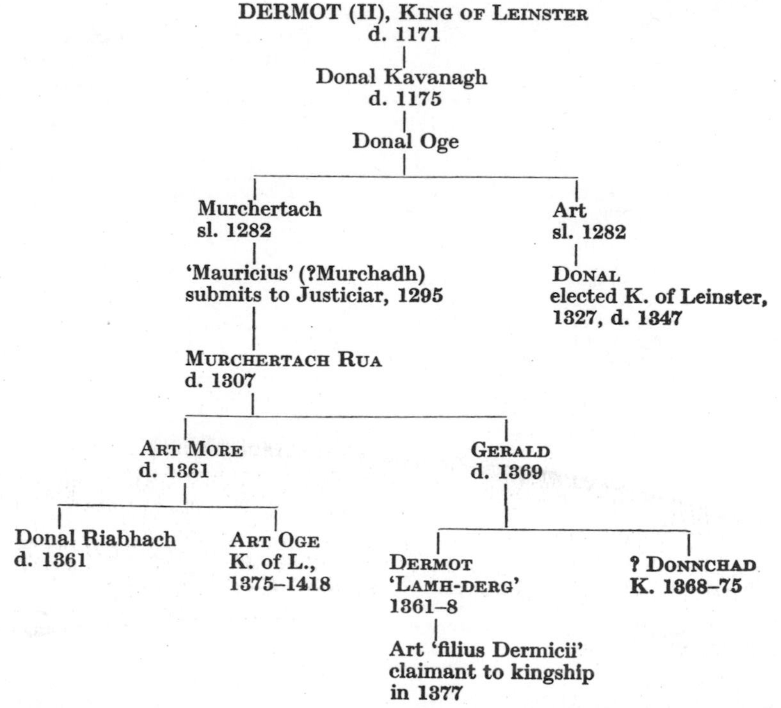

NOTE.—Hughes, 'Fall of Clan Kavanagh' in *R.S.A.I.* (1872–3), pp. 282–305, gives a full pedigree of the royal line, but it is not fully convincing. The above pedigree is a reconstruction, but Donnchad, who died in 1375, is hard to place.

THE LINE OF MACMURROUGH KAVANAGH
FROM 1376 TO 1522

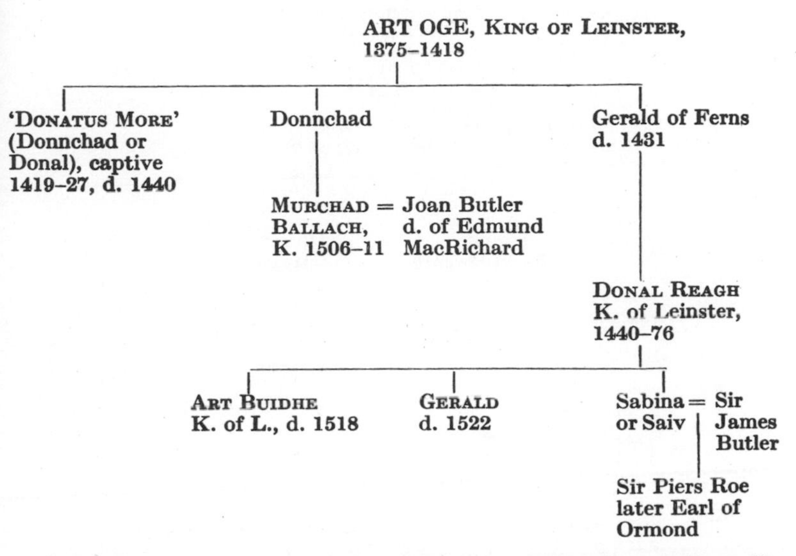

NOTE.—The later MacMurrough pedigree is particularly puzzling. The above is the best that can be made of it; Hughes, op. cit., renders it differently.

THE O'BRIEN KINGS OF THOMOND TO 1306

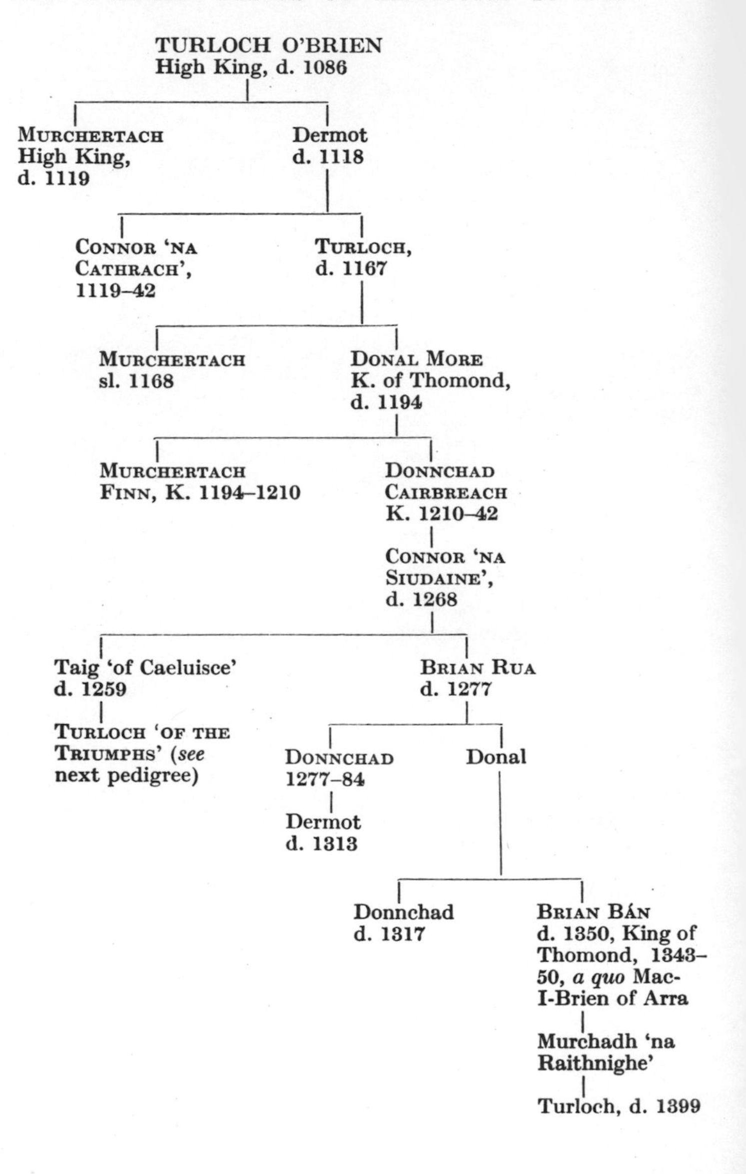

THE O'BRIENS OF THOMOND TO 1540

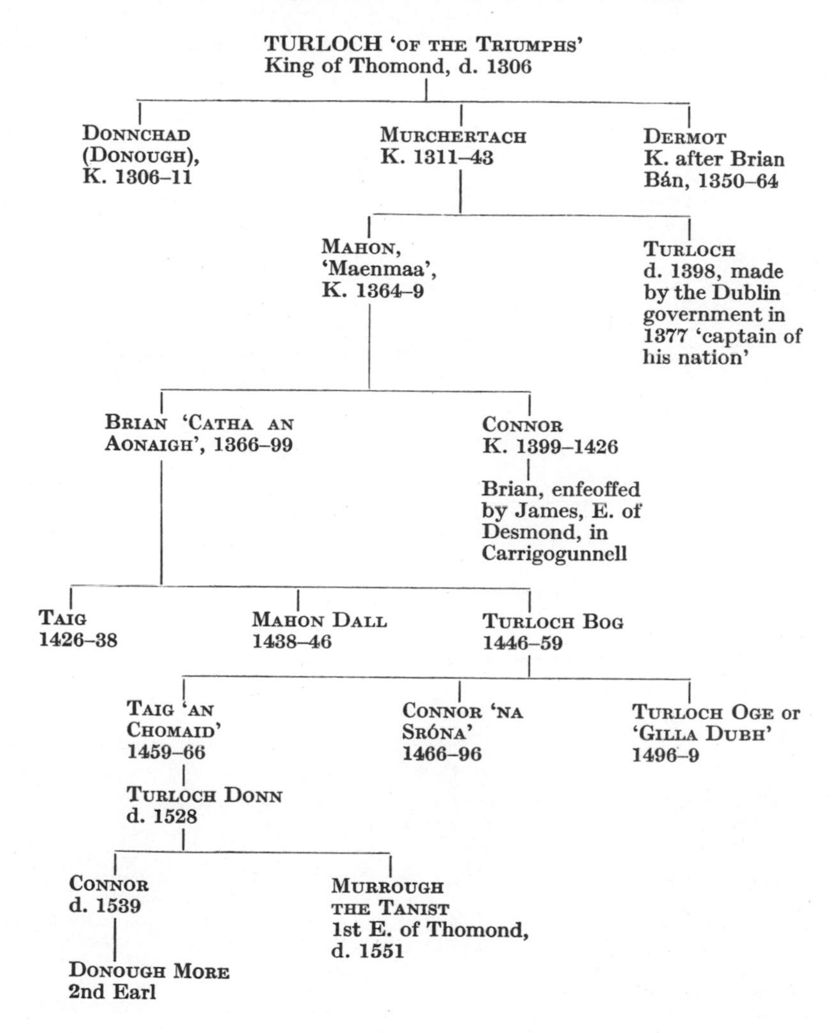

O'CONNOR KINGS OF CONNACHT TO 1324

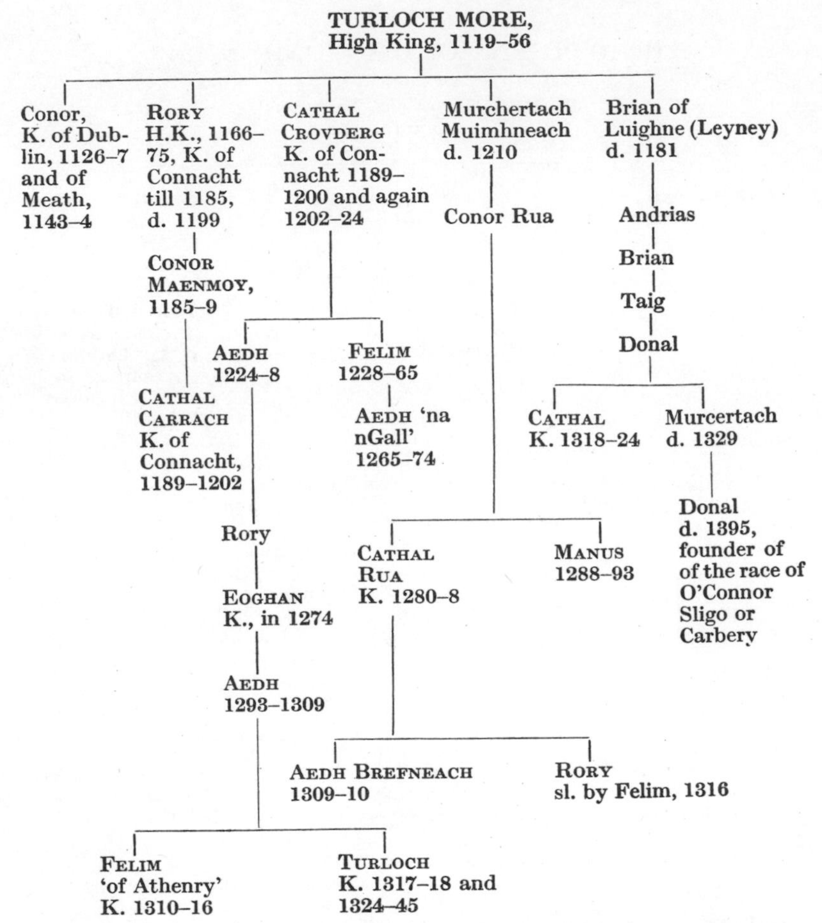

Note.—It is not altogether certain that Felim of Athenry was senior to his brother Turloch. Orpen makes him senior (which seems most probable), but Charles O'Conor Don in his *O'Conors of Connaught* (pedigrees given) makes him younger, in which case O'Connor Don's line is senior to O'Connor Roe. Mr. A. M. Freeman (who is editing the *Annals of Connacht*) kindly writes: 'I know nothing of the ages of Felim and Turloch, but Felim was foster-son of MacDermot (the historic kingmaker throughout almost the whole period) and was made king by him. He was evidently the approved candidate.' 'MacDermot later supported the O'Connor Roe line after the schism of 1384 and Keating draws the pedigree of O'Connor Roe, not O'Connor Don.' The evidence thus seems to favour Felim as senior and to support O'Connor Roe's branch as the senior line subsequently. For a fuller pedigree of the O'Connors *see* Orpen, *Normans*, IV, p. 127. The O'Connor Sligo descent is also somewhat uncertain, and Taig may be the son of Andrias instead of Brian.

O'CONNOR DON AND O'CONNOR ROE TO 1500

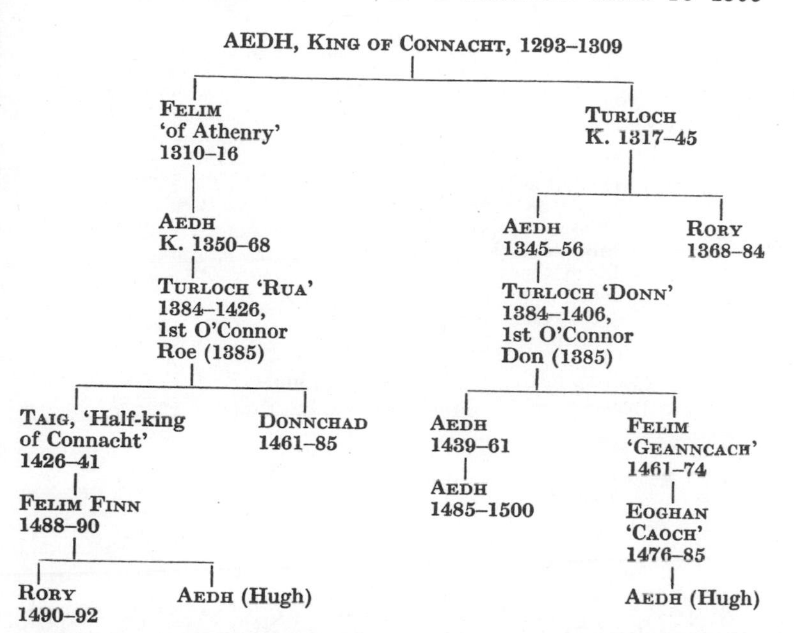

NOTE.—The O'Connor descent from 1310, and indeed from 1274, is most perplexing and intricate owing to the number of succession disputes between *rigdomnas*. Not all the collaterals are given here. After the race of Murchertach Muimhneach was eliminated and that of Brian Luighneach (O'Connor Sligo) relegated to the north, the race of Cathal Crovderg itself split and in 1385 a permanent division was made between O'Connor Don and O'Connor Roe, after which the title 'King of Connacht' was the emptiest of names.

THE O'DONNELL KINGS OF TYRCONNELL

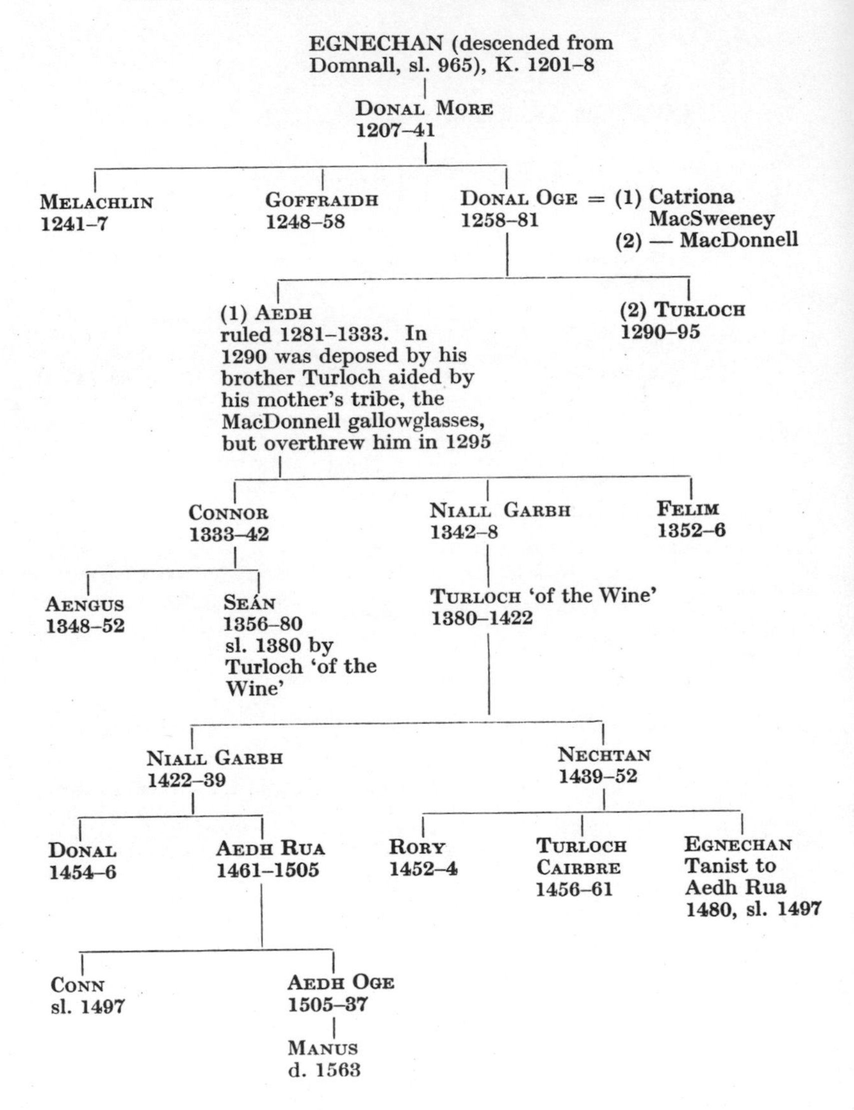

THE O'NEILL KINGS OF CINEL EOGHAIN (TYRONE)

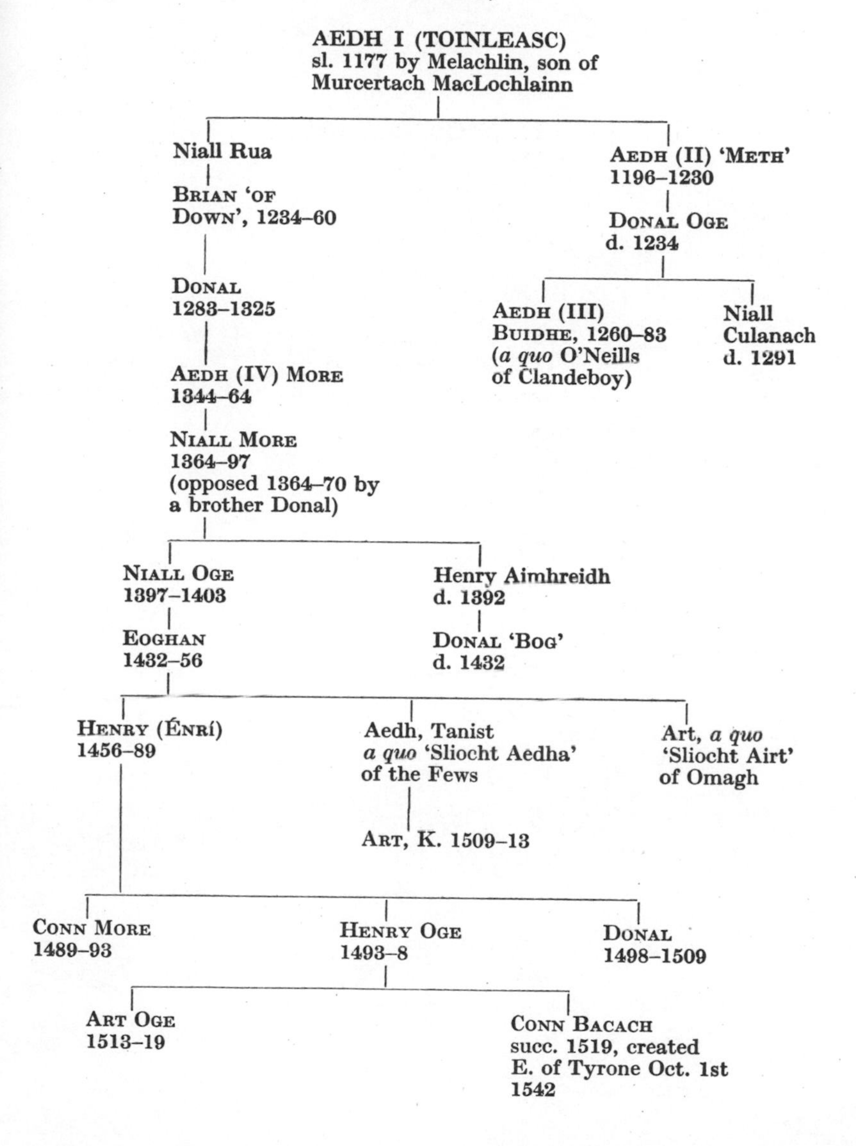

O'NEILLS OF CLANDEBOY

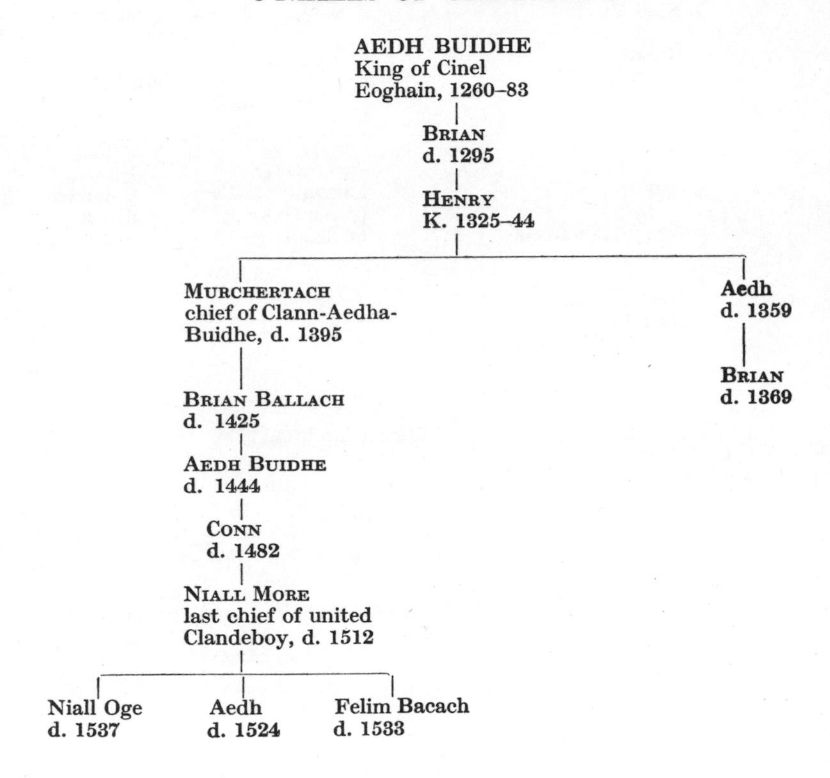

APPENDIX II

THE OSTMEN AFTER 1172

THE following (A) is a summary of the evidence collected on this question in the first edition of this book, which can be referred to under 'Ostmen' in the Index. My paper on 'English and Ostmen in Medieval Ireland' in *English Historical Review* (1908), contains a good deal of the evidence. In (B) I add some material collected since the first edition.

(A)

THE OSTMEN OF DUBLIN

After Henry II granted Dublin to his 'men of Bristol' in 1172, the Ostman population in general migrated to the suburb north of the river called Ostmaneby or Ostmantown, still commemorated in the name Oxmantown Green. The first roll of Dublin freemen, *circa* 1172, out of 148 names contains only 10 which seem to be Ostman. Among these are Walter and Siward Suaitman; this name as Sweetman (Suatgarman, 'man of the black spear') is henceforth frequent in Anglo-Irish records.

Owing to the loss of our records and non-publication of what formerly existed, evidence for the Ostmen after 1300 is and must remain very scanty. Naturally in the towns they soon blended with the English, in the country with the Irish. No doubt many Scandinavian-looking names came in also with the English, which cannot be reckoned Irish-Ostman.

Ostmen continue to appear in civic records of Dublin in later times (see Berry, *Catalogues of the Mayors etc. of Dublin, 1229–1447*). In Dublinshire the ruling MacTorcaill family had most of its lands confiscated by Strongbow. These were mainly in Fingall, i.e. north Dublin. Hamund, Sigrith, and Torphin Mac Torkil's lands are named. There seems to have been a Ballymagogan in Fingall in later times, hence my conjecture on 'Magoghdane' (p. 83 first, edition) is perhaps unwarranted and the hero's name more likely was 'Mag Eochagain' or 'Mag Eachdonn'. In the south of the county and along the Liffey there seems to have been an Ostman rural population. The 'land of Odurchil' may indicate the 'Ui Torcaill', and Mr. L. Price tells me of a townland near Blessington called Rathturtle, or formerly Rathtorkel. The 'land of Bren' as granted to De Ridlesford (p. 80, first edition) seems to contain some Ostman-named districts. A Pipe Roll of 1229 names 'Thurkil and Arphin' as headmen responsible for rents of the Ostmen in Annaliffey, but these are not mentioned again (*35th Report D.K. App.*, III, pp. 29–32). The MacTorcaill family evidently lingered on as small owners.

In a law-case in 1302 we find Hamo McTorkil. Ballymakartle (formerly Ballymakarkill) and Hamonstown in Fingall record this race.

In 1350 the viceroy confirms the election of a 'captain of the Harolds' and 'a captain of the Archbolds' in south county Dublin; these appear to be Ostman names (pp. 196 and 275, first edition). The late Dr. Sigerson suggested to me that Archbold is *recte* 'Aspoll', a Norse name which in a Christchurch deed is given as 'Absolea'.

THE OSTMEN OF WATERFORD

These formed the second-largest Ostman city and contado in Ostman Ireland. The ruling race in 1170 was MacGillamaire, and its two chiefs were brothers, Ragnall and Sitric. The former probably built the well-known 'Reginald's Tower' in the city.

When Strongbow and Dermot took Waterford in 1170, Ragnall was spared but we hear no more of him; Sitric was executed. From Ragnall or some other member of the stock came a later family of MacGillemory, from a Sitric a family called Makshiterok by the English [(?) MacSiocradha]. When Henry II in 1171 landed at Crook his entry into Waterford was resisted by a section of the Ostmen. Henry outlawed some for this, but granted his protection to most of them (see p. 65, first edition) in a charter beginning 'Houstmanni de Waterford ligei mei homines sunt'. Henceforth the Waterford coast was royal demesne.

The Crown was interested in this rich and important old Scandinavian element. In 1310–11 (p. 119, first edition), in an interesting case at Waterford in which a colonist had killed one John, son of Yvor MacGillemory, and pleaded that he was a 'mere Irishman' and not of free blood, John le Poer, acting for the Crown, produced a grant of liberty made to Gillecrist, William and John MacGillemory (apparently by King Henry) of whose race John, son of Yvor, was.

The 'liberties' of the Ostmen of Waterford are illustrated again in the following. In 1290 Philip MacGothmond, describing himself as 'an Ostman and Englishman (i.e. entitled to English law) of the city of Waterford', prays remedy against persons emulous of him and greedy of his demesne in Ireland, who exact five marks payment when a man is killed (i.e. by one of MacGothmond's men), and exact also his chattels and land, clearly usurping the King's liberties, and striving to prove that Philip and his race to the number of nearly four hundred are Irishmen, whereas they are English and Ostmen as appears by letters of the bailiffs and citizens of Waterford. As it belongs to the King to correct that from English and Ostman he should be turned into an Irishman, and as it is useful that there should be more English than Irish, he prays licence to use and enjoy the liberties and customs of the English in Ireland. The royal answer was: 'As Philip has from the commonalty of Waterford the charter which he now prays from the King, let it be shown to the King.' Philip's petition is granted because the Escheator testifies that it would be to the King's advantage. For this see p. 199 of my first edition, *E.H.R.* (1908), and *C.D.I.*, III, 305–6.

It looks as if the MacGillemory charter (previously referred to) is the one which the corporation of Waterford now produces.

In 1236 the Justiciar, Maurice Fitzgerald, is ordered to confiscate to the King's use the lands which MakShiteroc, an Irishman, had held near Waterford (pp. 120, 137, first edition). In 1283 Edward I confirmed English liberty to the Ostmen of Waterford ('Custumanni' is *recte* 'Oustmanni'), see *C.D.I.*, II, No. 2315. In 1290 William MacGilmory holds one and a half carucates of land at Duflagh near Dungarvan of Thomas Fitzmaurice, Lord of Desmond. In 1316 Edward II grants English law to Richard son of John MacShiterok. (*Cal. Pat. Rolls* (1313–17), p. 463.) Evidently the MacGillamaire family had been left a certain amount of land in their old estates.

The attempt to prove such Ostmen to be Irish (see Ardfinan case later) is significant of the rightless condition of the latter, and also shows how hibernicized most of the Ostmen had become in speech and names. Ballykilmury in the neighbourhood of Dungarvan seems to commemorate the MacGillamaire race. The name is found after 1300 in *Calendar of the Patent Rolls of Ireland* and in my *Calendar of the Ormond Deeds* (vol. I). The Ostmen both of the city of Waterford and of Dungarvan appear in the Pipe Rolls up to 1270 or so, and in 1280–92 'the vill of the Ostmen near Waterford' pays rent to Thomas, Lord of Desmond (p. 169). Ballytruckle near Waterford probably represents this place, and means 'Thorgils town'.

THE OSTMEN OF LIMERICK

The most interesting record of these is the 'Liberties of the Ostmen'. John, as Prince or King (for Henry is too early), perhaps at the same time as he granted charters of municipal liberties to Limerick (1197 and 1210), seems to have confirmed the Ostmen (the MacMagnus race) there in their rights of freedom and freehold status. But there is no other evidence for this than the interesting case of 1295. This is summarized formerly on pp. 106–7, but I give here a fuller rendering and translation taken from Plea Roll (*anno* 23 Edw. I) membrane 23, in the Public Record Office, Dublin (the original was destroyed in 1922).

'At Limerick, a jury to decide whether Henry and John le Norreys and Robert le Burdun unlawfully disseised William le Teynturer (the Dyer) of Ardfinan county of his free holding and a messuage in Ardfinan. Robert did not come and was not attachable because not found. Henry and John came and said no assize (jury) ought to be held because William was *hibernicus* and of servile condition. Asked what Irish surname and status William had, they say O'Moleyn and that his father was O'Moleyn born at Inishennan. William replied that he was not *hibernicus* but *Houstmannus*, viz. a MacMackus of the city of Limerick of free status and right to plead at law. Henry and John reiterate that he is *purus hibernicus* and say, if he is Ostman, he never had his little holding (*feodulum*) free in aforesaid messuage by which he could be disseised. Jury finds that Thomas, father of William, was held all his life to be an Irishman and after his death Olyva his widow, mother of said William, fearing that her son would be reduced to the servitude of his father, went to Limerick and there obtained "the liberty of the Ostmen" for her son, whereby William claims that as an Ostman he has always been free to reply to a suit and has enjoyed their liberty.'

Finally William recovered seisin in his freehold and messuage, and Henry, John, and Robert are fined for disseisin.

No better instance can be shown of the fact that while in general the old Scandinavian element in Ireland was held to be free in law and rights, the lesser Irish, in so far as the colonists could ensure, were held to be not. It had to be *proved* that an Ostman was Irish and not free; it was *assumed* that an *hibernicus* (Irishman) was not free, i.e. that he was a serf and devoid of freehold status, and could therefore be lawfully dispossessed by any Englishman.

The MacGothmond case (see 'The Ostmen of Waterford') is almost equally to the point.

An interesting petition to the Crown against Anglo-Irish oppression is that of Maurice Macotere, who in 1290 writing 'from the world's end' describes how he 'and three hundred of his race' suffer from the English who try to rob and dispossess them as Irish. My friend Mr. D. J. Gleeson believes 'the world's end' here refers to the Limerick district, perhaps as far as Ostman settlement went north or west. (See for this petition *E.H.R.*, 1908.) Macotere is from the Norse 'Ottir'. Cotter is still common in Munster. *C.D.I.*, II, No. 959 says that David archbishop of Cashel has the goods of Reginald Macotere a usurer. Perhaps then Maurice and his race were somewhere in Tipperary. For this Macotere case see pp. 199 and 210, first edition. My paper in *P.R.I.A.* (1929) on 'Sheriffs' Accounts of County Waterford, the Honour of Dungarvan etc.' adds a reference to the usurer Macotere; his goods are worth the large sum of four hundred pounds. (See *Analecta Hibernica*, vol V (1934)). Maurice's petition declares that the King in one day made three thousand pounds by conferring English liberty by letters patent.

THE OSTMEN OF WEXFORD

In 1283 a group of Ostmen still survived on the Wexford coast, for in that year William de Valence, Lord of Wexford, ordered an inquest into the services, etc. of his Ostmen at Rosslare, and the jury found that in the time of the Marshals there were in county Wexford 'a hundred forensic Ostmen very rich who used to pay to the reeves of Wexford certain money rents and commutation for harvest dues, but now there are only forty having little gear, and twelve more who serve the English and others for a living, having naught themselves'. The Lord therefore frees them from all burdens, rents, and services which the dead were wont to bear, and restores to them their former liberties.

This interesting document was for the first time published by me in 1908 in the *English Historical Review.* We can gather from it that in 1172 there must have been a large rural population of Ostmen outside the walls of Wexford, and dwelling in the Rosslare peninsula. When we put this beside the MacGothmond and the Macotere petitions we see that when the English came there must have been numerous 'pockets' of Ostmen all over Munster and Leinster, but mainly on the coasts, quite apart from the still more numerous town-populations and well colonized areas, such as Fingall and Gall-tir.

They were destined to disappear for various reasons, they blended with either English and Irish and dropped their old surnames, but there can be no doubt that the southern coast from Dublin round to Limerick contains much old Scandinavian blood.

(B)

Since the first edition of this book appeared, Miss Walsh has published a little work on *Scandinavian Relations with Ireland* (1924) which has much merit. But it must be said that the subject of Scandinavian Ireland has not yet been thoroughly dealt with. The *Calendar of Ormond Deeds* (vols. I and II) contains some new material. It is clear that as the Normans occupied the land, the Ostmen took opportunity to settle in the manors and in the new towns of the conquerors. *The Red Book of Ormond* (ed. N. B. White) similarly has new evidence for Tipperary, Kilkenny, and Carlow. The most intriguing entry I find in this is: 'An extent of the manor of Cloncurry' (in Kildare) in 1305. Among the cottars appear two McLothyrs, and there is Ballymcloth[yr] where apparently this sept dwells. It looks like an hibernicized Scandinavian sept. 'Lodher' in Norse would be 'Lothar'. An Ormond deed of *circa* 1210 mentions the 'Castellum quod Machen Lodher antiquitus fundavit' at Cloncurry.[1] That is, some Norseman of long ago, the son of one Lothar, had built some kind of a fortress in this Kildare locality and his descendants still lived there in a humble way. Perhaps the Ostmen spread further along the Liffey than Leixlip.

[1] *Cal. Ormond Deeds*, I, p. 19, in a grant by William, Earl of Pembroke; among the lands, etc. granted is the 'castle that Macenlodher first built, which is in the commote of Owaltan'.

APPENDIX III

THE TOWNS OF IRELAND

BEFORE 1170 our existing towns were either monastic 'civitates' such as Glendaloch and Clonmacnois, or the walled places which the Norsemen had built at Dublin and round the coast to Limerick. The latter were true self-governing towns but could show no charter, for their autonomy was popular in origin and derived from beneath.

The English arrived here when the communal movement was in full flow in their own country, and they introduced the medieval type of incorporated borough, owing its charter of self-government to some superior lord. The new ones began so; the older Ostman or monastic ones had to seek a charter establishing them as such. For now in the Roman-feudal order all authority had to come from above.

The new type of town was soon in full growth, and King, bishops, lords, all favoured them as guarantees for the Conquest, as centres of English rule, life, and civilization, and as providing them rents, customs, services, man-power.[1]

DUBLIN AND THE ROYAL TOWNS

The three chief types of town were to be distinguished by their chief officer. The mayor represents full self-government as a city; government by a sovereign ('superior') is the next highest type; underneath these the 'reeve' or 'praepositus' represents the small open town of different degrees of liberty.

Henry II granted Dublin the 'liberties of the men of Bristol' with free trade throughout his empire. A charter of John in 1192 granted the citizens a court of their own, freedom from extern manor courts, a merchant gild, and trading monopolies, such as that 'no stranger shall buy corn, wool, etc. in the city save from a burgess, or stay to trade more than forty days, or have a tavern for wine save in his ship where the Lord of Ireland may take for custom two hogsheads valued at twenty shillings each'. In 1215 as King he allowed the 'reeve' to be freely elected and the feefarm i.e. the composition for all royal dues, to be fixed at two hundred marks. Another charter from Henry III in 1229 allowed the Dubliners to elect a mayor who should rule with the aid of a council.

Henry II and John both took the Ostmen alike of town and country under their protection and the 'Ostmanni Domini Regis' in various places

[1] For charters to Irish towns, see *Chartae Privilegia et Immunitates* (*1171–1195*); also for general history of the towns, Gilbert's *Anc. Records of Dublin*, and *Hist. and Mun. Docs.*; Gale's *Ancient Corporate System of Ireland*; Webb's *Mun. Government in Ireland* (1918); and the standard works of Hore (Wexford), Hardiman (Galway), D'Alton (Drogheda), Ryland, Caulfield, etc.

are mentioned for over a century. We cannot doubt that in these ancient towns, which now became 'royal towns', the old Scandinavian element was the basis of the later population. In 1215 King John gave Waterford the liberties of Dublin, and the right to a reeve, who was to be chosen by twenty-four citizens forming a council; a charter of 1222 gave trading privileges and free trade through the Angevin empire and fixed the feefarm at a hundred marks. The mayor of Waterford is first heard of in 1289.

Cork already had a reeve in 1199, when John granted to it the liberties of Bristol; in 1241 its feefarm was fixed at eighty marks; its burgesses were freed from villein status and extern courts; and given a hundred court, a merchant gild, and a council of twenty-four. By the time of Edward II Cork had a mayor of its own.

Limerick was granted the 'liberties of Bristol' in 1197 by Prince John, who later in 1210 conferred on the burgesses forty carucates of land from the 'Cantred of the Ostmen', and by the end of the thirteenth century Limerick was a royal city ruled by its own freemen meeting in a common court. The 'liberties of Bristol', the summit of civic independence under a mayor, were finally enjoyed by the five royal cities of Dublin, Waterford, Cork, Limerick, and Galway, who held directly to the Crown. But the last city did not get them till 1484. Drogheda later got the same status, but indirectly.

Of the old Ostman towns, Wexford did not become a royal town. Passing from Strongbow to his heirs, it was not till 1317 that its lord Aymer de Valence granted it the 'liberties of Breteuil'.

LORDS' TOWNS AND THE 'CONSUETUDINES DE BRITOIL'[1]

A form of municipal self-government, less advanced than that of Bristol, was 'the free law of Breteuil'. William FitzOsbern enfranchized this little town of his in Normandy in 1060. After the Conquest, when he became Earl of Hereford, he granted the same liberties to the town of Hereford, and the first conquerors of Ireland brought them as a model to this country. In a few cases the Crown granted these rights, but in general they were given by charter of lay or ecclesiastical lords, by which 'liberty towns' were created in which the burgesses secured low rents and fines and yet retained the protection of the lord.

In 1194 Walter de Lacy, Earl of Meath, gave the laws of Breteuil to that part of Drogheda which was called 'towards Meath' or 'south of

[1] For these laws see Bateson in the *English Historical Review* (1900–3). They must not be confused with the laws of Bristol. By the 'free law of Breteuil' burgesses were freed from villein status and given a certain self-government under a reeve and a hundred court. Fines were limited to a shilling for ordinary offences, burgage rents were fixed at a shilling, a frontage and a few acres in the common field were attached to every tenement, there was free grinding at the lord's mill, and limitations upon the fines he could impose.

Some twenty places in Ireland received these rights. The chief officer in some of the Breteuil towns is called 'sovereign', e.g. Clonmel, New Ross, and Kilkenny.

the Boyne', and in 1213 King John confirmed them to Drogheda 'on both sides of the river'. By successive charters of Henry III the 'two Droghedas' got full 'liber burgus' rights and a mayor, and so the original Breteuil rights were expanded into the rights of a royal town like Dublin.

Dungarvan got Breteuil liberties from King John, and Wexford in 1317 from Aymer de Valence, Earl of Pembroke. Hugh de Lacy or his son Walter, earls of Meath, gave them to Kells, Duleek, and Trim. By the Marshal earls or their seneschals and vassals they were granted to Kilkenny, Kells in Ossory, New Ross, and other places.

In the Vale of Liffey or the plain of Kildare before 1240 were thus incorporated Ballymore, Naas, Rathcoole, Rathmore, Tallaght, and Kildare, by Fitzgerald or other lords or the archbishops. In 1297 we find the little town of Kildare claiming to have the correction of all trespasses within the boundaries by charter of the lord of the liberty; save the four chief pleas, robbery and other felonies, and breaches of the assize of wine.

On the Ulster border, Dundalk got them from Theobald de Verdun.

In the south Archbishop Donat O'Lonergan (1206–17) endowed Cashel with the rights of a 'burgus', a reeve of its own, and fifteen hundred acres of common land. His successor, Marianus O'Brien, in 1230 granted them a hundred court, keeping, however, manorial rights and rents. Marianus also endowed Fethard in Tipperary with rights like those of Cashel. The little town of Mungret in Limerick got Breteuil rights from Bishop Robert, who ruled from 1251 to 1272, and Daniel, bishop of Cloyne, about 1270 gave a charter of liberties to the burgesses of his cathedral town whether Irish or English. (See Laffan, *Records of Cashel*, *R.S.A.I.* (1904 and 1906); Berry, *Statutes*, III; 'Pipa Colmani' in *Cork Arch. Soc.* (1915).)

BURGAGES AND MANOR TOWNS

In addition to the true chartered boroughs, numerous open places, market towns, semi-urban centres, and manor-towns at first dotted the whole country as far as Sligo, Tralee, and Dingle. Such were the Butler towns at Nenagh and Thurles. The Irish place-name Borris (*buirgéis* from 'burgus'), commemorated in Borris-in-Ossory, Burrishoole, and Burriscarra, attest old Norman attempts at town-building as far as the remote shores of Mayo.

Meath had no large town save Drogheda, yet Ardee, Kells, Mullingar, Athboy, Navan, and a few other places had urban liberties from their lords, and up to the age of the Tudors the Justiciar could call out for military service the militia of the fourteen towns of Meath under their portreeves (Harris, *Collectanea*, IV, p. 154 (1 Hen. IV)).

Ossory and nearer Munster had incorporate or privileged towns at Nenagh, Cashel, Fethard, Gowran, Callan, Dungarvan, Youghal, Carrick-on-Suir, and Athmetum (Affane). The liberties of Kilkenny were conferred on Clonmel by William de Burgo, and it had a sovereign by 1300.

Next came Cork and Kinsale, which Andrew le Blund chartered in 1333. Thence stretched an unconquered country as far round the coast as Dingle, where began the Geraldine lordship, which stretched round the coast to Limerick, and here was a fresh chain of towns including Tralee and Kilmallock. Though many of these Munster towns were but unwalled urban settlements, yet the greater ones were prosperous places with many streets and numerous inhabitants, Irish as well as English. Dingle and Tralee flourished by trading Irish wool and hides against Spanish and French wines and cloth, and Kilmallock, for example, had in 1300 four streets, twenty-seven burgages on the main street, was ruled by a provost, and in 1300 paid to a State subsidy the handsome sum of twenty pounds.

CONNACHT

Connacht was ill fitted to sustain on its remote shores prosperous centres of English citizens and craftsmen. Yet around the old O'Connor fortress on the Corrib arose De Burgo's town of Galway, which grew rich on the fishery of the bay and the lake, and on the wines and stuffs which its traders carried from Europe to the inland chiefs. In 1270 began the building and enwalling of the remotest town of European civilization. For over a century Galway was a De Burgo town, and its lord named the magistrates, till in 1396 Richard II, putting aside the claims of the Clanrickard Burke, gave it a sovereign, made it a royal town, and endowed it with the liberties of Drogheda.

Some twelve miles inland, at the 'Ford of the Kings', the Berminghams founded a Dominican priory and built the town of Athenry. But not till 1310 did it get its charter of incorporation, nor till 1316 its defences, when it was walled with the spoils of the Irish slain at the battle of Athenry.

Sligo marked the furthest limit of the burghal movement. Fitz-Maurice built a castle here in 1245, but his race lost its Connacht lands before the century ended. The Red Earl de Burgo laid out a town in 1310, but it could not stand against the attacks of O'Donnell, and after 1400 it became the seat of O'Connor Sligo.

Inland, the thirteenth century saw Ballinrobe, Dunmore, and a few other attempts on the part of Burgos, Berminghams, and Fitzgeralds to found permanent Anglo-Irish boroughs, which failed in the next century.

It is to be noted that while the Norman conquerors attempted to create urban centres in Connacht and failed save for Galway and Athenry, not a single town-foundation was attempted in all the coast-country from Sligo round the north coasts to Coleraine.

THE TOWNS AT THEIR HEIGHT

The towns were the only consistently loyal element in medieval Ireland. Their blood was very mixed, Ostman, Irish, English, Flemish, French, but their tradition was at first sound Anglo-saxon, industrial, and middle-class. Enemies of feudalism and chieftainship, they allied with the State against 'English rebels and Irish enemies'. In the battle of Down, in the Bruce war, and in the Yorkist times they undoubtedly saved the English government in Ireland. They had therefore to be rewarded, and allowed to maintain their own defence by the State, which could do nothing for them, and so the Lord of Ireland showered on them abundant rights and responsibilities. They were ordered to keep galleys and weapons of offence and defence, given murage grants, had taxes remitted, wide admiralty and contado jurisdictions given, and had the highest local powers vested in their mayors and sovereigns.

The year 1300 shows them in their most numerous and prosperous state. In that year the Justiciar Wogan visited the chief towns and counties of Meath, Louth, Dublin, Wexford, Kilkenny, Kildare, Waterford, Tipperary, and Limerick raising a State subsidy. Thirty-three towns are named, and fourteen pay sums ranging from Cork (£174) to Kilmedan (£5). These fourteen towns are: Cork, Drogheda, Dublin, Waterford, Youghal, Kilkenny, Limerick, New Ross, Kilmallock, Cashel, Dungarvan, Emly, Kilmedan, and Athmetum (*Calendar of Justiciary Rolls*, I, p. 304).

In this prosperous period, while the State was still potent, we find in 1252 Dublin and Drogheda making a compact by which the men of Dublin are made free of Drogheda, disputes shall be settled by a common council, there shall be mutual aid against enemies, and petitions to the King and others shall be by joint assent. In 1285 a league was made which included Dublin, Waterford, Cork, and the two Droghedas, whose envoys shall meet annually at Kilkenny to discuss common affairs, and if any of the leagued towns shall fail to observe the treaty thus made and signed at Kilkenny under common seal, they shall suffer heavy penalties.

THE IRISH IN THE TOWNS

In their beginning the towns did not share the anti-Irish spirit of the rural colonists. The earliest population of many of them was itself Irish, especially in ancient seats such as Cashel, Cloyne, Kells, Downpatrick, Trim, Kilkenny, and Kildare. The earliest civic records show many Gaelic names. Later, Irishmen obtained the civic freedom with the approbation of all. The general medieval 'year and a day rule' enabled many 'betaghs' and poor tenants to escape from manor servitude. Thus an early Dublin bylaw of 1305 says: 'Villeins and betaghs who by permission of the mayor and commonalty remain in the city for a year and a day, are thereby freed from their lords.' The charter granted to Drogheda 'towards Oriel' in 1253 allowed that if any held a tenement for a year and a day it was his against all others thereafter. In 1307 the burgesses of Drogheda declared: 'Irishmen by custom of Irish towns being burgesses are as free as Englishmen.'

After the democratic beginning, the towns in the fourteenth century became steadily oligarchic. The dividing line may be found in the complaint of the poorer citizens of Dublin in 1316 (see Gilbert, *Ancient*

Records of Dublin, I, pp. 132–5). And as oligarchy grew, so an anti-Irish spirit grew. Partly under suggestion from the State and partly by racial antipathy, Galway, Limerick, Waterford, and other towns passed many bylaws against 'Irish enemies', and everyone has heard of the famous one, 'that no O' or Mac strut or swagger through the streets of Galway'. But the warlike rural lord and his retainers, whether Gael or Norman, were naturally offensive to peaceful burghers.

Peaceful and industrial Irish seem to have got civic freedom on easy terms, and the maintenance of English as the official language is not to be wondered at. Anti-Irish Acts were, it would appear, negligently enforced, and many charters of admission to 'English law and liberty' and so to burgess opportunities are recorded.[1]

On the Ostman element in the towns see Appendix II on the Ostmen. The Irish element is conspicuous from the first and appears often in the civic records. In Galway, even among the famous 'Tribes' of that city, Lynch is Irish ('Loingsech'—a mariner), in Limerick, Meagh ('Midheach', a Meathman), in Cork, Mead (the same), Ronayne, and Morrogh were leading names. In Kilkenny there was great race-equality, the bishop's vill of Irishtown just across the Nore had burgess liberties, and there was a *Villa Flamingorum*, or quarter for Flemish weavers in the city, where a street was still called in Irish in 1846 Sráid na mBodach (Street of the Boors); see Prim in *Kilk. Arch. Soc.* (1849–51), p. 37.

In 1375 at request of the Earl of Desmond the viceroy De Windsor at Clonmel enfranchises Molrony Ó Griffa, captain of his nation, his two brothers, and his son Molrony. In 1537 among the chief citizens of Clonmel are Molrony, Laynagh, Fagan, Quirk, all Irish. In Henry V's time 'Clonmel is inhabited by English merchants and burgesses who have lately constructed walls, and who, observing English laws, are a great succour to the Government' (W. P. Burke, *History of Clonmel*).

THE TOWNS AFTER 1366

After the Irish revival and decay of the State in the fourteenth century the only towns of importance that survived and continued their municipal organization would be about twenty, of which Dublin, Waterford, Drogheda, Wexford, Cork, Limerick, Dungarvan, Kilkenny, Galway were chief. Coleraine was lost in the north and Sligo in the west. Statutes against trading with the 'Irish enemy' in accord with the spirit of the Kilkenny statutes were fatal for the towns. In 1428 (see p. 299) they were forbidden to sell corn, salt, iron, and victuals to the Irish enemies without licence. An Act of 1431 forbade Irish merchants to frequent Irish fairs and markets and buy and sell merchandise, 'whereby the enemy take great customs and profits to the

[1] Gilbert, *Hist. and Mun. Docs.*, p. 453, records that in 1291 English freedom is granted to Robert de Bree and his five daughters. Hugh Kent of Galway petitions for the same and it is granted. The answer says: 'The King commanded his Great Council held of late in London that this grant should be made to all those who demand it, for his Council showed him it would be greatly to his advantage.' (See also for Bree, *C.D.I.*, III, p. 525 and No. 924.)

depression of the boroughs and trading towns' (Berry, *Statutes*, II, pp. 11–43).

In Connacht Galway, following the usual wish to be a 'royal' rather than a lord's town, got a charter from Richard II, making it a self-governing town with a mayor. But the Clanrickard Burke still exercised some unwelcome domination, and in 1484 Richard II gave it a final charter making it a self-governing town with a mayor, and forbade Clanrickard to exercise sovereignty there.

The triumph of oligarchy and the monopoly of town-offices, and privileges by a small group of hereditary families is best and familiarly illustrated in Galway, whose 'Tribes' in the sixteenth century were 'Athy, Bodkin, Blake, Browne, Darcy, Deane, Font, French, Joyce, Kirwan, Lynch, Martin, Morris, Skerrit'.

By this time the surviving towns, hemmed in by Norman lords gone Irish and by Irish chiefs, had a constant fight to survive and maintain both prosperity and self-government.

In the old Ulster earldom nothing north of Carrickfergus lasted till the sixteenth century, while Downpatrick remained an episcopal town still under the English, but by 1400 Armagh was entirely an Irish town, which the archbishop who resided at Termonfechin *inter anglicos* seldom visited, and subject to O'Neill. About 1416 (it was a common cry of distress), the provost and commons of Carlingford wrote to the King: 'Our town lies in a valley between mountains and sea, facing the marches of Louth, and contains only twenty carucates of lowland, and is often plundered by Irish and Scots.' The King therefore freed them for a number of years from subsidies and military service (D'Alton's *Drogheda*, II, p. 114).

The Irish revival and the going over of the old Normans, once friends of the towns, to Irish habit, with the devastating raids of the chiefs and weakness of State, had by the Tudor time wiped out the majority of the small towns so cheerfully and widely founded in the first century or so.

In west Munster and north Ormond the disappearance was very marked. Save for Kinsale no borough survived west of Buttevant (Barrymore's town) and Mallow; west of that was MacCarthy's country, until Dingle was reached. This continued under the Knight of Kerry to be a merchant town for trade with Spain; so did Tralee under the Earl of Desmond, and as the capital of his palatinate.

We have seen that in 1484 Richard III finally made Galway a city with a mayor of its own. The only other Connacht town that survived was Bermingham's foundation of Athenry. How far self-government of the municipal type continued in it is not clear, but Sir Henry Sidney in Elizabeth's time declared its walls were as great as those of Calais.

It became the constant complaint of the Anglo-Irish towns that they were in imminent peril from 'Irish enemies and English rebels'. The coast towns in particular were in danger from the pirates, Spanish, French, and Scottish, who roamed the seas and whom the State did nothing to suppress. No wonder that when the Tudor régime began the Irish towns were all for the Government, and that their loyalty won them the official praise that they were 'the sheet-anchor of the State'.

Waterford offers the most striking picture of a city beset at once by irishized Normans and Gaelic chiefs.[1] It had a long feud with the Poers of Donohill, 'degenerate' descendants of that Robert le Poer whom Henry II had made 'Custos' of all this coast. In 1345, says Clyn, 'the Poerini burnt and destroyed almost the whole country round Waterford, and some of them were taken and hanged, drawn and quartered in the city'. Later these Norman gentlemen threw in their lot with the strong maritime clan of O'Driscoll of Baltimore, and in 1368 assailed the city, routed the civic array, and slew the mayor, sheriff, thirty-six burgesses, and sixty strangers then trading in the city, losing on their own side the Baron of Donohill, his brother, and many more.

But the burghers of Irish towns had sturdy hearts and good armour to buckle upon them, as they showed against O'Neill, Bruce, and many an Irish king. Waterford might well boast that it was the *urbs intacta* which was never taken by Irish chief or Norman earl all through the Butler-Geraldine wars and the age of the Tudors. But it was hard to shake off the local tyrant, and we find in 1475 that Richard Poer had been sheriff of the city for twenty years and 'has inflicted great injuries by land and sea on the citizens and strangers resorting there, and since in all the counties round the said city there live no lords, gentlemen or commons arrayed in English habit, or submitting to the King's obedience, or governed by any other laws save those called Brehon . . . therefore, as the mayor and commons of the said city are faithful subjects, it is enacted by this present parliament that henceforth they elect the sheriffs of the said city'. (Dalton's *Drogheda*, II, p. 169, from an unpublished statute.)

The worst period for the towns was the Lancastrian, from 1400 to 1460; it improved under aristocratic Home Rule, and many of them, such as Clonmel, Kilkenny, New Ross, Limerick, Cork, were glad to put themselves under the patronage of the great earls of Ormond and Desmond and other magnates who now ruled Ireland. But for all that, while 'the March English' and even many in the Pale adopted Irish speech and culture, the towns remained the only strongholds of Englishism.

Oligarchy grew steadily in them, and even the resident families could not always keep the monopoly. In many cases the local gentry got freeman rights, enlisted the burgesses in their wars, and put the town government into their pockets, so that Acts of Poynings' parliament had to prohibit citizens of any town from receiving livery or wages of any lord or gentleman, and forbade admission of any one as alderman, juror, or freeman, save he had been an apprentice or inhabitant of the town.

[1] See for the feud of Waterford against Poers and O'Driscolls the first edition of this work, pp. 362–4.

These oligarchies were officially supposed to be anti-Irish, but there is plenty of evidence that members of the Irish race were numerous and prosperous in the boroughs. By 1350 we find many Irish names among the officers of the boroughs, and later some of the most famous civic names were of Gaelic origin, such as Lynch, Kirwan, Nolan, Fallon, Tully of Galway, Creagh of Limerick, and Meagh of Cork.

The towns being so favoured by Government, the civic rulers were bound officially to put anti-Irish statutes such as those of Kilkenny into effect. Waterford and Dublin being the most English did this with readiness and added ordinances of their own. In Waterford, by ordinance of 1384, it was an offence to call another citizen 'Irishman', the punishment being fine of a mark, to be paid to the victim. In a later ordinance of 1482 it was enacted that 'no manere man, free or foreigner, shall plead or defend in the Irish tongue', but must have an interpreter, 'except one party be of the countrye, then every such dweller shall be at liberty to speak Yrish'. (For such statutes see *The Red Book of Kilkenny*, and *Statutes of Waterford* and of *Galway* in *Historical MSS. Commission, 10th Report*, app. pt. v, also *Liber Primus Kilkenniensis* (ed. Charles MacNeill), *Irish MSS. Commission.*)

These enactments indeed suggest that the use of Irish and intercourse with the native race were becoming so common that hostile legislation, though considered the thing, was perfunctory. There was clearly no hostility to peaceful domiciled or naturalized Irishmen. In 1460 the Irish parliament enacted that civic freedom and admission to trades could only be obtained by Irishmen after they had got English liberty from the King, and had undertaken to be of English array, habit and apparel. This was not an unreasonable demand.

Acquaintance with the Irish language must have begun early among the rulers in the towns, and at the submissions of the Irish chiefs to Richard II (see p. 270) the mayor of Limerick, the Earl of Ormond, and two Anglo-Irish knights of Kildare alike can act as interpreters.

Later, owing to constant infusion of Irish blood and still more to anti-English feeling kindled by the religious question even in the loyal towns, this knowledge of Irish turned into a positive preference for it. In James I's reign Fynes Moryson wrote in his *Commonwealth of Ireland* thus: 'The English-Irish and the very citizens, excepting those of Dublin where the Lord Deputy resides, though they could speak English as well as we, yet commonly speak Irish among themselves, and were hardly induced by our familiar conversation to speak English with us.' This was the culmination of the flood-tide of Irish revival which, beginning in the fourteenth century, reached the towns last of all.

APPENDIX IV

THE BETAGH CLASS AND THE LEGAL TREATMENT OF THE IRISH IN MEDIEVAL IRELAND

(A) UP TO 1366

In the settled or conquered areas which at first covered most of Ireland the Anglo-Normans had to deal with two elements of simple tenants or cultivators, namely the ordinary free class of Irish law, and the serf class, called 'betaghs' (in Latin *betagii,* a word derived from the Irish *biatach,* a 'food-provider').

The position of the former may be briefly dealt with. The colonists tried to reduce numbers of them to the condition of serfs, a position described legally as *hibernicus servilis status et condicionis,* so that they could be ousted from their holdings or as villeins become the property of Anglo-Irish lords. The Crown, which was aware of the scandal, made several attempts to emancipate them. These attempts begin with Edward I, and finish with the Statutes of Kilkenny.[1]

The attempt at a general emancipation and admittance of the Irish race as a whole to English law finally failing, emancipation (naturalization or denization) by individual charter or grant made from the Exchequer on payment of a fee became the usual method right up to Elizabeth's reign.[2]

The reduction of the small freemen class to serfdom by the Normans is illustrated in Appendix II on the Ostmen.

According to Edward III's edict of emancipation in 1331 (see p. 205) 'the betaghs are in Ireland as the villeins are in England'. But in fact the betaghs were worse off, and more tied to the soil which they were bought and sold with, than the English villeins. They had existed long before the English came, and, as we have seen in the pages on the Conquest, the colonists were most anxious to keep them on their estates, for which their labour was necessary.

Within a century after the Invasion, and on all the conquered land, we have abundant evidence of communal betagh groups living under headmen, cultivating the lord's demesne and having their own *terra betagiorum* in common. They might be king's, lord's, or bishop's *betagii.* Their lot was not a happy one. They were bought and sold with the land, they had no right in the soil, their goods and chattels were the lord's nor could they dispose of them, they were subject to heavy

[1] See for the whole question the first edition of this work, pp. 114–19, 128, 136–7, 155, 169, 189, 200–10, 220, 238–40, 246, 256, 277.

[2] For the Crown attempts to emancipate the Irish see pp. 190, 197, 205. At the end of this Appendix I give two specimens of a charter of emancipation.

labour services, and subject solely to the lord's court. The law of the State took no concern of them, any more than it did of the English villein. But the communal tie did something to make their lot tolerable. They could by the accepted 'year and a day rule' get away to the towns, though by the writ 'De nativo habendo' or 'De fugitivis' the lord might recover them as runaways.

Betaghry, however, in general died out by the fourteenth century and for the same reasons as in England. It was a pious deed to free one's serfs. It was a good bargain to let them pay in money rather than in services. Rentals of Edward I's time and later often say, 'Here are no works of the betaghs because they are charged with rent.'

The decay of betaghry coincides with the Statutes of Kilkenny, and with a general change from tillage to pasturage, for the betaghs were corn-growers. There were, however, survivals up to early Tudor times. 'The serjeantry of the betaghry of the manor of Trim' is mentioned in an Act of Parliament in 1468.

In my first edition (pp. 203–4) I summarize the description of the episcopal estates of the see of Cloyne in the *Pipa Colmani*, a document drawn up under Bishop Swaffham (1363–76). In this we find thirteen betagh groups with clan-names living at Ballyonan near Cloyne, 'who are *hibernici* (serfs) of the church of Colman and born in servitude'. At Donoughmore in Muskerry four other such septs cannot remove or be removed without the lord bishop's permission. The O'Helghys (Healys), 'homines Sancti Colmani', told Bishop Synge who gave them a charter in 1639 that they had been there for five hundred years, probably underestimating the antiquity of their tenure. My paper on 'The Manor of Lisronagh with notes on Betagh Tenure' (*P.R.I.A.*, 1936) gives a formerly unknown description of betagh services (no such full description exists) from the *Ormond Deeds*. I reproduce it here.

Lisronagh (now a parish about four miles north of Clonmel in Tipperrary) was in 1333 a manor of Lady Elizabeth de Burgo, and the rental and extent of it make one of our fullest and most illuminating pictures of Anglo-Irish manors. Among the other tenants are given the betaghs on six separate granges with their surnames, and their services and works are as follows:

'THE WORKS OF THE BETAGHS

'Each betagh who has a plough shall plough one acre of wheat and the ploughing of the acre is worth 6*d*. Also he shall plough one acre of oats and the ploughing is worth 8*d*. Whoever of them has not [a whole plough] shall join his plough animals to those of his fellow-betaghs until they have a whole plough-team for doing the said work. So that each of the said ploughs shall plough one acre of wheat and one of oats as aforesaid. And they shall have for each crop of the lord 2*s*. Whosoever holds 30 acres shall find for each three acres 3 men in autumn for one day to reap the wheat and 2 men to reap the oats, and the work of each man is worth for the day 1½*d*. And all other betaghs shall reap for one day at wheat and so much at oats as above and the value of the day's work is as above. And also all betaghs who have one farm-beast shall carry wheat from day to day with the wagons or carts of the lord to the haggard until all is carted in and they shall have food and drink once a day and the day's work with man and beast apart from food is 1½*d.* And they shall ted [spread] the lord's meadow and make hay thereof and stack it in the meadow and carry it to the lord's haggard and shall have nothing therefor. Those who have horses shall do carriage for the lord at their own expense, provided they are able to return home that night and if they cannot they shall be at the lord's costs, and they shall carry the lord's letters or those of his ministers touching the state of the manor within the county at their own proper cost. And they shall find fuel for the lord or his chief ministers until they shall be residing in the said manor. Also whatsoever victuals may be in their possession, viz. gross meat, geese and hens, and provision of this kind or of corn and straw, the lord or his chief minister shall have the right to purchase such for money at a reasonable estimate. And they shall do services at the will of the lord; and of those who have 3 animals the lord shall have the best of them as heriot and of those who have less 12*d.* for heriot. Also they shall come to the lord's court as often as [unstated].'

The subsequent records of the manor make no mention of this betagh class.

The position of the betaghs was intimately connected with the manorial system which the Norman invaders at first organized over half the country, but which died out as the Irish revived. The liberties of the feudal class in Ireland were very extensive, ranging down from palatine regalities such as those of Ormond to the manorial rights of local lords.[1]

(B) AFTER 1366

After the Statutes of Kilkenny (see pp. 232–4) the 'mere Irish', those namely who remained under their own chiefs and law, were put as a community outside the English law that ruled the colonists. The betagh class gradually disappeared and other forms of farming took their place.

As for the chiefs, even the Five Bloods 'lost their right to plead in and be answerable in the royal courts'. An outstanding case of their rightlessness in the eyes of the English law is that of Art MacMurrough (p. 264). They needed royal charters or an Act of Parliament to admit them to 'English liberty'. (See the case of Conn O'Neill and

[1] For great franchises on Church lands see those of Cashel even under Henry VI (Laffan's *Cashel*, p. 33). *Gormanston Reg.*, p. 17—the court of the lay fief of Herbardestown, county Dublin, still had in 1410: View of frankpledge, waifs, strays, wrecks, infangthef, utfangthef (the right to hang thieves caught stealing, inside or outside your liberties), prison, irons, stocks, gallows, and pillory—the lord has all plaints in his court to determine as in court baron.

Saiv Kavanagh, pp. 319, 338.) Occasional treaties either by King or earls are made with them (see Index under 'MacMahon', 'O'Byrne', 'O'Neill', etc.), accompanied by submissions on their part. Till 1603, however, the Irish no matter how great remain legally outside the law, though under the Tudors many accepted tenure under the Crown. At the best they were vassals owing *simple* homage, never subjects owing *liege* homage.

As to the extension of English law and liberty, I look on the dividing line as the failure of the royal edict of 1331, the exclusion of the Irish from State office by the act of 1361 (p. 225), and finally the Kilkenny statutes. Thereafter individual charters of emancipation or naturalization are the only device. Numbers of these had begun before 1300, and numerous examples occur up to 1603; they are granted to great chiefs such as MacCarthy Reagh and O'Dwyer (see p. 205). I add here one preserved in the Harris *Collectanea* and another granted in 1542 by the Earl of Ormond, who as a palatine lord was able to exercise a royal prerogative and admit to English liberty.

GRANTS OF ENGLISH LAW AND LIBERTY

(1) A grant of English liberty made in 1403 to Maurice Sydrack, Irishman, and his issue by the Lord Deputy, Thomas of Lancaster, at Howth on November 8th, 5 Hen. IV (Harris, *Collectanea*, vol. IV, p. 135):

> 'We have granted to Maurice S. who is of Irish nation (*de nacione sanguinis hibernicalis*) that he and all his issue born or to be born shall be of free status and condition and free and quit of all Irish servitude. And that they may answer in the courts of Ireland and acquire lands and possessions and have hold possess and enjoy them, succeed in them and dispose of them at their will. Also they may be promoted to all ecclesiastical benefices.'

The rights to which under such grants Sydrack is admitted with his issue are significant of those from which the mere Irish were excluded under the Statutes of Kilkenny and earlier custom. It is probable that Sydrack was really of Ostman descent (Sigurd or Sitric), and possibly the Fingall name Segrave comes from him.

(2) Grant of English liberty to Dermot O'Hogan in 1542 (original in Latin):

> 'James, Earl of Ormond and Ossory, Lord of the Liberty and Regality of the county of Tipperary, to all to whom these our present letters shall come greeting. Know that We, wishing to extend our special favour to Dermot O'Hogan of Milodeston, husbandman, by whatsoever name or surname of Irish nation and blood he is known, have granted to him that he and all his issue both born and to be born shall be of free status, and condition, free and quit of all yoke of

Irish servitude. And that he and his issue may use and enjoy the English laws in all things in the same measure in which Englishmen within the said our Liberty of Tipperary have, enjoy and use them. And that he and they shall plead and be impleaded in all our courts whatsoever and those of others within the said Liberty. And that he and they may acquire and have lands and tenements and other possessions and offices and retain, occupy and enjoy the same for himself and his heirs and assigns for ever and succeed in and have them in heritage. Also that they may be promoted and admitted to all ecclesiastical benefices and offices whatsoever and have, accept, retain, occupy and enjoy them as Englishmen within the said Liberty do, without any impediment of Us and our heirs, successors, officers and ministers whatsoever, notwithstanding any Irish condition or any statutes, ordinances, or restrictions made to the contrary up to this time: To last as long as said Dermot and his issue shall, like the faithful lieges of the Lord King, behave and bear themselves well towards Us, our heirs and the King's lieges.

'In witness whereof We have had these our letters patent made. Witness myself at Crompeston on the 17th day of October in the 34th year of the reign of Henry VIII.

(This deed is for the first time printed in my *Calendar of Ormond Deeds*, vol. IV, p. 236. Another excellent example is the grant by Henry VII in 1502 to William Casshene, Irishman, given in volume III of the same, No. 306.)

INDEX

Abbreviations in Index

Abp.	= Archbishop.	K.	= King.	I.	= Ireland.
Bp.	= Bishop.	H.K.	= High King.	m.	= married.
Bk.	= Book.	Kdom.	= Kingdom.	k.	= killed.
E.	= Earl.	Ld.	= Lord.	anc.	= ancestor.
		B.	= Baron.		

IRELAND
DIVIDED INTO GREAT LORDSHIPS
CIRCA 1500
Miles
0
20
40
Rathlin I.
Ballycastle
Coleraine
THE ROUTE
GLENS OF ANTRIM
MAC DONNELL
CLAN DEBOY
THE EARLDOM OF ULSTER
Bangor
THE ARDS
INISHOWEN
O'DOHERTY
Fahan
Aileach
Derry
O'CAHAN
SUPREMACY OF O'NEILL
Lifford
L. Neagh
Tullahogue
DOE
Kilmacrenan
MACSWEENY
TYRCONNELL SUPREMACY OF O'DONNELL
Raphoe
BANAGH MACSWEENY
Donegal
L. Derg
Assaroe
L. Erne
FERMANAGH
Enniskillen
O'HANLON
Armagh
O'NEILL OF THE FEWS
MAGENNIS
IVEAGH
Downpatrick
Newry
Monaghan
MAGUIRE
OF TYRONE
MACMAHON
Killala Bay
BARRET
TIRAWLEY
THE LOWER MACWILLIAM OR BURKE OF MAYO
L. Conn
Burrishoole
O'MALLEY
L. Mask
O'DOWD
O'HARA
O'CONNOR
Sligo
O'RUAIRC
L. Gill
L. Allen
OF W. BREFNI
MACDONAGH
Boyle
Carrick-on-Shannon
O'REILLY
Cavan
OF E. BREFNI
L. Sheelin
Dundalk
Louth
Ardee
Siddan
Mellifont
O'GARA
L. Gara
MACDERMOT
Elphin
COSTELLO
Rathcroghan
O'FARRELL OF ANNALY
Longford
LIBERTY OF TRIM
Kells
Athboy
Slane
Drogheda
Navan
Tara
O' CONNOR DON
Dunmore
Roscommon
Athliag
L. Ree
L. Owel
O'MELACHLIN
L. Ennell
Mullingar
Trim
THE ENGLISH PALE
Skerries
IAR CONNACHT
O'FLAHERTY
L. Corrib
Tuam
THE UPPER MACWILLIAM OR CLANRICKARD BURKE
HYMANY
Athlone
O'MOLLOY
Clonard
O'CONNOR
Kilcock
EARLDOM
Clane
Swords
Howth
Dublin
Dalkey
Tallaght
Ballinasloe
Athenry
O'KELLY
O'MADDEN
Clonmacnois
Tullamore
FALY
O'DUNN
O'DEMPSEY
Rathcoole
Naas
O'TOOLE
Bray Head
Galway
Loughrea
Clonfert
Birr
Kildare
OF KILDARE
Kilcullen
Ballymore
Glendalough
O'LOCHLIN
THOMOND SUPREMACY OF O'BRIEN
O'CARROLL OF ELY
Slieve Bloom Mts.
LORDSHIP OF LEIX
O'MORE
O'KENNEDY OF ORMOND
Roscrea
MACGILLA PATRAIC
SLIEVE MARGY
SUPREMACY O'BYRNE
Wicklow
Ennis
Kincora
Nenagh
Silvermine Mts.
EARLDOM AND SUPREMACY OF ORMOND
Carlow
MACMURROUGH
Tullow
OF Shillelagh
Arklow
MACNAMARA
Bunratty
MACMAHON
Limerick
BURKE
Thurles
Holycross
Leighlin
Kilkenny
MACMURROUGH KAVANAGH
Ferns
KNIGHT OF GLIN
Adare
Croom
Callan
Thomastown
Newcastle
WHITE KNIGHT
Tipperary
Cashel
Kells
Jerpoint
Enniscorthy
LORD OF KERRY
Kilmallock
Galtees
Caher
Clonmel
Carrick-on-Suir
New Ross
LORDSHIP OF WEXFORD
Wexford
Mt. Brandon
KNIGHT OF KERRY
Tralee
EARLDOM AND SUPREMACY OF DESMOND
Corcaguiney
Dingle
Mallow
ROCHE
FITZGERALD
Lismore
Waterford
LE POER
Killorglin
L. Lene
Dungarvan
DECIES
Valencia I.
Iveragh
MAC CARTHY MORE
MACCARTHY OF MUSKERRY
Youghal
BARRY MORE
O'SULLIVAN MORE
Cork
Bandon
O'SULLIVAN BEARE
MAC CARTHY REAGH
Berehaven
CARBERY
Kinsale Head
O'DRISCOL
J. T. RANKIN